W9-AOM-049

my
Perspectives
ENGLISH LANGUAGE ARTS

Pearson

New York, New York   Boston, Massachusetts
Chandler, Arizona   Glenview, Illinois

ABOUT THE COVERS: *myPerspectives, Texas,* covers are designed to be fun, interesting, and inspiring. We want you to think differently about learning, make connections to the world around you, and bring in your own ideas, creativity, and perspectives. These illustrations highlight aspects of Texas that might be familiar to you and use art styles similar to those of famous painters such as Van Gogh, Matisse, and Seurat.

ISBN-13: 978-0-32-899133-4
ISBN-10: 0-32-899133-3

📍 Welcome!

Set goals. Share your ideas. Collaborate with your peers. Reflect on your learning... myPerspectives is about YOU!

You will:

» *come up with your own perspectives on essential questions*
» *engage in thoughtful discussions with your peers*
» *make choices in what you read*
» *and maybe, even, re-examine your own thinking as a result!*

Contents

In the myPerspectives learning community, you explore essential questions, watch videos, read texts, listen to audio, collaborate with your peers, write about interesting topics – and more.

Above all, **YOU** are at the center of your learning – sharing your perspectives, listening to others, and developing the skills and desire to learn that will last a lifetime!

Setting Goals

Self-Motivation

Organizational Skills

READING

Respecting Others

RESEARCH

Sharing Perspectives

Responsible Behavior

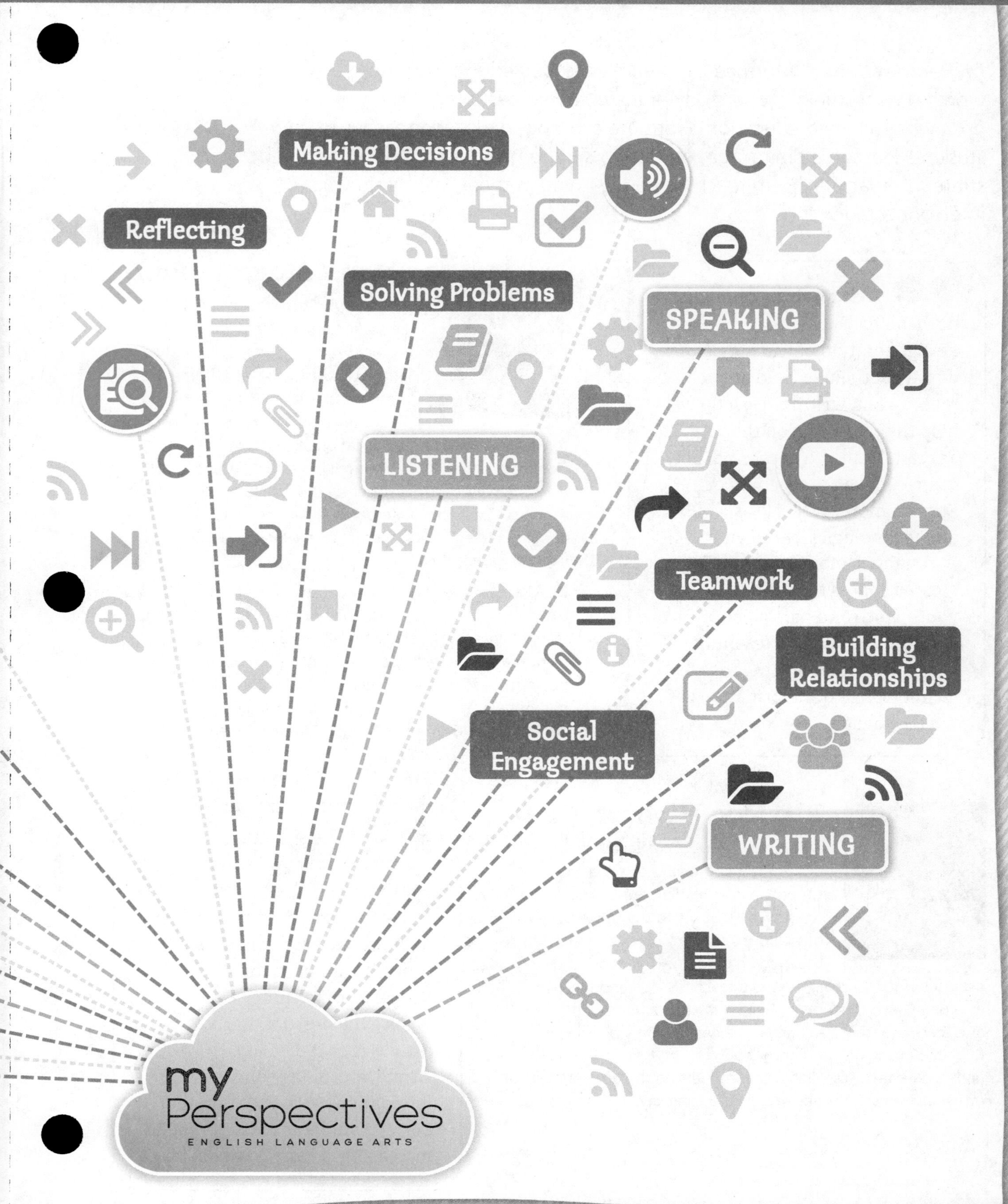

Making Decisions

Reflecting

Solving Problems

SPEAKING

LISTENING

Teamwork

Building Relationships

Social Engagement

WRITING

my Perspectives
ENGLISH LANGUAGE ARTS

Experts' Perspectives

myPerspectives is informed by a team of respected experts whose experiences working with students and study of instructional best practices have positively impacted education. From the evolving role of the teacher to how students learn in a digital age, our authors bring new ideas, innovations, and strategies that transform teaching and learning in today's competitive and interconnected world.

> "The teaching of English needs to focus on engaging a new generation of learners. How do we get them excited about reading and writing? How do we help them to envision themselves as readers and writers? And, how can we make the teaching of English more culturally, socially, and technologically relevant? Throughout the curriculum, we've created spaces that enhance youth voice and participation and that connect the teaching of literature and writing to technological transformations of the digital age."

Ernest Morrell, Ph.D.

is the Coyle Professor of Literacy Education and the Inaugural Director of the Center for Literacy Education at the University of Notre Dame. He was formerly Macy Professor of English Education and Director of the Institute for Urban and Minority Education at Teachers College, Columbia University. Dr. Morrell is also past-president of the National Council of Teachers of English, a Fellow of the American Educational Research Association (AERA), and an appointed member of International Literacy Association's Literacy Research Panel.

Dr. Morrell works with schools, districts, and families across the country to infuse social and emotional learning, digital technologies, project based learning, and multicultural literature into literacy practices aimed at developing powerful readers and writers among all students. Dr. Morrell has influenced the development of *my*Perspectives in Assessment, Writing & Research, Student Engagement, and Collaborative Learning.

Elfrieda Hiebert, Ph.D.

is President and CEO of TextProject, a nonprofit that provides resources to support higher reading levels. She is also a research associate at the University of California, Santa Cruz. Dr. Hiebert has worked in the field of early reading acquisition for 45 years, first as a teacher's aide and teacher of primary-level students in California and, subsequently, as a teacher and researcher. Her research addresses how fluency, vocabulary, and knowledge can be fostered through appropriate texts. Dr. Hiebert has influenced the development of *my*Perspectives in Vocabulary, Text Complexity, and Assessment.

> "The signature of complex text is challenging vocabulary. In the systems of vocabulary, it's important to provide ways to show how concepts can be made more transparent to students. We provide lessons and activities that develop a strong vocabulary and concept foundation—a foundation that permits students to comprehend increasingly more complex text."

Kelly Gallagher, M.Ed.

teaches at Magnolia High School in Anaheim, California, where he is in his thirty-third year. He is the former co-director of the South Basin Writing Project at California State University, Long Beach and the former president of the Secondary Reading Group for the International Literacy Association. Kelly is the author of several books on adolescent literacy, most notably *Readicide: How Schools Are Killing Reading and What You Can Do About It* and *Write Like This*. Kelly's latest book, co-written with Penny Kittle, is *180 Days: Two Teachers and the Quest to Engage and Empower Adolescents.* Mr. Gallagher has influenced the development of *my*Perspectives in Writing, Close Reading, and the Role of Teachers.

❝ The *my*Perspectives classroom is dynamic. The teacher inspires, models, instructs, facilitates, and advises students as they evolve and grow. When teachers guide students through meaningful learning tasks and then pass them ownership of their own learning, students become engaged and work harder. This is how we make a difference in student achievement—by putting students at the center of their learning and giving them the opportunities to choose, explore, collaborate, and work independently.❞

❝ It's critical to give students the opportunity to read a wide range of highly engaging texts and to immerse themselves in exploring powerful ideas and how these ideas are expressed. In *my*Perspectives, we focus on building up students' awareness of how academic language works, which is especially important for English language learners.❞

Jim Cummins, Ph.D.

is a Professor Emeritus in the Department of Curriculum, Teaching and Learning of the University of Toronto. His research focuses on literacy development in multilingual school contexts as well as on the potential roles of technology in promoting language and literacy development. In recent years, he has been working actively with teachers to identify ways of increasing the literacy engagement of learners in multilingual school contexts. Dr. Cummins has influenced the development of *my*Perspectives in English Language Learner and English Language Development support.

UNIT INTRODUCTION

WHOLE-CLASS LEARNING

PERFORMANCE TASK

PEER-GROUP LEARNING

Comparing Within Genre

PERFORMANCE TASK

👤 INDEPENDENT LEARNING

These selections are available on Pearson Realize.

SHARE YOUR INDEPENDENT LEARNING

☑ PERFORMANCE-BASED ASSESSMENT

UNIT REFLECTION

PEARSON
realize.
Go ONLINE for
all lessons

 AUDIO

 VIDEO

 NOTEBOOK

 ANNOTATE

 INTERACTIVITY

 DOWNLOAD

 RESEARCH

BOOK CLUB

The novels below
align to this unit.

HISTORICAL FICTION
Bud, Not Buddy
Christopher Paul Curtis

REALISTIC FICTION
Raymie Nightingale
Kate DiCamillo

 These activities include items in TEKS Test format.

UNIT 2 Natural Allies

🧑 INDEPENDENT LEARNING

POETRY
A Blessing
James Wright

MEDIA: VIDEO
The Secret Life of the Dog
British Broadcasting Company

REFLECTIVE ESSAY
All the Pretty Ponies
Oscar Cásares

INFORMATIONAL TEXT
The Girl Who Gets Gifts From Birds
Katy Sewall

INFORMATIONAL TEXT
Pet Therapy: How Animals and Humans Heal Each Other
Julie Rovner

These selections are available on Pearson Realize.

☑ PERFORMANCE-BASED ASSESSMENT

UNIT REFLECTION

PEARSON realize.
Go ONLINE for all lessons

 AUDIO

 VIDEO

 NOTEBOOK

 ANNOTATE

 INTERACTIVITY

 DOWNLOAD

 RESEARCH

BOOK CLUB

The novels below align to this unit.

HISTORICAL FICTION
Where the Red Fern Grows
Wilson Rawls

FANTASY
The Magician's Elephant
Kate DiCamillo

 These activities include items in TEKS Test format.

UNIT 3 Technology and Society

INDEPENDENT LEARNING

NEWS ARTICLE
7-Year-Old Girl Gets New Hand From 3-D Printer
John Rogers

NEWS ARTICLE
High-Tech Backpacks Open World of Whales to Deaf Students
Associated Press

POETRY COLLECTION
All Watched Over by Machines of Loving Grace
Richard Brautigan

Sonnet, Without Salmon
Sherman Alexie

NEWS ARTICLE
Teen Researchers Defend Media Multitasking
Sumathi Reddy

These selections are available on Pearson Realize.

SHARE YOUR INDEPENDENT LEARNING

☑ PERFORMANCE-BASED ASSESSMENT

UNIT REFLECTION

PEARSON
realıze™
Go ONLINE for all lessons

- AUDIO
- VIDEO
- NOTEBOOK
- ANNOTATE
- INTERACTIVITY
- DOWNLOAD
- RESEARCH

BOOK CLUB

The novels below align to this unit.

FANTASY
A Wrinkle in Time
Madeleine L'Engle

SCIENCE FICTION
Sky Jumpers
Peggy Eddleman

These activities include items in TEKS Test format.

UNIT 4 The Power of Imagination

👤 INDEPENDENT LEARNING

These selections are available on Pearson Realize.

SHARE YOUR INDEPENDENT LEARNING

☑ PERFORMANCE-BASED ASSESSMENT

UNIT REFLECTION

PEARSON
realize.
Go ONLINE for
all lessons

 AUDIO

 VIDEO

 NOTEBOOK

 ANNOTATE

 INTERACTIVITY

 DOWNLOAD

 RESEARCH

BOOK CLUB

The novels below
align to this unit.

FANTASY
**Charlie and
the Chocolate
Factory**
Roald Dahl

**REALISTIC
FICTION**
**Bridge to
Terabithia**
*Katherine
Paterson*

 These activities include items in TEKS
Test format.

UNIT 5 Exploration

INDEPENDENT LEARNING

These selections are available on Pearson Realize.

SHARE YOUR INDEPENDENT LEARNING

☑ PERFORMANCE-BASED ASSESSMENT

UNIT REFLECTION

PEARSON realize™

Go ONLINE for all lessons

 AUDIO

 VIDEO

 NOTEBOOK

 ANNOTATE

 INTERACTIVITY

 DOWNLOAD

 RESEARCH

BOOK CLUB

The novels below align to this unit.

SCIENCE FICTION
Journey to the Center of the Earth
Jules Verne

ADVENTURE
Navigating Early
Clare Vanderpool

 These activities include items in TEKS Test format.

You will continue your journey toward college and career readiness as you read, write, discuss, and reflect on the texts in this program. The following listing provides you with an overview of the knowledge and skills you will gain over the course of the year.

	Texas Essential Knowledge and Skills: Grade 6
1	**Developing and sustaining foundational language skills: listening, speaking, discussion, and thinking—oral language.** The student develops oral language through listening, speaking, and discussion. The student is expected to:
A	listen actively to interpret a message, ask clarifying questions, and respond appropriately;
B	follow and give oral instructions that include multiple action steps;
C	give an organized presentation with a specific stance and position, employing eye contact, speaking rate, volume, enunciation, natural gestures, and conventions of language to communicate ideas effectively; and
D	participate in student-led discussions by eliciting and considering suggestions from other group members, taking notes, and identifying points of agreement and disagreement.
2	**Developing and sustaining foundational language skills: listening, speaking, reading, writing, and thinking—vocabulary.** The student uses newly acquired vocabulary expressively. The student is expected to:
A	use print or digital resources to determine the meaning, syllabication, pronunciation, word origin, and part of speech;
B	use context such as definition, analogy, and examples to clarify the meaning of words; and
C	determine the meaning and usage of grade-level academic English words derived from Greek and Latin roots such as *mis/mit, bene, man, vac, scrib/script*, and *jur/jus*.
3	**Developing and sustaining foundational language skills: listening, speaking, reading, writing, and thinking—fluency.** The student reads grade-level text with fluency and comprehension. The student is expected to adjust fluency when reading grade-level text based on the reading purpose.
4	**Developing and sustaining foundational language skills: listening, speaking, reading, writing, and thinking—self-sustained reading.** The student reads grade-appropriate texts independently. The student is expected to self-select text and read independently for a sustained period of time.

5	**Comprehension skills: listening, speaking, reading, writing, and thinking using multiple texts.** The student uses metacognitive skills to both develop and deepen comprehension of increasingly complex texts. The student is expected to:
A	establish purpose for reading assigned and self-selected text;
B	generate questions about text before, during, and after reading to deepen understanding and gain information;
C	make, correct, or confirm predictions using text features, characteristics of genre, and structures;
D	create mental images to deepen understanding;
E	make connections to personal experiences, ideas in other texts, and society;
F	make inferences and use evidence to support understanding;
G	evaluate details read to determine key ideas;
H	synthesize information to create new understanding; and
I	monitor comprehension and make adjustments such as re-reading, using background knowledge, asking questions, and annotating when understanding breaks down.
6	**Response skills: listening, speaking, reading, writing, and thinking using multiple texts.** The student responds to an increasingly challenging variety of sources that are read, heard, or viewed. The student is expected to:
A	describe personal connections to a variety of sources, including self-selected texts;
B	write responses that demonstrate understanding of texts, including comparing sources within and across genres;
C	use text evidence to support an appropriate response;
D	paraphrase and summarize texts in ways that maintain meaning and logical order;
E	interact with sources in meaningful ways such as notetaking, annotating, freewriting, or illustrating;
F	respond using newly acquired vocabulary as appropriate;
G	discuss and write about the explicit or implicit meanings of text;
H	respond orally or in writing with appropriate register, vocabulary, tone, and voice; and
I	reflect on and adjust responses as new evidence is presented.

7	**Multiple genres: listening, speaking, reading, writing, and thinking using multiple texts—literary elements.** The student recognizes and analyzes literary elements within and across increasingly complex traditional, contemporary, classical, and diverse literary texts. The student is expected to:
A	infer multiple themes within and across texts using text evidence;
B	analyze how the characters' internal and external responses develop the plot;
C	analyze plot elements, including rising action, climax, falling action, resolution, and non-linear elements such as flashback; and
D	analyze how the setting, including historical and cultural settings, influences character and plot development.
8	**Multiple genres: listening, speaking, reading, writing, and thinking using multiple texts—genres.** The student recognizes and analyzes genre-specific characteristics, structures, and purposes within and across increasingly complex traditional, contemporary, classical, and diverse texts. The student is expected to:
A	demonstrate knowledge of literary genres such as realistic fiction, adventure stories, historical fiction, mysteries, humor, and myths;
B	analyze the effect of meter and structural elements such as line breaks in poems across a variety of poetic forms;
C	analyze how playwrights develop characters through dialogue and staging;
D	analyze characteristics and structural elements of informational text, including:
	i. the controlling idea or thesis with supporting evidence;
	ii. features such as introduction, foreword, preface, references, or acknowledgements to gain background information; and
	iii. organizational patterns such as definition, classification, advantage, and disadvantage;
E	analyze characteristics and structures of argumentative text by:
	i. identifying the claim;
	ii. explaining how the author uses various types of evidence to support the argument;
	iii. identifying the intended audience or reader; and
F	analyze characteristics of multimodal and digital texts.

9	**Author's purpose and craft: listening, speaking, reading, writing, and thinking using multiple texts.** The student uses critical inquiry to analyze the authors' choices and how they influence and communicate meaning within a variety of texts. The student analyzes and applies author's craft purposefully in order to develop his or her own products and performances. The student is expected to:
A	explain the author's purpose and message within a text;
B	analyze how the use of text structure contributes to the author's purpose;
C	analyze the author's use of print and graphic features to achieve specific purposes;
D	describe how the author's use of figurative language such as metaphor and personification achieves specific purposes;
E	identify the use of literary devices, including omniscient and limited point of view, to achieve a specific purpose;
F	analyze how the author's use of language contributes to mood and voice; and
G	explain the differences between rhetorical devices and logical fallacies.

continued on next page

10	**Composition: listening, speaking, reading, writing, and thinking using multiple texts—writing process.** The student uses the writing process recursively to compose multiple texts that are legible and uses appropriate conventions. The student is expected to:
A	plan a first draft by selecting a genre appropriate for a particular topic, purpose, and audience using a range of strategies such as discussion, background reading, and personal interests;
B	develop drafts into a focused, structured, and coherent piece of writing by:
	i. organizing with purposeful structure, including an introduction, transitions, coherence within and across paragraphs, and a conclusion; and
	ii. developing an engaging idea reflecting depth of thought with specific facts and details;
C	revise drafts for clarity, development, organization, style, word choice, and sentence variety;
D	edit drafts using standard English conventions, including:
	i. complete complex sentences with subject-verb agreement and avoidance of splices, run-ons, and fragments;
	ii. consistent, appropriate use of verb tenses;
	iii. conjunctive adverbs;
	iv. prepositions and prepositional phrases and their influence on subject-verb agreement;
	v. pronouns, including relative;
	vi. subordinating conjunctions to form complex sentences and correlative conjunctions such as *either/or* and *neither/nor*;
	vii. capitalization of proper nouns, including abbreviations, initials, acronyms, and organizations;
	viii. punctuation marks, including commas in complex sentences, transitions, and introductory elements; and
	ix. correct spelling, including commonly confused terms such as *its/it's, affect/effect, there/their/they're,* and *to/two/too*; and
E	publish written work for appropriate audiences.

11	**Composition: listening, speaking, reading, writing, and thinking using multiple texts—genres.** The student uses genre characteristics and craft to compose multiple texts that are meaningful. The student is expected to:
A	compose literary texts such as personal narratives, fiction, and poetry using genre characteristics and craft;
B	compose informational texts, including multi-paragraph essays that convey information about a topic, using a clear controlling idea or thesis statement and genre characteristics and craft;
C	compose multi-paragraph argumentative texts using genre characteristics and craft; and
D	compose correspondence that reflects an opinion, registers a complaint, or requests information in a business or friendly structure.
12	**Inquiry and research: listening, speaking, reading, writing, and thinking using multiple texts.** The student engages in both short-term and sustained recursive inquiry processes for a variety of purposes. The student is expected to:
A	generate student-selected and teacher-guided questions for formal and informal inquiry;
B	develop and revise a plan;
C	refine the major research question, if necessary, guided by the answers to a secondary set of questions;
D	identify and gather relevant information from a variety of sources;
E	differentiate between primary and secondary sources;
F	synthesize information from a variety of sources;
G	differentiate between paraphrasing and plagiarism when using source materials;
H	examine sources for:
	i. reliability, credibility, and bias; and
	ii. faulty reasoning such as hyperbole, emotional appeals, and stereotype;
I	display academic citations and use source materials ethically; and
J	use an appropriate mode of delivery, whether written, oral, or multimodal, to present results.

Growing Up

PEARSON
realize

Go ONLINE for
all lessons

 AUDIO

 VIDEO

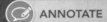 NOTEBOOK

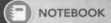 ANNOTATE

 INTERACTIVITY

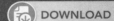 DOWNLOAD

 RESEARCH

WATCH THE VIDEO

Best of the Bee

DISCUSS IT Do you think competition should be part of everyone's childhood?

Write your response before sharing your ideas.

UNIT 1

UNIT INTRODUCTION

Essential Question

What are some of the challenges and triumphs of growing up?

MENTOR TEXT:
NONFICTION
NARRATIVE
Wagon Train at Dusk

WHOLE-CLASS LEARNING

MEMOIR

from Brown Girl Dreaming
Jacqueline Woodson

MEDIA: COMIC STRIP

Gallery of *Calvin and Hobbes* Comics
Bill Watterson

SCIENCE FICTION

The Sand Castle
Alma Luz Villanueva

PERFORMANCE TASK

WRITING PROCESS
Write a Personal Narrative

PEER-GROUP LEARNING

MEMOIR

from Bad Boy
Walter Dean Myers

MEDIA: ORAL STORYTELLING

The Moth Presents:
Aleeza Kazmi

COMPARE WITHIN GENRE

REALISTIC SHORT STORY

Prince Francis
Roddy Doyle

REALISTIC SHORT STORY

The Sound of Summer Running
Ray Bradbury

PERFORMANCE TASK

SPEAKING AND LISTENING
Present a Narrative

INDEPENDENT LEARNING

FANTASY

from Peter Pan
J.M. Barrie

POETRY COLLECTION

Oranges
Gary Soto

I Was a Skinny Tomboy Kid
Alma Luz Villanueva

PERSONAL ESSAY

The Boy Nobody Knew
Faith Ringgold

REALISTIC FICTION

Eleven
Sandra Cisneros

REALISTIC FICTION

Raymond's Run
Toni Cade Bambara

SHARE INDEPENDENT LEARNING

Share • Learn • Reflect

PERFORMANCE-BASED ASSESSMENT

Personal Narrative

You will write a personal narrative that explores the Essential Question for the unit.

UNIT REFLECTION

Goals • Texts • Essential Question

Unit Goals

▶ VIDEO

Throughout this unit, you will deepen your perspective about growing up by reading, writing, speaking, listening, and presenting. These goals will help you succeed on the Unit Performance-Based Assessment.

👆 INTERACTIVITY

SET GOALS Rate how well you meet these goals right now. You will revisit your ratings later when you reflect on your growth during this unit.

SCALE

1	2	3	4	5
NOT AT ALL WELL	NOT VERY WELL	SOMEWHAT WELL	VERY WELL	EXTREMELY WELL

ESSENTIAL QUESTION	Unit Introduction	Unit Reflection
I can read selections that illustrate the challenges and triumphs people experience while growing up.	1 2 3 4 5	1 2 3 4 5

READING	Unit Introduction	Unit Reflection
I can understand and use academic vocabulary words related to personal narratives.	1 2 3 4 5	1 2 3 4 5
I can recognize elements of different genres, especially narrative essays, realistic fiction, and memoirs.	1 2 3 4 5	1 2 3 4 5
I can read a selection of my choice independently and make meaningful connections to other texts.	1 2 3 4 5	1 2 3 4 5

WRITING	Unit Introduction	Unit Reflection
I can write a focused, well-organized personal narrative.	1 2 3 4 5	1 2 3 4 5
I can complete Timed Writing tasks with confidence.	1 2 3 4 5	1 2 3 4 5

SPEAKING AND LISTENING	Unit Introduction	Unit Reflection
I can prepare and present a nonfiction narrative.	1 2 3 4 5	1 2 3 4 5

🟊 **TEKS**

2.C. Determine the meaning and usage of grade-level academic English words derived from Greek and Latin roots such as *mis/mit, bene, man, vac, scrib/script,* and *jur/jus.*

6.F. Respond using newly acquired vocabulary as appropriate.

Academic Vocabulary: Nonfiction Narrative

Many English words have roots, or key parts, that come from ancient languages, such as Latin and Greek. Learn these roots and use the words as you respond to questions and activities in this unit.

 INTERACTIVITY

PRACTICE Academic terms are used routinely in classrooms. Build your knowledge of these words by completing the chart.

1. **Review** each word, its root, and the mentor sentences.

2. **Determine** the meaning and usage of each word using the mentor sentences and a dictionary, if needed.

3. **List** at least two related words for each word.

WORD	MENTOR SENTENCES	PREDICT MEANING	RELATED WORDS
reflect Latin Root: **-flect-** "bend"	1. Nathan needs time to *reflect* on his actions before he apologizes. 2. I could see the image of the tree *reflect* on the nearby window.		reflection; reflective
mission Latin Root: **-mis-/-mit-** "let go"; "send"	1. The museum's *mission* is to give local artists more attention. 2. If your *mission* is clear, your chances of success are better.		
contribute Latin Root: **-trib-** "pay"; "give"	1. You can *contribute* to the discussion by voicing your thoughts on the subject. 2. John was asked to *contribute* money for the annual picnic.		
recognize Latin Root: **-cogn-** "know"	1. Shay and Brooke did not *recognize* their cousin because he had grown so much since they last saw him. 2. We *recognize* our veterans by honoring them with a parade.		
memorize Latin Root: **-mem-** "mind"	1. It is difficult to *memorize* all of the different grammar rules for a foreign language. 2. The actors must *memorize* their lines before the opening night of the play.		

This selection is an example of a **nonfiction narrative**, a type of writing in which an author tells a true story. This is the type of writing you will develop in the Performance-Based Assessment at the end of the unit.

READ IT As you read, look at the way the author describes events and experiences. Mark the text to help you answer this question: What descriptive details make this narrative realistic and memorable?

Wagon Train at Dusk

 AUDIO

 ANNOTATE

1   Sometimes you just have to laugh," I tell my daughter, who is having an especially bad day. She's lost her favorite bracelet, she turned in the wrong homework assignment, and she just found out she would be playing Marshmallow #2 in the class play.

2   "Oh, you wouldn't understand," Sarah says, sulkily.

3   I ask her if I've ever told her the story of the diorama.

4   "Yes, Dad. More than once," she says.

5   That doesn't stop me. "When I was in the sixth grade," I say in my storyteller's voice, "we had to make shoebox dioramas of a scene from American history. I decided to do a wagon train traveling across the Great Plains in the mid-1800s."

6   Sarah pretends she isn't rolling her eyes, but I keep going. "I wanted it to be great. A diorama to end all dioramas! I wanted to be famous. I wanted to be on the local news. But what I really wanted was to show up Jorge Nuñez," I say.

7   "Jorge and I had been in the same class since fourth grade. We were pretty evenly matched when it came to test scores and homework, but for hands-on projects, there was no one like Jorge. He always came up with these unique creations, beautifully conceived and executed. Jorge's mom and dad were architects, so maybe he had a leg up, but who knows."

8   Sarah shrugs in sympathy—which I take as permission to continue. "As soon as I heard Jorge announce that he was making a shoebox diorama of a log cabin, I decided to go one better. I'd create a fleet of Conestoga wagons in a circle formation around a campfire at dusk, with miniature people and horses and dogs made of pipe cleaners, and children running around playing

hoops. It would be a masterpiece. And that's just how it turned out: a masterpiece! I carried it upstairs to my room and that night I went to sleep with a smile on my face, imagining Jorge's reaction."

9   "Then," I go on, "in the middle of the night I was jolted awake by a ripping sound. My heart stopped. I felt sick. *I know that sound*, I thought. There was no mistaking what it was—Lucy was demolishing my masterpiece! You couldn't even tell what it was supposed to be! I lay there in a stupor of self-pity and the sense that nothing in the world would ever be right again. *The dog ate my diorama*, I thought, and I pictured myself saying this in class. I pictured the hoots and guffaws and hollers. I pictured my teacher's puzzled expression as she tried to work out if I was being serious." I make the expression myself, and Sarah smiles.

10   "Then I said it out loud: *The dog ate my diorama*. It was funny, actually. The more I said it, the funnier it got. I started laughing. I laughed until my sides hurt. I couldn't stop laughing."

11   "And then?" Sarah says, knowing what comes next.

12   "Well," I say, "I picked up all the pieces and put them in the box and took the whole thing to school. I called it 'Wagon Train After a Tornado.' The teacher loved it. Everyone enjoyed my story. I think Jorge was actually jealous."

13   Sarah gives a reluctant smile, like she's supposed to. "So," she says, remembering that there's a lesson in there somewhere, "you learned to laugh at bad things. Right?"

14   I shake my head. "Nope," I tell her. "I learned that some things aren't so bad." ❧

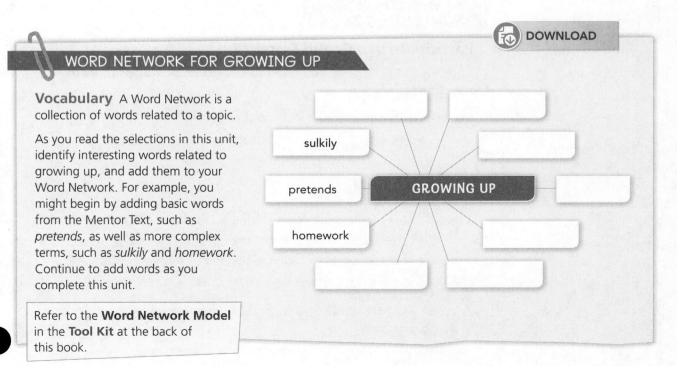

DOWNLOAD

WORD NETWORK FOR GROWING UP

Vocabulary A Word Network is a collection of words related to a topic.

As you read the selections in this unit, identify interesting words related to growing up, and add them to your Word Network. For example, you might begin by adding basic words from the Mentor Text, such as *pretends*, as well as more complex terms, such as *sulkily* and *homework*. Continue to add words as you complete this unit.

sulkily

pretends

homework

GROWING UP

Refer to the **Word Network Model** in the **Tool Kit** at the back of this book.

Summary

A **summary** is a brief, complete overview of a text that maintains the meaning of the original work and presents ideas in a logical order. It should not include your personal opinions.

📓 NOTEBOOK

WRITE IT ▶ Write a summary of "Wagon Train at Dusk."

Launch Activity

Participate in a Group Discussion

Consider this statement: **You need to overcome obstacles to learn new things.**

Record your position on the statement and explain your thinking.

◯ Strongly Agree   ◯ Agree   ◯ Disagree   ◯ Strongly Disagree

1. Form a small group with other students. Discuss questions related to the statement, such as the following:
   • Have you ever faced a challenge that led to success?
   • Does learning new things have to be challenging?

2. When you have finished your discussion, write a summary of the main points you covered.

3. Share the summary of your discussion with the class.

✪ TEKS
6.D. Paraphrase and summarize texts in ways that maintain meaning and logical order.

QuickWrite

Consider class discussions, the video, and the Mentor Text as you think about the Essential Question.

Essential Question

What are some of the challenges and triumphs of growing up?

At the end of the unit, you will respond to the Essential Question again and see how your perspective has changed.

NOTEBOOK

WRITE IT Record your first thoughts here.

DOWNLOAD

EQ Notes What are some of the challenges and triumphs of growing up?

As you read the selections in this unit, use a chart like the one shown to record your ideas and list details from the texts that support them. Taking notes as you go will help you clarify your thinking, gather relevant information, and be ready to respond to the Essential Question.

TITLE	MY IDEAS / OBSERVATIONS	TEXT EVIDENCE / INFORMATION

Refer to the **EQ Notes Model** in the **Tool Kit** at the back of this book.

Essential Question

What are some of the challenges and triumphs of growing up?

You deal with challenges every day. Some are big challenges, while others are small. Whatever the challenge is, you learn and grow from that experience. As you read, you will work with your whole class to explore the ways that people can learn from and triumph over childhood challenges.

 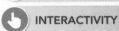

▶ VIDEO

👆 INTERACTIVITY

Whole-Class Learning Strategies

Throughout your life, in school, in your community, and in your career, you will continue to learn and work in large-group environments.

Review these strategies and the actions you can take to practice them as you work with your whole class. Add ideas of your own for each strategy. Get ready to use these strategies during Whole-Class Learning.

STRATEGY	MY ACTION PLAN
Listen actively • Put away personal items to avoid becoming distracted. • Try to hear the speaker's full message before planning your own response.	
Demonstrate respect • Show up on time and make sure you are prepared for class. • Avoid side conversations while in class.	
Show interest • Be aware of your body language. For example, sit up in your chair. • Respond when the teacher asks for feedback.	
Interact and share ideas • If you're confused, other people probably are, too. Ask a question to help your whole class. • Build on the ideas of others by adding details or making a connection.	

CONTENTS

from BROWN GIRL DREAMING

The selection you are about to read is an excerpt from a memoir.

Reading Memoirs

In a **memoir**, a writer tells a true story from a specific period in his or her own life. The writer's story is true—or true as the writer remembers it—but it may be told in an artistic way that uses elements of short stories or poems.

MEMOIR

Author's Purpose
- to share memories from the writer's life

Characteristics
- written from the first-person point of view
- presents a strong example of a writer's distinct sound, or voice
- expresses a controlling idea about an event in the writer's life
- has characters—although the characters are real people
- takes place in a certain setting, or time and place

Structure
- usually written in prose, or regular paragraphs
- may be broken into chapters or sections
- tends to tell of life events in time order

TEKS

2.A. Use print or digital resources to determine the meaning, syllabication, pronunciation, word origin, and part of speech.

8.A. Demonstrate knowledge of literary genres such as realistic fiction, adventure stories, historical fiction, mysteries, humor, and myths.

8.D. Analyze characteristics and structural elements of informational text.

Take a Minute!

 NOTEBOOK

FIND IT Perform a quick search to find the word history of *memoir*. What language is the word from, and what does it mean in that language? In what way does the word's meaning relate to the type of writing you are about explore? Jot down your ideas.

Genre / Text Elements

First-Person Point of View and Voice Memoirs are autobiographical because the writer tells his or her own story. Memoir writers almost always use the **first-person point of view**, referring to themselves with first-person pronouns, such as *I, me,* and *mine.* First-person point of view has specific effects.

- The reader sees through the author's eyes.

- The thoughts and feelings of others in the story remain hidden.

First-person narration may also make the writer's voice obvious. **Voice** is the way a writer "sounds" on the page. It is a sense the reader gets of a real person behind the words. The writer's attitude and word choices create his or her unique voice.

> **TIP:** In first-person narratives, the narrator is part of the story. With other points of view, the narrator tells the story but isn't part of it.

NARRATOR OF A MEMOIR	EXAMPLE
The writer is the main character, telling about his or her own life.	The morning before our vacation I got a horrible summer cold.
The writer provides an inside look at his or her thoughts and feelings.	I felt my face grow hot and red with embarrassment.
The writer's attitude and word choices create a unique voice.	I was content to be idle under the shade of the apple tree, and was as happy as the grass was green.

🖱 **INTERACTIVITY**

PRACTICE Read each item and determine whether it is written in the first-person. Mark your answers.

EXAMPLE	FIRST-PERSON POINT OF VIEW?	
	YES	NO
1. She bent to pet the little puppy, and laughed when he licked her face.	○	○
2. I felt all eyes staring at me.	○	○
3. There was only one person who knew Kirk's secret: me, and I'm not about to tell anyone else.	○	○

About the Author

Jacqueline Woodson
(b. 1964) was born in
Columbus, Ohio. She recalls
being happiest as a child
when she was writing:
"I wrote on paper bags and
my shoes and denim
binders." A 2008 Newbery
Honor winner, Woodson
believes that writers need
to be honest and to listen
to the voices of young
people.

from Brown Girl Dreaming

Concept Vocabulary

You will encounter the following words as you read the excerpt from
Brown Girl Dreaming. Before reading, note how familiar you are with
each word. Then, rank the words in order from most familiar (1) to least
familiar (6).

INTERACTIVITY

WORD	YOUR RANKING
squish	
humming	
twist	
twirl	
shushes	
feathery	

Comprehension Strategy

 ANNOTATE

Create Mental Images

Creating mental images, or picturing scenes in your mind as you
read, helps you better understand a text. As you read, take note of
words and phrases that describe colors, shapes, locations, and how
people and things look.

> **EXAMPLE**
> Notice the words related to colors and movement in these lines from
> *Brown Girl Dreaming*. Use them to see this scene in your mind.
>
> watch / the *gray sidewalk grow darker*, / watch / the *drops
> slide down the glass pane*

PRACTICE As you read, look for words and phrases that help you
create mental images. Mark those details or jot down notes about them
in the open space next to the text.

 TEKS
5.D. Create mental images to
deepen understanding.

from
Brown Girl Dreaming

Jacqueline Woodson

BACKGROUND

As a child in the 1960s, Jacqueline Woodson moved with her family from Greenville, South Carolina, to Brooklyn, in New York City. Her memoir *Brown Girl Dreaming* tells of her childhood experiences growing up in both places. In a memoir, an author recalls important events in his or her life. *Brown Girl Dreaming* is unique as a memoir because it is written in verse, or as poetry.

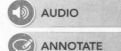

AUDIO

ANNOTATE

brooklyn rain

The rain here is different than the way
it rains in Greenville. No sweet smell of honeysuckle.
No soft **squish** of pine. No slip and slide through grass.
Just Mama saying, *Stay inside today. It's raining,*
5 and me at the window. Nothing to do but
watch
the gray sidewalk grow darker,
watch
the drops slide down the glass pane,
10 watch
people below me move fast, heads bent.

Already there are stories
in my head. Already color and sound and words.

squish (skwihsh) *n.* spongy, cushioned feeling when walking on a flexible surface

humming (HUHM ihng) *v.*
singing with closed lips
and without words

Already I'm
15 drawing circles on the glass, **humming**
myself someplace far away from here.

Down south, there was always someplace else to go
you could step out into the rain and
Grandma would let you
20 lift your head and stick out your tongue
be happy.

Down south already feels like a long time ago
but the stories in my head
take me back there, set me down in Daddy's garden
25 where the sun is always shining.

* * *

another way

While our friends are watching TV or playing outside,
we are in our house, knowing that begging our mother
to turn the television on is useless, begging her for
ten minutes outside will only mean her saying,
5 No. Saying,
You can run wild with your friends anytime. Today
I want you to find another way to play.

And then one day my mother
comes home with two shopping bags
10 filled with board games—Monopoly, checkers, chess,
Ants in the Pants, Sorry, Trouble,
just about every game we've ever seen
in the commercials between
our Saturday morning cartoons.

15 So many games, we don't know
where to begin playing, so we let Roman choose.
And he chooses Trouble
because he likes the sound the die makes
when it pops inside
20 its plastic bubble. And for days and days,
it is Christmas in November,
games to play when our homework is done,
Monopoly money to count
and checkers to slam down on boards, ants to flip
25 into blue plastic pants,
chess pieces to practice moving until we understand
their power
and when we don't, Roman and I argue
that there's another way to play

called *Our Way*. But Hope and Dell tell us
that we're too immature to even begin to understand
then bend over the chessboard in silence, each becoming
the next chess champ of the house, depending on the day
and the way the game is played.

35 Sometimes, Roman and I leave Hope and Dell alone
go to another corner of the room and become
what the others call us—*the two youngest*,
playing games we know the rules to
tic-tac-toe and checkers,
40 hangman and connect the dots

but mostly, we lean over their shoulders
as quietly as we can, watching
waiting
wanting to understand
45 how to play another way.

* * *

gifted

Everyone knows my sister
is brilliant. The letters come home folded neatly
inside official-looking envelopes that my sister proudly
hands over to my mother.
5 Odella has achieved
Odella has excelled at
Odella has been recommended to
Odella's outstanding performance in

She is gifted
10 we are told.
And I imagine presents surrounding her.

I am not gifted. When I read, the words **twist**
twirl across the page.
When they settle, it is too late.
15 The class has already moved on.

I want to catch words one day. I want to hold them
then blow gently,
watch them float
right out of my hands.

* * *

CLOSE READ

ANNOTATE: In "gifted," mark the words that are repeated in lines 5–7.

QUESTION: Why has the poet chosen to repeat these words?

CONCLUDE: What effect does this repetition have on the reader?

twist (twihst) *v.* wind or spin around one another

twirl (twurl) *v.* turn around and around quickly

sometimes

There is only one other house on our block
where a father doesn't live. When somebody asks why,
the boy says, *He died.*
The girl looks off, down the block, her thumb
5　slowly rising to her mouth. The boy says,
I was a baby. Says, *She doesn't remember him*
and points to his silent sister.

Sometimes, I lie about my father.
He died, I say, *in a car wreck* or
10　*He fell off a roof* or maybe
He's coming soon.
Next week and
next week and
next week . . . but
15　if my sister's nearby
she shakes her head. Says,
She's making up stories again.
Says,
We don't have a father anymore.
20　Says,
Our grandfather's our father now.
Says,
Sometimes, that's the way things happen.

* * *

uncle robert

Uncle Robert has moved to New York City!

I hear him taking the stairs
two at a time and then
he is at our door, knocking loud until our mother
　　opens it,
5　curlers in her hair, robe pulled closed, whispering,
It's almost midnight, don't you wake my children!

But we are already awake, all four of us, smiling
　　and jumping around
my uncle: *What'd you bring me?*

Our mama **shushes** us, says,
10　*It's too late for presents and the like.*
But we want presents and the like.
And she, too, is smiling now, happy to see her
　　baby brother who lives all the way over
in Far Rockaway where the ocean is right there
if you look out your window.

CLOSE READ

ANNOTATE: Mark the words Woodson and her sister say out loud in lines 9–23 of "sometimes."

QUESTION: What can you tell about Woodson from these lines? What can you tell about her sister?

CONCLUDE: How does this dialogue help you understand the differences between Woodson and her sister?

shushes (SHUHSH ihz) *v.* tells or signals someone to be quiet

15 Robert opens his hand to reveal a pair of silver earrings,
says to my sister, *This is a gift for how smart you are.*
I want
to be smart like Dell, I want
someone to hand me silver and gold
20 just because my brain clicks into thinking whenever
it needs to but
I am not smart like Dell so I watch her press
     the silver moons into her ears
I say, *I know a girl ten times smarter than her. She gets*
     diamonds every time she gets a hundred on a test.
     And Robert looks at me, his dark eyes smiling, asks,
     Is that something you made up? Or something real?
In my own head,
25 it's real as anything.

In my head
all kinds of people are doing all kinds of things.
I want to tell him this, that
the world we're living in right here in Brownsville isn't
30 the only place. But now my brothers are asking,

What'd you bring me, and my uncle is pulling gifts
     from his pockets,
from his leather briefcase, from inside his socks.
     He hands
my mother a record, a small 45—James Brown,[1]
     who none of us
like because he screams when he sings. But my mother
     puts it on the record player, turned way down low
     and then even us kids are dancing around—
     Robert showing us the steps he learned
     at the Far Rockaway parties. His feet are magic
35 and we all try to slide across the floor like he does,
our own feet, again and again,
betraying us.

Teach us, Robert! we keep saying. Teach us!

❋ ❋ ❋
_____
1. **James Brown** (1933–2006) American singer and dancer, and founding father of funk music.
   He is often referred to as the "Godfather of Soul."

CLOSE READ

ANNOTATE: Mark details in lines 15–23 of "uncle robert" that show what the poet is thinking.

QUESTION: Why might the poet have included these details?

CONCLUDE: What do these details suggest about the poet's character?

feathery (FEH<u>TH</u> uhr ee) *adj.*
light and airy, like the
touch of a feather

CLOSE READ

ANNOTATE: Mark details
in lines 4-8 of "wishes"
that refer to things you
can touch. Mark other
words that refer to things
you can feel or think, but
cannot touch.

QUESTION: Why does the
poet use these different
kinds of details?

CONCLUDE: How do
these details help the
reader understand what
the wishes mean to the
children?

wishes

When he takes us to the park, Uncle Robert tells us,
If you catch a dandelion puff, you can make a wish.
Anything you want will come true, he says as
we chase the **feathery** wishes around swings,
5   beneath sliding boards,
until we can hold them in our hands,
close our eyes tight, whisper our dream
then set it floating out into the universe hoping
our uncle is telling the truth,
10 hoping each thing we wish for
will one day come true.

* * *

believing

The stories start like this—

Jack and Jill went up a hill, my uncle sings.
I went up a hill yesterday, I say.
What hill?
5   *In the park.*
What park?
Halsey Park.
Who was with you?
Nobody.
10 *But you're not allowed to go to the park without anyone.*
I just did.
Maybe you dreamed it, my uncle says.
No, I really went.

And my uncle likes the stories I'm making up.

15 *. . . Along came a spider and sat down beside her.*
I got bit by a spider, I say.
When?
The other day.
Where?
20 *Right on my foot.*
Show us.
It's gone now.

But my mother accuses me of lying.
If you lie, she says, *one day you'll steal.*

25 *I won't steal.*
It's hard to understand how one leads to the other,
how stories could ever
make us criminals.

It's hard to understand
30 the way my brain works—so different
from everybody around me.
How each new story
I'm told becomes a thing
that happens,
35 in some other way
to me . . . !

Keep making up stories, my uncle says.
You're lying, my mother says.

Maybe the truth is somewhere in between
40 all that I'm told
and memory.

CLOSE READ

ANNOTATE: In lines 23–38 of "believing," mark words that show how the poet's mother reacts to her stories. Then, mark words that show how her uncle reacts.

QUESTION: Why does the poet include these different reactions?

CONCLUDE: How does this contrast help the reader better understand the poet's struggle?

BUILD INSIGHT

 NOTEBOOK

Response

1. **Personal Connections** Did the ideas and events remind you of any experiences in your own life or in the lives of people you know? Explain.

> Answer the questions in your notebook. Use text evidence to support your responses.

Comprehension

2. **Reading Check** **(a)** In "brooklyn rain," what does Woodson want to do and why? **(b)** What does Woodson tell people who ask about her father? **(c)** How does Woodson respond when Uncle Robert gives her sister Dell a pair of silver earrings?

3. **Strategy: Create Mental Images** **(a)** Which passages in the memoir were you able to picture most clearly? Why? **(b)** In what ways did this strategy add to your reading experience? Explain.

EQ Notes

What are some of the challenges and triumphs of growing up?

What ideas about growing up are suggested by this memoir? Go to your Essential Question Notes and record your observations and thoughts about *Brown Girl Dreaming.*

Analysis

4. **Speculate** Why do you think Woodson likes to make up stories so much?

5. **Make a Judgment** Woodson's mother worries that if her daughter lies, she will eventually steal. Do you think this is a reasonable worry? Explain.

6. **Make Inferences** What kind of child do you think Woodson was? Use three pieces of evidence from the poems to support your answer.

 TEKS
6.C. Use text evidence to support an appropriate response.

from Brown Girl Dreaming **21**

from BROWN GIRL DREAMING

Close Read

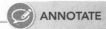 ANNOTATE

1. The model passage and annotation show how one reader analyzed lines 1–6 of "brooklyn rain." Find another detail in the passage to annotate. Then, write your own question and conclusion.

CLOSE-READ MODEL

The rain here is different than the way/it rains in Greenville. No sweet smell of honeysuckle./No soft squish of pine. No slip and slide through grass./Just mama saying, *Stay inside today. It's raining,*/and me at the window. Nothing to do but/watch . . .

ANNOTATE: The word *No* repeats.

QUESTION: Why does Woodson repeat the word *No*?

CONCLUDE: The repetition emphasizes the ways in which Woodson's life in Brooklyn is different from her life in Greenville.

MY **QUESTION:**

MY **CONCLUSION:**

2. For more practice, answer the Close-Read notes in the selection.

3. Choose a section of the memoir you found especially important. Mark important details. Then, jot down questions and write your conclusions in the open space next to the text.

Inquiry and Research

 RESEARCH

 NOTEBOOK

Research and Extend This excerpt from *Brown Girl Dreaming* tells of the writer's childhood in 1970s Brooklyn. Take some time to learn more about the time and place described in the memoir. Then, jot down ways in which your research helped you to more deeply understand and appreciate the text.

 TEKS

6.E. Interact with sources in meaningful ways such as notetaking, annotating, freewriting, or illustrating.

9.F. Analyze how the author's use of language contributes to mood and voice.

Genre / Text Elements

First-Person Point of View and Voice Most memoirs are written in the **first-person point of view** because the author is telling his or her own story. The reader sees events through the author's eyes. The choices the author makes about how to tell the story create a unique **voice**, or personality. In life, people express their personalities through what they do and say. In writing, an author's voice emerges through the way he or she uses language.

> **TIP:** When someone refers to the unique way a writer "sounds" or "speaks," they are talking about voice.

Look at how two writers describe the same event but have very different voices.

PASSAGE	USES OF LANGUAGE	VOICE
I crept out of the barn and stared at the green sky. Uh-oh. . . . No time to think. No time to call for help. No time to panic. I made a dead run for the cellar. I wrenched open the hatch doors and stumbled down the stairs. Safe! At least for now!	simple words punchy, short sentences and some fragments inner thoughts shown in quick bursts	The voice is straightforward. Plain, focused language creates a sense of a practical, no-nonsense person.
The barn was warm with the smells of hay and animals and I didn't want to leave. But I could see the sky turning a violent green, and that meant it was here, the storm we had feared. "Please, please, please, be unlocked," I chanted as I raced to the shelter. "Please, please, please...Dad, be there."	long sentences sensory details and repetition inner thoughts shown through dialogue	The voice is poetic. Sensory details and repetition create a sense of an imaginative, sensitive person.

 NOTEBOOK

PRACTICE Answer the questions.

1. **(a) Distinguish** Identify one example of a private thought or feeling Woodson shares in her memoir. **(b) Analyze** Explain how the use of first-person point of view allows her to share this detail.

2. **(a) Interpret** In "sometimes," Woodson's sister says "Sometimes, that's the way things happen." What does this detail suggest about the sister's view of life? **(b) Speculate** How might the stories of Woodson's childhood be different if they included the sister's inner thoughts? Explain.

3. **(a) Analyze** Choose a passage from the memoir in which you think Woodson's voice is very strong. **(b) Support** Explain the reasons for your choice, citing specific language. **(c) Describe** In your own words, describe Woodson's voice.

from BROWN GIRL DREAMING

Concept Vocabulary

 NOTEBOOK

Why These Words? The vocabulary words are examples of sensory language, or words that appeal to the five senses: touch, sight, smell, hearing, and taste. In *Brown Girl Dreaming*, Woodson uses sensory words to create imagery, or vivid word pictures. Imagery helps readers understand ideas in a deeper way than plain explanations might allow.

squish	twist	shushes
humming	twirl	feathery

PRACTICE Answer the questions.

1. How do the vocabulary words help you understand the concept of sensory language?

2. Find three other examples of sensory language in the excerpt from *Brown Girl Dreaming*.

3. What might *squish* if you step on it?

4. How is *humming* both similar to and different from singing?

5. How might you feel if you go on an amusement park ride that *twists* and *twirls*?

6. Write a sentence using the word *shushes*.

7. Describe what happens to a *feathery* object when the wind blows it.

 WORD NETWORK

Add words related to the idea of growing up from the text to your Word Network.

Word Study

 NOTEBOOK

Onomatopoeia The vocabulary words *squish, humming,* and *shushes* are examples of **onomatopoeia,** or words that sound like the object or action to which they refer. For example, the letters *sh* in *shushes* create the sound people make when they hush, or *shush,* someone.

1. Use each onomatopoeic vocabulary word in a sentence of your own.

2. Jot down other examples of onomatopoeia that you have come across in your own experience or in the selection. Explain your choices.

 TEKS
9.B. Analyze how the use of text structure contributes to the author's purpose.

Author's Craft

Text Structure and Purpose Memoirs are usually written in **prose,** or complete sentences and paragraphs. In this memoir, Jacqueline Woodson takes a different approach. Instead of prose, she tells her story in a series of poems that include these elements:

- **lines,** or horizontal groupings of words

- **stanzas,** or groups of lines

- poetic devices, such as **repetition,** or the deliberate re-use of certain words and phrases

- structures such as sentence fragments that break grammatical rules

In this memoir, Woodson explores the role of imagination in her childhood. Consider how her use of poetic text structures helps her achieve that purpose.

> **TIP:** Sentence fragments are groups of words that are punctuated like sentences but lack either a subject or a verb. Writers may use them for effect, such as to show a character's quick thoughts.

 NOTEBOOK

PRACTICE Respond to these questions.

1. **(a) Analyze** Identify the sentence fragments in lines 2–3 of "brooklyn rain." **(b) Connect** Explain how these fragments help to create a vivid picture of the rain in Greenville.

2. **(a) Analyze** In lines 4–11 of "brooklyn rain," what word appears on its own line three times? **(b) Draw Conclusions** Read the lines aloud. What purpose might Woodson have had in setting this word apart in this way?

3. **Analyze** In "sometimes," Woodson repeats the phrase *next week* three times in as many lines. How does the repetition affect what readers understand about the situation? Explain.

4. **(a) Compare** Rewrite the poem "sometimes" as a prose paragraph and compare it with the original. **(b) Analyze** Use your comparison and your answers to questions 1–3 to explain why the author chose to use poetic structures rather than prose in this memoir. What purpose does poetry serve?

from BROWN GIRL DREAMING

Composition

A **poem** is a form of writing that has lines that are organized into stanzas. Poems often use **sensory language**, or words and phrases that appeal to the senses.

EDITING TIP
Read your draft and make sure you have used repetition effectively. Don't simply repeat random words; repeat the ones that add meaning.

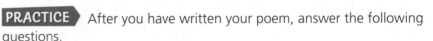

ASSIGNMENT

Write a brief **poem** in which you use Woodson's memoir as inspiration.

- Choose a single moment from your life on which to focus. The moment can be as small as looking out your window. Then, using sensory language, write a prose paragraph describing the moment.

- Change your paragraph into a poem by applying poetic elements. For example, break up sentences to make lines, or repeat an important word or phrase.

- Once your poem is organized, add dialogue or descriptive details. Work to make your poem fresh and alive for readers.

Use New Words
Try to use one or more of the vocabulary words in your writing: *squish, twist, shushes, humming, twirl, feathery*

 NOTEBOOK

Reflect on Your Writing

PRACTICE After you have written your poem, answer the following questions.

1. What was the most challenging part of the assignment?

2. What poetic elements did you use? How did they help you bring your ideas to life?

3. WHY THESE WORDS? The words you choose make a difference in your writing. Which words did you choose to create a vivid picture for your readers?

⊕ TEKS
1.D. Participate in student-led discussions by eliciting and considering suggestions from other group members, taking notes, and identifying points of agreement and disagreement.

6.F. Respond using newly acquired vocabulary as appropriate.

11.A. Compose literary texts such as personal narratives, fiction, and poetry using genre characteristics and craft.

Speaking and Listening

A **partner discussion** is a focused conversation with one other person.

ASSIGNMENT

Hold a **partner discussion** to talk about these questions:

In telling stories, do you think Woodson is just using her imagination? Is there a point at which the use of imagination can become a lie?

After you and your partner talk, regroup with the class and share highlights of your discussion.

DISCUSSION GUIDELINES

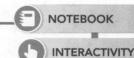

NOTEBOOK

INTERACTIVITY

Prepare for the Discussion Reread the text, using the chart to take notes about details that relate to the questions. Then, decide your position. You can also add examples from your own experience.

DETAILS / EXAMPLES	NOTES

EQ Notes Before moving on to a new selection, go to your EQ Notes and record any additional thoughts or observations you may have about *Brown Girl Dreaming*.

Discuss With Your Partner Use your notes as you share your ideas. Take additional notes as you discuss the following questions:

• Do you and your partner agree on your basic position?

• If so, how do your reasons and examples compare?

• If not, do the reasons your partner offers change your opinion?

Discuss With Your Class During the class discussion, take turns offering ideas about Woodson's use of imagination. When other partners share, listen politely and take notes. After everyone has shared their ideas, discuss similarities and differences in one another's points of view.

Reflect on the Discussion Did your initial position change as a result of the discussions? Why or why not?

About the Author

The cartoonist **Bill Watterson** (b. 1958) is the creator of the popular *Calvin and Hobbes* comic strip and a two-time recipient of the Reuben Award for Outstanding Cartoonist of the Year. He graduated from Kenyon College in Ohio, and he had his first *Calvin and Hobbes* strip published at the age of twenty-seven. Watterson fought against the commercialization and merchandising of his comics.

Gallery of *Calvin and Hobbes* Comics

Media Vocabulary

These words describe characteristics of comic strips, a type of multimodal text. Use them as you analyze, discuss, and write about the selection.

panel: individual frame of a comic, depicting a single moment	• Panels work together to tell a story. • Panels cannot show everything that happens, so readers must use their imaginations to fill in the blanks.
encapsulation: choice of scenes to display in each panel	• The layout of each scene influences readers' interpretations. • Comic strip writer/illustrators use size and shape to give more or less weight, or importance, to different elements in a scene.
speech balloon: graphic display, usually in an oval or circular shape, that shows what a character is saying	• The size, shape, and color of the speech balloon can show the emotion of the speaker. • Variations, such as a cloudy border or dotted lines, may show that a character is thinking rather than speaking.

Comprehension Strategy

 ANNOTATE

Make Inferences

Inferences are guesses readers make based on evidence in a text. These clues help readers fill in ideas the author doesn't state. Comic strip writers, for example, don't explain the humor in a set of panels. Instead, readers make inferences, filling in unstated connections between the drawings and the words in order to "get" the joke.

> **EXAMPLE** Here is an inference you might make about the *Calvin and Hobbes* comic strip titled "Ghosts."
>
> **Evidence:** In the first three panels, Calvin and Hobbes are camping at night. One mentions ghosts. In the fourth panel, they're outside at dawn, bug-eyed and clutching baseball bats.
>
> **Inference:** Spooked by the idea of ghosts, Calvin and Hobbes sat outside all night, too afraid to go to sleep.

PRACTICE As you read the comic strips, use evidence to make inferences. Write your notes in the open space.

 TEKS

5.F. Make inferences and use evidence to support understanding.

8.F. Analyze characteristics of multimodal and digital texts.

Gallery of *Calvin and Hobbes* Comics

Bill Watterson

BACKGROUND

Calvin and Hobbes was a highly popular comic strip that ran from 1985 to 1995. It follows the adventures of Calvin, a clever six-year-old with a wild imagination, and his stuffed tiger and imaginary friend, Hobbes. *Calvin and Hobbes* has appeared in thousands of newspapers worldwide and has attracted fans of all ages.

 AUDIO

 NOTEBOOK

Cartoon 1: Ghosts

Cartoon 2: Do You Like Her?

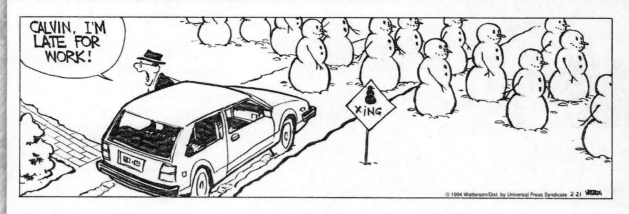

Cartoon 3: Snowman Xing

TAKE NOTES

BUILD INSIGHT

 NOTEBOOK

Response

1. Personal Connections Which comic strip did you find funniest? Why?

Comprehension

2. Reading Check (a) In "Ghosts," where are Calvin and Hobbes? **(b)** In "Do You Like Her?" what are Calvin and Hobbes doing? **(c)** In "Snowmen Xing," why does Calvin's dad yell to Calvin that he's late for work?

3. Strategy: Make Inferences Explain the inferences you made to unlock meaning in one strip. What evidence supports your inference?

Analysis

4. Interpret What insight about the power of the imagination does "Ghosts" express? Explain.

5. Make Inferences In "Do You Like Her?" why do you think Calvin refuses to answer Hobbes's questions? Explain.

6. Draw Conclusions What can you tell about the relationship between Calvin and Hobbes? Explain.

Answer the questions in your notebook. Use text evidence to support your responses.

EQ Notes

What are some of the challenges and triumphs of growing up?
What have you learned about growing up from these comics? Go to your Essential Question Notes and record your thoughts.

⊕ TEKS
5.F. Make inferences and use evidence to support understanding.

GALLERY OF *CALVIN AND HOBBES* COMICS

Close Review

 ANNOTATE

Read the comic strips again and note interesting details. Record any new observations that seem important to you. Then, write a question and your conclusion.

MY **QUESTION:**

MY **CONCLUSION:**

NOTEBOOK

LANGUAGE STUDY

Media Vocabulary

These words describe characteristics of multimodal texts. Practice using them in your responses.

| panel | encapsulation | speech balloon |

1. Why might Watterson have included only one panel in "Snowman Xing"?

2. In "Do You Like Her?" how does Watterson indicate that a character is speaking with emotion?

3. In "Ghosts," some of the panels include dialogue, whereas others do not. Why do you think Watterson chose to have panels without dialogue in this comic strip?

 TEKS

6.F. Respond using newly acquired vocabulary as appropriate.

8.F. Analyze characteristics of multimodal and digital texts.

Response

1. Personal Connections What experience would you miss most if Earth became either too hot or too cold to go outside without special gear?

I would miss the experience of going out to the beach if it was too cold and If it were to be to hot, then I would maybe miss the ~~exp~~ experience of playing in the snow.

> Answer the questions in your notebook. Use text evidence to support your responses.

Comprehension

2. Reading Check (a) Where does this story take place? **(b)** In the world of the story, what precautions do people have to take when they go outside? **(c)** What experience did Masha have as a child that she wants to recreate for her grandchildren? *In the beach, people have to* (protective clothing) *wear goggles and gloves, and Marisha wants her grandchildren to have ~~Tot To~~ experience of having fun at the beach with sand castles.*

3. Strategy: Make Predictions (a) How did you use the characteristics of science fiction to make predictions about the story? **(b)** Were you able to confirm your predictions or did you have to correct them? Explain.

I used the characteristics of science fiction by creating a plot like what I predicted that was the mom would not open the door. I was able to confirm this while reading because of how the heat has raised is caused by what happens with not being able to use the machine. ~~....~~

Analysis

4. Compare and Contrast How was the seashore of Masha's childhood different from the seashore her grandchildren experience? Explain, citing text evidence. *During Mashas childhood, they didn't have the types of problems they have ~~have~~ from her grandchildrens exprience with the is the Solar problems have increases more or the enviormental problems.*

5. (a) Distinguish Identify details in the story that relate to real science.
(b) Interpret In what ways do these details add to the story's impact? Explain. *The details of the which add to the problems is ~~....~~ during Mashas grans childrens time, ~~....~~ the sun is overheating the Earth. The impact created is that Marshas grandchildren cannot have the*

6. (a) Make Inferences Reread paragraphs 35 and 36. What do details in these paragraphs suggest about what the shells mean to Masha and why? *type of childhood that Marsh once had.*
(b) Analyze Why does Masha give up the shells in order to decorate her grandchildren's sand castle? *It suggests that the shells were kept as memories of the past when the enviormental problems of solar problem weren't so serious ~~....~~ and what ~~....~~ man she had during those times. She gave up her shells so that her grandchildren could have the same experience that Masha once had.*

EQ Notes
What are some of the challenges and triumphs of growing up?

What have you learned about growing up from reading this story? Go to your Essential Question Notes and record your observations and thoughts about "The Sand Castle."

⭕ **TEKS**

5.C. Make, correct, or confirm predictions using text features, characteristics of genre, and structures.

6.A. Describe personal connections to a variety of sources, including self-selected texts.

6.C. Use text evidence to support an appropriate response.

THE SAND CASTLE

Close Read

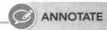 ANNOTATE

1. The model passage and annotation show how one reader analyzed part of paragraph 3 of the story. Find another detail in the passage to annotate. Then, write your own question and conclusion.

CLOSE-READ MODEL

She remembered the ride to the sea, the silence when the first shimmers of water became visible. Her father had always been first into the chilly water. "Good for the health!" he'd yell as he dove into it, swimming as far as he could, then back. Then he'd lie exhausted on the sand, stretched to the sun. Such happiness to be warmed by the sun.

ANNOTATE: Many words in the passage contain an *s* or *sh* sound.

QUESTION: Why has the writer chosen to repeat these sounds?

CONCLUDE: The repetition of the *s* and *sh* sounds mimics the sound of the ocean and creates a soothing effect. This suggests the character's love and longing for the ocean.

MY **QUESTION:**

MY **CONCLUSION:**

2. For more practice, answer the Close-Read notes in the selection.

3. Choose a section of the story you found especially important. Mark important details. Then, jot down questions and write your conclusions in the open space next to the text.

Inquiry and Research

 RESEARCH

 NOTEBOOK

Research and Extend In paragraph 7 of the story, the author names ozone-depleting chemicals as a reason for the global problem. Generate two questions you can use to guide brief research about chemicals that affect Earth's ozone layer. Then, do some informal research and jot down the answers you find. How does your research shed light on the situation the characters in the story are experiencing?

 TEKS

7.C. Analyze plot elements including rising action, climax, falling action, resolution and non-linear elements such as flashback.

12.A. Generate student-selected and teacher-guided questions for formal and informal inquiry.

Genre / Text Elements

Plot and Flashback A **flashback** is a break in the time order of a plot that shows a scene from the past. Flashbacks may take the forms of memories, dreams, or actual shifts in time. Signal words may help readers know when a flashback begins and when it ends.

- **Flashback Begins:** Look for signal words *(years ago, in the past, I remember)*, verbs in the past tense, dates, or references to characters' ages.
- **Flashback Ends:** Look for words that signal the story's current time *(now, today, these days, when I woke up from my dream)*.

> **TIP:** A story's plot centers on a conflict that develops in stages (exposition, rising action, climax, falling action, and resolution). A flashback adds information about the characters and conflict.

 NOTEBOOK

 INTERACTIVITY

PRACTICE Answer the questions and complete the activity.

1. **(a) Analyze** How do you know that paragraphs 1–2 are part of the story's exposition? Explain. **(b) Analyze** Explain how the story's conflict comes into focus in paragraph 7. **(c) Interpret** How does Masha's mood change at the end of the story? Why?

2. **Analyze** Reread the paragraphs from the story listed in the chart. Decide whether each passage contains a flashback or is set mainly in the story's present day. List details from each passage that support your response.

PASSAGES	FLASHBACK OR PRESENT?	DETAILS
Paragraphs 3 through 5		
Paragraphs 9 and 10		
Paragraph 28		

3. **(a) Analyze** Reread paragraph 30. Which part is present day? Which part is a flashback? **(b) Interpret** What information about the story's characters and conflict does this flashback provide? **(c) Analyze** How does the author signal the switch from the story's present to the past?

4. **(a) Speculate** How else might the author have conveyed the information she reveals in flashbacks? **(b) Interpret** Why do you think she chose flashbacks instead?

THE SAND CASTLE

Concept Vocabulary

 NOTEBOOK

Why These Words? The vocabulary words are all related to the concept of a lack of safety or protection. For example, you might feel *unprotected* in a *hostile* place.

scorched	unprotected	cumbersome
hostile	forlorn	drained

PRACTICE Answer the questions.

1. How do the vocabulary words sharpen your understanding of the story's setting and the characters' feelings?

2. Find three other words in the story that relate to lack of safety or protection.

3. Describe a garden that has been *scorched* by the sun.

4. Name two synonyms for *unprotected*.

5. Give an example of an object that would be *cumbersome* to carry.

6. Write a sentence using the word *hostile* as it is used in the story.

7. Name two words that mean the opposite of *forlorn*.

8. Write a sentence explaining what might make someone feel *drained*.

WORD NETWORK

Add words related to the idea of growing up from the text to your Word Network.

Word Study

 NOTEBOOK

Prefix: *un-* The prefix *un-* means "not." Adding *un-* to a word creates a new word with an opposite meaning. For example, *protected* means "kept safe." Adding the prefix *un-* creates the vocabulary word *unprotected,* which means "not kept safe."

PRACTICE Complete the following items:

1. Write a sentence that correctly uses the word *unprotected*.

2. Use a dictionary to identify two other words to which the prefix *un-* can be added to create new words with different meanings. Record the definition of each word. Then, write a sentence that correctly uses each word.

 TEKS

6.F. Respond using newly acquired vocabulary as appropriate.

10.D.ii. Edit drafts using standard English conventions, including consistent and appropriate use of verb tenses.

Conventions

Verb Tenses A **verb** is a word that expresses an action or a state of being. A verb's **tense** indicates when an action happens or a state exists. There are three simple verb tenses.

PAST TENSE *happened in the past*	PRESENT TENSE *happens now*	FUTURE TENSE *has not yet happened*
I <u>looked</u>.	I <u>look</u>.	I <u>will look</u>.
We <u>walked</u>.	We <u>walk</u>.	We <u>will walk</u>.
He <u>cried</u>.	He <u>cries</u>.	He <u>will cry</u>.

- To form the past tense of regular verbs, add *-ed* or *-d* to the base verb. For words that end in *y*, change the *y*, to *i*, and add *-ed*.
- To form the present tense of regular verbs, add *-s* or *-es* to the base word. For words that end in *y*, change the *y*, to *i*, and add *-es*.
- To form the future tense of regular verbs, use the base form of the verb preceded by *will*.

When you write about events that occur in a single time period, use the appropriate verb tense consistently.

> **TIP:** Note that irregular verbs, such as *see* and *know*, don't follow these rules, or don't follow them all the time. Use a dictionary to check your use of irregular verbs.

INTERACTIVITY

NOTEBOOK

READ IT Mark the verbs in each of the sentences. Then, label each verb as past, present, or future.

1. Masha remembered the beach as a young girl. _____

2. Together, Masha and the kids will build a sand castle. _____

3. The sun warmed Masha's skin. _____

4. The kids remove their goggles and gloves on the bus. _____

WRITE IT In the following paragraph, verb tenses are not used consistently. Edit the paragraph to make them consistent and appropriate.

Yesterday, Declan walked to school. He turns around and will observe his

mom watching him. His mom had waved. Declan sighed and rolls his

eyes. He will wonder if she would ever stop treating him like a baby.

THE SAND CASTLE

Composition

A **short story** is a brief work of fiction. A short story has a plot that centers on at least one character who faces a conflict.

> **EDITING PRACTICE**
> Review your draft and check that you have used verb tenses consistently, especially at points where you shift into or out of a flashback.

ASSIGNMENT

Imagine one of Masha's grandchildren as a grown up. Write a **short story** in which he or she tells what the world is like now, many years after that day on the beach with Masha.

- Decide whether the scientists' remedies were or were not successful. In your story, is the world better, the same, or worse than it is in "The Sand Castle"?

- Introduce a conflict that your character faces. Show how it develops, reaches a point of greatest intensity, and then ends, or resolves.

- Use flashbacks to relate your narrator's memories of his or her day at the beach with Masha.

Use New Words
Try to use one or more of the vocabulary words in your writing: *scorched, unprotected, cumbersome, hostile, forlorn, drained*

 NOTEBOOK

Reflect on Your Writing

PRACTICE Think about the choices you made as you wrote. Also consider what you learned by writing. Share your experiences by responding to these questions.

1. Which part of the assignment did you find most challenging?

2. In your story, did the world improve, stay the same, or get worse? How might your story have been different if you had made a different choice?

3. **WHY THESE WORDS?** The words you choose make a difference in your writing. Which words helped you describe what you wanted your readers to imagine as they read?

TEKS

1.A. Listen actively to interpret a message, ask clarifying questions, and respond appropriately.

1.C. Give an organized presentation with a specific stance and position, employing eye contact, speaking rate, volume, enunciation, natural gestures, and conventions of language to communicate ideas effectively.

2.A. Use print or digital resources to determine the meaning, syllabication, pronunciation, word origin, and part of speech.

10.D.ii. Edit drafts using standard English conventions, including consistent and appropriate use of verb tenses.

11.A. Compose literary texts such as personal narratives, fiction, and poetry using genre characteristics and craft.

Speaking and Listening

When you give an **oral reading**, you read a work of literature expressively for others to hear. An oral reading shows your stance on the literature you present. This is your interpretation.

ASSIGNMENT

Deliver the story you wrote earlier as an **oral reading** to your class. First, rehearse your reading, making sure that your voice and gestures show your stance on the story.

- Practice reading your story aloud. Mark sections that you find difficult and give them extra attention.

- Read with expression, allowing your voice to rise and fall in volume.

- Look up occasionally from your text to make eye contact with your listeners. Don't mumble. Instead, enunciate, pronouncing each word clearly, so that listeners can understand you.

When it's your turn to listen, be an attentive audience member:

- Listen actively, giving the reader your full attention.

- Once the reading is over, ask questions to clarify anything you didn't understand. Respond politely.

DICTIONARY PRACTICE You may have used a word in your story that you're not sure how to pronounce. If so, use a dictionary to find the pronunciation so you can say the word correctly.

 INTERACTIVITY

Evaluate Presentations

Use a presentation evaluation guide like the one shown to evaluate both your own and your classmates' oral readings. Invite feedback on your presentation, and provide feedback after others present.

PRESENTATION EVALUATION GUIDE

Rate each statement on a scale of 1 (not demonstrated) to 5 (demonstrated).

	1	2	3	4	5
The story held the audience's interest.	○	○	○	○	○
The speaker made periodic eye contact with the audience.	○	○	○	○	○
The speaker read clearly and with expression.	○	○	○	○	○
The speaker read loudly and slowly enough to be understood.	○	○	○	○	○

EQ Notes Before moving on to a new selection, go to your Essential Question Notes and record any additional thoughts or observations you may have about "The Sand Castle."

Write a Personal Narrative

A **personal narrative** is a true story in which a writer relates a meaningful experience from his or her own life. A personal narrative usually makes a point, like an essay, but reads like a story.

Write a **personal narrative** in which you relate an experience that answers the following question:

When did you use your imagination to solve a problem?

Provide details about the problem you faced and how you solved it. Use the elements of a personal narrative in your writing.

ELEMENTS OF A PERSONAL NARRATIVE

Purpose: to share a real-life story that has a deeper meaning or point

Characteristics

➔ a clear focus on a specific event or time in your life

➔ a conflict, or problem, related to the experience

➔ characters who are real people and settings that are real places

➔ first-person point of view, with you as the narrator

➔ an answer to a question or an insight

➔ narrative techniques such as dialogue and description

➔ standard English conventions

Structure

➔ a well-organized structure that includes
  • an interesting beginning that introduces the people, place, and conflict
  • a sequence of events that unfolds logically
  • a conclusion that offers an insight

⊕ TEKS

10.A. Plan a first draft by selecting a genre appropriate for a particular topic, purpose, and audience using a range of strategies such as discussion, background reading, and personal interests.

11.A. Compose literary texts such as personal narratives, fiction, and poetry using genre characteristics.

Take a Closer Look at the Assignment

 NOTEBOOK

1. What is the assignment asking me to write about, in my own words? Use a dictionary or ask your teacher if any of the words in the assignment are unclear to you.

2. Is a specific **audience** mentioned in the assignment?

○ Yes   If "yes," who is my main audience?

○ No   If "no," who do I think my audience is or should be?

3. Is my **purpose** for writing specified in the assignment?

○ Yes   If "yes," what is the purpose?

○ No   If "no," why am I writing this narrative (not just because it's an assignment)?

4. Does the assignment require that I use specific **narrative characteristics?**

○ Yes   If "yes," what are they?

○ No   If "no," what narrative characteristics do I think I need?

5. Does the assignment ask me to organize my ideas a certain way?

○ Yes   If "yes," what structure does it require?

○ No   If "no," how can I best order my ideas?

AUDIENCE

Always keep your **audience,** or reader, in mind.

- Choose an event that will engage readers' curiosity.
- Explain details that may be unfamiliar to readers.

PURPOSE

A specific **purpose,** or reason for writing, will help you focus your narrative.

General Purpose: *I'll write about a time I solved a problem.*

Specific Purpose: *I'll write about the time we made up games to get through the storm.*

NARRATIVE CHARACTERISTICS

Narrative characteristics are the main elements of a story.

- **Setting:** the place and time
- **Characters:** people who take part in the action
- **Conflict:** problem people face
- **Sequence of Events:** related moments described in time order

Use narrative techniques, such as dialogue and description, to make the elements of your story come alive for readers.

Planning and Prewriting

Before you draft, discover the narrative you want to tell. Complete the activities to get started.

Discover Your Thinking: Freewrite!

Think of times when you felt good about the way in which you solved a problem. Then, write quickly and freely about those experiences for at least three minutes without stopping.

- Grammar and spelling mistakes are okay. This is just for your eyes.
- When time is up, read what you wrote.
- Mark ideas you find interesting and want to develop more. Write quickly and freely as many times as needed to get all your ideas out. Each time, focus on the ideas you marked the time before.

NOTEBOOK

WRITE IT When did you use your imagination to solve a problem?

⭐ TEKS

10.B.i. Develop drafts into a focused, structured, and coherent piece of writing by organizing with purposeful structure, including an introduction, transitions, coherence within and across paragraphs, and a conclusion.

Structure Your Narrative

 NOTEBOOK

A. Choose a Focus Review the ideas you marked in your freewriting. Which experience is the most meaningful to you?

_____

_____

B. Clarify the Situation List the people involved in the events (the characters), the setting, and the main **conflict.** Also, list strong details you want to make sure to include.

Characters: _____

_____

_____

Setting: _____

_____

_____

Conflict: _____

_____

_____

C. Plan a Structure Plan how you will describe the **sequence of events** so that readers understand the conflict and how you solved it.

I. Beginning Plan how you'll engage your reader. Consider starting with a dramatic moment or the conflict's **inciting incident.**

II. Middle Think about how you'll build the tension till it reaches the **climax.** Keep readers wondering how the conflict will end.

III. End Show how the conflict resolves. Include a reflection, or thoughtful conclusion, about the deeper meaning of the experience.

_____

_____

_____

_____

_____

_____

_____

CONFLICT

The **conflict,** or problem you face in your narrative, is the force that makes everything happen. Clarify the conflict by writing it in one sentence. For example, "My bike got a flat tire while I was riding on a deserted road."

SEQUENCE OF EVENTS

The **sequence of events** should show how the conflict begins, gets more intense, and ends.

- **Inciting Incident:** event that makes people aware of the conflict
- **Rising Action:** events show how the conflict gets more intense
- **Climax:** point at which the conflict is most intense
- **Falling Action:** events in which the conflict gets less intense
- **Resolution:** point at which the conflict is over

As you write, show readers how you reacted to the conflict. Include details about what you saw, heard, felt, thought, said, and did.

Drafting

Apply the planning work you've done so far to write a first draft. Start with the beginning, which should grab readers' attention.

Read Like a Writer

Reread the first few paragraphs of the Mentor Text. Mark elements you think engage readers' interest. One observation has been done for you.

MENTOR TEXT

from Wagon Train at Dusk

"Sometimes you just have to laugh,"I tell my daughter, who is having an especially bad day. She's lost her favorite bracelet, she turned in the wrong homework assignment, and she just found out she would be playing Marshmallow #2 in the class play.

"Oh, you wouldn't understand,"Sarah says, sulkily.

I ask her if I've ever told her the story of the diorama.

"Yes, Dad. More than once,"she says.

That doesn't stop me."When I was in the sixth grade,"I say in my storyteller's voice...

> The narrative starts with dialogue, which places readers in the center of the action.

> Which details in the text grab your attention? Mark them.

📓 **NOTEBOOK**

WRITE IT Write your beginning. Follow the Mentor Text structure by using dialogue to engage readers' interest.

_____

_____

_____

_____

_____

_____

_____

_____

_____

_____

DEPTH OF THOUGHT

As you draft the rest of your narrative, use details to make your writing vivid and precise.

- **Characters** Describe how people look and act. Let them speak for themselves in dialogue.

- **Setting** Use details related to sight, sound, smell, and touch to help readers picture places in your story.

- **Development** Create a clear sequence of events. For each new moment or event, start a new paragraph.

 TEKS

10.B.i. Develop drafts into a focused, structured, and coherent piece of writing by developing an engaging idea reflecting depth of thought with specific facts and details.

Create Coherence

In a personal narrative, **narration** is the written voice of the author. **Dialogue** is the spoken words of the author (narrator) and other people. You can use dialogue for different purposes:

- **Develop Conflict** Allow characters to comment on or describe the problem they face.

- **Develop Portrayals** Part of what makes people unique is the way they speak. Show what people in your story say and indicate how they say it.

A **coherent** narrative integrates different elements, such as dialogue and narration, without confusing readers. To create coherence when switching between narration and dialogue, follow the rules shown here.

> **TIP** Dialogue can make the action of your story more vivid and realistic, which will make your reader feel more involved.

Integrate Dialogue with Narration

Rule	Example
Place every word spoken aloud inside quotation marks.	*"I love going to the movies," he said, "especially on a rainy day."*
Set a new paragraph for each new speaker.	*"What a great idea," he said. "Isn't it?" she answered.*
If the dialogue requires punctuation, place it inside the quotation mark.	*"Are you sure about that?" he asked. "I'm positive!" she exclaimed.*
Use a comma to separate dialogue from narration.	*She asked him, "Can this be the last rule we learn for now?"*

📓 NOTEBOOK

WRITE IT Write a paragraph of your narrative and include dialogue. Make sure to punctuate it correctly to create coherence within and across paragraphs.

_____
_____
_____
_____
_____
_____
_____
_____

VARY PUNCTUATION

Use punctuation to show nuances in how people speak.

- An ellipsis (…) can show a person speaking slowly.

EXAMPLE:
"Well…I'm not…I don't really know…how to answer that…"

- A dash (—) can show an interruption.

EXAMPLE:
"It's already 9:00! Did you—"
"Yes! I fed the dogs!"

Revising

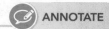 **ANNOTATE**

Now that you have your first draft, revise it to be sure it is interesting and detailed. Check for the following elements:

Clarity: sharpness of your ideas

Development: full descriptions with vivid and precise details

Organization: logical flow of events

Style and Tone: variety of sentences and precision of word choices; a level of formality that suits your audience and purpose

Read Like a Writer

Review the revisions made to the Mentor Text. Then, answer the questions in the white boxes.

MENTOR TEXT

from Wagon Train at Dusk

Sarah pretends she isn't rolling her eyes, but ~~she is and~~ I keep going.

"I wanted it to be great. A diorama to end all dioramas! ~~The greatest diorama ever!~~ I wanted to be famous. I wanted to be on the local news. But what I really wanted was to show up Jorge Nuñez," I say.

"Jorge and I had been in the same class since fourth grade. ~~As soon as I heard Jorge announce that he was making a shoebox diorama of a log cabin, I decided to go one better.~~ We were pretty evenly matched when it came to test scores and homework, but for hands-on projects, there was no one like Jorge. He always came up with these unique creations, beautifully conceived and executed. Jorge's mom and dad were architects, so maybe he had a leg up, but who knows."

Sarah shrugs, *in sympathy—which I take as permission to* ~~so I~~ continue. *"As soon as I heard Jorge announce that he was making a shoebox diorama of a log cabin, I decided to go one better."* ~~"~~I'd create *a fleet of* Conestoga wagons in a circle formation around a campfire *at dusk* with miniature people and ~~some animals~~ *horses and dogs* made of pipe cleaners, and children running around playing hoops. It would be a masterpiece. And that's just how it turned out: a masterpiece! I carried it upstairs to my room and that night ~~when I went to sleep~~, I went to sleep with a smile on my face, *imagining Jorge's reaction.*"

> Why do you think the author deleted this sentence?

> This sentence was moved to a place where it makes more sense.

> Descriptive details make the scene more vivid.

> Why did the writer change "some animals" to "horses and dogs"?

🌐 TEKS

10.C. Revise drafts for clarity, development, organization, style, word choice, and sentence variety.

Take a Closer Look at Your Draft

Now, revise your draft. Use the Revision Guide for Narratives to evaluate and strengthen your personal narrative.

REVISION GUIDE FOR NARRATIVES

EVALUATE	TAKE ACTION
Clarity	
Is the conflict clear?	If the conflict isn't clear, **add** details that show what you, as the main character, want and what is stopping you.
Is the sequence of events clear?	**Number** each event and see if the sequence follows time order. If it doesn't, **rearrange** the sequence in your narrative.
Have you expressed a deeper meaning or point?	If not, **add** sentences that show what you thought and felt. End with a paragraph of reflection.
Development	
Have you shown an inciting incident? Does the conflict clearly intensify and resolve?	**Mark** the inciting incident. Then, mark passages that show how that incident leads to other events. If you see too few marked passages, **add** details that show how the conflict gets worse and then ends.
Organization	
Does the narrative flow from beginning through to the end?	**Add** transition words (such as, *next, then, finally*) to make sure the sequence of events is clear.
Does the conclusion tie up any loose ends?	**Add** details to answer any questions that remain at the end of the narrative.
Style and Tone	
Does dialogue sound realistic and believable?	**Read** the dialogue aloud. If it doesn't sound natural, **say** it in your own words and use them instead.
Are word choices precise and descriptive?	**Scan** your draft for vague words, such as *some, thing, very, many, cute, great,* or *nice.* **Replace** them with precise choices that accurately describe what you want readers to see.
Are sentence types and lengths varied?	If your sentences are too similar (all short or all long) create variety: 1. **Break** a long, confusing sentence into two shorter sentences. 2. **Combine** two short sentences into one longer sentence. 3. **Rewrite** some sentences as questions or exclamations.

Editing

ANNOTATE

Don't let errors weaken the power of your story. Reread your draft and fix mistakes to create a finished narrative.

Read Like a Writer

Look at how the writer of the Mentor Text edited the draft. Then, follow the directions in the white boxes.

MENTOR TEXT

from Wagon Train at Dusk

"Then," I go on, ~~in~~ "*in* the middle of the night I was jolted awake by a ripping sound. My heart stopped. I felt sick. *I knows that sound,* I thought. There was no mistaking what it was—Lucy was demolishing my masterpiece! You couldn't even tell what it was supposed too be! I lay there in a ~~feeling~~ *stupor* of self-pity and the sense that nothing in the world would ever be right again…"

> The writer fixed a punctuation error in the dialogue.

> Find and fix an error in subject-verb agreement.

> The writer chose a more precise word.

> Find and fix a common usage error.

Focus on Sentences

Subject-Verb Agreement Singular subjects take singular verbs. Plural subjects take plural verbs. When a prepositional phrase comes between the subject and the verb, it can make subject-verb agreement harder to identify.

EXAMPLES

Singular Subject and Verb: Mike likes apples.

Plural Subject and Verb: They like apples.

With a Prepositional Phrase:

Incorrect: The apples *on the top* is the reddest.

Correct: The apples *on the top* are the reddest.

> **EDITING TIPS**
> 1. Mark the subject of each sentence.
> 2. Mark the verb of each sentence.
> 3. If the agreement isn't correct, fix it.
> 4. If a prepositional phrase makes it harder to check a sentence's subject-verb agreement, read the sentence without the phrase.

PRACTICE Fix the subject-verb agreement in this paragraph. Then, check your own draft for correctness.

Dakota wait at the edge of the ocean. *Soon,* she think, *the waves will swell.*

Her surfboard with its colorful stripes sit beside her. She begin pulling on

her wetsuit when a sudden tap on her shoulder distract her.

⊕ TEKS

10.D. Edit drafts using standard English conventions, including: **10.D.iv.** Prepositions and prepositional phrases and their influence on subject-verb agreement; **10.D.ix.** Correct spelling, including commonly confused terms such as *its/it's, affect/effect, there/their/they're,* and *to/two/too.*
10.E. Publish written work for appropriate audiences.

Focus on Spelling and Punctuation

Spelling: Commonly Confused Words Words that sound the same but have different meanings and spellings are called **homophones.** They are often confused. Make sure your narrative is free of these common errors.

- *Its / It's* *Its* shows possession. *It's* is a contraction for *it is*.
  EXAMPLE: The bear forgot *its* blanket. *It's* cold in the woods during the winter.

- *To/two/too* *To* indicates a direction. *Two* is the number after *one*. *Too* means "also."
  EXAMPLE: Lisa is going *to* the mall again. She has been there *two* times. She's going to the movie theater, *too*.

Punctuation: Dialogue Make sure you have punctuated dialogue correctly throughout your narrative.

- Use a comma to set off dialogue from narration.
  EXAMPLE: He yelled, "I love tigers!"

- A line of dialogue may be a complete sentence, which you would normally end with a period. If the dialogue is part of a sentence that includes narration, replace the period with a comma.
  EXAMPLE: "I love tigers," he admitted.

- If dialogue ends with a question mark or an exclamation point, place the punctuation inside the quotation marks.
  EXAMPLE: "Is there any animal better than a tiger?" he asked.

PRACTICE In the following sentences, correct spelling and punctuation errors. Then, check your own draft for correctness.

1. "Wagon trains", he told her, "weren't actually trains."

2. "I told the story too my teacher." he said.

3. "Did the dog eat your diorama, to"? she asked.

Publishing and Presenting

Make It Multimodal

Share your narrative with your class or school community. Choose one of these two options:

OPTION 1 Participate in an open mic storytelling event. Read your narrative to the class and listen to those of your classmates.

OPTION 2 Work with a partner to make videos based on your narratives. Include music and images. Post your videos to a class or school web site.

Essential Question

What are some of the challenges and triumphs of growing up?

Growing up isn't always easy. Some challenges are difficult to overcome, but learning how to persevere through hardships can be a triumph in itself. It is a triumph because every new experience is a lesson learned. You will work in a group to continue your exploration of some of these challenges and triumphs.

 VIDEO

 INTERACTIVITY

Peer-Group Learning Strategies

Throughout your life, in school, in your community, and in your career, you will continue to learn and work with others.

Review these strategies and the actions you can take to practice them as you work in small groups. Add ideas of your own for each category. Use these strategies during Peer-Group Learning.

STRATEGY	MY PEER-GROUP ACTION PLAN
Prepare • Complete your assignments so that you are prepared for group work. • Take notes on your reading so that you can share ideas with others in your group.	
Participate fully • Make eye contact to signal that you are paying attention. • Use text evidence when making a point.	
Support others • Build off ideas from others in your group. • Ask others who have not yet spoken to do so.	
Clarify • Paraphrase the ideas of others to be sure that your understanding is correct. • Ask follow-up questions.	

CONTENTS

PERFORMANCE TASK: SPEAKING AND LISTENING

Present a Nonfiction Narrative

The peer-group readings present different perspectives on the challenges of growing up. After reading, your group will plan and deliver a retelling of the childhood experiences explored in one of the selections.

Working as a Group

 NOTEBOOK

1. Take a Position
Discuss the following question with your group:

> What ideas and experiences about growing up can young people share with one another?

As you take turns sharing your ideas, be sure to provide reasons and examples. After all group members have shared, note where you agree and disagree, and discuss some of the reasons why.

2. List Your Rules
As a group, decide on the rules that you will follow as you work together. Elicit, or invite, suggestions from everyone in the group and consider which ones will help you the most. Two samples are provided. Add two more that make sense for your group.

- Everyone should participate in group discussions.
- People should not interrupt.

_____

_____

3. Apply the Rules
Share what you have learned about growing up. Make sure each person in the group contributes. Take notes and be prepared to share with the class one thing that you heard from another member of your group.

4. Name Your Group
Choose a name that reflects the unit topic.

Our group's name: _____

5. Create a Communication Plan
Decide how you want to communicate with one another. For example, you might use online collaboration tools, email, or instant messaging.

Our group's plan:

_____

_____

 TEKS

1.D. Participate in student-led discussions by eliciting and considering suggestions from other group members, taking notes, and identifying points of agreement and disagreement.

6.C. Use text evidence to support an appropriate response.

Making a Schedule

First, find out the due dates for the Peer-Group activities. Then, preview the texts and activities with your group and make a schedule for completing the tasks.

SELECTION	ACTIVITIES	DUE DATE
from Bad Boy		
The Moth Presents: Aleeza Kazmi		
Prince Francis		
The Sound of Summer Running		

Using Text Evidence

When you respond to literature, you use text evidence to support your ideas. Apply these tips to choose the right text evidence for any purpose.

Understand the Question: Different kinds of questions call for different kinds of evidence. For example, if you are *analyzing,* you are looking for specific details. If you are *interpreting,* you are looking for specific details that connect to build a larger meaning.

Notice Key Details: Notice details that stand out and make you feel strongly about a character or an idea. These details are probably important and may become evidence for your position or interpretation.

Evaluate Your Choices: The evidence you use should clearly relate to the question you are answering. For example, if a question asks about a character's motivations, choose evidence that shows *why* he or she felt, thought, and acted a certain way. Other details may be interesting, but are not relevant.

Use strong and effective text evidence to support your responses as you read, discuss, and write about the selections.

from BAD BOY

The selection you are about to read is an excerpt from a memoir.

Reading Memoirs

A **memoir** is a nonfiction narrative, or true story, in which the author writes about a specific aspect of his or her life.

MEMOIR

Author's Purpose
- ➲ to share memories and insights about an experience, moment, or period of time

Characteristics
- ➲ usually written from a first-person point of view
- ➲ conveys a controlling idea that is supported by evidence
- ➲ may include dialogue or other fiction-like storytelling elements
- ➲ shares the innermost thoughts and feelings of the author
- ➲ features characters who are real people and settings that are real places

Structure
- ➲ often, though not always, presents events in chronological, or time order

Take a Minute!

 NOTEBOOK

WRITE IT With a partner, discuss this question: Would you rather tell your own life story or have someone else tell it? Give reasons for your response. Then, use the space here to record your response.

✪ TEKS
8.D.i. Analyze characteristics and structural elements of informational text, including the controlling idea or thesis with supporting evidence.

Genre / Text Elements

Controlling Idea and Supporting Evidence The **controlling idea** is the message expressed in a work of nonfiction. Most memoir writers don't just state a controlling idea. Instead, they use **evidence** from their experiences to build meaning. This evidence appears in various ways:

- as **anecdotes**, or brief stories

- as **details** and **descriptions** of people, places, and feelings

- as **dialogue**, or conversations

- as **reflections**, thoughts, and questions

> **TIP:** A controlling idea is not the same as a topic. A topic is the "what;" a controlling idea is "what does it mean?"

Consider how the details in these two passages create different controlling ideas.

PASSAGE 1	PASSAGE 2
My first <u>challenge</u> came when I was twelve as a trip to the store to buy shallots for my mom. I <u>tried to look cool</u>, like the <u>girl I wanted to be</u>. But, <u>inside I was quaking</u>: *What on Earth are shallots?*	I <u>wanted to prove</u> that I could take care of myself. So, I went to the store to buy food (spinach) that I <u>knew I'd never eat</u>. A <u>child no more!</u> I'd soon find out <u>I was wrong.</u>
Controlling Idea: Taking on a new responsibility can be scary.	**Controlling Idea:** As we grow up, we may fool ourselves at times.

 NOTEBOOK

PRACTICE Work on your own to read the passage and answer the questions.

My sister and I spent hours looking at photos of young Cara. "Remember how she loved that dress?" Or, "She was such a great swimmer, but look at that crazy bathing cap!" There were photos of her made-up holidays: Curly Hair Day! Banjo Day! Great-aunt, best friend, gone now forever. Would we ever stop missing her?

1. What is the topic of the passage?

2. What is the controlling idea? Cite two pieces of evidence from the passage that support your answer.

By the age of five, **Walter Dean Myers** (1937–2014) was reading daily newspapers. Despite this impressive start with words, Myers did not think writing would be his career. However, in his twenties, he won a writing contest and went on to find success as an author of young adult books. Myers often wrote about his African American heritage and his life growing up in Harlem, a part of New York City.

from Bad Boy

Concept Vocabulary

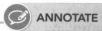 ANNOTATE

As you read the excerpt from *Bad Boy*, you will encounter these words.

respected	desperate	disgusted

Context Clues The **context** of a word is the other words and phrases that appear close to it in a text. Clues in the context can help you figure out word meanings.

Definition context clues provide a word's meaning—its definition—right in the text.

EXAMPLE Marcus *cherishes* his baseball collection, <u>valuing it above everything else he owns</u>.

Analysis: *Cherishes* is a verb that means "loves; prizes, or values" as the context clue shows.

PRACTICE As you read the excerpt from *Bad Boy*, study the context to clarify the meanings of unfamiliar words. Mark your observations in the open space next to the text.

Comprehension Strategy

 ANNOTATE

Make Connections

When you **make connections to society** while reading, you look for relationships between ideas in a text and your experiences of the larger world. For example, you might consider how details relate to local or national problems.

EXAMPLE

Here is an example of how you might make connections to society while reading the excerpt from *Bad Boy*.

Passage: *I could never have afforded to buy the books and was pleased to have the library with its free supply.*

Connection to Society: I have noticed that libraries are important to many people, but especially to those who have little money.

PRACTICE As you read, note connections between story events and your prior experience in society. Jot down your thoughts in the open space next to the text.

TEKS

2.B. Use context such as definition, analogy, and examples to clarify the meaning of words.

5.E. Make connections to personal experiences, ideas in other texts, and society.

from **Bad Boy**

Walter Dean Myers

BACKGROUND

In his memoir, Walter Dean Myers describes his childhood growing up in Harlem, New York, in the 1940s and 1950s. This excerpt takes place when Myers is in elementary school. Earlier in the chapter, his teacher, Mrs. Conway, lent him books to read after noticing his interest in reading.

 AUDIO

ANNOTATE

1   There were two categories of friends in my life: those with whom I played ball and everyone else. Athletes were highly **respected** in the black community, and boys my age were encouraged to play some sport. I loved playing ball. I would play basketball in the mornings with the boys who were just reaching their teens, and then stoop ball or punchball on the block with boys my age. Sometimes Eric and I would go down to the courts on Riverside Drive and play there. And I was a bad, bad loser. Most of my prayers, when they weren't for the Dodgers,[1] were quick ones in the middle of a game, asking God to let me win. I liked other sports as well and even followed the New York Rangers hockey team in the papers for a while until I found out that all the references to ice meant just that, that they were skating on ice. There wasn't any ice to skate on in Harlem, so I gave up hockey.

2   With school out and me not having access to Mrs. Conway's cache[2] of books, I rediscovered the George Bruce Branch of the public library on 125th Street. Sometimes on rainy days I would sit

Mark context clues or indicate another strategy you used that helped you determine meaning.

respected (rih SPEHK tihd) *adj.*

MEANING:

---

1. **Dodgers** Brooklyn Dodgers, an American professional baseball team, which moved to Los Angeles, California, after the 1957 season.
2. **cache** (kash) *n.* hidden supply.

© Pearson Education, Inc., or its affiliates. All rights reserved.

from Bad Boy **67**

in the library and read. The librarians always suggested books that were too young for me, but I still went on a regular basis. I could never have afforded to buy the books and was pleased to have the library with its free supply.

3   Being a boy meant to me that I was not particularly like girls. Most of the girls I knew couldn't play ball, and that excluded them from most of what I wanted to do with my life. Dorothy Dodson, daughter of the Wicked Witch,[3] read books, and I knew she did, but she couldn't stand me and was more than happy to tell me so on a number of occasions. Sometimes I would see other children on the trolley with books under their arms and suspected that they were like me somehow. I felt a connection with these readers but didn't know what the connection was. I knew there were things going on in my head, a fantasy life, that somehow corresponded to the books I read. I also felt a kind of comfort with books that I did not experience when I was away from them. Away from books I was, at times, almost **desperate** to fill up the spaces of my life. Books filled those spaces for me.

Mark context clues or indicate another strategy you used that helped you determine meaning.

desperate (DEHS puhr iht) *adj.*

MEANING:

4   As much as I enjoyed reading, in the world in which I was living it had to be a secret vice.[4] When I brought a book home from the library, I would sometimes run into older kids who would tease me about my reading. It was, they made it clear, not what boys did. And though by now I was fighting older boys and didn't mind that one bit, for some reason I didn't want to fight about books. Books were special and said something about me that I didn't want to reveal. I began taking a brown paper bag to the library to bring my books home in.

5   That year I learned that being a boy meant that I was supposed to do certain things and act in a certain way. I was very comfortable being a boy, but there were times when the role was uncomfortable. We often played ball in the church gym, and one rainy day, along with my brother Mickey and some of "my guys," I went to the gym, only to find a bevy of girls exercising on one half of the court. We wanted to run a full-court game, so we directed a few nasty remarks to the other side of the small gym. Then we saw that the girls were doing some kind of dance, so we imitated them, cracking ourselves up.

6   When the girls had finished their dancing, they went through some stretching exercises. A teenager, Lorelle Henry, was leading the group, and she was pretty, so we sent a few woo-woos her way.

7   "I bet you guys can't even do these stretching exercises," Lorelle challenged.

8   We scoffed, as expected.

9   "If you can do these exercises, we'll get off the court," Lorelle said. "If not, you go through the whole dance routine with us."

---

3. **Wicked Witch** Walter's nickname for Mrs. Dodson, a neighbor he dislikes.
4. **vice** (vys) *n.* bad habit.

10   It was a way to get rid of the girls, and we went over to do the exercises. Not one of us was limber enough to do the stretching exercises, and soon we were all trying to look as **disgusted** as we could while we hopped around the floor to the music.

11   They danced to music as a poem was being read. I liked the poem, which turned out to be "The Creation" by James Weldon Johnson. I liked dancing, too, but I had to pretend that I didn't like it. No big deal. I was already keeping reading and writing poems a secret; I would just add dancing.

BUILD INSIGHT

Response

1. Personal Connections If young Myers were your friend, what advice would you give him? Explain.

Comprehension

2. Strategy: Make Connections to Society (a) Cite one connection to society you made as you read this memoir. **(b)** In what ways was this strategy useful? Explain.

Analysis and Discussion

3. (a) Make Inferences Why do you think Myers pretends he doesn't like dancing? **(b) Draw Conclusions** What do you think it was like to grow up in Myers's neighborhood? Explain.

4. (a) Distinguish In young Myers's mind, which interests are acceptable and which are not? **(b) Analyze** Explain why Myers feels that he has to keep so many of his interests a secret.

5. (a) Hypothesize If Myers had been honest about his interests, how might his childhood have been different? **(b) Make a Judgment** Do you agree with Myers' decision to hide his passion for reading? Explain.

6. Get Ready for Close Reading Choose a passage from the text that you find especially interesting. You'll discuss the passage with your group during Close-Read activities.

EQ Notes What are some of the challenges and triumphs of growing up?

What ideas about growing up are suggested by this excerpt? Go to your Essential Question Notes and record your observations and thoughts about the excerpt from *Bad Boy*.

NOTEBOOK

Work on your own to answer the questions in your notebook. Use text evidence to support your responses.

WORKING AS A GROUP
Discuss your responses to the Analysis and Discussion questions with your group.

As you exchange ideas, practice using routine words, such as *conflict, analyze, similar,* and *different.*

 TEKS
5.E. Make connections to personal experiences, ideas in other texts, and society.

6.G. Discuss and write about the explicit or implicit meanings of text.

from BAD BOY

Close Read

ANNOTATE

PRACTICE Complete the following activities. Use text evidence to support your responses.

1. **Present and Discuss** With your group, share the passages from the memoir that you found especially interesting. Discuss what you notice, the questions you have, and the conclusions you reach. For example, you might focus on the following passages:

   • Paragraph 1: Discuss young Myers's idea of "categories." Who and what does he categorize in this paragraph? Where else in the excerpt does he categorize people or activities?

   • Paragraph 11: Discuss the use of the first-person point of view. How might your understanding of young Myers be different if his story had been told by someone else?

2. **Reflect on Your Learning** What new ideas or insights did you uncover during your second reading of the text?

WORD NETWORK

Add words related to the idea of growing up from the text to your Word Network.

NOTEBOOK

LANGUAGE STUDY

Concept Vocabulary

Why These Words? The vocabulary words are related.

| respected | desperate | disgusted |

1. With your group, determine what the words have in common. Write your ideas.

2. Add another word that fits the category: _____

3. Use each vocabulary word in a sentence. Include context clues that hint at each word's meaning.

Word Study

Latin Root: -spec- The word *respected* is formed from the Latin prefix *re-*, which means "back," and the Latin root *-spec-*, which means "look" or "see." The root meaning suggests that when you *respect* someone, you *see* him or her in a new way. Use a digital dictionary to find two other words formed from the root *-spec-*. Explain how each word involves the idea of seeing.

⚙ TEKS
2.A. Use print or digital resources to determine the meaning, syllabication, pronunciation, word origin, and part of speech.

2.C. Determine the meaning and usage of grade-level academic English words derived from Greek and Latin roots such as *mis/mit, bene, man, vac, scrib/script,* and *jur/jus*.

8.D.i. Analyze characteristics and structural elements of informational text, including the controlling idea or thesis with supporting evidence.

Genre / Text Elements

Controlling Idea and Supporting Evidence The **controlling idea** of an informational text is the main message that the author wants readers to understand. Sometimes the controlling idea is stated directly. However, in narrative nonfiction like a memoir, the controlling idea is usually suggested, not stated explicitly. To identify the controlling idea, readers examine **supporting evidence** or details and draw a conclusion.

> **TIP:** A topic can be stated in a word or phrase ("change"). A controlling idea must be stated in a sentence ("Change can be difficult.")

 NOTEBOOK

 INTERACTIVITY

PRACTICE Work with your group to complete the activity and answer the questions.

1. Connect Explain how each detail listed in the chart contributes to the controlling idea in *Bad Boy*—that boys are often expected to behave in certain ways.

EVIDENCE	HOW IT SUPPORTS THE CONTROLLING IDEA
...boys my age were encouraged to play some sport.	
Being a boy meant to me that I was not particularly like girls.	
It was, they made it clear, not what boys did.	
I was very comfortable being a boy, but there were times when the role was uncomfortable.	

2. Evaluate Which detail in the chart do you think most effectively supports the controlling idea? Explain.

3. Analyze Find two more details in the memoir that support the controlling idea. Explain each choice.

4. Extend If you were writing a text with the same controlling idea as in *Bad Boy*, what evidence from today's world would you use as support?

from BAD BOY

Conventions

Pronoun Case **Pronouns** are words that can replace nouns in a text. They can also replace other pronouns. **Pronoun case** is the form a pronoun takes that shows how it is being used in a sentence.

PRONOUN CASE	FUNCTION	PRONOUNS	EXAMPLES FROM *BAD BOY*
Subjective	names the subject of a verb	*I, you, he, she, it, we, they*	**We** scoffed **They** danced
Objective	names the object of a verb or preposition	*me, you, him, her, it, us, them*	so we imitated **them** (*Imitated* is the verb; *them* is the object.) Books filled those spaces for **me**. (*For* is the preposition; *me* is the object.)
Possessive	shows ownership	*my, mine, your, yours, his, her, hers, its, our, ours, their, theirs*	to bring **my** books sent a few woo-woos **her** way

 ANNOTATE

 NOTEBOOK

READ IT Mark the pronoun(s) in each passage. Label the case of each pronoun.

1. The girls I knew couldn't play ball.

2. The books they suggested were too young for me.

3. I knew there were things going on in my head.

4. Older kids would tease me about my reading.

WRITE IT Edit the following paragraph. Replace the underlined nouns with appropriate pronouns. Then, write two more sentences of your own using correct pronouns.

Maya heard about a song writing competition. Maya decided to perform a song Maya had written with friends. When Maya told Maya's friends, Maya's friends shocked Maya. Maya's friends couldn't go, so Maya's friends wanted Maya to stay home, too. Maya's friends said they didn't trust Maya to give Maya's friends credit. Maya later wrote a new song, which Maya called "Friends?"

 TEKS

6.E. Interact with sources in meaningful ways such as notetaking, annotating, freewriting, or illustrating.

10.D.v. Edit drafts using standard English conventions, including pronouns, including relative.

Composition

When you write a **response to literature** you explain what a text made you think about, and how the author's ideas affected you as a reader.

Write a **response to literature,** focusing on one of these key ideas expressed in *Bad Boy*:

○ Do people's characters—the qualities that make them who they are—change depending on who they are with?

○ Can people have different but equally true parts of their personalities?

Include details and examples from the text as well as your own thoughts and insights. Work independently to write and edit your response. Then, share your favorite ideas with your group.

Draft Your Response Balance supporting evidence from *Bad Boy* with your own observations and ideas.

Use Conventions for Clarity You have already learned about pronoun case. Make sure you also apply **pronoun-antecedent agreement**. The word a pronoun stands for, or refers to, is the **antecedent**. Pronouns must agree with, or match, their antecedents in number and person.

Pronoun-Antecedent Agreement: Number and Person

- Number can be singular (one person or thing) or plural (two or more people or things).

Singular: *Mrs. Conway* understood <u>her</u> students.
Plural: Other *boys* liked sports, but *they* did not care for books.

- Person tells to whom or what a pronoun refers.

First person: the person speaking
Example: *Jill* and *I* like to dance, but *we* can't dance well.

Second person: the person being spoken to
Example: *Jules*, what is *your* favorite thing to do?

Third person: person, place or thing being spoken about
Example: *Mickey* was laughing, but *he* should have kept quiet.

EQ Notes Before moving on to a new selection, go to your Essential Question Notes and record any additional thoughts or observations you may have about the excerpt from *Bad Boy*.

Edit Your Response Review your draft for spelling, punctuation, and grammatical errors. Focus especially on making sure your use of pronoun-antecedent agreement is correct.

At the time she told this story, **Aleeza Kazmi** was a student at the Beacon School in New York City. She is currently a student at Stony Brook University, where she is majoring in journalism and political science.

The Moth Presents:
Aleeza Kazmi

Media Vocabulary

These words will be useful to you as you analyze, discuss, and write about multimodal texts, such as an oral storytelling video.

performance: entertainment presented before an audience	• Storytelling is the oldest form of performance art. • A storyteller can perform live or on a recording, from notes or without notes. • Stories can be rehearsed or improvised.
personal account: account of a personal experience, told from the first-person point of view	• A personal account can be written, performed live, or recorded. • When telling about a personal experience in front of a live audience, the storyteller (and audience) can get caught up in emotion.
volume and pacing: softness or loudness of one's voice and the rate at which one speaks (e.g., quickly or slowly)	• A speaker may vary the volume of his or her voice to convey emotion and to keep the audience's attention. • A speaker may also change his or her pacing to emphasize ideas or express emotion.

Comprehension Strategy   NOTEBOOK

Listen Actively

To get the most out of a spoken-word performance like the one shown in this video, **listen actively** to interpret the speaker's message. This means you pay close attention, noting important details that develop the speaker's ideas.

Here are some ways to listen actively in order to interpret the message of a spoken-word performance:

• Listen for details that show why the speaker is sharing the information—what makes it important.
• Listen for words and phrases that show the speaker's feelings.
• Listen for words and phrases that make different kinds of connections, such as cause-and-effect or similarity-and-difference.
• If necessary, pause the video and use a dictionary to clarify the meanings of any words you don't know.

PRACTICE As you watch this video, listen actively. Use the Notes section to jot down key ideas while keeping your attention on the speaker.

⊕ TEKS

1.A. Listen actively to interpret a message, ask clarifying questions, and respond appropriately.

8.F. Analyze characteristics of multimodal and digital texts.

The Moth Presents: Aleeza Kazmi

BACKGROUND

The Moth is a nonprofit organization devoted to the art and craft of storytelling. Established in 1997, The Moth has featured thousands of stories that showcase a wide range of human experiences. The Moth's storytellers present their narratives live and without notes to standing-room-only crowds throughout the world. Each of The Moth's shows centers around a different theme, which the featured storytellers explore in distinct, and often unexpected, ways. Some of the storytellers are experienced in the art and craft of narration, whereas others have never told a story in performance before. The stories featured in The Moth's shows are recorded for broadcast and can be heard on many National Public Radio radio stations.

AUDIO

NOTEBOOK

TAKE NOTES As you listen, take notes about ideas that interest you and questions you have.

Work on your own to answer the questions in your notebook. Use text evidence to support your responses.

Response

1. Personal Connections What did you find most interesting about Aleeza Kazmi's experience? Explain.

Comprehension

2. (a) What did Miss Harrington do that upset Aleeza? **(b)** How does Aleeza finally take a stand?

3. Strategy: Listen Actively (a) Why do the experiences Kazmi relates in this video matter to her? **(b)** How did listening actively help you better appreciate her message?

WORKING AS A GROUP

Discuss your responses to the Analysis and Discussion questions with your group.

If necessary, revise your original answers to reflect what you learn from your discussion.

Analysis and Discussion

4. (a) Analyze Why does using the broken brown crayon make Aleeza feel so upset? **(b) Interpret** What might the crayon symbolize, or represent, to her?

5. (a) Distinguish How would you describe Kazmi's manner of speaking? For example, is it formal or informal, sincere or insincere? Explain. **(b) Analyze** How does her manner of speaking help viewers understand her experience and message? Explain.

6. Essential Question: *What are some of the challenges and triumphs of growing up?* What have you learned about the challenges and triumphs of growing up from this video?

MEDIA VOCABULARY

Use these words as you discuss and write about the video.

performance
personal account
volume and pacing

Close Review

Watch the video again. As you watch, take notes about important details and jot down your observations. Note time codes so you can find information later. Then, write a question and your conclusion. Share your notes and observations with your group.

MY QUESTION:

MY CONCLUSION:

 TEKS
5.E. Make connections to personal experiences, ideas in other texts, and society.

6.F. Respond using newly acquired vocabulary as appropriate.

8.F. Analyze characteristics of multimodal and digital texts.

Speaking and Listening

A **group discussion** is a conversation among three or more people.

THE MOTH PRESENTS:
ALEEZA KAZMI

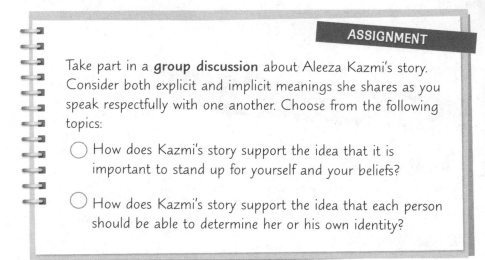

ASSIGNMENT

Take part in a **group discussion** about Aleeza Kazmi's story. Consider both explicit and implicit meanings she shares as you speak respectfully with one another. Choose from the following topics:

○ How does Kazmi's story support the idea that it is important to stand up for yourself and your beliefs?

○ How does Kazmi's story support the idea that each person should be able to determine her or his own identity?

Prepare for the Discussion Watch the video again, and take notes about details that relate to the topic you chose:

- Note details that relate to **explicit meanings**. These are insights Kazmi states directly.
- Note details that relate to **implicit meanings**. These are insights that Kazmi suggests through details but doesn't state directly.
- Jot down details that seem interesting even if you're not sure why. Use these details to formulate questions during the discussion.

Conduct the Discussion Listen closely to your group members and share your ideas in a respectful way.

- Use your notes to remind yourself of points you want to raise.
- Note where you agree and disagree with others. Do you agree for the same or different reasons? What are the reasons you disagree?
- Offer and accept suggestions that clarify ideas.

Use these sentence frames as a guide for responding appropriately.

TIP: Find implicit meanings by thinking about details. Look for positive or negative words, descriptions, and dialogue that hint at bigger ideas.

EQ Notes Before moving on to a new selection, go to your Essential Question Notes and record what you learned from the video.

SENTENCE FRAMES FOR GROUP DISCUSSION

Could you explain what you mean by _____?

I agree with what you said about _____, but I'm not sure about _____. Could you go into that some more?

Why do you think that about _____?

TEKS

1.A. Listen actively to interpret a message, ask clarifying questions, and respond appropriately.

1.D. Participate in student-led discussions by eliciting and considering suggestions from other group members, taking notes, and identifying points of agreement and disagreement.

6.G. Discuss and write about the explicit or implicit meanings of text.

Fiction

A **short story** is a brief work of fiction. A **realistic short story** features characters and situations like those in real life but is still a work of the writer's imagination.

PRINCE FRANCIS

THE SOUND OF SUMMER RUNNING

REALISTIC SHORT STORY

Author's Purpose
➔ to tell a brief story that entertains while providing an insight about life

Characteristics
➔ settings that seem like those one could experience in real life

➔ characters that seem like real people

➔ conflicts, or problems, like those people actually face

➔ a narrator that tells the story using a specific point of view

➔ descriptions of settings, scenes, and characters

➔ dialogue (words characters speak) that sounds natural

Structure
➔ a series of related events (the plot) that could actually happen

© Pearson Education, Inc., or its affiliates. All rights reserved.

⬡ TEKS
8.A. Demonstrate knowledge of literary genres such as realistic fiction, adventure stories, historical fiction, mysteries, humor, and myths.

9.E. Identify the use of literary devices, including omniscient and limited point of view, to achieve a specific purpose.

Take a Minute!

 NOTEBOOK

FIND IT With a partner, list two examples of realistic stories you have read. You can also consider TV shows or movies. What qualities do these stories have that make them seem like real life?

Genre / Text Elements

Narrative Point of View and Purpose A **narrator** is the voice that tells a story. The narrator's point of view is the perspective from which the story is told. There are three basic types of point of view.

NARRATIVE POINTS OF VIEW		
FIRST PERSON	**THIRD-PERSON LIMITED**	**THIRD-PERSON OMNISCIENT**
narrator is a character in the story	narrator is a voice outside the story and not a character	narrator is an all-knowing observer and not a character
reader sees through the narrator's eyes	reader sees through one character's eyes	reader sees through multiple characters' eyes
uses first-person pronouns (*I, me, mine*) to refer to him- or herself	uses third-person pronouns (*he, she, his, her*) to refer to all characters	uses third-person pronouns to refer to all characters

An author may choose a specific point of view to achieve a particular purpose. For example, he or she may want to emphasize one character's experience over others (first-person or third-person limited) or show how a situation affects a larger group of people (omniscient.)

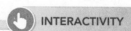 INTERACTIVITY

PRACTICE Work with your group to complete the activity and answer the question.

1. Identify the point of view used in each passage. Explain your thinking.

PASSAGE	POINT OF VIEW/EXPLANATION
I blame the apple core left on the cafeteria floor. When I slipped on it, I went down hard. My tray clattered and my lunch splattered. It seemed like time had stopped until I heard Sara's voice.	
Abel didn't see the apple core. When he fell, it hurt. As his tray clattered and his lunch splattered, it seemed to Abel that time had stopped. Then, he heard Sara's voice.	
Abel didn't see the apple core. As he fell, he imagined how foolish he looked. His tray clattered and his lunch splattered. Sara got hit with the soup. "Abel, you okay?" she said. "My new boots!" she thought.	

2. Discuss the different purpose each point of view serves. How does each one affect what readers know?

PRINCE FRANCIS

Compare Fiction

In this lesson, you will read and compare two realistic short stories. The stories feature similar main characters but use different points of view.

THE SOUND OF SUMMER RUNNING

About the Author

Roddy Doyle (b. 1958) is an Irish novelist, dramatist, and screenwriter best known for his realistic depictions of Irish working-class life. Doyle spent several years teaching English and geography before turning to full-time writing. Doyle is the author of ten novels for adults, seven books for children, seven plays and screenplays, and dozens of short stories. In 1993 Doyle won the Booker Prize for his novel, *Paddy Clarke Ha Ha Ha.*

Prince Francis

Concept Vocabulary

 ANNOTATE

As you read the short story, you will encounter these words.

envied	malice	admired

Print Resources A **dictionary** provides a great deal of information about words. A typical entry includes the word's part of speech, syllabication, and pronunciation. It also provides a word's definitions and history. Consider the example.

EXAMPLE

This entry shows that *agile* is an adjective with two syllables that can be pronounced in two different ways. It comes from the Latin word for "swift." Find and mark the definition.

agile (AJ uhl; AJ yl) *adj.,* [L. *agilis,* swift], able to move quickly and easily

PRACTICE As you read, use a print dictionary to determine meanings and other information about unfamiliar words.

Comprehension Strategy

 ANNOTATE

Make Inferences

An **inference** is a guess you make about unstated information in a text. To make inferences, connect details in a text with what you know about people. Use that combination of information to better understand what you read.

EXAMPLE PASSAGE

"All right," said Sir. *"Ciúnas."*

Francis knew that *ciúnas* meant "quiet" in Irish. He knew some other Irish words too.

Possible Inference: Francis is new to Ireland and has a lot to learn.

PRACTICE As you read "Prince Francis," write your inferences next to the text. Mark the text evidence that supports each one.

 TEKS

2.A. Use print or digital resources to determine the meaning, syllabication, pronunciation, word origin, and part of speech.

5.F. Make inferences and use evidence to support understanding.

Prince Francis

Roddy Doyle

BACKGROUND

This story comes from an anthology of short stories for young people, *Free? Stories About Human Rights*, which celebrates the Universal Declaration of Human Rights. Each story focuses on a different article, or statement, that is part of this important United Nations document. In this story, a child who had to leave his home in Africa hopes to make real friends in Ireland, where he now lives.

AUDIO

ANNOTATE

1   It was very exciting. The whole class was going to be interviewed, as if they were on television. In fact, they were on television.

2   The camera was in position, at the top of the classroom. Daragh was the cameraman.

3   Francis **envied** Daragh. He had wanted to be the cameraman. He had put his hand up. "Sir! Sir! Sir, me!" But Sir had chosen Daragh.

4   That was OK. Francis didn't really mind. He liked Daragh.

5   "All right," said Sir. "*Ciúnas.*"

6   Francis knew that *ciúnas* meant "quiet" in Irish. He knew some other Irish words too. *Buachaill* meant "boy." And *leithreas* meant "toilet."

7   "We're all set," said Sir. "Where's our first celebrity?"

8   They laughed and looked at one another. This was going to be fun.

9   One of the girls, Alice, was the interviewer. She was wearing a black dress that had once belonged to her grandmother, and black eyeshadow that made her blink. She had a clipboard on her lap, with her questions.

10   "Kevin," said Sir. "You're first."

Use a print dictionary, or indicate another strategy you used that helped you determine meaning.

envied (EHN veed) *v.*

MEANING:

11   Kevin went up to the top of the classroom and sat in the chair beside Alice.

12   "How's it going, Alice?" he said.

13   They laughed. Alice blinked.

14   "OK," said Sir. "Daragh, are we rolling?"

15   Daragh nodded. "Yes, sir."

16   "Good man," said Sir. "And . . ."

17   "Action!" shouted the rest of the class.

18   "Good evening," said Alice into the camera. "And welcome to *Back Chat*. My name is Alice and this is my first guest."

19   She was very good, although her blinking was quite strange to look at. It was almost as if she were trying to swim, but using her eyelids instead of her arms.

20   "What's your name?" she asked.

21   "Kevvo," said Kevin.

22   "And where are you from?"

23   "Here," said Kevin.

24   "My goodness," said Alice. "You were born in this classroom?"

25   "No way," said Kevin. "That'd be stupid."

26   Everyone laughed. Sir was laughing, too.

27   "Where were you born, then, Mister Kevvo?"

28   "Outside," said Kevin. "I mean, down the road. I mean—I don't know. In a hospital."

29   "And what are your interests, Kevvo?"

30   "Football."

31   "And?"

32 "GAA."

33 "*Gaah*?" said Alice. "What is *gaah*?"

34 "Gaelic[1] football," said Kevin.

35   Francis played on the same team as Kevin. He had joined the team when he came to the school, four years ago, when he was seven. He remembered he had been very surprised the first time he'd played, when one of the boys picked up the ball. Handling the ball was permitted in Gaelic football. In fact, handling the ball was important.

36   Kevin's interview was over. It was Jane's turn. She sat in the chair, in front of Alice. She was wearing a green wig.

37 "Good evening," said Alice.

38 "Good morning," said Jane.

39 "And who are you?"

40 "Jane."

41 "Jane," said Alice. "What a lovely name. It rhymes with 'pain.'"

42 "Take it easy, Alice," warned Sir.

43 "It's OK," said Jane. "Alice rhymes with '**malice**.'"

44 "And where are you from, Pain—sorry—Jane?"

45 "Ireland," said Jane.

46 "That explains your green hair."

47 "Yes," said Jane. "It's the same color as your snot."

48 "Hold on!" said Sir. He jumped in front of the camera. "Stop!"

49 "Do you mean 'cut,' sir?" Daragh asked.

50 "Yes," said Sir. "Yes. Cut." He turned to the two girls.

51 "Girls," he said.

52   Francis was surprised by what had happened. Alice and Jane were best friends.

53 "I was only joking, sir," protested Jane.

54 "Me as well," said Alice.

55 "Pain is my nickname, sir," said Jane.

56 "Yes," said Alice.

57   Francis wondered if he would ever have a nickname. He hoped so. He had been here four years. He had no enemies, but also no close friends. The other children were quite friendly, but none of them had given him a name that meant strong friendship.

58   Alice and Jane were ready again.

59 "And . . ."

60 "Action!"

61 "Now, Jane," said Alice. "Tell us a bit about yourself. Tell us about the *real* Jane."

62 "Well—"

63 "Do you have a pony?"

64 "No!"

Use a print dictionary, or indicate another strategy you used that helped you determine meaning.

malice (MAL ihs) *n.*

MEANING:

---

1. **Gaelic** (GAY lihk) *adj.* having to do with the Irish people or Irish language.

Use a print dictionary, or indicate another strategy you used that helped you determine meaning.

admired (ad MYRD) *v.*

MEANING:

65 "What about a donkey?"

66 Alice was funny. Francis **admired** her confidence.

67 "I like Harry Potter," said Jane.

68 "Oh," said Alice. "Is he your boyfriend?"

69 Francis had read, so far, three of the Harry Potter books. The lady in the hostel,[2] Mary, had given them to him. He had read each of them twice. There was a small shelf, between his bed and his mother's, that he used for his things. The books were on his shelf, his first books in this country.

70 Jane stood up, and Derek took her place.

71 "Hello, you," said Alice.

72 Sir laughed, and everybody else laughed. Francis could tell that Derek was embarrassed.

73 "Hello," said Derek.

74 "And you are who?"

75 "Derek," said Derek.

76 "Derek," said Alice. "And tell us, Derek, where are you from?"

77 "The UK," said Derek.

78 Francis was surprised again. He had thought that Derek, like the other children, was Irish. He certainly looked Irish. He was the only person in the class with red hair and freckles.

79 "Britain," said Derek. "England, like."

80 "You're English," said Alice.

81 "I was born there," said Derek. "So, yeah. I suppose." He shrugged.

82 "How interesting," said Alice. "Why did you come here? To Ireland."

83 "My dad's Irish," said Derek. "And my mum got a job here. So we moved."

84 "When?"

85 "When I was six."

86 "In a plane?"

87 "No," said Derek. "Boat."

88 "Do you remember it?"

89 "Yeah," said Derek. "'Course. We drove to the boat from our house in London. Then the boat. Then we drove again. To our house here, like."

90 Francis remembered his own journey here, to Dublin. He had traveled on a train from Belfast, in the north of Ireland—he had seen it since, on a map. But before that, he had been on a plane. Before that, there had been a long wait, in a very hot room with no windows. With his mother. And with many other people. Before that, there had been another plane. And before that, a bumpy journey in the back of a truck, when he lay beside his mother and there was a dusty canvas cover over them and the other people

_____

2. **hostel** (HAHS tuhl) *n.* lodging place; inn.

hiding with them. It was very frightening. His mother sang, but she sounded frightened, too. Before that, he remembered walking. A long distance, at nighttime. And before that, he remembered running—he thought he did. And gunshots. It was a long time ago; he was not sure.

91   "Francis?"

92   Everybody was looking at him. The chair beside Alice was empty. It was Francis's turn.

93   He stood up. He had been looking forward to this. From where he had been sitting, it had looked like great fun. Now he was not so sure. His legs felt rubbery and he walked to the chair.

94 "Hurry up, Francis!"

95 "Quiet," said Sir. "OK, Francis?"

96 Francis nodded. "Yes, sir."

97 "Good man. And . . ."

98 "Action!"

99 "Good evening," said Alice. She was blinking even faster.

100 "Good evening," said Francis. He wasn't nervous now.

101 "And who are *you*?"

102 Francis waited until the laughter had died down. Then:

103 "Francis," he said, quite loudly.

104 "Francis or Frances?" said Alice. "Boy or girl?"

105 "Alice," Sir warned.

106 "Boy," said Francis.

107 "Sure?"

108 "Alice!"

109 "Very sure," said Francis. "I am, without doubt, a boy."

110 And something wonderful happened. Everybody laughed. Francis had decided to make his classmates laugh, and he had done it. This was a great day.

111 Francis laughed, too, then stopped.

112 "So," said Alice. "You're a boy."

113 "Yes."

114 "What sort of a boy?"

115 "A most ordinary boy."

116 Again he heard the laughter. Alice blinked and blinked and blinked.

117 "What's the most ordinary thing about you?" she asked.

118 "My hands," said Francis. He showed them to her. "And my feet." He held them up, and put them back down on the floor. "I have two of each," he said, "which is very ordinary, I think you will agree."

119 "Yes," said Alice. "And ears."

120 "Yes," said Francis. "Two of them. And eyes."

121 "And nostrils."

122 "Absolutely."

123 "Very ordinary."

124 "Yes," said Francis. He wanted the next question, he was enjoying himself so much. He even leant forward, as if to catch the question as it came out of Alice's mouth.

125 "So, Francis," she said. "Where are you from?"

126 And Francis answered quickly. "Pikipiki."

127 The name was there in his head, suddenly, big and glowing.

128 Everybody laughed. This time the laughter surprised Francis— at first.

129 "There's no such place as Picky-Picky," said Alice.

130 "Yes," said Francis. "There is."

131   "No, there isn't," said Alice.

132   "Yes, there is," said Francis. He had forgotten all about Pikipiki. But it was the first place he'd thought of when Alice asked the question.

133   "There can't be," said Alice. "It's too mad. What is it again?"

134   "Pikipiki," said Francis.

135   He liked saying it again. It was like seeing someone he loved, from far away, coming closer. His father. He had not thought about his father in a long, long time.

136   "Sir?" said a boy, Liam.

137   "What?"

138   "There's no country in Africa called Picky-Picky," said Liam. "I know them all. Morocco, Tunisia, Libya—"

139   "Thanks, Liam," said Sir. He looked at Francis. "Where's Picky-Picky, Francis?" he asked. "Do you want to talk about it?"

140   Francis turned to face the teacher. "Yes, sir," he said. "It is where I lived with my father."

141   "Before you came to Dublin?"

142   "Yes, sir," said Francis.

143   "Is it the name of your village?"

144   "Oh, no, sir," said Francis. "We did not live in a village."

145   "A city, then," said Sir.

146   "There's no city in Africa called Picky-Picky, sir," said Liam. "I know them all. There's Alexandria, and—"

147   "Thanks, Liam," said Sir. "So, Francis. Is it a city?"

148   "No, sir."

149   "It's a country?"

150   "Yes, sir."

151   Francis heard several children groaning, an oh-no-here-we-go-again kind of groan.

152   "Bo-ring!"

153   "Someone else's turn."

154   "Quiet!" said Sir loudly. He turned back to Francis. "Where, Francis? Where's Picky-Picky?"

155   Francis put a finger to the side of his head. "In here, sir."

156   "In your head?"

157   "Yes, sir," said Francis. "In my head. And in my father's head."

158   "So it's an imaginary place?"

159   "No, sir," said Francis. "It is real."

160   Then they heard Alice.

161   "Ahem."

162   Everybody laughed. Francis laughed, too. He turned back to face Alice.

163   "I *am* supposed to be the interviewer, you know," said Alice. "It *is* a chat show and I do have the biggest mouth in the class. You said that, sir."

164   "You're right, Alice," said Sir. "You take over from here."

165   Alice looked at the camera and blinked. "Welcome back," she said. "So, Francis. Tell us a bit about Piggy-Piggy."

166   "Pikipiki," said Francis.

167   "Whatever," said Alice. "Tell us all about it."

168   Francis sat up straight. "My father knew many languages." He stopped. He started again. "My father *knows* many languages," he said.

169   It was five years since Francis had seen his father.

170   "One day," he said, "a man passed us by on a motorbike. And my father told me the word for motorbike in eleven different languages."

171   "*Eleven*?"

172   "Yes," said Francis. "And the one that made me laugh was *pikipiki*."

173   "So," said Alice. "'Picky-Picky' means 'motorbike'?"

174   "Yes," said Francis.

175   "In what language?"

176   "Swahili," said Francis.

177   "You're telling us you lived in a country called Motorbike?"

178   "Yes," said Francis. "We made it up, my father and I. On the street. My father was—*is*—the king, and I am the prince."

179   "Prince Francis."

180   "Yes," said Francis. "When I was with my father—when we were together—we lived in Pikipiki. When he came home from work. When I woke up in the morning. He would say, 'How is the prince of Pikipiki?' It was our country. We had our own money. And our own food. And everything. We made it up."

181   "Is your father still there?"

182   Francis nodded.

183   "Does he phone you?"

184   Francis shook his head. "My mother says they will not let him phone."

185   "Who are 'they'?"

186   "The soldiers," said Francis.

187   It was five years since Francis and his mother had had to leave their country, in the time of shooting and fires. In those years, since he had come to Dublin, Francis had forgotten much. He had been a little boy when he left. He could not remember everything—it could not be expected. But he remembered, today, Pikipiki, the Kingdom of the Motorbike.

188   He sat up. He'd remembered something else.

189   "In Pikipiki," he said, "the mobile phones have wheels."

190   "Cool," said Alice. "That makes sense."

191   "Yes," said Francis. "You speak into the phone and put it on the ground. Then it goes away very quickly to whoever you are talking to and comes back with the message."

192   Everybody laughed. They loved the idea of the wheelie mobile phones.

193   "Well, thank you, Francis," said Alice.

194   "*Prince* Francis, you mean," said Liam.

195   "Cool!"

196   From that day on, everybody called him Prince Francis. And Francis was very pleased, because it meant he was their friend. Every time he heard the word "prince," he thought of his father, the king, and it made him feel that his father was near. Francis was a prince now in his two homes, Pikipiki and Ireland. And his father was very proud of him.

ARTICLE 15[3]
WE ALL HAVE THE RIGHT TO BELONG TO A COUNTRY.

---

3. **Article 15** reference to Article 15 of the Universal Declaration of Human Rights, which was adopted by the United Nations General Assembly in 1948.

NOTEBOOK

Work on your own to answer the questions in your notebook. Use text evidence to support your responses.

Response

1. Personal Connections Did anything about this story surprise you? Explain.

Comprehension

2. Reading Check (a) What is Francis's class doing on the day the story takes place? **(b)** Why does Francis want a nickname? **(c)** What is Pikipiki?

3. Strategy: Make Inferences (a) Cite an inference you made while reading this story and the text evidence that supports it. **(b)** How did making inferences help you develop a more complete picture of Francis's life? Explain.

WORKING AS A GROUP

Discuss your responses to the Analysis and Discussion questions with your group.

- Note agreements and disagreements.
- Summarize insights.
- Consider changes of opinion.

If necessary, revise your original answers to reflect what you learn from your discussion.

Analysis and Discussion

4. (a) Analyze Cause and Effect Why does the class laugh at Kevin's simple question—"How's it going, Alice?"—in paragraph 12? **(b) Draw Conclusions** What does their reaction suggest about the mood in the classroom?

5. Interpret In paragraph 168, why does Francis say, "My father knew many languages," but then correct himself to say, "My father *knows* many languages"?

6. Draw Conclusions Why do you think Francis moved to Ireland? Explain.

7. (a) Analyze Why don't the other students give Francis a nickname until the interview? **(b) Interpret** How does the nickname make Francis feel?

8. Get Ready for Close Reading Choose a passage from the text that you find especially interesting or important. You'll discuss the passage with your group during Close-Read activities.

⚙ TEKS

1.D. Participate in student-led discussions by eliciting and considering suggestions from other group members, taking notes, and identifying points of agreement and disagreement.

5.F. Make inferences and use evidence to support understanding.

EQ Notes What are some of the challenges and triumphs of growing up?

What have you learned about growing up from reading this story? Go to your Essential Question Notes and record your observations and thoughts about "Prince Francis."

ANALYZE AND INTERPRET

Close Read

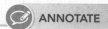 ANNOTATE

PRINCE FRANCIS

PRACTICE Complete the following activities. Use text evidence to support your responses.

1. Present and Discuss With your group, share passages from the story that you found especially interesting. Discuss what you notice, the questions you have, and the conclusions you reach. For example, you might focus on the following passages:

- Paragraphs 130–156: Discuss how Francis's thoughts of Pikipiki make him feel.

- Paragraphs 176–186: Discuss what Francis means when he says he "lived" in Pikipiki with his father.

2. Reflect on Your Learning What new ideas or insights did you uncover during your second reading of the text?

NOTEBOOK

LANGUAGE STUDY

Concept Vocabulary

Why These Words? The vocabulary words are related.

malice	envied	admired

1. With your group, discuss what the words have in common. Write your ideas.

2. Add another word that fits the category. _____

3. Use each vocabulary word in a sentence. Include context clues that hint at each word's meaning. Share and discuss your sentences.

WORD NETWORK

Add words related to the idea of growing up from the text to your Word Network.

Word Study

Latin Prefix: *mal-* The word *malice* incorporates the Latin prefix *mal-* which means "bad," or "evil." Many English words include this prefix. The word *malnourished*, for example, means "poorly—or badly—nourished." Use a dictionary to look up two more words that include *mal-*. Define each word.

 TEKS

6.F. Respond using newly acquired vocabulary as appropriate.

Genre / Text Elements

Narrative Point of View A **narrator** is the voice that tells a story.
Narrative point of view refers to the type of narrator telling the
tale. "Prince Francis" uses the **third-person limited point of view.**

TIP A third-person
limited narrator is just
that—*limited* to one
character's viewpoint.
An omniscient narrator
reveals the thoughts
and feelings of all the
characters.

THIRD-PERSON LIMITED POINT OF VIEW	
The narrator...	is not a character; it is a voice from outside the story.
	sees through the main character's eyes.
	reveals only the main character's private thoughts and feelings.
	speaks in the third person (using the pronouns *he*, *she*, *they*, and so on).

The point of view in a story is important because it determines
what readers learn about the characters and situation.

 NOTEBOOK

PRACTICE Work with your group to discuss and answer the
questions. Use new vocabulary you have learned, such as *third-person
limited*, in your responses.

1. Throughout this story, which character's private thoughts and feelings
   does the narrator share? Cite specific examples.

2. **(a) Categorize** Note two details about Alice's appearance and
   behavior. **(b) Analyze** Explain how the reader's knowledge of Alice is
   controlled by the narrative point of view.

3. **(a) Make Inferences** When Francis starts to talk about Pikipiki, why
   do you think Sir gets so interested? **(b) Speculate** How might that
   scene be different if the reader knew what Sir was thinking?

4. **(a)** In paragraph 90, what does Francis remember his mother doing as
   they traveled in the back of a truck? **(b) Infer** Why do you think she
   did this? **(c) Evaluate** Does the reader know with certainty why she
   did this? Explain.

5. **Evaluate** Writers use the third-person limited point of view to achieve
   various purposes. Which one do you think is *most important* in this
   story? Mark that item and explain your choice.

   • It emphasizes how the main character changes.

   • It keeps the motivations of other characters hidden.

   • It allows the reader to feel close to the main character.

TEKS
6.F. Respond using newly acquired
vocabulary as appropriate.
9.E. Identify the use of literary
devices, including omniscient and
limited point of view, to achieve a
specific purpose.

Author's Craft

PRINCE FRANCIS

Literary Devices and Character Development Writers use a variety of literary devices to show how characters look, act, think, and feel. They may also explain why characters think or feel as they do.

- **Dialogue:** conversations among characters
- **Description:** details that relate to the senses (sight, hearing, touch, taste, smell) and help readers picture characters and scenes
- **Direct Characterization:** statements about characters' traits

Consider these examples from "Prince Francis."

EXAMPLES: LITERARY DEVICES AND CHARACTER DEVELOPMENT

DIALOGUE	DESCRIPTION	DIRECT CHARACTERIZATION
"Good evening," said Alice. "Good morning," said Jane. "And who are you?" "Jane." "Jane," said Alice. "What a lovely name. It rhymes with 'pain.'"	One of the girls, Alice, was the interviewer. She was wearing a black dress that had once belonged to her grandmother, and black eyeshadow that made her blink.	Alice was funny.

 **NOTEBOOK**

 **INTERACTIVITY**

PRACTICE Work on your own to complete the activity and answer the questions. Then, discuss your responses with your group.

1. **Analyze** Reread the passages from the story listed in the chart. Identify the literary device or devices used in each example and explain what they tell you about characters.

PASSAGE	DEVICE	WHAT IT TELLS YOU
Paragraph 19		
Paragraphs 36–47		
Paragraphs 102–115		

2. **(a) Analyze** Identify the two passages of dialogue in which Francis changes the verb tense he uses to talk about his father. **(b) Interpret** What do these details tell you about Francis?

3. **Interpret** How does Francis change from the beginning of the story to the end? Cite one example each of dialogue and description that supports your answer.

EQ Notes Before moving on go to your Essential Question Notes and record any additional thoughts you may have about "Prince Francis."

Compare Fiction

In this lesson, you have read "Prince Francis," the first of two realistic short stories. Now you will read and compare "The Sound of Summer Running."

PRINCE FRANCIS

THE SOUND OF SUMMER RUNNING

The Sound of Summer Running

About the Author

As a boy, **Ray Bradbury** (1920–2012) loved magicians, circuses, and science-fiction stories. He began writing at the age of 12 and went on to become one of the most celebrated writers of science fiction and fantasy. *The Martian Chronicles*, a collection of Bradbury's stories about Earth's colonization of Mars, was published in 1950 and is considered a classic today.

Concept Vocabulary

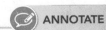 ANNOTATE

As you read the story, you will encounter these words.

| suspended | detached | abandoned |

Digital Resources Resources you use online or with a device can help you learn new words. A **digital dictionary** entry provides a word's definition, part of speech, pronunciation, syllabication, and word origin. Many digital dictionaries also include links to useful information, such as example sentences and audio pronunciations.

> **EXAMPLE** This entry shows that *solitary* is an adjective with three syllables. Find and mark information about the word's origin.
>
> **sol•i• tary** *adjective*
> 1. being, living, or going alone
> **Origin:** Latin, from *solus,* "alone"
> **Pronunciation:** SOHL ih tehr ee

PRACTICE As you read, use a digital dictionary to determine the meanings and pronunciations of unfamiliar words.

Comprehension Strategy

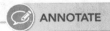 ANNOTATE

Fluency: Read in Phrases

When we speak, most of us don't pause after each word. Instead, we speak in phrases, or sets of words. Apply the same idea when you read by reading in phrases.

> **EXAMPLE** Each caret (^) ends a phrase. Read the passage to yourself, focusing on the phrases rather than on separate words.
>
> They felt ^ like it feels ^ sticking your feet ^ out of the hot covers…

PRACTICE Increase your fluency by reading this story in phrases.

TEKS
2.A. Use print or digital resources to determine the meaning, syllabication, pronunciation, word origin, and part of speech.

-year, you always found out, you always knew, you couldn't really jump over rivers and trees and houses in them, and they were dead. But this was a new year, and he felt that this time, with this new pair of shoes, he could do anything, anything at all.

16   They walked up on the steps to their house. "Save your money," said Dad. "In five or six weeks—"

17   "Summer'll be over!"

18   Lights out, with Tom asleep, Douglas lay watching his feet, far away down there at the end of the bed in the moonlight, free of the heavy iron shoes, the big chunks of winter fallen away from them.

19   "Reasons. I've got to think of reasons for the shoes."

20   Well, as anyone knew, the hills around town were wild with friends putting cows to riot, playing barometer[6] to the atmospheric changes, taking sun, peeling like calendars each day to take more sun. To catch those friends, you must run much faster than foxes or squirrels. As for the town, it streamed with enemies grown irritable with heat, so remembering every winter argument and insult. *Find friends, ditch enemies!* That was the Cream-Sponge Para Litefoot motto. *Does the world run too fast? Want to be alert, stay alert? Litefoot, then! Litefoot!*

21   He held his coin bank up and heard the faint small tinkling, the airy weight of money there.

22   Whatever you want, he thought, you got to make your own way. During the night now, let's find that path through the forest . . . .

23   Downtown, the store lights went out, one by one. A wind blew in the window. It was like a river going downstream and his feet wanting to go with it.

24   In his dreams he heard a rabbit running running running in the deep warm grass.

25   Old Mr. Sanderson moved through his shoe store as the proprietor[7] of a pet shop must move through his shop where are kenneled animals from everywhere in the world, touching each one briefly along the way. Mr. Sanderson brushed his hands over the shoes in the window, and some of them were like cats to him and some were like dogs; he touched each pair with concern, adjusting laces, fixing tongues. Then he stood in the exact center of the carpet and looked around, nodding.

26   There was a sound of growing thunder.

27   One moment, the door to Sanderson's Shoe Emporium was empty. The next, Douglas Spaulding stood clumsily there, staring

---

6. **barometer** (buh RAHM uh tur) *n.* tool that measures changes in air pressure and can help predict storms.
7. **proprietor** (pruh PRY uh tuhr) *n.* owner.

down at his leather shoes as if these heavy things could not be pulled up out of the cement. The thunder had stopped when his shoes stopped. Now, with painful slowness, daring to look only at the money in his cupped hand, Douglas moved out of the bright sunlight of Saturday noon. He made careful stacks of nickels, dimes, and quarters on the counter, like someone playing chess and worried if the next move carried him out into sun or deep into shadow.

28   "Don't say a word!" said Mr. Sanderson.

29   Douglas froze.

30   "First, I know just what you want to buy," said Mr. Sanderson. "Second, I see you every afternoon at my window; you think I don't see? You're wrong. Third, to give it its full name, you want the Royal Crown Cream-Sponge Para Litefoot Tennis Shoes: 'LIKE MENTHOL[8] ON YOUR FEET!' Fourth, you want credit."

31   "No!" cried Douglas, breathing hard, as if he'd run all night in his dreams. "I got something better than credit to offer!" he gasped. "Before I tell, Mr. Sanderson, you got to do me one small favor. Can you remember when was the last time you yourself wore a pair of Litefoot sneakers, sir?"

32   Mr. Sanderson's face darkened. "Oh, ten, twenty, say, thirty years ago. Why. . . ?"

8. **menthol** (MEHN thawl) *n.* substance that has cooling properties similar to mint.

33   "Mr. Sanderson, don't you think you owe it to your customers, sir, to at least try the tennis shoes you sell, for just one minute, so you know how they feel? People forget if they don't keep testing things. United Cigar Store man smokes cigars, don't he? Candy-store man samples his own stuff, I should think. So . . . ."

34   "You may have noticed," said the old man, "I'm wearing shoes."

35   "But not sneakers, sir! How you going to sell sneakers unless you can rave about them and how you going to rave about them unless you know them?"

36   Mr. Sanderson backed off a little distance from the boy's fever, one hand to his chin. "Well . . . ."

37   "Mr. Sanderson," said Douglas, "you sell me something and I'll sell you something just as valuable."

38   "It is absolutely necessary to the sale that I put on a pair of the sneakers, boy?" said the old man.

39   "I sure wish you could, sir!"

40   The old man sighed. A minute later, seated panting quietly, he laced the tennis shoes to his long narrow feet. They looked **detached** and alien[9] down there next to the dark cuffs of his business suit. Mr. Sanderson stood up.

41   "How do they *feel?*" asked the boy.

42   "How do they feel, he asks; they feel fine." He started to sit down.

43   "Please!" Douglas held out his hand. "Mr. Sanderson, now could you kind of rock back and forth a little, sponge around, bounce kind of, while I tell you the rest? It's this: I give you my money, you give me the shoes, I owe you a dollar. But, Mr. Sanderson, *but*—soon as I get those shoes on, you know what *happens?*"

44   "What?"

45   "Bang! I deliver your packages, pick up packages, bring you coffee, burn your trash, run to the post office, telegraph office, library! You'll see twelve of me in and out, in and out, every minute. Feel those shoes, Mr. Sanderson, *feel* how fast they'd take me? All those springs inside? Feel all the running inside? Feel how they kind of grab hold and can't let you alone and don't like you just *standing* there? Feel how quick I'd be doing the things you'd rather not bother with? You stay in the nice cool store while I'm jumping all around town! But it's not me really, it's the shoes. They're going like mad down alleys, cutting corners, and back! There they go!"

46   Mr. Sanderson stood amazed with the rush of words. When the words got going the flow carried him; he began to sink deep in the

Use a digital dictionary, or indicate another strategy you used that helped you determine meaning.

detached (dih TACHT) *adj.*

MEANING:

---

9. **alien** (AY lee uhn) *adj.* foreign in nature, wholly different from others.

shoes, to flex his toes, limber[10] his arches, test his ankles. He rocked softly, secretly, back and forth in a small breeze from the open door. The tennis shoes silently hushed themselves deep in the carpet, sank as in a jungle grass, in loam and resilient clay. He gave one solemn bounce of his heels in the yeasty dough, in the yielding[11] and welcoming earth. Emotions hurried over his face as if many colored lights had been switched on and off. His mouth hung slightly open. Slowly he gentled and rocked himself to a halt, and the boy's voice faded and they stood there looking at each other in a tremendous and natural silence.

47   A few people drifted by on the sidewalk outside, in the hot sun. Still the man and boy stood there, the boy glowing, the man with revelation[12] in his face.

48   "Boy," said the old man at last, "in five years, how would you like a job selling shoes in this emporium?"

49   "Gosh, thanks, Mr. Sanderson, but I don't know what I'm going to be yet."

50   "Anything you want to be, son," said the old man, "you'll be. No one will ever stop you."

51   The old man walked lightly across the store to the wall of ten thousand boxes, came back with some shoes for the boy, and wrote up a list on some paper while the boy was lacing the shoes on his feet and then standing there, waiting.

52   The old man held out his list. "A dozen things you got to do for me this afternoon. Finish them, we're even Stephen, and you're fired."

53   "Thanks, Mr. Sanderson!" Douglas bounded away.

54   "Stop!" cried the old man.

55   Douglas pulled up and turned.

56   Mr. Sanderson leaned forward. "How do they *feel?*"

57   The boy looked down at his feet deep in the rivers, in the fields of wheat, in the wind that already was rushing him out of the town. He looked up at the old man, his eyes burning, his mouth moving, but no sound came out.

58   "Antelopes?" said the old man, looking from the boy's face to his shoes. "Gazelles?"

59   The boy thought about it, hesitated, and nodded a quick nod. Almost immediately he vanished. He just spun about with a whisper and went off. The door stood empty. The sound of the tennis shoes faded in the jungle heat.

60   Mr. Sanderson stood in the sun-blazed door, listening. From a long time ago, when he dreamed as a boy, he remembered the sound. Beautiful creatures leaping under the sky, gone through

10. **limber** (LIHM buhr) *v.* make flexible.
11. **yielding** (YEEL dihng) *adj.* not stiff or hard.
12. **revelation** (reh vuh LAY shuhn) *n.* act of realizing a truth for the first time.

brush, under trees, away, and only the soft echo their running left behind.

61   "Antelopes," said Mr. Sanderson. "Gazelles."

62   He bent to pick up the boy's **abandoned** winter shoes, heavy with forgotten rains and long-melted snows. Moving out of the blazing sun, walking softly, lightly, slowly, he headed back toward civilization . . . .

Use a digital dictionary, or indicate another strategy you used that helped you determine meaning.

abandoned (uh BAN duhnd)
adj.
MEANING:

NOTEBOOK

Work on your own to answer the questions in your notebook. Use text evidence to support your responses.

Response

1. **Personal Connections** Is Douglas someone you admire? Explain.

Comprehension

2. **Reading Check (a)** What does Douglas want more than anything? **(b)** What arrangement does he make to get what he wants?

3. **Fluency: Read in Phrases** Did reading in phrases help you read with greater flow and understanding? Explain.

WORKING AS A GROUP

Discuss your responses to the Analysis and Discussion questions with your group.

- Note agreements and disagreements.
- Summarize insights.
- Consider changes of opinion.

If necessary, revise your original answers to reflect what you learn from your discussion.

Analysis and Discussion

4. **Interpret** Why does Douglas feel that his old sneakers are "dead inside"?

5. **(a) Make Inferences** Why does Douglas want Mr. Sanderson to try on the sneakers? Cite evidence to support your inference. **(b) Interpret** After Mr. Sanderson tries on the sneakers, what new understanding does he gain? Explain.

6. **Make a Judgment** Does Douglas offer proof of his own statement, "Whatever you want, you've got to make your own way"? Explain.

7. **Interpret** In the story's final paragraph, Mr. Sanderson heads "back to civilization." How is that possible when he never left the shoe store? Explain.

8. **Get Ready for Close Reading** Choose a passage from the text that you find especially interesting or important. You'll discuss the passage with your group during Close-Read activities.

EQ Notes What are some of the challenges and triumphs of growing up?

What have you learned about growing up from reading this story? Go to your Essential Question Notes and record your observations and thoughts about "The Sound of Summer Running."

TEKS

3. Adjust fluency when reading grade-level text based on the reading purpose.

5.F. Make inferences and use evidence to support understanding.

Close Read

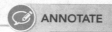 **ANNOTATE**

THE SOUND OF SUMMER RUNNING

PRACTICE Complete the following activities. Use text evidence to support your responses.

1. **Present and Discuss** With your group, share the passages from the short story that you found especially interesting. Discuss what you notice, the questions you have, and the conclusions you reach. For example, you might focus on the following passages:

   • Paragraphs 8 and 10: Discuss Douglas's reasons for wanting new sneakers.

   • Paragraph 14 and 15: Discuss Douglas's feeling that his old shoes are "dead inside."

   • Paragraph 25: Discuss the way Mr. Sanderson behaves in his store and how he treats the shoes.

2. **Reflect on Your Learning** What new ideas or insights did you uncover during your second reading of the text?

NOTEBOOK

LANGUAGE STUDY

Concept Vocabulary

Why These Words? The vocabulary words are related.

| suspended | detached | abandoned |

1. With your group, determine what the words have in common. Write your ideas.

2. Add another word that fits the category. _____

3. Write a paragraph about growing up that includes basic words as well as the vocabulary words you have just learned.

Word Study

Multiple-Meaning Words In paragraph 40 of the story, Mr. Sanderson thinks the sneakers make his feet look *detached* from his body. The word *detached* can have a physical meaning, as it does here, or an emotional meaning. Use a dictionary to find the definition for each meaning of *detached*. Then, propose at least one synonym for each definition you find.

WORD NETWORK

Add words related to the idea of growing up from the text to your Word Network.

 TEKS
6.F. Respond using newly acquired vocabulary as appropriate.

Genre / Text Elements

Narrative Point of View A **narrator** is the voice that tells a story. **Narrative point of view** refers to the type of narrator telling the tale. "The Sound of Summer Running" uses the **third-person omniscient point of view.**

THIRD-PERSON OMNISCIENT POINT OF VIEW	
The narrator…	is not a character; it is a voice from outside the story.
	reveals the unspoken thoughts and feelings of at least two characters.
	could reveal the unspoken thoughts and feelings of *every* character in a story.
	speaks in the third person (using the pronouns *he, she, they,* and so on).

The point of view in a story is important because it determines what readers learn about the characters and situation.

 INTERACTIVITY

NOTEBOOK

PRACTICE Work with your group to answer the questions.

1. Use the chart to cite three examples of unspoken thoughts or feelings for each character.

DOUGLAS	MR. SANDERSON

2. **(a)** Whose thoughts and feelings does the narrator share in paragraphs 1 through 24? **(b) Analyze** Explain why paragraph 25 shows that the story uses the omniscient point of view.

3. **Interpret** Reread paragraphs 60–62—the story's ending. Could the ending have happened in this way if the story did not use an omniscient narrator? Explain.

4. **Evaluate** Writers use the third-person omniscient point of view to achieve various purposes. Which one do you think is *most important* in this story? Mark that item and explain your choice.

   • It allows readers to feel that the version of events is accurate and not affected by one character's perspective.

   • It lets the writer show how characters truly feel about one another.

   • It helps the author make the world of the story more complex.

 TEKS
9.E. Identify the use of literary devices, including omniscient and limited point of view, to achieve a specific purpose.

Author's Craft

Literary Devices: Symbol A **symbol** is anything that stands for something else. In literature, symbols stand for ideas, such as a character's desire for freedom or love. In this story, Douglas's sneakers are a symbol. The author builds the symbolic meaning of the sneakers by using **sensory language,** or details that relate to sight, hearing, touch, taste, and smell.

THE SOUND OF SUMMER RUNNING

EXAMPLE: SENSORY LANGUAGE AND SYMBOL

In this passage from the story's first paragraph, the underlined words relate to touch, or physical sensations.

He glanced quickly away, but <u>his ankles were seized, his feet suspended, then rushed. The earth spun</u>; the shop awnings slammed their canvas wings overhead with <u>the thrust of his body running</u>.

TIP In the example, sensory details show how intensely Douglas is affected by the sneakers. His longing for them seems to grab him physically.

  INTERACTIVITY

NOTEBOOK

PRACTICE Work together as a group to complete the activity and answer the questions.

1. **(a) Distinguish** Cite at least three passages in which the narrator describes leather or winter shoes. **(b) Compare** What qualities do these descriptions share?

2. **Analyze** Identify details in the text that connect the sneakers to nature or to speed and lightness. Note these details in the chart.

EQ Notes Before moving on to a new selection, go to your Essential Question Notes and record any additional thoughts or observations you may have about "The Sound of Summer Running."

NATURE	SPEED AND LIGHTNESS

3. **(a) Generalize** What kinds of places do the sneakers make both Douglas and Mr. Sanderson imagine? **(b) Connect** What emotions do both characters associate with the sneakers?

4. **(a)** In paragraphs 60–61, what dream does Mr. Sanderson remember and from what time of his life? **(b) Interpret** How does this detail add meaning to the symbol of the sneakers? Explain.

5. **Summarize** Using your analysis of the story's details, explain what the sneakers in this story symbolize.

PRINCE FRANCIS

THE SOUND OF SUMMER RUNNING

Compare Fiction

Multiple Choice

 NOTEBOOK

These questions are based on "Prince Francis" and "The Sound of Summer Running." Choose the best answer for each question.

1. Which statement is true about both Francis and Douglas?

  A Douglas and Francis have both just started new jobs.

  B Douglas knows his town well, but Francis is new to his.

  C Francis knows his town well, and Douglas is new to his.

  D Both boys traveled from Africa to live in Ireland.

2. Read the passages from the stories. Which answer choice is an accurate statement about the challenges both boys face?

The Sound of Summer Running	Prince Francis
"Dad!"He blurted it out."Back there in that window, those Cream-Sponge Para Litefoot Shoes . . ." His father didn't even turn."Suppose you tell me why you need a new pair of sneakers. Can you do that?"	Francis wondered if he would ever have a nickname. He hoped so. He had been here four years. He had no enemies, but also no close friends. The other children were quite friendly, but none of them had given him a name that meant strong friendship.

  F Both Francis and Douglas must deal with strict fathers.

  G Both Francis and Douglas need money.

  H Both Francis and Douglas want something very deeply.

  J Both Francis and Douglas must get used to a new country.

3. How are the two boys' solutions to their challenges different?

  A Francis solves his without a plan, while Douglas needs a plan.

  B Francis solves his problem, but Douglas does not.

  C Douglas uses trickery, but Francis is honest.

  D Douglas doesn't need help, but Francis does.

 TEKS

6.B. Write responses that demonstrate understanding of texts, including comparing sources within and across genres.

9.E. Identify the use of literary devices, including omniscient and limited point of view, to achieve a specific purpose.

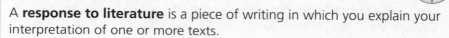
NOTEBOOK

Short Response

1. (a) Compare and Contrast In what ways are the conflicts Francis and Douglas face similar and different? **(b) Evaluate** Do you think the conflicts in both stories are realistic? Explain.

2. Interpret Do you think Douglas's sense of summer shares any similarities with Francis's imaginary country of Pikipiki? Explain.

3. (a) Draw Conclusions In "The Sound of Summer Running," why does Mr. Sanderson decide to help Douglas? **(b) Deduce** In "Prince Francis," do you think Sir wants to help Francis? Explain. **(c) Analyze** Explain how the use of the limited point of view in "Prince Francis" and the omniscient point of view in "The Sound of Summer Running" affect what readers learn about Sir and Mr. Sanderson.

> Answer the questions in your notebook. Use text evidence to support your responses.

Timed Writing

A **response to literature** is a piece of writing in which you explain your interpretation of one or more texts.

ASSIGNMENT

Write a **response to literature** in which you discuss the effects of the narrative points of view in these two stories. Explain how the points of view affect what you learn about the main characters and one other character in each story.

> **TIP** Add a sense of authority to your writing by using content vocabulary related to literature. For example, use words like *interpretation, source,* and *narrative.*

5-MINUTE PLANNER

1. Read the assignment carefully and completely.
2. Decide what you want to say about the points of view and their effects on your understanding of the characters in each story. This is your controlling idea.
3. Decide which examples you'll use from the two sources.
4. Organize your ideas, making sure to answer these questions:
   - What details does the point of view in each story allow me to see, and what does it keep hidden?
   - How does the point of view affect the way I feel about the characters in both stories?

- from *Bad Boy*
- The Moth Presents: Aleeza Kazmi
- Prince Francis
- The Sound of Summer Running

Present a Narrative: Retelling

A **retelling** is a new version of a text that changes elements of the original. For example, it may use a different perspective or change the setting. With your group, organize and deliver a **retelling** of one of the selections in this section of the unit, whether the memoir, the oral storytelling, or one of the short stories.

Plan With Your Group

 **INTERACTIVITY**

Analyze the Texts With your group, review the texts you have read during Peer-Group Learning. Consider the elements you might want to keep and the ones you might want to change. For example, you might want to have a different narrator or move the setting to the future. Capture your ideas in the chart.

SELECTION	ELEMENTS TO KEEP OR CHANGE
from *Bad Boy*	
The Moth Presents: Aleeza Kazmi	
Prince Francis	
The Sound of Summer Running	

Choose an Interpretation, Position, or Stance As a group, choose one text on which to focus. As you plan your retelling, keep this idea in mind: A successful retelling is true to the ideas in the original but presents them in a way that is new or fresh. It offers the reteller's viewpoint—his or her stance or position—on the original work.

Organize and Draft Now that you have chosen a text to retell and decided how you'll change the original story, write your new version. Choose a form. For example, you may want to create a script with a part for each group member, or plan a choral reading.

Rehearse and Present

Practice With Your Group Before you present your retelling to the class, practice delivering it.

- Choose language that reflects your interpretation, stance, or position. In general, use correct language conventions. However, your dialogue can show how characters speak, which may not always follow the rules.

- As you speak, don't look down at your feet or away from the audience. Make periodic eye contact with your listeners.

- Speak at a conversational rate and use gestures that enhance your meaning and are natural or unforced.

- Speak loudly and clearly enough to be understood by everyone in the room.

Use this checklist to evaluate your rehearsal. Then, revise your approach and fix your delivery to strengthen any elements that need improvement.

CONTENT	PRESENTATION TECHNIQUES
◯ The retelling presents characters and events vividly and clearly.	◯ Each speaker enunciates clearly and uses an appropriate volume and rate.
◯ The retelling presents a clear interpretation, stance, or position on the original story.	◯ Each speaker makes appropriate eye contact with the audience.
◯ The retelling uses language conventions correctly.	◯ Each speaker uses natural gestures that reinforce meaning.

Fine-Tune the Content Check to be sure you have emphasized key events in the original text. Also, review details that describe characters and situations. Add descriptive details as needed.

Brush Up on Your Presentation Techniques Avoid speaking in a flat, uninterested, or bored tone. Instead, vary your tone and speak with enthusiasm and liveliness. Consider having a peer film you as you speak so that you can sharpen your presentation skills.

Listen and Evaluate

Remember that you are delivering this retelling as a group. Everyone is equally important, and each person represents the entire group.

- Pay attention when members of your group are speaking.

- Give other groups your full attention when they are presenting.

- Listen actively and respond appropriately as others ask questions and contribute their ideas. For example, follow up on a comment another student makes, or answer a question in a thoughtful, respectful way.

⬥ TEKS

1.A. Listen actively to interpret a message, ask clarifying questions, and respond appropriately.

1.C. Give an organized presentation with a specific stance and position, employing eye contact, speaking rate, volume, enunciation, natural gestures, and conventions of language to communicate ideas effectively.

Essential Question

What are some of the challenges and triumphs of growing up?

People have many different ideas about what it means to grow up. In this section, you will choose a selection about growing up to read independently. Get the most from this section by establishing a purpose for reading. Ask yourself, "What do I hope to gain from my independent reading?" Here are just a few purposes you might consider:

Read to Learn Think about the selections you have already read. What questions do you still have about the unit topic?

Read to Enjoy Read the descriptions of the texts. Which one seems most interesting and appealing to you?

Read to Form a Position Consider your thoughts and feelings about the Essential Question. Are you still undecided about some aspect of the topic?

Reading Digital Text

Digital texts like the ones you will read in this section are electronic versions of print texts. They have a variety of characteristics:

- can be read on various devices
- text can be resized
- may include highlighting or other annotation tools
- may have bookmarks, audio links, and other helpful features

Independent Learning Strategies

 VIDEO

 INTERACTIVITY

Throughout your life, in school, in your community, and in your career, you will need to rely on yourself to learn and work on your own. Use these strategies to keep your focus as you read independently for sustained periods of time. Add ideas of your own for each category.

STRATEGY	MY ACTION PLAN
Create a schedule • Be aware of your deadlines. • Make a plan for each day's activities.	
Read with purpose • Use a variety of comprehension strategies to deepen your understanding. • Think about the text and how it adds to your knowledge.	
Take notes • Record key ideas and information. • Review your notes before sharing what you've learned.	

🔄 TEKS

4. Self-select text and read independently for a sustained period of time; **5.A.** Establish purpose for reading assigned and self-selected text; **8.F.** Analyze characteristics of multimodal and digital texts.

CONTENTS

 AUDIO   ANNOTATE   DOWNLOAD

Choose one selection. Selections are available online only.

SHARE YOUR INDEPENDENT LEARNING

Reflect on and evaluate the information you gained from your Independent Reading selection. Then, share what you learned with others.

Close-Read Guide

Tool Kit
Close-Read Guide and
Model Annotation

Establish your purpose for reading. Then, read the selection through at least once. Use this page to record your close-read ideas.

Selection Title: _____   Purpose for Reading: _____

Minutes Read: _____

 INTERACTIVITY

Close Read the Text

Zoom in on sections you found interesting. **Annotate** what you notice. Ask yourself **questions** about the text. What can you **conclude**?

_____

_____

_____

_____

_____

Analyze the Text

1. Think about the author's choices of literary elements, techniques, and structures. Select one and record your thoughts.

_____

_____

_____

2. What characteristics of digital texts did you use as you read this selection, and in what ways? How do the characteristics of a digital text affect your reading experience? Explain.

_____

_____

QuickWrite

Choose a paragraph from the text that grabbed your interest. Explain the power of this passage.

_____

_____

_____

_____

_____

_____

_____

Share Your Independent Learning

What are some of the challenges and triumphs of growing up?

When you read something independently, your understanding continues to grow as you share what you have learned with others.

 NOTEBOOK

Prepare to Share

CONNECT IT One of the most important ways to respond to a text is to notice and describe your personal reactions. Think about the text you explored independently and the ways in which it connects to your own experiences.

- What similarities and differences do you see between the text and your own life? Describe your observations.

- How do you think this text connects to the Essential Question? Describe your ideas.

Learn From Your Classmates

DISCUSS IT Share your ideas about the text you explored on your own. As you talk with others in your class, take notes about new ideas that seem important.

Reflect

EXPLAIN IT Review your notes, and mark the most important insight you gained from these writing and discussion activities. Explain how this idea adds to your understanding of childhood challenges and triumphs.

 TEKS

6.A. Describe personal connections to a variety of sources, including self-selected texts.
6.E. Interact with sources in meaningful ways such as notetaking, annotating, freewriting, or illustrating.

Personal Narrative

ASSIGNMENT

In this unit, you read about the challenges and triumphs of growing up from different perspectives. You also practiced writing personal narratives. Now, apply what you have learned.

Write a **personal narrative** that reflects your new understanding of the Essential Question:

Essential Question
What are some of the challenges and triumphs of growing up?

Review and Evaluate Your EQ Notes

INTERACTIVITY

Review your Essential Question Notes and your QuickWrite from the beginning of the unit. Have your ideas changed?

● Yes	● No
Identify at least three pieces of evidence that made you think differently about growing up.	Identify at least three pieces of evidence that reinforced your ideas about growing up.
1.	1.
2.	2.
3.	3.

State your ideas now:

How might you reflect your thinking about growing up in a personal narrative?

Share Your Perspective

The **Personal Narrative Checklist** will help you stay on track.

PLAN Before you write, read the Checklist and make sure you understand all the items.

DRAFT As you write, pause occasionally and make sure you're meeting the Checklist requirements.

Use New Words Refer to your Word Network to vary your word choice. Also, consider using one or more of the Academic Vocabulary terms you learned at the beginning of the unit: *reflect, mission, contribute, recognize, memorize.*

REVIEW AND EDIT After you have written a first draft, evaluate it against the Checklist. Make any changes needed to strengthen its structure, descriptions, and overall impact. Then, reread your narrative and fix any errors you find.

EQ Notes Make sure you have pulled in details from your Essential Question Notes to support your insights.

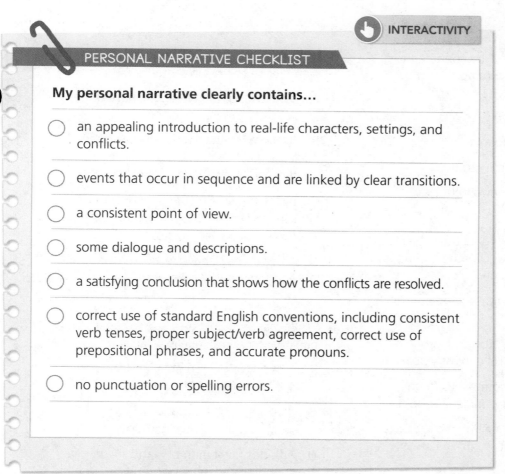

INTERACTIVITY

PERSONAL NARRATIVE CHECKLIST

My personal narrative clearly contains...

- ○ an appealing introduction to real-life characters, settings, and conflicts.

- ○ events that occur in sequence and are linked by clear transitions.

- ○ a consistent point of view.

- ○ some dialogue and descriptions.

- ○ a satisfying conclusion that shows how the conflicts are resolved.

- ○ correct use of standard English conventions, including consistent verb tenses, proper subject/verb agreement, correct use of prepositional phrases, and accurate pronouns.

- ○ no punctuation or spelling errors.

TEKS
10.D. Edit drafts using standard English conventions, including:
10.D.ii. Consistent and appropriate use of verb tenses.
10.D.iv. Prepositions and prepositional phrases and their influence on subject-verb agreement.
10.D.v. Pronouns, including relative.
11.A. Compose literary texts such as personal narratives, fiction, and poetry using genre characteristics and craft.

Revising and Editing

Read this draft and think about corrections the writer might make.
Then, answer the questions that follow.

[1] This year, Amy and I decide she's going to go see the rain-swelled streams at night, to. [2] Every spring, the other kids in our neighborhood talks endlessly about it. [3] Just another thing they've all done together that we two haven't. [4] When dinner ends, I demand of my mother: "We want to go to the brook *tonight*. [5] Everyone else gets to."

[6] "Too dangerous," my mom answers, "I'll bring you girls tomorrow." [7] She ruffles my hair but I dodge away. [8] By morning, the water will have gone, leaving a mess.

[9] "It's not fair I mumble, and she begins sponging the table vigorously. [10] She swipes a hand across her forehead. [11] Her ring has some sort of food stuck in it. [12] I notice her blink fast, then briskly shake her head. [13] No. [14] I know she's afraid for Amy, so I back down.

1. How should sentence 1 be corrected to replace one or more commonly confused words?

A Replace the first *to* with *too*.

B Replace *night* with *knight*.

C Replace the first *to* with *two*.

D Replace the second *to* with *too*.

2. What is the BEST way to fix the subject-verb agreement in sentence 2 without changing the meaning?

F Every spring, the other people talks endlessly about it.

G Every spring, the other kid in our neighborhood talks endlessly about it.

H Every spring, the other kids in our neighborhood talk endlessly about it.

J Every spring, our neighborhood talks endlessly about it.

3. Which revision BEST replaces vague words with precise choices in sentence 8?

A By morning, the water will have gone, leaving a smelly mess.

B By morning, the water will have receded, leaving behind a dead mess of sticky mud, drenched leaves, and broken branches.

C By the time the night has ended and the sun has started to come up, the water will have gone leaving a mess.

D The water will have receded by morning, and the world will be normal again.

4. What change should be made to correct the punctuation of dialogue in sentence 9?

F "It's not fair" I mumble, and she begins sponging the table vigorously.

G "It's not fair," I mumble, and she begins sponging the table vigorously.

H "It's not fair, I mumble, and she begins sponging the table vigorously.

J "It's not fair", I mumble, and she begins sponging the table vigorously.

Reflect on the Unit

NOTEBOOK

INTERACTIVITY

Reflect On the Unit Goals

Review your Unit Goals chart from the beginning of the unit. Then, complete the activity and answer the question.

1. In the Unit Goals chart, rate how well you meet each goal now.

2. In which goals were you most and least successful?

Reflect On the Texts

RATE! Choose three selections you most liked reading. For each, pick a favorite part and describe it in the chart. Explain why it appealed to you or how it related to your life. Then, discuss your choices.

SELECTION BALLOT

Selection Title	Favorite Part	Reason
from *Brown Girl Dreaming*		
Gallery of *Calvin and Hobbes* Comics		
The Sand Castle		
from *Bad Boy*		
The Moth Presents: Aleeza Kazmi		
Prince Francis		
The Sound of Summer Running		

Reflect On the Essential Question

Viewing/Listening List Make a list of media that you've seen or listened to that explore the Essential Question:

What are some of the challenges and triumphs of growing up?

- List at least three movies, TV shows, songs, podcasts, or other media you've enjoyed that speak to the experience of childhood.

- Briefly summarize each item you list, and explain how it relates to the Essential Question.

Tip: You may want to do a quick Internet search to jump start your list of media.

 TEKS

10.C. Revise drafts for word choice; **10.D.** Edit drafts using standard English conventions, including: **10.D.i.** subject-verb agreement; **10.D.ii.** consistent, appropriate use of verb tenses; **10.D.ix.** correct spelling, including commonly confused terms such as *to/two/too*.

Natural Allies

PEARSON
realize
Go ONLINE for
all lessons

AUDIO

VIDEO

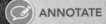

NOTEBOOK

ANNOTATE

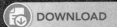

INTERACTIVITY

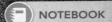

DOWNLOAD

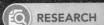

RESEARCH

WATCH THE VIDEO

People of the Horse:
Special Bond

DISCUSS IT Is the relationship between animals and people truly a special bond?

Write your response before sharing your ideas.

UNIT INTRODUCTION

Essential Question

How do animals and people interact?

MENTOR TEXT:
INFORMATIONAL ESSAY
Reading Buddies

 WHOLE-CLASS LEARNING

AUTOBIOGRAPHY
from My Life With the Chimpanzees
Jane Goodall

COMPARE WITHIN GENRE

SCIENCE ARTICLE
How Smart Are Animals?
Dorothy Hinshaw Patent

SCIENCE ARTICLE
So What Is a Primate?
Faith Hickman Brynie

 PEER-GROUP LEARNING

POETRY COLLECTION
Predators
Linda Hogan

The Naming of Cats
T. S. Eliot

Nikita
Alberto Ríos

MYTH
The Tale of the Hummingbird
Pura Belpré

BIOGRAPHY
Black Cowboy, Wild Horses
Julius Lester

INDEPENDENT LEARNING

POETRY
A Blessing
James Wright

MEDIA: VIDEO
The Secret Life of the Dog
British Broadcasting Company

REFLECTIVE ESSAY
All the Pretty Ponies
Oscar Cásares

INFORMATIONAL TEXT
The Girl Who Gets Gifts From Birds
Katy Sewall

INFORMATIONAL TEXT
Pet Therapy: How Animals and Humans Heal Each Other
Julie Rovner

PERFORMANCE TASK
WRITING PROCESS
Informational Essay

PERFORMANCE TASK
SPEAKING AND LISTENING
Give and Follow Oral Instructions

SHARE INDEPENDENT LEARNING
Share • Learn • Reflect

PERFORMANCE-BASED ASSESSMENT

Informational Essay

You will write an informational essay in response to the Essential Question for the unit.

UNIT REFLECTION

Goals • Texts • Essential Question

Unit Goals

 VIDEO

Throughout this unit, you will deepen your understanding of the ways that people and animals can relate to each other by reading, writing, speaking, listening, and presenting. These goals will help you succeed on the Unit Performance-Based Assessment.

👆 **INTERACTIVITY**

SET GOALS Rate how well you meet these goals right now. You will revisit your ratings later when you reflect on your growth during this unit.

SCALE

1	2	3	4	5
NOT AT ALL WELL	NOT VERY WELL	SOMEWHAT WELL	VERY WELL	EXTREMELY WELL

ESSENTIAL QUESTION	Unit Introduction	Unit Reflection
I can read texts that illustrate the different ways animals and people interact and compare it to my own experiences.	1 2 3 4 5	1 2 3 4 5

READING	Unit Introduction	Unit Reflection
I can understand and use academic vocabulary words related to informational texts.	1 2 3 4 5	1 2 3 4 5
I can recognize elements of different genres, especially science writing, poetry, and informational texts.	1 2 3 4 5	1 2 3 4 5
I can read a selection of my choice independently and make meaningful connections to other texts.	1 2 3 4 5	1 2 3 4 5

WRITING	Unit Introduction	Unit Reflection
I can write a focused, well-organized informational essay.	1 2 3 4 5	1 2 3 4 5
I can complete Timed Writing tasks with confidence.	1 2 3 4 5	1 2 3 4 5

SPEAKING AND LISTENING	Unit Introduction	Unit Reflection
I can prepare and deliver an informational presentation.	1 2 3 4 5	1 2 3 4 5

⊕ **TEKS**
2.C. Determine the meaning and usage of grade-level academic English words derived from Greek and Latin roots such as *mis/mit, bene, man, vac, scrib/script,* and *jur/jus.*

Academic Vocabulary: Informational Text

Many English words have roots, or key parts, that come from ancient languages, such as Latin and Greek. Learn these roots and use the words as you respond to questions and activities in this unit.

 INTERACTIVITY

PRACTICE Academic terms are used routinely in classrooms. Build your knowledge of these words by completing the chart.

1. Review each word, its origin, and the mentor sentences.

2. With a partner, read the words and mentor sentences aloud. Then, **determine** the meaning and usage of each word. Use a dictionary, if needed.

3. List at least two related words for each word.

WORD	MENTOR SENTENCES	PREDICT MEANING	RELATED WORDS
exclude LATIN ROOT: **-clud-** "shut"	1. He prefers to invite his entire class to his birthday party rather than *exclude* anyone. 2. To *exclude* people from the club based on their age would be unfair.		include; conclusive
illustrate LATIN ROOT: **-lus-** "shine"	1. Can you give me an example to *illustrate* that idea? I'm confused. 2. I gathered pictures of my family to *illustrate* my autobiographical narrative.		
benefit LATIN WORD PART: **bene-** "well"	1. One *benefit* of daily exercise is a healthier heart. 2. The concert was a *benefit* to raise money for a woman who needs an expensive operation.		
elaborate LATIN ROOT: **-lab-** "work"	1. Because Sara's instructions were hard to understand, Frank asked her to *elaborate* in detail. 2. You may first create an outline to list the key points, but then you must support and *elaborate* on your ideas with examples.		
objective LATIN ROOT: **-ject-** "throw"	1. The *objective* in a soccer game is to score goals by putting the ball in the other team's net. 2. When Mike drafted his resume, he made sure to state his *objective* for career success.		

MENTOR TEXT | INFORMATIONAL ESSAY

This selection is an example of an **informational essay**, a type of nonfiction in which an author presents facts, details, and explanations that help readers understand a topic or process. This is the type of writing you will develop in the Performance-Based Assessment at the end of the unit.

READ IT As you read, notice how the author introduces and explains new information. Mark the text to help you determine key ideas and details.

Reading Buddies

AUDIO

ANNOTATE

1 In a school library across town, a third-grade boy is reading his favorite book to a dog named Theo. The boy is petting the dog as he reads, and the dog has its paw on the boy's foot. Both seem relaxed and happy, but what is a dog doing in a school library?

2 Theo, a five-year-old border collie, is one of more than 2,300 dogs around the country that have been trained to listen to people read aloud. He is part of a program that began in Utah in 1999. Through this program, teams of dogs and their handlers were sent out to schools and libraries to serve as reading companions for kids who were having trouble reading. Since then, similar reading programs have popped up in every region of the United States. They have helped thousands of kids improve not only their reading skills but also their attitudes about reading.

3 There are many reasons kids can have trouble reading. Some have learning disabilities. Some think it's boring. Some are new to English. Others just haven't found a book they like.

4 Whatever the cause, struggling readers have one thing in common: They lack confidence. Learning to read is often less about reading skills than it is about confidence. To a struggling reader, an animal listener can produce less anxiety than a human listener.

5 Dogs are the ideal reading companions. They aren't in a hurry, so you can read at your own pace. They won't stop you when

you've pronounced something wrong. They won't laugh at you or make you feel self-conscious. When you read to a dog, you are not as likely to feel judged. You get a chance to focus on the book you're reading rather than your performance.

6   "I never finished a whole book before," said a 10-year-old girl who participated in the program. She had been reading at a first-grade level and hardly ever practiced, because she was too shy to read aloud. But after a few weeks of reading to a dog companion, she finished the book. She was proud of herself for having overcome such a major hurdle!

7   Reading is like any other skill—the more you practice, the better you get. But it's hard to find someone who has the time to sit down and listen. Readers can also feel nervous about making mistakes. "But if you're practicing with a dog," said one reading specialist, "you don't mind making the mistake. In fact, you'll probably correct it."

8   More and more libraries and schools are using dogs to help kids improve their reading skills and confidence level. Sometimes, when people read to dogs, it's the dogs that benefit. For example, the Arizona Animal Welfare League & Society for Prevention of Cruelty to Animals is using reading as a tool to help shelter animals become happier, more well-adjusted pets. Program volunteers spend time reading to dogs and cats who are waiting to be adopted. Reading calms the animals down and makes them more comfortable around people.

9   Through the experience of reading, humans and animals are helping each other develop the skills they need to take on life's challenges—whatever those challenges happen to be. ❧

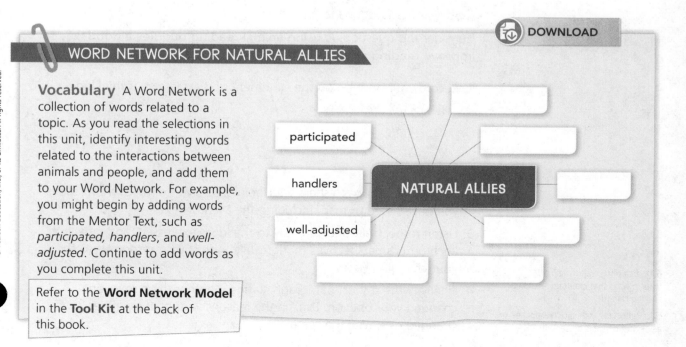

🔽 DOWNLOAD

WORD NETWORK FOR NATURAL ALLIES

Vocabulary A Word Network is a collection of words related to a topic. As you read the selections in this unit, identify interesting words related to the interactions between animals and people, and add them to your Word Network. For example, you might begin by adding words from the Mentor Text, such as *participated, handlers*, and *well-adjusted*. Continue to add words as you complete this unit.

Refer to the **Word Network Model** in the **Tool Kit** at the back of this book.

participated

handlers

well-adjusted

NATURAL ALLIES

Summary

A **summary** is a brief, complete overview of a text that maintains the meaning and logical order of the original work. It should not include your personal opinions.

🗐 NOTEBOOK

WRITE IT Write a summary of "Reading Buddies."

_____
_____
_____
_____
_____
_____
_____
_____
_____
_____
_____

Launch Activity

Conduct a Discussion

Consider this question: Is using animal reading buddies a good way to improve reading skills?

1. Record your position on the statement and explain your thinking.

   ◯ Yes   ◯ No

   _____

2. Form small groups to share your opinions. Give examples from stories you have heard or read, including the Mentor Text.

3. Listen respectfully and carefully to the ideas expressed, and reflect on each other's perspectives thoughtfully. Adjust your responses to show your changing views.

4. Finally, write a short paragraph stating whether the discussion changed your opinion. Explain the reasons your opinion either changed or stayed the same.

⭐ TEKS

6.D. Paraphrase and summarize texts in ways that maintain meaning and logical order.

6.I. Reflect on and adjust responses as new evidence is presented.

QuickWrite

Consider class discussions, the video, and the Mentor Text as you think about the prompt.

Essential Question

How do animals and people interact?

At the end of the unit, you will respond to the Essential Question again and see how your perspective has changed.

NOTEBOOK

WRITE IT Record your first thoughts here.

DOWNLOAD

EQ Notes ▸ How do animals and people interact?

As you read the selections in this unit, use a chart like the one shown to record your ideas and list details from the texts that support them. Taking notes as you go will help you clarify your thinking, gather relevant information, and be ready to respond to the Essential Question.

TITLE	MY IDEAS / OBSERVATIONS	TEXT EVIDENCE / INFORMATION

Refer to the **EQ Notes Model** in the **Tool Kit** at the back of this book.

Essential Question

How do animals and people interact?

Over thousands of years people and animals have formed important relationships. For example, people often rely on animals to help with farmwork, rescue, or transportation; many animals rely on humans for protection, shelter, and food. The selections you are going to read present insights into the bonds that exist between people and animals.

▶ VIDEO

👆 INTERACTIVITY

Whole-Class Learning Strategies

Throughout your life, in school, in your community, and in your career, you will continue to learn and work in large-group environments.

Review these strategies and the actions you can take to practice them as you work with your whole class. Add ideas of your own for each category. Get ready to use these strategies during Whole-Class Learning.

STRATEGY	MY ACTION PLAN
Listen actively • Put away personal items to avoid becoming distracted. • Try to hear the speaker's full message before planning your own response.	
Demonstrate respect • Show up on time and make sure you are prepared for class. • Avoid side conversations while in class.	
Show interest • Be aware of your body language. For example, sit up in your chair. • Respond when the teacher asks for feedback.	
Interact and share ideas • If you're confused, other people probably are, too. Ask a question to help your whole class. • Build on the ideas of others by adding details or making a connection.	

CONTENTS

PERFORMANCE TASK: WRITING PROCESS

Write an Informational Essay
The Whole-Class readings explore aspects of animal behavior and intelligence. After reading, you will write an informational essay in which you explain which traits animals and humans share.

Reading Autobiographies

from MY LIFE WITH THE CHIMPANZEES

The selection you are about to read is an excerpt from an autobiography.

An **autobiography** is a nonfiction narrative, or true story, in which the author relates events from his or her own life.

AUTOBIOGRAPHY

Author's Purpose
- to tell the author's life story in a meaningful way

Characteristics
- features characters who are real people and settings that are real places
- written from the first-person point of view
- uses storytelling techniques, including dialogue and description
- offers insight into the writer's life

Structure
- may describe the full sweep of the author's life or focus on a specific time period
- usually presents events in chronological order

Take a Minute!

 NOTEBOOK

LIST IT Identify a famous person whose autobiography you would be interested in reading. What types of information would you want to learn if that person were to tell his or her own life story? Jot down your ideas.

TEKS

8.D. Analyze characteristics and structural elements of informational text.

9.A. Explain the author's purpose and message within a text.

Genre / Text Elements

Author's Purpose and Message There are four broad purposes for writing—to describe, to inform, to narrate (tell a story), and to persuade. An autobiography is written to tell a story—the story of the writer's own life. The main purpose of autobiography is to narrate. However, by telling his or her own life story, the author of an autobiography also expresses insights and shares a message. Consider these examples:

- Author is a leader whose life shows how society has changed.

- Author played a role in historic events and has a unique point of view.

- Author is an artist or inventor who explores the imagination.

- Author struggled with personal difficulties and is now a role-model.

- Author was the first to study a topic and see its importance.

TIP: In some autobiographies, the writer simply states his or her purpose and message. More often, you need to notice details, think about them, and draw conclusions about the message.

 NOTEBOOK

PRACTICE Read the passage from an autobiography. Then, answer the questions.

It was my aunt's love that saved me. One evening, as the family gathered for supper, my heart was burning in rage. My aunt motioned for me to sit next to her, and she took my hand in hers. My first impulse was to yank it back, for I was angry with the world, but there was a look of kindness in her eyes that drew me to her. I calmed down, and as we ate and spoke quietly, bitterness left my heart. Peace took hold of me, and I was quite another child by the time the meal was done.

1. Explain the message the writer expresses in this passage. Cite details that support your answer.

2. In your view, what is the author's purpose for writing this text? Explain.

About the Author

Dame **Jane Goodall** (b. 1934) is the most celebrated primatologist, or researcher of primates (which includes apes, chimpanzees, and monkeys), of the twentieth century. She spent extended periods living with and observing chimpanzees in the wild. Dr. Goodall did most of her research in Tanzania at the Gombe Stream Game Reserve (now a national park), where she lived from 1960 to 1975. In 1977, she co-founded the Jane Goodall Institute for Wildlife Research, Education, and Conservation.

from My Life With the Chimpanzees

Concept Vocabulary

You will encounter the following words as you read this excerpt from *My Life With the Chimpanzees*. Before reading, note how familiar you are with each word. Then, rank the words in order from most familiar (1) to least familiar (6).

INTERACTIVITY

WORD	YOUR RANKING
vanished	
miserable	
irritable	
threateningly	
impetuous	
dominate	

Comprehension Strategy

ANNOTATE

Establish Purpose for Reading

Active readers **set a purpose**, or reason, for reading. For example, you might read for pleasure, to learn something new, or to solve a problem. Setting a purpose will help you focus your reading and get more from a text.

Answer these questions to set a purpose for reading:

- **What is the genre?** Your purpose should reflect the type of text you are reading.
- **What is the title?** The title can help you get a sense of what a text is about and set your purpose.
- **What else do I know about the text?** A quick scan of the text can help you set your purpose. Look for pictures, subheads, and other text features.

PRACTICE Before you begin to read this excerpt, establish your purpose. Write it here.

TEKS
5.A. Establish purpose for reading assigned and self-selected text.

from
My Life With the **Chimpanzees**

Jane Goodall

BACKGROUND

Gombe Stream National Park in Tanzania, Africa, is best known as the site of Jane Goodall's groundbreaking chimpanzee research. The park covers only about 20 square miles, but is home to a great variety of animals. Dr. Goodall's research in Gombe was supported by the famous paleontologist Louis Leakey. In this account, Dr. Goodall occasionally refers to Dr. Leakey by his first name only.

 AUDIO

 ANNOTATE

1   July 16, 1960, was a day I shall remember all my life. It was when I first set foot on the shingle and sand beach of Chimpanzee Land—that is, Gombe National Park. I was twenty-six years old.

2   Mum and I were greeted by the two African game scouts who were responsible for protecting the thirty square miles of the park. They helped us to find a place where we could put up our old ex-army tent.

3   We chose a lovely spot under some shady trees near the small, fast-flowing Kakombe Stream. In Kigoma (before setting out), we had found a cook, Dominic. He put up his little tent some distance from ours and quite near the lake.

4   When camp was ready I set off to explore. It was already late afternoon, so I could not go far. There had been a grass fire not long before, so all the vegetation of the more open ridges and peaks had burned away. This made it quite easy to move around, except that the slopes above the valley were very steep in places, and I slipped several times on the loose, gravelly soil.

5   I shall never forget the thrill of that first exploration. Soon after leaving camp I met a troop of baboons. They were afraid of the strange, white-skinned creature (that was I) and gave their barking alarm call, "Waa-hoo! Waa-hoo!" again and again. I left them, hoping that they would become used to me soon—otherwise, I thought, all the creatures of Gombe would be frightened. As I crossed a narrow ravine crowded with low trees and bushes I got very close to a beautiful red-gold bushbuck—a forest antelope about the size of a long-legged goat. I knew it was female because she had no horns. When she scented me she kept quite still for a moment and stared toward me with her big dark eyes. Then, with a loud barking call, she turned and bounded away.

6   When I got to one of the high ridges I looked down into the valley. There the forest was dark and thick. That was where I planned to go the next day to look for chimpanzees.

7   When I got back to camp it was dusk. Dominic had made a fire and was cooking our supper. That evening, and for the next four days, we had fresh food from Kigoma, but after that we ate out of cans. Louis had not managed to find very much money for our expedition, so our possessions were few and simple—a knife, fork, and spoon each, a couple of tin plates and tin mugs. But that was all we needed. After supper, Mum and I talked around our campfire, then snuggled into our two cots in the tent.

8   Early the next morning I set out to search for chimpanzees. I had been told by the British game ranger in charge of Gombe not to travel about the mountains by myself—except near camp. Otherwise, I had to take one of the game scouts with me. So I set off with Adolf. That first day we saw two chimps feeding in a tall tree. As soon as they saw us they leapt down and **vanished**. The next day we saw no chimps at all. Nor the day after. Nor the day after that.

9   A whole week went by before we found a very big tree full of tiny round red fruits that Adolf told me were called *msulula*. From the other side of the valley we could watch chimps arriving at the tree, feeding, then climbing down and vanishing into the forest. I decided to camp in the best viewing site so that I could see them first thing in the morning. I spent three days in that valley and I saw a lot of chimps. But they were too far away and the foliage of the tree was too thick. It was disappointing and frustrating, and I didn't have much to tell Mum when I got back.

10   There was another problem that I had to cope with—Adolf was very lazy. He was almost always late in the morning. I decided to try another man, Rashidi. He was far better and helped me a lot, showing me the trails through the forests and the best ways to move from one valley to the next. He had sharp eyes and spotted chimps from far away.

11   But even after several months, the chimps had not become used to us. They ran off if we got anywhere near to them. I begged the game ranger to let me move about the forests by myself. I promised that I would always tell Rashidi in which direction I was going, so that he would know where to look for me if I failed to turn up in the evening. The game ranger finally gave in. At last I could make friends with the chimpanzees in my own way.

12   Every morning I got up when I heard the alarm clock at 5:30 A.M. I ate a couple of slices of bread and had a cup of coffee from the Thermos flask. Then I set off, climbing to where I thought the chimps might be.

13   Most often, I went to the Peak. I discovered that from this high place I had a splendid view in all directions. I could see chimps moving in the trees and I could hear if they called. At first I watched from afar, through my binoculars, and never tried to get close. I knew that if I did, the chimps would run silently away.

14   Gradually I began to learn about the chimps' home and how they lived. I discovered that, most of the time, the chimps wandered about in small groups of six or less, not in a big troop like the baboons. Often a little group was made up of a mother with her children, or two or three adult males by themselves. Sometimes many groups joined together, especially when there was delicious ripe fruit on one big tree. When the chimps got together like that, they were very excited, made a lot of noise, and were easy to find.

15   Eventually I realized that the chimps I watched from the Peak were all part of one group—a community. There were about fifty chimps belonging to this community. They made use of three of the valleys to the north of the Kakombe Valley (where our tent was) and two valleys to the south. These valleys have lovely sounding names: Kasakela, Linda, and Rutanga in the north, Mkenke and Nyasanga in the south.

16   From the Peak I noted which trees the chimps were feeding in and then, when they had gone, I scrambled down and collected some of the leaves, flowers, or fruits so they could be identified later. I found that the chimps eat mostly fruits but also a good many kinds of leaves, blossoms, seeds, and stems. Later I would discover that they eat a variety of insects and sometimes hunt and kill prey animals to feed on meat.

17   During those months of gradual discovery, the chimps very slowly began to realize that I was not so frightening after all. Even so, it was almost a year before I could approach to within one hundred yards, and that is not really very close. The baboons got used to me much more quickly. Indeed, they became a nuisance around our camp by grabbing any food that we accidentally left lying on the table.

CLOSE READ

ANNOTATE: In paragraph 17, mark details that show how the chimps behave. Mark other details that show how the baboons behave.

QUESTION: Why does Goodall contrast the chimps' and baboons' behavior?

CONCLUDE: What does this contrast reveal about the chimps?

18   I began to learn more about the other creatures that shared the forests with the chimpanzees. There were four kinds of monkeys in addition to the baboons, and many smaller animals such as squirrels and mongooses. There was also a whole variety of nocturnal (nighttime) creatures: porcupines and civets (creatures looking rather like raccoons) and all manners of rats and mice. Only a very few animals in the forests at Gombe were potentially dangerous—mainly buffalo and leopards. Bush pigs can be dangerous too, but only if you threaten them or their young. And, of course, there are poisonous snakes—seven different kinds.

19   Once, as I arrived on the Peak in the early morning before it was properly light, I saw the dark shape of a large animal looming in front of me. I stood quite still. My heart began to beat fast, for I realized it was a buffalo. Many hunters fear buffalo more than lions or elephants.

20   By a lucky chance the wind was blowing from him to me, so he couldn't smell me. He was peacefully gazing in the opposite direction and chewing his cud. He hadn't heard my approach—always I try to move as quietly as I can in the bush. So, though I was only ten yards from him, he had no idea I was there. Very slowly I retreated.

21   Another time, as I was sitting on the Peak, I heard a strange mewing sound. I looked around and there, about fifteen yards away, a leopard was approaching. I could just see the black and white tip of its tail above the tall grass. It was walking along the little trail that led directly to where I sat.

22   Leopards are not usually dangerous unless they have been wounded. But I was frightened of them in those days—probably as a result of my experience with the leopard and the wolfhound[1] two years before. And so, very silently, I moved away and looked for chimps in another valley.

23   Later I went back to the Peak. I found that, just like any cat, that leopard had been very curious. There, in the exact place where I had been sitting, he had left his mark—his droppings.

24   Most of the time, though, nothing more alarming than insects disturbed my vigils on the Peak. It began to feel like home. I carried a little tin trunk up there. In it I kept a kettle, some sugar and coffee, and a tin mug. Then, when I got tired from a long trek to another valley, I could make a drink in the middle of the day. I kept a blanket up there, too, and when the chimps slept near the Peak, I slept there, so that I could be close by in the morning. I loved to be up there at night, especially when there was a moon. If I heard the coughing grunt of a leopard, I just prayed and pulled the blanket over my head!

---

1. **leopard and the wolfhound** Previously, Goodall saw a leopard kill a large hunting dog.

25   Chimps sleep all night, just as we do. From the Peak I often watched how they made their nests, or beds. First the chimp bent a branch down over some solid foundation, such as a fork or two parallel branches. Holding it in place with his feet, he then bent another over it. Then he folded the end of the first branch back over the second. And so on. He often ended up by picking lots of small, soft, leafy twigs to make a pillow. Chimps like their comfort! I've learned over the years that infants sleep in their nest with their mothers until they are about five years old or until the next baby is born and the older child has to make its own bed.

26   I never returned to camp before sunset. But even when I slept on the Peak, I first went down to have supper with Mum and tell her what I had seen that day. And she would tell me what she had been doing.

27   Mum set up a clinic. She handed out medicine to any of the local Africans, mostly fishermen, who were sick. Once she cured an old man who was very ill indeed. Word about this cure spread far and wide, and sometimes patients would walk for miles to get treatment from the wonderful white woman-doctor.

28   Her clinic was very good for me. It meant that the local people realized we wanted to help. When Mum had to go back to England after four months to manage things at home, the Africans wanted, in turn, to help me.

29   Of course, Mum worried about leaving me on my own. Dominic was a wonderful cook and great company. He was not really reliable. So Louis Leakey asked Hassan to come all the way from Lake Victoria to help with the boat and engine. It was lovely to see his handsome, smiling face again, and his arrival relieved Mum's mind no end.

30   Of course, I missed her after she'd gone, but I didn't have time to be lonely. There was so much to do.

31   Soon after she'd left, I got back one evening and was greeted by an excited Dominic. He told me that a big male chimp had spent an hour feeding on the fruit of one of the oil-nut palms growing in the camp clearing. Afterward he had climbed down, gone over to my tent, and taken the bananas that had just been put there for my supper.

32   This was fantastic news. For months the chimps had been running off when they saw me—now one had actually visited my camp! Perhaps he would come again.

33   The next day I waited, in case he did. What a luxury to lie in until 7:00 A.M. As the hours went by I began to fear that the chimp wouldn't come. But finally, at about four in the afternoon, I heard a rustling in the undergrowth opposite my tent, and a black shape appeared on the other side of the clearing.

CLOSE READ

ANNOTATE: In paragraph 32, mark the punctuation that Dr. Goodall uses to describe her reaction to the news about the chimpanzee visit.

QUESTION: Why might she have chosen to use this punctuation?

CONCLUDE: What does the punctuation reveal about her reaction?

Dr. Goodall was the first person to observe chimps like this one using grass and sticks to "fish" for termites.

34   I recognized him at once. It was the handsome male with the dense white beard. I had already named him David Greybeard. Quite calmly he climbed into the palm and feasted on its nuts. And then he helped himself to the bananas I had set out for him.

35   There were ripe palm nuts on that tree for another five days, and David Greybeard visited three more times and got lots of bananas.

36   A month later, when another palm tree in camp bore ripe fruit, David again visited us. And on one of those occasions he actually took a banana from my hand. I could hardly believe it.

37   From that time on things got easier for me. Sometimes when I met David Greybeard out in the forest, he would come up to see if I had a banana hidden in my pocket. The other chimps stared with amazement. Obviously I wasn't as dangerous as they had thought. Gradually they allowed me closer and closer.

38   It was David Greybeard who provided me with my most exciting observation. One morning, near the Peak, I came upon him squatting on a termite mound. As I watched, he picked a blade of grass, poked it into a tunnel in the mound, and then withdrew it. The grass was covered with termites all clinging on with their jaws. He picked them off with his lips and scrunched them up. Then he fished for more. When his piece of grass got bent, he dropped it, picked up a little twig, stripped the leaves off it, and used that.

39   I was really thrilled. David had used objects as tools! He had also changed a twig into something more suitable for fishing termites. He had actually *made* a tool. Before this observation, scientists had thought that only humans could make tools. Later I would learn that chimpanzees use more objects as tools than any creature except for us. This finding excited Louis Leakey more than any other.

40   In October the dry season ended and it began to rain. Soon the golden mountain slopes were covered with lush green grass. Flowers appeared, and the air smelled lovely. Most days it rained just a little. Sometimes there was a downpour. I loved being out in the forest in the rain. And I loved the cool evenings when I could lace the tent shut and make it cozy inside with a storm lantern. The only trouble was that everything got damp and grew mold.

Scorpions and giant poisonous centipedes sometimes appeared in the tent—even, a few times, a snake. But I was lucky—I never got stung or bitten.

41   The chimpanzees often seemed **miserable** in the rain. They looked cold, and they shivered. Since they were clever enough to use tools, I was surprised that they had not learned to make shelters. Many of them got coughs and colds. Often, during heavy rain, they seemed **irritable** and bad tempered.

42   Once, as I walked through thick forest in a downpour, I suddenly saw a chimp hunched in front of me. Quickly I stopped. Then I heard a sound from above. I looked up and there was a big chimp there, too. When he saw me he gave a loud, clear wailing *wraaaah*—a spine-chilling call that is used to threaten a dangerous animal. To my right I saw a large black hand shaking a branch and bright eyes glaring **threateningly** through the foliage. Then came another savage *wraaaah* from behind. Up above, the big male began to sway the vegetation. I was surrounded. I crouched down, trying to appear as nonthreatening as possible.

43   Suddenly a chimp charged straight toward me. His hair bristled with rage. At the last minute he swerved and ran off. I stayed still. Two more chimps charged nearby. Then, suddenly, I realized I was alone again. All the chimps had gone.

44   Only then did I realize how frightened I had been. When I stood up my legs were trembling! Male chimps, although they are only four feet tall when upright, are at least three times stronger than a grown man. And I weighed only about ninety pounds. I had become very thin with so much climbing in the mountains and only one meal a day. That incident took place soon after the chimps had lost their initial terror of me but before they had learned to accept me calmly as part of their forest world. If David Greybeard had been among them, they probably would not have behaved like that, I thought.

45   After my long days in the forests I looked forward to supper. Dominic always had it ready for me when I got back in the evenings. Once a month he went into Kigoma with Hassan. They came back with new supplies, including fresh vegetables and fruit and eggs. And they brought my mail—that was something I really looked forward to.

46   After supper I would get out the little notebook in which I had scribbled everything I had seen while watching the chimps during the day. I would settle down to write it all legibly into my journal. It was very important to do that every evening, while it was all fresh in my mind. Even on days when I climbed back to sleep near the chimps, I always wrote up my journal first.

47   Gradually, as the weeks went by, I began to recognize more and more chimpanzees as individuals. Some, like Goliath, William, and

miserable (MIHZ uhr uh buhl) *adj.* extremely unhappy or uncomfortable

irritable (IHR uh tuh buhl) *adj.* easily annoyed or angered

threateningly (THREHT uhn ihng lee) *adv.* in a frightening or alarming way

ANNOTATE: In paragraphs 48–49, mark the words that describe how the chimps look and behave.

QUESTION: Why do you think Dr. Goodall chose to include these descriptions of the chimps and their behavior?

CONCLUDE: How do these descriptions help the reader better understand the chimps?

impetuous (ihm PEHCH yoo uhs) *adj.* acting suddenly with little thought

old Flo, I got to know well, because David Greybeard sometimes brought them with him when he visited camp. I always had a supply of bananas ready in case the chimps arrived.

48 Once you have been close to chimps for a while they are as easy to tell apart as your classmates. Their faces look different, and they have different characters. David Greybeard, for example, was a calm chimp who liked to keep out of trouble. But he was also very determined to get his own way. If he arrived in camp and couldn't find any bananas, he would walk into my tent and search. Afterward, all was chaos. It looked as though some burglar had raided the place! Goliath had a much more excitable, **impetuous** temperament. William, with his long-shaped face, was shy and timid.

49 Old Flo was easy to identify. She had a bulbous nose and ragged ears. She came to camp with her infant daughter, whom I named Fifi, and her juvenile son, Figan. Sometimes adolescent Faben came, too. It was from Flo that I first learned that in the wild, female chimps have only one baby every five or six years. The older offspring, even after they have become independent, still spend a lot of time with their mothers, and all the different family members help one another.

50 Flo also taught me that female chimps do not have just one mate. One day she came to my camp with a pink swelling on her rump. This was a sign that she was ready for mating. She was followed by a long line of suitors. Many of them had never visited my camp before, and they were scared. But they were so attracted to Flo that they overcame their fear in order to keep close to her. She allowed them all to mate with her at different times.

51 Soon after the chimps had begun to visit my camp, the National Geographic Society, which was giving Louis money for my research, sent a photographer to Gombe to make a film. Hugo van Lawick was a Dutch baron. He loved and respected animals just as I did, and he made a wonderful movie. One year later, in England, we got married.

52 By then I had left Gombe for a while, to start my own studies at Cambridge University. I hated to leave, but I knew I would soon be back. I had promised Louis that I would work hard and get my Ph.D. degree.

53 After I got the degree, Hugo and I went back to Gombe together. It was a very exciting time, as Flo had just had a baby, little Flint. That was the first wild chimpanzee infant that I ever saw close up, nearly four years after I had begun my research.

54 Flo came very often to camp looking for bananas. Fifi, now six years old, and Figan, five years older, were still always with her. Fifi loved her new baby brother. When he was four months old

she was allowed to play with and groom him. Sometimes Flo let her carry him when they moved through the forest. During that time, Fifi learned a lot about how to be a good mother.

55   Flint learned to walk and climb when he was six months old. And he learned to ride on his mother's back during travel, instead of always clinging on underneath. He gradually spent more time playing with his two older brothers. They were always very gentle with him. So were other youngsters of the community. They had to be, for if Flo thought any other chimps were too rough, she would charge over and threaten or even attack them.

> Gradually, as the weeks went by, I began to recognize more and more chimpanzees as individuals.

56   I watched how Flint gradually learned to use more and more of the different calls and gestures that chimpanzees use to communicate with each other. Some of these gestures are just like ours— holding hands, embracing, kissing, patting one another on the back. They mean about the same, too. And although they do not make up a language the way human words do, all the different calls do help the chimpanzees know what is happening, even if they are far away when they hear the sounds. Each call (there are at least thirty, perhaps more) means something different.

57   Flo was the top-ranked female of her community and could **dominate** all the others. But she could not boss any of the males. In chimpanzee society, males are the dominant sex. Among the males themselves, there is a social order, and one male at the top is the boss.

dominate (DOM uh nayt) *v.* rule or control

58   The first top-ranking male I knew was Goliath. Then, in 1964, Mike took over. He did this by using his brain. He would gather up one or two empty kerosene cans from my camp and hit and kick them ahead of him as he charged toward a group of adult males. It was a spectacular performance and made a lot of noise. The other chimps fled. So Mike didn't need to fight to get to the top—which was just as well, as he was a very small chimp. He was top male for six years.

59   The adult males spend a lot of time in each other's company. They often patrol the boundaries of their territory and may attack chimpanzees of different communities if they meet. These conflicts are very brutal, and the victim may die. Only young females can move from one community to another without being hurt. In fact, the big males sometimes go out looking for such females and try to take them back into their own territory.

This photo from 1965 shows Dr. Goodall in her Gombe Stream camp with the chimp she named David Greybeard.

60   As the months went by, I learned more and more. I recorded more and more details when I watched the chimpanzees. Instead of writing the information in notebooks, I started to use a little tape recorder. Then I could keep my eyes on the chimps all the time. By the end of each day there was so much typing to be done that I found I couldn't do it all myself. I needed an assistant to help. Soon, with even more chimps coming to camp, I needed other people to help with the observations.

61   There were always more fascinating things to watch and record, more people to help write everything down. What had started as a little camp for Mum and me ended up, six years later, as a research center, where students could come and collect information for their degrees. I was the director. ⚘

Reprinted with the permission of Simon & Schuster Books for Young Readers, an imprint of Simon & Schuster Children's Publishing Division from *My Life With the Chimpanzees* by Jane Goodall. Copyright 1988, 1996 Byron Preiss Visual Publications, Inc. Text copyright © 1998, 1996 Jane Goodall.

Response

1. **Personal Connections** What part of Goodall's work do you find most interesting? Cite a specific passage or detail that led to your response.

Answer the questions in your notebook. Use text evidence to support your responses.

Comprehension

2. **Reading Check (a)** At first, how do the chimpanzees react to Goodall? **(b)** Why does Goodall first leave Gombe? **(c)** How long does it take for Goodall's camp to grow into a research center?

3. **Strategy: Establish Purpose for Reading (a)** How did establishing a purpose for reading help you better understand the text? **(b)** Would you recommend this strategy to others? Why or why not?

Analysis

4. **Make Inferences** What do David Greybeard's visits to Goodall's camp suggest about the chimpanzees' changing response to her presence? Cite text evidence that supports your response.

5. **(a)** What happens to Goodall in paragraphs 42–44? **(b) Analyze** What do you learn about chimps in this passage? **(c) Make Inferences** What can you infer about Goodall based on her reactions to the incident?

6. **Evaluate** In this text, does Goodall focus more on herself or on the chimps? What does this choice reveal about Goodall's interests?

EQ Notes How do animals and people interact?

What have you learned about how animals and people interact from reading this section of an autobiography? Go to your Essential Question Notes and record your observations and thoughts about this excerpt from *My Life with the Chimpanzees*.

 TEKS

6.C. Use text evidence to support an appropriate response.

6.G. Discuss and write about the explicit or implicit meanings of text.

Close Read

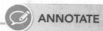 **ANNOTATE**

1. The model passage and annotation show how one reader analyzed part of paragraph 42 of the excerpt. Find another detail in the passage to annotate. Then, write your own question and conclusion.

CLOSE-READ MODEL

Once, as I walked through thick forest in a downpour, I suddenly saw a chimp hunched in front of me. Quickly I stopped. Then I heard a sound from above. I looked up and there was a big chimp there, too.

ANNOTATE: The writer has included a series of phrases that describe her actions.

QUESTION: What effect is created by these word choices?

CONCLUDE: The phrases help to create a feeling of suspense.

MY QUESTION:

MY CONCLUSION:

2. For more practice, answer the Close-Read notes in the selection.

3. Choose a section of the excerpt that you found especially important. Mark important details. Then, jot down questions and write your conclusions in the open space next to the text.

Inquiry and Research

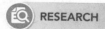 **RESEARCH**

 **NOTEBOOK**

Research and Extend As you go through school, you will need to follow your own curiosity and write your own research questions. Practice by generating your own questions about ideas or situations you read about in this text. Write an "I want to know more" statement about an aspect of the text that interests you. Then, change that statement into a question. One example has been done for you.

Statement: I want to know more about *what Jane Goodall did later in life.*

Research Question: *What did Jane Goodall do later in life?*

Statement: I want to know more about _____.

Research Question: _____.

Write as many statements and questions as you wish. Then, use one as the focus for a brief, informal inquiry. Jot down the answers you find.

 TEKS

9.A. Explain the author's purpose and message within a text.

12.A. Generate student-selected and teacher-guided questions for formal and informal inquiry.

Genre / Text Elements

Author's Purpose and Message An **author's purpose** is his or her main reason for writing. An **author's message** is the "big idea" or point that he or she communicates. Even though an autobiography is true, the author makes choices about how to tell his or her story and which details to include. Those choices shape the message.

To understand the message of an autobiography, identify key details and think about how they connect. Consider the following types of details:

- words and phrases that show strong feelings
- descriptions of people (or animals) and places
- episodes that show how a situation changes or develops

TIP: The four broad purposes for writing are to describe, to narrate, to inform, and to persuade. Every writer also has a specific purpose for writing a given text. For example, he or she wants to tell a certain story to convey a particular insight.

 NOTEBOOK

 INTERACTIVITY

PRACTICE Complete the activity and answer the questions.

1. **Analyze** Reread the passages listed in the chart and take notes about details in each one that seem important.

PASSAGE	NOTES
Paragraph 32: "This was fantastic news ... he would come again."	
Paragraph 37: "From that time ... they allowed me closer and closer."	
Paragraph 56: "I watched how Flint ... mean about the same, too."	
Paragraph 61: "There were always more fascinating things ... the director."	

2. **Connect** How do the passages noted in the chart relate to each other? Cite details from your chart to support your answer.

3. **Interpret** What is Goodall's message, or "big idea," in this excerpt? Explain, citing details from your chart or elsewhere in the autobiography to support your answer.

4. **Connect** What does the title of the autobiography tell you about Goodall's purpose and message? Explain.

from MY LIFE WITH THE
CHIMPANZEES

Concept Vocabulary

 **NOTEBOOK**

Why These Words? The vocabulary words describe different aspects of the chimpanzees' behavior or emotions. For example, the chimpanzees appear *miserable* and *irritable* in the rain.

vanished	irritable	impetuous
miserable	threateningly	dominate

PRACTICE

1. How do the vocabulary words sharpen the reader's understanding of chimpanzees' behavior?

2. What other words in the selection connect to this concept?

3. Use each vocabulary word in a sentence that shows the word's meaning. Then, use a dictionary or thesaurus to find at least one **synonym** (word with a similar meaning) and one **antonym** (word with an opposite meaning) for each vocabulary word.

Word Study

 **NOTEBOOK**

Latin Suffix: -able The Latin suffix *-able* means "capable of, given to, or tending to," and it usually indicates that a word is an adjective. In *My Life With the Chimpanzees*, the word *irritable* means "tending to be irritated," or "tending to be easily annoyed."

PRACTICE Complete the following items:

1. The word *miserable* is related to the word *misery*. How does knowing the meaning of the suffix *-able* help you understand the meaning of *miserable*?

2. Explain how the addition of the suffix *-able* changes the meaning of the first word in each pair:

notice / noticeable

believe / believable

WORD NETWORK

Add words that describe interactions between animals and people from the text to your Word Network.

⭐ TEKS

6.F. Respond using newly acquired vocabulary as appropriate.

10.D.viii. Edit drafts using standard English conventions, including punctuation marks, including commas in complex sentences, transitions, and introductory elements.

Conventions

Commas A **comma** is a punctuation mark that signals readers to pause. It is used in a variety of ways.

- to set off transitional words or phrases
  EXAMPLE: *Other chimps, however, followed Greybeard's lead.*

- after introductory elements, such as prepositional phrases
  EXAMPLE: *After several months, the chimps were still nervous.*

- to separate three or more words in a series
  EXAMPLE: *The chimps ate fruit, insects, and leaves.*

- to set off nonessential, or nonrestrictive, elements
  A nonessential, or nonrestrictive, element is one that can be removed from a sentence without changing its basic meaning.
  EXAMPLE: *David Greybeard, the boldest chimp, was the first one Dr. Goodall met.*

Commas are also used between clauses in compound and complex sentences. A **compound sentence** contains two independent clauses. A **complex sentence** contains an independent clause and one or more dependent clauses.

> **TIP:** An independent clause has a subject and a verb and can stand on its own as a sentence. A dependent clause also has a subject and a verb but cannot stand on its own.

SENTENCE TYPE AND RULES	EXAMPLE
Compound Sentence Separate the independent clauses with a comma and a coordinating conjunction, such as *and, or,* or *but.*	She thought primates were interesting, and she wanted to learn about them
Complex Sentence When the dependent clause comes before the independent clause, separate them with a comma. When the dependent clause comes after the independent clause, no comma is needed.	Because she thought primates were interesting, she wanted to learn about them. She wanted to learn about primates because she thought they were interesting.

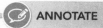 **ANNOTATE**

READ IT Reread paragraph 30 of the autobiography. Mark the commas and explain how each one is being used.

WRITE IT Edit this paragraph by adding commas correctly.

> After arriving in Africa Jane Goodall began her chimpanzee research. Because the chimpanzees did not yet trust her she spent months observing them from afar. It took more than a year but she finally gained their acceptance. Eventually her methods became models for other research.

from MY LIFE WITH THE CHIMPANZEES

Composition

A **how-to essay** is a type of explanatory essay that provides step-by-step instructions for how to do or make something.

TIP: As you draft your essay, remember to use commas correctly in complex sentences and with transitions and introductory elements.

ASSIGNMENT

Write a **how-to essay** that uses Dr. Goodall's process as a model and tells readers how they, too, can earn an animal's trust. Review the text, and record details related to Dr. Goodall's process. Then, plan and write your essay so that it has a logical structure.

- Introduce your topic and thesis, or controlling idea, in the first paragraph. This should define the overall approach you want readers to take to earn an animal's trust.

- Devote one body paragraph to each step in the process. Describe each step in complete sentences. Use transitions such as *first, next, then,* and *finally* to create a clear sequence for your readers to follow.

- Write a conclusion that restates your thesis and sums up the process.

 NOTEBOOK

Reflect on Your Writing

PRACTICE Think about the choices you made as you wrote. Also consider what you learned by writing. Share your experiences by responding to these questions.

1. How did explaining the steps in Dr. Goodall's process help you better understand her research?

2. Which details from the excerpt did you include in your writing? How did they help to convey the steps of the process?

3. **WHY THESE WORDS?** The words you choose make a difference in your writing. Which words did you specifically choose to clarify the steps in the process?

TEKS

1.A. Listen actively to interpret a message, ask clarifying questions, and respond appropriately.

10.B.i. Develop drafts into a focused, structured, and coherent piece of writing by organizing with purposeful structure, including an introduction, transitions, coherence within and across paragraphs, and a conclusion.

10.D.viii. Edit drafts using standard English conventions, including punctuation marks, including commas in complex sentences, transitions, and introductory elements.

11.B. Compose informational texts, including multi-paragraph essays that convey information about a topic, using a clear controlling idea or thesis statement, genre characteristics and craft.

Speaking and Listening

A **class discussion** is a conversation that takes place among an entire class in an academic setting.

ASSIGNMENT

Dr. Goodall describes several chimpanzee behaviors that are similar to human behaviors. Participate in a **class discussion** in which you compare and contrast these behaviors.

- **Use Text Evidence:** Think about details from the autobiography, and use them as evidence. Include examples from your own experience.

- **Listen Actively:** During the discussion, listen actively, giving your full attention to each speaker. Avoid interrupting one another. Instead, focus on interpreting each person's message. Ask questions to clarify any points or ideas that you find confusing or don't fully understand.

- **Speak Respectfully:** If you disagree with a statement, express your reasons respectfully. Consider using language such as the following:

    I want to understand your point of view better. Can you explain why you feel this way?

    I see your point. However, I disagree because . . .

 **INTERACTIVITY**

Evaluate the Class Discussion

Use a presentation evaluation guide like the one shown to evaluate the class discussion.

PRESENTATION EVALUATION GUIDE

Rate each statement on a scale of 1 (not demonstrated) to 5 (demonstrated).

	1	2	3	4	5
Each class member contributed ideas.	○	○	○	○	○
Class members listened actively as each person spoke and did not interrupt one other.	○	○	○	○	○
Class members asked clarifying questions and expressed disagreements respectfully.	○	○	○	○	○

EQ Notes ▶ Before moving on to a new selection, go to your Essential Question Notes and record any additional thoughts or observations you may have about the excerpt from *My Life with the Chimpanzees*.

HOW SMART ARE ANIMALS?

Nonfiction

A **science article** is a type of journalism, or nonfiction reporting, that presents scientific information for nonscientists.

SO WHAT IS A PRIMATE?

SCIENCE ARTICLE

Author's Purpose
➔ to communicate information about science topics in a way that nonscientists can understand

Characteristics
➔ provides factual information, often from scientific studies and experts

➔ expresses a controlling idea, or main point

➔ presents information in an engaging way, often with anecdotes, or brief stories

➔ supports conclusions with evidence from multiple sources

Structure
➔ may use a specific organizational pattern, such as classification or definition

Take a Minute!

 NOTEBOOK

FIND IT Work with a partner to find two other examples of science articles online or in this program. Jot down the titles.

Where did you find the two articles?

⭐ **TEKS**
8.D.iii. Analyze characteristics and structural elements of informational text, including organizational patterns such as definition, classification, advantage, and disadvantage.

Genre/Text Elements

Organizational Patterns The arrangement of information in an article is its structure. Sometimes, the structure follows a specific **organizational pattern**, or order. That pattern helps to show certain types of relationships among the parts of a topic.

> **TIP:** Some writers will use more than one organizational pattern in the same article.

TYPE OF PATTERN	HOW IT ORGANIZES INFORMATION	SIGNAL WORDS
Classification	divides a complex topic into smaller classes—categories, or groups	*type, kind, first, second, example*
Definition	shows how the writer views, or defines, a complex idea, especially one that is open to interpretation or not generally known	*is called, refers to, consists of*

 **INTERACTIVITY**

PRACTICE Answer the questions.

1. Read the excerpts from two science articles. Determine whether the full article most likely uses mainly classification or definition. Note your answers in the chart.

2. Then, in the third column, explain which details in each excerpt helped you make your choice.

PASSAGE	TYPE OF PATTERN	DETAILS
from "Kinds of Cats" All cats, from jungle cats to house cats, belong to the cat family, *Felidae*. The *Felidae* family includes two subfamilies, the *Pantherine* and *Felinae*. These subfamilies include approximately thirty-six separate species.		
from "Reptiles are Amazing" The scientific name "reptiles" refers to an animal that has cold blood, lays eggs, and has a body that is covered with scales or hard parts. Snakes, lizards, and turtles are reptiles.		

HOW SMART ARE
ANIMALS?

Compare Nonfiction

In this lesson, you will read two science articles,
"How Smart Are Animals?" and "So What
Is a Primate?" You will then compare the
two texts.

SO WHAT IS A PRIMATE?

About the Author

Dorothy Hinshaw Patent
(b. 1940) has always loved
animals and nature; her
childhood bedroom was
lined with aquariums
containing pet snakes,
frogs, lizards, and tropical
fish. Not surprisingly, her
books focus on science and
nature. Her many books
include *Dog on Board*, the
true story of Eclipse, the
bus-riding dog of Seattle.

How Smart Are Animals?

Concept Vocabulary

INTERACTIVITY

You will encounter the following words as you read the science article.
Before reading, note how familiar you are with each word. Using a scale
of 1 (do not know it at all) to 5 (know it very well), indicate your
knowledge of each word.

WORD	YOUR RATING
evaluate	
observing	
investigation	
phenomenon	
interpret	
measurable	

Comprehension Strategy

ANNOTATE

Monitor Comprehension: Reread

As you read a text, monitor your comprehension by noticing how well
you are taking in information and understanding ideas. If you need to
clarify any aspect of a text, make adjustments. For example, you might
reread a sentence, passage, or larger section. Follow these steps to
reread:

- Pause at the end of a paragraph, section, or chapter.
- Think about what you have just read.
- State what you've just read in your own words.
- If you cannot remember or do not understand what you read,
  reread the text again, more slowly this time.

PRACTICE As you read this article, monitor your comprehension
and make adjustments, rereading if necessary.

TEKS
5.I. Monitor comprehension
and make adjustments such as
re-reading, using background
knowledge, asking questions, and
annotating when understanding
breaks down.

How Smart Are Animals?

Dorothy Hinshaw Patent

∧ Villa, a Newfoundland dog like this one, saved a child caught in a snowdrift.

BACKGROUND

Do animals have emotions? Can a monkey have morals? Can a dog plan ahead? Questions like these have long been on the minds of those who study and research animal behavior. However, determining clear answers to these questions and others like them has proved to be a challenge.

AUDIO

ANNOTATE

How Smart Is Smart?

1   The blizzard came on suddenly, with no warning. Eleven-year-old Andrea Anderson was outside near her home when the storm struck. The sixty- to eighty-mile-an-hour winds drove her

into a snowdrift, and the snow quickly covered her up to her waist. Unable to get out, she screamed desperately for help. Through the swirling wind, Villa, a year-old Newfoundland dog belonging to Andrea's neighbors, heard her cries. Villa had always been content to stay inside her dog run, but now she leapt over the five-foot fence and rushed to Andrea's side. First she licked the girl, then began circling around her, packing down the snow with her paws. Next, Villa stood still as a statue in front of the girl with her paws on the packed snow. The dog waited until Andrea grabbed her, then strained forward, pulling the girl from the drift. As the storm raged around them, Villa led the way back to Andrea's home.

2   Villa won the Ken-L Ration Dog Hero of the Year award in 1983 for her bravery, loyalty, and intelligence. Her feat was truly impressive—understanding that Andrea needed help and performing the tasks necessary to save her. We can all admire Villa and envy Andrea for having such a loyal friend. But did Villa's heroic behavior exhibit intelligence? Some scientists would say that, while Villa certainly is a wonderful animal, her behavior was unthinking, perhaps an instinctive holdover from the protective environment of the wolf pack, where the adult animals defend the pups against danger. After all, dogs evolved from wolves, which are highly social animals. They would say that Villa just acted, without really understanding the concept of danger or thinking about what she was doing. Up until the 1960s, this view of animals prevailed among scientists studying animal behavior. But nowadays, a variety of experiments and experiences with different creatures are showing that some animals have impressive mental abilities.

Do Animals Think?

3   If dogs might think, what about bees, rats, birds, cats, monkeys, and apes? How well do animals learn? How much of their experiences can they remember? Can they apply what they may have learned to new challenges in their lives? Are animals aware of the world around them? How might it be possible to learn about and evaluate the intelligence of different animals?

4   It is easy to confuse trainability with thinking. But just because an animal can learn to perform a trick doesn't mean that it knows what it is doing. In the IQ Zoo in Hotsprings, Arkansas, for example, animals perform some amazing tasks. A cat turns on the lights and then plays the piano, while a duck strums on the guitar with its bill. Parrots ride tiny bicycles and slide around on roller

evaluate (ih VAL yoo ayt) *v.* determine the value or condition of someone or something in a careful and thoughtful way

skates. At John F. Kennedy Airport in New York, beagles work for the Food and Drug Administration, sniffing at luggage and signaling when they perceive drugs or illegal foods in the baggage. Dolphins and killer whales at marine parks perform some spectacular feats, and their behavior is often linked into a story line so that it appears they are acting roles, as humans would in a movie or play. These animals may seem to be behaving in an intelligent fashion, but they are just repeating behavior patterns they have been trained to perform for food rewards. The drug-sniffing beagle has no concept of drug illegality, and the duck doesn't understand or appreciate music. They aren't thinking and then deciding what to do.

CLOSE READ

ANNOTATE: Mark the examples of animal behavior mentioned in Paragraph 4.

QUESTION: Why has the writer included these examples?

CONCLUDE: How do these examples relate to the idea of "trainability"?

5   Studying the intelligence of animals is very tricky. During the nineteenth and early twentieth centuries, people readily attributed human emotions and mental abilities to animals. Even learned scientists had great faith in animal minds—"An animal can think in a human way and can express human ideas in human language," said the respected Swiss psychiatrist Gustav Wolff in the early 1900s.

6   Wolff's statement was inspired by Clever Hans, a horse that appeared to show remarkable intelligence. A retired schoolteacher trained Hans as he would a child, with blackboards, flash cards, number boards, and letter cards. After four years of training, Hans was ready to perform in public. When asked to solve a numerical problem, Hans would paw the answer with his hoof. He shook his head "yes" and "no," moved it "up" and "down," and turned it "right" or "left." Hans would show his "knowledge" of colors by picking up a rag of the appropriate shade with his teeth. Many scientists of the time came to watch Hans and tried to figure out how he performed his amazing feats; they went away impressed. Hans appeared to understand human language and to have mastered arithmetic.

7   Then Oskar Pfungst, a German experimental psychologist, uncovered Hans's secret by using what is now a standard scientific method—the double blind experiment.[1] When the horse was asked a question, no one in his presence knew the answer. Under these conditions, Clever Hans was no longer so "smart"; he couldn't come up with the correct responses. By **observing** the horse and the audience when the answer was known, Pfungst discovered that Hans was very sensitive to the smallest movements of the people watching. They would lean ever so slightly forward until he had

observing (uhb ZUHR vihng) v. watching carefully

---

1. **double blind experiment** testing procedure or study in which neither the subjects nor the experimenters know which participants are being tested and which are serving as a "control" group until after the experiment is over.

^ This photograph shows the horse Clever Hans with his owner, Wilhelm von Osten, and a worker. The wooden boards show some of the math Hans was supposedly calculating.

investigation (ihn vehs tuh GAY shuhn) *n.* careful examination of something, especially to discover the truth about it

phenomenon (fuh NAH muh nahn) *n.* rare or important fact or event

pawed the correct number of times, then relax. He watched for that sign of relief, then stopped pawing. His trainer unknowingly moved his head from side to side or up and down just enough for Hans to take a cue as to what to do. At the end of his **investigation**, Pfungst was able to prove his point. He stood in front of Hans without asking any questions. He nodded his head slightly, and the horse began to tap his hoof. When Pfungst straightened his head, Hans stood at attention.

8   Ever since the embarrassment of Clever Hans, psychologists have been extremely wary of falling into the same trap. They are ready to call upon the "Clever Hans **phenomenon**" whenever an animal seems to be exhibiting intelligent behavior. Clever Hans taught psychology some important lessons, but the incident may also have made behavioral scientists too cautious about the mental abilities of animals.

9   Animals that are easy to train may also be very intelligent. Some of the most trainable creatures, such as dolphins, are also the most likely candidates for genuine animal thinking. But finding ways to get at animals' real mental capacity can be very difficult.

What Is Intelligence?

10   We humans recognize a "smart" person when we meet one; we know who is a "brain" and who is not. In school, we take IQ tests, which are supposed to give a numerical measure of our "intelligence." But these days, the whole concept of intelligence is being reevaluated. The older, standard IQ tests measure only a limited range of mental abilities, concentrating on mathematics and language skills. Creativity, which most people would agree is a critical element in the meaningful application of intelligence, has not traditionally been evaluated by such tests, and other important mental skills have also been ignored. But things are changing. Many scientists believe that dozens of different talents are a part of intelligence. In fact, more than a hundred factors of intelligence have been written about in scientific literature. Psychologists are now developing tests that measure intelligence more accurately and more broadly. The SOI (Structure of Intellect) test, for example, evaluates five main factors of intelligence: cognition (comprehension), memory, evaluation (judgment, planning, reasoning, and critical decision making), convergent production (solving problems where answers are known), and divergent production (solving problems creatively). Each of these is broken down further into many subcategories.

11   But what about animals? We can't hand them a pencil and paper and give them a test, and we can't ask them what they're thinking. We must find other ways of measuring their "smarts." And that's not the only problem. Since the lives of animals are so different from ours, we can't apply human standards to them. We must develop different ideas of what animal intelligence might be.

12   The concept of intelligence was thought up by humans, and our thinking about it is tied up with our own human system of values. The things that are important to animals can be different from those that matter to humans. When studying animals, we must test them in situations that have meaning for their lives, not ours, and not just look to see how much they resemble us.

Studying Animal Thought

13   Many pitfalls await the scientist trying to **interpret** animals' behavior and make inferences about their intelligence. One is inconsistency. An animal might breeze through what we consider a difficult learning task and then fail when presented with what seems obvious to us. When an animal can't perform well, we don't know if it really cannot solve the problems put to it or if it just doesn't want to. Sometimes the difficulty lies in the perceptive abilities of the animals. The animal may have the mental ability and the desire to solve the problem but is unable to make the

CLOSE READ

ANNOTATE: Mark the five factors of intelligence that are listed in Paragraph 10.

QUESTION: Why does the author list and define these terms?

CONCLUDE: What point is the author making about intelligence by including this list?

interpret (ihn TUR pruht) *v.* explain the meaning of something

discriminations being asked of it. For example, a researcher using colored objects to compare learning in a cebus monkey and in a rhesus monkey[2] first found that the rhesus scored much better than the cebus. But rhesus monkeys have color vision that is essentially the same as ours, while the cebus's is significantly different. When the design of the experiment was changed and gray objects were substituted for the colored ones, the cebus monkeys actually did a little better than the rhesus.

14   Scientists studying animals in nature can run into difficulties in interpreting their results if they don't pay very close attention to what they see and hear. C. G. Beer of Rutgers University in New Jersey spent long hours studying laughing gull behavior. Early on, he interpreted what he called the "long call" as a signal that was the same for each bird and that was made on all occasions. But when he recorded a variety of long calls and played them back to the gulls, he noticed that the birds didn't always respond in the same way. There were differences in the calls that were hard for a human researcher to hear. Beer then realized that the long call was actually so individualized that it helped distinguish one bird from another! The more carefully he listened to the calls and watched the gulls' reactions to them, the more complexity and variety he found in both the calls and the responses. From this work Beer concluded: "We may often misunderstand what animals are doing in social interaction because we fail to draw our distinctions where the animals draw theirs."

Measuring Animal Intelligence

measurable (MEH zhur uh buhl) *adj.* able to determine size or quantity

15   Keeping all these concerns in mind, we can list some factors of intelligence that might be **measurable** or observable in animals—speed of learning, complexity of learned tasks, ability to retrieve information from long-term memory, rule learning, decision-making and problem-solving capacity, counting aptitude, understanding of spatial relations, and ability to learn by watching what others do. More advanced signs of intelligence are tool manufacture and use, symbolic communication,[3] and ability to form mental concepts.

16   With such a list of capabilities that might be involved with intelligence, it seems that scientists should be able to analyze and compare the intelligence of animals. But it's one thing to decide to

---

2. **cebus monkey… rhesus monkey** *Cebus* and *rhesus* are the scientific names for two types of monkeys. Both types are often used in research.
3. **symbolic communication** using objects that represent words to interact and share ideas. Symbolic language can include sign language, written words, and pictures.

test intelligence and another to design experiments that will measure it. You may read somewhere that rats, for example, are smarter than pigeons. But finding ways to compare the accomplishments of different species is virtually impossible. Animals are just too varied in their physical makeup and in their life styles. Scientists have found that different kinds of animals learn better under different sorts of conditions, so the same experiment usually can't be used meaningfully on a rat and a pigeon. In addition, some animals have evolved special mental skills to deal with their particular environments. They might appear especially intelligent on one measure of brain power and very dull on another.

17   Dealing with wild animals presents new problems. Laboratory pigeons and rats have been bred for many generations in captivity. They are used to cages and to humans, and large numbers are easy to acquire. Wild animals may not perform well in the

∧ A trained beagle identifies a suspicious piece of luggage in the airport.

laboratory because they are afraid or because the setting is so strange to them. And because wild animals are often hard to come by, the experimenter must usually work with only a small number of individuals. Variations of "intelligence" from one individual to the next can significantly affect the results. Primates—apes and monkeys—are among the most intelligent animals, and apes seem closer to our idea of "smart" than monkeys. But a bright monkey may score as well on a test as an ape, while a dull one may be outclassed by a rat. For these reasons, behavioral scientists have realized that trying to compare the intelligence of different animals is a very challenging problem.

18   That doesn't mean, however, that trying to find out how animal minds function is not worth the effort. We can learn a great deal through studying how various kinds of animals solve problems and how they use their mental abilities to survive in their natural environments.

Response

 NOTEBOOK

1. Personal Connections Which animals in this article would you most like to see in action? Explain.

> Answer the questions in your notebook. Use text evidence to support your responses.

Comprehension

2. Reading Check (a) What did the Newfoundland dog, Villa, do that was remarkable? **(b)** Did Hans the horse really solve numerical problems? **(c)** The author lists a number of qualities that show true intelligence and that might be measurable in animals. Cite two of these.

3. Strategy: Monitor Comprehension Were you able to monitor your comprehension and notice where your understanding broke down? Explain. In what ways did rereading affect your comprehension?

Analysis

4. (a) What is the SOI test? **(b) Connect** In what ways does this test show how scientific understanding of intelligence has changed since the early twentieth century? Explain.

5. (a) Analyze Cause and Effect How did the Clever Hans double-blind experiment affect the study of animal intelligence? **(b) Evaluate** Why were these changes important? Explain.

6. Distinguish What is the difference between trainability and true intelligence? Cite text evidence to support your response.

7. Take a Position Do you think a deeper understanding of animal intelligence affects people? Explain your thinking, citing details from the article.

EQ Notes ▸ How do animals and people interact?

What have you learned about interactions between people and animals from reading this article? Go to your Essential Question Notes and record your observations and thoughts about "How Smart Are Animals?"

⊙ TEKS
5.I. Monitor comprehension and make adjustments such as re-reading, when understanding breaks down.

HOW SMART ARE ANIMALS?

Close Read

 ANNOTATE

1. The model passage and annotation show how one reader analyzed paragraph 3 of the article. Find another detail in the passage to annotate. Then, write your own question and conclusion.

CLOSE-READ MODEL

If dogs might think, what about bees, rats, birds, cats, monkeys, and apes? How well do animals learn? How much of their experiences can they remember? Can they apply what they may have learned to new challenges in their lives? Are animals aware of the world around them? How might it be possible to learn about and evaluate the intelligence of different animals?

ANNOTATE: This paragraph is made up entirely of questions.

QUESTION: What is the effect of this long list of questions?

CONCLUDE: The writer may be providing questions that the rest of the article will address and answer.

MY **QUESTION:**

MY **CONCLUSION:**

2. For more practice, answer the Close-Read notes in the selection.

3. Choose a section of the article you found especially important. Mark important details. Then, jot down questions and write your conclusions in the open space next to the text.

Inquiry and Research

 RESEARCH

 NOTEBOOK

Research and Extend The article states that some of the most trainable animals are also the most intelligent. Conduct research to find a type of animal, other than a dolphin, that is considered highly trainable. What does the research say about this animal's intelligence? Write down one interesting fact or observation you find and the source that provided the information.

 TEKS

8.D.iii. Analyze characteristics and structural elements of informational text, including organizational patterns such as definition, classification, advantage, and disadvantage.

9.B. Analyze how the use of text structure contributes to the author's purpose.

Genre / Text Elements

Organizational Patterns In most science articles, the author's purpose is to explain a complex topic in a way that readers can grasp. The author chooses an **organizational pattern**, or text structure, that suits that purpose and creates a clear flow of ideas. With **definition,** the writer explains what a topic is or what it means—he or she *defines* that topic. Specific text features may indicate the use of definition pattern or structure.

> **TIP:** Writers often use definition text structure to analyze abstract ideas, such as freedom, justice, or intelligence.

TEXT FEATURE	EXAMPLES
Title: may state the idea or subject the writer will define	*What is Freedom?*
Subheads: show how the author has separated a topic into smaller parts that can be more easily defined	First subhead: *Freedom in America* Second subhead: *Freedom Around the World*

 NOTEBOOK

PRACTICE Answer the questions.

1. **Evaluate** In the third subhead, the author asks, "What is Intelligence?" Does she fully answer that question? Explain.

2. **(a) Distinguish** What differences does the author see between animals' instincts, trainability, and intelligence? Explain.
   (b) Analyze Why are these distinctions important to the author's effort to define intelligence?

3. **Generalize** When defining a concept, why might it be important to explain what it is *not*, as well as what it is? Cite details from the article to support your answer.

4. **(a) Connect** How does the title of the article suggest that the author is using a definition text structure or pattern? **(b) Make a Judgment** Do you think the author's use of this structure or pattern helps her achieve her purpose for writing? Explain.

HOW SMART ARE ANIMALS?

Concept Vocabulary

 NOTEBOOK

Why These Words? The vocabulary words are associated with scientific study and experimentation. For example, during an *investigation* a scientist hopes to find *measurable* results.

investigation	phenomenon	observing
evaluate	measurable	interpret

PRACTICE

1. How do the vocabulary words clarify your understanding about the ways in which scientists work?

WORD NETWORK

Add words that describe interactions between animals and people animals from the text to your Word Network.

2. Find three other words in the selection that relate to scientific study and experimentation.

3. Use each vocabulary word in a sentence that shows your understanding of its meaning.

Word Study

NOTEBOOK

Spelling Patterns: The *f* Sound In English, the initial *f* sound can be spelled with either an *f* or a *ph*, as in the vocabulary word *phenomenon*. Most words that use the letter pattern *ph* for the *f* sound come from ancient Greek.

PRACTICE
Label the spelling of each of the following words as *correct* or *incorrect*. Then, fix any incorrect spellings. Use a dictionary to check your work.

family	fotograph	phraction
physical	phind	fireworks

© Pearson Education, Inc., or its affiliates. All rights reserved.

TEKS

6.F. Respond using newly acquired vocabulary as appropriate.

8.D.i. Analyze characteristics and structural elements of informational text, including the controlling idea or thesis with supporting evidence.

10.D.ix. Edit drafts using standard English conventions, including correct spelling, including commonly confused terms such as *its/it's, affect/effect, there/their/they're,* and *to/two/too.*

Author's Craft

Controlling Idea and Supporting Evidence The **controlling idea** is the thesis or main point a writer communicates in a work of nonfiction. The writer develops and supports that idea by using **supporting evidence**, or proof. There are different types of evidence:

TIP: The controlling idea helps an author decide how to structure a text. Clues to the controlling idea may appear in the title, subheads, and other text features.

CONTROLLING IDEA: Training a dog takes time, but the results are worth it.	
TYPE OF EVIDENCE	EXAMPLE
Anecdote: brief story that illustrates an idea	Kim spent four weeks at obedience school with her puppy Roscoe. At first, he just played, but he soon learned to follow commands. He's still playful, but now he obeys.
Example: specific instance of a general idea	Apply basic commands in different situations. For instance, when it's dinner time for the dog, have him sit, walk away, sit again, and then eat.
Expert Quotation: statement from someone with special knowledge	"Keep sessions brief, but train several times every day," advises Juan Padilla, founder of K-9 Training, Inc.
Fact: provable statement	Most trainers use food treats to reward a dog's good behavior.

NOTEBOOK

INTERACTIVITY

PRACTICE Complete the activity and answer the questions.

1. **Classify** Identify one example of each type of evidence used in the article. Record each item in the chart.

TYPE OF EVIDENCE	EXAMPLE
Anecdote	
Example	
Expert Quotation	
Fact	

2. **(a) Interpret** In your own words, state the controlling idea or thesis of this article. **(b) Analyze** Explain how each item of evidence you listed in your chart helps to develop or support that idea.

3. **Analyze** In what ways do the text features in this article help to clarify and develop the controlling idea? In particular, consider the subheads.

HOW SMART ARE ANIMALS?

Compare Nonfiction

Both of these science articles focus on different aspects of animals. "How Smart Are Animals?" discusses the intelligence of animals in general. "So What Is a Primate?" shows how scientists classify one group of animals, primates.

SO WHAT IS A PRIMATE?

So What Is a Primate?

About the Author

Faith Hickman Brynie (b. 1946) is the author of numerous books focusing on science and health for children, teens, and adults, and regularly writes articles for websites and magazines. Brynie is a former laboratory scientist, medical technician, teacher, and university professor. She lives in Bigfork, Montana.

Concept Vocabulary

INTERACTIVITY

You will encounter the following words as you read the article. Before reading, note how familiar you are with each word. Using a scale of 1 (do not know it at all) to 5 (know it very well), indicate your knowledge of each word.

WORD	YOUR RANKING
agile	
prehensile	
sensitive	
keen	
opposable	
intelligent	

Comprehension Strategy

ANNOTATE

Generate Questions

Generating questions can help you deepen your understanding of a text and gain more information. Before you read, scan the title, text features, and images. Notice the questions that come into your mind. Use those questions to guide your reading.

EXAMPLE
Question: The title of this article is "So What Is a Primate?" Why is the author, a science writer, asking this question? Don't we already know what primates are?

PRACTICE Before you read the article, scan the introduction, acknowledgements, and images. Generate questions and write them in the open space next to the text. As you read, look for answers that deepen your understanding and help you gain more information.

TEKS
5.B. Generate questions about text before, during, and after reading to deepen understanding and gain information.

So What Is a Primate?

Faith Hickman Brynie

The cebus monkey, or capuchin, lives mainly in Central and South America.

BACKGROUND

Much of what we know about primates we owe to the scientists who have studied them. Some of these scientists, known as primatologists, study primates in their natural habitat. Others study primates in labs, in part, to find out more about their biological traits. This article addresses some of the similarities and differences in traits among the members of this group of mammals.

 AUDIO

 ANNOTATE

INTRODUCTION

1 *Just as cats, lizards, birds, spiders, and fish are all members of the animal kingdom, so are people. We humans like to think of ourselves as special, and in many ways we are. However, we also have a great deal in common with other animals. As a science writer, I'm fascinated by these similarities and differences and seek to understand them more deeply. The more we know about our kinship with all animals, the better guardians of our planet we will be.*

2   What do you have in common with the aye-aye, sifaka, siamang, and potto? If you said your collarbone, you're probably a *primatologist*—a person who studies primates. If you're not, read on.

3   Just like those animals with the weird names, you belong to the group of mammals called primates. (By the way, the group also includes the more commonly known monkeys, chimps, and gorillas.) Among other things, it's the structure of your shoulder that earns you membership in that club. In primates, the upper arms are linked to the chest by the collarbone (also called the *clavicle*). That construction allows you and other primates to do something most mammals can't: hang by your arms. Watch kids crossing a jungle gym hand-over-hand. They share that ability with monkeys and apes, but don't expect rabbits, goats, or polar bears to perform such a feat!

4   The ability to swing isn't the only adaptation to life in the trees, where most primates live. Eyes face forward, encased in bony sockets. That lets the view from one eye overlap the other. The result is three-dimensional or stereoscopic vision— the perfect tool for judging both depth and distance.

5   Primates have **agile** arms *and* legs. Apes have no tails, but monkeys use their long, flexible tails for balance. Many New World monkeys have **prehensile** tails that wrap around branches and act as an extra hand or foot. Some can support their entire weight using only their tails.

6   Primate fingers are flexible with **sensitive** ends, giving them a **keen** sense of touch. Except for marmosets and tamarins, all primates have flat fingernails and toenails instead of claws. Many primates, like humans, have a thumb that can bend to meet the other fingers or toes. This **opposable** thumb makes grasping small objects easy and paves the way for using and making tools. Tool use is aided by another very special primate feature—a large brain in relation to body size.

7   Many primates, especially those that are diurnal (active during the day), live in social groups. Some of the smaller, nocturnal (active at night) primates live alone. Like all mammals, primates have hair or fur. They nurse their young with milk from mammary glands. Compared to other mammals, however, primates have few offspring, and the babies take a long time to mature.

8   That growth and maturation varies greatly among species. The largest primate, the lowland gorilla, can achieve an adult weight of up to about 500 pounds. The smallest, the pygmy mouse lemur of Madagascar, tips the scales at about one ounce when fully grown.

agile (AJ uhl) *adj.* able to move quickly and easily

prehensile (pree HEHN suhl) *adj.* able to grab or hold something by wrapping around it

sensitive (SEHN suh tihv) *adj.* able to easily detect stimulation

keen (keen) *adj.* extremely clear or sharp in perception

opposable (uh POH zuh buhl) *adj.* able to be placed against one or more of the other fingers on the same hand or foot

This adult male orangutan lives in Borneo, a large island in the South Pacific.

9   Scientists group the more than 200 living species of primates into two main categories. The first are the *prosimians*, or "primitive" primates. This group includes lemurs, pottos, lorises, and tarsiers. Mostly, the prosimians are small in size. They have long whiskers and pointed snouts. Their senses of hearing and smell are keen. They have moist noses and mobile ears. Many are nocturnal and have only black-and-white vision.

10   The second group is the *anthropoids*, which contains nearly three times as many species as the prosimians. Anthropoids include monkeys, marmosets, tamarins, siamangs, and gibbons.

11   The "Great Apes" are another major group of anthropoids. That group includes our closest cousins, the gorilla, chimpanzee, orangutan, and bonobo. (Recently, many scientists have also started to classify humans as a fifth species of great ape.) Most anthropoids have flat faces, keen color vision, and a relatively poor sense of smell. Anthropoids are **intelligent** and quick to learn. Many use and make tools and set up social systems.

intelligent (ihn TEL uh juhnt) *adj.* able to learn and understand things

12   Where's the single best place to find one-quarter of primate species? On the "Red List" of critically endangered, or vulnerable, species published by the International Union for Conservation of Nature and Natural Resources (IUCN). Today's world is a dangerous place for primates, and when we lose them, we'll lose these amazing creatures—including our closest cousins—forever.

CLOSE READ

ANNOTATE: Mark the phrase in paragraph 13 that explains why Madagascar's forests are disappearing.

QUESTION: Why does the author include information about forests in an article about primates?

CONCLUDE: What point does this detail support?

13 One of the most dangerous areas for the world's primates is Madagascar. Some species of forest-dwelling lemurs found there live nowhere else in the world, but their homes are nearly all gone. Between 1950 and 1985 (say researchers at American University in Washington, D.C.), half of all Madagascar's forests disappeared, as people cut the trees to grow coffee, mine the earth, and raise cattle. Between 1990 and 1995, the island continued to lose nearly 320 acres of its forest land annually, according to estimates from the World Resources Institute.

Acknowledgements

I am grateful to the International Union for Conservation of Nature (IUCN). The staff were enormously helpful in my research. Thanks also go to graduate students in the Biology department at American University, who helped me better understand the effects of environmental change on primates. I am also grateful to the World Resources Institute for providing excellent public information about the threat of extinction in primate populations. I consulted their web site and other materials frequently during my research for this article. I am also thankful to my editor for her insights and feedback.

The Bengal Slow Loris is a small primate. These animals live mainly in India and other parts of Asia.

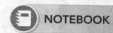

Response

1. Personal Connections Choose one detail from this article that you found surprising. Explain your choice.

Answer the questions in your notebook. Use text evidence to support your responses.

Comprehension

2. Reading Check (a) What key physical feature distinguishes primates from other mammals? **(b)** What are prosimians and anthropoids? **(c)** What is the "Red List"?

3. Strategy: Generate Questions (a) Write two questions you generated before reading the article. **(b)** In what ways did this strategy affect your reading experience?`

Analysis

4. (a) How do the offspring of primates differ from those of other mammals? **(b) Speculate** How might this difference affect the ways in which primates live? Explain your thinking.

5. (a) What is the main idea in paragraph 12? **(b) Draw Conclusions** Why do you think the author includes this information? Explain.

6. Extend Paragraph 13 sends a warning about the fate of primates that live in Madagascar. What steps might people take to reverse the situation described by the author?

EQ Notes How do animals and people interact?

What have you learned about interactions between people and animals from reading this article? Go to your Essential Question Notes and record your observations and thoughts about "So What Is a Primate?"

 TEKS

5.B. Generate questions about text before, during, and after reading to deepen understanding and gain information.

SO WHAT IS A PRIMATE?

Close Read

 ANNOTATE

1. The model passage and annotation show how one reader analyzed part of paragraph 11 in "So What Is a Primate?" Find another detail in the passage to annotate. Then, write your own question and conclusion.

CLOSE-READ MODEL

(Recently, many scientists have also started to classify humans as a fifth species of great ape.) Most anthropoids have flat faces, keen color vision, and a relatively poor sense of smell. Anthropoids are intelligent and quick to learn. Many use and make tools and set up social systems.

ANNOTATE: This passage describes characteristics of anthropoids.

QUESTION: Why did the author include this description immediately after the sentence in parentheses?

CONCLUDE: The author is providing support for a statement that some readers might find startling.

MY **QUESTION:**

MY **CONCLUSION:**

2. For more practice, answer the Close-Read notes in the selection.

3. Choose a section of the article you found especially important. Mark important details. Then, jot down questions and write your conclusions in the open space next to the text.

Inquiry and Research

 RESEARCH

 NOTEBOOK

Often, you have to generate your own research questions. Sometimes, however, your teacher will give you research questions to explore. Practice responding to teacher-guided questions by conducting a brief, informal inquiry to find facts about efforts to protect the types of primates discussed in this article:

- *What efforts are being made to protect primates in Madagascar?*
- *What other efforts to protect primates are being made around the world?*

Cite at least three facts you discover during your research.

 **TEKS**

8.D.iii. Analyze characteristics and structural elements of informational text, including organizational patterns such as definition, classification, advantage, and disadvantage.

Genre / Text Elements

Organizational Patterns In most science writing, the author chooses an **organizational pattern,** or structure, that helps create a clear and logical flow of ideas.

With **classification,** the writer breaks a broad topic down into smaller, related subtopics. These may be broken down further into even more focused categories. This pattern is useful when a single topic includes different parts.

EXAMPLE: Classification Pattern
Broad Topic: Types of <u>Dogs</u>

- Subtopic 1: Dog <u>Groups</u> / Sporting, Hound, Working, Terrier, Toy, Non-Sporting, <u>Herding</u>

  - <u>Herding Dogs</u> / Bearded Collie, Belgian Sheepdog, Collie, Icelandic Sheepdog

TIP: A writer could discuss even more specific categories, such as types of sheepdogs.

 NOTEBOOK

 INTERACTIVITY

PRACTICE Answer the questions and complete the activity.

1. **Analyze** The chart lists the subtopics into which the article's broad topic is broken down. For each subtopic, identify one feature that the author says separates it from others.

SUBTOPIC	DISTINGUISHING FEATURE
Primates	
Apes	
Monkeys	
Prosimians	
Anthropoids	
Great Apes	

2. **Evaluate** Is classification a useful pattern for the broad topic of this article? Explain your thinking, citing details from the text.

3. **(a) Analyze** In what ways does the use of classification support the author's purpose? **(b) Evaluate** Do you think the author achieves her purpose? Explain.

SO WHAT IS A PRIMATE?

Concept Vocabulary

Why These Words? The vocabulary words are associated with primate traits. For example, having an *opposable* thumb allows a primate's hand to be *prehensile*.

agile	prehensile	sensitive
keen	opposable	intelligent

PRACTICE **Answer the questions.**

1. How do the vocabulary words extend your knowledge of primates?

2. Find three other words in the article that relate to primate traits.

3. How might an *agile* dog behave?

4. Why would an elephant's trunk be considered *prehensile*?

5. Why might *sensitive* fingers be important to an artist?

6. What advantage comes from having an *opposable* thumb?

7. What traits make a person seem *intelligent*?

8. Why might a *keen* sense of smell be useful for animals in the wild?

WORD NETWORK

Add words that describe interactions between animals and people from the text to your Word Network.

Word Study

Multiple-Meaning Words The vocabulary word *keen* has two distinct meanings. In the selection, the word means "extremely clear or sharp in perception." *Keen* can also mean "eager," as in this sentence: *The group was keen on the idea of seeing a movie.*

Look up these multiple-meaning words from "What Is a Primate?" and write two definitions for each:

club   share   face

TEKS

8.D.ii. Analyze characteristics and structural elements of informational text, including features such as introduction, foreword, preface, references, or acknowledgements to gain background information.

Author's Craft

Text Features: Introductions and Acknowledgements Introductions and **acknowledgements** are text features that may appear in a book or other piece of writing. The author usually writes an introduction, although an editor or another person may write one. The author always writes an acknowledgements section. Each type of feature serves specific purposes.

TIP: Introductions are always at the beginning of a reading selection. Acknowledgements can come at the beginning or end.

PURPOSES OF INTRODUCTIONS AND ACKNOWLEDGEMENTS	
INTRODUCTION	ACKNOWLEDGEMENTS
• provides background information about the text • may explain the author's interest in the topic or the reasons it merits readers' attention • engages readers' interest and prepares them for reading the text	• expresses thanks to people or organizations who helped the author with research, editing, and other tasks • provides background about people who contributed to the published work • often, used to recognize the use of source texts

The introduction and acknowledgements refer to ideas in the larger work and help to establish the author as an expert on the topic. They may also reveal background information about how the author conducted research and the process he or she used to write a work.

 NOTEBOOK

PRACTICE Reread the Introduction and Acknowledgements sections of the article. Then, answer the questions.

1. **Make Inferences** What background information about the author's research process do you learn from the Acknowledgements? Explain.

2. **(a) Distinguish** Cite two pieces of information that the Introduction and Acknowledgements sections offer that the article itself does not. **(b) Analyze** How does this information provide background, or otherwise add to a reader's understanding and appreciation of the article?

3. **Generalize** In what ways do both the Introduction and the Acknowledgements help you know that the author of this article is a credible authority on the topic? Explain.

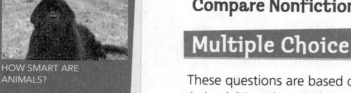

HOW SMART ARE ANIMALS?

SO WHAT IS A PRIMATE?

Compare Nonfiction

Multiple Choice

NOTEBOOK

These questions are based on the two science articles "How Smart Are Animals?" and "So What Is a Primate?" Choose the best answer to each question.

1. What is a key difference between "How Smart Are Animals?" and "So What Is a Primate?"

A "How Smart Are Animals?" is fiction, but "So What Is a Primate?" is nonfiction.

B "How Smart Are Animals?" begins with a story, but "So What Is a Primate?" begins with questions.

C "How Smart Are Animals?" focuses on animals' intelligence, but "So What Is a Primate?" does not mention animals' intelligence at all.

D "How Smart Are Animals?" is about many kinds of animals, but "So What Is a Primate?" is about one group of animals.

2. Read the passages from the two articles. What idea do both passages suggest?

from "How Smart Are Animals?"	from "So What Is a Primate?"
More advanced signs of intelligence are tool manufacture and use, symbolic communication, and ability to form mental concepts.	Many primates, like humans, have a thumb that can bend to meet the other fingers or toes. This opposable thumb makes grasping small objects easy and paves the way for using and making tools. Tool use is aided by another very special primate feature—a large brain in relation to body size.

F Animals and humans have very little in common.

G An opposable thumb indicates higher intelligence.

H It is impossible to assess animals' intelligence.

J Tool use and intelligence are related.

3. With which statement would the authors of both articles most likely agree?

A Animals are fascinating creatures.

B It is easy to test animal intelligence.

C Primates are the best laboratory animals.

D Animals deserve rewards for brave actions.

 TEKS
6.B. Write responses that demonstrate understanding of texts, including comparing sources within and across genres.

NOTEBOOK

Short Response

1. (a) Analyze Which article relies more on numerical data, and which relies more on expert quotations? **(b) Evaluate** Which article seems more "scientific"? Explain, citing details as support.

2. Make a Judgment Review the authors' word choices in each article. Which article seems written for an audience of middle-school students? Explain, citing examples to support your judgment.

3. Compare and Contrast Do you think the two authors see the relationship between human beings and animals in mostly similar or mostly different ways? Explain.

Answer the questions in your notebook. Use text evidence to support your responses.

Timed Writing

A **comparison-and-contrast essay** is a piece of writing in which you discuss similarities and differences among two or more topics.

ASSIGNMENT

Write a **comparison-and-contrast essay** in which you explain the similarities and differences between the organizational structures of "How Smart Are Animals?" and "So What Is a Primate?" In your conclusion, make a judgment about which article's organizational pattern is more effective, and explain why.

5-MINUTE PLANNER

1. Read the assignment carefully and completely.
2. Decide what you want to say—your controlling idea, or thesis.
3. Decide which examples you'll use from each article.
4. Organize your ideas:
   - Plan what to say in your introduction and conclusion.
   - Plan the order in which to present the examples from both articles.

Write an Informational Essay

Informational essays are short nonfiction works that present facts, details, and explanations about a topic or process.

Write an **informational essay** in which you share information that answers the following question:

What qualities do people and animals share?

You can choose to write about the qualities that one particular kind of animal shares with humans. Or, you can write about the qualities animals in general share with humans. Use the elements of informational essays in your writing.

ELEMENTS OF INFORMATIONAL ESSAYS

Purpose: to inform or educate readers about a topic

Characteristics

➔ engaging controlling idea that shows depth of thought

➔ varied evidence, including specific facts, details, and examples

➔ elements of craft, including precise word choices and explanations of unfamiliar terms

➔ well-chosen transitions that link sentences and paragraphs

➔ standard English conventions, including correct subject-verb agreement, spelling, and punctuation

Structure

➔ a well-organized structure that includes

- an interesting introduction
- a logical flow of ideas from paragraph to paragraph
- a strong conclusion

 TEKS

11.B. Compose informational texts, including multi-paragraph essays that convey information about a topic, using a clear controlling idea or thesis statement and genre characteristics and craft.

Take a Closer Look at the Assignment

1. What does the assignment want me to do (in my own words)? What choices can I make as I choose my topic?

2. Is a specific **audience** mentioned in the prompt?

   ○ Yes   If "yes," who is my main audience?

   ○ No   If "no," who do I think my audience is or should be?

3. Is my **purpose** for writing included in the assignment?

   ○ Yes   If "yes," what is the purpose?

   ○ No   If "no," why do I think I am writing this informational essay (not just because it's an assignment)?

4. (a) Does the assignment ask me to use specific **types of evidence**?

   ○ Yes   If "yes," what are they?

   ○ No   If "no," what types of evidence do I think I need?

   (b) Where will I get the evidence? What details can I pull from my EQ notes?

5. Does the assignment ask me to organize my ideas in a certain way?

   ○ Yes   If "yes," what structure does it require?

   ○ No   If "no," how can I best order my ideas?

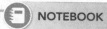
NOTEBOOK

AUDIENCE

You are writing to inform your **audience**, or readers, so make sure to define unfamiliar terms and explain new ideas.

PURPOSE

Knowing your **purpose**, or reason for writing, will help you write a stronger essay.

General Purpose: *I want to share information about people and animals.*

Specific Purpose: *I want to show that all mammals, not just humans, feel affection.*

EVIDENCE

Use different kinds of **evidence** to make your ideas clear. Many types of evidence can come from your reading.

- **Facts:** statements that can be proved true
- **Expert Opinions:** statements by people who have studied the topic
- **Anecdote:** brief story that makes a point
- **Examples:** specific instances of a general idea
- **Numbers:** distances, times, amounts, percentages, etc.

Planning and Prewriting

Before you draft your essay, decide what you want to say and how you want to say it. Complete the activities to get started.

Discover Your Thinking: Freewrite!

Keep the general topic in mind as you write quickly and freely for at least three minutes. Don't stop writing! You can even write down questions you want to research later.

- Don't worry about your spelling or grammar—just get your ideas out.
- After three minutes, read what you wrote. Mark ideas or points that seem strong or interesting.
- Repeat the process several times. When you begin a new round, start with the strong ideas you marked earlier.

NOTEBOOK

WRITE IT What qualities do people and animals share?

 TEKS

10.B.i. Develop drafts into a focused, structured, and coherent piece of writing by organizing with purposeful structure, including an introduction, transitions, coherence within and across paragraphs, and a conclusion.

Structure Your Essay: Create a Logical Flow

A. Collect Your Ideas Look again at your freewriting pages. Decide which ideas you want to explore in your essay. For now, don't worry about the order.

CONTROLLING IDEA

A **controlling idea** is the main idea or point of your essay. Start with a preliminary idea that you can state in one sentence. As you draft, your focus may become sharper and your controlling idea may change.

B. Write Your Controlling Idea

C. Plan a Structure Figure out what you want to say in each part of your essay.

I. Introduction Plan how you'll get your readers' attention and make them want to keep reading. Think about starting with an anecdote or a surprising fact about the topic.

II. Body Explain your ideas in a logical order. Decide the evidence you'll use to develop or support each idea.

III. Conclusion Remind readers of your controlling idea and leave them with a strong impression.

STRUCTURE

An effective **structure**, or organization of ideas and evidence, helps readers follow your thinking. These two types of structures work well with informational writing:

- **Classification:** Sort your topic into classes, or smaller groups. Explain the traits that define each class.

- **Comparison and Contrast:** Explore similarities and differences between two topics or aspects of a topic.

Drafting

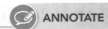 ANNOTATE

Apply the planning work you've done and write a first draft. Begin with your introduction, which should engage readers and make them want to read your essay.

Read Like a Writer

Reread the beginning of the Mentor Text. Mark details that make you want to read more. One observation has been done for you.

MENTOR TEXT

from **Reading Buddies**

In a school library across town, a third-grade boy is reading his favorite book to a dog named Theo. The boy is petting the dog as he reads, and the dog has its paw on the boy's foot. Both seem relaxed and happy, but what is a dog doing in a school library?

Theo, a five-year-old border collie, is one of more than 2,300 dogs around the country that have been trained to listen to people read aloud. He is part of a program that began in Utah in 1999. . . .

> Which details catch your interest? Mark them.

> This scene is surprising. Readers will want to learn the answer to the question.

NOTEBOOK

WRITE IT Write your introduction. Follow the Mentor Text example by asking a question that will spark readers' curiosity.

DEPTH OF THOUGHT

As you draft the rest of your essay, use strong evidence to develop your controlling idea.

- **Specific Facts** Include names, places, and other facts that validate your ideas, or prove them true.
- **Descriptive Details** Use clear, vivid language to describe situations or scenes.
- **Examples** Describe specific events or situations that illustrate a general concept.

⭐ TEKS
10.B.ii. Develop drafts into a focused, structured, and coherent piece of writing by developing an engaging idea reflecting depth of thought with specific facts and details.

Create Coherence

A coherent essay has a clear flow of ideas. Even if a topic is complex, readers can follow the logic. Use these strategies to help make your essay coherent:

- Write a **topic sentence for each paragraph.** The topic sentence states the paragraph's most important, or main, idea. Every topic sentence should relate to the controlling idea of the essay.

- Include **supporting details.** The supporting details in each paragraph should explain or illustrate the topic sentence.

- Use **transitions** to link the ideas in your essay.

Sample Transitions

Relationship Between Ideas	Transitional Word or Phrase
cause and effect	*as a result; so that*
example	*for example; as an example*
comparison	*also; similarly; likewise*
contrast	*although; instead; on the other hand; however*
importance	*mainly; more importantly*

TRANSITIONS

Transitions are words and phrases that join sentences and paragraphs. They help readers follow a writer's thoughts and reasons. Choose transitions that show how one idea leads to the next.

 NOTEBOOK

WRITE IT Write a paragraph of your essay here. Add transitions that show the connections between sentences. Then, write the first sentence of the next paragraph, including a a transition.

_____
_____
_____
_____
_____
_____
_____
_____
_____
_____
_____
_____
_____
_____

INCLUDE EVIDENCE

Use transitions to shift between ideas and evidence.

- Introduce an expert you will quote.

EXAMPLE
Similarly, Albus Hardwick, owner of a local pet store, no longer sells puppies. "I'll stick to fish," he said.

- Present an example.

EXAMPLE
For example, Albus Hardwick, owner of Hardwick's Pets, no longer sells puppies.

Remember to place a comma after a transition that starts a sentence.

PERFORMANCE TASK

Revising

NOTEBOOK

Now that you have a first draft, revise it to be sure it is as informative as possible. When you revise, you "re-see" your writing, checking for the following elements:

Clarity: sharpness of your ideas

Development: full explanations with strong and varied evidence

Organization: logical flow of ideas

Style and Tone: well-constructed sentences with well-chosen words; a tone that suits your audience and purpose

Read Like a Writer

Review the revisions made to the Mentor Text. Then, answer the questions in the white boxes.

MENTOR TEXT

from **Reading Buddies**

There are many reasons ~~individuals~~ *kids* can have trouble reading. Some have learning disabilities. Some think it's boring. Some are new to English. *Others just haven't found a book they like.*

Whatever the cause, struggling readers have one thing in common: They lack confidence. Learning to read is often less about reading skills than it is about confidence. To a struggling reader, an animal listener can ~~be easier to read to~~ *produce less anxiety* than a human listener.

Dogs are the ideal reading companions. They aren't in a hurry, so you can read at your own pace. They won't stop you when you've pronounced something wrong. They won't laugh at you or make you feel self-conscious. When you read to a dog, you are not as likely to feel judged. *You get a chance to focus on the book you're reading rather than your performance.* ~~It really helps if you have chosen an interesting book, too!~~

"I never finished a whole book before," said a 10-year-old girl who participated in the program. She had been reading at a first-grade level and hardly ever ~~practiced. She~~ *practiced, because she* was too shy to read aloud. But after a few weeks of reading to a dog companion, she finished the book. She was proud of herself for having overcome such a major hurdle!

Why do you think the writer replaced this word?

An additional example shows a wider range of reasons.

The transitional phrase clarifies the flow of ideas between paragraphs.

How does the addition of this sentence strengthen the paragraph?

Why do you think the author deleted this sentence?

TEKS
10.C. Revise drafts for clarity, development, organization, style, word choice, and sentence variety.

Take a Closer Look at Your Draft

Now, revise your draft. Use the Revision Guide for Informational Essays to evaluate and strengthen your work.

REVISION GUIDE FOR INFORMATIONAL ESSAYS

EVALUATE	TAKE ACTION
Clarity	
Is my controlling idea clear and engaging?	If your controlling idea isn't clear, **restate** it as a question. Then, answer the question with a single clear statement.
Have I used correct pronoun-antecedent agreement?	**Mark** pronouns you used and **trace** each one back to its antecedent. Make sure the two agree in number, person, and gender. For example, a sentence should read *The dog shows his feelings,* and not *The dog shows their feelings.*
Development	
Have I provided enough supporting evidence for every idea?	**List** your main ideas—the topic sentence of each paragraph. **Add** evidence for ideas that need more support. **Delete** details that are not relevant
Have I used varied evidence?	**Add** facts or expert statements to further support your controlling idea. **Add** anecdotes or examples to illustrate your facts.
Have I ended my essay in an effective way?	**Add** a reference to your best example, a quotation, or a strong statement to make a lasting impression on your reader.
Organization	
Have I organized my ideas in a logical way?	If the flow of ideas is confusing, **reorder** paragraphs. If you are working on a computer, save your essay with a new name. Then, experiment with the order of paragraphs until you find a better sequence.
Do the sentences in each paragraph all relate to the topic sentence?	**Mark** the topic sentence in each paragraph. **Analyze** the other sentences to make sure they relate to the topic sentence. **Delete** any sentences that don't belong, or **move** them to another paragraph.
Style and Tone	
Is my introduction interesting?	**Add** a question, anecdote, quotation, or interesting detail to engage your audience.
Is my tone suitable for an informational essay?	**Replace** any words that seem too casual or too formal.
Are my word choices precise?	**Replace** any vague words (*good, okay, nice*) with more precise, accurate terms (*noble, welcoming, polite*).

Editing

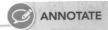 ANNOTATE

Don't let errors distract readers from your ideas. Reread your draft and fix mistakes to create a finished informative work.

Read Like a Writer

Look at how the writer of the Mentor Text edited the draft. Then, follow the directions in the white boxes.

> The writer corrected two spelling errors.

MENTOR TEXT

from **Reading Buddies**

More and more libraries and schools are using dogs to help kids improve ~~they're~~ *their* reading skills and confidence level. Sometimes when people read to dogs ~~its~~ *it's* the *dogs* that benefit. For ~~example the~~ *example, the* Arizona Animal Welfare League & Society for Prevention of Cruelty to Animals is using reading as a tool to help shelter animals become happier, more well-adjusted pets. Program volunteers spend time reading to dogs and ~~cats. Who~~ *cats, who* are waiting to be adopted.

> Add the missing comma in the second sentence.

> Why did the writer add a comma after "For example"?

> The writer fixed a sentence fragment.

Focus on Sentences

Complete Sentences A **complete sentence** expresses one or more complete thoughts, punctuated correctly. Three common errors are sentence fragments, run-on sentences, and comma splices.

- A **sentence fragment** does not express a complete thought, but it is punctuated as if it does.

  Incorrect: Volunteers read to dogs. <u>Because listening calms them</u>.

  Correct: Volunteers read to dogs because listening calms them.

- A **run-on sentence** runs two complete thoughts (independent clauses) together, without punctuation between them.

  Incorrect: The clock struck <u>one the</u> crowd left.

  Correct: When the clock struck one, the crowd left.

- A **comma splice** incorrectly connects two complete thoughts (independent clauses) with just a comma.

  Incorrect: The shoes were <u>old, they</u> were very nice.

  Correct: Although the shoes were old, they were very nice.

PRACTICE Check your draft, and fix any fragments, run-ons, or comma splices you find.

> **EDITING TIPS**
>
> To fix a run-on or splice, first identify the two independent clauses that are incorrectly joined. Then, choose one of these solutions to separate the clauses: 1. Add a semicolon; 2. Add a comma and a conjunction; 3. Add a period to the end of the first clause, and start the second clause with a capital letter.

🌐 TEKS

10.D.i. Edit drafts using standard English conventions, including complete complex sentences with subject-verb agreement and avoidance of splices, run-ons, and fragments. **10.D.viii.** Edit drafts using standard English conventions, including punctuation marks, including commas in complex sentences, transitions, and introductory elements. **10.D.ix.** Edit drafts using standard English conventions, including correct spelling, including commonly confused terms such as *its/it's*, *affect/effect*, *there/their/they're*, and *to/two/too.*

Focus on Spelling and Punctuation

Spelling: Commonly Confused Words The words *their, there,* and *they're* are homophones; they sound alike but have different meanings and spellings.

- *Their* is a possessive pronoun that refers to something that belongs to a group.
  EXAMPLE: The dogs ran off with *their* toys.

- *There* refers to a place.
  EXAMPLE: We keep the dog treats in *there.*

- *They're* is a contraction for *they are.*
  EXAMPLE: *They're* planning to bring the dogs tomorrow.

Punctuation: Commas Check your punctuation after transitions.

- Put a comma after a conjunctive adverb that begins a sentence.
  EXAMPLE: *Unfortunately, the dogs are not here today.*

- Put a comma after a transitional phrase.
  EXAMPLE: *Mark and Molly forgot to buy dog treats. As a result, they couldn't reward Spot's excellent behavior.*

EDITING TIPS
- Trade essays with a partner to look for spelling and punctuation errors.
- Proofread your paper at least twice. First, look for spelling errors; then, focus on punctuation.

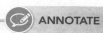 ANNOTATE

PRACTICE In the following sentences, correct spelling and punctuation errors. Then, review your own draft for correctness.

1. There eager to learn more about how pets can help people.

2. The boys want to bring they're pets to the library, but dogs are not allowed their.

3. Eventually all of the children will read with dogs.

4. More importantly they are improving there reading skills.

Publishing and Presenting

Make It Multimodal

Share your essay with your class or school community. Choose one of these options:

OPTION 1 Print your class's essays, and then assemble them into a book. Add a blank page after each essay for comments. Circulate the book among the class and write positive comments about each other's essays.

OPTION 2 Record your essay as a podcast. If possible, post the podcasts on your school website.

Essential Question

How do animals and people interact?

Sometimes animals communicate with other kinds of animals. Other times, they communicate with people. How is the relationship between different animal species similar to and different from the relationship between animals and people? You will work in a group to continue your exploration of these interactions.

▶ VIDEO

INTERACTIVITY

Peer-Group Learning Strategies

Throughout your life, in school, in your community, and in your career, you will continue to learn and work with others.

Review these strategies and the actions you can take to practice them as you work in small groups. Add ideas of your own for each step. Use these strategies during Peer-Group Learning.

STRATEGY	MY ACTION PLAN
Prepare • Complete your assignments so that you are prepared for group work. • Take notes on your reading so that you can share ideas with others in your group.	
Participate fully • Make eye contact to signal that you are paying attention. • Use text evidence when making a point.	
Support others • Build off ideas from others in your group. • Ask others who have not yet spoken to do so.	
Clarify • Paraphrase the ideas of others to be sure that your understanding is correct. • Ask follow-up questions.	

CONTENTS

PERFORMANCE TASK: SPEAKING AND LISTENING

Give and Follow Oral Instructions

The Peer-Group readings explore ways in which people and animals interact with one another. After reading, your group will give and follow oral instructions to complete an animal-related project.

Working as a Group

 NOTEBOOK

1. Take a Position

Discuss the following question with your group:

> Are animals better at communicating with people, or are people better at communicating with animals?

As you take turns sharing your ideas, elicit suggestions from everyone in the group and consider their ideas. Use the "round-robin" strategy to get everyone talking:

- Sit in a circle. Have a volunteer start the conversation and pass it to the person on his or her right.
- Each person in turn considers what the person on the left said, adds an idea, and passes the conversation to the next person.
- After everyone has spoken, follow up on interesting ideas by eliciting and considering additional insights from the group. Record the group's conclusions by taking notes.

2. List Your Rules

As a group, decide on the rules that you will follow as you work together. Two examples are provided. Add two more of your own. You may add or revise rules as you work through the readings and activities together.

- Everyone should participate in group discussions.
- People should not interrupt.

_____

_____

3. Name Your Group

Choose a name that reflects the unit topic.

Our group's name: _____

4. Create a Communication Plan

Decide how you want to share information with one another. For example, you might use online collaboration tools, email, or instant messaging.

Our group's plan:

_____

_____

 TEKS

1.D. Participate in student-led discussions by eliciting and considering suggestions from other group members, taking notes, and identifying points of agreement and disagreement; **6.G.** Discuss and write about the explicit or implicit meanings of text.

Making a Schedule

First, find out the due dates for the Peer-Group activities. Then, preview the texts and activities with your group and make a schedule for completing the tasks.

SELECTION	ACTIVITIES	DUE DATE
Predators		
The Naming of Cats		
Nikita		
The Tale of the Hummingbird		
Black Cowboy, Wild Horses		

Analyzing Explicit and Implicit Meanings

Literature is rich in meanings that are both explicit and implicit. You will be asked to discuss and write about both types of meaning as you work with your group.

Explicit meanings don't require interpretation. They are directly stated. Many informational texts and arguments convey explicit meanings more than implicit ones.

Implicit meanings are suggested by details. Readers make inferences and draw connections to figure them out. Literary genres may include some explicit meanings, but the key meanings are usually implicit.

Apply these strategies to identify and interpret both kinds of meaning:
- *To identify explicit meanings,* mark passages that directly state or explain ideas. **Paraphrase** these ideas, restating them in your own words, to make sure you understand them.
- *To interpret implicit meanings,* mark details that stand out. Then, consider what they are like and not like, and whether other details have similar or different qualities. Make inferences about the deeper ideas the details suggest.

The selections you are about to read are lyric poems.

Reading Lyric Poetry

Lyric poetry expresses the thoughts and feelings of a single speaker and often has a musical quality.

LYRIC POETRY

Author's Purpose
➔ to use focused, imaginative language to describe the experience of a particular moment

Characteristics
➔ describes a moment in time

➔ may have characters and settings, but does not tell a complete story

➔ expresses an insight or new understanding

➔ has a speaker who "tells" the poem

➔ uses language, including figures of speech and imagery, that has layers of meaning

Structure
➔ divided into lines, or horizontal groups of words

➔ lines may be organized into separate stanzas

➔ may have set patterns of stanza length, rhyme, or meter (formal poems)

➔ may not have any set patterns (free verse poems)

Take a Minute!

 NOTEBOOK

DISCUSS IT With a partner, discuss poems you have enjoyed. Are any of them lyrical? How do you know?

⬤ TEKS

8.B. Analyze the effect of meter and structural elements such as line breaks in poems across a variety of poetic forms.

Genre / Text Elements

Structural Elements of Poetry The basic unit of meaning in a poem is the **line**, or horizontal set of words. Lines can break, or end, in two different ways.

TIP: Structural elements affect how you read a poem. They also emphasize certain words or phrases, which affects a poem's meaning.

TYPE OF LINE BREAK	EXPLANATION	EXAMPLE
End-stopped	• end of the line matches the completion of a thought or meaning • may end with a comma, period, or other punctuation	*Fame is a bee.* *It has a song.* —Emily Dickinson
Enjambed	• thought or meaning continues past the end of the line to the next line or lines	*O world! O life! O time* *On whose last steps I climb,...* —from "A Lament," Percy Bysshe Shelley

Lines can be grouped into **stanzas**, which function like paragraphs in prose. A stanza may have a **rhyme scheme**, or pattern of rhyming sounds at the ends of lines. Letters (*abc*) indicate the same rhyming sounds.

EXAMPLE: RHYME SCHEME

Sleep, sleep, beauty bright,	*a*
Dreaming in the joys of night;	*a*
Sleep, sleep; in thy sleep	*b*
Little sorrows sit and weep	*b*

—from "Cradle Song," William Blake

 NOTEBOOK

PRACTICE Read the stanza from "The Courage That My Mother Had" by Edna St. Vincent Millay. Then, work with a partner to answer the questions.

> The golden brooch my mother wore
> She left behind for me to wear;
> I have no thing I treasure more:
> Yet, it is something I could spare.

1. (a) What type of line break is used in line 1? **(b)** What type of line break is used in line 3? Explain.

2. Mark the set of letters that accurately shows the rhyme scheme of the stanza.
   aabb   abab   abca   abba

3. Read the stanza aloud. What effect do the line breaks and rhyme scheme have? Explain.

POETRY COLLECTION

Predators

The Naming of Cats

Nikita

Concept Vocabulary ANNOTATE

As you read these poems, you will encounter these words.

domesticated	sensible	dignified

Context Clues To find the meaning of unfamiliar words, look for clues in the context—the words that surround the unknown word. There are different types of context clues that can help you. Here are two examples:

Definition: The dogs **gazed**, watching intensely as the foxes walked into the woods.

Elaborating Details: The painting's **indistinct** figures as well as the foggy colors and vague shapes suggest that the artist was losing his sight.

PRACTICE As you read the poems, study the context to determine the meanings of unfamiliar words. Mark your observations in the open space next to the text.

Comprehension Strategy NOTEBOOK

Adjust Fluency

Reading fluently means reading with accuracy, understanding, and expression. It also means that you read at an appropriate speed, which may change depending on the type of text and the reading purpose. To improve your fluency as you read poetry, follow the punctuation to see where to pause or stop.

- comma (,) or semicolon (;) = brief pause
- period (.) = full stop
- question mark (?) = full stop with a slight lift
- ellipses (…) = extended pause
- dash (—) = abrupt interruption

PRACTICE As you read and analyze these poems, follow the punctuation and adjust your fluency to fit your reading purpose.

 TEKS
3. Adjust fluency when reading grade-level text based on the reading purpose.

2.B. Use context such as definition, analogy, and examples to clarify the meaning of words.

About the Poems

Predators

BACKGROUND
Habitat loss is a major threat to wildlife in the United States. As people use more land and alter natural environments, wild animals are forced to move into places where people and domestic animals live. Foxes are one type of wild animal that has been seen in residential neighborhoods in increasing numbers. A female fox is called a "vixen."

Linda Hogan (b. 1947) is an award-winning Chickasaw novelist, essayist, environmentalist, and poet. Her writing often addresses topics such as the environment and Native American history. An activist and educator, Hogan has been a featured speaker at numerous international conferences and events on the environment and literature. She lives in the Colorado mountains and is currently the Chickasaw Nation's writer-in-residence.

The Naming of Cats

BACKGROUND
Unlike dogs, that often behave as our obedient servants, cats seem to have minds of their own. As a result, we tend to think of them as proud and mysterious. This famous poem by T. S. Eliot suggests that there are some essential things about these fascinating creatures that we will never be able to know.

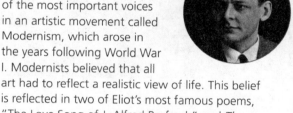

T. S. Eliot (1888-1965) is one of the most important voices in an artistic movement called Modernism, which arose in the years following World War I. Modernists believed that all art had to reflect a realistic view of life. This belief is reflected in two of Eliot's most famous poems, "The Love Song of J. Alfred Prufrock" and *The Waste Land*. Eliot also wrote a book of lighter verse, entitled *Old Possum's Book of Practical Cats,* which includes "The Naming of Cats." This book became the basis for the wildly successful musical, *Cats.* In 1948, Eliot received the Nobel Prize in Literature.

Nikita

BACKGROUND
Cats have been part of human communities ever since wild cats started living near farms in the Middle East about 8,000 years ago. It is believed that cats were welcomed in agricultural areas because they helped control mice and other rodents that ate crops. Today, Americans own 74 million cats, valuing these unique animals more for their companionship than for their usefulness. In this poem, a cat plays an important role in its owner's emotional life.

Alberto Ríos was born in Nogales, Arizona in 1952. He grew up in a Spanish-speaking family, but spoke English in school. After college, Ríos entered law school, then left after one year to pursue creative writing. He earned a Master of Fine Arts in creative writing from the University of Arizona. Ríos's poems and short stories are lyrical and use language in unexpected ways. He was named Arizona's first Poet Laureate in 2013.

Predators

Linda Hogan

 AUDIO

 ANNOTATE

I cannot smell the scent of the cat
who slept on this sweater, but do know
how the garden swells with old
and pungent herb art. In sun the fox

5 bows to my feline and her good
dog friends who rule this land. I hoe
and cultivate, find my dead aim
in the trust that many tales spun

this tract long before I came.
10 The dogs do not understand wild nature.
I also was **domesticated**.
Oh, give me strength to watch their sorry
looks as a bevy of vixen[1]

feed on a much smaller body
15 not the cat's . . . But it could be.

Mark context clues or indicate another strategy you used that helped you determine meaning.

domesticated (duh MEHS tuh kay tuhd) *adj.*

MEANING:

---

1 **bevy of vixen** a group of female foxes.

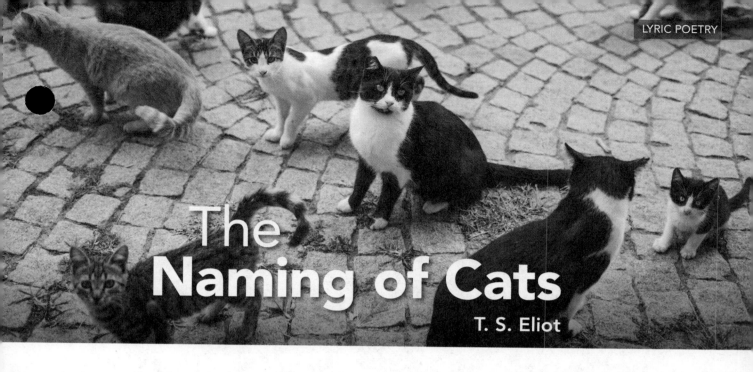

The Naming of Cats

T. S. Eliot

You may think at first I'm as mad as a hatter
When I tell you, a cat must have THREE DIFFERENT NAMES.
First of all, there's the name that the family use daily,
Such as Peter, Augustus, Alonzo or James,
5   Such as Victor or Jonathan, George or Bill Bailey—
All of them **sensible** everyday names.
There are fancier names if you think they sound sweeter,
Some for the gentlemen, some for the dames:
Such as Plato, Admetus, Electra, Demeter—
10   But all of them sensible everyday names.
But I tell you, a cat needs a name that's particular,
A name that's peculiar, and more **dignified**,
Else how can he keep up his tail perpendicular,
Or spread out his whiskers, or cherish his pride?
15   Of names of this kind, I can give you a quorum,
Such as Munkustrap, Quaxo, or Coricopat,
Such as Bombalurina, or else Jellylorum—
Names that never belong to more than one cat.
But above and beyond there's still one name left over,
20   And that is the name that you never will guess;
The name that no human research can discover—
But THE CAT HIMSELF KNOWS, and will never confess.
When you notice a cat in profound meditation,
The reason, I tell you, is always the same:
25   His mind is engaged in a rapt contemplation
Of the thought, of the thought, of the thought of his name:
His ineffable effable
Effanineffable
Deep and inscrutable singular Name.

Mark context clues or indicate another strategy that you used that helped you determine meaning.

sensible (SEHN suh buhl) *adj.*

MEANING:

dignified (DIHG nuh fyd) *adj.*

MEANING:

Nikita

Alberto Ríos

Under a heavy wire milk case,
A piece of concrete foundation
On top, in summer, in her backyard,
Mrs. Russo keeps the cat Nikita safe
5   From birds, from dogs, from eating
Johnson grass,[1] which he throws up.
Nikita waits for ants to wander in
And for the sun to leave.
Instead, she comes to keep him
10 Company, saying You look fat
And that her son died,
Remember I told you?
Walking thin in his uniform
On a road.

1. **Johnson grass** is a common plant in many states. It is considered a weed, and under certain conditions it can be poisonous to animals.

Response

 NOTEBOOK

1. Personal Connections Which poem did you most enjoy reading? Explain your choice.

> Work on your own to answer the questions in your notebook. Use text evidence to support your responses.

Comprehension

2. Reading Check (a) What is the setting for "Predators"? **(b)** Where is the cat in "Nikita" being kept? **(c)** According to the speaker in "The Naming of Cats," how many names does a cat have?

3. Strategy: Adjust Fluency (a) In what ways did following the punctuation of the poems help you better understand them? Explain. **(b)** Would you recommend this strategy to others? Why or why not?

Analysis and Discussion

4. (a) Make Inferences In "Predators," do the predators the speaker refers to include cats and dogs? Explain. **(b) Make Inferences** Reread the last four lines of the poem. What is the speaker worried about? Cite text evidence to support your inference.

5. Analyze In "The Naming of Cats," how is a cat's secret name different from its other names? Explain.

6. (a) In "Nikita," what happened to Mrs. Russo's son? **(b) Make Inferences** Why does Mrs. Russo want to protect the cat? Explain.

7. Get Ready for Close Reading Choose a passage from the text that you find especially interesting or important. You'll discuss the passage with your group during Close-Read activities.

> **WORKING AS A GROUP**
> Discuss your responses to the Analysis and Discussion questions with your group.
> • Note agreements and disagreements.
> • Summarize insights.
> • Consider changes of opinion.
> If necessary, revise your original answers to reflect what you learn from your discussion.

 EQ Notes How do animals and people interact?

What has reading these poems taught you about the ways animals and people interact? Go to your Essential Question Notes and record your observations and thoughts about the poems.

⭐ TEKS
3. Adjust fluency when reading grade-level text based on the reading purpose.

5.F. Make inferences and use evidence to support understanding.

POETRY COLLECTION

Close Read

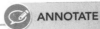 ANNOTATE

PRACTICE Complete the following activities. Use support from your peers and teacher to enhance and confirm your understanding of the poems.

1. **Present and Discuss** With your group, share the passages from the lyric poems that you found especially interesting. Discuss what you notice, the questions you have, and the conclusions you reach. For example, you might focus on the following passages:

   • "Predators," lines 12 and 15: Discuss why the speaker needs "strength" to watch the dogs as they watch the foxes.

   • "The Naming of Cats," lines 11–18: Discuss the unique qualities of the cats' "particular" names.

   • "Nikita," lines 9–14: Discuss what Mrs. Russo says to the cat and what it shows about Mrs. Russo's life.

2. **Reflect on Your Learning** What new ideas or insights did you uncover during your second reading of the text?

WORD NETWORK

Add words that describe interactions between animals and people from the text to your Word Network.

NOTEBOOK

LANGUAGE STUDY

Concept Vocabulary

Why These Words? The vocabulary words are related.

domesticated	sensible	dignified

1. With your group, determine what the words have in common. Write your ideas.

2. Add another word that fits the category. _____

3. Work on your own to write sentences for each word in which you describe someone or something. Share and discuss your sentences with your group.

- -

Word Study

Latin Root: -dom- The speaker in "Predators" recognizes a difference between creatures who are *domesticated* and those who are wild. The word *domesticated* is formed from the Latin root *-dom-*, which means "home" or "house." Use a dictionary to find the meanings of the words *domain* and *dome*. Explain how the meaning of the root *-dom-* is evident in each word.

⭐ TEKS

2.C. Determine the meaning and usage of grade-level academic English words derived from Greek and Latin roots such as *mis/mit, bene, man, vac, scrib/script,* and *jur/jus.*

6.F. Respond using newly acquired vocabulary as appropriate.

8.B. Analyze the effect of meter and structural elements such as line breaks in poems across a variety of poetic forms.

Genre / Text Elements

Structural Elements of Poetry Lines, line breaks, stanzas, and rhyme scheme are structural elements of poetry. The poets in this collection use these tools to give their poems shape, order, and emotional impact.

EXAMPLE: Effects of Poetic Structure

STRUCTURES	EXAMPLE FROM "THE NAMING OF CATS"	EXPLANATION
Lines and Line Breaks	*His mind is engaged in a rapt contemplation* *Of the thought, of the thought, of the thought of his name:* *His ineffable effable* *Effanineffable* *Deep and inscrutable singular Name.*	Long and short lines and both types of line breaks add dramatic pauses and emphasize words.

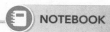 NOTEBOOK

PRACTICE With your group, read the poems aloud and listen for the effects of poetic structures. Then, answer the questions.

1. Analyze Answer the questions in the chart.

Predators In "Predators," what type of line break does the poet mainly use?	
How are lines 10 and 11 different from the other lines?	
How does the last line of each stanza connect to the next stanza?	
The Naming of Cats Which lines are not end-stopped?	
Nikita Which lines in "Nikita" are enjambed?	

2. Interpret Consider the use of line breaks in the three poems. In general, how do line breaks add to a poem's effect and meaning? Cite examples from the poems to support your answer.

3. (a) Analyze In "The Naming of Cats," which rhyming sound from the first four lines appears throughout the poem? **(b) Analyze** Using the *abc* system, write out the rhyme scheme of the poem as a whole. **(c) Interpret** How does this rhyme scheme add to the poem's humor? Explain.

4. (a) Contrast Explain how the experience of reading "The Naming of Cats" is different from that of the other two poems in this collection. **(b) Analyze** Which structural elements contribute most to those differences? Explain.

POETRY COLLECTION

Author's Craft

Language and Voice Poets use language with great precision. Their word choice, or **diction**, conveys layers of meaning and creates the music of a poem. A poet's diction also contributes to his or her **voice.** In life, peoples' personalities come through in how they speak and the words they use. The same idea applies in literature. Voice is a writer's sound, his or her personality on the page. Here are strategies for identifying voice:

• Read the poem aloud, and listen for the emotions it conveys.

• Do any words leap out at you? Which ones, and why?

• How would you describe the speaker's personality? What specific words or details make you think that?

Just as people's personalities can be described in many different ways, so can literary voice. Try to hear how details in a work create a unique sense of a person behind the words.

 NOTEBOK

PRACTICE Work together to read the poems aloud and discuss the voice each one creates.

POEM	DESCRIPTION OF VOICE	LANGUAGE THAT CREATES VOICE
Predators		
The Naming of Cats		
Nikita		

 TEKS

9.F. Analyze how the author's use of language contributes to mood and voice.

11.D. Compose correspondence that reflects an opinion, registers a complaint, or requests information in a business or friendly structure.

Composition

A **friendly letter** is a written message to a particular person or group of people. It includes an address, date, greeting, body, closing, and signature.

ASSIGNMENT

Choose a cat from one of the poems in this collection. Then, write a **friendly letter** from the cat to the poem's speaker. Express an opinion, from the cat's viewpoint, to the speaker of the poem. Choose one of the following options or come up with your own:

○ Explain to the speaker of "Predators" how you feel about foxes roaming near your home and what should be done about them.

○ Explain to the speaker of "The Naming of Cats" how you feel about your various names and whether they suit you.

○ Share with the speaker of "Nikita" your feelings about being kept under a milk crate while outside.

Work on your own to do this assignment. Then, share and discuss your letter with your group.

TIP: Include the elements of a friendly letter as you write.

- Place the address in the top right corner of the page.
- Include a greeting such as "Dear Owner," followed by a comma.
- End with a closing, such as "Yours Truly," on its own line followed by a comma.
- Add a signature, or signed name of the letter writer.

Plan Your Letter Choose the cat you will represent. Think about an opinion the cat wants to share with the speaker. How might the cat express itself and support its opinion? Use the chart to record your ideas.

INTERACTIVITY

OPINION	SUPPORT

EQ Notes Before moving on to a new selection, go to your Essential Question Notes and record any additional thoughts or observations you may have about this poetry collection.

Draft Your Letter State the cat's opinion clearly and respectfully, and give reasons that support it. Be sure to include the necessary parts of an informal letter including the address, date, greeting, body, closing, and signature.

Reflect on Your Writing Share your final letters as a group and discuss whether any of the letters expressed similar opinions.

The selection you are about to read is a myth.

Reading Myths

A **myth** is a traditional story that explains how some aspect of the world came to be. Myths are part of the oral tradition, but modern writers sometimes retell them.

MYTHS

Author's Purpose
- to tell a story that explains an aspect of the world and conveys the values of a culture

Characteristics
- characters who may be gods or goddesses, or have supernatural abilities
- settings that may be imaginary places, or real places that are important to a culture or religion
- theme, or insight about life, that is important to a culture

Structure
- a plot, or a related series of events, driven by a conflict

Take a Minute!

 NOTEBOOK

CHOOSE IT Choose three words or phrases from the list that you would most likely find in a myth. Share and discuss your choices with a partner.

came to be	automobile	mathematics
flight	golden	breakfast
computer	monster	goddess

TEKS

7.A. Infer multiple themes within and across texts using text evidence.

8.A. Demonstrate knowledge of literary genres such as realistic fiction, adventure stories, historical fiction, mysteries, humor, and myths.

Genre / Text Elements

Multiple Themes A **theme** of a story is a message or insight about life that it expresses. In myths, themes focus on big ideas such as love or the battle between good and evil. In most stories, themes are not directly stated. Instead, readers figure out themes by examining details, such as the ones listed here, and seeing how they build toward larger ideas:

> **TIP:** A theme can't be stated in a single word or phrase. It is a deeper message that must be expressed in a sentence. Many stories have more than one theme.

- **Characters' Qualities:** characters' actions, statements, and feelings; the ways in which characters grow or change; what characters learn

- **Conflicts:** types of problems characters face and the ways they resolve them

- **Setting:** important or dramatic places in a story

A theme is not a summary or a retelling of the main elements of a story. It is a deeper message that can be applied to life in general. Readers may interpret themes differently. Likewise, many stories express multiple themes. In order for an interpretation to be valid, it must take into account all of a story's important details.

 NOTEBOOK

PRACTICE Read the passage. Then, answer the questions.

When people first came to this land, it was harsh and dry. The people could not grow food. They blamed the Sky but were too proud to ask for help. One day, a child called to the Sky. "Please," she pleaded. "Save our land. Send rain and green plants." The Sky listened, but did not reply. "Please," the child cried, "Our people will die!" The Sky was moved to tears, which fell to Earth in great rainstorms. Plants sprouted and the people rejoiced.

1. Which statement best expresses a theme of this passage? Explain your thinking.

◯ You must try to help yourself before you seek help from others.

◯ You must put aside pride and seek help when you need it.

◯ The Sky is responsible for the people's survival.

2. What other theme might this brief passage express? Explain your thinking.

About the Author

Pura Belpré (1899–1982) was the first Puerto Rican librarian in New York City. She was also a writer and puppeteer. As a writer, Belpré re-interpreted many Puerto Rican folk tales; her story "Perez and Martina" is a classic of children's literature. Established in 1996, the Pura Belpré Award is presented annually to a Latino/Latina writer whose work portrays and affirms the Latino cultural experience.

The Tale of the Hummingbird

Concept Vocabulary

 ANNOTATE

As you read "The Tale of the Hummingbird," you will encounter these words.

swiftly	darting	hover

Use a Print Thesaurus A **thesaurus** is a reference book about words. A typical thesaurus entry indicates a word's part of speech and lists synonyms, or words with the same or similar meanings. The entry may also list antonyms, or words with opposite meanings.

In this example, notice that synonyms (*cold, distant*) and antonyms (*friendly, kind*) can help you determine the meaning of the more challenging word *aloof.*

SAMPLE THESAURUS ENTRY

aloof *adj.* synonyms: cold, indifferent, detached, distant, haughty

antonyms: warm, friendly, kind, compassionate

PRACTICE As you read, use a print thesaurus to determine the meanings of unfamiliar words.

Comprehension Strategy

 NOTEBOOK

Evaluate Details to Determine Key Ideas

The details in a text are not all of equal importance. When you **evaluate details to determine key ideas,** you assess which ones help to develop a central idea or theme. Mark details the author emphasizes or repeats, and details that relate to a single concept. Follow these tips:

• There are no right or wrong details to mark. Simply mark the ones that seem interesting or important to you.

• Review the details you marked and look for patterns or connections among them.

• Think about those connections and consider the key idea they help to express.

PRACTICE As you read the myth, mark details that seem important. Then, evaluate them to determine key ideas or themes.

 TEKS

2.A. Use print or digital resources to determine the meaning, syllabication, pronunciation, word origin, and part of speech.

5.G. Evaluate details read to determine key ideas.

The Tale of the Hummingbird
Pura Belpré

BACKGROUND

This traditional tale about the origin of the hummingbird is from the Caribbean island of Puerto Rico. This mountainous island, which is a territory of the United States, contains many rare plants and animals. El Yunque National Forest, the only tropical rain forest in the U.S. Forest System, gets its name from an Indian spirit—Yuquiye—whose name means "Forest of Clouds."

 AUDIO

 ANNOTATE

1   BETWEEN THE TOWNS of Cayey and Cidra, far up in the hills, there was once a small pool fed by a waterfall that tumbled down the side of the mountain. The pool was surrounded by pomarosa trees, and the Indians used to call it Pomarosa Pool. It was the favorite place of Alida, the daughter of an Indian chief, a man of power and wealth among the people of the hills.

2   One day, when Alida had come to the pool to rest after a long walk, a young Indian came there to pick some fruit from the trees. Alida was surprised, for he was not of her tribe. Yet he said he was no stranger to the pool. This was where he had first seen Alida, and he had often returned since then to pick fruit, hoping to see her again.

3   He told her about himself to make her feel at home. He confessed, with honesty and frankness, that he was a member of the dreaded Carib tribe that had so often attacked the island of Borinquen.[1] As a young boy, he had been left behind after one of those raids, and he had stayed on the island ever since.

4   Alida listened closely to his story, and the two became friends. They met again in the days that followed, and their friendship grew stronger. Alida admired the young man's courage in living

---
1 **Borinquen** alternative name for Puerto Rico.

among his enemies. She learned to call him by his Carib name, Taroo, and he called her Alida, just as her own people did. Before long, their friendship had turned into love.

5   Their meetings by the pool were always brief. Alida was afraid their secret might be discovered, and careful though she was, there came a day when someone saw them and told her father. Alida was forbidden to visit the Pomarosa Pool, and to put an end to her romance with the stranger, her father decided to marry her to a man of his own choosing. Preparations for the wedding started at once.

6   Alida was torn with grief, and one evening she cried out to her god: "O Yukiyú, help me! Kill me or do what you will with me, but do not let me marry this man whom I do not love!"

7   And the great god Yukiyú took pity on her and changed her into a delicate red flower.

8   Meanwhile Taroo, knowing nothing of Alida's sorrow, still waited for her by the Pomarosa Pool. Day after day he waited. Sometimes he stayed there until a mantle of stars was spread across the sky.

9   One night the moon took pity on him. "Taroo," she called from her place high above the stars. "O Taroo, wait no longer for Alida! Your secret was made known, and Alida was to be married to a man of her father's choosing. In her grief she called to her god, Yukiyú; he heard her plea for help and changed her into a red flower."

10   "Ahee, ahee!" cried Taroo. "O moon, what is the name of the red flower?"

11   "Only Yukiyú knows that," the moon replied.

12   Then Taroo called out: "O Yukiyú, god of my Alida, help me too! Help me to find her!"

13   And just as the great god had heard Alida's plea, he listened now to Taroo and decided to help him. There by the Pomarosa Pool, before the moon and the silent stars, the great god changed Taroo into a small many-colored bird.

14   "Fly, Colibrí[2], and find your love among the flowers," he said.

15   Off went the Colibrí, flying **swiftly**, and as he flew his wings made a sweet humming sound.

16   In the morning the Indians saw a new bird **darting** about among the flowers, swift as an arrow and brilliant as a jewel. They heard the humming of its wings, and in amazement they saw it **hover** in the air over every blossom, kissing the petals of the flowers with its long slender bill. They liked the new bird with the music in its wings, and they called it Hummingbird.

17   Ever since then the little many-colored bird has hovered over every flower he finds, but returns most often to the flowers that are red. He is still looking, always looking, for the one red flower that will be his lost Alida. He has not found her yet.

---

2. **Colibrí** (koh lee BREE) *n.* Spanish word for *hummingbird.*

Use print resources or indicate another strategy you used that helped you determine meaning.

swiftly (SWIFT lee) *adv.*

MEANING:

darting (DART ihng) *v.*

MEANING:

hover (HUHV ur) *v.*

MEANING:

 **NOTEBOOK**

Response

1. Personal Connections Describe how you feel about the ending of the myth. Explain your response.

Work on your own to answer the questions in your notebook. Use text evidence to support your responses.

Comprehension

2. Reading Check (a) Where do Alida and Taroo meet? **(b)** Why does Alida's father forbid her to see Taroo? **(c)** What new forms does Yukiyú give Alida and Taroo?

3. Strategy: Evaluate Details to Determine Key Ideas (a) Cite one example of a detail you evaluated that helped you determine a key idea in this myth. **(b)** Would you recommend this strategy to other readers? Why, or why not?

Analysis and Discussion

4. (a) Analyze What does the information in paragraph 3 reveal about Taroo's character? **(b) Make a Judgment** Do you think Taroo is a worthy suitor for Alida? Explain.

5. Connect What unique qualities of the hummingbird does this myth explain? Cite specific details that support your answer.

6. Make Inferences What do Yukiyú's interactions with the characters in this story suggest about the ways in which ancient Puerto Rican culture viewed its gods? Explain.

7. (a) Analyze Cause and Effect In this myth, how do Taroo and Alida's transformations change the world? **(b) Take a Position** Do you think the world's gain justifies the loss they suffered? Explain.

8. Get Ready for Close Reading Choose a passage from the text that you find especially interesting or important. You'll discuss the passage with your group during Close-Read activities.

WORKING AS A GROUP

Discuss your responses to the Analysis and Discussion questions with your group.

- Note agreements and disagreements.
- Summarize insights.
- Consider changes of opinion.

If necessary, revise your original answers to reflect what you learn from your discussion.

 EQ Notes How do animals and people interact?

What have you learned about how animals and people interact from reading this myth? Go to your Essential Question Notes and record your observations and thoughts about "The Tale of the Hummingbird."

 TEKS

5.F. Make inferences and use evidence to support understanding.

6.A. Describe personal connections to a variety of sources, including self-selected texts.

6.C. Use text evidence to support an appropriate response.

THE TALE OF THE HUMMINGBIRD

Close Read

ANNOTATE

PRACTICE Complete the following activities. Use text evidence to support your responses.

1. **Present and Discuss** With your group, share the passages from the myth that you found especially interesting. Discuss what you notice and why you chose the passage. If you have difficulty expressing yourself, use gestures or make a drawing to get your ideas across. You may choose to focus on the following passages:

   • Paragraphs 2–3: Discuss Taroo's past and details that suggest what his life has been like.

   • Paragraphs 5–7: Discuss how the god Yukiyú chooses to help Alida and whether this is what she would have wanted.

2. **Reflect on Your Learning** What new ideas or insights did you uncover during your second reading of the text?

NOTEBOOK

WORD NETWORK

Add words that describe interactions between animals and people from the text to your Word Network.

LANGUAGE STUDY

Concept Vocabulary

Why These Words? The vocabulary words are related.

swiftly	darting	hover

1. With your group, determine what the words have in common. Write your ideas.

2. Add another word that fits the category. _____

3. Write a description of an animal using all three of the vocabulary words.

- -

Word Study

Synonyms Words that have the same basic meanings are called **synonyms**. Synonyms often have small differences in meaning. These differences affect the word choices a writer might make.

1. The words *hastily* and *promptly* are synonyms for the vocabulary word *swiftly*. Explain how the meanings of all three words are both similar and different.

2. Write a sentence for each of the three synonyms. Make sure each sentence reflects the specific meaning of each word.

TEKS
6.F. Respond using newly acquired vocabulary as appropriate.

7.A. Infer multiple themes within and across texts using text evidence.

Genre / Text Elements

Multiple Themes A **theme** of any story, including a myth, is a message or insight about life that it expresses. Many stories have more than one, or multiple, themes. Usually, the author does not state the theme directly. Instead, he or she builds the theme through details. Readers must examine the story closely and use connections among details to infer the theme or themes.

INTERACTIVITY

NOTEBOOK

PRACTICE Work with your group to answer the questions and complete the activity.

1. **Interpret** Consider this possible theme for the story: *We all have to learn to live with our choices.* Cite at least three details from the story that support this theme. Explain your choices.

2. **Interpret** Consider this possible theme for the story: *Society judges people unfairly.* Cite at least three details from the story that support this theme. Explain your choices.

3. **(a) Evaluate Key Details** Use the chart to explain how Taroo and Alida change over the course of the story, and how the actions of others affect them. Identify key details from the myth that support your explanations. **(b) Interpret** What theme about love is suggested by these details?

EXPLANATION	KEY DETAILS
beginning of story:	
effects of Alida's father:	
effects of Yukiyú:	
effects of the Moon:	
end of story:	

THE TALE OF THE HUMMINGBIRD

Conventions

Sentence Structures A sentence can be classified according to the number and kinds of clauses it contains.

- An **independent, or main, clause** has a subject and verb, and can stand alone as a sentence.
- A **dependent clause** also has a subject and verb, but cannot stand alone as a sentence; it must be joined with a main clause to complete its meaning.

In the examples in the chart, independent clauses are underlined once, and dependent clauses are underlined twice.

TIP A dependent clause usually begins with a relative pronoun, such as *that, which,* or *who,* or a subordinating conjunction, such as *after, because,* or *when.*

SENTENCE TYPE	EXAMPLE
Simple: a single independent clause	Their meetings by the pool were always brief.
Compound: two or more independent clauses joined by a coordinating conjunction (*and, but, for, or, nor, so, yet*) and a comma, or by a semicolon	The pool was surrounded by pomarosa trees, and the Indians used to call it Pomarosa Pool.
Complex: one independent clause and one or more dependent clauses	When Alida came to the pool, a young man fell in love with her.
Compound-Complex: two or more independent clauses and one or more dependent clauses	Hummingbirds are brightly colored, and they move very quickly when they fly from flower to flower.

 ANNOTATE

 NOTEBOOK

READ IT Label each sentence as simple, compound, complex, or compound-complex.

1. Alida listened closely to his story, and the two became friends.

2. As the stars spread across the sky, he waited for her.

3. Alida admired the young man's courage.

4. The moon took pity on Taroo, who was broken-hearted, and it reached out to him with its light.

WRITE IT Work with a partner to write three new sentences—one compound, one complex, and one compound-complex—using the following simple sentence as a main clause: *Taroo became a hummingbird.*

 TEKS

12.A. Generate student-selected and teacher-guided questions for formal and informal inquiry.

12.J. Use an appropriate mode of delivery, whether written, oral, or multimodal, to present results.

Research

In a **research report,** you use facts, details, and explanations gathered from research to explain a topic.

ASSIGNMENT

Research and prepare a **research report** about one of the following topics:

○ Option 1: Hummingbirds

○ Option 2: Puerto Rican Cultural Sites

Work with a partner to generate questions, conduct formal research, and prepare the report. Decide how best to share the information you find. For example, you might choose to create a written report, an oral presentation, or a multimodal text.

Generate Research Questions Begin by generating questions to guide research on your topic. Start with the questions given here, and add two more of your own.

- Hummingbirds:

  1. Is the depiction of hummingbirds in the myth accurate?

  2. _____

  3. _____

- Puerto Rican Sites

  1. What is the Pomarosa Pool and why is it an important place?

  2. _____

  3. _____

Conduct a Formal Inquiry Work with your partner to identify sources you will use to learn about the topic. Read the relevant information in each source, and take notes in an organized way. For example, you might use note cards or create a chart. Make sure to capture complete citation information for every source you consult.

Choose a Mode of Delivery Once you have gathered information, decide which mode of delivery will let you present it in the best way. Consider these options:

- Prepare a **written text** if your information needs detailed explanations. Share your work by posting it to a website or blog.

- Deliver an **oral report** if your information needs thorough, but briefer, explanations. Deliver your report to the class.

- Present a **multimodal text,** either orally or in a digital format, if visuals or other media you found are very vivid and instructive. Make sure the media doesn't overwhelm your explanations.

Choose the most appropriate mode of delivery and prepare your text.

EQ Notes Before moving on to a new selection, go to your Essential Question Notes and record any additional thoughts or observations you may have about "The Tale of the Hummingbird."

BLACK COWBOY, WILD HORSES

The selection you are about to read is a biography.

Reading Biographies

A **biography** is a type of nonfiction narrative in which a writer tells the story of another person's life.

BIOGRAPHY

Author's Purpose
- to tell the true story of an important or interesting person's life

Characteristics
- includes facts and personal details about the subject

- paints a vivid picture of the subject's life, including the places and people in his or her world

- describes events from the subject's life; the author may imagine or re-create some scenes and details, but these are based on factual information

Structure
- tells a clear story, or related sequence of events, usually in chronological order

- may include the author's explanations, summaries, or reflections

Take a Minute!

 NOTEBOOK

LIST IT List the names of two people whose biographies you would enjoy reading. Jot down the reasons why you think their life stories would be interesting. Share your list and reasons with a partner.

⚙ TEKS

6.G. Discuss and write about the explicit or implicit meanings of text.

8.D. Analyze characteristics and structural elements of informational text.

9.A. Explain the author's purpose and message within a text.

Genre / Text Elements

Author's Purpose and Message The **author's purpose** is his or her reason for writing. The author's **message** is the deeper meaning he or she expresses. In a biography, the author's purpose and message are closely linked; an author chooses a subject because he or she sees meaning in the person's life and wants to share that insight. Consider these examples.

PURPOSE	SUBJECT	MESSAGE
share new ideas about a familiar person	Abraham Lincoln: president dealt with personal tragedies and political turmoil	The presidents' private life was full of sorrows that his public life did not show.
explain the contributions of an ordinary person	Irena Sendler: unknown woman saved 2,500 Jewish children from the Nazis	This regular person is a hero whose actions should be celebrated.
set the record straight about someone	Vincent Van Gogh: artist painted beauty while suffering from mental illness	The greatness of the artist's work came from creativity and not madness.

Sometimes, a biographer states an **explicit message**—directly expressing his or her interpretation of the subject's life. More often, the biographer relates events and details that combine to build an **implicit message,** or one that is suggested but not directly stated.

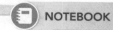 NOTEBOOK

PRACTICE Read the passage from a biography. Then, answer the questions.

from *The Most Famous Filmmaker You've Never Heard Of*

During the long summers of Nicholas's childhood, there were no games or TV. Instead, Nicholas wrote elaborate scripts and used the neighborhood as the set for films starring his siblings and their friends. In this atmosphere of pure play, one of the world's greatest movie directors found his voice.

1. What is the author's likely purpose for writing?

2. What is the author's message, or insight, in this passage? Explain. Is that message explicit or implicit? Explain.

About the Author

Julius Lester (1939–2018), a native of St. Louis, Missouri, has been a folk singer, a civil rights photographer, a writer, and a professor of African American Studies and Judaic Studies. His works include novels, stories, poetry, nonfiction, and a memoir.

Black Cowboy, Wild Horses

Concept Vocabulary

 ANNOTATE

As you read "Black Cowboy, Wild Horses," you will encounter these words.

milled	skittered	quivering

Context Clues The words that surround another word in a text are its *context*. The context can provide clues to the meaning of an unfamiliar word. There are different types of context clues.

With **example context clues,** details in the text provide specific examples of the word.

SAMPLE PASSAGE Her music was an **amalgam** of genres, mixing jazz, rock, and hip-hop.

> **Analysis:** The sentence lists different musical styles that are combined into one person's music. *Amalgam* must mean "a combination or mixture."

SAMPLE PASSAGE Many **celebrities,** including movie stars, singers, and best-selling authors, have appeared on the cover of this magazine.

> **Analysis:** The examples are all people who would be easily recognized, so *celebrities* must be another word for "famous people."

PRACTICE As you read "Black Cowboy, Wild Horses," study the context to determine the meanings of unfamiliar words. Mark your observations in the open space next to the text.

Comprehension Strategy

 NOTEBOOK

Paraphrase

When you **paraphrase** something you've read, you restate it in your own words while maintaining its meaning and logical order. Paraphrasing is especially useful for understanding challenging text and for clarifying figurative, or non-literal, language. Consider this example from "Black Cowboy, Wild Horses":

Passage: Far, far away, at what looked to be the edge of the world, land and sky kissed … (paragraph 1)

Paraphrase: In the far distance, the land and sky seemed to meet.

PRACTICE Read the third paragraph of the biography. Then, write a paraphrase in the open space next to the text. Check that your paraphrase maintains the meaning and order of the original text.

 TEKS

2.B. Use context such as definition, analogy, and examples to clarify the meaning of words.

6.D. Paraphrase and summarize text in ways that maintain meaning and logical order.

Black Cowboy, Wild Horses

Julius Lester

BACKGROUND

When Spanish explorers came to the Americas, they brought domesticated horses with them. Over time, some of these horses escaped into the wild, where they formed untamed herds and eventually spread west across the Great Plains. These wild horses became known as mustangs. Born a slave in 1848, Texas cowboy Robert Lemmons became a legend in his day by developing and perfecting his unique method of catching these wild horses.

 AUDIO

 ANNOTATE

1   First Light. Bob Lemmons rode his horse slowly up the rise. When he reached the top, he stopped at the edge of the bluff.[1] He looked down at the corral[2] where the other cowboys were beginning the morning chores, then turned away and stared at the land stretching as wide as love in every direction. The sky was curved as if it were a lap on which the earth lay napping like a curled cat. High above, a hawk was suspended on cold threads of unseen winds. Far, far away, at what looked to be the edge of the world, land and sky kissed.

2   He guided Warrior, his black stallion, slowly down the bluff. When they reached the bottom, the horse reared, eager to run across the vastness of the plains until he reached forever. Bob smiled and patted him gently on the neck. "Easy. Easy," he whispered. "We'll have time for that. But not yet."

3   He let the horse trot for a while, then slowed him and began peering intently at the ground as if looking for the answer to a question he scarcely understood.

4   It was late afternoon when he saw them—the hoofprints of mustangs, the wild horses that lived on the plains. He stopped, dismounted, and walked around carefully until he had seen all the prints. Then he got down on his hands and knees to examine them more closely.

---

1. **bluff** *n.* cliff.
2. **corral** (kuh RAL) *n.* fenced area for horses and cattle.

5   Some people learned from books. Bob had been a slave and never learned to read words. But he could look at the ground and read what animals had walked on it, their size and weight, when they had passed by, and where they were going. No one he knew could bring in mustangs by themselves, but Bob could make horses think he was one of them—because he was.

6   He stood, reached into his saddlebag, took out an apple, and gave it to Warrior, who chewed with noisy enthusiasm. It was a herd of eight mares, a colt, and a stallion. They had passed there two days ago. He would see them soon. But he needed to smell of sun, moon, stars, and wind before the mustangs would accept him.

7   The sun went down and the chilly night air came quickly. Bob took the saddle, saddlebag, and blanket off Warrior. He was cold, but could not make a fire. The mustangs would smell the smoke in his clothes from miles away. He draped a thick blanket around himself, then took the cotton sack of dried fruit, beef jerky, and nuts from his saddlebag and ate. When he was done, he lay his head on his saddle and was quickly asleep. Warrior grazed in the tall, sweet grasses.

8   As soon as the sun's round shoulders came over the horizon, Bob awoke. He ate, filled his canteen, and saddling Warrior, rode away. All day he followed the tracks without hurrying.

9   Near dusk, clouds appeared, piled atop each other like mountains made of fear. Lightning flickered from within them like candle flames shivering in a breeze. Bob heard the faint but distinct rumbling of thunder. Suddenly lightning vaulted from cloud to cloud across the curved heavens.

10   Warrior reared, his front hooves pawing as if trying to knock the white streaks of fire from the night sky. Bob raced Warrior to a nearby ravine[3] as the sky exploded sheets of light. And there, in the distance, beneath the ghostly light, Bob saw the herd of mustangs. As if sensing their presence, Warrior rose into the air once again, this time not challenging the heavens but almost in greeting. Bob thought he saw the mustang stallion rise in response as the earth shuddered from the sound of thunder.

11   Then the rain came as hard and stinging as remorse. Quickly Bob put on his poncho, and turning Warrior away from the wind and the rain, waited. The storm would pass soon. Or it wouldn't. There was nothing to do but wait.

12   Finally the rain slowed and then stopped. The clouds thinned, and there, high in the sky, the moon appeared as white as grief. Bob slept in the saddle while Warrior grazed on the wet grasses.

13   The sun rose into a clear sky and Bob was awake immediately. The storm would have washed away the tracks, but they had been going toward the big river. He would go there and wait.

14   By mid-afternoon he could see the ribbon of river shining in the distance. He stopped, needing only to be close enough to see the

---

3. **ravine** (ruh VEEN) *n.* narrow canyon with steep sides.

horses when they came to drink. Toward evening he saw a trail of rolling, dusty clouds.

15   In front was the mustang herd. As it reached the water, the stallion slowed and stopped. He looked around, his head raised, nostrils flared, smelling the air. He turned in Bob's direction and sniffed the air again.

16   Bob tensed. Had he come too close too soon? If the stallion smelled anything new, he and the herd would be gone and Bob would never find them again. The stallion seemed to be looking directly at him. Bob was too far away to be seen, but he did not even blink his eyes, afraid the stallion would hear the sound. Finally the stallion began drinking and the other horses followed. Bob let his breath out slowly. He had been accepted.

17   The next morning he crossed the river and picked up the herd's trail. He moved Warrior slowly, without sound, without dust. Soon he saw them grazing. He stopped. The horses did not notice him. After a while he moved forward, slowly, quietly. The stallion raised his head. Bob stopped.

18   When the stallion went back to grazing, Bob moved forward again. All day Bob watched the herd, moving only when it moved but always coming closer. The mustangs sensed his presence. They thought he was a horse.

19   So did he.

20   The following morning Bob and Warrior walked into the herd. The stallion eyed them for a moment. Then, as if to test this newcomer, he led the herd off in a gallop. Bob lay flat across Warrior's back and moved with the herd. If anyone had been watching, they would not have noticed a man among the horses.

21   When the herd set out early the next day, it was moving slowly. If the horses had been going faster, it would not have happened.

22   The colt fell to the ground as if she had stepped into a hole and broken her leg. Bob and the horses heard the chilling sound of the rattles. Rattlesnakes didn't always give a warning before they struck. Sometimes, when someone or something came too close, they bit with the fury of fear.

23   The horses whinnied and pranced nervously, smelling the snake and death among them. Bob saw the rattler, as beautiful as a necklace, sliding silently through the tall grasses. He made no move to kill it. Everything in nature had the right to protect itself, especially when it was afraid.

24   The stallion galloped to the colt. He pushed at her. The colt struggled to get up, but fell to her side, shivering and kicking feebly with her thin legs. Quickly she was dead.

25   Already vultures circled high in the sky. The mustangs **milled** aimlessly. The colt's mother whinnied, refusing to leave the side of her colt. The stallion wanted to move the herd from there, and pushed the mare with his head. She refused to budge, and he

Mark context clues or indicate another strategy you used that helped you determine meaning.

milled (mihld) *v.*

MEANING:

nipped her on the rump. She **skittered** away. Before she could return to the colt, the stallion bit her again, this time harder. She ran toward the herd. He bit her a third time, and the herd was off. As they galloped away, Bob looked back. The vultures were descending from the sky as gracefully as dusk.

26   It was time to take over the herd. The stallion would not have the heart to fight fiercely so soon after the death of the colt. Bob galloped Warrior to the front and wheeled around, forcing the stallion to stop quickly. The herd, confused, slowed and stopped also.

27   Bob raised Warrior to stand high on his back legs, fetlocks pawing and kicking the air. The stallion's eyes widened. He snorted and pawed the ground, surprised and uncertain. Bob charged at the stallion.

28   Both horses rose on hind legs, teeth bared as they kicked at each other. When they came down, Bob charged Warrior at the stallion again, pushing him backward. Bob rushed yet again.

29   The stallion neighed loudly, and nipped Warrior on the neck. Warrior snorted angrily, reared, and kicked out with his forelegs, striking the stallion on the nose. Still maintaining his balance, Warrior struck again and again. The mustang stallion cried out in pain. Warrior pushed hard against the stallion. The stallion lost his footing and fell to the earth. Warrior rose, neighing triumphantly, his front legs pawing as if seeking for the rungs on which he could climb a ladder into the sky.

30   The mustang scrambled to his feet, beaten. He snorted weakly. When Warrior made as if to attack again, the stallion turned, whinnied weakly, and trotted away.

31   Bob was now the herd's leader, but would they follow him? He rode slowly at first, then faster and faster. The mustangs followed as if being led on ropes.

32   Throughout that day and the next he rode with the horses. For Bob there was only the bulging of the horses' dark eyes, the **quivering** of their flesh, the rippling of muscles and bending of bones in their bodies. He was now sky and plains and grass and river and horse.

33   When his food was almost gone, Bob led the horses on one last ride, a dark surge of flesh flashing across the plains like black lightning. Toward evening he led the herd up the steep hillside, onto the bluff, and down the slope toward the big corral. The cowboys heard him coming and opened the corral gate. Bob led the herd, but at the last moment he swerved Warrior aside, and the mustangs flowed into the fenced enclosure. The cowboys leaped and shouted as they quickly closed the gate.

34   Bob rode away from them and back up to the bluff. He stopped and stared out onto the plains. Warrior reared and whinnied loudly.

35   "I know," Bob whispered. "I know. Maybe someday."

36   Maybe someday they would ride with the mustangs, ride to that forever place where land and sky kissed, and then ride on. Maybe someday. ❧

NOTEBOOK

Response

1. Personal Connections Describe the part of Bob's job that you would most enjoy and the part that you would find most difficult.

> Work on your own to answer the questions in your notebook. Use text evidence to support your responses.

Comprehension

2. Reading Check (a) Who is Warrior? **(b)** Where does Bob take the mustangs?

3. Strategy: Paraphrase In what ways did paraphrasing challenging or non-literal language in the text affect your reading experience? Explain your answer.

Analysis and Discussion

4. (a) In paragraph 5, what does the author say Bob could make horses think? **(b) Connect** Cite at least two actions Bob takes later in the text that connect to that idea. **(c) Interpret** Note the single statement in paragraph 19. What point is the author making about Bob's abilities? Explain.

5. (a) In paragraph 2, where does Warrior want to go? **(b) Connect** How does this idea return at the end of the text? **(c) Interpret** Is this something that could really happen? Explain.

6. Evaluate How might the end of Bob's journey be described as both a success and a failure? Explain.

7. Get Ready for Close Reading Choose a passage from the text that you find especially interesting or important. You'll discuss the passage with your group during Close-Read activities.

> **WORKING AS A GROUP**
> Discuss your responses to the Analysis and Discussion questions with your group. Try to use increasingly sophisticated words as you discuss ideas and ask one another questions. Revise your original answers to include new words that express literary concepts more precisely.

EQ Notes How do animals and people interact?

What have you learned about how people and animals interact from this biography? Go to your Essential Question Notes and record your observations and thoughts about "Black Cowboy, Wild Horses."

TEKS

6.A. Describe personal connections to a variety of sources, including self-selected texts.

6.C. Use text evidence to support an appropriate response.

6.D. Paraphrase and summarize texts in ways that maintain meaning and logical order.

BLACK COWBOY, WILD HORSES

Close Read

 ANNOTATE

PRACTICE Complete the following activities. Use text evidence to support an appropriate response.

1. **Present and Discuss** With your group, share the passages from the biography that you found especially interesting. Discuss what you notice, the questions you have, and the conclusions you reach. For example, you might focus on the following passages:

   • Paragraphs 4–6: Discuss how Bob might have been able to figure out so much information about the horses.

   • Paragraphs 11–12: Discuss why Bob slept in his saddle.

   • Paragraphs 26–30: Discuss how Bob and Warrior took control of the herd.

2. **Reflect on Your Learning** What new ideas or insights did you uncover during your second reading of the text?

📓 NOTEBOOK

LANGUAGE STUDY

Concept Vocabulary

Why These Words? Complete the activities. Seek support from your peers or teacher as needed.

milled	skittered	quivering

1. With your group, determine what the words have in common. Write your ideas.

2. Add another word that fits the category. _____

3. Use each vocabulary word in a sentence. Include context clues that hint at the word's meaning.

Word Study

Multiple-Meaning Words Some words have more than one meaning. For instance, the word *mill*, the base word for the vocabulary word *milled*, has many different meanings and is used as several different parts of speech. Use a dictionary to look up two meanings for the noun *mill* and two meanings for the verb *mill*. Record your findings.

Genre / Text Elements

Author's Purpose and Message Every author has a **purpose**, or reason, for writing. He or she also has a **message**—an important idea or insight—to share. An author's message may be explicit or implicit.

- The author states an **explicit message** directly. For example, a biographer may simply tell the reader why the subject is interesting and worthy of attention.

- The author develops an **implicit message** but does not state it directly. Instead, he or she suggests it through details. In a biography, these details may describe the subject's thoughts, actions, behavior, and interactions with the larger world.

> **TIP** The *subject* of a biography is the person the work is about.

To determine the author's purpose and message in a biography, examine details about the subject's appearance, thoughts, actions, and reasons, and consider what each one shows you about the subject.

 **INTERACTIVITY**

PRACTICE Work on your own to complete the activity and answer the questions. Then, share your responses with your group.

1. **(a) Analyze** Reread the passages indicated in the chart and identify key details.
   (b) Interpret Explain what each passage tells you implicitly about Bob Lemmons.

PASSAGE	IMPORTANT DETAILS	WHAT DETAILS SHOW
Paragraph 5: *But he could look at the ground and ... where they were going.*		
Paragraph 7: *He was cold, but ... smoke in his clothes from miles away.*		
Paragraph 18: *The mustangs sensed his ... was a horse.*		

2. **(a)** In paragraph 5, what information about Bob Lemmons does the biographer *explicitly* state? **(b) Evaluate** Why is this information important for understanding Bob Lemmons?

3. **Draw Conclusions** Bob Lemmons was not a leader or celebrity. Why do you think Julius Lester chose to write about him? Explain.

4. **(a) Interpret** What is the "forever place"? Explain. **(b) Assess** Do you think the biographer sees a conflict for Bob in his work? Explain.

BLACK COWBOY, WILD HORSES

Author's Craft

Figurative Language Language that is meant to be understood imaginatively rather than literally is **figurative language**. Authors use figurative language—including similes, metaphors, and personification—for a variety of purposes. These literary devices create vivid word pictures, build mood, and express ideas in memorable ways.

TYPE OF FIGURATIVE LANGUAGE	EXAMPLES FROM THE TEXT
Simile: a comparison of two unlike things using the words *like, as, than,* or *resembles*	*horses… flashing across the plains like black lightning*
Metaphor: a comparison that speaks of one thing as if it *is* another thing	*cold threads of unseen winds*
Personification: an implied comparison that gives human traits to a nonhuman subject	*the sun's round shoulders*

 NOTEBOOK

 INTERACTIVITY

PRACTICE Work on your own to answer the questions. Then, discuss your responses with your group.

1. Use the chart to complete the activity. **(a) Classify** Name the type of figurative language used in each passage. **(b) Interpret** Explain the purpose of each passage—the word picture or emotion it conveys.

PASSAGE	TYPE OF FIGURATIVE LANGUAGE	PURPOSE OR EFFECT
the land stretching as wide as love in every direction		
Far, far away, at what looked to be the edge of the world, land and sky kissed.		
By mid-afternoon he could see the ribbon of river shining in the distance.		

2. **Generalize** How does the author's use of figurative language serve the purpose of showing what Bob Lemmons's world is like? Explain, citing specific examples from the biography.

⬮ TEKS

9.D. Describe how the author's use of figurative language such as metaphor and personification achieves specific purposes.

12.B. Develop and revise a plan.

12.G. Differentiate between paraphrasing and plagiarism when using source materials.

12.I. Display academic citations and use source materials ethically.

12.J. Use an appropriate mode of delivery, whether written, oral, or multimodal, to present results.

Research

An **informative report** presents facts and explanations to educate readers or listeners about a topic.

ASSIGNMENT

Work with your group to research and create an **informative report** on one of the following topics:

○ the real-life Bob Lemmons

○ another legendary cowboy or cowgirl

Decide which mode of delivery is the most appropriate way to share the information that you find. For example, you may want to write a written report or deliver an oral or multimodal presentation. Use information from a variety of sources, and credit each one accurately.

Develop a Research Plan Choose your topic. Then, assign each group member to specific research tasks. For example, one person might take responsibility for finding and gathering print sources, while others look for online information or media. Use notecards like the one shown to record information about each source you review.

○ Print   ○ Digital   ○ Text   ○ Media

Title: _____

Author/Publisher: _____

Date of Access/Copyright Date: _____

URL/Other Location Information: _____

EQ Notes ▶ Before moving on to a new selection, go to your Essential Question Notes and record any additional thoughts or observations you may have about "Black Cowboy, Wild Horses."

Organize Your Presentation After you have finished your research, organize the information, and decide how you will present it—as a written text, an oral report, or a multimodal presentation.

Use Source Materials Ethically Avoid plagiarism by citing the sources of the information you use. Display a list of all the sources you consulted at the end of your report or presentation.

AVOID PLAGIARISM Even if you paraphrase a text, you must still credit the source that provided the ideas.

- Predators
- The Naming of Cats
- Nikita
- The Tale of the Hummingbird
- Black Cowboy, Wild Horses

Give and Follow Oral Instructions

ASSIGNMENT

Origami is the Japanese art of folding paper to make different shapes and figures. With your group, research how to make an origami version of an animal you choose together. Then, write a set of **oral instructions** and deliver them so that classmates can follow them successfully. You will have a chance to both give and follow instructions.

Plan With Your Group

INTERACTIVITY

Analyze the Task As a group, discuss the animal you would like to learn to make as an origami figure. List everyone's suggestions in the left column of the chart. Then, narrow down the list to two or three different options. Research those options and decide which will work best. Consider the following questions:

- Is the origami process for the animal too simple to be interesting?
- Is it too complicated to be practical?
- Does one origami animal seem more fun to make than the others?

Capture your notes in the chart. Then, choose the animal you think will work best for this assignment.

SUGGESTIONS	NOTES

Write and Organize Work together to break down the origami process for your animal into clear steps. List those steps. Then, assign each step to a different group member. Write clear, focused instructions for each step. Regroup and read the instructions in sequence.

- Are they easy to follow? If not, add details that will clarify the process. For example, make sure you clearly indicate spatial relationships, using terms such as *behind, below, up, around*, or *in front*.
- Have you skipped any steps? If so, add necessary information.

Give Instructions

 **INTERACTIVITY**

Rehearse With Your Group Make sure every group member has a speaking role in the presentation and rehearse the delivery of your oral instructions. Practice giving the entire set of instructions a few times using basic to more abstract terms. Figure out which type of language works best and finalize your text. Use this checklist to evaluate your work.

CONTENT	PRESENTATION TECHNIQUES
◯ The instructions are broken down into manageable steps.	◯ Transitions from speaker to speaker are smooth and do not interrupt the flow of information.
◯ The transitions from step to step are easy to follow.	◯ The presenter speaks at an appropriate rate and with proper volume so that listeners can hear and understand.
◯ The instructions are complete and do not omit any necessary information.	◯ The speaker checks in with the audience, making sure everyone completes each step before moving on to the next one.
◯ Word choices are accurate and suited for your audience.	◯ The presenter enunciates clearly.

Brush Up on your Presentation Techniques Before you present your set of instructions, give your audience the materials they need, such as origami paper or any visual aids you made, to complete the task. As you speak, pause periodically to check in with your listeners, making sure they understand each step before you move on to the next one. Be prepared to clarify the steps if your audience has questions.

Follow Instructions

Listen Actively Groups will take turns delivering and following the oral instructions. When it's your turn to listen and create an origami animal, give the speakers your full attention. Do your best to follow each step accurately. If you need more information or find anything confusing, ask clarifying questions. Make sure your questions are clearly worded. Once all groups have finished giving and following the instructions, create a classroom display of everyone's origami animals.

 TEKS

1.A. Listen actively to interpret a message, ask clarifying questions, and respond appropriately.

1.B. Follow and give oral instructions that include multiple action steps.

Essential Question

How do animals and people interact?

Animals and people learn from each other in different ways. In this section, you will choose a text about the interactions between animals and people to read independently. Get the most from this section by establishing a purpose for reading. Ask yourself, "What do I hope to gain from my independent reading?" Here are just a few purposes you might consider.

Read to Learn Think about the selections you have already studied: What questions do you still have about the unit topic?

Read to Enjoy Read the descriptions of the texts. Which one seems most interesting and appealing to you?

Read to Form a Position Consider your thoughts and feelings about the Essential Question. Are you still undecided about some aspect of the topic?

Reading Digital Texts

Digital texts, like the ones you will read in this section, are electronic versions of print texts. They have a variety of characteristics:

- can be read on various devices
- text can be resized
- may include highlighting or other annotation tools
- may have bookmarks, audio links, and other helpful features

▶ VIDEO

👆 INTERACTIVITY

Independent Learning Strategies

Throughout your life, in school, in your community, and in your career, you will need to rely on yourself to learn and work on your own. Use these strategies to keep your focus as you read independently for sustained periods of time. Add ideas of your own for each category.

STRATEGY	MY ACTION PLAN
Create a schedule • Be aware of your deadlines. • Make a plan for each day's activities.	
Read with purpose • Use a variety of comprehension strategies to deepen your understanding. • Think about the text and how it adds to your knowledge.	
Take notes • Record key ideas and information. • Review your notes before sharing what you've learned.	

⭐ TEKS
4. Self-select text and read independently for a sustained period of time; **5.A.** Establish purpose for reading assigned and self-selected text; **8.F.** Analyze characteristics of multimodal and digital texts.

CONTENTS

 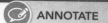 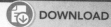

AUDIO ANNOTATE DOWNLOAD

Choose one selection. Selections are available online only.

SHARE YOUR INDEPENDENT LEARNING

Reflect on and evaluate the information you gained from your Independent Reading selection. Then, share what you learned with others.

Close-Read Guide

Tool Kit
Close-Read Guide and
Model Annotation

Establish your purpose for reading. Then, read the selection
through at least once. Use this page to record your close-read ideas.

Selection Title: _____   Purpose for Reading: _____

Minutes Read: _____

INTERACTIVITY

Close Read the Text

Zoom in on sections you found interesting.
Annotate what you notice. Ask yourself
questions about the text. What can you
conclude?

_____
_____
_____
_____
_____

Analyze the Text

1. Think about the author's choices of literary
elements, techniques, and structures. Select
one and record your thoughts.

_____
_____
_____
_____

2. What characteristics of digital texts did you use
as you read this selection, and in what ways?
How do the characteristics of a digital text
affect your reading experience? Explain.

_____
_____
_____

QuickWrite

Choose a paragraph from the text that grabbed your interest. Explain the power of this passage.

_____
_____
_____
_____
_____
_____
_____
_____

Share Your Independent Learning

How do animals and people interact?

When you read something independently, your understanding continues to grow as you share what you have learned with others.

 NOTEBOOK

Prepare to Share

CONNECT IT One of the most important ways to respond to a text is to notice and describe your personal reactions. Think about the text you explored independently and the ways in which it connects to your own experiences.

• What similarities and differences do you see between the text and your own life? Describe your observations.

• How do you think this text connects to the Essential Question? Describe your ideas.

Learn From Your Classmates

DISCUSS IT Share your ideas about the text you explored on your own. As you talk with others in your class, take notes about new ideas that seem important.

Reflect

EXPLAIN IT Review your notes, and mark the most important insight you gained from these writing and discussion activities. Explain how this idea adds to your understanding of the ways animals and people interact.

 TEKS

6.A. Describe personal connections to a variety of sources, including self-selected texts.
6.E. Interact with sources in meaningful ways such as notetaking, annotating, freewriting, or illustrating.

Informational Essay

In this unit, you read about interactions between animals and people from different perspectives. You also practiced writing informational essays. Now, apply what you have learned.

Write a structured and coherent **informational essay** in which you develop a thesis in response to the Essential Question:

Essential Question
How do animals and people interact?

Review and Evaluate Evidence

INTERACTIVITY

Review your Essential Question Notes and your QuickWrite from the beginning of the unit. Have your ideas changed?

Yes	No
Identify at least three pieces of evidence that made you think differently about the topic.	Identify at least three pieces of evidence that reinforced your ideas about the topic.
1.	1.
2.	2.
3.	3.

State your ideas now:

What other evidence might you need to support a thesis on the topic?

Share Your Perspective

The **Informational Essay Checklist** will help you stay on track.

PLAN Before you write, read the Checklist and make sure you understand all the items.

DRAFT Develop a structured and coherent draft. As you write, pause occasionally to make sure you're meeting the Checklist requirements.

Use New Words Refer to your Word Network to vary your word choice. Also, consider using one or more of the Academic Vocabulary terms you learned at the beginning of the unit: *exclude, illustrate, benefit, elaborate, objective.*

REVIEW AND EDIT After you have written a first draft, evaluate it against the Checklist. Make any changes needed to strengthen your controlling idea, structure, coherence and transitions, use of facts and details, and language. Then, reread your essay and fix any errors you find.

EQ Notes Make sure you have pulled in details from your Essential Question Notes to support your controlling idea.

INTERACTIVITY

INFORMATIONAL ESSAY CHECKLIST

My essay clearly contains . . .

○ a strong thesis, or controlling idea.

○ a variety of supporting evidence, including facts, details, and examples.

○ a purposeful structure that includes an introduction, coherence within and across paragraphs, and a strong conclusion.

○ use of transitional words and phrases that accurately show how ideas are related within and across paragraphs.

○ varied and precise word choice.

○ correct use of standard English conventions, including consistent verb tenses and correct subject-verb agreement in all sentence types.

○ no comma splices, run-on sentences, or sentence fragments; and no punctuation or spelling errors.

TEKS
10.B.i. Develop drafts into a focused, structured, and coherent piece of writing by organizing with purposeful structure, including an introduction, transitions, coherence within and across paragraphs, and a conclusion.
10.B.ii. Develop drafts into a focused, structured, and coherent piece of writing by developing an engaging idea reflecting depth of thought with specific facts and details.
11.B. Compose informational texts, including multi-paragraph essays that convey information about a topic, using a clear controlling idea or thesis statement and genre characteristics and craft.

Revising and Editing

 INTERACTIVITY

Read this draft and think about corrections the writer might make.
Then, answer the questions that follow.

Training My Friend

[1] When I turned ten my parents finally said I was old enough to have a dog. [2] I had wanted a puppy since I was little I was excited when Teddy joined our family! [3] I soon found out, however, that being a dog owner is a big responsibility. [4] One important part of that responsibility is training the dog.

[5] Dog training school, one of my parents' suggestions, was a good experience. [6] The main lesson I learned is to reward good behavior. [7] That means that Teddy gets a treat when he obeys my commands, such as sitting when I tell him to sit. [8] Otherwise, I don't want Teddy to jump up on me, so when he does that I turn away and ignore him. [9] He calms down. [10] I then pet him and tell him he is a good dog.

1. How should the punctuation in sentence 1 be corrected?

   A Quotation marks should be placed around *I was old enough to have a dog*.

   B A comma should be placed after *said*.

   C A comma should be placed after *ten*.

   D The period should be replaced with an exclamation mark.

2. Which answer choice BEST corrects the run-on in sentence 2?

   F I had wanted a puppy since I was little, so I was excited when Teddy joined our family!

   G I had wanted a puppy since I was little, I was excited when Teddy joined our family!

   H I had wanted a puppy since I was little. When Teddy joined our family!

   J No change should be made.

3. In sentence 8, which transitional word or phrase would be a better choice than *otherwise?*

   A In addition

   B Instead

   C Next

   D Therefore

4. Which revision BEST combines sentences 9 and 10 while maintaining their original meanings?

   A He calms down, I pet him, and I tell him he is a good dog.

   B After he calms down, I pet him and tell him he is a good dog.

   C He calms down because I then pet him and tell him he is a good dog.

   D Then, when he calms downs, I tell him he is a good dog.

Reflect on the Unit

Reflect On the Unit Goals

📓 NOTEBOOK

👆 INTERACTIVITY

🔍 RESEARCH

Review your Unit Goals chart from the beginning of the unit. Then, complete the activity and answer the question.

1. In the Unit Goals chart, rate how well you meet each goal now.

2. In which goals were you most and least successful?

Reflect On the Texts

RECOMMEND! Who do you think would love to read the texts in this unit? Use the chart to write in the names of people to whom you would recommend each selection. Then, discuss your responses.

SELECTION TITLE	
Title	Who might like to read it?
from *My Life with the Chimpanzees*	
How Smart Are Animals?	
So What Is a Primate?	
Predators / The Naming of Cats / Nikita	
The Tale of the Hummingbird	
Black Cowboy, Wild Horses	
Your Independent Reading Selection:	

Reflect On the Essential Question

Poster Make a poster to show different answers to the Essential Question: **How do animals and people interact?**

- Conduct research to find images that capture two to three answers to the question.

- If you are working digitally, use design or word-processing software to incorporate images and text into a document. If you are working on paper, paste images to a piece of poster board and add commentary.

- Share your posters and discuss them with your class.

⭐ TEKS

10.D.i. Edit drafts using standard English conventions, including complete complex sentences with subject-verb agreement and avoidance of splices, run-ons, and fragments; **10.D.viii.** Edit drafts using standard English conventions, including punctuation marks, including commas in complex sentences, transitions, and introductory elements.

Technology and Society

PEARSON
realıze™

Go ONLINE for all lessons

 AUDIO

 VIDEO

 NOTEBOOK

 ANNOTATE

 INTERACTIVITY

 DOWNLOAD

 RESEARCH

WATCH THE VIDEO

Dog Receives Prosthetic Legs
Made by 3-D Printer

DISCUSS IT How does modern technology help us solve problems in new ways?

Write your response before sharing your ideas.

UNIT 3

UNIT INTRODUCTION

Essential Question

Is technology helpful or harmful to society?

MENTOR TEXT:
ARGUMENT
That's Not Progress!

WHOLE-CLASS LEARNING

SCIENCE FICTION

Feathered Friend
Arthur C. Clarke

COMPARE ACROSS GENRES

INFORMATIONAL ARTICLE

The Biometric Body
Kathiann M. Kowalski

ARGUMENT

Biometrics Are Not Better
Reuben Lorre

MEDIA: VIDEO

The Internet of Things
IBM Social Media

PERFORMANCE TASK

WRITING PROCESS
Write an Argument

PEER-GROUP LEARNING

REFLECTIVE ESSAY

Is Our Gain Also Our Loss?
Cailin Loesch

PERSUASIVE ESSAY

The Black Hole of Technology
Leena Khan

SCIENCE FICTION

The Fun They Had
Isaac Asimov

MEDIA: PHOTO ESSAY

Mexico's Abandoned Railways and the SEFT-1
Ivan Puig Domene and Andrés Padilla Domene

MEDIA: PODCAST

Bored . . . and Brilliant? A Challenge to Disconnect From Your Phone
NPR

PERFORMANCE TASK

SPEAKING AND LISTENING
Conduct a Debate

INDEPENDENT LEARNING

NEWS ARTICLE

7-Year-Old Girl Gets New Hand From 3-D Printer
John Rogers

NEWS ARTICLE

High-Tech Backpacks Open World of Whales to Deaf Students
Associated Press

POETRY COLLECTION

All Watched Over by Machines of Loving Grace
Richard Brautigan

Sonnet, Without Salmon
Sherman Alexie

NEWS ARTICLE

Teen Researchers Defend Media Multitasking
Sumathi Reddy

SHARE INDEPENDENT LEARNING

Share • Learn • Reflect

PERFORMANCE-BASED ASSESSMENT

Argumentative Essay

You will write an essay in response to the Essential Question for the unit.

UNIT REFLECTION

Goals • Texts •
Essential Question

235

Unit Goals

 ▶ VIDEO

Throughout this unit, you will deepen your perspective about technology and society by reading, writing, speaking, listening, and presenting. These goals will help you succeed on the Unit Performance-Based Assessment:

👆 INTERACTIVITY

SET GOALS Rate how well you meet these goals right now. You will revisit your ratings later when you reflect on your growth during this unit.

SCALE

1	2	3	4	5
NOT AT ALL WELL	NOT VERY WELL	SOMEWHAT WELL	VERY WELL	EXTREMELY WELL

ESSENTIAL QUESTION	Unit Introduction	Unit Reflection
I can read selections that express different points of view about technology and society, and develop my own perspective.	1 2 3 4 5	1 2 3 4 5

READING	Unit Introduction	Unit Reflection
I can understand and use academic vocabulary words related to arguments.	1 2 3 4 5	1 2 3 4 5
I can recognize elements of different genres, especially science fiction, news articles, and argument.	1 2 3 4 5	1 2 3 4 5
I can read a selection of my choice independently and make meaningful connections to other texts.	1 2 3 4 5	1 2 3 4 5

WRITING	Unit Introduction	Unit Reflection
I can write a focused, well-organized argumentative essay.	1 2 3 4 5	1 2 3 4 5
I can complete Timed Writing tasks with confidence.	1 2 3 4 5	1 2 3 4 5

SPEAKING AND LISTENING	Unit Introduction	Unit Reflection
I can participate effectively in a debate.	1 2 3 4 5	1 2 3 4 5

🔵 **TEKS**
2.C. Determine the meaning and usage of grade-level academic English words derived from Greek and Latin roots such as *mis/mit, bene, man, vac, scrib/script,* and *jur/jus.*

Academic Vocabulary: Argument

Understanding and using academic terms can help you read, write, and speak with precision and clarity. Here are five academic words that will be useful in this unit as you analyze and write argumentative texts.

 **INTERACTIVITY**

PRACTICE Complete the chart.

1. **Review** each word, its root, and the mentor sentences.

2. **Predict** the meaning of each word using the information and your own knowledge.

3. **List** at least two related words for each word.

4. **Refer** to the dictionary or other resources if needed.

WORD	MENTOR SENTENCES	PREDICT MEANING	RELATED WORDS
convince LATIN ROOT: **-vict-/-vinc-** "conquer"	1. To *convince* the jury, the lawyer presented evidence of the woman's innocence. 2. I will try to *convince* my mother that I need new clothes, even though she bought me a new shirt last week.		convincingly; unconvincing
certain LATIN ROOT: **-cert-** "sure"	1. The band became famous for having a *certain* jangly sound in their music. 2. I will be *certain* to study before the next test.		
sufficient LATIN ROOT: **-fic-/-fac-** "make"; "do"	1. We brought a *sufficient* amount of food and water for a week's worth of camping. 2. Studying an hour a day during the week before the test is *sufficient* to do well.		
declare LATIN ROOT: **-clar-** "clear"	1. Many officials will *declare* their support of the mayor's campaign by speaking at the press conference. 2. Ruthie was about to *declare* her innocence, but the chocolate stain on her face and the empty cookie jar told the truth.		
justify LATIN ROOT: **-jur-/-jus-** "law"; "right"	1. I don't think there's anything you can say that will *justify* that bad behavior. 2. The student's excellent grades *justify* her promotion to advanced math.		

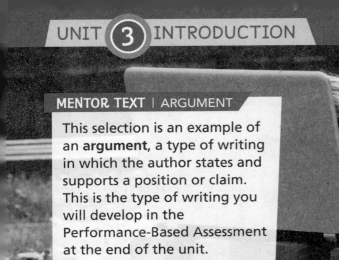

MENTOR TEXT | ARGUMENT

This selection is an example of an **argument**, a type of writing in which the author states and supports a position or claim. This is the type of writing you will develop in the Performance-Based Assessment at the end of the unit.

READ IT As you read, notice the way that the writer builds an argument. Mark the text to help answer this question: What is the author's position and how does the author support it?

That's Not Progress!

 AUDIO

 ANNOTATE

1 Social networking has become a big part of our lives, and its negative effects can be overlooked. But mental health experts are starting to notice—and what they are finding is disturbing.

2 As the popularity of social media skyrockets, so do reports of "Facebook depression." Like other kinds of depression, its common signs are anxiety, low self-confidence, and loneliness.

3 This form of depression hits those who worry too much about what others think. It largely affects young people because they tend to worry most about others' opinions. The constant need to see how they're "measuring up" can cause people to feel huge amounts of stress.

4 Studies have found that people who get their sense of self-worth from others are more likely to keep checking their status. They want to monitor their updates, wall posts, and photos to see how well or how poorly they're measuring up. The feeling that they're missing out on something makes it hard to take a break. And they don't have to—smartphones have made it possible to log in from any place at any time. The result is more stress.

5 Social networking can cause serious emotional problems. Everyone knows the effects of online bullying. There are other ways to damage a person's self-confidence. "When 'friends' upload unflattering photos and post mean comments, it can seriously damage a person's self-image," says one mental health

expert. In addition, getting no response to a post or not being "friended" can also be very painful.

6   The effects can be physical, too. Frequent users of social media often suffer from pain in their fingers and wrists. Blood vessels in their eyes and necks can narrow. Their backs can ache from being hunched over phones and computers for hours at a time.

7   Texting is another problem created by technology. Half the nation's youth send 50 or more text messages a day. One study found that young people send an average of 34 texts a night after they get into bed! This loss of sleep can affect the ability to concentrate, problem-solve, and learn.

8   Not all experts agree with this analysis. Some point to the benefits of social media. Dr. Megan Moreno is an assistant professor of pediatrics and adolescent medicine. She believes that social networking helps develop a young person's sense of community. She also believes that it can be used to identify youth who are most at risk for depression. "Our studies have found that adolescents often share feelings of depression on Facebook," she says. "Social media is a tool; it cannot in and of itself cause mental illness," says Dr. Moreno. She insists that young people had problems before computers came into being.

9   Maybe so. In the past, however, young people found ways to escape from their problems. Now, smartphones and other high-tech devices have made escape impossible. Is that progress?

10   Technology should simplify life, not complicate it. In a recent study, 76% of kids interviewed said they felt an obligation to respond to all social media notifications. The danger of social media is that young users can eventually lose their ability to focus on what is most important in life—no matter what path they choose to follow. ✍

DOWNLOAD

WORD NETWORK FOR TECHNOLOGY AND SOCIETY

Vocabulary A Word Network is a collection of words related to a topic. As you read the selections in this unit, identify interesting words related to the impact of technology, and add them to your Word Network. For example, you might begin by adding basic words from the Mentor Text, such as *stress*, as well as more complex terms, such as *status* and *community*. Continue to add words as you complete this unit.

stress

status

community

TECHNOLOGY AND SOCIETY

Refer to the **Word Network Model** in the **Tool Kit** at the back of this book.

Summary

A **summary** is a brief, complete overview of a text that maintains the meaning and logical order of ideas of the original. It should not include your personal opinions.

📝 **NOTEBOOK**

WRITE IT ▸ Write a summary of "That's Not Progress!"

Launch Activity

Conduct a Walk-Around Debate

Consider this statement: Technology improves our lives by providing us with access to large amounts of information quickly.

◯ Strongly Agree ◯ Agree ◯ Disagree ◯ Strongly Disagree

1. Prepare for the debate by thinking about the topic. Consider how access to smartphones and the Internet affects your life and the lives of people you know.
2. Jot down your ideas about the topic.
3. Decide whether you agree or disagree with the statement, and write your opinion on a sticky note that you stick to your clothes.
4. Walk around the room, and discuss your ideas about the topic with at least two people who do not share your opinion.
5. At the end of the debate, determine how many people in the room changed their opinions, and why.

✪ TEKS
6.D. Paraphrase and summarize texts in ways that maintain meaning and logical order.

QuickWrite

Consider class discussions, the video, and the Mentor Text as you think about the prompt. Record your first thoughts here.

Is technology helpful or harmful to society?

At the end of the unit, you will respond to the Essential Question again and see how your perspective has changed.

📔 NOTEBOOK

WRITE IT Record your first thoughts here.

_____
_____
_____
_____
_____
_____
_____
_____
_____
_____
_____

📥 DOWNLOAD

EQ Notes — Is technology helpful or harmful to society?

As you read the selections in this unit, use a chart like the one shown to record your ideas and list details from the texts that support them. Taking notes as you go will help you clarify your thinking, gather relevant information, and be ready to respond to the Essential Question.

TITLE	MY IDEAS / OBSERVATIONS	TEXT EVIDENCE / INFORMATION

Refer to the **EQ Notes Model** in the **Tool Kit** at the back of this book.

Is technology helpful or harmful to society?

Technology and social media have become central parts of today's world—but are they truly improving our lives? You will work with your whole class to explore the impact of modern technology on society. The selections you will read present insights into its positive and negative effects.

VIDEO

INTERACTIVITY

Whole-Class Learning Strategies

Throughout your life, in school, in your community, and in your career, you will continue to learn and work in large-group environments.

Review these strategies and the actions you can take to practice them as you work with your whole class. Add ideas of your own for each category. Get ready to use these strategies during Whole-Class Learning.

STRATEGY	MY ACTION PLAN
Listen actively • Put away personal items to avoid becoming distracted. • Try to hear the speaker's full message before planning your own response.	
Demonstrate respect • Show up on time and make sure you are prepared for class. • Avoid side conversations while in class.	
Show interest • Be aware of your body language. For example, sit up in your chair. • Respond when the teacher asks for feedback.	
Interact and share ideas • If you're confused, other people probably are, too. Ask a question to help your whole class. • Build on the ideas of others by adding details or making a connection.	

CONTENTS

PERFORMANCE TASK: WRITING PROCESS

Write an Argument
The Whole-Class selections illustrate ways in which technology has affected our everyday lives. After reading the texts and watching the video, you will write an argumentative essay about the impact of modern technology.

FEATHERED FRIEND

The selection you are about to read is a science-fiction short story.

Reading Science Fiction

Science fiction is a type of fiction in which real or imagined elements of science or advanced technology play a key role.

SCIENCE FICTION

Author's Purpose
> to tell an imaginative story

Characteristics
> a setting with imaginary elements, such as the future or another planet

> a plot and setting that feature elements of science or technology

> a theme, or message, about life

> characters that may be non-human, such as robots or aliens

> dialogue that reflects the imaginary setting and technology

Structure
> a plot, or sequence of related events, that involves technology or science

Take a Minute!

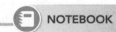 **NOTEBOOK**

DESCRIBE IT With a partner, jot down ideas for the setting of a science-fiction story. Where is it? Who lives there? What makes it the kind of setting you would expect to find in a science-fiction story?

 TEKS

7.A. Infer multiple themes within and across texts using text evidence.

8.A. Demonstrate knowledge of literary genres such as realistic fiction, adventure stories, historical fiction, mysteries, humor, and myths.

Genre / Text Elements

Multiple Themes The **theme** of a story is the insight or message about life that it expresses. Sometimes, a character or narrator directly states a theme. More often, the theme is implied by the story's details. You ask questions, connect details, and infer the larger ideas they express.

> **TIP:** You can identify a story's topic with a single word or phrase, such as "space travel." A theme is a message that you express in a complete sentence.

QUESTIONS FOR INFERRING THEMES	
Setting	• What is the setting like? • How does it affect the characters?
Conflicts	• What conflicts do characters face? • How do the conflicts end?
Characters	• What do characters say and do? • Do characters change? If so, how? • Do characters learn a lesson? If so, what is it?

Readers may view themes differently and a single story may have multiple themes. A valid interpretation must take into account all of a story's details.

 NOTEBOOK

PRACTICE Read the passage, noting text evidence that suggests one or more themes. Then, answer the question.

> K-Max balanced on one metallic leg. His arm was bent at an angle that made it look broken, and water streamed to the floor from the glass he was holding. This was his third lock-up that day.
>
> "K-Max, you froze up again? K-Max?" When he gets like this, his eyes are the only body part that works, and they were filled with robotic sadness. "Blink once if you can't move and twice if you can."
>
> One blink.
>
> "Okay, don't panic. Everyone makes mistakes."
>
> I headed for the laundry room to get a towel, glad to get some distance from those sad eyes.

Which statement best expresses your interpretation of the theme? Explain your thinking.

○ Future technology may be more trouble than it's worth.

○ People create technologies that mirror our own feelings and views.

About the Author

With more than one hundred million copies of his books in print worldwide, **Arthur C. Clarke** (1917–2008) may have been the most successful science-fiction writer of all time. He is known for combining his knowledge of technology and science with touches of poetry. Clarke once said, "The only way of finding the limits of the possible is by going beyond them into the impossible."

Feathered Friend

Concept Vocabulary

You will encounter the following words as you read "Feathered Friend." Before reading, note how familiar you are with each word. Then, rank the words in order from most familiar (1) to least familiar (5).

INTERACTIVITY

WORD	YOUR RANKING
pathetically	
distressed	
mournfully	
apologetically	
lamented	

Comprehension Strategy

ANNOTATE

Generate Questions

When you **generate questions** about a text, you engage your curiosity. You don't ignore details that interest, confuse, or surprise you. Instead, you ask questions about them and find answers that deepen your understanding and help you gain more information.

> **EXAMPLES** Here are examples of questions you might ask about this story:
>
> *Before Reading:* What type of friend would be feathered?
>
> *During Reading:* Are these details about life in space realistic?
>
> *After Reading:* Why does the narrator say the crew would have been "slightly dead"?

PRACTICE Write your questions in the open space next to the text. Do so before, during, and after you read. Then, jot down answers as you discover them.

 TEKS
5.B. Generate questions about text before, during, and after reading to deepen understanding and gain information.

Feathered Friend
Arthur C. Clarke

BACKGROUND

This story was written during the 1950s, a time of growth and technological advancement in the United States. The possibility of space exploration created a feeling of immense potential. This optimism about the future influenced all areas of the arts, especially popular literature, in what is now called the Golden Age of Science Fiction.

 AUDIO

 ANNOTATE

1   To the best of my knowledge, there's never been a regulation that forbids one to keep pets in a space station. No one ever thought it was necessary—and even had such a rule existed, I am quite certain that Sven Olsen would have ignored it.

2   With a name like that, you will picture Sven at once as a six-foot-six Nordic giant, built like a bull and with a voice to match. Had this been so, his chances of getting a job in space would have been very slim. Actually he was a wiry little fellow, like most of the early spacers, and managed to qualify easily for the 150-pound bonus that kept so many of us on a reducing diet.

3   Sven was one of our best construction men, and excelled at the tricky and specialized work of collecting assorted girders as they floated around in free fall, making them do the slow-motion, three-dimensional ballet that would get them into their right positions, and fusing the pieces together when they were precisely dovetailed into the intended pattern: It was a skilled and difficult job, for a spacesuit is not the most convenient of garbs in which to work. However, Sven's team had one great advantage over the

construction gangs you see putting up skyscrapers down on Earth. They could step back and admire their handiwork without being abruptly parted from it by gravity. . . .

4   Don't ask me why Sven wanted a pet, or why he chose the one he did. I'm not a psychologist, but I must admit that his selection was very sensible. Claribel weighed practically nothing, her food requirements were tiny—and she was not worried, as most animals would have been, by the absence of gravity.

5   I first became aware that Claribel was aboard when I was sitting in the little cubbyhole laughingly called my office, checking through my lists of technical stores to decide what items we'd be running out of next. When I heard the musical whistle beside my ear, I assumed that it had come over the station intercom, and waited for an announcement to follow. It didn't; instead, there was a long and involved pattern of melody that made me look up with such a start that I forgot all about the angle beam just behind my head. When the stars had ceased to explode before my eyes, I had my first view of Claribel.

6   She was a small yellow canary, hanging in the air as motionless as a hummingbird—and with much less effort, for her wings were quietly folded along her sides. We stared at each other for a minute; then, before I had quite recovered my wits, she did a curious kind of backward loop I'm sure no earthbound canary had ever managed, and departed with a few leisurely flicks. It was quite obvious that she'd already learned how to operate in the absence of gravity, and did not believe in doing unnecessary work.

7   Sven didn't confess to her ownership for several days, and by that time it no longer mattered, because Claribel was a general pet. He had smuggled her up on the last ferry from Earth, when he came back from leave—partly, he claimed, out of sheer scientific curiosity. He wanted to see just how a bird would operate when it had no weight but could still use its wings.

8   Claribel thrived and grew fat. On the whole, we had little trouble concealing our guest when VIPs from Earth came visiting. A space station has more hiding places than you can count; the only problem was that Claribel got rather noisy when she was upset, and we sometimes had to think fast to explain the curious peeps and whistles that came from ventilating shafts and storage bulkheads. There were a couple of narrow escapes—but then who would dream of looking for a canary in a space station?

9   We were now on twelve-hour watches, which was not as bad as it sounds, since you need little sleep in space. Though of course there is no "day" and "night" when you are floating in permanent sunlight, it was still convenient to stick to the terms. Certainly when I woke that "morning" it felt like 6:00 A.M. on Earth. I had

---

CLOSE READ

ANNOTATE: Mark details in paragraph 6 that describe the canary's appearance and movements.

QUESTION: Why does the author include so much descriptive detail about the canary?

CONCLUDE: What aspects of life in space does this description help readers imagine?

a nagging headache, and vague memories of fitful, disturbed dreams. It took me ages to undo my bunk straps, and I was still only half awake when I joined the remainder of the duty crew in the mess. Breakfast was unusually quiet, and there was one seat vacant.

10   ''Where's Sven?'' I asked, not very much caring.

11   "He's looking for Claribel," someone answered. "Says he can't find her anywhere. She usually wakes him up."

12   Before I could retort that she usually woke me up, too, Sven came in through the doorway, and we could see at once that something was wrong. He slowly opened his hand, and there lay a tiny bundle of yellow feathers, with two clenched claws sticking **pathetically** up into the air.

13   "What happened?" we asked, all equally **distressed**.

14   "I don't know," said Sven **mournfully**. "I just found her like this."

15   "Let's have a look at her," said Jock Duncan, our cook-doctor-dietitian. We all waited in hushed silence while he held Claribel against his ear in an attempt to detect any heartbeat.

16   Presently he shook his head. "I can't hear anything, but that doesn't prove she's dead. I've never listened to a canary's heart," he added rather **apologetically**.

17   "Give her a shot of oxygen," suggested somebody, pointing to the green-banded emergency cylinder in its recess beside the door. Everyone agreed that this was an excellent idea, and Claribel was tucked snugly into a face mask that was large enough to serve as a complete oxygen tent for her.

18   To our delighted surprise, she revived at once. Beaming broadly, Sven removed the mask, and she hopped onto his finger. She gave her series of "Come to the cookhouse, boys" trills—then promptly keeled over again.

19   "I don't get it," **lamented** Sven. "What's wrong with her? She's never done this before."

20   For the last few minutes, something had been tugging at my memory. My mind seemed to be very sluggish that morning, as if I was still unable to cast off the burden of sleep. I felt that I could do with some of that oxygen—but before I could reach the mask, understanding exploded in my brain. I whirled on the duty engineer and said urgently:

21   "Jim! There's something wrong with the air! That's why Claribel's passed out. I've just remembered that miners used to carry canaries down to warn them of gas."

22   "Nonsense!" said Jim. "The alarms would have gone off. We've got duplicate circuits, operating independently."

pathetically (puh THEHT ihk lee) *adv.* in a way that causes someone to feel pity

distressed (dih STREHST) *adj.* troubled; upset

mournfully (MAWRN fuh lee) *adv.* in a way that expresses grief or sadness

apologetically (uh pol uh JEHT ihk lee) *adv.* in a way that shows someone is sorry for having done or said something; regretfully

lamented (luh MEHN tihd) *v.* said in a way that showed sadness or sorrow

23   "Er—the second alarm circuit isn't connected up yet." His assistant reminded him. That shook Jim; he left without a word, while we stood arguing and passing the oxygen bottle around like a pipe of peace.

24   He came back ten minutes later with a sheepish expression. It was one of those accidents that couldn't possibly happen; we'd had one of our rare eclipses by Earth's shadow that night: Part of the air purifier had frozen up, and the single alarm in the circuit had failed to go off. Half a million dollars' worth of chemical and electronic engineering had let us down completely. Without Claribel, we should soon have been slightly dead.

25   So now, if you visit any space station, don't be surprised if you hear an inexplicable snatch of birdsong. There's no need to be alarmed; on the contrary, in fact. It will mean that you're being doubly safeguarded, at practically no extra expense. 🐦

Response

Answer the questions in your notebook. Use text evidence to support your responses.

1. Personal Connections Claribel saved the crew, but her presence on board was against the rules. Do you think Sven was wrong for sneaking her on board? Explain.

Comprehension

2. Reading Check (a) How does the narrator discover Claribel's presence? **(b)** Why does Sven bring Claribel on board? **(c)** What causes Claribel to pass out?

3. Strategy: Generate Questions (a) What is one question you generated as you read? **(b)** Were you able to answer your question? Explain. **(c)** How does asking and answering questions help you deepen your understanding and gain more from what you read?

Analysis

4. (a) Make Inferences How do the crew members feel about Claribel? **(b) Draw Conclusions** What is the benefit of having a pet in the space station?

5. (a) Synthesize What events or factors help the narrator figure out that something is wrong with the air? **(b) Make a Judgment** Who is responsible for saving the crew's lives: Claribel or the narrator? Explain.

6. (a) What causes the failure of the alarm that was intended to warn about air quality? **(b) Speculate** What are some potential problems with using a canary instead of an electronic alarm system? **(c) Evaluate** Which is a more reliable form of alarm? Explain.

EQ Notes Is technology helpful or harmful to society?

What have you learned about technology and society from reading this science-fiction story? Go to your Essential Question Notes and record your observations and thoughts about "Feathered Friend."

 TEKS

5.B. Generate questions about text before, during, and after reading to deepen understanding and gain information.

6.A. Describe personal connections to a variety of sources, including self-selected texts.

6.C. Use text evidence to support an appropriate response.

FEATHERED FRIEND

Close Read

 ANNOTATE

1. The model passage and annotation show how one reader analyzed paragraph 3 of the story. Find another detail in the passage to annotate. Then, write your own question and conclusion.

CLOSE-READ MODEL

Sven was one of our best construction men, and excelled at the tricky and specialized work of collecting assorted girders as they floated around in free fall, making them do the slow-motion, three-dimensional ballet that would get them into their right positions, and fusing the pieces together when they were precisely dovetailed into the intended pattern. . . .

ANNOTATE: The author combines familiar details of construction work with unfamiliar details of zero gravity.

QUESTION: Why does the author make this choice?

CONCLUDE: The combination of Earth-like details and space-related details creates a startling setting.

MY QUESTION:

MY CONCLUSION:

2. For more practice, answer the Close-Read notes in the selection.

3. Choose a section of the story you found especially important. Mark important details. Then, jot down questions and write your conclusions in the open space next to the text.

Inquiry and Research

 RESEARCH

 NOTEBOOK

Research and Extend In the Background section, you learned that this story was written during the mid-1900s. Briefly research a space mission that occurred during the 1950s or 1960s, taking note of your sources. Jot down the reason for the mission, the results, and why that mission was significant. Share what you learn with the class.

 TEKS

6.E. Interact with sources in meaningful ways such as notetaking, annotating, freewriting, or illustrating.

6.G. Discuss and write about the explicit or implicit meanings of text.

7.A. Infer multiple themes within and across texts using text evidence.

Genre / Text Elements

Multiple Themes In some stories, the narrator or a character simply states a theme. That is **explicit meaning.** More often, themes are not directly stated. Instead, they are **implicit,** or suggested through details. Readers examine the details, think about how they fit together, and infer the deeper meanings they convey.

> **TIP:** A single story may express multiple themes. Likewise, readers may interpret a story's theme in different ways.

STORY ELEMENT	KEYS TO THEME
Title	Do any words in the title suggest a theme?
Setting	• Are certain places important in the story? • How do characters feel about the setting?
Conflicts	• What types of conflicts do characters face? • Do different characters face conflicts in different ways?
Characters	• Do characters change? If so, how? • What, if anything, do characters learn?

 NOTEBOOK

 INTERACTIVITY

PRACTICE Complete the activity and answer the questions.

1. **Make Inferences** This diagram lists key details from "Feathered Friend" that suggest a theme. Consider the details. Then, write a theme they suggest.

Setting Detail: The station has advanced systems to protect air quality.		**Event 1:** One of the workers smuggles a canary onto the station.		**Event 2:** The canary alerts the men when the air quality gets bad.

Theme:

2. **Support** Here is another possible theme expressed in "Feathered Friend": *Advanced technology leaves a void that people try to fill with companionship.* Cite at least three details from the text that support this theme. Explain your choices.

3. **(a)** What is the setting of "Feathered Friend"? **(b) Analyze** How does the setting contribute to the multiple themes you explored in questions 1 and 2?

FEATHERED FRIEND

Concept Vocabulary

Why These Words? The vocabulary words relate to feelings of sadness, suffering, or regret. For example, crew members are *distressed*, and Claribel's owner speaks *mournfully*.

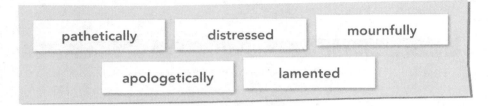

| pathetically | distressed | mournfully |
| apologetically | lamented |

WORD NETWORK

Add words that are related to technology and society from the text to your Word Network.

PRACTICE Answer the questions.

1. What other words in the selection relate to feelings of sadness, suffering, or regret?

2. What other words do you know that connect to this concept?

3. State whether the vocabulary word is used correctly in each sentence. Briefly explain your answers.

   (a) The frightened cat hid in the corner and mewed *pathetically*.

   (b) We *lamented* the loss of our favorite teacher when she moved away.

   (c) The baby was so *distressed* by the attention that she grinned widely and clapped her hands.

   (d) The dog was old and sick, but I still cried *mournfully* when she died.

   (e) "I'm so happy that I won!" Kara cheered *apologetically*.

Word Study

Greek Root: -path- The Greek root -path- means "feeling" or "suffering." In "Feathered Friend," when Claribel is unwell, her claws stick up *pathetically*, or in a way that causes others to feel sadness for her suffering.

1. Write a definition of the word *sympathy* that shows your understanding of the root -path-. Then, use the word *sympathy* correctly in a sentence.

2. Use a dictionary to find the meaning of *empathy*. Write the definition. Then, explain how the definition connects to the meaning of the root.

 TEKS

2.C. Determine the meaning and usage of grade-level academic English words derived from Greek and Latin roots such as *mis/mit, bene, man, vac, scrib/script*, and *jur/jus*.

6.F. Respond using newly acquired vocabulary as appropriate.

7.D. Analyze how the setting, including historical and cultural settings, influences character and plot development.

Author's Craft

Setting and Plot The **setting** is the time and place in which the events of the plot occur. It includes all the details of the physical location. It also includes cultural and historical elements, such as the rules and problems of a society, and the beliefs and values people hold. In some stories, the setting is merely a background for the action. In other stories, it influences the characters and plot.

NOTEBOOK

PRACTICE Answer the questions.

1. **(a)** What is the story's setting? **(b) Analyze** In what ways does the setting influence how characters live and the precautions they have to take? Explain, citing at least two story details in your response.

2. **(a) Analyze** How does the crew react when they find Claribel motionless, with her legs in the air? **(b) Analyze** How does the nature of the setting contribute to their reactions? Explain.
(c) Speculate How might this scene play out differently if it took place in a home on Earth? Explain.

3. **(a) Make Inferences** What does the crew's effort to save Claribel and their reaction to her revival show about their values? **(b) Speculate** How might this story be different if it took place in a setting where animals matter only as food or labor?

4. **(a) Analyze** How does the setting of this story influence the characters and plot? Explain, citing details from the story in your response. **(b) Draw Conclusions** Could this story have happened in any other historical or cultural setting? Why, or why not?

FEATHERED FRIEND

Composition

An **argumentative essay** is a brief nonfiction work in which a writer states a position (or claim) and defends it with reasons and evidence.

ASSIGNMENT

One theme of "Feathered Friend" is that it is risky for people to become dependent on technology. Write a brief **argumentative essay** in which you take a position on that theme. Do you think the story expresses valid concerns about the risks of technology?

- State a clear claim, or position, on the topic.
- Include evidence from the story that supports your claim.
- Set up a logical organization for your essay. Show how your claim, reasons, and evidence connect.
- Begin with an engaging introduction, and end with a memorable conclusion in which you restate your claim.

Use New Words

Try to use one or more of the vocabulary words in your writing: *pathetically, distressed, mournfully, apologetically, lamented.*

- NOTEBOOK

Reflect on Your Writing

PRACTICE Think about the choices you made as you wrote. Also consider what you learned by writing. Share your experiences by responding to these questions.

1. How did writing your argument strengthen your understanding of the story?

2. Is your argument clear and easy to follow? If not, how might you improve the organization and support?

3. **WHY THESE WORDS?** The words you choose make a difference in your writing. Which words did you specifically choose to make your argument persuasive, or convincing?

Speaking and Listening

A **multimedia presentation** is a work that you deliver orally to an audience while also sharing pictures, video, audio, or other media.

ASSIGNMENT

In this story, the author shows the benefits of combining low-tech methods like canaries with high-tech methods like sensors. Work with a partner to create a **multimedia presentation** in which you take a stance or position on another way in which high-tech and low-tech methods can be combined to help people.

Research the Topic Research other examples of high-tech and low-tech methods working in combination. Choose one that you think benefits society now or might do so in the future. In your presentation, explain your stance or position on the topic.

Choose and Organize Multimedia Choose media, such as photos and video, that will help listeners understand your ideas.

Rehearse Your Delivery Practice delivering your presentation with your partner. As you speak, make periodic eye contact with your audience. Enunciate, saying each word clearly, and speak loudly enough to be heard by everyone. Also, be aware of your speaking rate—don't speak too slowly and don't rush.

EQ Notes Before moving on to a new selection, go to your Essential Question Notes and record any additional thoughts or observations you may have about "Feathered Friend."

 INTERACTIVITY

Evaluate Presentations

Use an evaluation guide like the one shown to rate your classmates' deliveries. Listen closely, and then give constructive feedback.

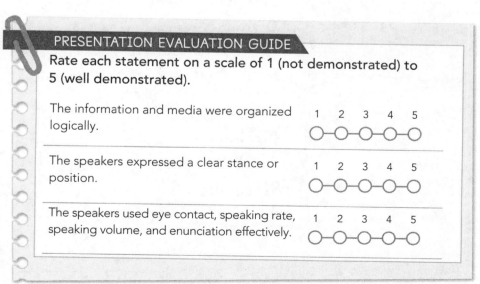

PRESENTATION EVALUATION GUIDE

Rate each statement on a scale of 1 (not demonstrated) to 5 (well demonstrated).

	1	2	3	4	5
The information and media were organized logically.	○	○	○	○	○
The speakers expressed a clear stance or position.	○	○	○	○	○
The speakers used eye contact, speaking rate, speaking volume, and enunciation effectively.	○	○	○	○	○

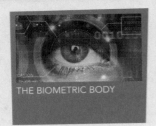

THE BIOMETRIC BODY

Informational Text and Argument

An **informational article** is a short nonfiction work that educates readers about a topic. An **argumentative essay** is a short nonfiction work in which the author attempts to convince the reader to think or do something specific.

BIOMETRICS ARE NOT BETTER

INFORMATIONAL ARTICLE

Author's Purpose
- to inform the reader about real people, situations, or events

Characteristics
- presents fact-based information on a topic
- expresses a controlling, or main, idea
- uses varied types of supporting evidence
- often makes use of text features such as diagrams
- often includes references to related texts

Structure
- uses an organizational pattern that clarifies ideas and information

ARGUMENTATIVE ESSAY

Author's Purpose
- to convince readers to take an action or think in a certain way

Characteristics
- expresses the writer's claim, or position
- provides reasons and evidence that support the claim
- appeals to readers' sense of reason; may also appeal to readers' emotions
- often, argues why other opinions or positions are wrong

Structure
- organizational pattern that clarifies connections between the claim and supporting information

Genre / Text Elements

Controlling Idea and Claim In both informational texts and arguments, the writer presents a main idea. This idea serves somewhat different roles in the two types of nonfiction, and is referred to in different terms.

- Informational texts feature a **controlling idea**, or thesis—the idea the writer explains.

- Arguments present a **claim**—the position the writer defends or attempts to prove.

Authors use supporting evidence, or reasons and information, to develop main ideas. They may also use a specific **organizational pattern**, or text structure, to connect ideas and evidence. Signal words provide clues to the type of organizational pattern being used.

TIP: Writers may use more than one organizational pattern in a single work.

EXAMPLES: Types of Organizational Patterns

ORGANIZATIONAL PATTERN	EXPLANATION	EXAMPLE SIGNAL WORDS
Comparison and Contrast	show similarities and differences among two or more topics	*alike, unlike, both, neither, although, same, different, by contrast, in comparison*
Cause and Effect	discuss the reasons a situation exists and the effects it has	*because of, as a result, the effect of, since*
Advantage/ Disadvantage	present the positive and negative sides of an issue or topic	*disadvantage, advantage, however, on one hand, on the other hand, better, worse*

 NOTEBOOK

PRACTICE Read each passage and analyze the organizational pattern it uses. Then, label it with one of the following patterns: comparison and contrast, cause and effect, or advantage/disadvantage.

1. To guard your health, learn the pros and cons of foods. For example, cheese has energy-giving protein. However, it also contains harmful saturated fats.

2. Cheese is a good source of protein, but it is high in fat. By contrast, beans are a better source of protein and contain no saturated fats.

3. Many Americans eat diets that are high in fat and sugar. As a result, certain illnesses, such as diabetes, are on the rise. This situation adds to the burden on our healthcare system.

 TEKS

8.D.iii. Analyze characteristics and structural elements of informational text, including organizational patterns such as definition, classification, advantage, and disadvantage.

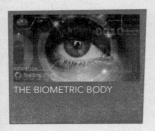

THE BIOMETRIC BODY

Compare Informational Text and Argument

In this lesson, you will read the informational article "The Biometric Body" and the argumentative essay "Biometrics Are Not Better." You will then compare the two texts.

BIOMETRICS ARE NOT BETTER

About the Author

Kathiann M. Kowalski (b. 1955) has written more than 625 books, articles, and stories. She once said, "The challenge of writing nonfiction is to both entertain and inform." In addition to writing, she spent 15 years practicing law with an emphasis on environmental issues.

The Biometric Body

Concept Vocabulary

INTERACTIVITY

You will encounter the following words as you read the article. Before reading, note how familiar you are with each word. Then, rank the words in order from most (1) to least (6) familiar.

WORD	YOUR RATING
fraud	
disguise	
masquerade	
criminals	
forged	
impostor	

Comprehension Strategy

ANNOTATE

Evaluate Details to Determine Key Ideas

When you **evaluate details to determine key ideas**, you figure out which details in a text are most important. Some may be interesting, but are less critical. As you read, mark details that seem important, and then evaluate them to see if they connect to a single key idea.

> **EXAMPLE** Here is an example of how you might apply the strategy to this article:
>
> **Marked Details:** *Thermal face images are not very reliable... Smell... is not a very reliable biometric.*
>
> **Evaluation for Key Idea:** These details relate to reliability. The key idea may be about whether the technology even works.

PRACTICE As you read each section, mark details that seem important and related to one idea. Then, evaluate the details to determine key ideas.

 TEKS
5.G. Evaluate details read to determine key ideas.

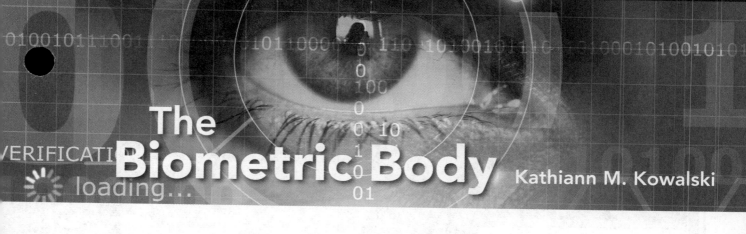

The Biometric Body

Kathiann M. Kowalski

BACKGROUND

The word *biometrics* comes from the Greek *bio*, meaning "life," and *metric*, meaning "to measure." Biometrics is the use of any part of the body for identification purposes. Just about everything on your body—including your face, eyes, voice, and walk—can be scanned, turned into digital data, and used to identify you.

1   YOU'LL NEED A TICKET and your fingertip to travel through the turnstiles at Walt Disney World in Orlando, Florida. A scanner captures an image of the index finger for guests aged 10 and up (Wyld). Then a computer calculates a number from minutiae points on the image. It compares that result with data stored in the resort's Ticket Tag system ("Biometrics").

2   "Preventing ticket **fraud** is something that benefits guests," explains Kim Prunty at Walt Disney World. If guests lose their tickets, other people can't use them and leave the real owners stranded. Having everyone show ID was another option. "But that would have been far more burdensome," says Prunty. With Ticket Tag, guests zip quickly into the Magic Kingdom or other parks.

3   Welcome to the world of biometrics!

Biology and Behavior

4   Computerized biometrics systems aim to recognize individuals automatically, based on the physical body and behavior. For most systems, information goes into a computer as images, recordings, or other data formats. A computer program, called an *algorithm*, performs mathematical calculations to convert the raw images or sound into numbers or features. The system then links the results with individuals.

5   Features used for biometrics should be distinctive. Ideally, a system's result will link to one and only one person. Since it's impossible to test everyone, scientists use statistics to see which traits are distinctive. Features should be stable, too. Your hair's appearance can change with a haircut, perm, or dyes. But you don't generally alter the shape of your hands or ears.

fraud (frawd) *n.* crime that involves deception and fakery

BIOMETRICS FROM HEAD TO TOE

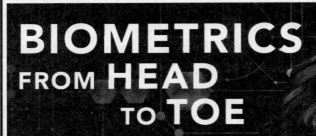

About Face

How do biometrics systems recognize your face? The holistic technique looks at the variation of light intensities over an image of the face. Using that data, it calculates a numerical description. "It turns out that the pattern of variation is distinctive to the subject," says Patrick Flynn, Professor and Chair of the Department of Computer Science and Engineering at the University of Notre Dame.

Another approach, called the local features technique, measures locations of the eyes, eyebrows, mouth, nose, and other facial features. The computer then analyzes the relationships between these various features. Collectively, they "form a signature for the face" (Flynn).

Three-dimensional images can be useful. But computers currently don't deal with them as well as two-dimensional color images, notes James Wayman, Senior Fellow in the Office of Research at San Jose State University and Director of the Biometric Identification Research Program. Thermal face images are not very reliable on their own, either. Think how fast your face heats up when you're embarrassed!

Sniff It Out

Although every person has a unique smell, it is not a very reliable biometric. If you've just eaten a taco, the extra food smell may mask your usual scent. However, smell sensing technology is becoming more advanced.

ID at Your Fingertips

Fingerprint identification examines patterns in friction ridges on the fingertips. The science of studying fingerprints' loops, arches, and whorls dates back to the late nineteenth century. The Federal Bureau of Investigation's fingerprint database of over 50 million records is an essential law enforcement tool.

Databases for biometrics systems used to enter a specific location are much smaller. Generally, they store records just for the authorized users. In the case of Walt Disney World's Ticket Tag system, the program just stores a set of numbers derived from the fingerprint image, not the actual fingerprints ("Privacy").

Ahem!

Speaker recognition systems classify a person's pattern of speech. "Voiceprints" look like waveforms and include information about the pitch, loudness, and duration of sounds in a spoken phrase. For most systems, a person tells it his or her username, then says a set word or phrase, like a password. After analysis, the system verifies if the speaker is an authorized user.

Your Genetic ID?

DNA would be "the ultimate biometric" (Flynn). Deoxyribonucleic Acid (DNA) encodes genetic information within our cells. Imagine touching a device that grabs a few skin cells. A computer would determine your DNA profile and search its database for a match. Certainly it would be difficult to **disguise** DNA or to **masquerade** as someone else. However, analysis could also reveal lots of private information: Whom are you related to? What diseases might you get? And so on. Privacy concerns make DNA the "most spooky biometric. . . . But we're decades away from having that. Doing rapid DNA assays [analyses within seconds] is something that's beyond the capabilities of current technology" (Flynn).

Walk This Way

Gait recognition systems analyze how people walk. Movements are recorded as video images. Computers analyze the patterns for distinctive images. "It can be applied when people don't know that they are being recognized," notes Mark Nixon, Professor in Computer Vision at the School of Electronics and Computer Science at the University of Southampton. Thus, while other biometric systems work to allow access, gait recognition could help facilities identify and keep out potential **criminals** ("Gait Biometrics").

Reading Environmental Print

"Biometrics From Head to Toe" is an informational graphic that includes text, heads, and images. Consider how all the elements work together to convey meaning.

disguise (dihs GYZ) *v.* change or hide appearance

masquerade (mas kuh RAYD) *v.* pretend to be someone or something else

criminals (KRIHM uh nuhlz) *n.* people who break the law

forged (fawrjd) *v.* illegally created fake copies or versions

---

Why Biometrics?

6   Biometric systems aren't perfect. In 2004, an innocent man spent two weeks in jail after the FBI's Automated Fingerprint Identification System (AFIS) mistakenly linked his fingerprint record with one found near a bombing scene. The FBI apologized afterward. People have also **forged** fingerprints, although usually with someone's cooperation.

7   Variability is another problem. Your face's appearance changes with your mood, lighting, the seasons, and so on. Programmers must decide how close a match is needed to accept someone.

8   "Often the application is going to tell you whether you want to minimize false accepts or false rejects. If you push one down, you

have to let the other one go up" (Flynn). If the program isn't careful enough, it might let an **impostor** through (a false accept). But it's also a problem if the program is too careful about matching patterns exactly. Then it might say no to a true match (a false reject).

9   People also change with age. "We don't have much information about how fingers grow. We don't have much information on aging" (Wayman). Some better programs update database records each time matches are made.

10   Systems might also link data for multiple features, like the face, ear, and gait. Mark Nixon says such "fusion" is the "state of the art in biometric research" (Nixon).

11   Biometrics systems aren't perfect. But they can improve security and save money. Systems offer conveniences to users, too. Biometrics systems already control access to restricted areas at various airports, defense facilities, companies, and some schools. Check-cashing services may use fingerprint scans to protect consumers and reduce fraud. At some stores, buyers even "pay by touch." Fingerprint scans work like debit cards.

12   And at Heathrow Airport, James Wayman says, "I don't wait in line." A machine scans his iris, and a printed slip welcomes him to the United Kingdom.

_____

References

"Biometrics." *Communications, Signal Processing, and Control,* U of Southampton, http://www.url-website. Accessed 19 Aug. 2017.

Flynn, Patrick J. Personal interview. 12 Aug. 2017.

"Gait Biometrics." *Communications, Signal Processing, and Control,* U of Southampton, http://www.url-website. Accessed 19 Aug. 2017

Nixon, Mark S. Personal interview. 14 Aug. 2017.

"Privacy Impact Assessment Integrated Automated Fingerprint Identification System National Security Enhancements." *Federal Bureau of Investigation,* http://www.url-website. Accessed 23 Aug. 2017.

Wayman, James. Personal interview. 12 Aug. 2017.

Wyld, David. "Biometrics at the Disney Gates." *SecureIDNews,* 2 Mar. 2006, http://www.url-website. Accessed 20 Aug. 2017.

Response

 NOTEBOOK

1. **Personal Connections** How would you feel if you always had to use your own biometrics as identification? Explain.

Answer the questions in your notebook. Use text evidence to support your responses.

Comprehension

2. **Reading Check** **(a)** What type of biometric identification was used as far back as the 19th century? **(b)** What information is included in a "voiceprint"? **(c)** Note two types of places where biometric systems are already being used for security.

3. **Strategy: Evaluate Details to Determine Key Ideas** Cite two details you marked in one section of the article. Did each one connect to a key idea? Explain.

Analysis

4. **(a) Define** In paragraph 5, Kowalski writes that features need to be distinctive and "stable." What does *stable* mean in this context? **(b) Analyze** Why are indistinct or unstable features problematic for biometrics? Explain, citing text evidence.

5. **(a)** What are false accepts and false rejects? **(b) Analyze Cause and Effect** Why are they an issue for biometric programmers, businesses, and customers? Explain.

6. **Speculate** Do you think biometrics will evolve to become a better option in the future? Explain your thinking, citing evidence from the article.

EQ Notes Is technology helpful or harmful to society?

What have you learned about technology and society from reading this article? Go to your Essential Question Notes and record your observations and thoughts about "The Biometric Body."

 TEKS

5.G. Evaluate details read to determine key ideas.

6.C. Use text evidence to support an appropriate response.

THE BIOMETRIC BODY

Close Read

 ANNOTATE

1. The model passage and annotation show how one reader analyzed part of the section entitled "Your Genetic ID?" Find another detail in the passage to annotate. Then, write your own question and conclusion.

CLOSE-READ MODEL

Imagine touching a device that grabs a few skin cells. A computer would determine your DNA profile and search its database for a match. Certainly it would be difficult to disguise DNA or to masquerade as someone else.

ANNOTATE: The writer asks me to imagine doing something.

QUESTION: Why does she speak directly to the reader in this way?

CONCLUDE: Her approach makes the ideas real and immediate; the reader can see him- or herself having this experience.

MY QUESTION:

MY CONCLUSION:

2. For more practice, answer the Close-Read notes in the selection.

3. Choose a section of the article you found especially important. Mark important details. Then, jot down questions and write your conclusions in the open space next to the text.

Inquiry and Research

 RESEARCH

 NOTEBOOK

Research and Extend Practice generating your own questions about ideas or situations you read about in this text. Write an "I want to know more" statement about an idea that interests you. Then, change that statement into a question. One example has been done for you.

Statement: I want to know more about _how biometric technology is being used in schools._

Research Question: _What biometric technology is being used in schools right now?_

Statement: I want to know more about _____.

Research Question: _____.

Write as many statements and questions as you wish. Then, use one as the focus for brief, informal inquiry. Jot down the answers you find.

 TEKS

8.D.i. Analyze characteristics and structural elements of informational text, including the controlling idea or thesis with supporting evidence.

8.D.iii. Analyze characteristics and structural elements of informational text, including organizational patterns such as definition, classification, advantage, and disadvantage.

12.A. Generate student-selected and teacher-guided questions for formal and informal inquiry.

Genre / Text Elements

Controlling Idea and Organizational Patterns In informational texts, the author expresses a **controlling idea**, or thesis, and supports it with evidence. The controlling idea guides the choices a writer makes about all the characteristics of a text, including the **organizational pattern**, or structure, he or she uses.

For example, in "The Biometric Body," the author uses an advantage/disadvantage pattern to explore a controlling idea about the pros and cons of biometric security. These pros and cons involve a variety of qualities, including the values most people hold.

> **TIP:** In informational writing, the author presents pros and cons in a balanced way. He or she will not directly state an opinion.

EXAMPLE: Advantage/Disadvantage Pattern in "The Biometric Body"

VALUE: PRIVACY	VALUE: CONVENIENCE
However, analysis could also reveal lots of private information: Whom are you related to?	*With Ticket Tag, guests zip quickly into the Magic Kingdom or other parks.*

 NOTEBOOK

PRACTICE Answer the questions.

1. **Analyze** Which sentence accurately states the controlling idea of this article? Explain your thinking.

   • Biometrics are a perfect solution to security needs.

   • Biometrics are too problematic to use for security needs.

   • Biometrics are promising but there are issues to work out.

2. **Evaluate** The author starts the article with an anecdote about biometrics' replacing tickets. Does this anecdote show an advantage or a disadvantage of biometrics? Explain.

3. **Distinguish** Do paragraphs 6 through 9 describe advantages or disadvantages to the use of biometrics? Explain your answer, citing specific details.

4. **Analyze** What competing values are represented in the problem of false accepts and false rejects? Explain.

5. **Evaluate** Do you think advantage/disadvantage organization is effective for the topic of biometrics? Explain your answer.

THE BIOMETRIC BODY

Concept Vocabulary

 NOTEBOOK

Why These Words? The vocabulary words are all related to deception. For example, an *impostor* commits fraud by pretending to be someone else.

fraud	disguise	masquerade
criminals	forged	impostor

PRACTICE Answer the questions.

1. How do the vocabulary words help you understand the concept of deception in this article?

2. Find two other words in the article that relate to deception.

3. Use the vocabulary words to complete the paragraph so that it makes sense. Use each word only once.

I think biometric security could prevent _____. After all, _____would have to work hard to _____their fingerprints or faces. It's just not that easy to make _____body parts! People think they're good at spotting others in _____, but a computer will do a better job identifying an _____.

Word Study

 NOTEBOOK

Synonyms and Nuance Words that have the same or similar meanings are **synonyms**. For example, the vocabulary words *disguise* and *masquerade* are synonyms. However, the two words have **nuances,** or differences, in meanings. *Masquerade* may suggest playfulness, while *disguise* does not.

PRACTICE Complete the activity.

1. What synonyms for *impostor* can you find in a thesaurus? Note two of them.

2. Write definitions for the two words that show nuances in their meanings. Which one has a more negative meaning?

3. Use a dictionary to confirm the nuances in meaning you describe.

★ TEKS
2.A. Use print or digital resources to determine the meaning, syllabication, pronunciation, word origin, and part of speech.

8.D.ii. Analyze characteristics and structural elements of informational text, including features such as introduction, foreword, preface, references, or acknowledgements to gain background information.

12.H.i. Examine sources for reliability, credibility, and bias.

Author's Craft

References in Informational Writing References, or citations, are characteristics and structures of informational texts that show the sources a writer used. These features are important to readers for a variety of reasons, including the following:

- indicate which ideas are the writer's and which came from others

- give readers details they need to verify information

- allow readers to gain background information

- depending on the quality of sources, either add to the writer's credibility or reveal bias and lack of credibility

TIP: Stronger sources include government and university publications, scholars, and major newspapers, magazines, or journals. Weaker sources include include biased publications, people with no credentials, and anyone who can't prove information.

References are characteristics of informational texts that can be structured in different ways. In-text citations appear in the text and show the source of specific details. A references page appears at the end of a text and gives complete bibliographic information about all the sources used.

EXAMPLE: Citation From "The Biometric Body"

IN-TEXT CITATION	REFERENCES PAGE ENTRY
A scanner captures an image of the index finger for guests aged 10 and up (Wyld).	Wyld, David. "Biometrics at the Disney Gates." *SecureIDNews*, 2 Mar. 2006, http://www.url-website. Accessed 20 Aug. 2017.

 NOTEBOOK

PRACTICE Answer the questions.

1. **Generalize** Why do you think it's customary to include both in-text citations and references pages in informational texts? What purpose does each type of structure serve? Cite examples from the article to support your answer.

2. **Draw Conclusions** What does the References list tell you about the writer's research process and the background information she used in her article?

3. **Analyze** In the "About Face" section, which details show that James Wayman is a credible reference?

4. **(a)** In the second paragraph of the section entitled "ID at Your Fingertips," what source is cited? **(b) Analyze** How does this reference add to the reader's sense that the information is reliable? Explain.

5. **Evaluate** Do the sources cited in this article add to or take away from its reliability and credibility? Explain.

Compare Informational Text and Argument

Both "The Biometric Body" and "Biometrics Are Not Better" focus on the subject of biometric security and identification. Notice similarities and differences between each author's approach and point of view on the subject.

THE BIOMETRIC BODY

BIOMETRICS ARE NOT BETTER

About the Author

Reuben Lorre has written articles for readers of all ages on a wide variety of topics, ranging from technology and mathematics to literature and culture. He splits his time between New York City and Buenos Aires, Argentina.

Biometrics Are Not Better

Concept Vocabulary

INTERACTIVITY

You will encounter the following words as you read the essay. Before reading, note how familiar you are with each word. Using a scale of 1 (do not know it at all) to 5 (know it very well), indicate your knowledge of each word.

WORD	YOUR RATING
security	
vulnerabilities	
exploiting	
bypassed	
breaches	
hacked	

Comprehension Strategy

ANNOTATE

Synthesize Information

When you **synthesize information**, you pull together different ideas in order to develop your own perspective. You allow your thinking to change and grow. To synthesize as you read, follow these steps:

- Identify important ideas and details in a text.
- Think about how those ideas and details connect with what you already know and whether they change your understanding.
- Use these sentence starters to organize the process:

  At first I, thought _____.
  Then, I learned _____.
  Now, I think _____.

PRACTICE > As you read the essay, synthesize information to develop a new understanding. Record your ideas in the open space next to the text.

TEKS
5.H. Synthesize information to create new understanding.

Biometrics Are Not Better

Reuben Lorre

BACKGROUND

Passwords are currently the most common way for individuals to identify themselves on their mobile devices or online. Over the past few years, however, biometric identification systems that use people's physical data have started to replace passwords. While some people welcome this trend, others are concerned that it may actually make all of us less safe.

1 New isn't always an improvement. We shouldn't assume that the latest technology is the best option. Using biometrics for **security** protection is a perfect example. This technology offers an excitingly modern experience, but it comes with unexpected **vulnerabilities**. In fact, the disadvantages of biometrics far outweigh potential gains.

2 Biometrics include any body measurements or calculations. Since every person is unique, measurements such as fingerprints, eye scans, facial patterns, heartbeats, or even DNA can be used to prove your identity. **Exploiting** an individual's unrepeatable features seems like a sure-fire way to prevent the wrong person from gaining access to cell phones, laptops, or other devices. The use of biometrics is booming. One research group estimates that about 650 million smartphones used biometrics in 2015. They predict users will increase to 2 billion by 2020. While companies and consumers rush to take advantage of this new technology, we must be careful that it isn't actually taking advantage of us.

security (sih KYOOR uh tee) *n.* protection; safety measure

vulnerabilities (vuhl nur uh BIHL ih teez) *n.* areas of weakness

exploiting (eks PLOYT ihng) *v.* taking unfair advantage of

AUDIO

ANNOTATE

ANNOTATE: Mark details in paragraph 4 that relate to places we leave our fingerprints.

QUESTION: Why do you think the author includes these details?

CONCLUDE: What does this help us understand about the use of fingerprints as a safe biometric?

bypassed (BY past) *v.* gotten around or avoided

breaches (BREE chuhz) *n.* gaps in a line of defense

hacked (hakt) *v.* gained illegal access to private information

3   Everyone is jumping on the biometrics bandwagon because of the perceived advantages. Users love the fact that the use of biometrics puts an end to confusing passwords. Unfortunately, biometrics can be unreliable. Many body measurements change over time or in specific situations. Fingerprints aren't useful if you cut yourself and need to wear a bandage. Voice recognition software can fail when you have a cold. Dim lighting can greatly reduce the ability of eye scanners to recognize users.

4   Promoters also emphasize that biometrics cannot be stolen as easily as passwords. However, almost any security system can be **bypassed** by determined crooks. For example, we leave our fingerprints everywhere: on tables, mirrors, cars, and the very smartphones they are increasingly being used to unlock. Thieves can transfer those fingerprints to molds and create models using household materials. Children's modeling clay can create a fake finger that's real enough to fool some biometric sensors. Eye scans are equally vulnerable. In a simple web search, Jan "Starbug" Krissler, a security researcher from Chaos Computer Club, found photographs of presidents and world politicians that were detailed enough to trick some iris scanners.

5   These biometric **breaches** pose a much more serious threat than password theft. What seems like an advantage turns out to be a huge weakness. If your password is **hacked**, you can easily change it. But if your biometric data is stolen, what are your choices? You can't replace your fingerprints, your eyes, or any of your biometric data.

6   The brightest promise of biometrics is freedom. Nothing could be easier than swiping your finger or blinking your eyes. However, that freedom comes at a heavy price. You could lose fundamental liberties, such as your right to privacy. When a device scans your body measurements, that data could be collected. A password says nothing about who you are; your fingerprints are much more revealing. With access to your biometric information, companies—or criminals—could easily identify you.

7   Another freedom you might give up is your right to keep your ideas private. According to United States laws, authorities with a warrant can force you to open a phone or computer with a fingerprint or other body scan. However, they can't make you provide mental information, such as a password. What you *know* is protected under the Fifth Amendment—what you *have*, including your personal biometrics, isn't.

8   Biometric technology is certainly cool. Using these new scanners can make you feel like you're living in a science fiction movie. But remember that not all movies end happily. We should be very cautious before giving in to this new technology. It may bring with it very unwelcome surprises.

NOTEBOOK

Answer the questions in your notebook. Use text evidence to support your responses.

Response

1. **Personal Connections** Do you think most people view biometrics as cool or scary? What do you think about this topic? Explain.

Comprehension

2. **Reading Check (a)** What do supporters of biometric security like about the technology? **(b)** Cite two examples of physical changes that might keep biometric identification from working properly.

3. **Strategy: Synthesize Information** In what ways did this article create a new understanding of the topic for you? Cite one example.

Analysis

4. **Analyze** Cite two kinds of reliability problems the author feels biometric security systems create.

5. **(a) Paraphrase** In your own words, state the two types of freedom the author says biometrics threaten. Stay true to the author's meaning and logic. **(b) Take a Position** Of the two, which do you think is more important? Explain your thinking.

6. **(a) Speculate** What might the author say to people who rush to embrace any new technology? Explain. **(b) Analyze** What attitude toward technology in general does the author express in this essay? Cite at least two details from the essay that support your response.

 EQ Notes Is technology helpful or harmful to society?

What have you learned about technology and society from reading this essay? Go to your Essential Question Notes and record your observations and thoughts about "Biometrics Are Not Better."

⚙ TEKS

5.H. Synthesize information to create new understanding.

6.A. Describe personal connections to a variety of sources, including self-selected texts.

6.D. Paraphrase and summarize texts in ways that maintain meaning and logical order.

BIOMETRICS ARE NOT BETTER

Close Read

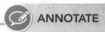
ANNOTATE

1. The model passage and annotation show how one reader analyzed part of paragraph 2 of the essay. Find another detail in the passage to annotate. Then, write your own question and conclusion.

CLOSE-READ MODEL

Biometrics include any body measurements or calculations. Since every person is unique, measurements such as fingerprints, eye scans, facial patterns, heartbeats, or even DNA can be used to prove your identity.

ANNOTATE: The author includes a list of specific body parts that can be used in biometrics.

QUESTION: Why does the author include this list?

CONCLUDE: The list further defines what biometrics are. The topic involves much more than people's fingerprints.

MY **QUESTION:**

MY **CONCLUSION:**

2. For more practice, answer the Close-Read notes in the selection.

3. Choose a section of the essay you found especially important. Mark important details. Then, jot down questions and write your conclusions in the open space next to the text.

TEKS

8.D.i. Analyze characteristics and structural elements of informational text, including the controlling idea or thesis with supporting evidence.

8.D.iii. Analyze characteristics and structural elements of informational text, including organizational patterns such as definition, classification, advantage, and disadvantage.

8.E. Analyze characteristics and structures of argumentative text by identifying the claim.

8.E.iii. Analyze characteristics and structures of argumentative text by identifying the intended audience or reader.

12.D. Identify and gather relevant information from a variety of sources.

Inquiry and Research

RESEARCH

NOTEBOOK

Research and Extend Lorre notes that millions of phones use biometrics. What other types of technology or businesses are currently using biometric systems for security? Identify four sources of different types that present information related to this question. Scan each source, and choose two that offer the most relevant details. Then, read those two sources more thoroughly. Write down at least two facts from each source that answer the question.

Genre / Text Elements

Claim and Organizational Patterns In an argument, the **claim** is the author's position, the idea he or she wants the **audience**, or readers, to accept. As an author builds an argument, he or she takes the audience into account and guides them through his or her thinking. The author:

- considers what readers may not know and explains unfamiliar words or ideas.

- gives reasons that connect to readers' beliefs or values.

- uses **organizational patterns**, or structures, that help readers follow the logic. For example, the author often presents the claim at the beginning, and then uses a logical pattern, such as cause-and-effect or advantage/disadvantage, that readers can recognize.

> **TIP:** The language and logic you might use to convince a child is different from the approach you would take with a peer. In a similar way, writers modify arguments to suit the needs of the audience.

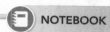

NOTEBOOK

INTERACTIVITY

PRACTICE Answer the questions and complete the activity.

1. **Analyze** What is the author's claim in this text? Cite two different pieces of evidence he uses to support that claim. Explain your choices.

2. **Analyze** In this essay, the author describes several advantages to biometrics, and then shows how each one is actually a disadvantage. Use the chart to explain the disadvantage he sees for each item, and list the reasons and evidence he uses to support his views.

ADVANTAGE	ACTUAL DISADVANTAGE	SUPPORTING REASONS AND EVIDENCE
ends the problem of forgetting passwords		
can't be stolen easily		
freedom (convenience and ease of use)		

3. **Analyze** What audience do you think the author is trying to reach—software engineers, politicians or other decision-makers, the general public, or another group? Explain your thinking, citing details from the essay.

4. **Evaluate** Do you think advantage/disadvantage organization is an effective way to present an argument? Explain, citing details from this essay as examples.

BIOMETRICS ARE NOT BETTER

Concept Vocabulary

 NOTEBOOK

Why These Words? The vocabulary words are related to weaknesses in a technological system. For example, *vulnerabilities* could result in a system's being *hacked*.

| security | vulnerabilities | exploiting |
| bypassed | breaches | hacked |

PRACTICE Answer the questions.

1. How do the vocabulary words sharpen your understanding of technological weaknesses?

2. Find two other words in the essay that relate to the concept of weakness in technological systems.

3. Why do people worry about online *vulnerabilities*?

4. Why might *exploiting* someone's weaknesses be unfair?

5. If you've been *bypassed* for an award, what happened?

6. Would anyone enjoy having his or her social media account *hacked*?

7. Why is online *security* important to preventing *breaches* of information?

WORD NETWORK

Add words that are related to technology and society from the text to your Word Network.

Word Study

 NOTEBOOK

Multiple-Meaning Words A **multiple-meaning word** has more than one definition. For example, the vocabulary word *hacked* is the past tense form of *hack,* a verb that has a number of meanings, including "illegally access" and "chop into pieces."

PRACTICE Complete the following items:

1. Use a dictionary to find a third, somewhat informal, meaning of *hack* as a verb. Write the definition.

2. *Hack* can also be a noun. Use a dictionary to find two of those meanings.

 TEKS

10.D.iv. Edit drafts using standard English conventions, including prepositions and prepositional phrases and their influence on subject-verb agreement.

10.D.viii. Edit drafts using standard English conventions, including punctuation marks, including commas in complex sentences, transitions, and introductory elements.

Conventions

Prepositions and Prepositional Phrases A **preposition** relates a noun or a pronoun that follows it to another word in the sentence. In the sentence *The book is on the table,* the preposition *on* relates the noun *table* to another word in the sentence, *book.* A **prepositional phrase** is a group of words that has certain qualities:

TIP: There are more than 100 prepositions in English. Some of the most-common ones are *at, after, between, for, from, in, of, on, to, through, above,* and *with.*

- begins with a preposition and ends with either a noun or a pronoun, which is the **object of the preposition**. The phrase may include modifiers.

- functions as an adjective by telling *what kind* or *which one*, or as an adverb by telling *how, when,* or *where*

Note that if a prepositional phrase begins a sentence, it must be followed by a comma. In addition, the verb of a sentence must always agree with the subject of the sentence, not with the object of the preposition.

EXAMPLES from "Biometrics Are Not Better"

SENTENCE	EXPLANATION
Fingerprints are one option *for* **identification.**	The prepositional phrase begins with the preposition *for* and ends with the noun *identification*, which is the object of the preposition.
Before the **Internet**, personal security was less risky.	The prepositional phrase begins with the preposition *before* and ends with the noun *Internet*, which is the object of the preposition.

NOTEBOOK

READ IT

Read the essay and mark at least three prepositional phrases. Identify the object of the preposition in each one. Use support from your peers or teacher if you need help.

WRITE IT

Draft a brief paragraph in which you explain any uses of biometric security you have personally experienced or seen in movies or on TV. Use at least two prepositional phrases. Then, edit your draft, making sure you have used commas correctly after any prepositional phrase at the beginning of a sentence and that you maintain correct subject-verb agreement.

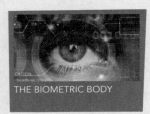

THE BIOMETRIC BODY

BIOMETRICS ARE NOT BETTER

Compare Informational Text and Argument

Multiple Choice

 **NOTEBOOK**

These questions are based on "The Biometric Body" and "Biometrics Are Not Better." Choose the best answer to each question.

1. What do the two selections have in common?

A Both selections are mainly informational texts.

B Both selections are mainly argumentative texts.

C Both selections address the topic of biometrics.

D Both selections express the author's deep feelings.

2. Read the passages from the two texts. Which answer choice BEST states a similarity between the two?

The Biometric Body	**Biometrics Are Not Better**
Variability is another problem. Your face's appearance changes with your mood, lighting, the seasons, and so on.	Many body measurements change over time or in specific situations. Fingerprints aren't useful if you cut yourself and need to wear a bandage.

F Both passages explain how biometric systems work.

G Both passages explain why biometrics are very reliable.

H Both passages highlight ways that biometric systems may be unreliable.

J Both passages describe an advantage to biometrics.

3. What point about privacy does the author of "Biometrics Are Not Better" make that the author of "The Biometric Body" does not?

A Most people are not that concerned about their privacy.

B Since biometrics aren't reliable, we'd be giving up our privacy for nothing.

C The use of biometrics may make private information available to criminals.

D If we give up passwords, we may also give up our rights to the privacy of our ideas.

 TEKS

6.B. Write responses that demonstrate understanding of texts, including comparing sources within and across genres.

NOTEBOOK

Short Response

1. Generalize Which author is more willing to accept the imperfections of biometric technology? Explain.

2. Evaluate Cite at least one piece of information from "The Biometric Body" that you could you use to argue against Lorre's claim that biometrics are not better than passwords. Explain your choice.

3. Compare and Contrast How are the two authors' conclusions about biometric security similar and different?

Answer the questions in your notebook. Use text evidence to support your responses.

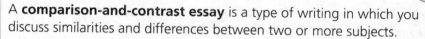

Timed Writing

A **comparison-and-contrast essay** is a type of writing in which you discuss similarities and differences between two or more subjects.

ASSIGNMENT

Write a **comparison-and-contrast essay** in which you take a position about which text, the informational article or the argument, you liked more and found more meaningful. Explain similarities and differences between the two texts, and cite examples that support your analysis.

5-MINUTE PLANNER

1. Read the assignment carefully and completely.
2. Decide what you want to say—your claim.
3. Decide which examples you'll use from each text.
4. Organize your ideas, keeping these points in mind:
   - Clearly explain your position and your reasons.
   - Accurately cite evidence from both texts.

EQ Notes Before moving on to a new selection, go to your EQ Notes and record any additional thoughts or observations you have about "The Biometric Body" and "Biometrics Are Not Better."

About IBM

International Business Machines Corporation (IBM) is one of the world's largest companies, employing nearly half a million people. In 1953, the company introduced its first computer, and in 1981 it introduced its version of the personal computer, a landmark event in the era of desktop computing.

The Internet of Things

Media Vocabulary

These words describe characteristics of animated videos, a type of multimodal text. Use them as you analyze, discuss, and write about the selection.

images or graphics: visual representations of people, places, objects, or ideas	• Images, such as photographs, show what people, objects, or places look like. • Graphics, such as charts or maps, show data and information in interesting ways.
animation: process of making films from still images	• Animators may use drawings, computer graphics, photos, or even objects to create moving images. • Animation can make certain scenes more lively or help an audience understand a process.
audio: recorded sound	• Audio that is part of a video or website allows listeners to hear actual sound effects or voices.
voiceover: off-camera voice	• The person delivering the voiceover may comment on the action or tell the story shown in the film. • Voiceovers may provide additional background information for viewers or listeners.
narrator: person who tells a story	• In an informational video, the narrator reads or relates descriptions or explanations.

Comprehension Strategy

 NOTEBOOK

Make Connections

When you watch media, such as an informational video, you can deepen your understanding by **making connections** to your personal experiences. This means you recognize how details in the media are similar to aspects of your own life.

EXAMPLES

Here are examples of ways in which you might make personal connections to this video:

• Notice activities in the video that remind you of things you do.
• Examine how issues explained in the video affect your life, too.
• Consider whether you share the attitudes, concerns, or feelings expressed in the video.

PRACTICE As you watch, use the Take Notes section to jot down connections to personal experiences you make. Think about ways in which those connections deepen your understanding of the information presented.

 TEKS

5.E. Make connections to personal experiences, ideas in other texts, and society.

8.F. Analyze characteristics of multimodal and digital texts.

The Internet of Things

IBM Social Media

BACKGROUND

The IBM "Smarter Planet" program promotes and discusses how global leaders can use new technologies and types of data to create a "smarter planet"—a world in which the smart use of information can matter as much as any other natural resource. This video was produced as part of their "Smarter Planet" series.

AUDIO

NOTEBOOK

TAKE NOTES As you watch, write down your observations and questions, making sure to note time codes so you can easily revisit sections later.

NOTEBOOK

Answer the questions in your notebook. Use text evidence to support your responses.

Response

1. **Personal Connections** Which technology mentioned in the video is the most surprising or interesting to you? Explain.

Comprehension

2. **Strategy: Make Connections to Personal Experiences** **(a)** Note one personal connection you made to this video. **(b)** In what ways did making personal connections help you better understand the ideas in the video?

Analysis

3. **Paraphrase** According to the video, how can connectivity, or "The Internet of Things," help create a smarter planet?

4. **(a) Analyze** Revisit the scene that shows the world map made up of devices. What does this scene add to the video? **(b) Evaluate** In your opinion, which images are most effective in helping the viewer understand the ideas? Explain.

5. **Interpret** The narrator explains that the planet has "grown a central nervous system." What does this statement mean?

6. **Essential Question** *Is technology helpful or harmful to society?* What have you learned about technology and society from this video? Go to your Essential Question Notes and record your observations and thoughts.

MEDIA VOCABULARY

Use these words as you discuss and write about the video.

images
graphics
animation
audio
voiceover
narrator

Close Review

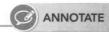 **ANNOTATE**

Watch the video again. As you watch, take notes about important details and jot down your observations. Note time codes so you can find information later. Then, write a question and your conclusion.

> **MY QUESTION:**
>
> **MY CONCLUSION:**

TEKS

5.E. Make connections to personal experiences, ideas in other texts, and society.

6.F. Respond using newly acquired vocabulary as appropriate.

8.F. Analyze characteristics of multimodal and digital texts.

Composition

A **summary** is a retelling of the most important ideas in a text in a way that maintains the meaning and logical order of information.

THE INTERNET OF THINGS

> **ASSIGNMENT**
>
> Write a **summary** of the video. Make sure to include key information from the beginning, middle, and end of the video.

To write a summary, follow these steps:

1. Watch the video, and take notes on the most important ideas.

2. Briefly restate the main ideas from the original. Don't add ideas or change the thinking of the original text.

3. Be sure to present ideas from the video in the same order as in the original.

4. Use an objective, or neutral tone. Don't include your own opinions or judgments.

Speaking and Listening

An **oral report** is an organized presentation of information that you deliver to a listening audience.

> **ASSIGNMENT**
>
> Prepare and deliver an **oral report**, retelling information from the video. Focus on the ideas and details you find most interesting.

EQ Notes Before moving on to a new selection, go to your Essential Question Notes and record what you learned from the video.

To prepare your oral report, answer these questions:

- Who is delivering the information in the video? What is the purpose of the message?
- Does the video present mostly facts or mostly opinions? A **fact** can be proved. An **opinion** can be supported, but not proved.
- What do the video makers want viewers to think or do?

To deliver your report, follow these steps:

- Organize your information into **talking points**—a list of brief statements.
- As you speak, glance at your talking points, but then make eye contact with your audience.
- Speak clearly, pausing to emphasize key words.
- Don't rush, and make sure to clearly pronounce, or enunciate, each word.

 TEKS

1.C. Give an organized presentation with a specific stance and position, employing eye contact, speaking rate, volume, enunciation, natural gestures, and conventions of language to communicate ideas effectively.

6.D. Paraphrase and summarize texts in ways that maintain meaning and logical order.

Write an Argumentative Essay

An **argumentative essay** is a brief nonfiction work in which an author presents a claim, or position, and supports it with reasons and evidence.

ASSIGNMENT

Write an **argumentative essay** in which you take a position on the following question:

Do mobile devices improve our lives?

Support your position with evidence from your reading, your background knowledge, and your own observations. Include the elements of an argumentative essay in your writing.

ELEMENTS OF AN ARGUMENTATIVE ESSAY

Purpose: to explain and defend a position, or claim

Characteristics

→ a clear claim that expresses an engaging idea and shows depth of thought

→ consideration of other opinions or positions

→ different types of evidence, including specific facts, details, and examples

→ clear examples of craft, including well-chosen transitions and language that connects to the reader

→ standard English conventions, including correct subject-verb agreement, especially within prepositional phrases

Structure

→ a well-organized structure that includes:

- an interesting introduction
- a logical flow of ideas from paragraph to paragraph
- a strong conclusion

 TEKS

11.C. Compose multi-paragraph argumentative texts using genre characteristics and craft.

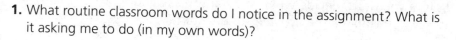

Take a Closer Look at the Assignment

1. What routine classroom words do I notice in the assignment? What is it asking me to do (in my own words)?

2. Is a specific **audience** mentioned in the assignment?

◯ Yes   If "yes," who is my main audience?

◯ No   If "no," who do I think my audience is or should be?

3. Is my **purpose** for writing specified in the assignment?

◯ Yes   If "yes," what is the purpose?

◯ No   If "no," why am I writing this argument (not just because it's an assignment)?

4. (a) Does the assignment require that I use specific **types of evidence**?

◯ Yes   If "yes," what are they?

◯ No   If "no," what types of evidence do I think I need?

(b) Where will I get the evidence? What can I pull from my EQ Notes?

5. Does the assignment ask me to organize my ideas in a certain way?

◯ Yes   If "yes," what structure does it require?

◯ No   If "no," how can I best order my ideas?

AUDIENCE

Keep your **audience**, or reader, in mind when you write.

- Explain any details they may not know.
- Take into account opinions they may already hold about your topic.

PURPOSE

A specific **purpose**, or reason for writing, will help you focus your argument.

- **General Purpose:** *In this argument, I'll talk about dogs in town.*
- **Specific Purpose:** *In this essay, I'll argue that we should let dogs run off-leash on beaches during the off-season.*

EVIDENCE

Varied **evidence**, or supporting details, will make your essay stronger.

- **Facts:** information that can be proved true
- **Expert Opinion:** words of people who have special knowledge
- **Personal Observation:** explanations of your own knowledge or experience
- **Anecdote:** brief story that illustrates a point
- **Examples:** specific instances of a general idea

Planning and Prewriting

Before you draft, decide what you want to say and how you want to say it. Complete the activities to get started.

Discover Your Thinking: Freewrite!

Freewriting can help you find a focus for your essay. Write quickly and freely for at least three minutes without stopping.

As you write, think about your own experiences with mobile devices, as well as your observations and information you have read or researched.

- Don't worry about grammar or spelling errors. Just write quickly and freely.
- When time is up, pause and read what you wrote. Mark ideas you find interesting.
- Repeat the process as many times as necessary to get all your ideas out. For each round, start with the strong ideas you marked before. Focus on those as you again write quickly and freely.

NOTEBOOK

WRITE IT Do mobile devices improve our lives?

 TEKS

10.A. Plan a first draft by selecting a genre appropriate for a particular topic, purpose, and audience using a range of strategies such as discussion, background reading, and personal interests; **10.B.i.** Develop drafts into a focused, structured, and coherent piece of writing by organizing with purposeful structure, including an introduction, transitions, coherence within and across paragraphs, and a conclusion.

Structure Ideas: Make a Plan

A. Focus Your Position Read the text you generated during freewriting and pull out your best ideas. Then, place the ideas into two lists—one for the benefits of mobile devices and one for the harms. Consider which list is stronger. Use this process to figure out your position.

_____

_____

_____

_____

B. Write a Claim

_____

_____

C. Plan a Structure Figure out the content for each section of your argumentative essay.

    I. Introduction: State your claim and show that your topic is important. Consider telling a story or describing a scene.

    II. Body: List your points and evidence in logical order.

    III. Conclusion: Plan how you can leave your reader with a strong impression. Consider including a statement about the possible future effects of a situation you describe.

_____

_____

_____

_____

_____

_____

_____

_____

_____

_____

CLAIM

A **claim** is your main idea, position, or point. Begin by writing a "working" claim—just one sentence. As you draft and revise, you may change or refine your claim.

STRUCTURE

A clear **structure**, or organization of ideas and evidence, helps you focus your thinking. Consider using this structure to build your argument:

- **Claim:** State your claim.
- **Support:** Present evidence and explain how it connects to your claim.
- **Counterclaim:** Describe a differing opinion that others might hold.
- **Rebuttal:** Give evidence that disproves the counterclaim and explain how your claim is stronger.

Drafting

Apply the planning work you've done so far to write a first draft. At some point in the body of your essay, introduce a counterclaim and evidence that disproves it.

Read Like a Writer

Reread these paragraphs from the body of the Mentor Text. Mark details that show how the writer considers other points of view.

MENTOR TEXT

from That's Not Progress!

Not all experts agree with this analysis. Some point to the benefits of social media. Dr. Megan Moreno is an assistant professor of pediatrics and adolescent medicine. She believes that social networking helps develop a young person's sense of community. … She insists that young people had problems before computers came into being.

Maybe so. In the past, however, young people found ways to escape from their problems. Now, smartphones and other high-tech devices have made escape impossible. Is that progress?

> The writer introduces a counterclaim and uses evidence to explain it.

> At what point does the writer begin to answer the counterclaim? Mark those details.

NOTEBOOK

WRITE IT Draft a paragraph of your essay here in which you explain a counterclaim. Then, add a sentence in which you transition back to your own argument.

_____
_____
_____
_____
_____
_____
_____
_____
_____
_____
_____

DEPTH OF THOUGHT

Keep these points in mind as you draft your essay.

- **Audience** Remember your audience and explain any details that may be unfamiliar to them.
- **Tone** Make sure your tone, or attitude, is serious and respectful.
- **Development** Use varied evidence to support your claim and disprove a counterclaim. For example, if you make an observation, back it up with facts.

 TEKS

10.B.ii. Develop drafts into a focused, structured, and coherent piece of writing by developing an engaging idea reflecting depth of thought with specific facts and details; **10.D.iv.** Edit drafts using standard English conventions, including prepositions and prepositional phrases and their influence on subject-verb agreement.

Create Coherence

A **preposition** is a word such as *of, in, to, for, over,* or *with* that relates a noun or a pronoun to another word in the sentence. A **prepositional phrase** is a group of words that begins with a preposition and ends with a noun or pronoun, called the *object of the preposition.*

Prepositional phrases may appear at different points in a sentence. When the phrase appears at the beginning of a sentence, follow it with a comma. When the phrase comes in the middle of a sentence, it can lead to errors in subject-verb agreement. Follow these rules to avoid errors:

- The subject of a sentence never appears in a prepositional phrase.
- The verb always agrees with the subject—not with the object of the preposition.

> **TIP:** A **coherent** piece of writing does not confuse readers. The correct use of prepositional phrases can make your writing more precise and, thus, more coherent.

EXAMPLES: Prepositional Phrases in Sentences

In the examples, the preposition is underlined once, and its object is underlined twice.

PLACE IN SENTENCE	EXAMPLE	EXPLANATION
Beginning	*After the storm, the sun shone brightly.*	A comma follows the phrase.
Middle	*Our analysis of the results shows progress.*	The verb *shows* agrees with *analysis*, which is the subject, and not with *results*, which is the object of the preposition. No comma is needed.
End	*Technology is a big part of our lives.*	*No comma is needed.*

 NOTEBOOK

WRITE IT Write or copy a paragraph of your essay here. Mark any prepositional phrases that appear in the middle of a sentence. Check that each verb agrees with the subject and not with the object of the preposition.

FUNCTIONS OF PREPOSITIONAL PHRASES

- may modify a noun or pronoun, telling *what kind* or *which one*

EXAMPLE:

Let's take a picture *of each other.* (modifies *picture,* telling *what kind*)

- may modify a verb, telling *where* or *in what way*

EXAMPLE:

She called me *on the phone.* (modifies *called,* telling *in what way*)

Revising

 ANNOTATE

Now that you have a first draft, revise it to be sure it is as persuasive as possible. When you revise, you "re-see" your writing, checking for the following elements:

Clarity: sharpness of your ideas

Development: full explanations with strong supporting details

Organization: logical flow of ideas

Style and Tone: quality and variety of sentences and precision of word choices; a level of formality that suits your audience and purpose

Read Like a Writer

Review the revisions made to the Mentor text. Then, answer the questions in the white boxes.

MENTOR TEXT

from That's Not Progress!

Social networking can cause serious emotional problems. The effects can be physical, too. Everyone knows the effects of online bullying. There are other ways to damage ~~someone.~~ *a person's self-confidence.* "When 'friends' upload unflattering photos and post mean comments, it can seriously damage a person's self-image," says one mental health expert. *In addition, getting* ~~Getting~~ no response to a post or not being "friended" can also be very painful.

Frequent users of social media often suffer from pain in their fingers and wrists. Blood vessels in their eyes and necks can narrow. Their backs can ache from being hunched over phones and computers for hours at a time.

Texting is another problem created by technology. *Half the nation's youth send 50 or more text messages a day.* ~~Students text a lot.~~ One study found that young people send an average of 34 texts a night after they get into bed! This loss of sleep can affect the ability to concentrate, problem-solve, and learn.

> Why did the writer move this sentence to the next paragraph?

> The writer replaced a vague word with more precise choices.

> The writer added a transition to clarify the flow of ideas.

> Why did the writer replace this sentence?

 TEKS

10.C. Revise drafts for clarity, development, organization, style, word choice, and sentence variety.

Take a Closer Look at Your Draft

Now, revise your draft. Use the Revision Guide for Argument to evaluate and strengthen your argumentative essay.

REVISION GUIDE FOR ARGUMENT

EVALUATE	TAKE ACTION
Clarity	
Is my claim strong and clear?	If your claim isn't clear, try saying what you mean out loud as if you were speaking to a friend. Then, **restate** your claim more simply in writing.
Development	
Have I given enough supporting evidence for every idea?	**Mark** each supporting detail and the idea it supports. Then, **move** any detail that is not in the same paragraph as the idea it supports. **Add** or **delete** details.
Have I used varied evidence?	• **Add** facts or expert statements to strengthen your opinions. • **Add** anecdotes or examples to illustrate your facts.
Organization	
Have I organized my ideas in a logical way?	If the structure doesn't work, **reorganize** ideas and details. Print your paper and then cut out the paragraphs. Physically **rearrange** them until you find a better order. Then, **add** transitions to make the flow of ideas clear.
Do all the sentences in each paragraph relate to the topic sentence?	Mark the topic sentence in each paragraph. Then, analyze each supporting sentence to make sure it relates directly to the topic sentence. Delete any sentences that are out of place.
Style and Tone	
Does my essay begin and end in memorable ways?	**Add** a question, anecdote, quotation, or strong detail to interest your audience.
Are my word choices precise and vivid?	Review your draft and mark any vague words, such as *nice, good, bad,* or *important.* Replace those words with vivid words that will make your ideas more interesting and persuasive.
Is my tone suitable for an essay, in which I attempt to persuade my audience?	Replace any overly casual language with more formal options. For example, instead of saying, "Technology is *alright,*" say, "Technology is *beneficial.*"
Are sentence types and lengths varied?	If your sentences are all short or all long, create variety: 1. **Break** a long, confusing sentence into two shorter sentences. 2. **Combine** two short sentences into one longer sentence. 3. **Rewrite** some sentences as questions or exclamations.

Editing

🖊 **ANNOTATE**

Don't let errors distract readers from your ideas. Reread your draft and fix mistakes to create a finished persuasive work.

Read Like a Writer

Look at how the writer of the Mentor Text edited the draft. Then, follow the directions in the white boxes.

MENTOR TEXT

from **That's Not Progress!**

Social networking has become a big part of our lives, *and* its negative effects can be overlooked. But mental health experts are starting to notice issues—and what they are finding is disturbing.

As the ~~The~~ popularity of social media skyrockets, so do reports of "facebook depression." Like other kinds of depression, its common signs are anxiety low self-confidence and loneliness.

> Find and fix a capitalization error.

> The writer added a prepositional phrase with correct punctuation to create a complex sentence.

> Insert the missing commas in a series of items.

Focus on Mechanics

Capitalization A proper noun names a specific person, place, or thing, and is always capitalized. Even when proper nouns appear in shortened forms—such as **abbreviations** or **initials**—they are capitalized. An **acronym** is a special type of abbreviation that uses the first letters of a long term to form a pronounceable word. Even if the long form is not a proper noun, most acronyms are capitalized.

TYPE OF TERM	FULL FORM	SHORTENED FORM
Proper Name	Clive Staples Lewis	Initials: C. S. Lewis
Company Name	International Business Machines	Abbreviation: IBM
Organization	National Aeronautics and Space Administration	Acronym: NASA
Science Terminology	rapid eye movement	Acronym: REM

> **EDITING TIPS**
>
> In your writing, whenever you refer to a specific person, company, organization, or even a brand name, use proper capitalization. Go through your draft and mark all the proper nouns, including any shortened versions. Make sure you have capitalized them correctly.

PRACTICE Fix the errors in capitalization in the following sentences. Then, check your own draft for correctness.

1. Arthur c. clarke won many awards given by sfwa, the science fiction and fantasy writers of america.

2. We used the Bay Area Rapid Transit System, which people call bart, to get around San Francisco.

🔄 **TEKS**

10.D.i. Edit drafts using standard English conventions, including complete complex sentences with subject-verb agreement and avoidance of splices, run-ons, and fragments. **10.D.viii.** Edit drafts using standard English conventions, including capitalization of proper nouns, including abbreviations, initials, acronyms, and organizations.

Focus on Spelling and Punctuation

Spelling: Q takes a U In English, the letter *q* always appears with a *u*. Together, *qu* usually represents the sound *kw*, as in *quick*. It may also represent a *k* sound as in *conquer*. If you see the letter *q* in a word without a *u*, the word comes from another language, such as Arabic. Check your essay for any q words and make sure you have spelled them correctly.

Punctuation: Commas Make sure you use commas correctly in your essay.

- Place a comma after a prepositional phrase at the beginning of a sentence.
  EXAMPLE: *After the rain, the sun shone brighter than before.*

- Use a comma before and after a nonrestrictive, or nonessential, element in the middle of a sentence. A nonrestrictive element can be deleted without changing the basic meaning of the sentence.
  EXAMPLE:

  Restrictive Element: The girl *who is wearing gold sneakers* is my friend.

  Nonrestrictive Element: Anna, *whom I've known for years,* is my friend.

- Use commas after each item in a list of more than two items.
  EXAMPLE: He owns a *computer, a tablet, and a cellphone.*

> **EDITING TIPS**
> - Read your essay aloud, listening for errors you might not catch while reading silently.
> - Look for spelling errors by reading your essay backwards, which lets you see words in a different way.

 ANNOTATE

PRACTICE In the following sentences, correct spelling and punctuation errors. Then, check your own draft for correctness.

1. I can text email, call or send you a chat.

2. On most days, I look at my phone and watch TV at the same time.

3. Call customer service to inqire about your account.

4. Technology which changes so fast has altered our lives.

Publishing and Presenting

Make It Multimodal

Share your essay with your class or school community. Choose one of these options:

OPTION 1 Post your essay to a class or school blog, or website. Respectfully comment on the essays of others, and respond politely to the comments your essay receives.

OPTION 2 Pair up with a classmate whose essay expresses a different point of view than yours. Take turns presenting your ideas to the class. After your presentation, answer questions from listeners.

Is technology helpful or harmful to society?

Modern technology has made our lives easier in many ways. It has also raised our expectations about how quickly tasks can be completed. You will read selections that examine the presence of technology and social media in our daily lives. You will work in a group to continue your exploration of living in a world that is increasingly dependent on technology.

 VIDEO

 INTERACTIVITY

Peer-Group Learning Strategies

Throughout your life, in school, in your community, and in your career, you will continue to learn and work with others.

Review these strategies and the actions you can take to practice them as you work in small groups. Add ideas of your own for each step. Use these strategies during Peer-Group Learning.

STRATEGY	MY PEER-GROUP ACTION PLAN
Prepare • Complete your assignments so that you are prepared for group work. • Take notes on your reading so that you can share ideas with others in your group.	
Participate fully • Make eye contact to signal that you are paying attention. • Use text evidence when making a point.	
Support others • Build off ideas from others in your group. • Ask others who have not yet spoken to do so.	
Clarify • Paraphrase the ideas of others to be sure that your understanding is correct. • Ask follow-up questions.	

CONTENTS

PERFORMANCE TASK: SPEAKING AND LISTENING

Conduct a Debate
After reading the selections, your group will plan and deliver a multimedia presentation about either the benefits or the disadvantages of technology.

Working as a Group

 NOTEBOOK

1. Take a Position

In your group, discuss the following question:

> Does having instant access to information always make our lives easier?

As you take turns sharing your positions, be sure to provide reasons or examples that support your ideas. Ask for clarification if you don't understand any words or ideas. After all group members have shared, discuss the ways in which instant access to information changes people's expectations.

2. List Your Rules

As a group, decide on the rules that you will follow as you work together. Elicit, or invite, suggestions from everyone in the group and consider which ones will help you the most. Two samples are provided. Add two more that make sense for your group.

- Everyone should participate in group discussions.
- People should not interrupt.

_____

_____

3. Apply the Rules

Share what you have learned about technology. Make sure each person in the group contributes. Take notes and be prepared to share with the class one thing that you heard from another member of your group.

4. Name Your Group

Choose a name that reflects the unit topic.

Our group's name: _____

5. Create a Communication Plan

Decide how you want to communicate with one another. For example, you might use online collaboration tools, email, or instant messaging.

Our group's plan:

_____

_____

 TEKS

1.D. Participate in student-led discussions by eliciting and considering suggestions from other group members, taking notes, and identifying points of agreement and disagreement; **6.I.** Reflect on and adjust responses as new evidence is presented.

Making a Schedule

First, find out the due dates for the peer-group activities. Then, preview the texts and activities with your group, and make a schedule for completing the tasks.

SELECTION	ACTIVITIES	DUE DATE
Is Our Gain Also Our Loss?		
The Black Hole of Technology		
The Fun They Had		
Mexico's Abandoned Railways and the SEFT-1		
Bored . . . and Brilliant? A Challenge to Disconnect From Your Phone		

 NOTEBOOK

Reflect and Adjust Your Responses

Literature can generate a wide variety of responses in different readers—and that can make your peer-group work exciting and fun. At the same time, it can be a challenge to engage in collaborative work with people who have many different opinions. Use these tips to get the most from your peer-group work:

Agree to disagree. Disagreement can be as important as agreement. It makes you focus on why you feel or think as you do and that can sharpen your reasoning.

Pause before you respond. Really reflect on what someone has said or written. Even if you agree, take a quick moment before you say something or give feedback.

Be open. In the end, you may not adjust your response, but be open to other points of view.

Other people's experiences and ways of seeing things can open your eyes to new understandings. If reflecting on evidence leads you to adjust your response, share your thinking. Your thought process may be instructive for everyone in your group.

Reading Reflective Essays

A **reflective essay** is a type of nonfiction in which an author presents his or her thoughts and feelings about an experience or an idea.

IS OUR GAIN ALSO OUR LOSS?
The selection you are about to read is a reflective essay.

REFLECTIVE ESSAY

Author's Purpose
➔ to express insights gained through experience or observation

Characteristics
➔ descriptions of a specific event, time period, or person
➔ often, dialogue and other storytelling elements
➔ language that captures the author's process of feeling and thinking
➔ a controlling idea involving lessons learned or insights gained
➔ a thoughtful tone, or attitude, and mood, or emotional quality

Structure
➔ an introduction that provides focus, body paragraphs that describe and explain, and a conclusion that summarizes insights

Take a Minute!

 NOTEBOOK

DISCUSS IT What kinds of objects are reflective? Why might this type of writing be called *reflective*? Discuss your ideas with a partner.

⟳ **TEKS**
8.D. Analyze characteristics and structural elements of informational text.

9.A. Explain the author's purpose and message within a text.

Genre / Text Elements

Author's Purpose and Message In reflective nonfiction, an **author's purpose**, or reason for writing, is to *reflect on* or think deeply about a topic. The writer explores the personal effects of experiences or situations. His or her **message** is the new insight or sense of truth gained as a result. To understand the writer's purpose and message in reflective writing, examine all the elements of the text:

- Consider the title.

- Notice the writer's direct statements about the meaning of an experience. These may appear at the beginning of the piece and again at the end in a slightly different way.

- Look for words and phrases that are emphasized or repeated.

Reflective writing is often very direct and the writer's purpose may be obvious. The author attempts to re-create an experience for the reader and show how it changed his or her understanding.

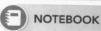

PRACTICE Work on your own to read the passage and answer the questions.

Some people feel they can't live without a phone, and maybe that's true. But it's not true for me. When I first bought a phone, I felt my world expand. I could post and text and chat in countless ways. But then I noticed something odd: I felt lonely. When I hung out with friends, we were distracted, disconnected. I asked myself, Why should a social media post matter more than the people I'm with? I saw that my phone had taken over my life. So, I got rid of it. Now, I'm back in the real world, and I like it here very much.

1.   Mark details that show the writer's thought process.

2.   Explain the author's purpose for writing this text.

3.   What message, or insight, does the author express in this passage?

About the Author

Cailin Loesch (b. 1997) is a web correspondent for *Teen Kids News*, which is an Emmy Award–winning television series.

Is Our Gain Also Our Loss?

Concept Vocabulary

 ANNOTATE

As you read the essay, you will encounter these words.

gradually	nostalgic	continuation

Base Words and Context A **base word** is the simplest form of a word. The addition of a prefix or suffix (or both) forms a new word. You can use base words along with context to figure out the meanings of unfamiliar words.

> **Unfamiliar Word:** *considerate*
>
> **Base:** *consider*, which means "think"
>
> **Context:** We were late, but Kitty was **considerate** and kind enough to drive us.
>
> **Analysis:** Kitty is described in a positive way, and *considerate* is paired with *kind*. *Considerate* might mean "thinking about the feelings of others."

PRACTICE As you read the essay, use your understanding of base words to determine the meanings of unfamiliar words. Mark your notes in the open space next to the text.

Comprehension Strategy

 ANNOTATE

Make Connections

When you **make connections** while reading, you look for relationships between ideas in a text and your personal experiences, other texts you have read, and society. To help make connections, ask questions like these as you read.

- What experiences have I had that relate to the situation being described?
- How are the ideas in this text similar to ideas I've read in other texts?
- How do the ideas in this text relate to the society I live in and the larger world?

Then, combine the connections you make, to create a deeper understanding.

© Pearson Education, Inc., or its affiliates. All rights reserved.

 TEKS
5.E. Make connections to personal experiences, ideas in other texts, and society.

PRACTICE As you read, mark details that connect to your personal experiences, other texts, and society. Note your observations in the open space next to the text.

Is Our Gain Also Our Loss?

Cailin Loesch

BACKGROUND

New technology changes our daily world with ever-increasing speed, often causing things to become obsolete, or out-of-date. These changes can leave older people longing for what they feel was the simpler, less complicated world of their youth. Is every generation destined to long for the past?

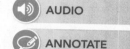

AUDIO

ANNOTATE

1   "When I was your age, I had to wait for the hourly report on TV in order to get the information that you have right at your fingertips. That's the problem with the world today."

2   It was the summer of 2012, and I was standing in the kitchen with my dad and sister—holding my iPhone—a towel and bathing suit thrown over my shoulder. I had just finished reading aloud the full-day weather report, and, until my dad spoke, had nothing on my mind but the gleaming pool water that seemed to be calling my name. I waited a moment for his comment to process, then looked down at my phone, analyzing it in a way that I had never before: feeling the cold, hard metal in my palm, and the smooth, sleek screen underneath my thumb.

3   I asked Dad to elaborate on his comment.

4   "When I was a young boy, we had a pool in our backyard. My brothers and I weren't allowed to go swimming until the temperature reached 75 degrees—not one degree less. And so we boys spent our summer mornings waiting by the TV for the hourly report that read the temperature, praying that it would say the number we wanted it to so that we could dive in. I have vivid memories of those mornings."

5   Suddenly, life in the 1970s seemed distant, and people detached. It occurred to me that my dad has experienced life like I will never know it, and that I have experienced life like my children will never know. I even started to think about how things have changed in the years that I've been alive. It's not just technology that's changing, either: It's our way of living. I've seen it with my own eyes, and it's only becoming clearer as the years go by.

gradually (GRAJ oo uhl
ee) *adv.*

MEANING:

6   **Gradually**, evenings spent doing homework at lamp-lit desks covered in pencils, paper, and textbooks are turning into late nights under bedsheets and blankets, a Google Docs page pulled up, fingers typing aggressively on a keyboard that can barely be seen in the dark. It seems as though I am part of the last generation that will know the satisfied feeling of stapling together a completed research paper, pages still warm from the printer. People of the next generation will never go on a family trip to the local Blockbuster[1] in search of candy and a comedy for movie night. They might miss out on handwritten letters from their grandparents, available to read and reread for years. Do we even realize what we're all leaving behind?

7   This morning, I was sitting at the breakfast table eating cereal when my dad came in to say goodbye before he left for work. When he saw that I was eating Life cereal, a huge smile immediately crept across his face, and he started excitedly reciting a commercial that he remembered from his childhood. He called me into his office, where he threw himself down in front of his desktop computer to search for the ad on YouTube,[2] eager to take me back in time with him.

8   Watching the commercial, my modernly-adjusted ears picked up on a faint hum in the background of the actor's voices. There were no snappy graphics or fast-paced cuts. In fact, the colors were a bit faded and the actors' faces were only highlighted in dim lighting. Then I turned to my dad, who was still beaming, as if all the happy memories from his childhood were flashing before his eyes. Judging by his enthusiastic clapping at the end, he sure didn't seem to miss modern technology during those 30 seconds.

9   In a world of iPhones and missions to Mars, is it even possible that my childhood will ever be looked at in the way that I look at my dad's? By then, will our TV shows be even crisper? Will it be unimaginable that we needed long, easily tangled wires in our ears in order to listen to music? Will my kids marvel at the idea of us old-fashioned teenagers having to wait by wall outlets for our phones to get out of the dreaded red battery zone before heading out for the night? Will they laugh at us for using pieces of green paper to buy things?

nostalgic (nuh STAL jihk) *adj.*

MEANING:

10   The thing that has really stayed with me, though, is my dad's comment about how all these new technologies are a "problem." One day, will we late-millennials[3] feel **nostalgic** as we look back on our simpler days, where we sometimes got a 10-minute homework break when our laptops lost battery life, giving us an excuse to sit in peace in front of a warm fire while we waited for them to charge? Will a lack of instant-charging mechanisms

---

1. **Blockbuster** chain of stores where people rented movies in the form of physical DVDs or VHS tapes.
2. **YouTube** video-sharing website.
3. **late-millennials** people born between the early 1990s and the early 2000s.

become the new lack of a weather.com app? Will we pull out our old Nintendo 3DS XLs to smile at what was once the hottest new piece of technology, recalling memories of online play with friends, in the same way that my dad smiled at an old commercial? Will we wish that things had never changed? They say that you should never try to fix what's not broken. Does the charm of the way things are now trump the need for things that are fresher, newer, and more advanced? Will we ever reach a point where there is no possible way to make any more "improvements"? And does this possibly inevitable peak signal impending doom or the continuation of tradition?

11   In my last-period sociology class the other day, the teacher ended a class discussion about the impact of changing technology on society with a statement that summarized my thoughts on the matter and left me with something to think about:

12   "I don't know how new technology will affect future generations, and I don't know if it will do more good or bad."

13   I couldn't have said it better myself. ✦

Mark the base word or indicate another strategy you used that helped you determine meaning.

continuation (kuhn tihn yoo AY shuhn) *n.*

MEANING:

BUILD INSIGHT

 NOTEBOOK

Response

1. Personal Connections The author mentions the saying "You should never try to fix what's not broken." Do you agree? Explain.

Comprehension

2. Strategy: Make Connections (a) Cite specific connections you made to your own experiences, other texts, and society as you read the essay. **(b)** How did these connections add to your understanding?

Analysis and Discussion

3. Analyze What is the author's attitude toward the technology of her youth? Explain, citing details from the text.

4. Interpret In paragraph 8, what idea is the author expressing when she says that her father "didn't seem to miss modern technology during those 30 seconds"? Explain.

5. Get Ready for Close Reading Choose a passage from the text that you find especially interesting or important. You'll discuss the passage with your group during Close-Read activities.

Work on your own to answer the questions in your notebook. Use text evidence to support your responses.

WORKING AS A GROUP
Discuss your responses to the Analysis and Discussion questions with your group. If necessary, revise your original answers to reflect what you learn from your discussion.

EQ Notes Is technology helpful or harmful to society?

What have you learned about technology and society from reading this essay? Go to your Essential Question Notes and record your observations and thoughts about "Is Our Gain Also Our Loss?"

⬡ TEKS
5.E. Make connections to personal experience, ideas in other texts, and society.

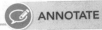

IS OUR GAIN ALSO OUR LOSS?

Close Read

ANNOTATE

PRACTICE Complete the following activities. Use text evidence to support your responses.

1. **Present and Discuss** With your group, share the passages from the selection that you found especially interesting. Discuss what you notice, the questions you have, and the conclusions you reach. For example, you might focus on the following passages:

   • Paragraph 5: Discuss what the author means in saying, "It's not just technology that's changing, either: It's our way of living."

   • Paragraphs 6–9: Discuss the author's conversations with her father.

   • Paragraph 10: Discuss the idea of a "continuation of tradition."

2. **Reflect on Your Learning** What new ideas or insights did you uncover during your second reading of the text?

NOTEBOOK

WORD NETWORK

Add words that are related to technology and society from the text to your Word Network.

LANGUAGE STUDY

Concept Vocabulary

Why These Words? The vocabulary words are related.

gradually	nostalgic	continuation

1. With your group, determine what the words have in common. Write your ideas.

2. Add another word that fits the category. _____

3. Confirm your understanding of these words by using them logically in a paragraph. Use each word only once.

Word Study

Latin Suffix: -ation The Latin suffix -ation means "the condition or process of." For example, the vocabulary word *continuation* is based on the verb *continue*. With your group, brainstorm for five other verbs that can be turned into nouns by adding the suffix -ation. Note that the e at the end of the word may drop to add the suffix. Then, scan the essay to find another noun that contains the suffix -ation.

TEKS
9.A. Explain the author's purpose and message within a text.

Genre / Text Elements

Author's Purpose and Message In a reflective essay, the **author's purpose** is to examine, or reflect on, an aspect of life. The author's **message** is the insight he or she gains from this reflection. The language the author uses fits this purpose and helps express the message. For example, in this essay, Cailin Loesch's diction and use of rhetorical questions reveal her purpose and help express her insight.

EXAMPLE: Language, Purpose, and Message

LANGUAGE	REFLECTIVE PURPOSE	EXAMPLES FROM THE ESSAY
Diction: types of words an author chooses	• shows what the writer felt • shows how he or she thought through an issue	*I waited a moment for his comment to process, then looked down at my phone, analyzing it in a way that I had never before…*
Rhetorical Questions: questions asked for effect or to raise a point, rather than to be answered	• pulls readers in • introduces issues • shows questions the author asked him- or herself	*Do we even realize what we're all leaving behind?*

 NOTEBOOK

PRACTICE Work on your own to answer the questions. Then, discuss your answers with your group.

1. **(a)** Identify at least three examples of diction in paragraph 2 that relate to the author's thought process—how she thinks about information. **(b) Analyze** What new understanding is she beginning to consider in this paragraph?

2. **(a) Analyze** Identify three additional examples of reflective diction in paragraph 5.
   (b) Interpret Explain how this diction helps the reader understand the writer's thinking.

3. **Interpret** What insight, or message, does the writer share in this essay? Explain.

4. **Interpret** How does the author's use of rhetorical questions in paragraphs 9–10 reveal her purpose for writing and help to express her message? Explain.

IS OUR GAIN ALSO OUR LOSS?

Conventions

Relative Clauses A dependent clause that acts as an adjective in a sentence is called a **relative clause** or an adjective clause. A relative clause begins with either a relative pronoun or a relative adverb. When a relative clause is connected to an independent clause, it creates a complex sentence.

- A **relative pronoun** relates the clause to the noun it modifies. Common relative pronouns are *who, whom, whose, that,* and *which.*

  EXAMPLE: The <u>firefighter</u> *who rescued the cats* <u>is</u> a hero.

- Relative clauses may also start with **relative adverbs:** *when, where,* or *why.* These types of relative clauses modify nouns that are places or times.

  EXAMPLE: The <u>cafe</u> *where we ate biscuits* <u>was</u> crowded.

Notice that in all of the examples, the relative clause appears immediately after the noun it modifies. In addition, the verb that follows the relative clause agrees with the subject of the sentence.

> **TIP:** In the examples, subjects are underlined once, verbs are underlined twice, and the relative clauses are set in italics.

INTERACTIVITY

NOTEBOOK

READ IT Mark the relative clause in each sentence from the essay. Then, mark the noun it modifies. State whether the clause begins with a relative pronoun or a relative adverb.

1. I even started to think about how things have changed in the years that I've been alive.

2. Then I turned to my dad, who was still beaming…

3. One day, will we late-millennials feel nostalgic as we look back on our simpler days, where we sometimes got a 10-minute homework break…

WRITE IT Write a paragraph in which you describe your favorite piece of technology. Then, edit it to create at least two complex sentences that use relative clauses. Make sure to maintain correct subject-verb agreement in the edited sentences.

TEKS

1.D. Participate in student-led discussions by eliciting and considering suggestions from other group members, taking notes, and identifying points of agreement and disagreement.

10.D.i. Edit drafts using standard English conventions, including complete complex sentences with subject-verb agreement and avoidance of splices, run-ons, and fragments.

10.D.v. Edit drafts using standard English conventions including pronouns, including relative.

Speaking and Listening

A **group discussion** is an informal exchange of ideas among three or more people.

Take part in a **group discussion** about ways in which our views of technology change. Choose one of the following options:

○ Identify a game, device, or other type of technology that you once thought was great but now think is outdated. Discuss the reasons your feelings about this technology changed.

○ Identify a game, device, or other type of technology that you think has stood the test of time. Explain why you think this example continues to be fun, useful, or current.

Take notes throughout the discussion, and identify points on which you agree and disagree. Once you feel you have fully explored everyone's ideas, write up a summary of the conversation.

Take Notes Before and During the Discussion Use the chart to gather ideas and examples you might share during the discussion. Add new ideas, questions, and thoughts to the chart as you participate in the discussion.

INTERACTIVITY

CHANGING VIEWS ON TECHNOLOGY	
What type of technology will you discuss?	
When was it most popular? What purpose did it serve? Does it still serve that purpose?	
How did you feel when you first heard about it or saw it?	
Have your feelings about it changed? In what way are they different? Why?	
Do you feel the technology left a lasting impact on you or on society? Why or why not?	

EQ Notes Before moving on to a new selection, go to your Essential Question Notes and record any additional thoughts or observations you may have about "Is Our Gain Also Our Loss?"

THE BLACK HOLE OF
TECHNOLOGY

The selection you are
about to read is a
persuasive essay.

Reading Persuasive Essays

A **persuasive essay** is a short nonfiction work in which a writer
presents an argument and attempts to convince readers to think a
certain way or take a certain action.

PERSUASIVE ESSAY

Author's Purpose
- to convince or persuade readers
- to argue for or against an idea

Characteristics
- statement of the writer's claim or position
- reasons and evidence that support the claim
- persuasive techniques, such as appeals to readers' emotions
- rhetorical devices, or special patterns of language, that add emotion or emphasis
- often, an opposing position that is presented and refuted

Structure
- an introduction, a body, and a conclusion that flow logically and make the author's ideas clear

⊛ TEKS

8.E.i. Analyze characteristics
and structures of argumentative
text by identifying the claim.

8.E.ii. Analyze characteristics
and structures of argumentative
text by explaining how the
author uses various types
of evidence to support the
argument.

8.E.iii. Analyze characteristics
and structures of argumentative
text by identifying the intended
audience or reader.

Take a Minute!

 NOTEBOOK

CHOOSE IT With a partner, decide which of the titles is most
likely a persuasive essay. Discuss your thinking.

Fighting for Breath: The Effects of Air Pollution

Too Much Money Can Ruin Your Life

The History of Submarines

Genre / Text Elements

Claim, Evidence, and Audience The **claim** is the writer's position, the idea he or she wants the **audience**, or readers, to accept. In effective persuasion, the writer is aware of the audience and what they know, think, and feel about a topic. He or she tailors the argument to the audience, using reasons and evidence that will convince them.

To identify the claim, look for direct statements of the writer's position. The author may or may not use signal phrases such as "I think" or "in my opinion."

> **TIP:** To clarify audience and argument, imagine that you must persuade a toddler and a teen to go to bed on time. In each case, the claim and reasons are similar, but the ways in which you present them would be different.

Persuasive writers use different types of **evidence** to develop the claim.

TYPE OF EVIDENCE	EXAMPLE
Facts: information, including dates and numerical data, that can be proved true	On August 21, 2017, North America experienced a solar eclipse.
Examples: specific instances of a general idea	To safely view the event, observers needed special equipment, such as eclipse glasses or pinhole projectors.
Personal Observations: explanations from the writer's experience or knowledge	To me, it looked like the moon was on fire just before and after totality.
Anecdotes: brief stories that illustrate a situation	For a moment, all of us were united and watching the sky. We cheered as the world went dark. It was an eclipse party!

 NOTEBOOK

PRACTICE Work on your own to identify the claim in each example and the type of evidence used as support.

1. Social media has changed our lives for the better. For example, in the past, most people only consumed media, but today millions actually create media, posting photos, cartoons, videos, and other products.

2. According to the study, teens spend more than eight hours a day consuming media of some kind. In my view, that time should be restricted and students should be reading instead.

About the Author

Leena Khan (b. 2001) is an aspiring author. Khan lives in Saudi Arabia.

The Black Hole of Technology

Concept Vocabulary

 ANNOTATE

As you read "The Black Hole of Technology," you will encounter these words.

devouring	process	consumed

Context Clues The **context** of a word is the other words and phrases that appear close to it in a text. You can use clues in the context to clarify the meanings of unfamiliar words.

> Antonym, or **contrast**, is a type of context clue that shows differences.
>
> **EXAMPLE** Amelia's **antiquated** computer is much slower than my <u>brand new</u> laptop.
>
> > **Analysis:** Since the capability of Amelia's antiquated computer is contrasted with that of a new one, *antiquated* probably means the opposite of *brand new*, or "outdated; old."

PRACTICE As you read "The Black Hole of Technology," study the context to clarify the meanings of unfamiliar words. Mark your observations in the open space next to the text.

Comprehension Strategy

 ANNOTATE

Summarize

A *summary* is a shorter version of a text that maintains the meaning and logical order of the original. When you **summarize**, you separate out the key ideas and details in a text and make sure you understand them. You may write a summary down, but you may also simply keep it in your mind as you read. Follow these steps to summarize:

- Pause after any section that you find confusing.
- Mark the subject and note details that show *what* it is, *why* it is important, and *how* it relates to other ideas.
- Restate the key ideas and details in your own words, maintaining the meaning and order of the original text.

PRACTICE As you read, summarize sections of the essay that may be unclear after a first reading. Write your summaries in the open space next to the text.

 TEKS

2.B. Use context such as definition, analogy, and examples to clarify the meaning of words.

6.D. Paraphrase and summarize texts in ways that maintain meaning and logical order.

The Black Hole of Technology

Leena Khan

BACKGROUND

The first smartphone was introduced in 1993. Since then, smartphones have become the fastest-selling devices in history. By 2013, 22% of the world's total population owned a smartphone. Although many people also own personal computers, the smartphone is a portable device that allows people to stay connected wherever they go.

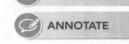

🔊 AUDIO

✏ ANNOTATE

1 The black hole of endless, unimportant streams of technology-enabled information is **devouring** everyone living in the twenty-first century. No matter how much people may look at information, it does not mean they are absorbing it. Equating quality with speed and volume, people may read thousands of news headlines broadcasted across the world daily, yet they will forget them in a couple of hours. No one stops to **process** information anymore to determine its significance or importance. No one appreciates the value of personal interaction or nature. Everything is go, go, go. Not once do we stop. Before being introduced to my phone and computer, I had been more appreciative of the world around me. Now, I'm always **consumed** by my "tech," and I never stop to take a break.

2 "Did you guys see what Miley Cyrus[1] posted?" My friend Fouly only peeled her eyes away from her iPhone screen to ask us that question. I glanced around at my friends, and they all quickly checked Instagram[2] in the hopes that they hadn't missed Miley's latest update. I, on the other hand, glanced out the window separating us from the beautiful weather outside. We were 15 friends sitting inside under artificial lighting and with our

Mark context clues or indicate another strategy you used that helped you determine meaning.

devouring (dih VOW rihng) *v.*

MEANING:

process (PRAH sehs) *v.*

MEANING:

consumed (kuhn SOOMD) *adj.*

MEANING:

1. **Miley Cyrus** celebrity who has achieved fame as an actress and a singer.
2. **Instagram** online social-media platform.

hands glued to our phones on a Friday, when the enticing warmth of the sun and delicate breeze were begging us to run around outside. Of course, our ears were deaf to nature's pleas, just like any other teenager nowadays. I put my phone down to shut the curtains, then I continued to mindlessly scroll through Miley's Instagram page.

3   I found myself longing for that Instagram page a week later, in an entirely different country. The scorching sun baked the back of my neck as my family and I walked along the wide, crowded dirt path on our way to visit yet another Cambodian temple. I slipped my phone out of my bag to check for a signal, but before I could even unlock it, it was snatched out of my hands.

4   "Leena, you're heading toward one of the most well preserved ancient wonders in the world. It would do you well to appreciate your surroundings!" my dad scolded.

5   My phone was wailing at me from the tight grip his hands had on it, but I had no choice but to ignore it, like I had been forced to do for the entire fall break. Huffing, I looked up and drank in our surroundings. There were tents perched on the sides of the sandy roads, and a couple of half-naked boys were jumping into a murky lake nearby. A toddler was laughing her head off, playing with an old man who I assumed was her grandfather. I missed all of this liveliness, the beauty of a community, because I was trapped in the black hole of technology. Everyone around me was smiling, despite having to live their lives in poverty. Then I noticed something I hadn't before: no one had a cellphone on them. There were no TVs, no radios, and their music came from live instruments instead of mp3 players and iPods. These people had nothing. Some of them were even walking around without shoes! How could they look so happy? Then I thought . . . Maybe it's because they don't have all that modern technology. They aren't subjected to the black hole of endless information.

6   I carried my insightful observations all the way to the temple, and my breath caught in my throat when we got there. It was stunning. When the guide started a long speech about the origin of the temple, I turned to face him. Then I realized I was inside of the black hole again. I was paying attention to the information the guide was throwing at me instead of also recognizing this once-in-a-lifetime experience. When would I be able to visit one of the seven wonders of the world again? The answer was pretty clear, so keeping one ear with the guide, and turning the rest of myself to the temple, I soaked in the extraordinary sight before me. For once, I wasn't digesting useless information. I wasn't typing into my phone, or watching any screen at all. In a life of go, go, go I had finally stopped.

7   It was then that I vowed that the next time my friends and I are absorbed in our phones on a sunny day, I won't close the curtains. Next time I'm walking along any road, I'll value my surroundings instead of texting on a device. From now on, I will make sure that the endless information flying my way won't go in one ear and out the other. I will find the significance in things and recognize it, because that's something many people fail to do—by falling into the technology trap. Escape the black hole of technology, because when you do . . . you feel free. ❧

BUILD INSIGHT

 NOTEBOOK

Response

1. **Personal Connections** Have you ever experienced—or been aware of others experiencing—a feeling of disconnection from the real world because of technology? Describe your experience.

Work on your own to answer the questions in your notebook. Use text evidence to support your responses.

Comprehension

2. **Reading Check (a)** What does the author do when a friend points out a new Miley Cyrus post? **(b)** Where do the author and her family go on vacation? **(c)** Why does the author's father take away her cell phone?

3. **Strategy: Summarize (a)** Identify a passage you summarized as you read. **(b)** How did summarizing help you better understand the text? Explain.

Analysis and Discussion

4. **Evaluate** Kahn says that both her cell phone and the guide at the temple are part of the same "black hole." Do you think that's true? Explain.

5. **Speculate** Do you think Kahn will be able to "find the significance in things" as she hopes to do after she returns home? Explain.

6. **Get Ready for Close Reading** Choose a passage from the text that you find especially interesting or important. You'll discuss the passage with your group during Close-Read activities.

WORKING AS A GROUP

Discuss your responses to the Analysis and Discussion questions with your group.

If necessary, revise your original answers to reflect what you learn from your discussion.

EQ Notes Is technology helpful or harmful to society?

What have you learned about technology and society from reading this essay? Go to your Essential Question Notes and record your observations and thoughts about "The Black Hole of Technology."

 TEKS

6.A. Describe personal connections to a variety of sources, including self-selected texts.

6.D. Paraphrase and summarize texts in ways that maintain meaning and logical order.

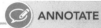

THE BLACK HOLE OF
TECHNOLOGY

Close Read

ANNOTATE

PRACTICE Complete the following activities. Use text evidence to support your responses.

1. **Present and Discuss** With your group, share the passages from the essay that you found especially interesting. Discuss what you notice, the questions you have, and the conclusions you reach. For example, you might focus on the following passages:

   • Paragraph 5: Discuss Kahn's analysis of the relationship between technology and unhappiness.

   • Paragraph 6: Discuss why Kahn turns away from the tour guide.

2. **Reflect on Your Learning** What new ideas or insights did you uncover during your second reading of the text?

NOTEBOOK

LANGUAGE STUDY

Concept Vocabulary

Why These Words? The vocabulary words are related.

devouring	process	consumed

1. With your group, determine what the words have in common. Write your ideas.

2. Add another word that fits the category. _____

3. Write a paragraph about your experiences with technology. Use all of the vocabulary words in the paragraph.

- -

Word Study

Multiple-Meaning Words A multiple-meaning word has more than one definition. For example, the vocabulary word *process* has many different meanings and may be a noun or a verb. You may have used context clues to determine which meaning applies in this essay. You can also use a dictionary to determine meaning. Complete this activity:

1. Use a digital dictionary (online or in an app) to find four meanings of *process*, two as a noun and two as a verb. **2.** Explain what *process* means in this essay. **3.** Write three sentences using the word *process* in each of the other three meanings you found.

WORD NETWORK

Add words that are related to technology and society from the text to your Word Network.

🟡 **TEKS**

2.A. Use print or digital resources to determine the meaning, syllabication, pronunciation, word origin, and part of speech.

6.F. Respond using newly acquired vocabulary as appropriate.

8.E.i. Analyze characteristics and structures of argumentative text by identifying the claim.

8.E.ii. Analyze characteristics and structures of argumentative text by explaining how the author uses various types of evidence to support the argument.

8.E.iii. Analyze characteristics and structures of argumentative text by identifying the intended audience or reader.

Genre / Text Elements

Claim, Evidence, and Audience In effective persuasive writing, an author states and defends a **claim**. He or she gives reasons to support the claim and **evidence** that shows the reasons are valid. In this essay, Kahn relies on two types of evidence that may be considered subjective, or personal.

> **TIP:** Subjective evidence, which can be perfectly valid, involves the writer's experiences or interpretations. Objective evidence is fact-based.

Subjective Types of Evidence

Personal Observations	remarks and explanations from the writer's own experience or knowledge
Anecdotes	brief stories that illustrate an idea or present an example

Strong persuasive writers also consider the **audience**, or readers, they are trying to reach, and what those people already know, think, and feel about a topic. They then tailor their ideas and evidence to convince that audience.

PRACTICE Work on your own to answer the questions. Then, share your responses with your group, using new vocabulary you have learned, such as *claim* or *persuasive*.

 NOTEBOOK

1. **Analyze** Record your answers in the chart. **(a)** Where does the author first state her claim? What is that claim? **(b)** Cite one example of each type of evidence listed and explain how each one supports the author's argument.

CLAIM:		
TYPE OF EVIDENCE	EXAMPLE	HOW IT SUPPORTS CLAIM
Personal Observation		
Anecdote		

2. **(a) Make Inferences** Who is Kahn's intended audience? For example, is she writing for other teens, the general public, her parents, or another group? Explain your thinking. **(b) Connect** Why does the author use the structure of a series of anecdotes to support her claim? Is that choice effective for her audience? Explain.

3. **(a) Assess** Do you think Kahn does a good job of persuading her intended audience? Why or why not? **(b) Evaluate** Do you find Kahn's argument personally convincing? Explain your answer.

THE BLACK HOLE OF
TECHNOLOGY

Author's Craft

Rhetorical Devices and Logical Fallacies **Rhetorical devices** are patterns of words that stress certain ideas and stir readers' feelings. These devices show correct reasoning. Writers may also use language that shows faulty, misleading reasoning. These are **logical fallacies**. Rhetorical devices strengthen arguments; logical fallacies weaken them.

TYPES OF RHETORICAL DEVICES AND LOGICAL FALLACIES

TERM AND DEFINITION	RHETORICAL DEVICE OR FALLACY?	EXAMPLES FROM THE ESSAY
Repetition: deliberate re-use of the same words or phrases	Rhetorical Device	*Everything is go, go, go.*
Charged Language: words with very strong positive or negative meanings	Can be either	*our ears were deaf to nature's pleas*
Overgeneralization: conclusion that is too broad and unsupported by facts	Fallacy	*Not once do we stop.*
Single Cause: assumption that one simple cause leads to a certain situation	Fallacy	*Before being introduced to my phone and computer, I had been more appreciative of the world…*

 NOTEBOOK

PRACTICE Work with your group to complete the activity and answer the questions.

1. **Analyze** Explain why each passage is an example of the type of rhetorical device indicated. Then, describe the effect of each.

   • **Charged Language:** *The black hole of endless, unimportant streams of technology-enabled information is devouring everyone…*

   • **Repetition:** *No one stops to process…No one appreciates the value…*

2. **Analyze** Explain why the first bulleted item is an overgeneralization and the second one is not. What is the difference?

   • No one appreciates the value of personal interaction or nature.

   • I will find the significance in things and recognize it, because that's something many people fail to do…

3. **(a) Summarize** In paragraph 5, why does the author think the people she observes are happy? **(b) Analyze** What logical fallacy does her conclusion represent? Explain.

4. **Analyze** Explain key differences between rhetorical devices and logical fallacies in this essay, especially in their effects on the strength of the argument.

 TEKS

9.G. Explain the differences between rhetorical devices and logical fallacies.

12.A. Generate student-selected and teacher-guided questions for formal and informal inquiry.

12.D. Identify and gather relevant information from a variety of sources.

12.H.i. Examine sources for reliability, credibility, and bias.

12.H.ii. Examine sources for faulty reasoning, such as hyperbole, emotional appeals, and stereotype.

Research

A **summary of research findings** is a document that lists research sources and briefly describes the most important ideas in each one.

ASSIGNMENT

In this essay, the author relies on personal observations to support her position that people are bombarded with too much information. Work with your group to conduct a formal inquiry into the accuracy of her argument. Find fact-based information that either proves or disproves her point. Identify at least three different relevant sources. Then, work together to gather information and write a **summary of research findings.**

Generate Questions Specific questions will help guide your research. Start with this question. Then, add two more of your own:

- *How much information does the average American take in daily?*

- _____

- _____

Conduct Research Use the checklist to make sure that all the sources you use are credible, reliable, and do not express bias or faulty reasoning.

INTERACTIVITY

EQ Notes Before moving on to a new selection, go to your Essential Question Notes and record any additional thoughts or observations you may have about "The Black Hole of Technology."

Source Checklist

Don't use any source that gets a "no" answer.

Credibility

- Is the author an authority on the subject?   yes ◯ no ◯
- Do at least two other sources agree with this source?   yes ◯ no ◯

Reliability

- Does the source go into depth?   yes ◯ no ◯
- Is the information current?   yes ◯ no ◯

Absence of Bias and Faulty Reasoning

Does the source:

- avoid hyperbole (excessive exaggeration)?   yes ◯ no ◯
- avoid stereotypes?   yes ◯ no ◯

THE FUN THEY HAD

The selection you are about to read is a science-fiction story.

Reading Science Fiction

Science fiction is a form of fiction that incorporates elements of actual or imagined science and technology. Science-fiction stories are often set in the future, in outer space, on other planets, or in a totally imaginary place.

SCIENCE FICTION

Author's Purpose
➔ to tell an imaginative story

Characteristics
➔ conveys a theme, or message about life

➔ features settings that are at least partly imaginary, such as the future, and that are often the source of conflict

➔ may have non-human characters, such as aliens or robots

➔ dialogue reflects details in the world of the story

Structure
➔ a sequence of related events (plot) that involves aspects of science or technology

Take a Minute!

 NOTEBOOK

CHOOSE IT! Choose at least three settings you would most likely find in a work of science fiction. Discuss your choices with a partner.

a colony on the moon

an ancient Aztec city

an American town right now

a galaxy far, far away

a freight-train in the 1930s

a traveling circus

Earth in a parallel universe

a science lab in the year 2000

⭐ TEKS

7.D. Analyze how the setting, including historical and cultural settings, influences character and plot development.

8.A. Demonstrate knowledge of literary genres such as realistic fiction, adventure stories, historical fiction, mysteries, humor, and myths.

Genre / Text Elements

Setting, Character, and Plot Development The **setting** of a story is the place and time in which it occurs. In some stories, the setting is merely a backdrop for the events. In science-fiction stories, however, the setting often influences the characters, creating conflicts that drive the plot.

> **TIP:** The cultural and historical aspects of a setting include a society's beliefs and traditions. These can be just as important as a story's physical setting.

EXAMPLE: Setting, Character, and Plot Development

- Place and Time: Earth, hundreds of years from now
- Historical/Cultural Details: The government has outlawed sleep. The people work every hour of every day. They never sleep, so they never dream.

Influence on Plot	Influence on Character
• Conflict Begins: Main character accidentally falls asleep and dreams. • Conflict Develops: After her dream, the main character is disturbed. She learns of others like her. Her actions lead to a rebellion.	By falling asleep illegally, the main character is awakened to the problems of her society. She stops being passive and becomes a leader.

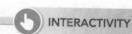 INTERACTIVITY

PRACTICE Work on your own to read the story information and answer the questions. Discuss your responses with your group.

Place: a spaceship on a 120-year journey to a distant planet

Time: the distant future

Plot Summary: When his hibernation pod opens early due to asteroid damage, the main character faces a conflict. Should he live alone on the ship for the rest of his life, or awaken another passenger? If he wakes her, he will doom her future. After much internal struggle, he wakes her up.

1. How does the setting influence the characters?

2. How does the setting create a conflict that drives the plot?

3. Could the same story take place on an airplane in the present day?

About the Author

Isaac Asimov (1920–1992) became a science-fiction fan after reading fantastic stories in magazines. Asimov's father discouraged his son's early interest, and described the magazines he loved as "junk." Still, Asimov's interest in science fiction continued, and he started writing his own stories at age eleven. At first, his stories were rejected, but Asimov developed into a visionary writer and became one of the most influential science-fiction authors of the twentieth century.

 TEKS

2.B. Use context such as definition, analogy, and examples to clarify the meaning of words.

5.F. Make inferences and use evidence to support understanding.

The Fun They Had

Concept Vocabulary

 ANNOTATE

As you read "The Fun They Had," you will encounter these words.

| sorrowfully | loftily | nonchalantly |

Context Clues The **context** of a word is the other words and phrases that appear close to it in a text. Clues in the context can help you figure out the meanings of unfamiliar words.

> **Synonyms** are context clues that show similarities.
>
> **EXAMPLE** Erin assumed her sister was **melancholy** and <u>sad</u> because her best friend had just moved away.
>
> **Analysis:** Erin refers to her sister as both *melancholy* and *sad*, so those words must have similar meanings. *Melancholy* must mean "gloomy; depressed."

PRACTICE As you read the story, study the context to determine the meanings of unfamiliar words. Make your observations in the open space next to the text.

Comprehension Strategy

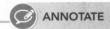 ANNOTATE

Make Inferences

An **inference** is an educated guess you make about aspects of a story that a writer hints at but doesn't state directly. To make inferences, connect evidence in a text with what you already know about life. Then, use that information to develop an informed idea about the story's characters, setting, and events.

> **EXAMPLE** This is an inference you might make as you read this story.
>
> **Passage:** *Margie even wrote about it that night in her diary. On the page headed May 17, 2155, she wrote, "'Today Tommy found a real book."*
>
> **Possible Inference:** Finding a "real" book seems to be an unusual event, so books are probably a thing of the past.

PRACTICE As you read the story, write your inferences in the open space next to the text. Mark the evidence you use to support each one.

The Fun They Had

Isaac Asimov

BACKGROUND

New methods of learning have been influenced by changes in technology. During ancient times, the Romans wrote on wax tablets. Children in the 1700s read and practiced writing on slates, or blackboards. In the 1900s, educational radio programs were introduced. In today's society, online education has become popular.

 AUDIO

 ANNOTATE

1   Margie even wrote about it that night in her diary. On the page headed May 17, 2155, she wrote, "Today Tommy found a real book."

2   It was a very old book. Margie's grandfather once said that when he was a little boy, his grandfather told him that there was a time when all stories were printed on paper.

3   They turned the pages, which were yellow and crinkly, and it was awfully funny to read words that stood still instead of moving the way they were supposed to—on a screen, you know. And then, when they turned back to the page before, it had the same words on it that it had had when they read it the first time.

4   "Gee," said Tommy, "what a waste. When you're through with the book, you just throw it away, I guess. Our television screen must have had a million books on it and it's good for plenty more. I wouldn't throw it away."

5   "Same with mine," said Margie. She was eleven and hadn't seen as many telebooks as Tommy had. He was thirteen.

6   She said, "Where did you find it?"

7   "In my house." He pointed without looking, because he was busy reading. "In the attic."

8   "What's it about?"

9   "School."

10   Margie was scornful. "School? What's there to write about school? I hate school." Margie always hated school, but now she hated it more than ever. The mechanical teacher had been giving her test after test in geography, and she had been doing worse and worse until her mother had shaken her head **sorrowfully** and sent for the county inspector.

11   He was a round little man with a red face and a whole box of tools with dials and wires. He smiled at her and gave her an apple, then took the teacher apart. Margie had hoped he wouldn't know how to put it together again, but he knew how all right and, after an hour or so, there it was again, large and ugly, with a big screen on which all the lessons were shown and the questions were asked. That wasn't so bad. The part she hated most was the slot where she had to put homework and test papers. She always had to write them out in a punch code[1] they made her learn when she was six years old, and the mechanical teacher calculated the mark in no time.

> **Why would anyone write about school?**

12   The inspector had smiled after he was finished and patted her head. He said to her mother, "It's not the little girl's fault, Mrs. Jones. I think the geography sector was geared a little too quick. Those things happen sometimes. I've slowed it up to an average ten-year level. Actually, the overall pattern of her progress is quite satisfactory." And he patted Margie's head again.

13   Margie was disappointed. She had been hoping they would take the teacher away altogether. They had once taken Tommy's teacher away for nearly a month because the history sector had blanked out completely.

14   So she said to Tommy, "Why would anyone write about school?"

---

1. **punch code** card containing data that was used to program computers during the 1950s, when this story was written.

15   Tommy looked at her with very superior eyes. "Because it's not our kind of school, stupid. This is the old kind of school that they had hundreds and hundreds of years ago." He added **loftily**, pronouncing the word carefully, "Centuries ago."

16   Margie was hurt. "Well, I don't know what kind of school they had all that time ago." She read the book over his shoulder for a while, then said, "Anyway, they had a teacher."

17   "Sure they had a teacher, but it wasn't a regular teacher. It was a man."

18   "A man? How could a man be a teacher?"

19   "Well, he just told the boys and girls things and gave them homework and asked them questions."

20   "A man isn't smart enough."

21   "Sure he is. My father knows as much as my teacher."

22   "He can't. A man can't know as much as a teacher."

23   "He knows almost as much I betcha."

24   Margie wasn't prepared to dispute that. She said, "I wouldn't want a strange man in my house to teach me."

25   Tommy screamed with laughter, "You don't know much, Margie. The teachers didn't live in the house. They had a special building and all the kids went there."

26   "And all the kids learned the same thing?"

27   "Sure, if they were the same age."

28   "But my mother says a teacher has to be adjusted to fit the mind of each boy and girl it teaches and that each kid has to be taught differently."

29   "Just the same, they didn't do it that way then. If you don't like it, you don't have to read the book."

30   "I didn't say I didn't like it," Margie said quickly. She wanted to read about those funny schools.

31   They weren't even half finished when Margie's mother called, "Margie! School!"

32   Margie looked up. "Not yet, Mamma."

33   "Now," said Mrs. Jones. "And it's probably time for Tommy, too."

34   Margie said to Tommy, "Can I read the book some more with you after school?"

35   "Maybe," he said, **nonchalantly**. He walked away whistling, the dusty old book tucked beneath his arm.

36   Margie went into the schoolroom. It was right next to her bedroom, and the mechanical teacher was on and waiting for her. It was always on at the same time every day except Saturday and Sunday, because her mother said little girls learned better if they learned at regular hours.

Mark context clues or indicate another strategy you used that helped you determine meaning.

loftily (LAWF tih lee) *adv.*

MEANING:

Mark context clues or indicate another strategy you used that helped you determine meaning.

nonchalantly (non shuh LONT lee) *adv.*

MEANING:

37   The screen was lit up, and it said: "Today's arithmetic lesson is on the addition of proper fractions. Please insert yesterday's homework in the proper slot."

38   Margie did so with a sigh. She was thinking about the old schools they had when her grandfather's grandfather was a little boy. All the kids from the whole neighborhood came, laughing and shouting in the schoolyard, sitting together in the schoolroom, going home together at the end of the day. They learned the same things so they could help one another on the homework and talk about it.

39   And the teachers were people. . . .

40   The mechanical teacher was flashing on the screen: "When we add the fractions ½ and ¼ . . . "

41   Margie was thinking about how the kids must have loved it in the old days. She was thinking about the fun they had. ❧

Response

1. Personal Connections Would you rather attend school the way you do today, or the way Margie and her brother do in the future? Explain.

Work on your own to answer the questions in your notebook. Use text evidence to support your responses.

Comprehension

2. Reading Check (a) What does Tommy find in the attic? **(b)** Why does Margie hate school now more than ever? **(c)** What surprises Margie about teachers of the past?

3. Strategy: Make Inferences (a) Give an example of an inference you made as you read this story. **(b)** Which text evidence helped you make that inference? **(c)** In what ways did making inferences affect your reading experience? Explain.

Analysis and Discussion

4. (a) Analyze How do Tommy and Margie feel about the book when they first look through it? **(b) Make a Judgment** Do their feelings change as the story progresses? Use evidence from the story to support your answer.

5. (a) Contrast In what ways is Margie's school different from school today? **(b) Compare** In what ways is it similar? **(c) Hypothesize** What aspects of this story do you think might actually occur in the future, and which do not seem likely? Explain.

6. Analyze Why do you think the author includes the description of the county inspector fixing Margie's teacher in paragraphs 11–13? What point does that scene make? Explain.

7. Get Ready for Close Reading Choose a passage from the text that you find especially interesting or important. You'll discuss the passage with your group during Close-Read activities.

WORKING AS A GROUP
Discuss your responses to the Analysis and Discussion questions with your group.
- Note agreements and disagreements.
- Summarize insights.
- Consider changes of opinion.

If necessary, revise your original answers to reflect what you learn from your discussion.

EQ Notes Is technology helpful or harmful to society?

What have you learned about technology and society from reading this story? Go to your Essential Question Notes and record your observations and thoughts about "The Fun They Had."

TEKS
5.F. Make inferences and use evidence to support understanding.

6.A. Describe personal connections to a variety of sources, including self-selected texts.

6.C. Use text evidence to support an appropriate response.

THE FUN THEY HAD

Close Read

 ANNOTATE

PRACTICE Complete the following activities. Use text evidence to support your responses.

1. **Present and Discuss** With your group, share the passages from the story that you found especially interesting. Discuss what you notice, the questions you have, and the conclusions you reach. For example, you might focus on the following passages:

   • Paragraph 4: Discuss Tommy's assessment of real books.

   • Paragraphs 17–32: Discuss Margie's attitude toward learning from Tommy and the book and how it compares to her attitude toward school.

2. **Reflect on Your Learning** What new ideas or insights did you uncover during your second reading?

 NOTEBOOK

WORD NETWORK

Add words that are related to technology and society from the text to your Word Network.

LANGUAGE STUDY

Concept Vocabulary

Why These Words? The vocabulary words are related.

| sorrowfully | loftily | nonchalantly |

1. With your group, determine what the words have in common. Write your ideas.

2. Add another word that fits the category. _____

3. With your group, write a sentence about the story. Then, have each person in your group choose one vocabulary word. Without telling which word you chose, take turns saying the sentence in a way that reflects the word. Discuss which vocabulary word each person meant to portray and how you know.

- -

Word Study

Sounds and Letters: the *sh* sound English words of French origin, such as the vocabulary word *nonchalant*, often use the letters *ch* to spell the *sh* sound. Write a paragraph in which you use all of the words listed here. Take turns reading your paragraphs aloud with your group.

machine   chef   mustache   parachute   ricochet

 TEKS

6.F. Respond using newly acquired vocabulary as appropriate.

7.D. Analyze how the setting, including historical and cultural settings, influences character and plot development.

Genre / Text Elements

Setting, Character, and Plot Development A story's **setting** is the time and place in which it occurs. It includes all the details of the physical location, as well as cultural and historical elements such as the following:

- the people's beliefs and values, and the traditions they think are important

- the ways in which the society is structured, including laws, rules, and common practices

In some stories, the setting is just a backdrop. In other stories, the setting is a source of conflicts. These conflicts influence the characters, causing them to react and change, which develops the plot.

PRACTICE Work on your own to complete the activity and answer the questions. Then, discuss your responses with your group, using new vocabulary, such as *cultural, setting* and *influence*.

1. **(a)** Where and when does the story take place? **(b) Compare and Contrast** In what ways is this setting similar to and different from a typical American town today? Explain.

2. **Analyze** Explain what each passage tells you about the cultural and historical setting of the story.

PASSAGES FROM "THE FUN THEY HAD"	CULTURAL AND HISTORICAL SETTING
Paragraph 1: Margie … book.	
Paragraph 2: It was … on paper.	
Paragraph 4: "Gee … away."	
Paragraph 10: The mechanical … inspector.	

3. **(a) Connect** Cite two conflicts the setting of the story creates for Margie.
   (b) Interpret How do these conflicts influence the development of Margie's character?

4. **(a) Analyze Cause and Effect** How does Margie change over the course of the story? What does she learn? **(b) Interpret** Do you think the conflicts she faces in the story end when the story ends? Explain.

THE FUN THEY HAD

Author's Craft

Multiple Themes A **theme** of a literary work is a message or insight about life that it expresses. A single work may express more than one theme. You may find clues to themes in all of a work's details:

- Look at the title. Does it make a direct statement? Does it have especially meaningful words?

- Figure out the situation. Is there a problem or struggle? How does it end? Is there a wish or hope? Is it fulfilled?

Two texts that share a basic topic may express similar themes. However, it's not unusual when two texts that share a topic convey surprisingly different themes.

> **TIP:** Theme is not a topic and can't be stated in one word or phrase. It is a statement that can be applied to life beyond the story you are reading.

 NOTEBOOK

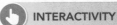 INTERACTIVITY

PRACTICE Work on your own to answer the questions. Then, discuss your responses with your group.

1. **Analyze** Note at least three details from "The Fun They Had" that support this theme: *Technology cannot replace human interaction.* Explain your choices.

2. Read the first stanza from the poem "All Watched Over By Machines of Loving Grace" (see the Independent Reading section of this unit for the full work). Then, answer the questions.

   > I like to think (and
   > the sooner the better!)
   > of a cybernetic meadow
   > where mammals and computers
   > live together in mutually
   > programming harmony
   > like pure water
   > touching clear sky.

   (a) Compare Do the characters in "The Fun They Had" find "harmony" in technology the way the speaker in the poem does? Explain. **(b) Make Inferences** What theme about the relationship between people and technology does this stanza of the poem begin to express? Explain. **(c) Compare and Contrast** In what ways is the theme of the poem similar to and different from the theme about technology expressed in "The Fun They Had"?

3. **(a) Analyze** What view of the future do both works express? **(b) Interpret** Formulate a theme that you think applies to both works. Explain your thinking.

⟳ TEKS

6.G. Discuss and write about the explicit or implicit meanings of text.

7.A. Infer multiple themes within and across texts using text evidence.

Composition

Dialogue is the conversations among characters in literary works. Authors use dialogue to move the plot forward, and to provide insights into characters' personalities.

ASSIGNMENT

With your group, write a **scene with dialogue** in which Margie describes finding the old book to one of her friends. Discuss each of the following genre options as a group. Together, decide which genre you will use:

◯ Write the scene in dramatic form with characters' names appearing at the beginning of each new line of dialogue. Place in brackets any descriptions or lines not spoken by the characters.

◯ Write the scene in short-story form. All descriptions will appear in paragraphs. Indicate who is speaking, and set lines of dialogue in quotation marks.

Discuss and Plan Discuss Margie's character and what her friends would be like. Then, describe how other aspects of this future time might be different from today and how to pull these ideas into the scene. Brainstorm for a few sample lines of dialogue that feel true to Margie's character and how you think her friend would react. Take notes during the discussion.

Draft Use your discussion notes and the story as background to develop the scene. Decide on a logical sequence of events. As you write, use precise words, vivid details, and descriptive language to show the setting and action.

Revise and Edit Work together to revise and edit the scene.

- Are the events arranged in a logical order?
- Are the word choices descriptive, and do they capture the futuristic setting in which the conversation takes place?
- Does the dialogue contribute to the reader's understanding of the characters and plot?

Present Present your group's scene to the class and answer any questions your classmates may have.

EQ Notes Before moving on to a new selection, go to your Essential Question Notes and record any additional thoughts or observations you may have about "The Fun They Had."

 TEKS

10.A. Plan a first draft by selecting a genre appropriate for a particular topic, purpose, and audience using a range of strategies such as discussion, background reading, and personal interests.

About the Authors

Brothers **Ivan Puig Domene** and **Andrés Padilla Domene** are artists living and working in Mexico. Ivan is a photographer and sculptor whose works have been exhibited in Germany, Canada, Brazil, Mexico, and the United States. Andrés is a filmmaker whose work includes documentaries, fiction films, and television shows.

Mexico's Abandoned Railways and the SEFT-1

Media Vocabulary

These words will be useful to you as you analyze, discuss, and write about photographs.

Composition: arrangement of the different elements in a work of art	• The composition may emphasize certain parts of a picture over others.
Background and Foreground: background is the part of an image that is furthest from the observer; foreground is the part of an image that is closest to the observer	• Background is usually the context, or setting, for the main subject of a photograph. • The subject usually appears in the foreground.
Camera Angle: position from which a photograph is taken	• Camera angles may be on-level with the subject, below it, or above it. • The angle may affect how much of a scene is visible in a photo. • The camera angle may add drama to a photo.

Comprehension Strategy

 NOTEBOOK

Synthesize Information

When you **synthesize information**, you pull together ideas from different sources in order to develop your own perspective. You allow your thinking about a topic to grow and change. To synthesize as you read, follow these steps:

- Notice important ideas and details in parts of a text or multiple texts on the same topic.
- Consider what you already know and how new information changes your thinking.
- Combine ideas and details to arrive at a new understanding.

PRACTICE As you study this photo essay, synthesize your observations of the photos with information in the captions to arrive at a new understanding. Use the Take Notes section to capture your ideas.

 TEKS

5.H. Synthesize information to create new understanding.

8.F. Analyze characteristics of multimodal and digital texts.

Mexico's Abandoned Railways and the SEFT-1

Ivan Puig Domene and Andrés Padilla Domene

BACKGROUND

In the late 1800s, Mexico's railroad system covered nearly 6,000 miles. Over the next century, the system went through two major upgrades. By 1995, however, the railroad was losing money and was largely abandoned. It soon fell into decay. Two brothers, Ivan Puig Domene and Andrés Padilla Domene, both artists, designed and built a vehicle that could travel on both the railroad tracks and open ground. They named the vehicle SEFT-1. In 2010, they set out to travel the abandoned rail line.

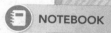 NOTEBOOK

IMAGE 1: Ivan and Andrés built the aluminum road and rail vehicle SEFT-1 themselves. Here, the SEFT-1 is pictured at the base of the Yuhualixqui volcano just outside Mexico City.

IMAGE 2: This photograph shows the SEFT-1 on the Metlac Bridge between Mexico City and Veracruz. In 1881, Mexican artist José María Velasco painted this same spot, creating "Curved Bridge of the Mexican Railway on the Metlac Ravine," a work that became extremely famous. Today, the bridge is in ruins.

TAKE NOTES

IMAGE 3: This photograph shows the interior of the SEFT-1, which is equipped with navigation tools the brothers used to determine the time and their location.

TAKE NOTES

IMAGE 4: Occasionally, the SEFT-1 met up with railways that are still in use. The brothers met some of the people working on the tracks and in the stations and often took their pictures. This photograph was taken near Durango, Mexico.

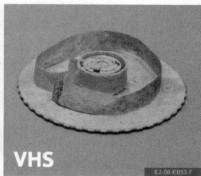

KCT   E7-04-FD164.1   VHS   E2-08-EB53.7   CD   E6-32-FP59.8

IMAGE 5: This combined photo shows an audio cassette tape, part of a VHS video cassette, and an audio CD. These are three of a collection of more than three hundred objects the brothers collected during their journey.

 **NOTEBOOK**

Work on your own to answer the questions in your notebook. Use text evidence to support your responses.

Response

1. **Personal Connections** How do you think you would react to an exploration of abandoned places like the Mexican railway? For example, would you find it exciting, frightening, uninteresting? Explain.

Comprehension

2. **Reading Check (a)** Where is the SEFT-1 in Image 1? **(b)** What similarity does Image 2 have to a famous Mexican painting? **(c)** What kind of decayed items appear in Image 5?

3. **Strategy: Synthesize Information** In what ways did reading the captions help you create a new understanding of the photographs? Cite one example.

WORKING AS A GROUP

Discuss your responses to the Analysis and Discussion questions with your group.

- Note agreements and disagreements.
- Summarize insights.
- Consider changes of opinion.

If necessary, revise your original answers to reflect what you learn from your discussion.

Analysis and Discussion

4. **Interpret** Study image 2 and read the caption. Why do you think the brothers chose to duplicate a classic painting with their new technology?

5. **Speculate** Why do you think the brothers collected and photographed lost and broken items, such as the ones in Image 5?

6. **Essential Question** *Is technology helpful or harmful to society?* What have you learned about technology and society from reading this photo essay? Go to your Essential Question notes and record your observations and thoughts about the photo essay.

Close Review

 NOTEBOOK

Review the photo essay again and note interesting details. Record any new observations that seem interesting to you. Then, write a question and your conclusion.

MY **QUESTION:**

MY **CONCLUSION:**

MEDIA VOCABULARY

Use these words as you discuss and write about the photo essay.

composition
background/foreground
camera angle

Composition

A **research report** is a type of nonfiction that presents information gathered from a variety of sources in a way that conveys a clear controlling idea, or thesis.

ASSIGNMENT

With a partner, prepare a **research report** about the SEFT-1. Choose one of the following options:

○ **Option 1:** design and construction of the vehicle
Conduct research about the brothers's design process and the materials they used, as well as the time it took to construct the vehicle and make it operational.

○ **Option 2:** route the brothers traveled
Locate information about the span of the railway before it was partially abandoned, which sections are still in use, and which portions the brothers traveled.

After you have gathered information, choose the best mode of delivery—written text, oral presentation, or multimodal presentation—and prepare your report.

TIP: You may find relevant information about the SEFT-1 project in Spanish. Invite any Spanish speakers in your class to translate, or seek out others in your school or community to help.

Choose a Mode of Delivery After you gather information, discuss the best way to organize and present it. Mark your choice.

○ **Written Report:** Write a polished text that includes an introduction in which you state your thesis, body paragraphs in which you present your findings, and a conclusion in which you restate your thesis.

○ **Oral Presentation:** Write a set of detailed notes you can use to deliver your findings orally.

○ **Multimodal Presentation:** Use slide presentation software or a set of posters to present verbal text. Enhance the information by including media elements, such as videos, music, photos, or maps.

EQ Notes Before moving on to a new selection, go to your Essential Question Notes and record what your learned from the photo essay.

Paraphrase, Don't Plagiarize Plagiarism is the act of using the language or ideas of another person without permission. Follow these steps to avoid plagiarism:

- Properly cite information and ideas that are not common knowledge. Use the citation style, such as MLA, that your teacher prefers.
- **Paraphrase**, or restate the ideas of others in your own words. Note that even when you paraphrase, you must still cite the source because the ideas are not your own.
- If you want to use an author's exact words, set them in quotation marks and cite the source accurately.

 TEKS

8.F. Analyze characteristics of multimodal and digital texts.

12.G. Differentiate between paraphrasing and plagiarism when using source materials.

12.J. Use an appropriate mode of delivery, whether written, oral, or multimodal, to present results.

About the Podcast

All Things Considered began airing in 1971 and was the first news program on National Public Radio (NPR). It has since won numerous awards for excellence. The daily radio show mixes news stories with interviews, analysis, and commentaries on the arts and culture. In 2005, NPR first started making its programs available in the form of podcasts.

Bored . . . and Brilliant?
A Challenge to Disconnect From Your Phone

Media Vocabulary

These words describe characteristics of podcasts, a type of multimodal text. Use them as you analyze, discuss, and write about the selection.

podcast: digital audio or video file or recording, usually part of a series, that can be downloaded from the Internet	• Many podcasts invite listeners to leave comments or share their thoughts about the shows. • Some podcasts are accompanied by a transcript, or the text of the spoken words.
host: someone who introduces and talks to the guests on a television or radio program	• Most hosts prepare for a program by researching the topic and the background of the guests.
interview: recorded conversation in which someone is asked questions about his or her life, experiences, or opinions	• An interesting interview usually reveals new information about the person being interviewed. • The interviewer usually creates a list of questions beforehand, but asks unplanned follow-up questions during the interview itself.

Comprehension Strategy

 NOTEBOOK

Notetaking

When you take notes while listening to an audio presentation, you jot down important details, your own thoughts, and questions. Taking notes can help you pay attention and remember information later. Apply these strategies to take effective notes:

- **Note timecodes:** Jot down the timecode so you can find sections later.
- **Use phrases and symbols:** Don't write full sentences. Jot down phrases and key details. If you hear a word you don't know, write it down and add a question mark.
- **Use abbreviations:** Create your own abbreviations. For example, replace "time code" with "TC."
- **Type your notes:** Type up your notes, adding more detail, as soon as possible after taking them.

PRACTICE As you listen to the podcast, take notes using the space on the page or your notebook.

 TEKS

6.E. Interact with sources in meaningful ways such as notetaking, annotating, freewriting, or illustrating.

8.F. Analyze characteristics of multimodal and digital texts.

Bored . . . and Brilliant?

A Challenge to Disconnect From Your Phone

BACKGROUND

According to a survey by the research group Flurry, which is cited in this podcast, smartphones have taken over television as the most-watched kind of screen in the United States. In 2014, the average American spent almost three hours a day on his or her phone, just a little more than the average American spent watching television.

AUDIO

NOTEBOOK

TAKE NOTES Pause the video if you find any language confusing. Use a dictionary or another strategy to clarify word meanings and then start the video again.

NOTEBOOK

Work on your own to answer the questions in your notebook. Use text evidence to support your responses.

WORKING AS A GROUP

Discuss your responses to the Analysis and Discussion questions with your group. Practice speaking using the Media Vocabulary as well as any new words you learned from the podcast.

If necessary, revise your original answers to reflect what you learn from your discussion.

MEDIA VOCABULARY

Use these words as you discuss and write about the podcast.

podcast
host
interview

Response

1. **Personal Connections** Have you ever discovered something surprising as a result of being bored?

Comprehension

2. **Strategy: Notetaking** How did notetaking while listening help you better understand the podcast? Explain.

Analysis and Discussion

3. **(a)** Where did the hosts conduct their interviews? **(b) Speculate** Why do you think they chose this location? Explain.

4. **(a)** Why do some scientists want to bring boredom back? **(b)** Do you agree? Explain.

5. **(a) Analyze** Why is putting down one's mobile device for a period of time a challenge? **(b) Interpret** What is "the lost art of spacing out"?

6. **Essential Question** *Is technology helpful or harmful to society?* What have you learned about technology and society from listening to this podcast? Go to your Essential Question Notes and record your observations and thoughts about the podcast.

Close Review

With your group, listen to the podcast again. Take notes about important details. Note time codes so you can find information later. Then, write a question and your conclusion.

MY QUESTION:

MY CONCLUSION:

TEKS

6.A. Describe personal connections to a variety of sources, including self-selected texts.

Research

A **multimodal text** combines words with another mode of communication, such as images or media.

BORED . . . AND BRILLIANT? A CHALLENGE TO DISCONNECT FROM YOUR PHONE

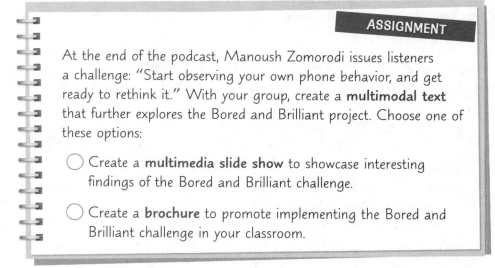

ASSIGNMENT

At the end of the podcast, Manoush Zomorodi issues listeners a challenge: "Start observing your own phone behavior, and get ready to rethink it." With your group, create a **multimodal text** that further explores the Bored and Brilliant project. Choose one of these options:

○ Create a **multimedia slide show** to showcase interesting findings of the Bored and Brilliant challenge.

○ Create a **brochure** to promote implementing the Bored and Brilliant challenge in your classroom.

Develop a Research Plan Start by identifying the types of information you will need and an initial list of sources you will consult. Conduct the research and take notes about the information you find.

INFORMATION WE NEED	SOURCES WE'LL USE	INFORMATION WE FOUND

EQ Notes Before moving on to a new selection, go to your Essential Question Notes and record any additional thoughts or observations you may have about the podcast.

Revise a Research Plan Evaluate your research plan so far and consider any changes you need to make. Ask the following types of questions:

- Should we narrow our focus?
- Should we broaden our focus?
- Should we consider different kinds of sources?

Synthesize Information from Sources Now that you have collected information, synthesize it, or pull it together to create a new understanding. This is the main point you will convey in your presentation.

Present and Discuss Share your multimedia slide show or brochure with the rest of the class. Give your classmates an opportunity to ask questions, and support your answers with evidence from both your research and the podcast.

 TEKS

12.D. Identify and gather relevant information from a variety of sources.

12.F. Synthesize information from a variety of sources.

Conduct a Debate

ASSIGNMENT

With your group, pair up with another group to conduct a **debate** in which each team takes a position or stance on this resolution:

The disadvantages of technology outweigh its benefits.

Prepare for the Debate

 INTERACTIVITY

Assign Teams There are two teams in a debate. The pro team supports the resolution and the con team opposes it. Assign at least two people to each team and one person to act as the debate judge. You don't have to personally agree with the position you are assigned.

Learn Debate Structure A formal debate has a set order:

1. Presentation of Opening Arguments: Each team speaks for an agreed-upon amount of time. This is followed by a short break that gives each team time to prepare a *rebuttal*, or argument against the points the other team made.
2. Presentation of Rebuttals
3. Presentation of Closing Statements

The judge decides which team won the debate.

Build Arguments and Gather Evidence With your team, discuss the texts from this section of the unit. Identify three clear reasons that support your position, or stance, and gather evidence from the texts that support each reason. Then, prepare for arguments against your position. Use the chart to organize your arguments and evidence, and decide which team members will present each stage of the debate.

POSITION (PRO OR CON)	
Reason 1:	Evidence:
Reason 2:	Evidence:
Reason 3:	Evidence:
Rebuttal	
Ideas for Closing Statement	

 TEKS

6.C. Use text evidence to support an appropriate response.

12.D. Identify and gather relevant information from a variety of sources.

12.F. Synthesize information from a variety of sources.

Rehearse

 INTERACTIVITY

Practice With Your Group With your team, practice delivering the points you will make during the debate. Use the checklist to evaluate the quality of your arguments and evidence, and the effectiveness of your speaking style. Then, use your evaluation and the instruction to improve your ideas, evidence, or presentation.

DEBATE CHECKLIST		
CONTENT	**DEBATE TECHNIQUE**	**PRESENTATION TECHNIQUE**
◯ Reasons and evidence clearly support the pro or con argument. ◯ Opposing arguments are anticipated and addressed effectively.	◯ Each speaker keeps within agreed-upon set time limits. ◯ Each speaker presents ideas in an organized way.	Each team member communicates effectively: ◯ enunciates, pronouncing words clearly ◯ speaks loudly enough to be heard and uses highs and lows of vocal register to emphasize meaning ◯ makes periodic eye contact with listeners ◯ seems engaged but relaxed, and uses natural gestures ◯ speaks formally, using the conventions of language

Hold the Debate

Speak Effectively When it is your team's turn to speak, present your position in a clear, organized manner. Avoid rushing through your explanations, and speak loudly enough to be heard by everyone in the room. Use a forceful, steady tone that shows you are in control of your ideas. Choose precise, accurate vocabulary that helps you communicate exactly what you mean to say.

Listen Attentively While the other team presents their arguments, listen attentively. Plan how you will respond appropriately during the rebuttal or closing statement. Jot down questions that you think the opposing team leaves unanswered and take notes about points you can challenge.

Discuss and Evaluate

Once both teams have presented, allow time for discussion so that listeners can ask questions and contribute their own ideas. Provide sufficient time for the judge to decide which team had the strongest arguments and speaking skills.

🟢 TEKS

1.A. Listen actively to interpret a message, ask clarifying questions, and respond appropriately.

1.C. Give an organized presentation with a specific stance and position, employing eye contact, speaking rate, volume, enunciation, natural gestures, and conventions of language to communicate ideas effectively.

6.H. Respond orally or in writing with appropriate register, vocabulary, tone and voice.

Essential Question

Is technology helpful or harmful to society?

People use and rely on technological devices every day in different ways. In this section, you will choose a selection about technology and society to read independently. Get the most from this section by establishing a purpose for reading. Ask yourself, "What do I hope to gain from my independent reading?" Here are just a few purposes you might consider:

Read to Learn Think about the selection you have already read. What question do you still have about the unit topic?

Read to Enjoy Read the descriptions of the texts. Which one seems more interesting and appealing to you?

Read to Form a Position Consider your thoughts and feelings about the Essential Question. Are you still undecided about some aspect of the topic?

Reading Digital Texts

Digital texts, like the ones you will read in this section, are electronic versions of print texts. They have a variety of characteristics:

- can be read on various devices
- text can be resized
- may include highlighting or other annotation tools.
- may have bookmarks, audio links, and other helpful features.

Independent Learning Strategies

Throughout your life, in school, in your community, and in your career, you will need to rely on yourself to learn and work on your own. Use these strategies to keep your focus as you read independently for sustained periods of time. Add ideas of your own for each category.

STRATEGY	MY ACTION PLAN
Create a schedule • Be aware of your deadlines. • Make a plan for each day's activities.	
Read with purpose • Use a variety of comprehension strategies to deepen your understanding. • Think about the text and how it adds to your knowledge.	
Take notes • Record key ideas and information. • Review your notes before sharing what you've learned.	

 TEKS

4. Self-select text and read independently for a sustained period of time;

5.A. Establish purpose for reading assigned and self-selected; 8.F. Analyze characteristics of multimodal and digital texts.

CONTENTS

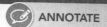 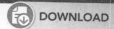
Choose one selection. Selections are available online only.

SHARE INDEPENDENT LEARNING

Reflect on and evaluate the information you gained from your Independent Reading selection. Then, share what you learned with others.

Close-Read Guide

Tool Kit
Close-Read Guide and
Model Annotation

Establish your purpose for reading. Then, read the selection through at least once. Use this page to record your close-read ideas.

Selection Title: _____   Purpose for Reading: _____

Minutes Read: _____

INTERACTIVITY

Close Read the Text

Zoom in on sections you found interesting. **Annotate** what you notice. Ask yourself **questions** about the text. What can you **conclude**?

_____

_____

_____

_____

_____

_____

_____

_____

Analyze the Text

1. Think about the author's choices of literary elements, techniques, and structures. Select one and record your thoughts.

_____

_____

_____

_____

2. What characteristics of digital texts did you use as you read this selection, and in what ways? How do the characteristics of a digital text affect your reading experience? Explain.

_____

_____

_____

_____

QuickWrite

Choose a paragraph from the text that grabbed your interest. Explain the power of this passage.

_____

_____

_____

_____

_____

_____

Share Your Independent Learning

Essential Question

Is technology helpful or harmful to society?

When you read something independently, your understanding continues to grow as you share what you have learned with others.

 NOTEBOOK

Prepare to Share

CONNECT IT One of the most important ways to respond to a text is to notice and describe your personal reactions. Think about the text you explored independently and the ways in which it connects to your own experiences.

- What similarities and differences do you see between the text and your own life? Describe your observations.

- How do you think this text connects to the Essential Question? Describe your ideas.

Learn From Your Classmates

DISCUSS IT Share your ideas about the text you explored on your own. As you talk with others in your class, take notes about new ideas that seem important.

Reflect

EXPLAIN IT Review your notes, and mark the most important insight you gained from these writing and discussion activities. Explain how this idea adds to your understanding of how technology affects society.

 TEKS

6.A. Describe personal connections to a variety of sources, including self-selected texts.
6.E. Interact with sources in meaningful ways such as notetaking, annotating, freewriting, or illustrating.

Argumentative Essay

ASSIGNMENT

In this unit, you read about technology and society from different perspectives. You also practiced debating and writing arguments. Now, apply what you have learned.

Write an **argumentative essay** in which you state and defend a claim in response to the Essential Question:

Essential Question
Is technology helpful or harmful to society?

Review and Evaluate Evidence

Review your Essential Question Notes and your QuickWrite from the beginning of the unit. Has your position changed?

⬤ Yes	⬤ No
Identify at least three pieces of evidence that convinced you to change your mind.	Identify at least three pieces of evidence that reinforced your initial position.
1.	1.
2.	2.
3.	3.

State your position now:

What other evidence might you need to support your position?

Share Your Perspective

The **Argumentative Essay Checklist** will help you stay on track.

PLAN Before you write, read the Checklist and make sure you understand all the items.

DRAFT As you write, pause occasionally to make sure you're meeting the Checklist requirements.

Use New Words Refer to your Word Network to vary your word choice. Also, consider using one or more of the Academic Vocabulary terms you learned at the beginning of the unit: *convince, certain, sufficient, declare, justify.*

REVIEW AND EDIT After you have written a first draft, evaluate it against the Checklist. Make any changes needed to strengthen your claim, structure, transitions, and language. Then, reread your essay and fix any errors you find.

EQ Notes Make sure you have pulled in details from your Essential Question Notes to support your claim.

🔘 INTERACTIVITY

ARGUMENTATIVE ESSAY CHECKLIST

My essay clearly contains . . .

○ a claim that shows depth of thought.

○ varied types of supporting evidence, including facts, details, and examples.

○ a purposeful structure that includes an introduction, logical connections among body paragraphs, and a strong conclusion.

○ varied sentence length and style, including complex sentences and sentences with prepositional phrases.

○ varied and precise word choices.

○ correct use of standard English conventions, including proper subject-verb agreement and use of commas.

○ no punctuation or spelling errors.

⬢ TEKS

10.B.i. Develop drafts into a focused, structured, and coherent piece of writing by organizing with purposeful structure, including an introduction, transitions, coherence within and across paragraphs, and a conclusion.
10.B.ii. Develop drafts into a focused, structured, and coherent piece of writing by developing an engaging idea reflecting depth of thought with specific facts and details.
10.D.viii. Edit drafts using standard English conventions including punctuation marks including commas in complex sentences, transitions, and introductory elements.
11.C. Compose multi-paragraph argumentative texts using genre characteristics and craft.

Revising and Editing

Read this paper and think about corrections the writer might make.
Then, answer the questions that follow.

[1] After welcoming a refugee into our home, I strongly believe that technology can be a tool for healing. [2] Along with several other boys our "little brother," as we called him, had escaped his village during a violent civil war. [3] The "Lost Boys" from his village was traveling on foot for many hungry months, moving only under the cover of night.

[4] In the beginning, a stovetop to cook food was a mystery a wall switch was magic. [5] Because of this, some people thought that introducing him to computers would be overwhelming. [6] These people didn't know him. [7] However, we saw how his eyes lit up with reflected light and amazement the first time he opened a laptop. [8] He used it to find games movies and songs in his native language, which he loved.

1. Which change corrects an error in comma usage in sentence 2?

  A Add a comma after *boys*.

  B Remove the comma after *brother*.

  C Remove the comma after *him*.

  D Add a comma after *village*.

2. Which answer choice correctly fixes the subject-verb agreement error in sentence 3?

  F Change *months* to *month*.

  G Change *village* to *villages*.

  H Change *was* to *were*.

  J Change *foot* to *feet*.

3. Which revision correctly uses a relative pronoun to combine sentences 5 and 6?

  F Because of this, some people thought that introducing him to computers would be overwhelming, but these people didn't know him.

  G Because of this, some people thought that introducing him to computers would be overwhelming that didn't know him.

  H Because of this, some people thought that introducing him to computers would be overwhelming, and these people didn't know him.

  J Because of this, some people who didn't know him thought that introducing him to computers would be overwhelming.

4. Which answer choice corrects comma usage in sentence 8?

  A Remove the comma after *language*

  B insert a comma after *games* and *movies*

  C insert a comma after *to*

  D insert a comma after *movies*

Reflect on the Unit

📓 NOTEBOOK

👆 INTERACTIVITY

Reflect On the Unit Goals

Review your Unit Goals chart from the beginning of the unit. Then, complete the activity and answer the question.

1. In the Unit Goals chart, rate how well you meet each goal now.

2. In which goals were you most and least successful?

Reflect On the Texts

CHOOSE! When you look back on the entire unit, which selection do you find most memorable? Use the Selection List to make your choice. Then, discuss your reasons.

Selection Title	Most Memorable
Feathered Friend	
The Biometric Body	
Biometrics Are Not Better	
The Internet of Things	
Is Our Gain Also Our Loss?	
The Black Hole of Technology	
The Fun They Had	
Mexico's Abandoned Railways and the SEFT-1	
Bored…and Brilliant? A Challenge to Disconnect from Your Phone	
Your Independent Reading Selection:	

Reflect On the Essential Question

Going Away Card Send this unit off with a going away card from the class. Invite everyone in the class to contribute a final thought, joke, saying, quotation, or other brief message that relates to the unit or its Essential Question: **Is technology helpful or harmful to society?**

 TEKS

10.D.iv. Edit drafts using standard English conventions, including prepositions and prepositional phrases and their influence on subject-verb agreement.
10.D.v. Edit drafts using standard English conventions, including pronouns, including relative.

UNIT ④
The Power of Imagination

PEARSON
realize™

Go ONLINE for
all lessons

 AUDIO

 VIDEO

 NOTEBOOK

 ANNOTATE

 INTERACTIVITY

 DOWNLOAD

 RESEARCH

WATCH THE VIDEO

Yo Ho Ho and a Rubber Ducky

DISCUSS IT Do you think children use their imaginations more often than adults?

Write your response before sharing your ideas.

UNIT INTRODUCTION

Essential Question

What is the purpose of imagination?

MENTOR TEXT:
FICTION
The Great Universal Undo

WHOLE-CLASS LEARNING

DRAMA

The Phantom Tollbooth, Act I
play by Susan Nanus, based on the book by Norton Juster

DRAMA

The Phantom Tollbooth, Act II
play by Susan Nanus, based on the book by Norton Juster

PEER-GROUP LEARNING

RETELLING

from **The Misadventures of Don Quixote**
Miguel de Cervantes, retold by Tom Lathrop

COMPARE WITHIN GENRE

NARRATIVE POEM

Jabberwocky
from **Through the Looking-Glass**
Lewis Carroll

▶ MEDIA CONNECTION
Alice in Wonderland (1983): Jabberwocky

SONG

The Mock Turtle's Song
from **Alice's Adventures in Wonderland**
Lewis Carroll

REFLECTIVE ESSAY

The Importance of Imagination
Esha Chhabra

INDEPENDENT LEARNING

FANTASY

from **The Wonderful Wizard of Oz**
L. Frank Baum

POETRY COLLECTION

Our Wreath of Rose Buds
Corrinne

Fantasy
Gwendolyn Bennett

NOVEL EXCERPT

The Shah of Blah
from Haroun and the Sea of Stories
Salman Rushdie

FANTASY

from **Alice's Adventures in Wonderland**
Lewis Carroll

PERFORMANCE TASK

WRITING PROCESS
Write a Short Story

PERFORMANCE TASK

SPEAKING AND LISTENING
Present a Short Story

SHARE INDEPENDENT LEARNING

Share • Learn • Reflect

PERFORMANCE-BASED ASSESSMENT

Short Story

You will write a short story that explores the Essential Question for the unit.

UNIT REFLECTION

Goals • Texts • Essential Question

Unit Goals

▶ VIDEO

Throughout this unit, you will deepen your understanding of imagination by reading, writing, speaking, listening, and presenting. These goals will help you succeed on the Unit Performance-Based Assessment.

👆 INTERACTIVITY

SET GOALS ▸ Rate how well you meet these goals right now. You will revisit your ratings later, when you reflect on your growth during this unit.

SCALE

1	2	3	4	5
NOT AT ALL WELL	NOT VERY WELL	SOMEWHAT WELL	VERY WELL	EXTREMELY WELL

ESSENTIAL QUESTION	Unit Introduction	Unit Reflection
I can read selections that explore the purposes of imagination and develop my own perspectives.	1 2 3 4 5	1 2 3 4 5

READING	Unit Introduction	Unit Reflection
I can understand and use academic vocabulary words related to fiction.	1 2 3 4 5	1 2 3 4 5
I can recognize elements of different genres, especially drama, fantasy, and poetry.	1 2 3 4 5	1 2 3 4 5
I can read a selection of my choice independently and make meaningful connections to other texts.	1 2 3 4 5	1 2 3 4 5

WRITING	Unit Introduction	Unit Reflection
I can write an imaginative and creative short story.	1 2 3 4 5	1 2 3 4 5
I can complete Timed Writing tasks with confidence.	1 2 3 4 5	1 2 3 4 5

SPEAKING AND LISTENING	Unit Introduction	Unit Reflection
I can prepare and deliver a short story.	1 2 3 4 5	1 2 3 4 5

🌐 **TEKS**

2.C. Determine the meaning and usage of grade-level academic English words derived from Greek and Latin roots such as *mis/mit, bene, man, vac, scrib/script,* and *jur/jus.*

Academic Vocabulary: Fiction

Many English words have roots, or key parts, that come from ancient languages, such as Latin and Greek. Learn these roots and use the words as you respond to questions and activities in this unit.

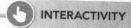 INTERACTIVITY

PRACTICE Academic terms are used routinely in classrooms. Build your knowledge of these words by completing the chart.

1. **Review** each word, its root, and the mentor sentences.

2. With a partner, read the words and mentor sentences aloud. Then, **determine** the meaning and usage of each word. Use a dictionary, if needed.

3. **List** at least two related words for each word.

WORD	MENTOR SENTENCES	PREDICT MEANING	RELATED WORDS
dialogue GREEK ROOT: **-log-** "speech"	1. The *dialogue* in this story sounds very authentic. 2. They had a useful *dialogue* about how to solve the problem.		monologue; travelogue
transform LATIN ROOT: **-form-** "shape"	1. The clay was soft and easy to *transform* from a lump into the shape of a vase. 2. The caterpillar will *transform* into a butterfly.		
novelty LATIN ROOT: **-nov-** "new"	1. Having grown up in the city, riding a horse was a *novelty* for Ben. 2. The shop was full of *novelty* items that tourists would buy.		
consequently LATIN ROOT: **-sequ-** "follow"	1. The pothole in the road was fixed, and *consequently* it was much easier to drive. 2. Kayla missed the bus and *consequently* was late for practice.		
description LATIN ROOT: **-script-** "write"	1. The writer's vivid *description* of the setting helps me picture the action. 2. If you give me a *description*, I can help you find your missing cat.		

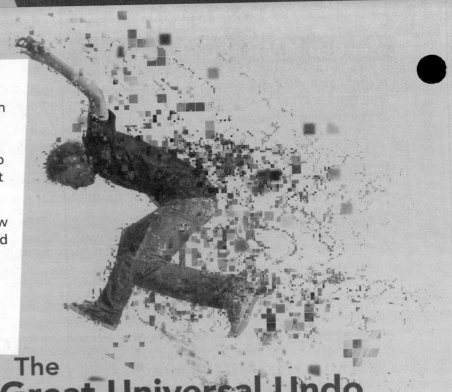

This selection is an example of a **fictional narrative**, a type of writing in which the author tells a story about made-up characters and events. This is the type of writing you will develop in the Performance-Based Assessment at the end of the unit.

READ IT As you read, consider how the author makes the characters and situation interesting. Mark the text to help answer this question: How does the author keep the reader interested and make the flow of events clear?

The Great Universal Undo

 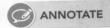

AUDIO

ANNOTATE

1   If Alexander Dillahunt wasn't the world's worst typist, he was close. But that was okay. Fixing mistakes on a computer was a snap—especially if you caught them right away. That was the beauty of the Undo, Alexander thought: a tiny backwards arrow at the top of the screen that performed magic, allowing the user to go back to a more perfect, mistake-free moment in time.

2   That's how Alexander Dillahunt got it into his head to create the Universal Undo. The Universal Undo would do nothing short of "taking back" the last thing a person did.

3   Making a working model was simple. All Alexander needed to do was figure out how to take something in 2-D and make it 4-D (skipping over 3-D completely) and then get the whole thing to fit inside his smartphone. Finally, after a few weeks of trial and error, the Universal Undo was ready for a test run.

4   Alexander went into the kitchen and stood in front of the refrigerator. From there he walked to the cupboard. He waited a few seconds, then hit Universal Undo on his smartphone. Presto! Alexander was back at the refrigerator. He walked to the stove. He waited, hit Universal Undo—and there he was, back at the refrigerator again. Action undone!

5   Alexander took his new invention outside. By the traffic lights, he ran into Mrs. Bieberman, who was carrying a bag of groceries and holding the hand of her 3-year-old son Tommy.

6   "Hello Mrs. Bieberman! Hi Tommy!" Alexander called out. He smiled. "That's a really silly hat you're wearing, Mrs. Bieberman!"

Then he tapped his smartphone. If everything worked, his last comment would be Undone.

7 "Hello yourself, Alexander!" exclaimed Mrs. Bieberman.

8 *Good!* thought Alexander. *She hadn't heard it!* Flushed with excitement, he continued. "You know, your little boy looks like a toad." He paused, waiting for a response.

9 "I do *not* not look like a toe!" Tommy wailed and, still blubbering, started to play his video game. Had Alexander tapped Undo—or just imagined it? He couldn't remember.

10 "He can't go long without his game," Mrs. Bieberman said, sighing. "And only three years old." Alexander hadn't started playing video games until he was nine.

11 "I want a cookie!" said Tommy suddenly, and he began tugging at the hem of his mother's skirt. Mrs. Bieberman reached into a bag of cookies and pulled one out. She declared, "I'll give you just one, Tommy." Tommy grabbed it and stuffed it in his mouth.

12 "How's your mother?" asked Mrs. Bieberman. "I should call her."

13 Alexander, even though Tommy was loudly crunching the cookies, was aware of a *tap tapping* sound.

14 Mrs. Bieberman reached into a bag of cookies and pulled one out. "I'll give you just one, Tommy."

15 Alexander froze. *How could he have missed it?* He'd read all about multiple discovery—the idea that most inventions are made by a number of different people in different places at the same time. *How could he have thought he was the only one?*

16 "'Bye Mrs. Bieberman, Tommy" said Alexander in a shaky voice.

17 Tommy, his mouth crammed with cookie, looked into Alexander's eyes and hit a button on his video game. *Tap, tap-tap.*

18 Mrs. Bieberman reached into a bag of cookies and pulled one out. "I'll give you just one, Tommy." ❧

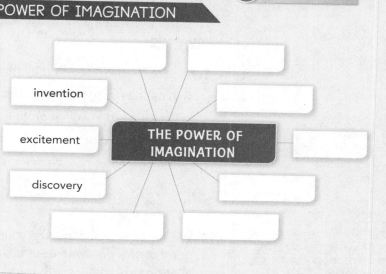

DOWNLOAD

WORD NETWORK FOR THE POWER OF IMAGINATION

Vocabulary A Word Network is a collection of words related to a topic. As you read the selections in this unit, identify interesting words related to the idea of imagination and add them to your Word Network. For example, you might begin by adding words from the Mentor Text, such as *invention, excitement,* and *discovery.* Continue to add words as you complete this unit.

Refer to the **Word Network Model** in the **Tool Kit** at the back of this book.

invention

excitement

discovery

THE POWER OF IMAGINATION

Summary

A **summary** is a brief, complete overview of a text that maintains the meaning and logical order of ideas of the original. It should not include your personal opinions.

WRITE IT Write a summary of "The Great Universal Undo."

_____

_____

_____

_____

_____

_____

_____

_____

_____

_____

_____

Launch Activity

Participate in a Group Discussion

Consider this statement: **Imagination is more important than knowledge.**

1. Prepare for the discussion by thinking about these related questions:
   - What has imagination led people to achieve?
   - Do we need imagination to learn?

2. Mark your position and briefly explain your reasons.

   ○ Strongly Agree   ○ Agree   ○ Disagree   ○ Strongly Disagree

_____

3. With a small group, discuss your responses to the statement and questions. Then, write a summary of the main points you covered. Share your summary with the class.

 TEKS
6.D. Paraphrase and summarize texts in ways that maintain meaning and logical order.

QuickWrite

Consider class discussions, the video, and the Mentor Text as you think about the prompt.

Essential Question

What is the purpose of imagination?

At the end of the unit, you will respond to the Essential Question again and see how your perspective has changed.

NOTEBOOK

WRITE IT Record your thoughts here.

DOWNLOAD

EQ Notes What is the purpose of imagination?

As you read the selections in this unit, use a chart like the one shown to record your ideas and list details from the texts that support them. Taking notes as you go will help you clarify your thinking, gather relevant information, and be ready to respond to the Essential Question.

TITLE	MY IDEAS / OBSERVATIONS	TEXT EVIDENCE / INFORMATION

Refer to the **EQ Notes Model** in the **Tool Kit** at the back of this book.

What is the purpose of imagination?

When you use your imagination, the possibilities are endless. You might explore an unusual place or daydream about an exciting activity. But what lessons about yourself and your world did you learn from your imagined experience? You will work with your whole class to explore the concept of imagination and its purpose. The selections you read will present insights into how people use their imaginations.

▶ VIDEO

👆 INTERACTIVITY

Whole-Class Learning Strategies

Throughout your life, in school, in your community, and in your career, you will continue to learn and work in large-group environments. Review these strategies and the actions you can take to practice them as you work with your whole class. Then, add ideas of your own for each category. Get ready to use these strategies during Whole-Class Learning.

STRATEGY	MY ACTION PLAN
Listen actively • Put away personal items to avoid becoming distracted. • Try to hear the speaker's full message before planning your own response.	
Demonstrate respect • Show up on time and make sure you are prepared for class. • Avoid side conversations while in class.	
Describe personal connections • Recognize that literature explores human experience—the details may differ from your own life, but the emotions it expresses are universal. • Actively look for ways in which your personal experiences help you find meaning in a text. • Consider how your own experiences help you understand characters' actions and reactions.	

CONTENTS

PERFORMANCE TASK: WRITING PROCESS

Write a Short Story

The Whole-Class readings focus on one boy's amazing adventures. After reading the drama, you will write a short story about amazing events and characters from your own imagination.

THE PHANTOM TOLLBOOTH, ACT I

The selection you are about to read is a drama.

Reading Dramas

A **drama,** also called a *play*, is a story that's written to be performed by actors.

DRAMA

Author's Purpose
→ to tell a story meant to be performed by actors for an audience

Characteristics
→ characters who take part in the story's action

→ setting, or the time and place in which the action occurs; may have multiple settings

→ dialogue, monologues, and other types of dramatic speech

→ stage directions that describe how characters should deliver their lines and how a play should be staged, or presented

Structure
→ organized in sections called acts and scenes

→ plot, or related sequences of events, driven by one or more conflicts

Take a Minute!

 NOTEBOOK

LIST IT With a partner, make a list of plays you have seen performed—either at school or in another space. Discuss which plays were your favorite and what made watching them so memorable.

TEKS
8.A. Demonstrate knowledge of literary genres such as realistic fiction, adventure stories, historical fiction, mysteries, humor, and myths.

8.C. Analyze how playwrights develop characters through dialogue and staging.

Genre / Text Elements

Dialogue, Stage Directions, and Character Development Character development is the way an author shows what a character is like and how he or she changes. Playwrights use dialogue and stage directions to develop characters.

- **Dialogue:** conversations among characters; what they say out loud

- **Stage Directions:** playwright's instructions for how a drama should be **staged,** or presented. They include details about performance elements (set, lighting, costumes, props), and also tell actors how to speak their lines and move.

> **TIP:** Stage directions are visually set off from dialogue in some way. They may be set in italic text, placed in brackets, or both.

EXAMPLE: Consider how stage directions and dialogue develop the character.

PASSAGE	CHARACTER DEVELOPMENT
[A castle room. There is a large, fancy bed and a cold fireplace. The stone walls are hung with tattered tapestries. Ice is visible in the room.] **Ani.** *[rushing in and throwing herself on the bed]* What have I done? Why am I such a fool? She will never forgive me! *[She gestures at the fireplace.]* FLAME! *[A fire roars into place.]*	**Stage directions** show that Ani… • lives in a cold castle. • has magical skill (creates fire). • is very upset. **Dialogue** shows that Ani is upset by something she has done, perhaps by accident, to someone she cares about.

 NOTEBOOK

PRACTICE Read the passage and answer the questions.

[The same castle room, now covered in ice. ANI and MILLI face each other from opposite sides of the stage.]

    Ani. *[pleading]* You must believe me, Milli. I didn't know it was the golden apple. *[She reaches out.]* But I could tell King Roland no. I could say this is a terrible tradition! Why should a stupid golden apple rule us?

    Milli. *[coldly]* Accident or not, Roland gave you the apple. *[She has been standing stiffly. Now she sags.]* You were chosen, and you will be the one to lead the armies.

1. In what ways do dialogue and stage directions help to develop the characters? Cite details that support your answer.

2. How might this scene be presented, or staged, to develop the characters and show their differences? Explain your thinking.

About the Playwright

Susan Nanus has written plays, television scripts, and movie screenplays. Like other dramatists, she sometimes bases her plays or screenplays on novels or other existing works. Her script for *The Phantom Tollbooth* was based on the novel by Norton Juster.

For a biography of Norton Juster, see Act II.

The Phantom Tollbooth, Act I

Concept Vocabulary

You will encounter the following words as you read *The Phantom Tollbooth*, Act I. Before reading, note how familiar you are with each word. Using a scale of 1 (do not know it at all) to 5 (know it very well), indicate your knowledge of each word.

WORD	YOUR RANKING
ignorance	
surmise	
presume	
speculate	
consideration	
misapprehension	

Comprehension Strategy

ANNOTATE

Generate Questions

To deepen your understanding and gain more information from a text, **generate questions** about it before, during, and after reading.

- **Before you read a drama,** you might generate questions based on the title, illustrations, or character list.
- **During your reading,** you might generate questions about a specific event or character's actions.
- **After you read,** you might generate questions about the ending or how characters have changed.

PRACTICE Generate questions before, during, and after reading the play to deepen your understanding and gain more information. Jot your questions in the margins of the text.

 TEKS
5.B. Generate questions about text before, during, and after reading to deepen understanding and gain information.

The Phantom Tollbooth Act I

Susan Nanus • Based on the book by Norton Juster

BACKGROUND

The writer of a drama is called a *playwright* or a *dramatist*. Playwright Susan Nanus adapted Norton Juster's novel *The Phantom Tollbooth* into a drama with two acts, or main sections. You will read Act I in this lesson.

 AUDIO

 ANNOTATE

Cast (In order of appearance)

- The Clock
- Milo, A Boy
- The Whether Man
- Six Lethargarians
- Tock, The Watchdog (same as the Clock)
- Azaz the Unabridged, King of Dictionopolis
- The Mathemagician, King of Digitopolis
- Princess Sweet Rhyme
- Princess Pure Reason
- Gatekeeper of Dictionopolis
- Three Word Merchants
- The Letterman (fourth Word Merchant)
- Spelling Bee
- The Humbug

- The Duke of Definition
- The Minister of Meaning
- The Earl of Essence
- The Count of Connotation
- The Undersecretary of Understanding
- A Page
- Kakafonous A. Dischord, Doctor of Dissonance
- The Awful Dynne
- The Dodecahedron
- Miners of the Numbers Mine
- The Everpresent Wordsnatcher
- The Terrible Trivium
- The Demon of Insincerity
- Senses Taker

ignorance (IHG nuhr uhns) *n.* state of lacking knowledge, learning, or information

The Sets

1. MILO'S BEDROOM—with shelves, pennants, pictures on the wall, as well as suggestions of the characters of the Land of Wisdom.

2. THE ROAD TO THE LAND OF WISDOM—a forest, from which the Whether Man and the Lethargarians emerge.

3. DICTIONOPOLIS—a marketplace full of open air stalls as well as little shops. Letters and signs should abound.

4. DIGITOPOLIS—a dark, glittering place without trees or greenery, but full of shining rocks and cliffs, with hundreds of numbers shining everywhere.

5. THE LAND OF IGNORANCE—a gray, gloomy place full of cliffs and caves, with frightening faces. Different levels and heights should be suggested through one or two platforms or risers, with a set of stairs that lead to the castle in the air.

⌘ ⌘ ⌘

Act I

Scene i

1 [*The stage is completely dark and silent. Suddenly the sound of someone winding an alarm clock is heard, and after that, the sound of loud ticking is heard.*]

2 [*LIGHTS UP on the* Clock, *a huge alarm clock. The* Clock *reads 4:00. The lighting should make it appear that the* Clock *is suspended in mid-air (if possible). The* Clock *ticks for 30 seconds.*]

3 **Clock.** See that! Half a minute gone by. Seems like a long time when you're waiting for something to happen, doesn't it? Funny thing is, time can pass very slowly or very fast, and sometimes even both at once. The time now? Oh, a little after four, but what that means should depend on you. Too often, we do something simply because time tells us to. Time for school, time for bed, whoops, 12:00, time to be hungry. It can get a little silly, don't you think? Time is important, but it's what you do

with it that makes it so. So my advice to you is to use it. Keep your eyes open and your ears perked. Otherwise it will pass before you know it, and you'll certainly have missed something!

4 Things have a habit of doing that, you know. Being here one minute and gone the next.

5 In the twinkling of an eye.

6 In a jiffy.

7 In a flash!

8 I know a girl who yawned and missed a whole summer vacation. And what about that caveman who took a nap one afternoon, and woke up to find himself completely alone. You see, while he was sleeping, someone had invented the wheel and everyone had moved to the suburbs. And then of course, there is Milo. [*LIGHTS UP to reveal* Milo's *Bedroom. The* Clock *appears to be on a shelf in the room of a young boy—a room filled with books, toys, games, maps, papers, pencils, a bed, a desk. There is a dartboard with numbers and the face of the* Mathemagician, *a bedspread made from* King Azaz's *cloak, a kite looking like the* Spelling Bee, *a punching bag with the* Humbug's *face, as well as records, a television, a toy car, and a large box that is wrapped and has an envelope taped to the top. The sound of FOOTSTEPS is heard, and then enter* Milo *dejectedly. He throws down his books and coat, flops into a chair, and sighs loudly.*] Who never knows what to do with himself—not just sometimes, but always. When he's in school, he wants to be out, and when he's out he wants to be in. [*During the following speech,* Milo *examines the various toys, tools, and other possessions in the room, trying them out and rejecting them.*] Wherever he is, he wants to be somewhere else—and when he gets there, so what. Everything is too much trouble or a waste of time. Books—he's already read them. Games—boring. T.V.—dumb. So what's left? Another long, boring afternoon. Unless he bothers to notice a very large package that happened to arrive today.

9 **Milo.** [*Suddenly notices the package. He drags himself over to it, and disinterestedly reads the label.*] "For Milo, who has plenty of time." Well, that's true. [*Sighs and looks at it.*] No. [*Walks away.*] Well . . . [*Comes back. Rips open envelope and reads.*]

10 **A Voice.** "One genuine turnpike tollbooth,[1] easily assembled at home for use by those who have never traveled in lands beyond."

11 **Milo.** Beyond what? [*Continues reading.*]

ANNOTATE: In paragraphs 4–7, mark expressions that mean "very quickly."

QUESTION: Why does the playwright have the Clock repeat the same idea in different ways?

CONCLUDE: What is the effect of this quick series of expressions?

1. **turnpike tollbooth** A turnpike is a road that people pay a fee, or toll, to use. A tollbooth is the booth or gate at which tolls are collected.

© Pearson Education, Inc., or its affiliates. All rights reserved.

The Phantom Tollbooth, Act I **365**

12 **A Voice.** "This package contains the following items:" [Milo *pulls the items out of the box and sets them up as they are mentioned.*] "One (1) genuine turnpike tollbooth to be erected according to directions. Three (3) precautionary² signs to be used in a precautionary fashion. Assorted coins for paying tolls. One (1) map, strictly up to date, showing how to get from here to there. One (1) book of rules and traffic regulations which may not be bent or broken. Warning! Results are not guaranteed. If not perfectly satisfied, your wasted time will be refunded."

13 **Milo.** [*Skeptically.*] Come off it, who do you think you're kidding? [*Walks around and examines tollbooth.*] What am I supposed to do with this? [*The ticking of the* Clock *grows loud and impatient.*] Well . . . what else do I have to do. [Milo *gets into his toy car and drives up to the first sign.*]

14 **Voice.** "HAVE YOUR DESTINATION IN MIND."

15 **Milo.** [*Pulls out the map.*] Now, let's see. That's funny. I never heard of any of these places. Well, it doesn't matter anyway. Dictionopolis. That's a weird name. I might as well go there. [*Begins to move, following map. Drives off.*]

16 **Clock.** See what I mean? You never know how things are going to get started. But when you're bored, what you need more than anything is a rude awakening.

17 [*The ALARM goes off very loudly as the stage darkens. The sound of the alarm is transformed into the honking of a car horn, and is then joined by the blasts, bleeps, roars and growls of heavy traffic. When the lights come up, Milo's bedroom is gone and we see a lonely road in the middle of nowhere.*]

Scene ii • The Road to Dictionopolis

1 [*Enter* Milo *in his car.*]

2 **Milo.** This is weird! I don't recognize any of this scenery at all. [*A SIGN is held up before* Milo, *startling him.*] Huh? [*Reads.*] WELCOME TO EXPECTATIONS. INFORMATION, PREDICTIONS AND ADVICE CHEERFULLY OFFERED. PARK HERE AND BLOW HORN. [Milo *blows horn.*]

3 **Whether Man.** [*A little man wearing a long coat and carrying an umbrella pops up from behind the sign he was holding. He speaks very fast and excitedly.*] My, my, my, my, my, welcome, welcome, welcome, welcome to the Land of Expectations, Expectations,

Expectations! We don't get many travelers these days; we certainly don't get many travelers. Now what can I do for you? I'm the Whether Man.

4 **Milo.** [*Referring to the map.*] Uh . . . is this the right road to Dictionopolis?

5 **Whether Man.** Well now, well now, well now, I don't know of any wrong road to Dictionopolis, so if this road goes to Dictionopolis at all, it must be the right road, and if it doesn't, it must be the right road to somewhere else, because there are no wrong roads to anywhere. Do you think it will rain?

6 **Milo.** I thought you were the Weather Man.

7 **Whether Man.** Oh, no, I'm the Whether Man, not the weather man. [*Pulls out a SIGN or opens a FLAP of his coat, which reads: "WHETHER."*] After all, it's more important to know whether there will be weather than what the weather will be.

8 **Milo.** What kind of place is Expectations?

9 **Whether Man.** Good question, good question! Expectations is the place you must always go to before you get to where you are going. Of course, some people never go beyond Expectations, but my job is to hurry them along whether they like it or not. Now what else can I do for you? [*Opens his umbrella.*]

10 **Milo.** I think I can find my own way.

11 **Whether Man.** Splendid, splendid, splendid! Whether or not you find your own way, you're bound to find some way. If you happen to find my way, please return it. I lost it years ago. I imagine by now it must be quite rusty. You did say it was going to rain, didn't you? [*Escorts* Milo *to the car under the open umbrella.*] I'm glad you made your own decision. I do so hate to make up my mind about anything, whether it's good or bad, up or down, rain or shine. Expect everything, I always say, and the unexpected never happens. Goodbye, goodbye, goodbye, good . . .

12 [*A loud CLAP OF THUNDER is heard.*] Oh dear! [*He looks up at the sky, puts out his hand to feel for rain, and RUNS AWAY.* Milo *watches puzzledly and drives on.*]

13 **Milo.** I'd better get out of Expectations, but fast. Talking to a guy like that all day would get me nowhere for sure. [*He tries to speed up, but finds instead that he is moving slower and slower.*] Oh, oh,

CLOSE READ

ANNOTATE: In paragraph 9, mark the **pun**, or play on words, that Whether Man makes about Expectations.

QUESTION: Why does the playwright include this pun?

CONCLUDE: What double meaning does the pun have? How does the double meaning add to the scene?

ANNOTATE: In paragraphs 14 and 15, mark the punctuation that separates characters' words.

QUESTION: Why does the author include ellipses in the Lethargarians' dialogue?

CONCLUDE: What does this punctuation show about how the Lethargarians speak?

now what? [*He can barely move. Behind* Milo, *the* LETHARGARIANS *begin to enter from all parts of the stage. They are dressed to blend in with the scenery and carry small pillows that look like rocks. Whenever they fall asleep, they rest on the pillows.*] Now I really am getting nowhere. I hope I didn't take a wrong turn. [*The car stops. He tries to start it. It won't move. He gets out and begins to tinker with it.*] I wonder where I am.

14 **Lethargarian 1.** You're . . . in . . . the . . . Dol . . . drums . . . [Milo *looks around.*]

15 **Lethargarian 2.** Yes . . . the . . . Dol . . . drums . . . [*A YAWN is heard.*]

16 **Milo.** [*Yelling.*] WHAT ARE THE DOLDRUMS?

17 **Lethargarian 3.** The Doldrums, my friend, are where nothing ever happens and nothing ever changes. [*Parts of the Scenery*

stand up or Six People come out of the scenery colored in the same colors of the trees or the road. They move very slowly and as soon as they move, they stop to rest again.] Allow me to introduce all of us. We are the Lethargarians at your service.

18 **Milo.** [*Uncertainly.*] Very pleased to meet you. I think I'm lost. Can you help me?

19 **Lethargarian 4.** Don't say think. [*He yawns.*] It's against the law.

20 **Lethargarian 1.** No one's allowed to think in the Doldrums. [*He falls asleep.*]

21 **Lethargarian 2.** Don't you have a rule book? It's local ordinance 175389-J. [*He falls asleep.*]

22 **Milo.** [*Pulls out rule book and reads.*] Ordinance 175389-J: "It shall be unlawful, illegal and unethical to think, think of thinking, **surmise**, **presume**, reason, meditate, or **speculate** while in the Doldrums. Anyone breaking this law shall be severely punished." That's a ridiculous law! Everybody thinks.

23 **All The Lethargarians.** We don't!

24 **Lethargarian 2.** And most of the time, you don't, that's why you're here. You weren't thinking and you weren't paying attention either. People who don't pay attention often get stuck in the Doldrums. Face it, most of the time, you're just like us. [*Falls, snoring, to the ground. Milo laughs.*]

25 **Lethargarian 5.** Stop that at once. Laughing is against the law. Don't you have a rule book? It's local ordinance 574381-W.

26 **Milo.** [*Opens rule book and reads.*] "In the Doldrums, laughter is frowned upon and smiling is permitted only on alternate Thursdays." Well, if you can't laugh or think, what can you do?

27 **Lethargarian 6.** Anything as long as it's nothing, and everything as long as it isn't anything. There's lots to do. We have a very busy schedule . . .

28 **Lethargarian 1.** At 8:00 we get up and then we spend from 8 to 9 daydreaming.

29 **Lethargarian 2.** From 9:00 to 9:30 we take our early mid-morning nap . . .

30 **Lethargarian 3.** From 9:30 to 10:30 we dawdle and delay . . .

surmise (suhr MYZ) *v.* guess, using only intuition or imagination

presume (prih ZOOM) *v.* take for granted; assume something to be the case

speculate (SPEHK yuh layt) *v.* guess, using information that is uncertain or incomplete

31 Lethargarian 4. From 10:30 to 11:30 we take our late early morning nap . . .

32 Lethargarian 5. From 11:30 to 12:00 we bide our time and then we eat our lunch.

33 Lethargarian 6. From 1:00 to 2:00 we linger and loiter . . .

34 Lethargarian 1. From 2:00 to 2:30 we take our early afternoon nap . . .

35 Lethargarian 2. From 2:30 to 3:30 we put off for tomorrow what we could have done today . . .

36 Lethargarian 3. From 3:30 to 4:00 we take our early late afternoon nap . . .

37 Lethargarian 4. From 4:00 to 5:00 we loaf and lounge until dinner . . .

38 Lethargarian 5. From 6:00 to 7:00 we dilly-dally . . .

39 Lethargarian 6. From 7:00 to 8:00 we take our early evening nap and then for an hour before we go to bed, we waste time.

40 Lethargarian 1. [*Yawning.*] You see, it's really quite strenuous doing nothing all day long, and so once a week, we take a holiday and go nowhere.

41 Lethargarian 5. Which is just where we were going when you came along. Would you care to join us?

42 Milo. [*Yawning.*] That's where I seem to be going, anyway. [*Stretching.*] Tell me, does everyone here do nothing?

43 Lethargarian 3. Everyone but the terrible Watchdog. He's always sniffing around to see that nobody wastes time. A most unpleasant character.

44 Milo. The Watchdog?

45 Lethargarian 6. THE WATCHDOG!

46 All The Lethargarians. [*Yelling at once.*] RUN! WAKE UP! RUN! HERE HE COMES! THE WATCHDOG! [*They all run off and ENTER a large dog with the head, feet, and tail of a dog, and the body of a clock, having the same face as the character the Clock.*]

47 Watchdog. What are you doing here?

48 Milo. Nothing much. Just killing time. You see . . .

49 Watchdog. KILLING TIME! [*His ALARM RINGS in fury.*] It's bad enough wasting time without killing it. What are you doing in the Doldrums, anyway? Don't you have anywhere to go?

50 Milo. I think I was on my way to Dictionopolis when I got stuck here. Can you help me?

51 Watchdog. Help you! You've got to help yourself. I suppose you know why you got stuck.

52 Milo. I guess I just wasn't thinking.

53 Watchdog. Precisely. Now you're on your way.

54 Milo. I am?

55 Watchdog. Of course. Since you got here by not thinking, it seems reasonable that in order to get out, you must start thinking. Do you mind if I get in? I love automobile rides. [*He gets in. They wait.*] Well?

56 Milo. All right. I'll try. [*Screws up his face and thinks.*] Are we moving?

57 Watchdog. Not yet. Think harder.

58 Milo. I'm thinking as hard as I can.

59 Watchdog. Well, think just a little harder than that. Come on, you can do it.

60 Milo. All right, all right . . . I'm thinking of all the planets in the solar system, and why water expands when it turns to ice, and all the words that begin with "q," and . . . [*The wheels begin to move.*] We're moving! We're moving!

61 Watchdog. Keep thinking.

62 Milo. [*Thinking.*] How a steam engine works and how to bake a pie and the difference between Fahrenheit and Centigrade . . .

63 Watchdog. Dictionopolis, here we come.

64 Milo. Hey, Watchdog, are you coming along?

65 Tock. You can call me Tock, and keep your eyes on the road.

66 Milo. What kind of place is Dictionopolis anyway?

67 Tock. It's where all the words in the world come from. It used to be a marvelous place, but ever since Rhyme and Reason left, it hasn't been the same.

68 **Milo.** Rhyme and Reason?

69 **Tock.** The two princesses. They used to settle all the arguments between their two brothers who rule over the Land of Wisdom. You see, Azaz is the king of Dictionopolis and the Mathemagician is the king of Digitopolis and they almost never see eye to eye on anything. It was the job of the Princesses Sweet Rhyme and Pure Reason to solve the differences between the two kings, and they always did so well that both sides usually went home feeling very satisfied. But then, one day, the kings had an argument to end all arguments . . .

70 [*The LIGHTS DIM on* Tock *and* Milo, *and come up on* King Azaz *of Dictionopolis on another part of the stage.* Azaz *has a great stomach, a grey beard reaching to his waist, a small crown, and a long robe with the letters of the alphabet written all over it.*]

71 **Azaz.** Of course, I'll abide by the decision of Rhyme and Reason, though I have no doubt as to what it will be. They will choose *words*, of course. Everyone knows that words are more important than numbers any day of the week.

72 [*The* Mathemagician *appears opposite* Azaz. *The* Mathemagician *wears a long flowing robe covered entirely with complex mathematical equations, and a tall pointed hat. He carries a long staff with a pencil point at one end and a large rubber eraser at the other.*]

73 **Mathemagician.** That's what you think, Azaz. People wouldn't even know what day of the week it is without *numbers*. Haven't you ever looked at a calendar? Face it, Azaz. It's numbers that count.

74 **Azaz.** Don't be ridiculous. [*To audience, as if leading a cheer.*] Let's hear it for WORDS!

75 **Mathemagician.** [*To audience, in the same manner.*] Cast your vote for NUMBERS!

76 **Azaz.** A, B, C's!

77 **Mathemagician.** 1, 2, 3's! [*A FANFARE is heard.*]

78 **Azaz and Mathemagician.** [*To each other.*] Quiet! Rhyme and Reason are about to announce their decision.

79 [Rhyme *and* Reason *appear.*]

CLOSE READ

ANNOTATE: In paragraphs 74–78, mark details that show to whom the characters are speaking.

QUESTION: Why does the playwright include this information?

CONCLUDE: How might these details affect how actors deliver their lines, and how an audience might respond?

80 **Rhyme.** Ladies and gentlemen, letters and numerals, fractions and punctuation marks—may we have your attention, please. After careful **consideration** of the problem set before us by King Azaz of Dictionopolis [Azaz *bows.*] and the Mathemagician of Digitopolis [Mathemagician *raises his hands in a victory salute.*] we have come to the following conclusion:

81 **Reason.** Words and numbers are of equal value, for in the cloak of knowledge, one is the warp and the other is the woof.

82 **Rhyme.** It is no more important to count the sands than it is to name the stars.

83 **Rhyme and Reason.** Therefore, let both kingdoms, Dictionopolis and Digitopolis, live in peace.

84 [*The sound of* CHEERING *is heard.*]

85 **Azaz.** Boo! is what I say. Boo and Bah and Hiss!

86 **Mathemagician.** What good are these girls if they can't even settle an argument in anyone's favor? I think I have come to a decision of my own.

87 **Azaz.** So have I.

88 **Azaz and Mathemagician.** [*To the Princesses.*] You are hereby banished from this land to the Castle-in-the-Air. [*To each other.*] And as for you, KEEP OUT OF MY WAY! [*They stalk off in opposite directions.*]

89 [*During this time, the set has been changed to the Market Square of Dictionopolis. LIGHTS come UP on the deserted square.*]

90 **Tock.** And ever since then, there has been neither Rhyme nor Reason in this kingdom. Words are misused and numbers are mismanaged. The argument between the two kings has divided everyone and the real value of both words and numbers has been forgotten. What a waste!

91 **Milo.** Why doesn't somebody rescue the Princesses and set everything straight again?

92 **Tock.** That is easier said than done. The Castle-in-the-Air is very far from here, and the one path which leads to it is guarded by ferocious demons. But hold on, here we are. [*A Man appears, carrying a Gate and a small Tollbooth.*]

93 **Gatekeeper.** AHHHHREMMMM! This is Dictionopolis, a happy kingdom, advantageously located in the foothills of Confusion

consideration (kuhn sihd uh RAY shuhn) *n.* careful thought

and caressed by gentle breezes from the Sea of Knowledge. Today, by royal proclamation, is Market Day. Have you come to buy or sell?

94 **Milo.** I beg your pardon?

95 **Gatekeeper.** Buy or sell, buy or sell. Which is it? You must have come here for a reason.

96 **Milo.** Well, I . . .

97 **Gatekeeper.** Come now, if you don't have a reason, you must at least have an explanation or certainly an excuse.

98 **Milo.** [*Meekly.*] Uh . . . no.

99 **Gatekeeper.** [*Shaking his head.*] Very serious. You can't get in without a reason. [*Thoughtfully*] Wait a minute. Maybe I have an old one you can use. [*Pulls out on old suitcase from the tollbooth and rummages through it.*] No . . . no . . . no . . . this won't do . . . hmmm . . .

100 **Milo.** [*To* Tock.] What's he looking for? [Tock *shrugs.*]

101 **Gatekeeper.** Ah! This is fine. [*Pulls out a Medallion on a chain. Engraved in the Medallion is: "WHY NOT?"*] Why not. That's a good reason for almost anything . . . a bit used, perhaps, but still quite serviceable. There you are, sir. Now I can truly say: Welcome to Dictionopolis.

102 [*He opens the Gate and walks off.* Citizens *and* Merchants *appear on all levels of the stage, and* Milo *and* Tock *find themselves in the middle of a noisy marketplace. As some people buy and sell their wares, others hang a large banner which reads: WELCOME TO THE WORD MARKET.*]

103 **Milo.** Tock! Look!

104 **Merchant 1.** Hey-ya, hey-ya, hey-ya, step right up and take your pick. Juicy tempting words for sale. Get your fresh-picked "ifs," "ands," and "buts"! Just take a look at these nice ripe "wheres" and "whens."

105 **Merchant 2.** Step right up, step right up, fancy, best-quality words here for sale. Enrich your vocabulary and expand your speech with such elegant items as "quagmire," "flabbergast," or "upholstery."

106 **Merchant 3.** Words by the bag, buy them over here. Words by the bag for the more talkative customer. A pound of "happys" at a very reasonable price. . . . very useful for "Happy Birthday," "Happy New Year," "happy days," or

"happy-go-lucky." Or how about a package of "goods," always handy for "good morning," "good afternoon," "good evening," and "goodbye."

107 **Milo.** I can't believe it. Did you ever see so many words?

108 **Tock.** They're fine if you have something to say. [*They come to a Do-It-Yourself Bin.*]

109 **Milo.** [*To* Merchant 4 *at the bin.*] Excuse me, but what are these?

110 **Merchant 4.** These are for people who like to make up their own words. You can pick any assortment you like or buy a special box complete with all the letters and a book of instructions. Here, taste an "A." They're very good. [*He pops one into* Milo's *mouth.*]

111 **Milo.** [*Tastes it hesitantly.*] It's sweet! [*He eats it.*]

misapprehension (mihs ap ree HEHN shuhn) *n.* incorrect understanding; wrong idea

112 **Merchant 4.** I knew you'd like it. "A" is one of our bestsellers. All of them aren't that good, you know. The "Z," for instance—very dry and sawdusty. And the "X"? Tastes like a trunkful of stale air. But most of the others aren't bad at all. Here, try the "I."

113 **Milo.** [*Tasting.*] Cool! It tastes icy.

114 **Merchant 4.** [*To* Tock] How about the "C" for you? It's as crunchy as a bone. Most people are just too lazy to make their own words, but take it from me, not only is it more fun, but it's also *de*-lightful. [*Holds up a "D."*] *e*-lating. [*Holds up an "E."*] and extremely useful! [*Holds up a "U."*]

115 **Milo.** But isn't it difficult? I'm not very good at making words.

116 [*The* Spelling Bee, *a large colorful bee, comes up from behind.*]

117 **Spelling Bee.** Perhaps I can be of some assistance . . . a-s-s-i-s-t-a-n-c-e. [*The Three turn around and see him.*] Don't be alarmed . . . a-l-a-r-m-e-d. I am the Spelling Bee. I can spell anything. Anything. A-n-y-t-h-i-n-g. Try me. Try me.

118 **Milo.** [*Backing off,* Tock *on his guard.*] Can you spell goodbye?

119 **Spelling Bee.** Perhaps you are under the **misapprehension** . . . m-i-s-a-p-p-r-e-h-e-n-s-i-o-n that I am dangerous. Let me assure you that I am quite peaceful. Now, think of the most difficult word you can, and I'll spell it.

120 **Milo.** Uh . . . o.k. [*At this point,* Milo *may turn to the audience and ask them to help him choose a word or he may think of one on his own.*] How about . . . "Curiosity"?

121 **Spelling Bee.** [*Winking.*] Let's see now . . . uh . . . how much time do I have?

122 **Milo.** Just ten seconds. Count them off, Tock.

123 **Spelling Bee.** [*As* Tock *counts.*] Oh dear, oh dear. [*Just at the last moment, quickly.*] C-u-r-i-o-s-i-t-y.

124 **Merchant 4.** Correct! [ALL *Cheer.*]

125 **Milo.** Can you spell anything?

126 **Spelling Bee.** [*Proudly.*] Just about. You see, years ago, I was an ordinary bee minding my own business, smelling flowers all day, occasionally picking up part-time work in people's bonnets. Then one day, I realized that I'd never amount to anything without an education, so I decided that . . .

127 **Humbug.** [*Coming up in a booming voice.*] BALDERDASH! [*He wears a lavish coat, striped pants, checked vest, spats and a derby hat.*] Let me repeat . . . BALDERDASH! [*Swings his cane and clicks his heels in the air.*] Well, well, what have we here? Isn't someone going to introduce me to the little boy?

128 **Spelling Bee.** [*Disdainfully.*] This is the Humbug. You can't trust a word he says.

129 **Humbug.** NONSENSE! Everyone can trust a Humbug. As I was saying to the king just the other day . . .

130 **Spelling Bee.** You've never met the king. [*To Milo.*] Don't believe a thing he tells you.

131 **Humbug.** Bosh, my boy, pure bosh. The Humbugs are an old and noble family, honorable to the core. Why, we fought in the Crusades with Richard the Lionhearted, crossed the Atlantic with Columbus, blazed trails with the pioneers. History is full of Humbugs.

132 **Spelling Bee.** A very pretty speech . . . s-p-e-e-c-h. Now, why don't you go away? I was just advising the lad of the importance of proper spelling.

133 **Humbug.** BAH! As soon as you learn to spell one word, they ask you to spell another. You can never catch up, so why bother? [*Puts his arm around Milo.*] Take my advice, boy, and forget about it. As my great-great-great-grandfather George Washington Humbug used to say . . .

134 **Spelling Bee.** You, sir, are an impostor i-m-p-o-s-t-o-r who can't even spell his own name!

135 **Humbug.** What? You dare to doubt my word? The word of a Humbug? The word of a Humbug who has direct access to the ear of a King? And the king shall hear of this. I promise you . . .

136 **Voice 1.** Did someone call for the King?

137 **Voice 2.** Did you mention the monarch?

138 **Voice 3.** Speak of the sovereign?

139 **Voice 4.** Entreat the Emperor?

140 **Voice 5.** Hail his highness?

141 [*Five tall, thin gentlemen regally dressed in silks and satins, plumed hats, and buckled shoes appear as they speak.*]

142 **Milo.** Who are they?

143 **Spelling Bee.** The King's advisors. Or in more formal terms, his cabinet.

144 **Minister 1.** Greetings!

145 **Minister 2.** Salutations!

146 **Minister 3.** Welcome!

147 **Minister 4.** Good Afternoon!

148 **Minister 5.** Hello!

149 **Milo.** Uh . . . Hi.

150 [*All the* Ministers, *from here on called by their numbers, unfold their scrolls and read in order.*]

3. **unabridged** (uhn uh BRIHJD) *adj.* complete; not shortened.

151 **Minister 1.** By the order of Azaz the Unabridged . . .[3]

152 **Minister 2.** King of Dictionopolis . . .

153 **Minister 3.** Monarch of letters . . .

154 **Minister 4.** Emperor of phrases, sentences, and miscellaneous figures of speech . . .

155 **Minister 5.** We offer you the hospitality of our kingdom . . .

156 **Minister 1.** Country.

157 **Minister 2.** Nation.

158 **Minister 3.** State.

159 **Minister 4.** Commonwealth.

160 **Minister 5.** Realm.

161 **Minister 1.** Empire.

162 **Minister 2.** Palatinate.

163 **Minister 3.** Principality.

164 **Milo.** Do all those words mean the same thing?

165 **Minister 1.** Of course.

166 **Minister 2.** Certainly.

167 **Minister 3.** Precisely.

168 **Minister 4.** Exactly.

169 **Minister 5.** Yes.

170 **Milo.** Then why don't you use just one? Wouldn't that make a lot more sense?

171 **Minister 1.** Nonsense!

172 **Minister 2.** Ridiculous!

173 **Minister 3.** Fantastic!

174 **Minister 4.** Absurd!

175 **Minister 5.** Bosh!

176 **Minister 1.** We're not interested in making sense. It's not our job.

177 **Minister 2.** Besides, one word is as good as another, so why not use them all?

178 **Minister 3.** Then you don't have to choose which one is right.

179 **Minister 4.** Besides, if one is right, then ten are ten times as right.

180 **Minister 5.** Obviously, you don't know who we are.

181 [*Each presents himself and* Milo *acknowledges the introduction.*]

182 **Minister 1.** The Duke of Definition.

183 **Minister 2.** The Minister of Meaning.

184 **Minister 3.** The Earl of Essence.

185 **Minister 4.** The Count of Connotation.

186 **Minister 5.** The Undersecretary of Understanding.

187 **All Five.** And we have come to invite you to the Royal Banquet.

188 **Spelling Bee.** The banquet! That's quite an honor, my boy. A real h-o-n-o-r.

189 **Humbug.** DON'T BE RIDICULOUS! Everybody goes to the Royal Banquet these days.

190 **Spelling Bee.** [To *the* Humbug] True, everybody does go. But some people are invited and others simply push their way in where they aren't wanted.

191 **Humbug.** HOW DARE YOU? You buzzing little upstart, I'll show you who's not wanted . . . [*Raises his cane threateningly.*]

CLOSE READ

ANNOTATE: In paragraphs 182–186, mark the letters that start the two main words of each character's title.

QUESTION: Why do both main words of each character's title begin with the same letters?

CONCLUDE: What effect do these repeated sounds create?

192 **Spelling Bee.** You just watch it! I'm warning w-a-r-n-i-n-g you! [*At that moment, an ear-shattering blast of TRUMPETS, entirely* off-key, *is heard, and* a page *appears.*]

193 **Page.** King Azaz the Unabridged is about to begin the Royal banquet. All guests who do not appear promptly at the table will automatically lose their place. [*A huge Table is carried out with* King Azaz *sitting in a large chair, carried out at the head of the table.*]

194 **Azaz.** Places. Everyone take your places. [*All the characters, including the* Humbug *and the* Spelling Bee, *who forget their quarrel, rush to take their places at the table.* Milo *and* Tock *sit near the king.* Azaz *looks at* Milo.] And just who is this?

195 **Milo.** Your Highness, my name is Milo and this is Tock. Thank you very much for inviting us to your banquet, and I think your palace is beautiful!

196 **Minister 1.** Exquisite.

197 **Minister 2.** Lovely.

198 **Minister 3.** Handsome.

199 **Minister 4.** Pretty.

200 **Minister 5.** Charming.

201 **Azaz.** SILENCE! Now tell me, young man, what can you do to entertain us? Sing songs? Tell stories? Juggle plates? Do tumbling tricks? Which is it?

202 **Milo.** I can't do any of those things.

203 **Azaz.** What an ordinary little boy. Can't you do anything at all?

204 **Milo.** Well . . . I can count to a thousand.

205 **Azaz.** AARGH, numbers! Never mention numbers here. Only use them when we absolutely have to. Now, why don't we change the subject and have some dinner? Since you are the guest of honor, you may pick the menu.

206 Milo. Me? Well, uh . . . I'm not very hungry. Can we just have a light snack?

207 Azaz. A light snack it shall be!

208 [Azaz *claps his hands. Waiters* rush in with covered trays. When they are uncovered, Shafts of Light pour out. The light may be created through the use of battery-operated flashlights which are secured in the trays and covered with a false bottom. The Guests help themselves.*]

209 Humbug. Not a very substantial meal. Maybe you can suggest something a little more filling.

210 Milo. Well, in that case, I think we ought to have a square meal . . .

211 Azaz. [*Claps his hands.*] A square meal it is! [*Waiters serve trays of Colored Squares of all sizes. People serve themselves.*]

212 Spelling Bee. These are awful. [*Humbug coughs and all the Guests do not care for the food.*]

213 Azaz. [*Claps his hands and the trays are removed.*] Time for speeches. [*To Milo.*] You first.

214 Milo. [*Hesitantly.*] Your Majesty, ladies and gentlemen, I would like to take this opportunity to say that . . .

215 Azaz. That's quite enough. Mustn't talk all day.

216 Milo. But I just started to . . .

217 Azaz. NEXT!

218 Humbug. [*Quickly*] Roast turkey, mashed potatoes, vanilla ice cream.

219 Spelling Bee. Hamburgers, corn on the cob, chocolate pudding p-u-d-d-i-n-g. [*Each Guest names two dishes and a dessert.*]

220 Azaz. [*The last.*] Pâté de foie gras, soupe à l'oignon, salade endives, fromage et fruits et demi-tasse. [*He claps his hands. Waiters serve each Guest his Words.*] Dig in. [*To Milo.*] Though I can't say I think much of your choice.

221 Milo. I didn't know I was going to have to eat my words.

222 Azaz. Of course, of course, everybody here does. Your speech should have been in better taste.

223 Minister 1. Here, try some somersault. It improves the flavor.

224 Minister 2. Have a rigamarole. [*Offers breadbasket.*]

ANNOTATE: In paragraphs 223–226, mark the words that sound like but are not actually a seasoning or food.

QUESTION: Why does the playwright use this wordplay?

CONCLUDE: What is the effect of these and other examples of wordplay throughout this scene?

225 **Minister 3.** Or a ragamuffin.

226 **Minister 4.** Perhaps you'd care for a synonym bun.

227 **Minister 5.** Why not wait for your just desserts?

228 **Azaz.** Ah yes, the dessert. We're having a special treat today . . . freshly made at the half-bakery.

229 **Milo.** The half-bakery?

230 **Azaz.** Of course, the half-bakery! Where do you think half-baked ideas come from? Now, please don't interrupt. By royal command, the pastry chefs have . . .

231 **Milo.** What's a half-baked idea?

232 [Azaz *gives up the idea of speaking as a cart is wheeled in and the* Guests *help themselves.*]

233 **Humbug.** They're very tasty, but they don't always agree with you. Here's a good one. [Humbug *hands one to* Milo.]

234 **Milo.** [*Reads.*] "The earth is flat."

235 **Spelling Bee.** People swallowed that one for years. [*Picks up one and reads.*] "The moon is made of green cheese." Now, there's a half-baked idea.

236 [*Everyone chooses one and eats. They include: "It Never Rains But Pours, "Night Air Is Bad Air," "Everything Happens for the Best," "Coffee Stunts Your Growth."*]

237 **Azaz.** And now for a few closing words. Attention! Let me have your attention! [*Everyone leaps up and Exits, except for* Milo, Tock, *and the* Humbug.] Loyal subjects and friends, once again on this gala occasion, we have . . .

238 **Milo.** Excuse me, but everybody left.

239 **Azaz.** [*Sadly.*] I was hoping no one would notice. It happens every time.

240 **Humbug.** They're gone to dinner, and as soon as I finish this last bite, I shall join them.

241 **Milo.** That's ridiculous. How can they eat dinner right after a banquet?

242 **Azaz.** SCANDALOUS! We'll put a stop to it at once. From now on, by royal command, everyone must eat dinner before the banquet.

243 **Milo.** But that's just as bad.

244 **Humbug.** Or just as good. Things which are equally bad are also equally good. Try to look at the bright side of things.

245 **Milo.** I don't know which side of anything to look at. Everything is so confusing, and all your words only make things worse.

246 **Azaz.** How true. There must be something we can do about it.

247 **Humbug.** Pass a law.

248 **Azaz.** We have almost as many laws as words.

249 **Humbug.** Offer a reward. [Azaz *shakes his head and looks madder at each suggestion.*] Send for help? Drive a bargain? Pull the switch? Lower the boom? Toe the line?

250 [*As* Azaz *continues to scowl, the* Humbug *loses confidence and finally gives up.*]

251 **Milo.** Maybe you should let Rhyme and Reason return.

252 **Azaz.** How nice that would be. Even if they were a bother at times, things always went so well when they were here. But I'm afraid it can't be done.

253 **Humbug.** Certainly not. Can't be done.

254 **Milo.** Why not?

255 **Humbug.** [*Now siding with* Milo.] Why not, indeed?

256 **Azaz.** Much too difficult.

257 **Humbug.** Of course, much too difficult.

258 **Milo.** You could, if you really wanted to.

259 **Humbug.** By all means, if you really wanted to, you could.

260 **Azaz.** [*To* Humbug.] How?

261 **Milo.** [*Also to* Humbug.] Yeah, how?

262 **Humbug.** Why . . . uh, it's a simple task for a brave boy with a stout heart, a steadfast dog and a serviceable small automobile.

263 **Azaz.** Go on.

264 **Humbug.** Well, all that he would have to do is cross the dangerous, unknown countryside between here and Digitopolis, where he would have to persuade the Mathemagician to release the Princesses, which we know to be impossible because the Mathemagician will never agree with

Azaz about anything. Once achieving that, it's a simple matter of entering the Mountains of Ignorance from where no one has ever returned alive, an effortless climb up a two thousand foot stairway without railings in a high wind at night to the Castle-in-the-Air. After a pleasant chat with the Princesses, all that remains is a leisurely ride back through those chaotic crags where the frightening fiends have sworn to tear any intruder limb from limb and devour him down to his belt buckle. And finally after doing all that, a triumphal parade! If, of course, there is anything left to parade . . . followed by hot chocolate and cookies for everyone.

265 **Azaz.** I never realized it would be so simple.

266 **Milo.** It sounds dangerous to me.

267 **Tock.** And just who is supposed to make that journey?

268 **Azaz.** A very good question. But there is one far more serious problem.

269 **Milo.** What's that?

270 **Azaz.** I'm afraid I can't tell you that until you return.

271 **Milo.** But wait a minute, I didn't . . .

272 **Azaz.** Dictionopolis will always be grateful to you, my boy, and your dog. [Azaz *pats* Tock *and* Milo.]

273 **Tock.** Now, just one moment, sire . . .

274 **Azaz.** You will face many dangers on your journey, but fear not, for I can give you something for your protection. [Azaz *gives* Milo *a box.*] In this box are the letters of the alphabet. With them you can form all the words you will ever need to help you overcome the obstacles that may stand in your path. All you must do is use them well and in the right places.

275 **Milo.** [*Miserably.*] Thanks a lot.

276 **Azaz.** You will need a guide, of course, and since he knows the obstacles so well, the Humbug has cheerfully volunteered to accompany you.

277 **Humbug.** Now, see here . . . !

278 **Azaz.** You will find him dependable, brave, resourceful, and loyal.

279 **Humbug.** [*Flattered.*] Oh, your Majesty.

280 **Milo.** I'm sure he'll be a great help. [*They approach the car.*]

281 **Tock.** I hope so. It looks like we're going to need it.

282 [*The lights darken and the* king *fades from view.*]

283 **Azaz.** Good luck! Drive carefully! [*The three get into the car and begin to move. Suddenly a thunderously loud NOISE is heard. They slow down the car.*]

284 **Milo.** What was that?

285 **Tock.** It came from up ahead.

286 **Humbug.** It's something terrible, I just know it. Oh, no. Something dreadful is going to happen to us. I can feel it in my bones. [*The NOISE is repeated. They all look at each other fearfully as the lights fade.*] ❧

Response

NOTEBOOK

Answer the questions in your notebook. Use text evidence to support your responses.

1. Personal Connections Which character did you find most humorous? Cite specific details from the play that you especially enjoyed.

Comprehension

2. Reading Check **(a)** What do the merchants in the marketplace of Dictionopolis sell? **(b)** What does Azaz send Milo, Tock, and Humbug to do? **(c)** What does Azaz give Milo?

3. Strategy: Generate Questions **(a)** Cite one question you asked at each stage of the reading: before, during, and after. **(b)** Explain how at least one of these questions led to an answer that deepened your understanding and helped you gain more information.

Analysis

4. Interpret The Clock says, ". . . when you're bored, what you need more than anything is a rude awakening." What does this mean?

5. (a) Analyze What does the clock on Tock's body represent? Explain. **(b) Speculate** If Tock hadn't come along, would Milo still be in the Doldrums? Explain.

6. Make Inferences Milo's bedroom contains images of characters from the Land of Wisdom. What does this suggest about Milo's adventure?

7. Draw Conclusions At the end of Act I, is Milo still bored? Explain, citing text evidence.

EQ Notes > **What is the purpose of imagination?**

What have you learned about the purpose of imagination from reading Act I of the play? Go to your Essential Question Notes and record your observations and thoughts about Act I of *The Phantom Tollbooth*.

 TEKS
5.F. Make inferences and use evidence to support understanding.

6.C. Use text evidence to support an appropriate response.

THE PHANTOM TOLLBOOTH,
ACT I

Close Read

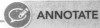
ANNOTATE

1. The model passage and annotation show how one reader analyzed part of paragraph 264 in Act I, Scene ii. Find another detail in the passage to annotate. Then, write your own question and conclusion.

CLOSE-READ MODEL

. . . it's a simple matter of entering the Mountains of Ignorance from where no one has ever returned alive, an effortless climb up a two thousand foot stairway without railings in a high wind at night to the Castle-in-the-Air. After a pleasant chat with the Princesses, all that remains is a leisurely ride back through those chaotic crags. . . .

ANNOTATE: These words suggest something easy and stress-free.

QUESTION: Why does the playwright use words that make the task sound so easy?

CONCLUDE: The contrast shows that Humbug is trying to play down the dangers. It also makes the passage funny.

MY **QUESTION:**

MY **CONCLUSION:**

2. For more practice, answer the Close-Read notes in the selection.

3. Choose a section of the drama that you found especially important. Mark important details. Then, jot down questions and write your conclusions in the open space next to the text.

RESEARCH

NOTEBOOK

Inquiry and Research

Research and Extend This play was adapted from the novel *The Phantom Tollbooth* by Norton Juster. Conduct research to find out when the novel was published and when Susan Nanus's dramatic adaptation was first performed. List the copyright dates and the sources that provided you with this information.

 TEKS
8.C. Analyze how playwrights develop characters through dialogue and staging.

Genre / Text Elements

Dialogue and Character Development In a novel or short story, a narrator may describe characters, explaining how they look and behave as well as what they think and feel. That type of information is called **character development.** In a drama, there is often no narrator. Instead, playwrights use **dialogue,** paired with stage directions, to show what characters are like, what they want, and how they think and feel.

EXAMPLE FROM THE PLAY

Milo. I think I was on my way to Dictionopolis when I got stuck here. Can you help me?

Watchdog. Help you! You've got to help yourself. I suppose you know why you got stuck.

TIP: In this example, we learn that Milo is confused. The Watchdog's surprised response suggests that Milo may be someone who gives up too easily.

NOTEBOOK

INTERACTIVITY

PRACTICE Complete the activity and answer the question. As you write your answers, use content-area vocabulary you have learned, such as *character development* and *playwright.*

1. **Interpret** Explain how each passage helps to develop Milo's character. Consider what the dialogue tells you about his feelings, thoughts, and overall personality. Record your responses in the chart.

DIALOGUE	WHAT IT TELLS YOU
Act I, Scene i, paragraph 13 (Come off it, who do you think you're kidding?… *up to the first sign.*])	
Act I, Scene i, paragraph 15 (I never heard … might as well go there.)	
Act I, Scene ii, paragraph 13 (I'd better get out of … didn't take a wrong turn.)	

2. **Summarize** Explain how Milo's character changes over the course of Act I. Cite specific details in the dialogue that support your summary.

THE PHANTOM TOLLBOOTH,
ACT I

Concept Vocabulary

 NOTEBOOK

Why These Words? These vocabulary words relate to knowledge and ways of thinking. For example, if you are *ignorant*, you lack knowledge.

ignorance	presume	misapprehension
surmise	speculate	consideration

PRACTICE Answer the question and complete the activities.

1. How do the vocabulary words sharpen your understanding of the ideas in the play?

2. Find three other words in the play that relate to knowledge and thinking.

3. Complete each sentence with a vocabulary word. Use each word once.

   (a) Monroe wanted to solve the problem, so he gave it _____.

   (b) Rather than _____, let's wait to see if we made the squad.

   (c) I thought the problem was solved, but that was a _____ on my part.

   (d) I _____ that it's raining since your coat is wet.

   (e) Leena was embarrassed about her _____ on the topic, so she decided to research it.

   (f) You should not _____ what I want; you should ask me.

WORD NETWORK

Add words that are related to imagination from the text to your Word Network.

Word Study

 NOTEBOOK

Denotation and Nuance The **denotation** of a word is its literal dictionary definition. Two words that have the same denotation may have different **nuances,** or shades of difference in meaning. For example, the vocabulary words *surmise* and *speculate* both mean "guess." However, *surmise* implies that the guess is based on a hunch, or feeling. In contrast, *speculate* implies that the guess is based on incomplete information.

PRACTICE Complete the activity.

Use a dictionary to look up these three words that have the same denotation: *stingy, economical, thrifty*. First, write down the denotation that they share. Then, explain the nuances in their meanings.

⭐ TEKS
6.F. Respond using newly acquired vocabulary as appropriate.
10.D.vi. Edit drafts using standard English conventions, including subordinating conjunctions to form complex sentences and correlative conjunctions such as *either/or* and *neither/nor*.

Conventions

Conjunctions Words that join other words, phrases, or clauses together are called **conjunctions.** There are three types of conjunctions: coordinating, subordinating, and correlative. In the sample sentences in the chart, the conjunctions are underlined.

TYPE OF CONJUNCTION	EXAMPLES	SAMPLE SENTENCES
Coordinating Conjunctions: join words or groups of words of equal importance	*and, or, but, nor, for, yet, so*	• Spelling Bee <u>and</u> Humbug quarrel. • They are different characters, <u>yet</u> they echo one another.
Subordinating Conjunctions: introduce a dependent clause in a complex sentence	*after, although, because, since, unless, when, while, where*	• <u>When</u> the banquet is over, everyone leaves. • Milo agrees to help, <u>although</u> he knows very little.
Correlative Conjunctions: come in pairs and join two equal grammatical terms	*both/and; either/or; neither/ nor; not only/but also; whether/or*	• <u>Both</u> Milo <u>and</u> Tock go on an adventure. • They cannot agree <u>whether</u> words <u>or</u> numbers matter more.

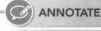

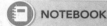

ANNOTATE

NOTEBOOK

READ IT Identify the conjunctions used in these passages from the play. Label each conjunction as coordinating, subordinating, or correlative.

1. You see, while he was sleeping, someone had invented the wheel and everyone had moved to the suburbs.

2. And ever since then, there has been neither Rhyme nor Reason in this kingdom.

3. The argument between the two kings has divided everyone and the real value of both words and numbers has been forgotten.

WRITE IT Write a paragraph about an imaginary adventure. Then, edit your draft to use at least one coordinating conjunction, one subordinating conjunction to create a complex sentence, and one set of correlative conjunctions.

DISCUSS IT Pair up with a partner and read your paragraphs aloud to each other. As you speak, emphasize the conjunctions. The listener should note the conjunctions the speaker uses. Then, trade places. Discuss ways in which conjunctions indicate specific relationships among ideas.

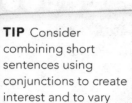

THE PHANTOM TOLLBOOTH,
ACT I

TIP Consider combining short sentences using conjunctions to create interest and to vary your sentence lengths and types.

Composition

A **profile** is a type of descriptive writing that provides details and explanations about a subject. Profiles are often written about people.

ASSIGNMENT

Write a casting **profile** in which you explain why an actor of your choice should play the role of Milo in a new production of this play. The actor could be a well-known film star or someone you know personally.

- In your introduction, state your purpose and main point.
- Continue focusing on your main point in one to two body paragraphs, including facts and descriptive details about the character of Milo. Make sure to explain why the actor you are recommending is a good match for Milo and could do a great job with the role.
- Use transitional words and phrases—such as *therefore*, or *in my opinion*—to lead readers through your thought process.
- Write a memorable conclusion in which you restate your main point.

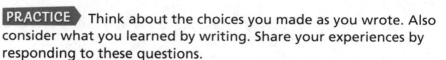

NOTEBOOK

Reflect on Your Writing

PRACTICE Think about the choices you made as you wrote. Also consider what you learned by writing. Share your experiences by responding to these questions.

1. What was the most challenging part of writing the profile? Explain.

2. How could you revise your profile to improve it?

3. WHY THESE WORDS? The words you choose make a difference in your writing. Which words helped you clearly state your purpose and main point in your profile?

TEKS

6.H. Respond orally or in writing with appropriate register, vocabulary, tone, and voice.

10.B.i. Develop drafts into a focused, structured, and coherent piece of writing by organizing with purposeful structure, including an introduction, transitions, coherence within and across paragraphs, and a conclusion.

10.B.ii. Develop drafts into a focused, structured, and coherent piece of writing by developing an engaging idea reflecting depth of thought with specific facts and details.

Speaking and Listening

A **dramatic reading** is an oral performance of a literary work. It shows a performer's interpretation of the text.

ASSIGNMENT

Conduct a **dramatic reading** of a scene from Act I of *The Phantom Tollbooth*. As a class, decide whether pairs or groups will work on the same scene or on different scenes. Then, decide who will play the different roles. If necessary, one person can play more than one role or you can divide a single role among several people. Also, decide who will read the stage directions.

EQ Notes Before moving on to a new selection, go to your Essential Question Notes and record any additional thoughts or observations you may have about Act I of the play.

Prepare and Deliver the Reading

Annotate the Text Reread the scene you will perform and take notes about the way you want to present it. Mark words and phrases you will emphasize to show how you interpret the text. Be clear about the reasons for your choices, so that you can discuss them after your reading.

Use Your Voice Effectively Decide how you will use your voice to capture characters' unique qualities.

- **Vocal register** refers to the highs and lows of your voice.

- **Speaking rate** is the speed at which you talk.

- **Tone** is the attitude you show when you speak.

Decide on the appropriate register, speaking rate, and tone to use. For example, if you are playing a Lethargarian, you might use a low register, speak slowly, and adopt an uncaring tone. Use the stage directions to help make your decisions.

Discuss and Evaluate

After you deliver your reading, discuss your choices with the audience. Accept and answer questions and be prepared to explain your interpretation of the characters.

BUILD YOUR SIGHT VOCABULARY

As you prepare to read aloud, make sure you are familiar with all the words in the text. Read it through, taking note of any words that are not part of your sight vocabulary. Listen to the selection audio as you read along to make sure you're comfortable with the words and their pronunciations.

The Phantom Tollbooth, Act II

Concept Vocabulary

You will encounter the following words as you read *The Phantom Tollbooth*, Act II. Before reading, note how familiar you are with each word. Using a scale of 1 (do not know it at all) to 5 (know it very well), indicate your knowledge of each word.

WORD	YOUR RANKING
suspiciously	
obstacle	
pessimistic	
malicious	
insincerity	
compromise	

Comprehension Strategy

ANNOTATE

Create Mental Images

When you **create mental images** as you read a play, you use visual clues in the text to imagine how characters look and behave. Picturing the characters, their actions, and the scenery can deepen your understanding of the play's events and ideas. Look for the following types of details to create mental images as you read this play:

- details that tell how characters act and move, and what they do on stage
- adjectives related to color, space, and shape
- verbs (such as *sprint* or *stroll*) and adverbs (such as *quickly* or *awkwardly*) that tell how characters move or react

PRACTICE As you read the play, mark details that help you create mental images and deepen your understanding. Jot down your notes in the open space next to the text.

 TEKS
5.D. Create mental images to deepen understanding.

The Phantom Tollbooth Act II

Susan Nanus
Based on the book by Norton Juster

REVIEW AND ANTICIPATE

In Act I, Milo is lifted from his boredom into a strange kingdom that is in conflict over the importance of letters and numbers. After traveling through Dictionopolis, he agrees to rescue Princesses Rhyme and Reason, who can settle the conflict. As Act II opens, Milo, Tock, and the Humbug arrive in the city of Digitopolis on their quest to rescue the princesses.

 AUDIO

 ANNOTATE

Act II

Scene i

1 *The set of Digitopolis glitters in the background, while Upstage Right near the road, a small colorful Wagon sits, looking quite deserted. On its side in large letters, a sign reads: "KAKAFONOUS A. DISCHORD Doctor of Dissonance."*[1] *Enter Milo, Tock, and Humbug,* fearfully. *They look at the wagon.*

1. **dissonance** (DIHS uh nuhns) *n.* harsh or unpleasant combination of sounds.

2 **Tock.** There's no doubt about it. That's where the noise was coming from.

3 **Humbug.** [*To* Milo.] Well, go on.

4 **Milo.** Go on what?

5 **Humbug.** Go on and see who's making all that noise in there. We can't just ignore a creature like that.

6 **Milo.** Creature? What kind of creature? Do you think he's dangerous?

7 **Humbug.** Go on, Milo. Knock on the door. We'll be right behind you.

8 **Milo.** O.K. Maybe he can tell us how much further it is to Digitopolis.

9 [*Milo tiptoes up to the wagon and KNOCKS timidly. The moment he knocks, a terrible CRASH is heard inside the wagon, and* Milo *and the others jump back in fright. At the same time, the Door Flies Open, and from the dark interior, a Hoarse* Voice *inquires.*]

10 **Voice.** Have you ever heard a whole set of dishes dropped from the ceiling onto a hard stone floor? [*The Others are speechless with fright.* Milo *shakes his head.* Voice *happily.*] Have you ever heard an ant wearing fur slippers walk across a thick wool carpet? [Milo *shakes his head again.*] Have you ever heard a blindfolded octopus unwrap a cellophane-covered bathtub? [Milo *shakes his head a third time.*] Ha! I knew it. [*He hops out, a little man, wearing a white coat, with a stethoscope around his neck, and a small mirror attached to his forehead, and with very huge ears, and a mortar and pestle in his hands. He stares at* Milo, Tock *and* Humbug.] None of you looks well at all! Tsk, tsk, not at all. [*He opens the top or side of his Wagon, revealing a dusty interior resembling an old apothecary shop, with shelves lined with jars and boxes, a table, books, test tubes, and bottles and measuring spoons.*]

11 **Milo.** [*Timidly.*] Are you a doctor?

12 **Dischord.** [Voice.] I am KAKAFONOUS A. DISCHORD. DOCTOR OF DISSONANCE! [*Several small explosions and a grinding crash are heard.*]

13 **Humbug.** [*Stuttering with fear.*] What does the "A" stand for?

14 **Dischord.** AS LOUD AS POSSIBLE! [*Two screeches and a bump are heard.*] Now, step a little closer and stick out your tongues. [Dischord *examines them.*] Just as I expected. [*He opens a large dusty book and thumbs through the pages.*] You're all suffering from a severe lack of noise. [Dischord *begins running around, collecting bottles, reading the labels to himself as he goes along.*] "Loud Cries."

"Soft Cries." "Bangs, Bongs, Swishes, Swooshes." "Snaps and Crackles." "Whistles and Gongs." "Squeaks, Squawks, and Miscellaneous Uproar." [*As he reads them off, he pours a little of each into a large glass beaker and stirs the mixture with a wooden spoon. The concoction smokes and bubbles.*] Be ready in just a moment.

15 **Milo.** [*Suspiciously.*] Just what kind of doctor are you?

16 **Dischord.** Well, you might say, I'm a specialist. I specialize in noises, from the loudest to the softest, and from the slightly annoying to the terribly unpleasant. For instance, have you ever heard a square-wheeled steamroller ride over a street full of hard-boiled eggs? [*Very loud CRUNCHING SOUNDS are heard.*]

17 **Milo.** [*Holding his ears.*] But who would want all those terrible noises?

18 **Dischord.** [*Surprised at the question.*] Everybody does. Why, I'm so busy I can hardly fill all the orders for noise pills, racket lotion, clamor salve, and hubbub tonic. That's all people seem to want these days. Years ago, everyone wanted pleasant sounds and business was terrible. But then the cities were built and there was a great need for honking horns, screeching trains, clanging bells, and all the rest of those wonderfully unpleasant sounds we use so much today. I've been working overtime ever since and my medicine here is in great demand. All you have to do is take one spoonful every day, and you'll never have to hear another beautiful sound again. Here, try some.

19 **Humbug.** [*Backing away.*] If it's all the same to you, I'd rather not.

20 **Milo.** I don't want to be cured of beautiful sounds.

21 **Tock.** Besides, there's no such sickness as a lack of noise.

22 **Dischord.** How true. That's what makes it so difficult to cure. [*Takes a large glass bottle from the shelf.*] Very well, if you want to go all through life suffering from a noise deficiency,[2] I'll just give this to Dynne for his lunch. [*Uncorks the bottle and pours the liquid into it. There is a rumbling and then a loud explosion accompanied by smoke, out of which* Dynne, *a smog-like creature with yellow eyes and a frowning mouth, appears.*]

23 **Dynne.** [*Smacking his lips.*] Ahhh, that was good, Master. I thought you'd never let me out. It was really cramped in there.

24 **Dischord.** This is my assistant, the awful Dynne. You must forgive his appearance, for he really doesn't have any.

25 **Milo.** What is a Dynne?

---

suspiciously (suh SPIHSH uhs lee) *adv.* based on a lack of trust or belief; disbelievingly; cautiously

2. **deficiency** (dih FIHSH uhn see) *n.* shortage or lack.

CLOSE READ

ANNOTATE: In paragraphs 22–24, mark details that show what Dynne looks like and how he behaves.

QUESTION: Why does the playwright include these details?

CONCLUDE: What is the effect of these details, especially when added to Dischord's statement that Dynne "doesn't have" an appearance?

26 **Dischord.** You mean you've never heard of the awful Dynne? When you're playing in your room and making a great amount or noise, what do they tell you to stop?

27 **Milo.** That awful din.

28 **Dischord.** When the neighbors are playing their radio too loud late at night, what do you wish they'd turn down?

29 **Tock.** That awful din.

30 **Dischord.** And when the street on your block is being repaired and the drills are working all day, what does everyone complain of?

31 **Humbug.** [*Brightly.*] The dreadful row.

32 **Dynne.** The Dreadful Rauw was my grandfather. He perished in the great silence epidemic of 1712. I certainly can't understand why you don't like noise. Why, I heard an explosion last week that was so lovely, I groaned with appreciation for two days. [*He gives a loud groan at the memory.*]

33 **Dischord**. He's right, you know! Noise is the most valuable thing in the world.

34 **Milo.** King Azaz says words are.

35 **Dischord.** NONSENSE! Why, when a baby wants food, how does he ask?

36 **Dynne.** [*Happily.*] He screams!

37 **Dischord.** And when a racing car wants gas?

38 **Dynne.** [*Jumping for Joy.*] It chokes!

39 **Dischord.** And what happens to the dawn when a new day begins?

40 **Dynne.** [*Delighted.*] It breaks!

41 **Dischord.** You see how simple it is? [*To Dynne.*] Isn't it time for us to go?

42 **Milo.** Where to? Maybe we're going the same way.

43 **Dynne.** I doubt it. [*Picking up empty sacks from the table.*] We're going on our collection rounds. Once a day, I travel throughout the kingdom and collect all the wonderfully horrible and beautifully unpleasant sounds I can find and bring them back to the doctor to use in his medicine.

44 **Dischord.** Where are you going?

45 **Milo.** To Digitopolis.

46 **Dischord.** Oh, there are a number of ways to get to Digitopolis, if you know how to follow directions. Just take a look at the sign at the fork in the road. Though why you'd ever want to go there, I'll never know.

47 **Milo.** We want to talk to the Mathemagician.

48 **Humbug.** About the release of the Princesses Rhyme and Reason.

49 **Dischord.** Rhyme and Reason? I remember them. Very nice girls, but a little too quiet for my taste. In fact, I've been meaning to send them something that Dynne brought home by mistake and which I have absolutely no use for. [*He rummages through the wagon.*] Ah, here it is . . . or maybe you'd like it for yourself. [*Hands* Milo *a package.*]

50 **Milo.** What is it?

51 **Dischord.** The sounds of laughter. They're so unpleasant to hear, it's almost unbearable. All those giggles and snickers and happy shouts of joy. I don't know what Dynne was thinking of when he collected them. Here, take them to the Princesses or keep them for yourselves, I don't care. Well, time to move on. Goodbye now and good luck! [*He has shut the wagon by now and gets in. LOUD NOISES begin to erupt as* Dynne *pulls the wagon offstage.*]

CLOSE READ

ANNOTATE: In paragraph 51, mark terms that identify different kinds of laughter.

QUESTION: Why does the playwright include these details?

CONCLUDE: What is the effect of these details, especially in helping to portray Dischord?

52 **Milo.** [*Calling after them.*] But wait! The fork in the road . . . you didn't tell us where it is . . .

53 **Tock.** It's too late. He can't hear a thing.

54 **Humbug.** I could use a fork of my own, at the moment. And a knife and a spoon to go with it. All of a sudden, I feel very hungry.

55 **Milo.** So do I, but it's no use thinking about it. There won't be anything to eat until we reach Digitopolis. [*They get into the car.*]

56 **Humbug.** [*Rubbing his stomach.*] Well, the sooner the better is what I say. [*A SIGN suddenly appears.*]

57 **Voice.** [*A strange voice from nowhere.*] But which way will get you there sooner? That is the question.

58 **Tock.** Did you hear something?

59 **Milo.** Look! The fork in the road and a signpost to Digitopolis! [*They read the Sign.*]

60 **Humbug.** Let's travel by miles, it's shorter.

61 **Milo.** Let's travel by half inches. It's quicker.

62 **Tock.** But which road should we take? It must make a difference.

63 **Milo.** Do you think so?

64 **Tock.** Well, I'm not sure, but . . .

65 **Humbug.** He could be right. On the other hand, he could also be wrong. Does it make a difference or not?

66 **Voice.** Yes, indeed, indeed it does, certainly, my yes, it does make a difference.

67 [*The Dodecahedron appears, a 12-sided figure with a different face on each side, and with all the edges labeled with a small letter and all the angles labeled with a large letter. He wears a beret and peers at the others with a serious face. He doffs his cap and recites:*]

68 **Dodecahedron.** *My angles are many.*

My sides are not few.

I'm the Dodecahedron.

Who are you?

69 **Milo.** What's a Dodecahedron?

70 **Dodecahedron.** [*Turning around slowly.*] See for yourself. A Dodecahedron is a mathematical shape with 12 faces. [*All his faces appear as he turns, each face with a different expression. He points to them.*] I usually use one at a time. It saves wear and tear. What are you called?

71 **Milo.** Milo.

72 **Dodecahedron.** That's an odd name. [*Changing his smiling face to a frowning one.*] And you have only one face.

73 **Milo.** [*Making sure it is still there.*] Is that bad?

74 **Dodecahedron.** You'll soon wear it out using it for everything. Is everyone with one face called Milo?

75 **Milo.** Oh, no. Some are called Billy or Jeffery or Sally or Lisa or lots of other things.

76 **Dodecahedron.** How confusing. Here everything is called exactly what it is. The triangles are called triangles, the circles are called circles, and even the same numbers have the same name. Can you imagine what would happen if we named all the twos Billy or Jeffery or Sally or Lisa or lots of other things? You'd have to say Robert plus John equals four, and if the fours were named Albert, things would be hopeless.

77 **Milo.** I never thought of it that way.

78 **Dodecahedron.** [*With an admonishing face.*] Then I suggest you begin at once, for in Digitopolis, everything is quite precise.

79 **Milo.** Then perhaps you can help us decide which road we should take.

80 **Dodecahedron.** [*Happily.*] By all means. There's nothing to it. [*As he talks, the three others try to solve the problem on a Large Blackboard that is wheeled onstage for the occasion.*] Now, if a small car carrying three people at 30 miles an hour for 10 minutes along a road 5 miles long at 11:35 in the morning starts at the same time as 3 people who have been traveling in a little automobile at 20 miles an hour for 15 minutes on another road exactly twice as long as half the distance of the other, while a dog, a bug, and a boy travel an equal distance in the same time or the same distance in an equal time along a third road in mid-October, then which one arrives first and which is the best way to go?

81 **Humbug.** Seventeen!

82 **Milo.** [*Still figuring frantically.*] I'm not sure, but . . .

83 **Dodecahedron.** You'll have to do better than that.

84 **Milo.** I'm not very good at problems.

85 **Dodecahedron.** What a shame. They're so very useful. Why, did you know that if a beaver 2 feet long with a tail a foot and a half long can build a dam 12 feet high and 6 feet wide in 2 days, all you would need to build Boulder Dam is a beaver 68 feet long with a 51 foot tail?

86 **Humbug.** [*Grumbling as his pencil snaps.*] Where would you find a beaver that big?

87 **Dodecahedron.** I don't know, but if you did, you'd certainly know what to do with him.

88 **Milo.** That's crazy.

89 **Dodecahedron.** That may be true, but it's completely accurate, and as long as the answer is right, who cares if the question is wrong?

90 **Tock.** [*Who has been patiently doing the first problem.*] All three roads arrive at the same place at the same time.

91 **Dodecahedron.** Correct! And I'll take you there myself. [*The blackboard rolls off, and all four get into the car and drive off.*] Now you see how important problems are. If you hadn't done this one properly, you might have gone the wrong way.

92 **Milo.** But if all the roads arrive at the same place at the same time, then aren't they all the right road?

93 **Dodecahedron.** [*Glaring from his upset face.*] Certainly not! They're all the wrong way! Just because you have a choice, it doesn't mean that any of them has to be right. [*Pointing in another direction.*] That's the way to Digitopolis and we'll be there any moment. [*Suddenly the lighting grows dimmer.*] In fact, we're here. Welcome to the Land of Numbers.

94 **Humbug.** [*Looking around at the barren landscape.*] It doesn't look very inviting.

95 **Milo.** Is this the place where numbers are made?

96 **Dodecahedron.** They're not made. You have to dig for them. Don't you know anything at all about numbers?

97 **Milo.** Well, I never really thought they were very important.

98 **Dodecahedron.** NOT IMPORTANT! Could you have tea for two without the 2? Or three blind mice without the 3? And how would you sail the seven seas without the 7?

99 **Milo.** All I meant was . . .

100 **Dodecahedron.** [*Continues shouting angrily.*] If you had high hopes, how would you know how high they were? And did you know that narrow escapes come in different widths? Would you travel the whole world wide without ever knowing how wide it was? And how could you do anything at long last without knowing how long the last was? Why, numbers are the most beautiful and valuable things in the world. Just follow me and I'll show you. [*He motions to them and pantomimes walking through rocky terrain with the others in tow. A Doorway similar to the Tollbooth appears and the* Dodecahedron *opens it and motions the others to follow him through.*] Come along, come along. I can't wait for you all day. [*They enter the doorway and the lights are dimmed very low, as to simulate the interior of a cave. The SOUNDS of scraping and tapping, scuffling and digging are heard around them. He hands them Helmets with flashlights attached.*] Put these on.

101 **Milo.** [*Whispering.*] Where are we going?

102 **Dodecahedron.** We're here. This is the numbers mine. [*LIGHTS UP A LITTLE, revealing Little Men digging and chopping, shoveling, and scraping.*] Right this way and watch your step. [*His voice echoes and reverberates. Iridescent*[3] *and glittery numbers seem to sparkle from everywhere.*]

103 **Milo.** [*Awed.*] Whose mine is it?

104 **Voice of Mathemagician.** By the four million eight hundred and twenty-seven thousand six hundred and fifty-nine hairs on my head, it's mine, of course! [*ENTER the Mathemagician, carrying his long staff which looks like a giant pencil.*]

105 **Humbug.** [*Already intimidated.*] It's a lovely mine, really it is.

106 **Mathemagician.** [*Proudly.*] The biggest number mine in the kingdom.

107 **Milo.** [*Excitedly.*] Are there any precious stones in it?

108 **Mathemagician.** Precious stones! [*Then softly.*] By the eight million two hundred and forty-seven thousand three hundred and twelve threads in my robe, I'll say there are. Look here. [*Reaches in a cart, pulls out a small object, polishes it vigorously, and holds it up to the light, where it sparkles.*]

109 **Milo.** But that's a five.

110 **Mathemagician.** Exactly. As valuable a jewel as you'll find anywhere. Look at some of the others. [*Scoops up others and pours*

3. **iridescent** (ihr uh DEHS uhnt) *adj.* showing different colors when seen from different angles.

CLOSE READ

ANNOTATE: In paragraph 104 and again in paragraph 108, mark the items the Mathemagician counts.

QUESTION: Why does the playwright indicate that he counts items that are so small and plentiful?

CONCLUDE: What is the effect of these details?

them into Milo's arms. They include all numbers from 1 to 9 and an assortment of zeros.]

111 **Dodecahedron.** We dig them and polish them right here, and then send them all over the world. Marvelous, aren't they?

112 **Tock.** They are beautiful. [*He holds them up to compare them to the numbers on his clock body.*]

113 **Milo.** So that's where they come from. [*Looks at them and carefully hands them back, but drops a few which smash and break in half.*] Oh. I'm sorry!

114 **Mathemagician.** [*Scooping them up.*] Oh, don't worry about that. We use the broken ones for fractions. How about some lunch? [*Takes out a little whistle and blows it. Two miners rush in carrying an immense cauldron which is bubbling and steaming. The workers put down their tools and gather around to eat.*]

115 **Humbug.** That looks delicious! [*Tock and Milo also look hungrily at the pot.*]

116 **Mathemagician.** Perhaps you'd care for something to eat?

117 **Milo.** Oh, yes, sir!

118 **Tock.** Thank you.

119 **Humbug.** [*Already eating.*] Ummm . . . delicious! [*All finish their bowls immediately.*]

120 **Mathemagician.** Please have another portion. [*They eat and finish.* Mathemagician *serves them again.*] Don't stop now. [*They finish.*] Come on, no need to be bashful. [*Serves them again.*]

121 **Milo.** [*To* Tock *and* Humbug *as he finishes again.*] Do you want to hear something strange? Each one I eat makes me a little hungrier than before.

122 **Mathemagician.** Do have some more. [*He serves them again. They eat frantically, until the* Mathemagician *blows his whistle again and the pot is removed.*]

123 **Humbug.** [*Holding his stomach.*] Uggghhh! I think I'm starving.

124 **Milo.** Me, too, and I ate so much.

125 **Dodecahedron.** [*Wiping the gravy from several of his mouths.*] Yes, it was delicious, wasn't it? It's the specialty of the kingdom . . . subtraction stew.

126 **Tock.** [*Weak from hunger.*] I have more of an appetite than when I began.

127 **Mathemagician.** Certainly, what did you expect? The more you eat, the hungrier you get, everyone knows that.

128 **Milo.** They do? Then how do you get enough?

129 **Mathemagician.** Enough? Here in Digitopolis, we have our meals when we're full and eat until we're hungry. That way, when you don't have anything at all, you have more than enough. It's a very economical system. You must have been stuffed to have eaten so much.

130 **Dodecahedron.** It's completely logical. The more you want, the less you get, and the less you get, the more you have. Simple arithmetic, that's all. [Tock, Milo *and* Humbug *look at him blankly.*] Now, look, suppose you had something and added nothing to it. What would you have?

131 **Milo.** The same.

132 **Dodecahedron.** Splendid! And suppose you had something and added less than nothing to it? What would you have then?

133 **Humbug.** Starvation! Oh, I'm so hungry.

134 **Dodecahedron.** Now, now, it's not as bad as all that. In a few hours, you'll be nice and full again . . . just in time for dinner.

135 **Milo.** But I only eat when I'm hungry.

136 **Mathemagician.** [*Waving the eraser of his staff.*] What a curious idea. The next thing you'll have us believe is that you only sleep when you're tired.

137 [*The mine has disappeared as well as the Miners.*]

138 **Humbug.** Where did everyone go?

139 **Mathemagician.** Oh, they're still in the mine. I often find that the best way to get from one place to another is to erase everything and start again. Please make yourself at home.

140 [*They find themselves in a unique room, in which all the walls, tables, chairs, desks, cabinets, and blackboards are labeled to show their heights, widths, depths, and distances to and from each other. To one side is a gigantic notepad on an artist's easel, and from hooks and strings hang a collection of rulers, measures, weights and tapes, and all other measuring devices.*]

141 **Milo.** Do you always travel that way? [*He looks around in wonder.*]

142 **Mathemagician.** No, indeed! [*He pulls a plumb line from a hook and walks.*] Most of the time I take the shortest distance between any two points. And of course, when I have to be in several places at

once . . . [*He writes 3 × 1 = 3 on the notepad with his staff.*] I simply multiply. [*Three Figures* looking like *the* Mathemagician *appear on a platform above.*]

143 **Milo.** How did you do that?

144 **Mathemagician** and **The Three.** There's nothing to it, if you have a magic staff. [*The Three Figures* cancel themselves out and disappear.]

145 **Humbug.** That's nothing but a big pencil.

146 **Mathemagician.** True enough, but once you learn to use it, there's no end to what you can do.

147 **Milo.** Can you make things disappear?

148 **Mathemagician.** Just step a little closer and watch this. [*Shows them that there is nothing up his sleeve or in his hat. He writes:*]

$$4 + 9 - 2 \times 16 + 1 = 3 \times 6 - 67 + 8 \times 2 - 3 + 26 - 1 - 34 + 3 - 7 + 2 - 5 = [\textit{He looks up expectantly.}]$$

149 **Humbug.** Seventeen?

150 **Milo.** It all comes to zero.

CLOSE READ

ANNOTATE: In paragraphs 151 and 158, mark the directions that suggest the characters speak directly to the audience.

QUESTION: Why does the playwright include these directions?

CONCLUDE: If the actors were to follow these directions, how might they affect the audience's response?

151 **Mathemagician.** Precisely. [*Makes a theatrical bow and rips off paper from notepad.*] Now, is there anything else you'd like to see? [*At this point, an appeal to the audience to see if anyone would like a problem solved.*]

152 **Milo.** Well . . . can you show me the biggest number there is?

153 **Mathemagician.** Why, I'd be delighted. [*Opening a closet door.*] We keep it right here. It took four miners to dig it out. [*He shows them a huge "3" twice as high as the* Mathemagician.]

154 **Milo.** No, that's not what I mean. Can you show me the longest number there is?

155 **Mathemagician.** Sure. [*Opens another door.*] Here it is. It took three carts to carry it here. [*Door reveals an "8" that is as wide as the "3" was high.*]

156 **Milo.** No, no, that's not what I meant either. [*Looks helplessly at* Tock.]

157 **Tock.** I think what you would like to see is the number of the greatest possible magnitude.

158 **Mathemagician.** Well, why didn't you say so? [*He busily measures them and all other things as he speaks, and marks it down.*] What's the

greatest number you can think of? [*Here, an appeal can also be made to the audience or* Milo *may think of his own answers.*]

159 **Milo.** Uh . . . nine trillion, nine hundred and ninety-nine billion, nine hundred ninety-nine million, nine hundred ninety-nine thousand, nine hundred and ninety-nine. [*He puffs.*]

160 **Mathemagician.** [*Writes that on the pad.*] Very good. Now add one to it. [Milo *or audience does.*] Now add one again. [Milo *or audience does so.*] Now add one again. Now add one again. Now add . . .

161 **Milo.** But when can I stop?

162 **Mathemagician.** Never. Because the number you want is always at least one more than the number you have, and it's so large that if you started saying it yesterday, you wouldn't finish tomorrow.

163 **Humbug.** Where could you ever find a number so big?

164 **Mathemagician.** In the same place they have the smallest number there is, and you know where that is?

165 **Milo.** The smallest number . . . let's see . . . one one-millionth?

166 **Mathemagician.** Almost. Now all you have to do is divide that in half and then divide that in half and then divide that in half and then divide that . . .

167 **Milo.** Doesn't that ever stop either?

168 **Mathemagician.** How can it when you can always take half of what you have and divide it in half again? Look. [*Pointing offstage.*] You see that line?

169 **Milo.** You mean that long one out there?

170 **Mathemagician.** That's it. Now, if you just follow that line forever, and when you reach the end, turn left, you will find the Land of Infinity. That's where the tallest, the shortest, the biggest, the smallest, and the most and the least of everything are kept.

171 **Milo.** But how can you follow anything forever? You know, I get the feeling that everything in Digitopolis is very difficult.

172 **Mathemagician.** But on the other hand, I think you'll find that the only thing you can do easily is be wrong, and that's hardly worth the effort.

173 **Milo.** But . . . what bothers me is . . . well, why is it that even when things are correct, they don't really seem to be right?

CLOSE READ

ANNOTATE: In paragraph 173, mark the ellipses, or punctuation that looks like three periods in a row.

QUESTION: Why does the author use ellipses here?

CONCLUDE: How might this punctuation affect the way in which an actor delivers this line?

174 **Mathemagician.** [*Grows sad and quiet.*] How true. It's been that way ever since Rhyme and Reason were banished. [*Sadness turns to fury.*] And all because of that stubborn wretch Azaz! It's all his fault.

175 **Milo.** Maybe if you discussed it with him . . .

176 **Mathemagician.** He's just too unreasonable! Why just last month, I sent him a very friendly letter, which he never had the courtesy to answer. See for yourself. [*Puts the letter on the easel. The letter reads:*]

177 4738 1919,

     667 394107 5841 62589 85371 14

     39588 7190434 203 27689 57131 481206.

       5864 98053,

         62179875073

178 **Milo.** But maybe he doesn't understand numbers.

179 **Mathemagician.** Nonsense! Everybody understands numbers. No matter what language you speak, they always mean the same thing. A seven is a seven everywhere in the world.

180 **Milo.** [*To* Tock *and* Humbug.] Everyone is so sensitive about what he knows best.

181 **Tock.** With your permission, sir, we'd like to rescue Rhyme and Reason.

182 **Mathemagician.** Has Azaz agreed to it?

183 **Tock.** Yes, sir.

184 **Mathemagician.** THEN I DON'T! Ever since they've been banished, we've never agreed on anything, and we never will.

185 **Milo.** Never?

186 **Mathemagician.** NEVER! And if you can prove otherwise, you have my permission to go.

187 **Milo.** Well then, with whatever Azaz agrees, you disagree.

188 **Mathemagician.** Correct.

189 **Milo.** And with whatever Azaz disagrees, you agree.

190 **Mathemagician.** [*Yawning, cleaning his nails.*] Also correct.

191 **Milo.** Then, each of you agrees that he will disagree with whatever each of you agrees with, and if you both disagree with the same thing, aren't you really in agreement?

192 **Mathemagician.** I'VE BEEN TRICKED! [*Figures it over, but comes up with the same answer.*]

193 **Tock.** And now may we go?

194 **Mathemagician.** [*Nods weakly.*] It's a long and dangerous journey. Long before you find them, the demons will know you're there. Watch out for them, because if you ever come face to face, it will be too late. But there is one other **obstacle** even more serious than that.

195 **Milo.** [*Terrified.*] What is it?

196 **Mathemagician.** I'm afraid I can't tell you until you return. But maybe I can give you something to help you out. [*Claps hands. ENTER the* Dodecahedron, *carrying something on a pillow. The* Mathemagician *takes it.*] Here is your own magic staff. Use it well and there is nothing it can't do for you. [*Puts a small, gleaming pencil in* Milo's *breast pocket.*]

197 **Humbug.** Are you sure you can't tell about that serious obstacle?

198 **Mathemagician.** Only when you return. And now the Dodecahedron will escort you to the road that leads to the Castle-in-the-Air. Farewell, my friends, and good luck to you. [*They shake hands, say goodbye, and the* Dodecahedron *leads them off.*] Good luck to you! [*To himself.*] Because you're sure going to need it. [*He watches them through a telescope and marks down the calculations.*]

199 **Dodecahedron.** [*He re-enters.*] Well, they're on their way.

200 **Mathemagician.** So I see . . . [Dodecahedron *stands waiting.*] Well, what is it?

201 **Dodecahedron.** I was just wondering myself, your Numbership. What actually is the serious obstacle you were talking about?

202 **Mathemagician.** [*Looks at him in surprise.*] You mean you really don't know?

203 # BLACKOUT

CLOSE READ

ANNOTATE: Mark the stage direction after paragraph 202 that tells what happens after the Dodecahedron asks about the obstacle.

QUESTION: Why does the playwright include this stage direction?

CONCLUDE: How might this stage direction, if followed, affect a viewing audience?

Scene ii • The Land of Ignorance

1   *LIGHTS UP on* Rhyme *and* Reason, *in their castle, looking out two windows.*

2   **Rhyme.** *I'm worried sick I must confess*

I wonder if they'll have success

All others tried in vain,

And were never seen or heard again.

3   **Reason.** Now, Rhyme, there's no need to be so **pessimistic**. Milo, Tock, and Humbug have just as much chance of succeeding as they do of failing.

4   **Rhyme.** *But the demons are so deadly smart*

They'll stuff your brain and fill your heart

With petty thoughts and selfish dreams

And trap you with their nasty schemes.

5   **Reason.** Now, Rhyme, be reasonable, won't you? And calm down, you always talk in couplets when you get nervous. Milo has learned a lot from his journey. I think he's a match for the demons and that he might soon be knocking at our door. Now, come on, cheer up, won't you?

6   **Rhyme.** I'll try.

7   [*LIGHTS FADE on the* Princesses *and COME UP on the little Car, traveling slowly.*]

8   **Milo.** So this is the Land of Ignorance. It's so dark. I can hardly see a thing. Maybe we should wait until morning.

9   **Voice.** They'll be mourning for you soon enough. [*They look up and see a large, soiled, ugly bird with a dangerous beak and a* **malicious** *expression.*]

10   **Milo.** I don't think you understand. We're looking for a place to spend the night.

11   **Bird.** [*Shrieking.*] It's not yours to spend!

12   **Milo.** That doesn't make any sense, you see . . .

13   **Bird.** Dollars or cents. It's still not yours to spend.

14   **Milo.** But I don't mean . . .

15   **Bird.** Of course you're mean. Anybody who'd spend a night that doesn't belong to him is very mean.

16   **Tock.** Must you interrupt like that?

17   **Bird.** Naturally, it's my job. I take the words right out of your mouth. Haven't we met before? I'm the Everpresent Wordsnatcher.

18 **Milo.** Are you a demon?

19 **Bird.** I'm afraid not. I've tried, but the best I can manage to be is a nuisance. [*Suddenly gets nervous as he looks beyond the three.*] And I don't have time to waste with you. [*Starts to leave.*]

20 **Tock.** What is it? What's the matter?

21 **Milo.** Hey, don't leave. I wanted to ask you some questions . . . Wait!

22 **Bird.** Weight? Twenty-seven pounds. Bye-bye. [*Disappears.*]

23 **Milo.** Well, he was no help.

24 **Man.** Perhaps I can be of some assistance to you? [*There appears a beautifully dressed man, very polished and clean.*] Hello, little boy. [*Shakes* Milo's *hand.*] And how's the faithful dog? [*Pats* Tock.] And who is this handsome creature? [*Tips his hat to* Humbug.]

25 **Humbug.** [*To others.*] What a pleasant surprise to meet someone so nice in a place like this.

26 **Man.** But before I help you out, I wonder if first you could spare me a little of your time, and help me with a few small jobs?

27 **Humbug.** Why, certainly.

28 **Tock.** Gladly.

29 **Milo.** Sure, we'd be happy to.

30 **Man.** Splendid, for there are just three tasks. First, I would like to move this pile of sand from here to there. [*Indicates through pantomime a large pile of sand.*] But I'm afraid that all I have is this tiny tweezers. [*Hands it to* Milo, *who begins moving the sand one grain at a time.*] Second, I would like to empty this well and fill that other, but I have no bucket, so you'll have to use this eyedropper. [*Hands it to* Tock, *who begins to work.*] And finally, I must have a hole in this cliff, and here is a needle to dig it. [Humbug *eagerly begins. The man leans against a tree and stares vacantly off into space. The LIGHTS indicate the passage of time.*]

31 **Milo.** You know something? I've been working steadily for a long time now, and I don't feel the least bit tired or hungry. I could go right on the same way forever.

32 **Man.** Maybe you will. [*He yawns.*]

33 **Milo.** [*Whispers to* Tock.] Well, I wish I knew how long it was going to take.

34 **Tock.** Why don't you use your magic staff and find out?

35 **Milo.** [*Takes out pencil and calculates. To* Man.] Pardon me, sir, but it's going to take 837 years to finish these jobs.

36 **Man.** Is that so? What a shame. Well then you'd better get on with them.

37 **Milo.** But . . . it hardly seems worthwhile.

38 **Man.** WORTHWHILE! Of course they're not worthwhile. I wouldn't ask you to do anything that was worthwhile.

39 **Tock.** Then why bother?

40 **Man.** Because, my friends, what could be more important than doing unimportant things? If you stop to do enough of them, you'll never get where you are going. [*Laughs villainously.*]

41 **Milo.** [*Gasps.*] Oh, no, you must be . . .

42 **Man.** Quite correct! I am the Terrible Trivium, demon of petty tasks and worthless jobs, ogre of wasted effort and monster of habit. [*They start to back away from him.*] Don't try to leave, there's so much to do, and you still have 837 years to go on the first job.

43 **Milo.** But why do unimportant things?

44 **Man.** Think of all the trouble it saves. If you spend all your time doing only the easy and useless jobs, you'll never have time to worry about the important ones which are so difficult. [*Walks toward them whispering.*] Now do come and stay with me. We'll have such fun together. There are things to fill and things to empty, things to take away and things to bring back, things to pick up and things to put down . . . [*They are transfixed[4] by his soothing voice. He is about to embrace them when a* Voice *screams.*]

45 **Voice.** Run! Run! [*They all wake up and run with the Trivium behind. As the voice continues to call out directions, they follow until they lose the Trivium.*] RUN! RUN! This way! This way! Over here! Over here! Up here! Down there! Quick, hurry up!

46 **Tock.** [*Panting.*] I think we lost him.

47 **Voice.** Keep going straight! Keep going straight! Now step up! Now step up!

48 **Milo.** Look out! [*They all fall into a Trap.*] But he said "up"!

49 **Voice.** Well, I hope you didn't expect to get anywhere by listening to me.

50 **Humbug.** We're in a deep pit! We'll never get out of here.

51 **Voice.** That is quite an accurate evaluation of the situation.

52 **Milo.** [*Shouting angrily.*] Then why did you help us at all?

4. **transfixed** *v.* made motionless by horror or fascination.

insincerity (ihn sihn SEHR uh tee) *n.* lack of honesty; untruthfulness

53 **Voice.** Oh, I'd do as much for anybody. Bad advice is my specialty. [*A Little Furry Creature appears.*] I'm the demon of **Insincerity**. I don't mean what I say; I don't mean what I do; and I don't mean what I am.

54 **Milo.** Then why don't you go away and leave us alone!

55 **Insincerity.** (VOICE) Now, there's no need to get angry. You're a very clever boy and I have complete confidence in you. You can certainly climb out of that pit . . . come on, try . . .

56 **Milo.** I'm not listening to one word you say! You're just telling me what you think I'd like to hear, and not what is important.

57 **Insincerity.** Well, if that's the way you feel about it . . .

58 **Milo.** That's the way I feel about it. We will manage by ourselves without any unnecessary advice from you.

59 **Insincerity.** [*Stamping his foot.*] Well, all right for you! Most people listen to what I say, but if that's the way you feel, then I'll just go home. [*Exits in a huff.*]

60 **Humbug.** [*Who has been quivering with fright.*] And don't you ever come back! Well, I guess we showed him, didn't we?

61 **Milo.** You know something? This place is a lot more dangerous than I ever imagined.

62 **Tock.** [*Who's been surveying the situation.*] I think I figured a way to get out. Here, hop on my back. [*Milo does so.*] Now, you, Humbug, on top of Milo. [*He does so.*] Now hook your umbrella onto that tree and hold on. [*They climb over* Humbug, *then pull him up.*]

63 **Humbug.** [*As they climb.*] Watch it! Watch it, now. Ow, be careful of my back! My back! Easy, easy . . . oh, this is so difficult. Aren't you finished yet?

64 **Tock.** [*As he pulls up* Humbug.] There. Now, I'll lead for a while. Follow me, and we'll stay out of trouble. [*They walk and climb higher and higher.*]

65 **Humbug.** Can't we slow down a little?

66 **Tock.** Something tells me we better reach the Castle-in-the-Air as soon as possible, and not stop to rest for a single moment. [*They speed up.*]

67 **Milo.** What is it, Tock? Did you see something?

68 **Tock.** Just keep walking and don't look back.

69 **Milo.** You *did* see something!

70 **Humbug.** What is it? Another demon?

71 **Tock.** Not just one, I'm afraid. If you want to see what I'm talking about, then turn around. [*They turn around. The stage darkens and hundreds of Yellow Gleaming Eyes can be seen.*]

72 **Humbug.** Good grief! Do you see how many there are? Hundreds! The Overbearing Know-it-all, the Gross Exaggeration, the Horrible Hopping Hindsight . . . and look over there! The Triple Demons of **Compromise**! Let's get out of here! [*Starts to scurry.*] Hurry up, you two! Must you be so slow about everything?

73 **Milo.** Look! There it is, up ahead! The Castle-in-the-Air! [*They all run.*]

74 **Humbug.** They're gaining!

75 **Milo.** But there it is!

76 **Humbug.** I see it! I see it!

77 [*They reach the first step and are stopped by a little man in a frock coat, sleeping on a worn ledger. He has a long quill pen and a bottle of ink at his side. He is covered with ink stains over his clothes and wears spectacles.*]

78 **Tock.** Shh! Be very careful. [*They try to step over him, but he wakes up.*]

79 **Senses Taker.** [*From sleeping position.*] Names? [*He sits up.*]

80 **Humbug.** Well, I . . .

81 **Senses Taker.** *NAMES?* [*He opens book and begins to write, splattering himself with ink.*]

82 **Humbug.** Uh . . . Humbug, Tock, and this is Milo.

83 **Senses Taker.** Splendid, splendid. I haven't had an "M" in ages.

84 **Milo.** What do you want our names for? We're sort of in a hurry.

85 **Senses Taker.** Oh, this won't take long. I'm the official Senses Taker and I must have some information before I can take your sense. Now if you'll just tell me: [*Handing them a form to fill. Speaking slowly and deliberately.*] When you were born, where you were born, why you were born, how old you are now, how old you were then, how old you'll be in a little while . . .

86 **Milo.** I wish he'd hurry up. At this rate, the demons will be here before we know it!

87 **Senses Taker.** . . . Your mother's name, your father's name, where you live, how long you've lived there, the schools you've attended, the schools you haven't attended . . .

compromise (KOM pruh myz) *n.* settlement of a disagreement in which each side gives up part of what it wanted

88 **Humbug.** I'm getting writer's cramp.

89 **Tock.** I smell something very evil and it's getting stronger every second. [*To Senses Taker.*] May we go now?

90 **Senses Taker.** Just as soon as you tell me your height, your weight, the number of books you've read this year . . .

91 **Milo.** We have to go!

92 **Senses Taker.** All right, all right. I'll give you the short form. [*Pulls out a small piece of paper.*] Destination?

93 **Milo.** But we have to . . .

94 **Senses Taker.** *DESTINATION?*

95 **Milo, Tock** and **Humbug.** The Castle-in-the-Air! [*They throw down their papers and run past him up the first few stairs.*]

96 **Senses Taker.** Stop! I'm sure you'd rather see what I have to show you. [*Snaps his fingers; they freeze.*] A circus of your very own. [*CIRCUS MUSIC is heard. Milo seems to go into a trance.*] And wouldn't you enjoy this most wonderful smell? [*Tock sniffs and goes into a trance.*] And here's something I know you'll enjoy hearing . . . [*To Humbug. The sound of CHEERS and APPLAUSE for Humbug is heard, and he goes into a trance.*] There we are. And now, I'll just sit back and let the demons catch up with you.

97 [*Milo accidentally drops his package of gifts. The Package of Laughter from* Dr. Dischord *opens and the Sounds of Laughter are heard. After a moment,* Milo, Tock, *and* Humbug *join in laughing and the spells are broken.*]

98 **Milo.** There was no circus.

99 **Tock.** There were no smells.

100 **Humbug.** The applause is gone.

101 **Senses Taker.** I warned you I was the Senses Taker. I'll steal your sense of Purpose, your sense of Duty, destroy your sense of Proportion—and but for one thing, you'd be helpless yet.

102 **Milo.** What's that?

103 **Senses Taker.** As long as you have the sound of laughter, I cannot take your sense of Humor. Agh! That horrible sense of humor.

104 **Humbug.** HERE THEY COME! LET'S GET OUT OF HERE!

105 [*The demons appear in nasty slithering hordes, running through the audience and up onto the stage, trying to attack* Tock, Milo, *and*

Humbug. *The three heroes run past the* Senses Taker *up the stairs toward the Castle-in-the-Air with the demons snarling behind them.*]

106 **Milo.** Don't look back! Just keep going! [*They reach the castle. The two princesses appear in the windows.*]

107 **Princesses.** Hurry! Hurry! We've been expecting you.

108 **Milo.** You must be the Princesses. We've come to rescue you.

109 **Humbug.** And the demons are close behind!

110 **Tock.** We should leave right away.

111 **Princesses.** We're ready anytime you are.

112 **Milo.** Good, now if you'll just come out. But wait a minute—there's no door! How can we rescue you from the Castle-in-the-Air if there's no way to get in or out?

113 **Humbug.** Hurry, Milo! They're gaining on us.

114 **Reason.** Take your time, Milo, and think about it.

115 **Milo.** Ummm, all right . . . just give me a second or two. [*He thinks hard.*]

116 **Humbug.** I think I feel sick.

117 **Milo.** I've got it! Where's that package of presents? [*Opens the package of letters.*] Ah, here it is. [*Takes out the letters and sticks them on the door, spelling:*] E-N-T-R-A-N-C-E. Entrance. Now, let's see. [*Rummages through and spells in smaller letters:*] P-u-s-h. Push. [*He pushes and a door opens. The* Princesses *come out of the castle. Slowly, the demons ascend the stairway.*]

118 **Humbug.** Oh, it's too late. They're coming up and there's no other way down!

119 **Milo.** Unless . . . [*Looks at* Tock.] Well . . . Time flies, doesn't it?

120 **Tock.** Quite often. Hold on, everyone, and I'll take you down.

121 **Humbug.** Can you carry us all?

122 **Tock.** We'll soon find out. Ready or not, here we go! [*His alarm begins to ring. They jump off the platform and disappear. The demons, howling with rage, reach the top and find no one there. They see the* Princesses *and the heroes running across the stage and bound down the stairs after them and into the audience. There is a mad chase scene until they reach the stage again.*]

123 **Humbug.** I'm exhausted! I can't run another step.

124 **Milo.** We can't stop now . . .

CLOSE READ

ANNOTATE: In the stage directions in paragraph 105, mark the word the playwright uses to refer to Milo, Tock, and Humbug.

QUESTION: Why does the playwright use this term at this point in the play?

CONCLUDE: What does this word suggest about ways in which the three characters have changed?

125 **Tock.** Milo! Look out there! [*The armies of Azaz and* Mathemagician *appear at the back of the theater, with the Kings at their heads.*]

126 **Azaz.** [*As they march toward the stage.*] Don't worry, Milo, we'll take over now.

127 **Mathemagician.** Those demons may not know it, but their days are numbered!

128 **Spelling Bee.** Charge! C-H-A-R-G-E! Charge! [*They rush at the demons and battle until the demons run off howling. Everyone cheers. The* Five Ministers of Azaz *appear and shake Milo's hand.*]

129 **Minister 1.** Well done.

130 **Minister 2.** Fine job.

131 **Minister 3.** Good work!

132 **Minister 4.** Congratulations!

133 **Minister 5.** CHEERS! [*Everyone cheers again. A fanfare interrupts. A* Page *steps forward and reads from a large scroll:*]

134 **Page.** *Henceforth, and forthwith,*

> *Let it be known by one and all.*

> *That Rhyme and Reason*

> *Reign once more in Wisdom.*

135 [*The* Princesses *bow gracefully and kiss their brothers, the Kings.*]

136 > *And furthermore,*

> *The boy named Milo,*

> *The dog known as Tock,*

> *And the insect hereinafter referred to as the Humbug*

> *Are hereby declared to be Heroes of the Realm.*

137 [*All bow and salute the heroes.*]

138 **Milo.** But we never could have done it without a lot of help.

139 **Reason.** That may be true, but you had the courage to try, and what you can do is often a matter of what you *will* do.

140 **Azaz.** That's why there was one very important thing about your quest we couldn't discuss until you returned.

141 **Milo.** I remember. What was it?

142 **Azaz.** Very simple. It was impossible!

143 **Mathemagician.** *Completely* impossible!

144 **Humbug.** Do you mean . . . ? [*Feeling faint.*] Oh . . . I think I need to sit down.

145 **Azaz.** Yes, indeed, but if we'd told you then, you might not have gone.

146 **Mathemagician.** And, as you discovered, many things are possible just as long as you don't know they're impossible.

147 **Milo.** I think I understand.

148 **Rhyme.** I'm afraid it's time to go now.

149 **Reason.** And you must say goodbye.

150 **Milo.** To everyone? [*Looks around at the crowd. To* Tock *and* Humbug.] Can't you two come with me?

151 **Humbug.** I'm afraid not, old man. I'd like to, but I've arranged for a lecture tour which will keep me occupied for years.

152 **Tock.** And they do need a watchdog here.

153 **Milo.** Well, O.K., then. [Milo *hugs the* Humbug.]

154 **Humbug.** [*Sadly.*] Oh, bah.

155 **Milo.** [*He hugs* Tock, *and then faces everyone.*] Well, goodbye. We all spent so much time together, I know I'm going to miss you. [*To the* Princesses.] I guess we would have reached you a lot sooner if I hadn't made so many mistakes.

156 **Reason.** You must never feel badly about making mistakes, Milo, as long as you take the trouble to learn from them. Very often you learn more by being wrong for the right reasons than you do by being right for the wrong ones.

157 **Milo.** But there's so much to learn.

158 **Rhyme.** That's true, but it's not just learning that's important. It's learning what to do with what you learn and learning why you learn things that matters.

159 **Milo.** I think I know what you mean, Princess. At least, I hope I do. [*The car is rolled forward and* Milo *climbs in.*] Goodbye! Goodbye! I'll be back someday! I will! Anyway, I'll try. [*As* Milo *drives the set of the Land of Ignorance move offstage.*]

160 **Azaz.** Goodbye! Always remember. Words! Words! Words!

161 **Mathemagician.** And numbers!

162 **Azaz.** Now, don't tell me you think numbers are as important as words?

163 **Mathemagician.** Is that so? Why I'll have you know . . . [*The set disappears, and* Milo's *Room is seen onstage.*]

164 **Milo.** [*As he drives on.*] Oh, oh. I hope they don't start all over again. Because I don't think I'll have much time in the near future to help them out. [*The sound of loud ticking is heard.* Milo *finds himself in his room. He gets out of the car and looks around.*]

165 **The Clock.** Did someone mention time?

166 **Milo.** Boy, I must have been gone for an awful long time. I wonder what time it is. [*Looks at the clock.*] Five o'clock. I wonder what day it is. [*Looks at calendar.*] It's still today! I've only been gone for an hour! [*He continues to look at his calendar, and then begins to look at his books and toys and maps and chemistry set with great interest.*]

167 **Clock.** An hour. Sixty minutes. How long it really lasts depends on what you do with it. For some people, an hour seems to last forever. For others, just a moment, and so full of things to do.

168 **Milo.** [*Looks at clock.*] Six o'clock already?

169 **Clock.** In an instant. In a trice. Before you have time to blink. [*The stage goes black in less than no time at all.*] 🐌

Response

📓 NOTEBOOK

1. Personal Connections Do you admire Milo and his companions? Explain your answer, citing details from the text.

Answer the questions in your notebook. Use text evidence to support your responses.

Comprehension

2. Reading Check (a) What gift does Dischord give Milo? **(b)** What does Mathemagican give Milo before he goes to the Land of Ignorance? **(c)** How does Tock help get everyone down from the Castle-in-the-Air?

3. Strategy: Create Mental Images (a) Cite two details that helped you create mental images as you read Act II. **(b)** In what ways did this strategy deepen your understanding and appreciation of the play? Explain.

Analysis

4. Analyze In what ways is the gift that Dischord gives to Milo and his companions valuable? Explain.

5. (a) What does the Terrible Trivium want Milo, Tock, and Humbug to do? **(b) Speculate** What will happen if they follow his directions? Explain. **(c) Interpret** What important lesson does Milo learn through his experience with the Terrible Trivium? Explain.

6. Deduce How do Milo's solutions for getting the princesses out of the Castle-in-the-Air show his growth from the beginning of the play?

7. (a) Paraphrase In your own words, restate Rhyme and Reason's advice to Milo at the end of Act II. **(b) Evaluate** Do you think this advice is reasonable and useful? Explain your thinking.

8. Interpret What is one theme, or deeper message, you think this play conveys? Explain your thinking, citing text evidence from both acts of the play.

EQ Notes ▶ **What is the purpose of imagination?**

What have you learned about the power of imagination from reading this play? Go to your Essential Question Notes and record your observations and thoughts about *The Phantom Tollbooth*, Act II.

 TEKS

5.D. Create mental images to deepen understanding.

6.C. Use text evidence to support an appropriate response.

THE PHANTOM TOLLBOOTH,
ACT II

Close Read

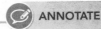 **ANNOTATE**

1. The model passage and annotation show how one reader analyzed paragraph 100 of Act II, Scene i. Find another detail in the passage to annotate. Then, write your own question and conclusion.

CLOSE-READ MODEL

Dodecahedron. [*Continues shouting angrily.*] If you had high hopes, how would you know how high they were? And did you know that narrow escapes come in different widths? Would you travel the whole world wide without ever knowing how wide it was? And how could you do anything at long last without knowing how long the last was?

ANNOTATE: Dodecahedron repeats the words *know* and *knowing*.

QUESTION: Why does the playwright have the character repeat these words?

CONCLUDE: The repetition emphasizes the importance of knowledge to Dodecahedron.

MY QUESTION:

MY CONCLUSION:

2. For more practice, answer the Close-Read notes in the selection.

3. Choose a section of the drama you found especially important. Mark important details. Then, jot down questions and write your conclusions in the open space next to the text.

Inquiry and Research

 RESEARCH

 NOTEBOOK

Research and Extend Conduct research to find the answer to this question: What inspired Norton Juster to write *The Phantom Tollbooth?* List the sources you use in your research.

 TEKS
8.C. Analyze how playwrights develop characters through dialogue and staging.

Genre / Text Elements

Stage Directions and Character Development In the script of a play, lines of dialogue tell readers what characters say. **Stage directions** are the words that the characters do not say. They provide details about **staging,** including what the scenery, lighting, and sound should be like. They also add to **character development** because they tell the actors how to move and the emotions to express as they speak their lines. Stage directions are usually printed in italics and set in brackets.

> **EXAMPLE FROM THE PLAY**
>
> **Dodecahedron.** [*Glaring from his upset face.*] Certainly not! They're all the wrong way! Just because you have a choice, it doesn't mean that any of them has to be right....

TIP: In the example, the stage direction tells the actor to show distress. Imagine the difference in character development if the stage direction were [*Breaking into a laugh.*].

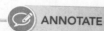 ANNOTATE

 INTERACTIVITY

PRACTICE Complete the activities.

1. **Analyze** Reread the passages from Act II listed in the chart. Explain how the stage directions in each passage develop Milo's character.

PASSAGE	INFORMATION ABOUT CHARACTER
Act II, Scene i, paragraphs 8–9 (O.K … *jump back in fright.]*)	
Act II, Scene i, paragraphs 71–73 (Milo … Is that bad?)	
Act II, Scene ii, paragraph 166 (Boy, I must have been gone … *set with great interest.]*)	

2. **Analyze** Explain how Milo has changed by the end of the play. Cite details of both dialogue and stage directions in Act II that support your answer.

3. **(a) Analyze** Mark a point in Act II in which stage directions help readers understand what characters are feeling or doing.
   (b) Interpret Explain how the stage directions in your example help to develop at least one character.

4. **(a) Compose** Find several lines in Act II that have no stage directions. Write your own stage directions for that section. **(b) Interpret** Explain how your stage directions add to the development of one or more characters.

THE PHANTOM TOLLBOOTH,
ACT II

Concept Vocabulary

 NOTEBOOK

Why These Words? The vocabulary words relate to negative emotions and lack of trust. For example, Milo *suspiciously* questions Dischord. He expresses doubt about Dischord's honesty.

suspiciously	pessimistic	insincerity
obstacle	malicious	compromise

PRACTICE Answer the question and complete the activities.

1. How do the vocabulary words sharpen your understanding of some of the conflicts in the play?

2. Find three other words in the selection that relate to negative emotions and doubt.

3. With a partner, list as many related words for each vocabulary word as you can. For example, for *suspiciously* you might list *suspicious*.

4. For each vocabulary word, write a sentence in which you use the word correctly. Include context clues that hint at the meaning of the word.

WORD NETWORK

Add words that are related to imagination from the text to your Word Network.

Word Study

 NOTEBOOK

Latin Suffix: -ity The Latin suffix *-ity* indicates that a word is a noun. It means "the state or quality of." The vocabulary word *insincerity* means "the state of being insincere."

PRACTICE Complete the following items.

1. Use your understanding of the suffix *-ity* to write a definition for the following words: *conformity* and *flexibility*.

2. Identify two other words that end with the suffix *-ity*. For each word, write a definition that demonstrates the meaning of the suffix. Then, consult a dictionary to check your work.

 TEKS
9.F. Analyze how the author's use of language contributes to mood and voice.

Author's Craft

Language and Mood It is impossible to read this play without noticing the unusual names of the places and characters Milo encounters and events he experiences. In many cases, these terms are **puns**—plays on words.

HOW PUNS WORK	EXAMPLE FROM THE PLAY	EXPLANATION
uses a word that sounds like another word but has a different meaning	**Milo.** …Maybe we should wait until *morning*. **Voice.** They'll be *mourning* for you soon enough.	*Morning* and *mourning* sound alike. *Mourning* means "grieving," so the pun is a threat.
applies a literal understanding to a nonliteral expression	**Dodecahedron.** …If you had *high hopes*, how would you know how high they were?…	The expression "high hopes" refers to happy possibilities. The pun turns it into actual height.
uses a word that has multiple meanings	**Dischord.** What happens to the dawn when a new day begins? **Dynne:** …It *breaks*!	*Breaks* means "smashes." In *dawn breaks*, it means "begins." The pun suggests dawn makes a loud sound.

In the play, the puns capture key qualities of characters, places, and events. They also help to create the play's **mood**, or emotional quality.

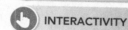

PRACTICE Complete the activities and answer the questions. Ask for support from peers or your teacher if you need help.

1. **(a) Define** Look up the words *cacophony* and *discord* in a dictionary and write their definitions. **(b) Analyze** Explain how Dr. Dischord's name is a pun. **(c) Connect** How does the pun fit the character?

2. **Analyze** Explain how the characters apply literal understandings to each expression listed in the chart to create puns.

EXPRESSION	EXPLANATION OF PUN
whole wide world (Act II, Scene i, paragraph 100)	
spend the night (Act II, Scene ii, paragraphs 10–15)	

3. **(a) Interpret** Which adjectives best describe the mood of this play? Choose two and explain your answers. **(b) Interpret** How does the playwright's use of puns add to this mood? Explain.

lighthearted   serious   humorous

scary   lonely   thoughtful

THE PHANTOM TOLLBOOTH,
ACT II

Composition

A **narrative retelling** is a new version of a story that changes a key element. For example, it may be told from a different character's point of view.

In *The Phantom Tollbooth*, readers see events from Milo's perspective. We are connected to the way Milo experiences the events. Choose a scene from the play and write a **narrative retelling** from Tock's perspective.

- Reread a scene from either Act I or Act II that you found memorable or interesting. Note important details that reveal Tock's personality and reasons for his actions. Use these details to help develop Tock's perspective.

- Retell the scene in story rather than play form.

- Write as if you were Tock. Include dialogue and description to show how Tock feels about other characters and the events taking place.

Use New Words

Try to use one or more vocabulary words in your writing:
suspiciously, pessimistic, insincerity, obstacle, malicious, compromise

 NOTEBOOK

Reflect on Your Writing

PRACTICE Think about the choices you made as you wrote your retelling. Then, answer the questions.

1. How did writing from Tock's perspective help you better understand both Tock and Milo?

2. What did you find most challenging about writing a retelling?

3. **WHY THESE WORDS?** The words you choose make a difference in your writing. Which words did you specifically choose to make Tock's point of view clear for readers?

 TEKS

1.A. Listen actively to interpret a message, ask clarifying questions, and respond appropriately.

1.C. Give an organized presentation with a specific stance and position, employing eye contact, speaking rate, volume, enunciation, natural gestures, and conventions of language to communicate ideas effectively.

6.H. Respond orally or in writing with appropriate register, vocabulary, tone, and voice.

11.A. Compose literary texts such as personal narratives, fiction, and poetry using genre characteristics and craft.

Speaking and Listening

A **speech** is a type of formal public speaking.

ASSIGNMENT

Write and deliver a **speech** that Milo might give after returning home from his adventure. In your speech, summarize Milo's experiences and clearly explain his stance or position on his adventures—the lessons he learned.

- Use formal vocabulary, but include humorous touches to create a **tone**, or attitude, that matches the playfulness of the drama.

- Make sure to include connecting words that clearly show the relationships between Milo's experiences and the lessons he learns.

- Make your speech sound like Milo. Recreate his **voice**, or personality.

Write and Analyze Your Speech Write a short speech, choosing words that continue the formal but playful tone of the script. Then, analyze your writing and note where you intend to pause, slow down, and speed up. Also, mark words you will emphasize as you speak. Pay special attention to your use of conjunctions, because they help listeners understand the flow of ideas.

Rehearse and Deliver the Speech Practice your speech to ensure the quality of your delivery. Check the items off on the Speaking Guide as you become satisfied with your results. Then, deliver your speech to the class.

SPEAKING GUIDE

◯ **Enunciation:** Don't mumble. Pronounce each word clearly.

◯ **Rate:** Speak with energy, but avoid rushing. Slow down for emphasis.

◯ **Volume and Register:** Don't shout, but speak loudly enough to be heard by all. Avoid speaking in a monotone; instead vary the highs and lows of your voice.

◯ **Words for Emphasis:** Give special attention to words that will help listeners follow your ideas. Conjunctions, for example, are important to emphasize as you speak because they help listeners understand relationships between ideas.

EQ Notes Before moving on to a new selection, go to your Essential Question Notes and record any additional thoughts or observations you may have about *The Phantom Tollbooth*, Act II.

Listen Actively As your classmates deliver their speeches, listen closely to interpret the message each person is conveying. Take notes about ideas or details that seem particularly interesting or unique. Then, as a class, discuss similarities and differences in everyone's interpretations of Milo's character and the lessons he learned.

Write a Short Story

Short stories are brief works of fiction that tell of characters and events from the writer's imagination.

ASSIGNMENT

Write a **short story** that centers on one or more characters from *The Phantom Tollbooth*. If you wish, use this story starter to begin:

One day in the Kingdom of Wisdom, ...

The type of short story you write is up to you. It can be realistic fiction, science fiction, adventure, or fantasy. Include the elements of a short story in your writing.

ELEMENTS OF A SHORT STORY

Purpose: to tell a story that entertains or expresses an insight

Characteristics

- well-developed, interesting characters
- a clear, well-described setting
- a deeper meaning, insight, or theme
- a consistent narrative point of view (first-person, third-person, or third-person omniscient)
- elements of craft, including vivid, precise word choices and descriptive details
- literary devices, including dialogue
- standard English conventions, including sentence variety

Structure

- a plot that centers on a conflict and includes a clear sequence of events

 TEKS

10.A. Plan a first draft by selecting a genre appropriate for a particular topic, purpose, and audience using a range of strategies such as discussion, background reading, and personal interests.

11.A. Compose literary texts such as personal narratives, fiction, and poetry using genre characteristics and craft.

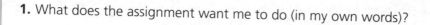
Take a Closer Look at the Assignment

 NOTEBOOK

1. What does the assignment want me to do (in my own words)?

2. What **mood**, or emotional quality, do I want my story to have? What is my **purpose** for telling this story?

3. (a) Which type of story, or **genre**, interests me the most—realistic, science fiction, adventure, or another genre? Why?

(b) Which genre will best help me create the mood I want and achieve my purpose?

4. What **point of view** do I want to use?

- ◯ Do I want a character to tell the story?
- ◯ Do I want an outside narrator to tell the story?
- ◯ Do I want the narrator to know what everyone in the story feels and thinks, or just what one character feels and thinks?

5. Does the assignment ask me to follow a specific structure?

- ◯ Yes   If "yes," what structure does it require?

- ◯ No   If "no," how can I best structure my story?

PURPOSE

Consider your **purpose,** for writing and the **mood** you want to create. For example, do you want readers to laugh? to cry? to be inspired? to ask questions? As you draft, your story may take you in surprising directions, but start out with a clear purpose.

GENRE

Choose a **genre,** or type of story, that will help you achieve your purpose.

- **Realistic fiction** mirrors the conflicts of real life.
- **Science fiction** focuses on the future or other worlds.
- **Adventure stories** feature physical danger and action.

POINT OF VIEW

Point of view refers to the type of narrator you use.

- **First-person:** narrator is a character in the story
- **Third-person:** narrator is not a character; shares the thoughts and feelings of one character only
- **Third-person omniscient:** narrator is not a character; shares the thoughts and feelings of all the characters

Planning and Prewriting

Before you start to draft, generate first thoughts for a story you truly want to tell. Complete the activities to get started.

Discover Your Thinking: Freewrite!

Think for a moment about the subject of your story, especially the main character and central conflict. Then, write quickly and freely for at least three minutes without stopping. If it helps you, fill in this sentence to start your freewrite:

What if [character] _____, suddenly [action] _____?

Don't worry about spelling and grammar—just jot down ideas. When time is up, read what you wrote and mark ideas that you want to develop. Repeat the process as many times as necessary to get all of your ideas out.

NOTEBOOK

WRITE IT Generate ideas for your story.

 TEKS

10.B.i. Develop drafts into a focused, structured, and coherent piece of writing by organizing with purposeful structure, including an introduction, transitions, coherence within and across paragraphs, and a conclusion.

Structure Ideas: Make a Plan

 NOTEBOOK

A. Collect Your Ideas Review your freewriting and pull out your most exciting ideas. Look for interesting words, phrases, characters, character traits, and descriptive details.

_____

_____

_____

_____

B. Focus on Character and Situation Write a sentence or two about the main **character,** the **setting,** and situation.

_____

_____

C. Plan a Structure A typical essay has a structure that includes an introduction, a body, and a conclusion. A typical short story follows a plot structure, that includes the exposition, rising action, climax, and resolution. Outline your story's structure, including its **conflict** and **plot.**

I. What event starts the conflict or makes my main character aware of the conflict?

II. How does the conflict build or develop?

III. At what point is the conflict most intense?

IV. How does the conflict end?

_____

_____

_____

_____

_____

_____

_____

_____

> ## CHARACTER
> Answer these questions to develop your main **character:**
> - What does he or she look like?
> - How does he or she think, feel, and behave?
> - What does he or she want?
> - What does he or she _not_ want?

> ## SETTING
> Answer these questions to create a vivid **setting:**
> - Where and when does your story take place?
> - What are the setting's most significant features?
> - Will this setting affect the action of the story?

> ## CONFLICT
> The **plot** of a story centers on a **conflict.** The story's events show how the conflict begins, develops, reaches a high point, and ends. Make sure the conflict you choose for your story is significant enough to keep readers' interest through all the stages of the plot.

Drafting

ANNOTATE

Use your planning work to write a first draft of your story. Consider starting by developing a key scene.

Read Like a Writer

Reread a scene from the Mentor Text. Mark details that make it come to life. One comment has been done for you.

MENTOR TEXT

from The Great Universal Undo

"I want a cookie!" said Tommy suddenly, tugging at the hem of his mother's skirt. Mrs. Bieberman reached into a bag of cookies and pulled one out. "I'll give you just one, Tommy." Tommy grabbed it and stuffed it in his mouth.

"How's your mother?" asked Mrs. Bieberman. "I should call her."

Alexander was aware of a *tap tapping* sound.

> Which details in the text grab your attention? Mark them.

> The author uses a sensory detail to show what Alexander sees and hears.

NOTEBOOK

WRITE IT Write a scene from your story. Use details to show what a character is seeing and feeling.

DEPTH OF THOUGHT

Keep these ideas in mind as you draft your story.

- **Audience** Grab your reader's attention. Begin with a vivid scene or an idea that makes readers curious.

- **Characters** Write dialogue that shows the unique way in which each character speaks.

- **Descriptive Details** Bring the story to life by using strong details that include factual or realistic aspects of a setting, vivid examples, and powerful sensory details.

⭐ TEKS

10.B.ii. Develop drafts into a focused, structured, and coherent piece of writing by developing an engaging idea reflecting depth of thought with specific facts and details; **10.D.i.** Edit drafts using standard English conventions, including complete complex sentences with subject-verb agreement and avoidance of splices, run-ons, and fragments; **10.D.iii.** Edit drafts using standard English conventions, including conjunctive adverbs; **10.D.vi.** Edit drafts using standard English conventions, including subordinating conjunctions to form complex sentences and correlative conjunctions such as *either/or* and *neither/nor.*

Create Coherence

You can create **coherence**, or a logical flow, in your writing by making clear connections among ideas. Different types of **conjunctions** and **conjunctive adverbs**, or connecting words and phrases, can help you join ideas in specific ways.

> **TIP:** Conjunctions create different logical relationships between parts of a sentence or paragraph. Choose conjunctions that show the specific relationships that you want to express.

TYPE OF CONJUNCTION	EXAMPLES	HOW IT'S USED
Conjunctive Adverbs: words or phrases that connect ideas within or between sentences or paragraphs—also known as **transitions**	*also, as a result, finally, however, indeed, instead, on the other hand, similarly, still, therefore*	At the beginning of a sentence: *I sprinted.* **Finally,** *I ran out of breath.* After a semicolon: *I sprinted;* **finally,** *I ran out of breath.*
Subordinating Conjunctions: words that begin a dependent clause and connect it to an independent clause to create a complex sentence	*after, although, because, before, even if, even though, in order that, so that, unless, until, when*	Before an independent clause: **Even though** the food was delicious, I couldn't eat any more. After an independent clause: I couldn't eat any more, **even though** the food was delicious.
Correlative Conjunctions: pairs of words used together to show a relationship between equal items in a sentence	*either/or, neither/nor, not only/ but also, whether/or*	**Neither** my sister **nor** I was willing to compromise. **Not only** were we stubborn **but also** we were spiteful.

 NOTEBOOK

WRITE IT Write a section of your story. Then, edit it to make clear connections using at least one conjunctive adverb, one subordinating conjunction, and one pair of correlative conjunctions.

_____

_____

_____

_____

_____

_____

_____

PUNCTUATION

Punctuate correctly:

- At the beginning of a sentence, place a comma after a subordinate clause.
- At the beginning of a clause, place a comma after a conjunctive adverb.
- In the middle of a clause, place commas before and after a conjunctive adverb.

Revising

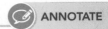 ANNOTATE

Now that you have a first draft, revise it to ensure that characters and other details come to life. Reread your story, checking for the following elements:

Clarity: the sharpness of your ideas

Development: vibrant characters; a conflict that builds and is resolved

Structure: a plot that shows a clear sequence of events

Style and Tone: varied sentence types and lengths, and precise word choices that create a strong mood; authentic dialogue

Read Like a Writer

Review the revisions made to the Mentor Text. Then, answer the questions in the white boxes.

MENTOR TEXT

from **The Great Universal Undo**

Alexander took his new invention outside. By the traffic lights, he ran into Mrs. Bieberman, who was carrying a bag of groceries and holding the hand of her 3-year-old son Tommy. ~~Alexander was outside now.~~

> The writer rewrote and moved a sentence to clarify the sequence of events.

"Hello, Mrs. Bieberman! Hi, Tommy!" Alexander called out ~~to the Beibermans.~~ He smiled. "That's a really silly hat you're wearing, Mrs. Bieberman!" Then he tapped his smartphone. If everything worked, his last comment would be Undone.

> Why did the author add dialogue?

"Hello yourself, Alexander!" exclaimed Mrs. Bieberman.

Good! thought Alexander. She hadn't heard it! Flushed with excitement, he continued. "You know, your little boy looks like a toad." He paused, waiting for a response.

> The addition of Alexander's thoughts develops the character and conflict.

"I do *not* look like a toe!" Tommy ~~said and~~ *wailed and, still blubbering,* started to play his video game. Had Alexander tapped Undo—or just imagined it? He couldn't remember.

> How does this revision make the scene more vivid?

 TEKS

10.C. Revise drafts for clarity, development, organization, style, word choice, and sentence variety.

Take a Closer Look at Your Draft

Now, revise your draft. Use the Revision Guide for Fiction to evaluate and strengthen your story.

REVISION GUIDE FOR FICTION

EVALUATE	TAKE ACTION
Clarity	
Does my story express an insight?	If your message is unclear, simply **say** it out loud. Then, look for points where characters can express that insight or details can suggest it.
Development	
Are my characters believable and well-drawn?	**List** each character's traits. **Mark** details and dialogue that reveal those traits. If there are too few, add telling details.
Do characters' actions and reactions fit their personalities?	Again, **list** each character's traits. Then, list what each character does. If any action or reaction does not reflect a character trait, **delete** or **change** it.
Structure	
Is the main conflict clear?	**Mark** the points at which the conflict begins and gets most intense. If those two points are not clear, **add** details that better show the problem.
Is the sequence of events logical?	**List** the events presented in the story. Do they happen in a logical order? If not, **reorder** them. If any events are missing, **add** them.
Style and Tone	
Does the beginning of the story engage readers?	**Begin** with an interesting detail or puzzling action to make your audience want to read more.
Have I used vivid sensory details to bring the characters and setting to life?	**Replace** any ordinary words with language that appeals to the senses of sight, hearing, taste, smell, or touch. For example, instead of saying, "The garage was messy," say, "The garage was piled with boxes, old oil cans, and parts of cars."
Does the dialogue sound authentic?	**Read aloud** sections of dialogue. If they sound unnatural, **adjust** by imagining how someone you know might speak the words.
Does my story contain sentences of varying lengths to create liveliness?	**Read your story aloud,** listening for sentence variety and lengths. If the story sounds dull, **combine** some short sentences to create longer ones or break some long sentences into shorter ones.

Editing

 ANNOTATE

Don't let errors distract readers from your story. Reread your draft and fix mistakes to create a finished narrative.

Read Like a Writer

Look at how the writer of the Mentor Text edited the draft. Then, follow the directions in the white boxes.

> **MENTOR TEXT**
>
> *from* The Great Universal Undo
>
> "He can't go long without his game," Mrs. Bieberman said, sighing. "And only three years old." Alexander ~~played video games, too. However, he~~ hadn't started playing ~~them~~ *video games* until he was nine.
>
> "I want a cookie!" said Tommy. He said it suddenly. He tugged at his mother's skirt. Mrs. Bieberman reached into a bag of cookies and pulled one out, *although she declared,* "I'll give you just one, Tommy." Tommy grabbed it and then stuffed it in his mouth.

> The writer combined two sentences into one complex sentence.

> Edit the first three sentences of the second paragraph to better connect ideas.

> The writer joined two sentences into a complex sentence.

Focus on Sentences

Sentence Fragments A **sentence fragment** is a group of words that is not a complete sentence but is punctuated as if it is. It may be missing a subject or a verb, or it may be a dependent clause that cannot stand on its own. You might use fragments on purpose in dialogue, but you should avoid them elsewhere.

Missing a Subject: Ran a great race and won.
Add a Subject: *Joseph* ran a great race and won.

Missing a Verb: Joseph at the track meet yesterday.
Add a Verb: Joseph *won* at the track meet yesterday.

Dependent Clause: Since Alice wasn't there.
Create a Complex Sentence: Since Alice wasn't there, *we went home.*

> **EDITING TIPS**
> As you review your draft, look for subordinating conjunctions (for example, *since*, *although*, *because*, *until*) and make sure they connect dependent clauses to independent clauses to create complex sentences.

PRACTICE Edit the paragraph to correct sentence fragments. Then, check your own draft and fix any fragments you find.

> Alexander walked home. Until he had more information about Tommy. Didn't know what he could do. At the end of his rope. Suddenly, an idea! Luckily, his neighbor was an inventor. Who could help if he asked.

⟳ TEKS
10.D.i. Edit drafts using standard English conventions, including complex sentences with subject-verb agreement and avoidance of splices, run-ons, and fragments; **10.D.viii.** Edit drafts using standard English conventions, including punctuation marks, including commas in complex sentences, transitions, and introductory elements; **10.E.** Publish written work for appropriate audiences.

Focus on Spelling and Punctuation

Spelling: Plurals of Words Ending in -f or -fe To form the plural of many nouns that end in -f or -fe, drop the -f or -fe and add -ves. This rule does not apply to words ending in -ff or -ffe. Look at these examples: *half/ halves; knife/knives; loaf/loaves.*

Note that there are exceptions to this rule. For example, the plural of *roof* is *roofs*. Check that you have correctly used the plural forms of any nouns ending in -f or -fe. If necessary, use a dictionary to find the correct spellings of specific words.

Punctuation: Commas Check your comma usage in compound and complex sentences.

- Put a comma before the conjunction that joins two independent clauses to form a compound sentence.
  EXAMPLE: *Alexander thought he had the only Undo button, but Tommy also had one.*

- Place a comma after a dependent clause at the beginning of a sentence.
  EXAMPLE: *While he was trying out his Undo button, Alexander had a great shock.*

- Use commas to set off dependent clauses that appear in the middle of a sentence.
  EXAMPLE: *Alexander, because he was so surprised, didn't even wonder how Tommy had gotten the button.*

> **EDITING TIPS**
> - Try reading your paper backward. Doing so can help you focus on each word and catch spelling errors.
> - Read your paper aloud to listen for choppy sentences or unintentional repetition.

> **PRACTICE** Correct any spelling or comma errors in the sentences. Then, review your own draft for correctness.
>
> **1.** She gave Tommy one cookie and then she put the jar away.
>
> **2.** Some of us might like to try the Great Undo as crazy as it seems ourselfs.
>
> **3.** Unfortunately thiefs could steal Alexander's idea and cause problems.

Publishing and Presenting

Make It Multimodal

Choose one of these options to share your work with a broader audience:

OPTION 1 Print your story and add illustrations. Choose one or two key moments to illustrate. Create drawings, photos, graphics, or other visuals to enhance your text.

OPTION 2 Record yourself reading your story. Then, link it to your school website or make a digital audio compilation of the stories written by classmates.

What is the purpose of imagination?

Imagination can lead to new hobbies and interests—even exciting adventures. You will read selections that examine how both fictional characters and real people use their imaginations to face challenges and discover new ideas. Work in a small group to continue your exploration of the purposes of imagination.

▶ VIDEO

👆 INTERACTIVITY

Peer-Group Learning Strategies

Throughout your life, in school, in your community, and in your career, you will continue to learn and work with others. Review these strategies and the actions you can take to practice them as you work in small groups. Add ideas of your own for each category. Use these strategies during Peer-Group Learning.

STRATEGY	MY PEER-GROUP ACTION PLAN
Prepare • Complete your assignments so that you are prepared for team work. • Take notes on your reading to share with your group.	
Participate fully • Volunteer information and use verbal and nonverbal forms of communication to get your points across. • Use text evidence when making a point.	
Support others • Build off ideas from others in your group. • Ask others who have not yet spoken to do so.	
Clarify • Paraphrase the ideas of others to check your own understanding. • Ask follow-up questions.	

CONTENTS

PERFORMANCE TASK: SPEAKING AND LISTENING

Present a Short Story

The Peer-Group readings focus on the role imagination plays in both fictional stories and real life situations. After reading, your group will write and present a short story in which you use your imagination to create a new adventure for a familiar character.

Working as a Group

1. Take a Position

In your group, discuss the following question:

| Can imaginary adventures be as important as real adventures?

As you take turns sharing your positions, provide reasons for your choice. After all group members have shared, discuss some specific examples of real and imaginary adventures.

2. List Your Rules

As a group, decide on the rules that you will follow as you work together. Two examples are provided. Add two more of your own. You may add or revise rules as you work through the readings and activities together.

- Everyone should participate in group discussions.
- People should not interrupt.

3. Apply the Rules

Practice working as a group. Share what you have learned about imagination. Make sure each person in the group contributes. Take notes, and be prepared to share with the class one thing that you heard from another member of your group.

4. Name Your Group

Choose a name that reflects the unit topic.

Our group's name: _____

5. Create a Communication Plan

Decide how you want to communicate with one another. For example, you might use online collaboration tools, email, or instant messaging.

Our group's plan:

 TEKS

1.D. Participate in student-led discussions by eliciting and considering suggestions from other group members, taking notes, and identifying points of agreement and disagreement.

INTERACTIVITY

Making a Schedule

First, find out the due dates for the peer-group activities. Then, preview the texts and activities with your group, and make a schedule for completing the tasks.

SELECTION	ACTIVITIES	DUE DATE
from The Misadventures of Don Quixote		
Jabberwocky The Mock Turtle's Song		
The Importance of Imagination		

NOTEBOOK

Build Your Vocabulary

As you work with your group to complete writing, speaking, and listening activities, you will use many kinds of vocabulary, ranging from sight words you already know, to basic terms, to academic words, to complex words for specialized ideas. The greater your vocabulary, the more clearly you will be able to express yourself, follow instructions, and comprehend others' ideas.

Use these strategies to expand your vocabulary:

Notice Routine Words: Many words in this text, such as *draft* or *tell*, appear over and over again. Build your vocabulary by learning and using other words that appear repeatedly.

Listen to Audio: Play the audio versions of the selections to hear words in context and how they are pronounced.

Use Resources: Regularly consult dictionaries and thesauri to build your word knowledge.

Keep Track: Use the Word Network chart to keep track of new words you learn or make another chart of your own. Go through your word lists periodically to remind yourself of word meanings and to see how much your vocabulary has grown.

from THE MISADVENTURES OF DON QUIXOTE

The selection you are about to read is an excerpt from a retelling of a classic Spanish novel.

Reading Retellings

A **retelling** is a new version of an existing story.

RETELLING

Author's Purpose
➔ to tell the same story as an older work while changing it in some meaningful way

Characteristics
➔ settings, conflicts, events, and themes based on those in the original work

➔ characters with distinct qualities that are shown, or developed, by what they think, feel, say, and do

Structure
➔ plot, or related series of events, based on that of an original narrative

➔ plot that centers on a conflict characters face

Take a Minute!

 NOTEBOOK

DISCUSS IT With a partner, discuss retellings that you have read or seen on television or at the movies. Such retellings might include fairy tales or other classic stories. Discuss whether you like the retelling or the original version better, and why.

 TEKS

7.B. Analyze how the characters' internal and external responses develop the plot.

8.A. Demonstrate knowledge of literary genres such as realistic fiction, adventure stories, historical fiction, mysteries, humor, and myths.

Genre / Text Elements

Character and Plot A **plot** is the sequence of related events in a story. Plots center on at least one conflict that characters face. **Character development** is how a writer shows what a character is like. A character's personality—including likes, dislikes, fears, and wishes—affects his or her responses to conflict. These responses lead to actions that become the events of the plot.

EXAMPLES: CHARACTERS' INTERNAL AND EXTERNAL RESPONSES

TYPE OF RESPONSE	HOW IT IS SHOWN	EXAMPLE
Internal: characters' thoughts and feelings	• narrator's direct statements • descriptions of characters' thoughts and feelings • characters' unspoken words (internal monologue)	After moving to a new town, Hannah feels lonely and shy in a way she never did before.
External: characters' behavior and actions	• characters' spoken words (dialogue) • descriptions of characters' appearance and actions	Hannah forces herself to say hello to a classmate she sees working at a local store.

INTERACTIVITY

NOTEBOOK

PRACTICE With a partner, mark each item as an example of an internal or an external response to a conflict. Then, using clues from Max's external and internal responses, explain what might happen next in the plot.

	EXTERNAL	INTERNAL
1. When the dragon roared, Max stood his ground and raised his sword.	○	○
2. He knew that his life—and those of the villagers— depended on what he did in the next seconds.	○	○

About the Author

Miguel de Cervantes (1547-1616) was born near Madrid, Spain. He became a soldier in 1570, and took part in the Battle of Lepanto in 1571. Cervantes then began a writing career, and, in 1605, published the first part of *Don Quixote*. The second part was published in 1615. *Don Quixote* is considered one of the greatest works of fiction ever published and has become one of the world's best-selling books. The reteller, **Tom Lathrop** (1942–2014), was a professor of romance languages at the University of Delaware for more than twenty-five years. He wrote many books, and edited numerous editions of Spanish and French classics for English readers.

🌐 TEKS

2.A. Use print or digital resources to determine the meaning, syllabication, pronunciation, word origin, and part of speech.

5.C. Make, correct, or confirm predictions using text features, characteristics of genre, and structures.

from The Misadventures of Don Quixote

Concept Vocabulary

 ANNOTATE

As you read the selection, you will encounter these words.

valiant	fearlessly	righteous

Digital Resources A **digital thesaurus** is a resource you access online or through a mobile device. Thesaurus entries show a word's part of speech and list synonyms and antonyms. A digital thesaurus often provides audio pronunciations, which clarify syllable breaks.

SAMPLE DIGITAL THESAURUS ENTRY

reverence [REV uh rens] 🔊 *noun*

synonyms: admiration, adoration, awe, devotion

antonyms: disdain, hate, disrespect, dishonor

<u>Related Words</u>   <u>Dictionary</u>

Analysis: This entry shows that *reverence* is a noun with three syllables. Judging from its synonyms and antonyms, you can determine that reverence means "great respect."

PRACTICE As you read, use a digital thesaurus to determine the meanings and syllabications of unfamiliar words.

Comprehension Strategy

 NOTEBOOK

Make Predictions

Predictions are logical guesses you make about a story, including what might happen and what kind of feeling, or mood, it will have. You can use text features and structures to make meaningful predictions about a narrative.

- Read the title and think about the kinds of characters and events it suggests.
- Scan illustrations and footnotes, and consider what they show about the story's characters, events, and mood—for example, will the story most likely be serious, funny, or scary?

PRACTICE Use text features—such as the title, illustrations, and footnotes—to make predictions. Then, correct or confirm your predictions as you read the full text.

from The Misadventures of Don Quixote

Miguel de Cervantes,
Retold by Tom Lathrop

 AUDIO

 ANNOTATE

BACKGROUND

The original version of this story is the Spanish novel *Don Quixote*, which was written in the early 1600s. This was a time when romantic tales of knights and their adventures were very popular. With its foolish, elderly hero and other unlikely characters, Cervantes' *Don Quixote* made fun of these popular works. The book was so successful that it was translated into English within seven years of its publication. The novel has since inspired many other works of art, and even given rise to English expressions, such as *tilting at windmills,* which means "attacking imaginary enemies."

1   Long ago, in a tiny Spanish village, an old country gentleman named Don Quixote lived with his young niece and faithful housekeeper. The village barber and priest were his best friends. Don Quixote dreamed of adventure and spent every spare moment reading old tales about **valiant** knights who wore splendid suits of armor, fought **fearlessly** in battle, and rescued beautiful princesses from danger.

2   He read these adventures day and night.

3   Through his reading, he came to know about a powerful and evil enchanter named Frestón,[1] who, in his mind, became his own

Use a thesaurus or indicate another strategy you used that helped you determine meaning.

valiant (VAL yuhnt) *adj.*

MEANING:

fearlessly (FEER lehs lee) *adv.*

MEANING:

---

1. **Frestón** (freh STOHN) *n.* name of a famous villain from a story about knightly adventures.

enemy. He also learned about Mambrino's[2] Magic Helmet, and that anyone who wore it could not be defeated. Oh, how he wanted that helmet!

4   Everybody knew those stories were just made up. But Don Quixote was sure the knights were real and had done exactly what the books described. Because his head was so full of the old stories, he began to think, "I, too, must become a knight!" He wanted to wear armor and travel around on horseback looking for adventures, just like the knights of old did, and so he set out to do just that.

5   In the old stories, knights had special ladies—sometimes even princesses—to love and serve faithfully. Alas! There was no lady in Don Quixote's life, and, of course, he didn't know any princesses, so he chose a young girl from a nearby village to be his lady. He'd never even met her. But in his imagination, she was a princess. He named her Dulcinea,[3] because *dulce* means "sweet" in Spanish. In his imagination she was the sweetest, most beautiful woman in the world.

6   Of course, a knight also had to have armor, a shield, a sword, and a lance. Don Quixote was lucky to find what he needed in his attic. He cleaned the rust and dirt from the ancient armor and weapons he found there. He had a tired old horse that couldn't run fast anymore, but when Don Quixote saw him in the corral, in his mind's eye, it was the finest horse any knight could want. He named his horse Rocinante,[4] because in Spanish *rocín* means "old nag," and *ante* means "before," signifying that his horse used to be an old nag but wasn't one anymore. Don Quixote exclaimed, "Oh, Rocinante, you mighty charger! What great battles we will win together!"

7   Don Quixote now had his lady, his armor, and his charger, but he wasn't quite finished yet. He still needed a squire. Who could do that job? He went to visit his neighbor, Sancho Panza, and said, "My friend, I am going to be a knight-errant, and I want you to be my squire."

---

2. **Mambrino** (mahm BREE noh) *n.* name of a character in an old tale of knightly adventure.
3. **Dulcinea** (duhl seeh NEH ah) *n.* name of a character. *Dulce* means "sweet" in Spanish.
4. **Rocinante** (ROH seeh nahn teh) *n.* name Don Quixote gives his horse.

8   "What's a knight-errant? What's a squire?" Sancho couldn't read so he had no idea what the knights and squires from the old books were.

9   "Sancho," Don Quixote said, "a long time ago there were knights-errant roaming about Spain wearing armor and helping ladies in distress, rescuing orphans, and fighting in important battles. Squires were their servants and companions. They helped knights put on their armor, and took care of them and their horses. When a knight-errant became an emperor, he could make his squire the governor of an island. I'll make you the governor of an island, too, as soon as I can!"

10   This seemed like a fine idea, and Sancho agreed to be his squire.

11   At last, the morning came when, with Sancho's help, Don Quixote put on his armor, took up his sword and lance, and mounted Rocinante. Sancho got on his donkey—he didn't have a horse—and the two of them rode off to begin their new life of adventure.

12   As soon as they were on the road, Sancho said to his master, "Look, Señor[5] Knight-errant, don't forget about the island you promised me. I'll be able to govern it, no matter how big it is."

13   Later that very morning, they came across a windmill. As soon as Don Quixote saw it, he said to Sancho, "Fortune is guiding us better than we could have ever hoped! Look over there, Sancho, my friend! Do you see that monstrous giant? I will do battle with him. This is righteous warfare, and it's a great good to rid the earth of such a wicked creature!"

Use a thesaurus or indicate another strategy you used that helped you determine meaning.

righteous (RY chuhs) *adj.*

MEANING:

14   "What giant?" said Sancho.

15   "The one you see over there," responded his master, "with the long arms."

16   "Look, Señor," said Sancho, "that's not a giant—it's a windmill. And what looks like his arms are sails that turn the millstone to grind wheat."

17   "No, Sancho," insisted Don Quixote, "it *is* a giant. It's your fear that makes him look like a windmill! Stay here while I go into fierce battle with him."

18   And saying this, he spurred Rocinante. He rode on shouting, "Do not flee, you cowardly and vile creature—it is but one lone knight attacking you!"

19   Just when Don Quixote thrust into the sail with his lance, there was a great gust of wind, and the sails sped up with such fury that they tossed him and his horse onto the ground, sorely battered.

---

5. **Señor** (seh NYOR) *n. Mister*, in Spanish.

20   Sancho went as fast as his donkey could take him to help his master. When he got there, he saw that Don Quixote couldn't move because Rocinante had landed on top of him. Sancho said, "Why didn't you listen to me, Señor? Didn't I tell you that it was just a windmill?"

21   "Keep still, Sancho, my friend," responded Don Quixote. "In war, things change constantly. Moreover, I believe—and it's true—that my enemy, Frestón, has changed this giant into a windmill to take away the glory of my having conquered him. If only I had Mambrino's Magic Helmet, the giant couldn't have harmed me!" Sancho had never heard of that magic helmet, and he had no idea who Frestón was. All he could do was help his master climb back onto Rocinante, and they continued their journey. ❧

Response

📓 **NOTEBOOK**

Work on your own to answer the questions in your notebook. Use text evidence to support your responses.

1. **Personal Connections** Would you want to go on an adventure with Don Quixote? Why or why not?

Comprehension

2. **Reading Check (a)** What does Don Quixote dream of becoming? **(b)** Who does Don Quixote enlist as his squire? **(c)** What does Don Quixote mistake for a giant?

3. **Strategy: Make Predictions (a)** Cite at least one prediction you made using text features and structures in this selection. **(b)** Were you able to confirm your prediction, or did you have to correct it? Explain.

Analysis and Discussion

4. **(a)** Before starting his adventure, what types of stories does Don Quixote read? **(b) Make Inferences** What qualities in these stories do you think capture his imagination? Explain, citing text evidence that supports your inference.

5. **Interpret** How does Don Quixote's fantasy change both his view of himself and the world around him? Explain, citing specific examples from the text.

6. **Compare and Contrast** In what ways does Sancho Panza both share and not share in Don Quixote's view of the world? Explain.

7. **Get Ready for Close Reading** Choose a passage from the text that you find especially interesting or important. You'll discuss the passage with your group during Close-Read activities.

WORKING AS A GROUP

Discuss your responses to the Analysis and Discussion questions with your group.

- Note agreements and disagreements.
- Summarize insights.
- Consider changes of opinion.

If necessary, revise your original answers to reflect what you learn from your discussion.

EQ Notes ▸ What is the purpose of imagination?

What have you learned about the power of imagination from reading this retelling? Go to your Essential Question Notes and record your observations and thoughts about the excerpt from *The Misadventures of Don Quixote*.

 TEKS

6.A. Describe personal connections to a variety of sources, including self-selected texts.

6.C. Use text evidence to support an appropriate response.

from THE MISADVENTURES
OF DON QUIXOTE

Close Read

 ANNOTATE

PRACTICE Complete the following activities.
Use text evidence to support your responses.

1. **Present and Discuss** With your group, share the passages from the retelling that you found especially interesting. Discuss what you notice, the questions you have, and the conclusions you reach. For example, you might focus on the following passages:

   • Paragraph 4: Discuss the qualities that distinguish Don Quixote from his neighbors.

   • Paragraphs 5 and 6: Discuss why Don Quixote's names for his princess and his horse are comical.

2. **Reflect on Your Learning** What new ideas or insights did you uncover during your second reading of the text?

 NOTEBOOK

LANGUAGE STUDY

Concept Vocabulary

Why These Words? The vocabulary words are related.

valiant	fearlessly	righteous

1. With your group, determine what the words have in common. Write your ideas.

2. Add another word that fits the category. _____

3. Write a paragraph in which you use all three words correctly.

- -

Word Study

Long i Spelling Pattern: *igh* In English, the long *i* sound can be spelled in six different ways. One way is with the letter sequence *igh*, as in the word *right*, which is the base word of the vocabulary word *righteous*. Label the spelling of each of the following words as *correct* or *incorrect*. Then, fix any incorrect spellings. Use a dictionary to check your work.

delite	nitegown	insight
high	fistfite	knight

Genre / Text Elements

Character and Plot A character's personality and situation in life affect how he or she responds to conflict. These responses lead to actions that become the events of the plot. Characters have both internal and external responses to conflicts and other aspects of their environments.

- **Internal Response:** what characters feel and think; their unspoken thoughts and emotions

- **External Response:** what characters say and do; their spoken statements and physical actions

TIP: Characters' external responses reflect their internal ones. You can make inferences about characters' feelings and thoughts by examining their actions.

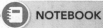 NOTEBOOK

PRACTICE Work with your group to answer the questions.

1. **(a) Analyze** Explain the internal response Don Quixote has to the old stories. **(b) Analyze Cause and Effect** Identify at least three actions Don Quixote takes as a result of his internal response to the stories. How do these responses develop the plot?

2. **Summarize** Briefly describe the plot of this narrative. In your summary, identify Don Quixote's internal and external responses that lead to specific plot events.

3. **Speculate** How might the events of this story have been different if Don Quixote had understood that the stories of knightly adventure were not real? Explain.

from THE MISADVENTURES OF DON QUIXOTE

Conventions

Subject-Verb Agreement in Complex Sentences A **complex sentence** is made up of an independent clause and one or more dependent clauses.

- An **independent clause** has a subject and a verb and can stand alone as a sentence.
- A **dependent clause** also contains a subject and a verb, but it cannot stand alone as a sentence. The thought it expresses is incomplete.

Managing subject-verb agreement in a complex sentence can be tricky. This is especially true when the dependent clause comes between the subject and the verb of the independent clause. In this example, the verb *decides* agrees with its subject, the singular noun *Sancho Panza*, rather than with the plural noun *rewards*:

Sancho Panza, only after he has been promised rewards, decides to be Don Quixote's squire.

> **TIP:** A clause has subject-verb agreement when its verb agrees with its subject in person and number.
> - **Person:** A first-person subject takes a first-person verb, and so on.
> - **Number:** A singular subject takes a singular verb. A plural subject takes a plural verb.

ANNOTATE

READ IT Mark the dependent clause in each complex sentence. Then, mark the subject and verb of the independent clause.

1. A knight, if he became an emperor, rewarded his squire with land.

2. Don Quixote, even though people tell him the truth, refuses to believe it.

WRITE IT Edit these complex sentences to correct subject-verb agreement errors.

1. A traditional squire, although he was supposed to be the knight's friend and guide, were often just an employee.

2. Don Quixote's friends, even after they listen to his explanations, thinks his mission is foolish.

TEKS

10.D.i. Edit drafts using standard English conventions, including complete complex sentences with subject-verb agreement and avoidance of splices, run-ons, and fragments.

12.B. Develop and revise a plan.

12.C. Refine the major research question, if necessary, guided by the answers to a secondary set of questions.

12.E. Differentiate between primary and secondary sources.

12.F. Synthesize information from a variety of sources.

12.J. Use an appropriate mode of delivery, whether written, oral, or multimodal, to present results.

Research

In a **research report,** you present facts, details, and examples gathered from research to support your own explanations and insights.

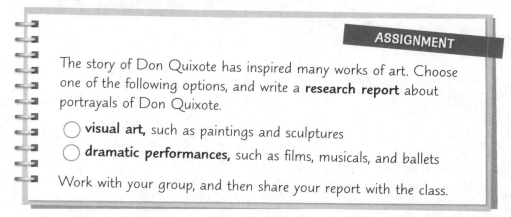

ASSIGNMENT

The story of Don Quixote has inspired many works of art. Choose one of the following options, and write a **research report** about portrayals of Don Quixote.

- ○ **visual art,** such as paintings and sculptures
- ○ **dramatic performances,** such as films, musicals, and ballets

Work with your group, and then share your report with the class.

Develop and Revise a Research Plan

Generate Research Questions With your group, brainstorm for questions to start your research process. Write your initial questions here:

🗐 NOTEBOOK

👆 INTERACTIVITY

Refine Research Questions Identify several sources to learn basic information about the topic. Take notes and discuss what you learned. Use this information to refine your research questions. You may need to broaden your inquiry if you have too few questions or if your questions are too narrow. You may need to focus your inquiry if you have too many questions or if your questions are too vague.

Gather and Synthesize Information

Use Relevant Sources Make a list of primary and secondary sources you will consult. When researching art, the works themselves are primary sources. Secondary sources are texts about the artists or the art works. Conduct research and take notes.

Synthesize Information When you synthesize information, you integrate ideas, examples, and facts from a variety of sources to offer your own new insight. That insight is your thesis. Work together to synthesize information and write your report, including a strong thesis.

Choose a Mode of Delivery Discuss the best way to organize and present your ideas. Mark your choice.

- ○ **Written Report:** Write a polished well-structured text.
- ○ **Oral Presentation:** Write a set of detailed notes you can use to deliver your findings orally.
- ○ **Multimodal Presentation:** Enhance the information by including media elements, such as videos, music, photos, or maps.

EQ Notes Before moving on to a new selection, go to your Essential Question Notes and record any additional thoughts or observations you may have about the excerpt from *The Misadventures of Don Quixote.*

JABBERWOCKY

Poetry

A **narrative poem** is a poem that tells a story. A **song** is a poem that is sung to music. The words to songs can also be recited without music.

THE MOCK TURTLE'S SONG

NARRATIVE POEM

Author's Purpose
- ⊙ to use highly focused, imaginative language and poetic form to tell a complete story

Characteristics
- ⊙ all the elements of a story, including setting, characters, and conflict
- ⊙ imagery, or sensory language
- ⊙ speaker, or voice that relates the story
- ⊙ language that emphasizes the sounds of words

Structure
- ⊙ lines of text that are organized into stanzas, or sections
- ⊙ may feature meter, or rhythmic patterns of stressed and unstressed syllables
- ⊙ plot that introduces, develops, and resolves a conflict

SONG

Author's Purpose
- ⊙ to use imaginative, rhythmic language and form to express ideas or feelings in a musical way

Characteristics
- ⊙ rhyme and other sound devices
- ⊙ speaker, or voice that relates the story
- ⊙ imagery that creates word pictures
- ⊙ repetition of words, phrases, and sections
- ⊙ may have characters, dialogue, and other story elements

Structure
- ⊙ verses and refrains, or repeated sections
- ⊙ meter, or rhythmic patterns of stressed and unstressed syllables

Genre / Text Elements

Structures in Poetry: Meter Language has natural rises and falls, peaks and valleys. Poets may use this quality of language to craft **meter**, or rhythmic patterns.

- The basic unit of meter is a **foot,** a group of stressed and unstressed syllables. A metrical foot may not match the syllables of words. One word may end one foot and begin another.
- The different patterns of stressed and unstressed syllables have specific definitions and names.

Meter has different effects. It contributes to a poem's emotional quality, or mood. It can also add to a poem's flow, unify the different parts of a poem, add humor, or create a sense of drama.

> **TIP:** Metrical names indicate the type of foot and number of feet per line. *Di-* = "two," so *dimeter* has two feet per line. If those feet are iambs, the meter is *iambic dimeter. Tri-* = three; *tetra-* = four; *penta-* = five; and so on.

TYPE OF FOOT	PATTERN	EXAMPLE
Iambic	one unstressed syllable, then one stressed syllable	To **strive**, | to **seek**, | to **find**
Trochaic	one stressed syllable, then one unstressed syllable	**Dou**ble, | **dou**ble, | **toil** and | **trou**ble
Anapestic	two unstressed syllables, then one stressed syllable	I must **fin** | ish my **jour** | ney a | **lone**

ANNOTATE

NOTEBOOK

PRACTICE Work together to read the poem and complete the activity.

> I saw a star slide down the sky,
> Blinding the north as it went by,
> Too burning and too quick to hold,
> Too lovely to be bought or sold,
> Good only to make wishes on
> And then forever to be gone.

1. **(a)** Mark the stressed and unstressed syllables in each line. Which line doesn't fit the overall pattern you marked? **(b)** Explain why this stanza is primarily iambic tetrameter.

2. Read the poem aloud. Then, decide which of the following effects the meter creates. Choose one or both of the answers listed, or add your own. Explain your choices.

- emphasizes key words, including *star, burning,* and *quick*
- emphasizes the rhyme and creates a songlike quality

TEKS

8.B. Analyze the effect of meter and structural elements such as line breaks in poems across a variety of poetic forms.

JABBERWOCKY

Compare Poetry

In this lesson, you will read the narrative poem, "Jabberwocky," and the song, "The Mock Turtle's Song"—both by Lewis Carroll. You will then compare the themes of the two works.

THE MOCK TURTLE'S SONG

Jabberwocky • The Mock Turtle's Song

Concept Vocabulary

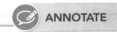 **ANNOTATE**

As you read the poems, you will encounter these words.

beware	shun	askance

Context Clues Clues in the context can help you narrow in on the meanings of unfamiliar words. For example, even if you cannot figure out a word's exact definition, you can usually determine its part of speech.

> **EXAMPLE**
>
> **Context:** The captain <u>countermanded</u> the officer's orders.
>
> **Analysis:** Even if you can't determine the exact meaning of *countermanded,* you can see that it ends in *-ed* and follows the subject of the sentence, *captain*. Therefore, it must be a verb.

PRACTICE "Jabberwocky" is famous for words the poet made up. You may not be able to determine exactly what they mean, but you can use context clues to figure out their parts of speech.

Comprehension Strategy

 ANNOTATE

Adjust Fluency

Poetry presents reading challenges that are different from those of prose. When your purpose is to read and understand poetry, **adjust your fluency** to better appreciate its imaginative language.

- As you read, look for complete thoughts, using punctuation as a guide.
- Don't automatically pause at the ends of lines; read on until the thought ends.
- Read aloud to appreciate how the words and lines fit together.

PRACTICE As you read and analyze these poems, use the strategies and adjust your fluency to fit your reading purpose.

 TEKS

3. Adjust fluency when reading grade-level text based on the reading purpose.

About the Poems

Jabberwocky

BACKGROUND
In the first chapter of *Through the Looking-Glass*, the sequel to *Alice's Adventures in Wonderland*, Alice encounters a creature called a Jabberwock. Many of the invented words in Carroll's imaginative poem are made up of two different words. For example, *brillig* is a combination of *brilliant* and *broiling*.

Lewis Carroll (1832–1898) is the pen name of Charles Lutwidge Dodgson, who was a British mathematics professor at Oxford University. Under his pen name, Dodgson wrote *Alice's Adventures in Wonderland* and *Through the Looking-Glass*. Like these classic novels, his poems are noted for their clever wordplay and delightfully zany word choices.

The Mock Turtle's Song

BACKGROUND
"The Mock Turtle's Song" is from *Alice's Adventures in Wonderland*. Also known as "The Lobster Quadrille," the poem is a parody, or comic reinvention, of an earlier poem. A quadrille is a difficult square dance that was popular when the poem was written. The original Alice, a young friend of Lewis Carroll's, had learned the quadrille from her dance teacher. In the original novel, the poem is recited by the Mock Turtle, who notes that he learned both the poem and the dance that goes with it from his teacher, Tortoise.

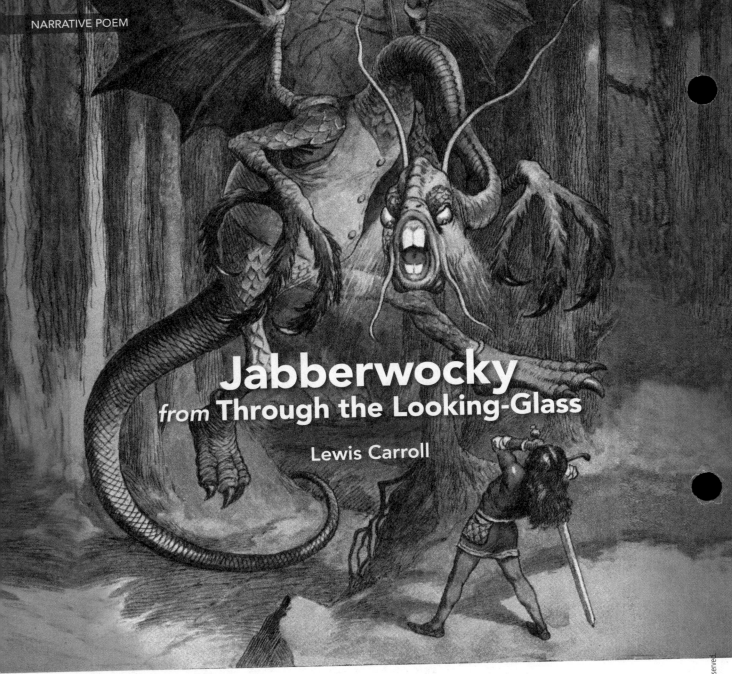

Jabberwocky
from Through the Looking-Glass

Lewis Carroll

 AUDIO

 ANNOTATE

Mark context clues or indicate another strategy you used that helped you determine meaning.

beware (bee WAIR) *v.*

MEANING:

shun (shuhn) *v.*

MEANING:

'Twas brillig, and the slithy toves
    Did gyre and gimble in the wabe;
All mimsy were the borogoves,
    And the mome raths outgrabe.

5 "**Beware** the Jabberwock, my son!
    The jaws that bite, the claws that catch!
Beware the Jubjub bird, and **shun**
    The frumious Bandersnatch!"

He took his vorpal sword in hand;
    Long time the manxome foe he sought—
10 So rested he by the Tumtum tree
    And stood awhile in thought.

And, as in uffish thought he stood,
    The Jabberwock, with eyes of flame,
15 Came whiffling through the tulgey wood,
    And burbled as it came!

One, two! One, two! And through and through
    The vorpal blade went snicker-snack!
He left it dead, and with its head
20   He went galumphing back.

"And hast thou slain the Jabberwock?
    Come to my arms, my beamish boy!
O frabjous day! Callooh! Callay!"
    He chortled in his joy.

25 'Twas brillig, and the slithy toves
    Did gyre and gimble in the wabe;
All mimsy were the borogoves,
    And the mome raths outgrabe.

MEDIA CONNECTION

 VIDEO

DISCUSS IT How does the performance of "Jabberwocky" in the video help you better understand the poem?

Write your response before sharing your ideas.

Alice in Wonderland (1983)

Jabberwocky

The Mock Turtle's Song

Lewis Carroll

"Will you walk a little faster?" said a whiting[1] to a snail.

"There's a porpoise close behind us, and he's treading on my tail.

See how eagerly the lobsters and the turtles all advance!

They are waiting on the shingle[2]—will you come and join the dance?

5 Will you, won't you, will you, won't you, will you join the dance?

Will you, won't you, will you, won't you, won't you join the dance?

"You can really have no notion how delightful it will be,

When they take us up and throw us, with the lobsters, out to sea!"

But the snail replied "Too far, too far!" and gave a look **askance**—

10 Said he thanked the whiting kindly, but he would not join the dance.

Would not, could not, would not, could not, would not join the dance.

Would not, could not, would not, could not, could not join the dance.

"What matters it how far we go?" his scaly friend replied.

"There is another shore, you know, upon the other side.

15 The further off from England the nearer is to France—

Then turn not pale, beloved snail, but come and join the dance?

Will you, won't you, will you, won't you, won't you join the dance?

Will you, won't you, will you, won't you, won't you join the dance?"

Mark context clues or indicate another strategy you used that helped you determine meaning.

askance (uh SKANTS) *adv.*

MEANING:

---

1. **whiting** (WY tihng) *n.* type of fish.
2. **shingle** (SHIHNG guhl) *n.* part of a beach that is covered with larger stones instead of sand.

 **NOTEBOOK**

Work on your own to answer the questions in your notebook. Use text evidence to support your responses.

Response

1. **Personal Connections** Which of these poems would you prefer to read to an audience of young children? Why?

Comprehension

2. **Reading Check (a)** In "Jabberwocky," what happens to the Jabberwock at the end of the poem? **(b)** Who is conversing in "The Mock Turtle's Song"? **(c)** Where does "The Mock Turtle's Song" take place?

3. **Strategy: Adjust Fluency** Which strategies did you use to adjust your fluency as you read the poems? How did adjusting your fluency affect your reading experience?

WORKING AS A GROUP

Discuss your responses to the Analysis and Discussion questions with your group.

- Note agreements and disagreements.
- Summarize insights.
- Consider changes of opinion.

If necessary, revise your original answers to reflect what you learn from your discussion.

Analysis and Discussion

4. **(a) Analyze** What phrases does the poet use to capture the Jabberwock's fierceness? **(b) Evaluate** How effective are these phrases in helping you imagine the Jabberwock? Explain.

5. **(a)** In "Jabberwocky," what does the hero do after being warned about the Jabberwock? **(b) Evaluate** Do you think the poem makes fun of typical portrayals of heroism? Explain.

6. **(a) Make Inferences** What is the relationship between the whiting and the snail in "The Mock Turtle's Song"? **(b) Analyze** Does the snail trust the whiting? Support your answer with text evidence.

7. **Get Ready for Close Reading** Choose a passage from the text that you find especially interesting or important. You'll discuss the passage with your group during Close-Read activities.

EQ Notes What is the purpose of imagination?

What have you learned about the purpose of imagination from reading these poems? Go to your Essential Question Notes and record your observations and thoughts about "Jabberwocky" and "The Mock Turtle's Song."

TEKS

5.F. Make inferences and use evidence to support understanding.

6.A. Describe personal connections to a variety of sources, including self-selected texts.

6.C. Use text evidence to support an appropriate response.

Close Read

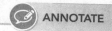 ANNOTATE

JABBERWOCKY

THE MOCK TURTLE'S SONG

PRACTICE Complete the following activities. Use text evidence to support your responses.

1. **Present and Discuss** With your group, share the passages from the two poems that you found especially interesting. Discuss what you notice, the questions you have, and the conclusions you reach. For example, you might focus on the following:

   • Lines 13–16 of "Jabberwocky": Discuss the poet's use of invented words, such as *uffish*, *whiffling*, and *burbled*.

   • Stanza 3 of "The Mock Turtle's Song": Discuss how the whiting tries to ease the snail's fears.

2. **Reflect on Your Learning** What new ideas or insights did you uncover during your second reading of the poem and song?

  NOTEBOOK

LANGUAGE STUDY

Concept Vocabulary

Why These Words? The vocabulary words are related.

beware	shun	askance

1. With your group, determine what the words have in common. Write your ideas.

2. Add another word that fits the category.

3. Write a paragraph in which you describe an imaginary scene. Use all three vocabulary words. Be sure to use context clues that hint at each word's meaning.

Word Study

Word Origins All three vocabulary words have Anglo-Saxon word origins. With your group, use print and digital resources to research what this means. Use these questions to guide your work:

   • What does the term Anglo-Saxon mean?

   • What other languages contributed to the development of modern English?

Discuss your findings with your group, and explain how your research adds to your understanding of word origins in general.

WORD NETWORK

Add words that are related to imagination from the text to your Word Network.

TEKS

2.A. Use print or digital resources to determine the meaning, syllabication, pronunciation, word origin, and part of speech.

6.F. Respond using newly acquired vocabulary as appropriate.

JABBERWOCKY

THE MOCK TURTLE'S SONG

Genre / Text Elements

Structures in Poetry: Meter Meter is the rhythm created by the pattern of stressed and unstressed syllables in each line of a poem. A **foot** is a unit of meter. There are different types of feet:

- **Iamb** = an unstressed syllable, followed by a stressed syllable
- **Trochee** = a stressed syllable, followed by an unstressed syllable
- **Anapest** = two unstressed syllables followed by one stressed syllable

In these poems, the poet uses two different meters in each stanza. In "Jabberwocky," the first three lines of each stanza have a slightly different meter than the fourth. In "The Mock Turtle's Song," the first four lines of each stanza have a very different meter than the last two lines. These choices add to the effect of each poem.

TIP: Even in poems that use a set meter throughout, the poet may stray from the pattern and then return to it. The difference may add humor or create drama.

ANNOTATE

NOTEBOOK

PRACTICE Work with your group to complete the activities. It may help you to take turns reading the poems aloud and listening for the effects of the meter.

1. **Analyze** Mark the stressed syllables in the first three lines of stanza two of "Jabberwocky." Then, answer these questions:

   (a) What type of metrical foot does the poet use?

   (b) How many metrical feet do these lines have?

2. **Analyze** Mark the stresses in the last line of stanza two of "Jabberwocky." Then, answer these questions:

   (a) What type of metrical foot does the poet use?

   (b) How many metrical feet does this line have?

3. **Interpret** Which item best states the effect of the change in meter in each stanza of "Jabberwocky"? Choose one or more of the answers listed, or add your own. Explain your choices.

   - makes the end of each stanza more dramatic
   - brings the reader to a slight pause before continuing
   - makes the beginning of the next stanza more dramatic

4. **Interpret** Read one stanza of "The Mock Turtle's Song" aloud and listen for the change in meter in the last two lines. Why do you think the poet makes this change? What is the effect? Explain.

⊕ TEKS

8.B. Analyze the effect of meter and structural elements such as line breaks in poems across a variety of poetic forms.

9.F. Analyze how the author's use of language contributes to mood and voice.

Author's Craft

Language and Mood Most **sound devices** are groupings of words that share certain sounds. They are sometimes called "musical devices," because they highlight the musical qualities of language. Rhyme is a sound device with which you are probably familiar. There are other types of sound devices that may be less obvious than rhyme. Sound devices contribute to the overall **mood**, or emotional quality, of a poem.

SOUND DEVICE	DEFINITION	EXAMPLE
Alliteration	repetition of the same consonant sound at the beginnings of stressed syllables in nearby words	*flurry of foam flew*
Consonance	the repetition of final consonant sounds in stressed syllables with different vowel sounds	*wonder, wind, and splendor*

PRACTICE Work with your group to complete the activities.

ANNOTATE

NOTEBOOK

1. **Analyze** Mark examples of alliteration and consonance in each passage shown in the chart, and explain the mood it helps create. You may also consider the use of rhyme and repetition.

PASSAGE FROM THE POEMS	EFFECTS ON MOOD
The jaws that bite, the claws that catch! ("Jabberwocky," line 6)	
O frabjous day! Callooh! Callay! ("Jabberwocky," line 23)	
Will you, won't you, will you, won't you, will you join the dance? ("The Mock Turtle's Song," refrain)	

2. **Interpret** Read the poems aloud. Do you think each poem has one dominant mood, or does the mood change? How do sound devices help to create the mood, or moods, you hear?

JABBERWOCKY

THE MOCK TURTLE'S SONG

Compare Poetry

Multiple Choice

 NOTEBOOK

These questions are based on "Jabberwocky" and "The Mock Turtle's Song." Choose the best answer to each question.

1. One way that the creatures in "Jabberwocky" and "The Mock Turtle's Song" are similar is that they all are

A very aggressive.

B very realistic.

C at least partly imaginary.

D very depressed.

2. Read these lines from both poems. Which answer choice best describes similarities between these lines of dialogue in the two poems?

---

from **"Jabberwocky"**

"Beware the Jabberwock, my son!
    The jaws that bite, the claws that catch!
Beware the Jubjub bird, and shun
    The frumious Bandersnatch!"

---

from **"The Mock Turtle's Song"**

"What matters it how far we go?" his
    scaly friend replied.
There is another shore, you know, upon
    the other side. …
Then turn not pale, beloved snail, but
    come and join the dance?"

F Both are expressing hope.

G Both are giving advice.

H Both are giving warnings.

J Both are expressing fear.

3. In both poems, what personal quality seems to be highly valued?

A a sense of humor

B bravery

C kindness

D physical strength

⭐ TEKS

6.B. Write responses that demonstrate understanding of texts, including comparing sources within and across genres.

7.A. Infer multiple themes within and across texts using text evidence.

Short Response

1. **Compare and Contrast** In what ways are the challenges the boy and the snail face in the two poems similar and different?

2. **Take a Position** Would you rather have the older character in "Jabberwocky" or the whiting in "The Mock Turtle's Song" as a friend? Explain your thinking, citing text evidence.

3. **(a) Analyze** What message do you think "Jabberwocky" might be expressing about facing challenges or fears? **(b) Compare and Contrast** Do you think "The Mock Turtle's Song" expresses a similar or a different message? Explain.

Timed Writing

In a **comparison-and-contrast essay,** you analyze and explain similarities and differences among two or more topics.

ASSIGNMENT

Write a **comparison-and-contrast essay** about the **themes** these poems express. Consider two themes: one about bravery and facing fears, and the other about relationships and how we interact with others.

5-MINUTE PLANNER

1. Read the assignment carefully and completely.

2. Decide what you want to say—your controlling idea.

3. Decide which text evidence you'll use from the poems. Make sure to balance your analysis of two different themes across both works.

4. Organize your ideas, by choosing an appropriate structure for your essay:

   • **Point-by-Point:** Discuss one theme in one poem, and then one theme in the other poem. Then, discuss the second theme in one poem, and the second theme in the other poem.

   • **Block:** Discuss both themes in one poem, and then both themes in the other poem.

EQ Notes Before moving on to a new selection, go to your Essential Question Notes and record what you learned from "Jabberwocky" and "The Mock Turtle's Song."

THE IMPORTANCE OF IMAGINATION

The selection you are about to read is a reflective essay.

Reading Reflective Essays

When you reflect, you look back on something to discover its deeper meaning. A **reflective essay** is a brief work of nonfiction in which an author shares newfound insights about an event from the past.

REFLECTIVE ESSAY

Author's Purpose

○ to express insights gained through experience and observation

Characteristics

○ contains a controlling idea and supporting evidence

○ explains insights and how the author gained them

○ includes words and phrases that relate to feeling and thinking

○ conveys a thoughtful tone, or attitude, and mood, or emotional quality

○ may contain dialogue or other storytelling elements

Structure

○ an introduction that provides focus, body paragraphs that describe and explain, and a conclusion that summarizes insights

Take a Minute!

 NOTEBOOK

LIST IT The word *reflect* has multiple meanings. With a partner, discuss the types of things that reflect. Why does the idea of reflection make sense for essays of this type?

Why might a person want to write a reflective essay?

 TEKS

8.D.i. Analyze characteristics and structural elements of informational text, including the controlling idea or thesis with supporting evidence.

Genre / Text Elements

Controlling Idea Reflective essays revisit real-life events through the lens of time. The writer describes experiences from the past with fresh eyes and a more mature perspective. Unlike a fictional narrative, which has a plot, essays are structured with an introduction, a body, and a conclusion. The author's main insight about those events is called a **controlling idea.**

EXAMPLE

PASSAGES FROM A REFLECTIVE ESSAY	DEVELOPMENT OF CONTROLLING IDEA
When I think about that day, I realize now that no amount of pleading could have changed Mom's mind. "Start fresh," she said. "Look forward, not back."	**Introduction:** establishes a place and time, and hints at the author's controlling idea
My sisters were quiet, but I could see they had been crying. Tomorrow we were moving away from everyone and everything we knew. To my nine-year-old self, it was tragic. "How could Mom ruin our lives like this," I thought.	**Body:** develops the controlling idea through evidence
What Mom knew then, and I didn't, was that starting over after tragedy can heal a family. It is never too late or too early to begin again.	**Conclusion:** reveals, restates, or summarizes the controlling idea

 INTERACTIVITY

PRACTICE Read this introduction of a reflective essay. Choose the item that best states its controlling idea. Then, mark evidence in the passage that supports your choice.

PASSAGE	CONTROLLING IDEA
The ragamuffin parade, held every year on the Saturday before Halloween, was a beloved tradition in my town. There I was, dressed in robes, light-saber in hand, ready to fight for right. Surrounded by ninjas, astronauts, and the occasional dinosaur, I felt so strong and powerful. When I examine my choice to become a first responder, I trace it back to that moment.	• A childhood event can shape your future. • Halloween can be important. • Children benefit from dressing in costume.

About the Author

Esha Chhabra (b. 1991) is a journalist who has written for *The New York Times*, *The San Francisco Chronicle,* and *The Guardian*. Chhabra is a graduate of Georgetown University and studied global politics at the London School of Economics.

The Importance of Imagination

Concept Vocabulary

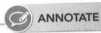 ANNOTATE

As you read "The Importance of Imagination," you will encounter these words.

template	parameters	model

Context Clues If these words are unfamiliar to you, try using **context clues**—other words and phrases that appear near the unfamiliar words—to help you determine their meanings. There are various types of context clues that may help you as you read. Here are two examples:

Definition: The palace was **magnificent,** <u>grand in its size and beauty</u>.

Analysis: "grand in its size and beauty" defines *magnificent*

Contrast of Ideas: The winners of the race **glided** across the finish line, while the remaining competitors <u>stumbled</u> behind them.

Analysis: *Glided* must mean the opposite of *stumbled,* or "moved smoothly."

PRACTICE As you read the essay, use context clues to clarify the meanings of new words. Mark your observations in the open space next to the text.

Comprehension Strategy

 NOTEBOOK

Establish a Purpose for Reading

When you **establish a purpose** for reading, you decide why you are reading a text and what you hope to get from it. To set a purpose for reading, ask yourself the following questions:

- **What's the genre?** You may set one purpose to read an essay and another to read a story. Decide how the genre affects your reading goals.
- **What do you already know and want to learn?** You may already have some knowledge of a topic. Decide whether you want to learn something specific or just add to your basic knowledge

PRACTICE Before you begin to read this essay, establish your purpose. Write it here.

 TEKS

2.B. Use context such as definition, analogy, and examples to clarify the meaning of words.

5.A. Establish purpose for reading assigned and self-selected text.

The Importance of Imagination

Esha Chhabra

BACKGROUND

A curriculum vitae, or CV, is a short account of a person's background, skills, education, and work experience. In the United States, a CV is similar to a résumé. Résumés are usually no longer than one page. Many employers require these documents for job applications and look at them carefully to decide who they should hire.

AUDIO

ANNOTATE

1   While growing up, I'd never really considered how important it is to be imaginative. It's a childhood profession, you could say. It comes naturally. Then we hit an age when we're presented with a scantron[1] of bubble-in options, a **template** for a CV that we need to create, and Excel.[2] At that point, our learning has to fit into certain **parameters**: within that little bubble, within the one page limit, and within a tiny digital graph. So, what happens to our imagination?

2   It seems to fade.

3   Being Asian (as I am) doesn't help. The assumption that you're more apt for engineering or medicine is like a nagging tail. We have a so-called fondness for numbers apparently. If you're Asian, you must be good at math—of course.

4   Well, then I turned out to be an oddball. I developed an affinity for words and images instead. At the age of 12, my dream was to be a professional doodler, which could turn into a career as a cartoonist, if it went well. And my parents indulged me in that dream. Unlike others, who may have thought that

Mark context clues or indicate another strategy you used to help you determine meaning.

template (TEHM pliht) *n.*

MEANING:

parameters (puh RAM uh tuhrz) *n.*

MEANING:

1. **scantron** refers to a paper form used for multiple-choice tests.
2. **Excel** widely used computer program for creating spreadsheets and graphs.

was ridiculous, they got me drawing books. When my mother saw me sitting idle, or falling asleep among a pile of school books, she'd suggest, "Why don't you draw for a bit?" Over a decade later, little has changed. She still chuckles at my drawings, tells me to draw more often, and has preserved that notebook.

5   As I grew older, as the reading list of books grew longer, the assignments tougher, and jobs took up any spare time as a student in college, that ability to just sit down and pour your imagination onto a blank canvas began to disappear. Rather, that creative side had to reinvent itself.

6   My high school history teacher once told me that history is not a timeline; it's a story. She threw out the linearity of history. She made what was dry and ancient, charming, engaging, and at times, even humorous. That was her imagination at work. And it helped me develop a love for the social sciences. Our imaginations can be quite contagious, I learned.

7   But can this love for the imaginative ever find a place in the real world? Certainly.

8   Imagination creates not just fairy tales and children's books but a new vision for the way we conduct our lives. Imaginations challenge the norm, push boundaries, and help us progress.

9   We need to encourage more creativity. Forget the CV for a bit.

10   If we encourage that brilliant math student to be imaginative as well, he could use those algorithms[3] to innovate. If we encourage the biology student to be imaginative as well, she could design a new sustainable fuel source for us. If we encourage that economics buff to be imaginative as well, he could build a new people-friendly business model. The tools are there. You just need to reorient them towards the unexpected. That's where creativity—at home, in the classroom, and in the workplace—is so essential.

11   That's why, last week I found myself, sitting with my mom late at night, rereading Shel Silverstein's poems for children. Turns out, they're just as good for adults, maybe even better. ❧

---

3. **algorithms** (AL guh rihth uhmz) *n.* steps for solving a problem, usually related to math.

Mark context clues or indicate another strategy you used to help you determine meaning.

model (MOD uhl) *n.*

MEANING:

Response

1. Personal Connections Do you agree that creativity should be encouraged? Cite the text in your response.

Comprehension

2. Reading Check (a) According to the author, what happens to our imagination when we grow up, and why? **(b)** What was the author's dream at age 12? **(c)** What did the author's history teacher say about history?

3. Establish Purpose for Reading Explain the purpose you established to read this essay. In what ways did having a specific purpose affect how you read and what you learned? Explain.

Analysis and Discussion

4. Analyze Causes and Effects What causes the author to doodle? What effect did her doodling have? Use text evidence to support your response.

5. (a) Connect How do the author's parents support her break with tradition? **(b) Speculate** Do you think the author would have broken with tradition if her parents had not supported her? Explain.

6. Evaluate Reread paragraph 10. Do you think these possible outcomes of encouraging creativity are convincing evidence for the author's thesis? Why or why not?

7. Get Ready for Close Reading Choose a passage from the text that you find especially interesting or important. You'll discuss the passage with your group during Close-Read activities.

WORKING AS A GROUP

Discuss your responses to the Analysis and Discussion questions with your group.

• Note agreements and disagreements.
• Summarize insights.
• Consider changes of opinion.

If necessary, revise your original answers to reflect what you learn from your discussion.

EQ Notes What is the purpose of imagination?

What have you learned about the power of imagination from reading this essay? Go to your Essential Question Notes and record your observations and thoughts about "The Importance of Imagination."

 TEKS

5.A. Establish purpose for reading assigned and self-selected text.

6.A. Describe personal connections to a variety of sources, including self-selected texts.

6.C. Use text evidence to support an appropriate response.

THE IMPORTANCE OF
IMAGINATION

Close Read

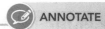 ANNOTATE

PRACTICE Complete the following activities. Use text evidence to support your responses.

1. **Present and Discuss** With your group, share the passages from the reflective essay that you found especially interesting. Discuss what you notice, the questions you have, and the conclusions you reach. For example, you might focus on the following passages:

   • Paragraph 3: Discuss how the author views the assumptions people make about Asians.

   • Paragraph 10: Discuss what the author means when she writes, "The tools are there. You just need to reorient them towards the unexpected."

2. **Reflect on Your Learning** What new ideas or insights did you uncover during your second reading of the text?

 NOTEBOOK

LANGUAGE STUDY

Concept Vocabulary

Why These Words? The vocabulary words are related.

template	parameters	model

1. With your group, determine what the words have in common. Write your ideas.

2. Add another word that fits the category. _____

3. Confirm your understanding of the vocabulary words by using all of them in a paragraph. Be sure to include context clues that hint at each word's meaning.

Word Study

Greek Prefix: *para-* The Greek prefix *para-*, which means "beside" or "alongside," contributes to the meanings of many English words. For example, *parallel* lines are lines that run alongside each other. Use a dictionary to look up these words related to careers: *paralegal, paramedic, paramilitary*. Discuss with your group how the prefix *para-* contributes to the meaning of each word.

WORD NETWORK

Add words that are related to imagination from the text to your Word Network.

 TEKS
8.D.i. Analyze characteristics and structural elements of informational text, including the controlling idea or thesis, with supporting evidence.

Genre / Text Elements

Controlling Idea and Supporting Evidence In a reflective essay, an author attempts to draw a larger and deeper meaning from personal experience. This meaning shapes the essay's **controlling idea,** which is the main message the author wishes to convey. The author provides different kinds of **evidence** to support the thesis. To identify a controlling idea, look for clues in both the structure and details of the essay:

- Examine the title of the work.
- Look for related ideas stated in the introduction and conclusion.
- Notice any words or ideas that are repeated.
- Pay attention to definitions, examples, contrasts, or other ways the author emphasizes one particular idea.

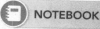 NOTEBOOK

PRACTICE Answer the questions on your own. Then, discuss your responses with your group.

1. **Interpret** What is the controlling idea of the essay? Support your response with evidence from the text.

2. **(a) Connect** Reread paragraph 1 of the essay. Where is the controlling idea introduced? **(b) Analyze** What purpose does paragraph 2 serve? Why do you think that paragraph is a single sentence?

3. **Interpret** In paragraph 8, how does the author redefine *imagination*?

4. **Distinguish** How are the examples used to support the controlling ideas in paragraph 10 different from the examples used earlier in the essay?

5. **Evaluate** Do you think the author's insights about life are valid and well supported? Support your response with details from the text.

THE IMPORTANCE OF
IMAGINATION

Author's Craft

Language and Voice When you talk with people, you get a sense of their personalities from the way they speak and the types of words they use. A written text conveys a similar sense of the author's personality. That quality is called **voice**. An author's voice is created mainly through diction and syntax.

- **Diction:** the types of words and phrases an author uses
- **Syntax:** the types of sentences an author uses

EXAMPLE: Notice how a similar moment is conveyed in two different voices.

PASSAGES	DICTION AND SYNTAX	VOICE
After what seemed like a million years, I got home. Safe! I mean, I made it to the door. There, to my horror, I was greeted by my dad's new alarm system. His new baby.	• informal words • dramatic exaggeration • sentence fragments	lighthearted; chatty
It took more than an hour to travel home. I was relieved, because home is where I feel safe. At my front door, however, my father's new alarm system was screaming, startling me greatly.	• formal words • restrained quality • longer sentences	analytical; serious

 INTERACTIVITY   NOTEBOOK

PRACTICE Work with your group to complete the activities.

1. **Analyze** Reread the passages indicated in the chart and jot down your observations about the author's diction and syntax.

PASSAGE FROM THE TEXT	DICTION AND SYNTAX
Well, then I turned out to be an oddball... if it went well. (from paragraph 4)	
My high school history teacher... imagination at work. (from paragraph 6)	

2. **Analyze** Review your completed chart. How would you describe Esha Chhabra's voice?

3. **Compare and Contrast** Rewrite paragraph 8 from the text with a specific voice in mind, choosing different words and altering sentence lengths and styles. What effect does this new voice create?

 TEKS

9.F. Analyze how the author's use of language contributes to mood and voice.

10.D.viii. Edit drafts using standard English conventions, including punctuation marks, including commas in complex sentences, transitions, and introductory elements.

11.B. Compose informational texts including multi-paragraph essays that convey information about a topic, using a clear controlling idea or thesis statement, genre characteristics, and craft.

Composition

An **explanatory essay** describes the author's thoughts about and position on a topic.

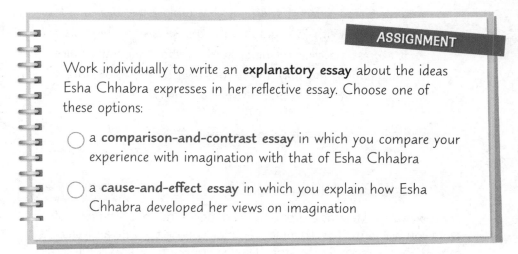

ASSIGNMENT

Work individually to write an **explanatory essay** about the ideas Esha Chhabra expresses in her reflective essay. Choose one of these options:

○ a **comparison-and-contrast essay** in which you compare your experience with imagination with that of Esha Chhabra

○ a **cause-and-effect essay** in which you explain how Esha Chhabra developed her views on imagination

Gather Text Evidence Review "The Importance of Imagination," looking for relevant details to support your writing task.

- If you chose a comparison-and-contrast essay, note your reaction to details from the essay: Did you identify with what the author said? Or, did you feel that you couldn't relate to her experience?

- If you chose a cause-and-effect essay, identify details that reveal what influenced the author's views on imagination. Then, connect each detail to her perspective.

Draft Your Essay As you draft your essay, use vivid details that help to explain your response. Organize your ideas clearly, using transitional words and phrases that make logical connections:

- **Comparison-and-Contrast:** Transitions, such as *likewise* and *however,* highlight similarities and differences.

- **Cause-and-Effect:** Transitions, such as *since* and *therefore,* help to show causes and effects.

Edit Your Essay Once you have a first draft, edit it for correct conventions. Pay particular attention to your use of punctuation with transitions.

- When you use a transition at the beginning of a sentence, follow it with a comma.

- When you use a transition in the middle of a sentence, set it off with commas.

Share and Revise Exchange your draft with a group member. Provide feedback to your classmate by noting places in which the ideas are unclear, disconnected, or need more support. Remember to be polite and offer helpful suggestions when giving feedback.

EQ Notes Before moving on to a new selection, go to your Essential Question Notes and record any additional thoughts or observations you may have about "The Importance of Imagination."

Present a Short Story

ASSIGNMENT

You have read different selections that explore the idea of imagination. With your group, write and present a **short story** that expresses a clear theme or position about the importance of imagination. You may invent your own character, or write a new adventure for a character from this unit.

Plan and Write

 **INTERACTIVITY**

Discuss Ideas Meet as a group to make decisions about the type of story you will write. For example, you may choose to write a mystery, a fantasy, or a science-fiction story. Discuss your options and come to a consensus, or agreement, about the genre you will use and the theme, or position, you will express.

Brainstorm for Characters and Conflict Generate ideas and make decisions about the characters, setting, and conflict of your story. Let your imaginations loose and have fun with your ideas. Capture your decisions in the chart.

STORY ELEMENT	DETAILS
Characters	
Setting	
Conflict	

Make a Plan You can organize group writing in different ways. For example, you may have one person write the beginning and then hand it to the next person who writes a scene, and so on. Alternatively, you may work together on each segment. Decide how you want to approach the task and make sure everyone has equal responsibility.

Draft the Story As you draft the story, show how a conflict begins, gets more intense, reaches a climax, and ends. Use dialogue and description to bring the characters to life. Make sure the story events and details work together to express the theme, or position, you chose.

Prepare to Share

Read With Fluency You will share your story with the class by reading it aloud, so practice reading with fluency. This means reading with expressiveness and clarity. As a group, decide how to divide the story. One way would be to take turns reading aloud by paragraphs. Another would be to assign some group members to read the narration and others to read dialogue.

Rehearse and Present

Practice With Your Group Work with your group to polish your story and your performance. As you read the story aloud, vary your voice, expressions, and gestures to portray characters and events in an engaging way. Remember to make eye contact with your audience at appropriate intervals. Use the checklist to evaluate your first rehearsal. Then, use your evaluation to guide additional rehearsals.

CONTENT	PRESENTATION TECHNIQUES
◯ The story expresses a clear theme, or position, on the idea of imagination.	◯ Speakers make eye contact with the audience at appropriate points in the performance.
◯ The story develops characters using dialogue and description.	◯ Speakers adjust their voices and use gestures and expressions to portray characters and events in an engaging way.
◯ The story uses sensory details to create a vivid setting.	◯ Readers use an appropriate speaking rate and volume.
◯ The story includes an entertaining plot that leads to a resolution.	◯ Readers speak clearly, enunciating each word.
◯ With the possible exception of dialogue, the story uses correct conventions of language.	

Fine-Tune the Content Sometimes it is hard to describe a setting in a way that makes it seem real. Consider adding more sensory details to help your audience visualize the setting.

Brush Up on Your Presentation Techniques Use your voice in ways that develop the characters' personalities and convey the mood of a scene. For example, if the setting is a dark, threatening forest, you may want to speak with a low, worried tone that conveys a sense of danger.

Listen and Evaluate

Present your story to the class. As you listen to other groups present, note differences in the ways they managed the task. Discuss your observations after all groups have shared their work.

 TEKS

1.C. Give an organized presentation with a specific stance and position, employing eye contact, speaking rate, volume, enunciation, natural gestures, and conventions of language to communicate ideas effectively.

3. Adjust fluency when reading grade-level text based on the reading purpose.

11.A. Compose literary texts such as personal narratives, fiction, and poetry using genre characteristics and craft.

Essential Question

What is the purpose of imagination?

Activating your imagination can teach you about the real world and about yourself. In this section, you will choose a selection about imagination to read independently. Get the most from this section by establishing a purpose for reading. Ask yourself, "What do I hope to gain from my independent reading?" Here are just a few purposes you might consider:

Read to Learn Think about the selections you have already read. What questions do you still have about the unit topic?

Read to Enjoy Read the descriptions of the texts. Which one seems most interesting and appealing to you?

Read to Form a Position Consider your thoughts and feelings about the Essential Question. Are you still undecided about some aspect of the topic?

Reading Digital Texts

Digital texts, like the ones you will read in this section, are electronic versions of print texts. They have a variety of characteristics:

- can be read on various devices
- text can be resized
- may include highlighting or other annotation tools
- may have bookmarks, audio links, and other helpful features

 VIDEO

 INTERACTIVITY

Independent Learning Strategies

Throughout your life, in school, in your community, and in your career, you will need to rely on yourself to learn and work on your own. Use these strategies to keep your focus as you read independently for sustained periods of time. Add ideas of your own for each category.

STRATEGY	MY ACTION PLAN
Create a schedule • Understand your goals and deadlines. • Make a plan for each day's activities.	
Read with purpose • Use a variety of comprehension strategies to deepen your understanding. • Think about the text and how it adds to your knowledge.	
Take notes • Record key ideas and information. • Review your notes before sharing what you've learned.	

⬟ **TEKS**

4. Self-select text and read independently for a sustained period of time; **5.A.** Establish purpose for reading assigned and self-selected text; **8.F.** Analyze characteristics of multimodal and digital texts.

CONTENTS

Choose one selection. Selections are available online only.

PERFORMANCE TASK

Share Your Independent Learning

Reflect on and evaluate the information you gained from your Independent Reading selection. Then, share what you learned with others.

Close-Read Guide

Tool Kit
Close-Read Guide and
Model Annotation

Establish your purpose for reading. Then, read the selection through at least once. Use this page to record your close-read ideas.

Selection Title: _____   Purpose for Reading: _____

Minutes Read: _____

INTERACTIVITY

Close Read the Text

Zoom in on sections you found interesting. **Annotate** what you notice. Ask yourself **questions** about the text. What can you **conclude?**

_____
_____
_____
_____
_____
_____
_____

Analyze the Text

1. Think about the author's choices of literary elements, techniques, and structures. Select one and record your thoughts.

_____
_____
_____

2. What characteristics of digital texts did you use as you read this selection, and in what ways? How do the characteristics of a digital text affect your reading experience? Explain.

_____
_____
_____

QuickWrite

Choose a paragraph from the text that grabbed your interest. Explain the power of this passage.

_____
_____
_____
_____
_____
_____

Share Your Independent Learning

© Pearson Education, Inc., or its affiliates. All rights reserved.

Essential Question

What is the purpose of imagination?

When you read something independently, your understanding continues to grow as you share what you have learned with others.

 NOTEBOOK

Prepare to Share

CONNECT IT One of the most important ways to respond to a text is to notice and describe your personal reactions. Think about the text you explored independently and the ways in which it connects to your own experiences.

- What similarities and differences do you see between the text and your own life? Describe your observations.

- How do you think this text connects to the Essential Question? Describe your ideas.

Learn From Your Classmates

DISCUSS IT Share your ideas about the text you explored on your own. As you talk with others in your class, take notes about new ideas that seem important.

Reflect

EXPLAIN IT Review your notes, and mark the most important insight you gained from these writing and discussion activities. Explain how this idea adds to your understanding of the purpose of imagination.

 TEKS
6.A. Describe personal connections to a variety of sources, including self-selected texts.
6.E. Interact with sources in meaningful ways such as notetaking, annotating, freewriting, or illustrating.

Short Story

In this unit, you read about imagination from different perspectives. You also practiced writing a short story. Now, apply what you have learned.

Imagine that one of the characters from this unit has found his or her way into the real world. What might happen? Write a **short story** that uses that premise and explores the Essential Question:

Essential Question
What is the purpose of imagination?

Review and Evaluate Your EQ Notes

INTERACTIVITY

Review your Essential Question Notes and your QuickWrite from the beginning of the unit and complete the chart. Have your ideas changed?

● Yes	● No
Identify at least three details that made you think differently about imagination.	Identify at least three examples or other details that reinforced your ideas about imagination.
1.	1.
2.	2.
3.	3.

State your ideas now:

How might you reflect your thinking about imagination in a short story?

Share Your Perspective

The **Short Story Checklist** will help you stay on track.

PLAN Before you write, read the Checklist and make sure you understand all the items.

DRAFT As you write, pause occasionally to make sure you're meeting the Checklist requirements.

Use New Words Refer to your Word Network to vary your word choice. Also, consider using one or more of the Academic Vocabulary terms you learned at the beginning of the unit: *dialogue, transform, novelty, consequently, description.*

REVIEW AND EDIT After you have written a first draft, evaluate it against the Checklist. Make any changes needed to clarify the sequence of events or to make your characters more vivid. Then, reread your story and fix any errors you find.

EQ Notes Make sure you have pulled in details from your Essential Question Notes to support your insights about imagination.

 INTERACTIVITY

SHORT STORY CHECKLIST

My story clearly contains . . .

◯ a believable, well-drawn main character and supporting characters.

◯ a well-structured plot centered on a clear conflict.

◯ a consistent narrative point of view, whether first-person, third-person limited, or third-person omniscient.

◯ dialogue that sounds natural and reveals what characters are like.

◯ use of transitional words and phrases that accurately show how ideas and events are related.

◯ varied and precise word choices.

◯ correct use of standard English conventions, including consistent verb tenses.

◯ no punctuation or spelling errors.

 TEKS

11.A. Compose literary texts such as personal narratives, fiction, and poetry, using genre characteristics and craft.

Revising and Editing

Read this draft and think about corrections the writer might make. Then, answer the questions that follow.

Guests

[1] Captain Miranda speaks to her crew from the main platform of the planet command station. [2] "As you know, we will be entertaining very important visitors from Ogdorf today. [3] Are the loafs of friendship bread ready?"

[4] Gerald, her second-in-command, motions to the spaceport. [5] While he speaks. [6] "Yes, Captain, although they won't arrive until Venus sets, everything is in readiness. [7] When the guests arrive, they will be greeted by the children of our planet, who have been waiting patiently to see the guests' scaly green skin. [8] The musicians, including the violinist who sings, is practicing the welcome march."

[9] Gerald takes a breath. [10] He continues with his speech. [11] "Our cook has prepared many delicacies, including Saturn-ring soup, Martian fowl, and Plutonian cake, which we will serve on the Sun terrace. [12] The food will be delicious, and the view will be beautiful. [13] They will easily be convinced to join forces with us, although something unexpected happens."

1. What spelling correction should be made in sentence 3?

  A Change *are* to *our.*

  B Change *loafs* to *loaves.*

  C Change *friendship* to *freindship.*

  D Change *ready* to *reddy.*

2. What change should be made to correct subject-verb agreement in sentence 8?

  F Change *sings* to *sing.*

  G Change *violinist* to *violinists.*

  H Change *is* to *are.*

  J Change *practicing* to *practice.*

3. Which revision to sentences 9 and 10 links the two ideas most effectively?

  A Unless Gerald takes a breath, he continues with his speech.

  B After Gerald takes a breath, he continues with his speech.

  C Gerald takes a breath, nor he continues with his speech.

  D Gerald takes a breath whether he continues with his speech.

4. What change should the writer make to improve the clarity of sentence 13?

  F Change *easily* to *easy.*

  G Delete the comma after *us.*

  H Change *although* to *unless.*

  J Add a comma after *although.*

Reflect on the Unit

NOTEBOOK

INTERACTIVITY

Reflect On the Unit Goals

Review your Unit Goals chart from the beginning of the unit. Then, complete the activity and answer the question.

1. In the Unit Goals chart, rate how well you meet each goal now.

2. In which goals were you most and least successful?

Reflect On the Texts

VOTE! In the chart below, write the character, scene, or idea from the selections in this unit that you find most memorable. Explain your reasons, and discuss your choice.

Title	Most Memorable
The Phantom Tollbooth, Act I	
The Phantom Tollbooth, Act II	
from The Misadventures of Don Quixote	
Jabberwocky	
The Mock Turtle's Song	
The Importance of Imagination	
Your Independent Reading Selection:	

Reflect On the Essential Question

Unit Memory Book Create a class memory book that shows what you learned from this unit about the Essential Question:
What is the purpose of imagination?

- You may create a hard copy book or a digital one. Each member of the class should make one page.

- Include passages from the texts you read, the writing tasks you completed, and the research you conducted. Also, include photos, drawings, or other images.

TIP: Make sure your page represents your individual thoughts about imagination. Include passages from the texts you read and researched, but also include your own reflections.

🌐 TEKS

10.D.i. Edit drafts using standard English conventions, including complete complex sentences with subject-verb agreement and avoidance of splices, run-ons, and fragments; **10.D.ix.** Edit drafts using standard English conventions, including correct spelling, including commonly confused terms such as *its/it's, affect/effect, there/their/they're,* and *to/two/too.*

Exploration

PEARSON
realıze™

Go ONLINE for
all lessons

 AUDIO

 VIDEO

 NOTEBOOK

 ANNOTATE

 INTERACTIVITY

 DOWNLOAD

 RESEARCH

WATCH THE VIDEO

Hang Son Doong

DISCUSS IT Why might explorers want to discover unknown places?

Write your response before sharing your ideas.

UNIT 5

Essential Question

What drives people to explore?

MENTOR TEXT:
INFORMATIONAL
TEXT–RESEARCH
**What on Earth Is
Left to Explore?**

 **WHOLE-CLASS
LEARNING**

MEMOIR

from **A Long Way
Home**
Saroo Brierley

MEDIA: VIDEO

**BBC Science Club: All
About Exploration**
narrated by Dara Ó Briain

PERFORMANCE TASK

WRITING PROCESS
Write a Formal Research Paper

 **PEER-GROUP
LEARNING**

BIOGRAPHY

**Ada and the Thinking
Machines**
Kathleen Krull

ADVENTURE STORY

**The King of Mazy
May**
Jack London

COMPARE ACROSS GENRES

HISTORICAL FICTION

from **Sacajawea**
Joseph Bruchac

MEDIA: GRAPHIC "NOVEL" HISTORY

from **Lewis & Clark**
Nick Bertozzi

PERFORMANCE TASK

SPEAKING AND LISTENING
Deliver a Research Presentation

 **INDEPENDENT
LEARNING**

BLOG POST

To the Top of Everest
Samantha Larson

NONFICTION NARRATIVE

from **Shipwreck at the
Bottom of the World**
Jennifer Armstrong

MAGAZINE ARTICLE

**Barrington Irving,
Pilot and Educator**
National Geographic

INFORMATIONAL ARTICLE

**The Legacy of Arctic
Explorer Matthew
Henson**
James Mills

MEDIA: GRAPHIC NOVEL

**The Hero Twins
Against the Lords of
Death: A Mayan Myth**
by Dan Jolley, illustrated by
David Witt

SHARE INDEPENDENT LEARNING

Share • Learn • Reflect

PERFORMANCE-BASED ASSESSMENT

Research-Based Essay

You will write a research-based essay that explores the Essential Question for the unit.

UNIT REFLECTION

Goals • Texts •
Essential Question

Unit Goals

 VIDEO

Throughout this unit, you will deepen your understanding of exploration by reading, writing, speaking, listening, and presenting. These goals will help you succeed on the Unit Performance-Based Assessment.

INTERACTIVITY

SET GOALS Rate how well you meet these goals right now. You will revisit your ratings later when you reflect on your growth during this unit.

SCALE	1	2	3	4	5
	NOT AT ALL WELL	NOT VERY WELL	SOMEWHAT WELL	VERY WELL	EXTREMELY WELL

ESSENTIAL QUESTION	Unit Introduction	Unit Reflection
I can read selections that express different points of view about exploration, and develop my own perspective.	1 2 3 4 5	1 2 3 4 5

READING	Unit Introduction	Unit Reflection
I can understand and use academic vocabulary words related to research.	1 2 3 4 5	1 2 3 4 5
I can recognize elements of different genres, especially informational texts, adventure stories, and historical fiction.	1 2 3 4 5	1 2 3 4 5
I can read a selection of my choice independently and make meaningful connections to other texts.	1 2 3 4 5	1 2 3 4 5

WRITING	Unit Introduction	Unit Reflection
I can write a focused, well-organized research report.	1 2 3 4 5	1 2 3 4 5
I can complete Timed Writing tasks with confidence.	1 2 3 4 5	1 2 3 4 5

SPEAKING AND LISTENING	Unit Introduction	Unit Reflection
I can prepare and deliver a research presentation.	1 2 3 4 5	1 2 3 4 5

⊕ TEKS
2.C. Determine the meaning and usage of grade-level academic English words derived from Latin roots such as *mis/mit, bene, man, vac, scrib/script*, and *jur/jus*

Academic Vocabulary: Informational Text

Many English words have roots, or key parts, that come from ancient languages, such as Latin and Greek. Learn these roots and use the words as you respond to questions and activities in this unit.

 **INTERACTIVITY**

PRACTICE Academic terms are used routinely in classrooms. Build your knowledge of these words by completing the chart.

1. Review each word, its root, and the mentor sentences.

2. With a partner, read the words and mentor sentences aloud. Then, **determine** the meaning and usage of each word. Use a dictionary, if needed.

3. List at least two related words for each word.

WORD	MENTOR SENTENCES	PREDICT MEANING	RELATED WORDS
critical LATIN ROOT: **-crit-** "judge"	1. I don't think she liked the story because she had many *critical* comments. 2. It is *critical* to follow the steps exactly, otherwise the experiment might fail.		critic; critically
manual LATIN ROOT: **-man-** "hand"	1. Digging and planting the garden is a type of *manual* labor that I love. 2. If you need to know how to use the new computer, consult the *manual*.		
omit LATIN ROOT: **-mit- / -mis-** "go"; "send"	1. If a detail does not support your thesis, *omit* it from your paper. 2. I didn't mean to *omit* that step, but I forgot to do it.		
valid LATIN ROOT: **-val-** "strong"	1. You need a *valid* password to log in to the network. 2. If you want to convince me, you had better use *valid* reasons.		
coherent LATIN ROOT: **-her- / -hes-** "cling"; "stick"	1. Present your information in a clear, *coherent* order so it is easy to understand. 2. Sam's speech was *coherent* because he used clear logic and evidence.		

MENTOR TEXT | INFORMATIONAL TEXT—RESEARCH

This selection is a **research-based essay**, a type of writing in which ideas are supported with researched information. This is the type of writing you will develop in the Performance-Based Assessment at the end of the unit.

READII As you read, notice how the author supports ideas with facts and specific details.

What on Earth Is Left to Explore?

 AUDIO

 ANNOTATE

1   At the beginning of the 1800s, the United States was a young country. Most people lived in small towns clustered on the Atlantic coast. To the west lay an entire continent, full of mystery and promise.

2   Government leaders believed that exploration of the continent was important. Exploration would bring knowledge and resources. Urged on by President Thomas Jefferson, Congress funded a small expedition to explore the lands west of the Mississippi River. The Lewis and Clark expedition became one of the most famous exploratory journeys in history.

3   In the modern world, the idea of exploration has changed. Cars, trains, and airplanes have made the world seem much smaller. People seem to be everywhere. Thousands have climbed Mount Everest, the world's highest mountain. There are even people living in Antarctica, the world's coldest continent. In addition, the Internet allows people to visit faraway places through the screens of their computers. Given these changes, some people may ask whether exploration matters anymore. Is there anything left to explore? The answer is simple: Exploration matters as much today as it ever has.

4   Let's start with ocean exploration. It is true that much of Earth has been visited and charted. However, we should remember that people actually live on less than twenty percent of the planet. We inhabit the land, but Earth is mostly ocean. Vast stretches of the oceans are hidden under miles of water. The little we do know

about these secret places is fascinating. For example, almost a quarter of Earth is made up of a single mountain range. It just happens to be under the sea! Consider the other wonders we might find as we explore.

5   Ocean exploration might help us solve tough problems. For example, it might lead to new food sources for the planet's growing population. It may also help us find ways to slow damage to the environment. These types of problems threaten all of us, and we need solutions. They make the need for ocean exploration more important than ever.

6   Space exploration is another area of great importance. Human beings have always been interested in the skies. We are curious about the stars and planets and the possibility that they hold other intelligent life. Satisfying that curiosity is one good reason to explore space. Another reason is that by exploring beyond Earth, we will answer essential questions about the history of our solar system and of the universe itself. This will help us understand our own planet and ourselves better. Human exploration of space also has practical benefits. According to NASA (National Aeronautics and Space Administration), space exploration pushes us to "expand technology, create new industries, and help to foster a peaceful connection with other nations."

7   Lewis and Clark did not know what they would find as they set out on their journey. They only knew that they would have an adventure. In the end, their efforts added to the country's territory and to people's knowledge and understanding. The results of exploration may not always be that impressive, but that may not be the point. The need to explore and extend the boundaries of knowledge remains vital and should continue. ❧

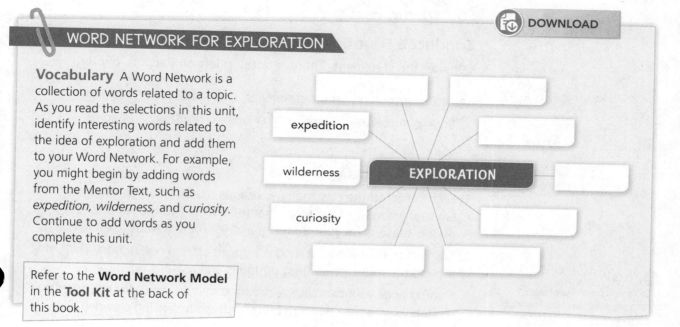

DOWNLOAD

WORD NETWORK FOR EXPLORATION

Vocabulary A Word Network is a collection of words related to a topic. As you read the selections in this unit, identify interesting words related to the idea of exploration and add them to your Word Network. For example, you might begin by adding words from the Mentor Text, such as *expedition, wilderness,* and *curiosity.* Continue to add words as you complete this unit.

expedition

wilderness

curiosity

EXPLORATION

Refer to the **Word Network Model** in the **Tool Kit** at the back of this book.

Summary

A **summary** is a brief, complete overview of a text that maintains the meaning and logical order of ideas of the original. It should not include your personal opinions.

NOTEBOOK

WRITE IT Write a summary of "What on Earth Is Left to Explore?"

_____
_____
_____
_____
_____
_____
_____
_____
_____
_____
_____
_____
_____
_____
_____

Launch Activity

Conduct a Four-Corner Debate

Consider this statement: There is nothing left on Earth to explore.

Record your position on the statement, and explain your thinking.

◯ Strongly Agree   ◯ Agree   ◯ Disagree   ◯ Strongly Disagree

_____
_____

1. Each corner of the classroom represents one position on the question. Go to the corner of the room that represents your position. Briefly discuss reasons for your thinking, and list the three strongest ones.

2. Start off the debate by stating your position and one reason. Then, go around the room, presenting positions and reasons.

3. If you change your mind as the debate continues, move to the corner that represents your new position. Explain why your thinking changed.

TEKS
6.D. Paraphrase and summarize texts in ways that maintain meaning and logical order.

QuickWrite

Consider class discussions, the video, and the Mentor Text as you think about the Essential Question.

Essential Question

What drives people to explore?

At the end of the unit, you will respond to the Essential Question again and see how your perspective has changed.

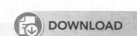 NOTEBOOK

WRITE IT Record your first thoughts here.

 DOWNLOAD

EQ Notes — What drives people to explore?

As you read the selections in this unit, use a chart like the one shown to record your ideas and list details from the texts that support them. Taking notes as you go will help you clarify your thinking, gather relevant information, and be ready to respond to the Essential Question.

TITLE	MY IDEAS / OBSERVATIONS	TEXT EVIDENCE / INFORMATION

Refer to the **EQ Notes Model** in the **Tool Kit** at the back of this book.

Essential Question

What drives people to explore?

Exploration may be physical, involving travel to unknown places. It may be mental, involving new ways of looking at a topic. In many cases, it requires both action and imagination. You will work with your whole class to learn more about explorers and exploration.

 VIDEO

 INTERACTIVITY

Whole-Class Learning Strategies

Throughout your life, in school, in your community, and in your career, you will continue to learn and work in large-group environments. Review these strategies and the actions you can take to practice them as you work with your whole class. Use a dictionary to check the meaning of any basic or academic vocabulary words you are unsure of. Add ideas of your own for each category. Get ready to use these strategies during Whole-Class Learning.

STRATEGY	MY ACTION PLAN
Listen actively • Put away personal items to avoid becoming distracted. • Try to hear the speaker's full message before planning your own response.	
Demonstrate respect • Show up on time and make sure you are prepared for class. • Avoid side conversations while in class.	
Describe personal connections • Recognize that literature explores human experience—the details may differ from your own life, but the emotions it expresses are universal. • Actively look for ways in which your personal experiences help you find meaning in a text. • Consider how your own experiences help you understand characters' actions and reactions.	

CONTENTS

PERFORMANCE TASK: WRITING PROCESS

Write a Formal Research Paper
The Whole-Class readings offer new ideas and perspectives on the topic of exploration. After reading the selection and watching the video, you will write a research paper in which you answer a question about an explorer from history or someone who is exploring new frontiers today.

from A LONG WAY HOME

The selection you are about to read is a memoir.

Reading Memoirs

A **memoir** is a type of autobiography. It is a work of narrative nonfiction in which a writer tells a true story about a period in his or her life.

MEMOIR

Author's Purpose
- to tell about important aspects of an author's life

Characteristics
- expresses the author's perspective on his or her experiences; often, this is the controlling idea, insight, or message.
- includes characters who are real people
- usually includes fiction-like elements, such as a setting, conflict, and plot
- contains descriptions, including sensory details

Structure
- usually presents events in chronological, or time, order
- often focuses on a single experience or small group of events, rather than a whole lifetime

Take a Minute!

 NOTEBOOK

LIST IT Work with a partner to make a list of three people whose memoirs you would like to read. Consider people in your own lives, as well as celebrities, historical figures, and other people in the news. Discuss why you chose each person.

⭐ TEKS
8.D.i. Analyze characteristics and structural elements of informational text, including the controlling idea or thesis with supporting evidence.

Genre / Text Elements

Controlling Idea and Evidence The **controlling idea** of an informational text is the message the author conveys. In some nonfiction, such as an explanatory essay or an argument, the author states the controlling idea directly and uses **evidence** to support it. In a memoir, the author may suggest but not state the controlling idea. The reader looks for evidence in the details and makes connections to infer the controlling idea.

Text Evidence in a Memoir
Ask questions to analyze the details in a memoir and determine the controlling idea.

Title	How does the title connect to the story the memoir tells?
Events	What events has the author chosen to write about? Why are they significant?
Descriptions	How does the author describe people, events, and places? How do these descriptions reveal the author's feelings?
Lessons Learned	What does the author learn? How does the author change?
Emotional Response	Which passages cause powerful emotional responses in you, the reader, signaling their importance?

 **INTERACTIVITY**

PRACTICE Read the title and passage from a memoir. Then, answer the questions.

My Unlikely Best Friend

After my stepfather lost his job, we moved to a dusty little town that the world seemed to have forgotten. I hated my new school—especially at lunchtime when I faced the cafeteria alone. Every day, I saw the same mangy stray cat on my way home. I ignored the ugly thing at first, thinking it probably had fleas. But one rainy day I saw Mangy, as I'd nicknamed him, huddling under a bush. I knelt down and called to him. He came out slowly, then cautiously rubbed his face against my knees, marking me as his. "If you're mine, I guess I'm yours, too," I said. And I let him follow me home.

1. How does the author change during the course of this passage? Explain.

2. Write a statement that expresses the controlling idea of the passage. Which evidence from the passage supports your thinking?

About the Author

Saroo Brierley (b. 1981) was born in a tiny village in India. At around the age of 5, he accidentally boarded a train alone and was whisked away from his family, hopelessly lost. He ended up at an orphanage in the West Bengal capital of Kolkata, formerly known as Calcutta. Brierley was eventually adopted by an Australian family and was raised in Tasmania. After twenty-five years of separation, Brierley finally succeeded in his quest to find his Indian family.

from A Long Way Home

Concept Vocabulary

You will encounter the following words as you read the memoir. Before reading, note how familiar you are with each word. Then, rank the words in order from most familiar (1) to least familiar (6).

INTERACTIVITY

WORD	YOUR RANKING
deliberate	
quest	
thorough	
obsessive	
intensity	
relentlessly	

Comprehension Strategy

 ANNOTATE

Make Predictions

Predictions are guesses you make about the types of ideas and information a writer will share in a text. The way in which a text, such as a memoir, is structured offers meaningful clues.

- **Time Order:** Most memoirs follow time order. You can predict that the beginning will focus on an early period of the writer's life and progress over a span of time.

- **Connections:** A memoir explores themes in the author's life. You can predict that related ideas will be repeated.

- **Sections:** Memoirs often devote sections to particular aspects of the author's life. You can scan a text and predict the focus of each section.

PRACTICE As you read, consider the text structures of memoir to make specific predictions about the content. Confirm or correct your predictions as you read on.

 TEKS
5.C. Make, correct, or confirm predictions using text features, characteristics of genre, and structures.

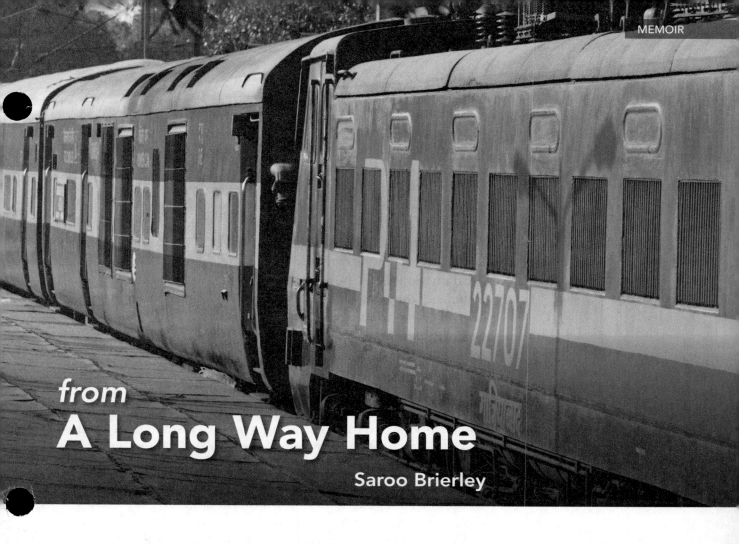

from
A Long Way Home

Saroo Brierley

BACKGROUND

In his memoir *A Long Way Home*, Saroo Brierley shares his memories of searching for his hometown and his birth family. He describes the detailed method he used to locate them after decades of separation. At this point in the memoir, Brierley has recently graduated from college and moved in with his friend Byron.

 AUDIO

 ANNOTATE

1   Alas, the new search didn't start out as an obsession.

2   If Byron wasn't home, I might spend a couple of hours musing over the various "B" towns[1] again. Or I might make a casual sweep down the east coast, to see what was there. I even checked out a Birampur in Uttar Pradesh, near Delhi, in the central north of India, but that was a ridiculously long way from Kolkata, and I couldn't have traveled that far in twelve or so hours. It turned out it doesn't even have a train station.

3   These occasional forays showed the folly of searching by town, particularly when I wasn't sure about the names. If I was going to do this, I needed to be strategic and methodical about it.

BUILD YOUR VOCABULARY

Concept and other higher-level words aren't the only ones that matter. As you read, actively build your understanding of sight and basic words. Listen to the audio and note words you've mastered and those you are still acquiring.

---

1. **"B" Towns** Brierley remembers that the name of the train station near his hometown begins with a "B." This is the station at which he boarded a train and became lost.

4   I went over what I knew. I came from a place where Muslims and Hindus lived in close proximity and where Hindi was spoken. Those things were true of most of India. I recalled all those warm nights outside, under the stars, which at least suggested it wouldn't be in the colder regions of the far north. I hadn't lived by the sea, although I couldn't rule out that I'd lived near it. And I hadn't lived in the mountains. My hometown had a railway station—India was riddled with train lines, but they didn't run through every single village and town.

5   Then there was the opinion of the Indians at college that I looked like someone from the east, perhaps around West Bengal. I had my doubts: in the eastern part of the country, the region took in some of the Himalayas,[2] which wasn't right, and part of the Ganges Delta, which looked much too lush and fertile to be my home. But as these were people who had firsthand experience of India, it seemed silly to dismiss their hunch.

6   I also thought I could remember enough landmark features to recognize my hometown if I came across it, or to at least narrow the field. I clearly recalled the bridge over the river where we played as kids and the nearby dam wall that restricted the river's flow below it. I knew how to get from the train station to our house, and I knew the layout of the station.

7   The other station I thought I remembered quite well was the "B" one, where I'd boarded the train. Although I'd been there quite a few times with my brothers, they'd never let me leave it, so I knew nothing of the town outside the station—all I'd ever seen beyond the exit was a sort of small ring road for horse carts and cars, and a road beyond it that led into the town. But still, there were a couple of distinguishing features. I remembered the station building and that it only had a couple of tracks, over the other side of which was a big water tank on a tower. There was also a pedestrian overpass across the tracks. And just before the train pulled into town from the direction of my home, it crossed a small gorge.

8   So I had some vague thoughts on likely regions, and some ways of identifying "Ginestlay"[3] and the "B" place if I found them. Now I needed a better search method. I realized that the names of places had been a distraction, or were at least not the right place to start. Instead, I thought about the end of the journey. I knew that train lines linked the "B" place with Kolkata. Logic dictated, then, that if I followed all the train lines out of Kolkata, I would eventually find my starting point. And from there, my hometown was itself up the line, not far away. I might even come upon my

---

2. **Himalayas** (hihm uh LAY uhz) tallest mountain range in the world.
3. **"Ginestlay"** Brierley remembered this as the name of his hometown, but no one he asked had heard of it and he could not find it on a map.

home first, depending on how the lines linked up. This was an intimidating prospect—there were many, many train lines from the national hub of Kolkata's Howrah Station, and my train might have zigzagged across any of the lines of the spider's web. It was unlikely to be a simple, straight route.

9   Still, even with the possibility of some winding, irregular paths out of Howrah, there was also a limit to how far I could have been transported in the time frame. I'd spent, I thought, a long time on the train—somewhere between twelve and fifteen hours. If I made some calculations, I could narrow the search field, ruling out places too far away.

10   Why hadn't I thought of the search with this clarity before? Maybe I had been too overwhelmed by the scale of the problem to think straight, too consumed by what I didn't know to focus on what I did. But as it dawned on me that I could turn this into a painstaking, **deliberate** task that simply required dedication, something clicked inside. If all it took were time and patience to find home, with the aid of Google Earth's[4] god's-eye view, then I would do it. Seeing it almost as much an intellectual challenge as an emotional **quest**, I threw myself into solving it.

11   First, I worked on the search zone. How fast could India's diesel trains travel, and would that have changed much since the eighties? I thought my Indian friends from college might be able to help, especially Amreen, whose father would likely have a more educated guess, so I got in touch with them. The general consensus was around seventy or eighty kilometers an hour. That seemed like a good start. Figuring I had been trapped on the train for around twelve to fifteen hours, overnight, I calculated how many kilometers I might have traveled in that time, which I put at around a thousand, or approximately 620 miles.

12   So the place I was looking for was a thousand kilometers along a train line out of Howrah Station. On Google Earth you can draw lines on the map at precise distances, so I made a circular boundary line of a thousand kilometers around Kolkata and saved it for my searches. That meant that as well as West Bengal, my search field included the states of Jharkhand, Chhattisgarh, and nearly half of the central state of Madhya Pradesh to the west, Orissa to the south, Bihar and a third of Uttar Pradesh to the north, and most of the northeastern spur of India, which encircles Bangladesh. (I knew I wasn't from Bangladesh, as I'd have spoken Bengali, not Hindi. This was confirmed when I discovered

---
4. **Google Earth** computer program that displays satellite images of the world.

CLOSE READ

ANNOTATE: In paragraph 8, mark details that describe the challenges Brierley faces in finding his hometown.

QUESTION: Why does Brierley provide so much detail about his thought process?

CONCLUDE: What can you conclude about Brierley and his mission from these details?

deliberate (dih LIHB uhr iht) *adj.* carefully thought over in advance; planned

quest (kwehst) *n.* long search undertaken in order to find or realize something

that a rail connection between the two countries had only been established a few years ago.)

13   It was a staggering amount of territory, covering some 962,300 square kilometers, over a quarter of India's huge landmass. Within its bounds lived 345 million people. I tried to keep my emotions out of the exercise, but I couldn't help but wonder: Is it possible to find my four family members among these 345 million? Even though my calculations were reliant on guesswork and were therefore very rough, and even though that still presented me with a huge field within which to search, it felt like I was narrowing things down. Rather than randomly throwing the haystack around to find the needle,[5] I could concentrate on picking through a manageable portion and set it aside if it proved empty.

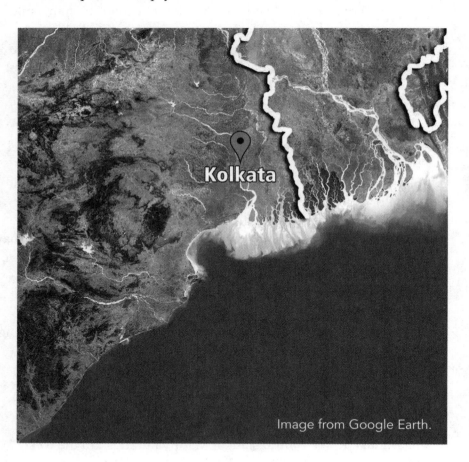

Image from Google Earth.

14   The train lines within the search zone wouldn't all simply stretch out to the edge in a straight radius, of course—there would be a lot of twists, turns, and junctions, as they wound around and traveled much more than a thousand kilometers before they

_____
5. **haystack . . . needle** the saying "finding a needle in a haystack" means looking for something almost impossible to find.

reached the boundary edge. So I planned to work outward from Kolkata, the only point of the journey I was certain about.

15   The first time I zoomed in on Howrah Station, looking at the rows of ridged gray platform roofs and all the tracks spilling out of it like the fraying end of a rope, I was amazed and shocked that I'd once trod barefoot along these walkways. I had to open my eyes wide to make sure what I was looking at was real. I was about to embark on a high-tech version of what I'd done in my first week there, twenty years ago, randomly taking trains out to see if they went back home.

16   I took a deep breath, chose a train line, and started scrolling along it.

17   Immediately, it became clear that progress would be slow. Even with broadband, my laptop had to render the image, which took time. It started a little pixelated, then resolved into an aerial photograph. I was looking for landmarks I recognized and paid particular attention to the stations, as they were the places I remembered most vividly.

18   When I first zoomed out to see how far I'd gone along the track, I was amazed at how little progress the hours of scrolling and studying had brought me. But rather than being frustrated and impatient, I found I had enormous confidence that I would find what I was looking for as long as I was **thorough**. That gave me a great sense of calm as I resumed my search. In fact, it quickly became compelling, and I returned to it several nights a week. Before I turned in each night, I'd mark how far I'd gone on a track and save the search, then resume from that point at the next opportunity.

19   I would come across goods yards, overpasses and underpasses, bridges over rivers and junctions. Sometimes I skipped along a bit but then nervously went back to repeat a section, reminding myself that if I wasn't methodical, I could never be sure I'd looked everywhere. I didn't jump ahead to look for stations in case I missed a small one—I followed the tracks so I could check out anything that came along. And if I found myself reaching the edge of the boundary I'd devised, I'd go back along the train line to a previous junction and then head off in another direction.

20   I remember one night early on, following a line north, I came to a river crossing not far outside a town. I caught my breath as I zoomed in closer. The dam wall was decaying, but maybe the area had since been reconstructed? I quickly dragged the cursor to roll the image along. Did the countryside look right? It was quite green, but there were a lot of farms on the outskirts of my town. I watched as the town unpixelated before my eyes. It was quite small. Too small, surely. But with a child's perspective . . .

CLOSE READ

ANNOTATE: A **simile** compares two unlike things using the word *like* or *as*. Mark the simile in paragraph 15.

QUESTION: Why might the author have used a simile to describe what he was viewing on his computer screen?

CONCLUDE: How does the simile help the reader to better understand the challenges the author is facing?

thorough (THUR oh) *adj.* including everything possible; careful and complete

And there was a high pedestrian overpass across the tracks near the station! But what were the large blank areas dotted around the town? Three lakes, four or five even, within the tiny village's bounds—and it was suddenly obvious that this wasn't the place. You didn't clear whole neighborhoods to put in lakes. And of course, many, many stations were likely to have overpasses, and many towns would be situated near life-giving rivers, which the tracks would have to cross. How many times would I wonder if all the landmarks aligned, only to be left with tired, sore eyes and the realization that I was mistaken again?

21   Weeks and then months passed with my spending hours at a time every couple of nights on the laptop. Byron made sure I spent other nights out in the real world so I didn't become an Internet recluse. I covered the countryside of West Bengal and Jharkhand in these early stages without finding anything familiar, but at least it meant that much of the immediate vicinity of Kolkata could be ruled out. Despite the hunch of my Indian friends, I'd come from farther away.

22   Several months later, I was lucky enough to meet someone with whom I started a new relationship, which made the search less of a priority for a while. Lisa and I met in 2010 through a friend of Byron's and mine. We became friends on Facebook, and then I asked her for her phone number. We hit it off immediately; Lisa's background is in business management and she is smart, pretty, and can hold a great conversation. However, we had an unsettled start together, with a couple of breakups and reunions, which meant there was a similar inconsistency in the periods I spent looking on the Internet, before we finally settled into the lasting relationship we have today.

23   I didn't know how a girlfriend would take to the time-consuming quest of her partner staring at maps on a laptop. But Lisa understood the personal and growing importance of the search, and was patient and supportive. She was as amazed as anyone about my past, and wanted me to find the answers I was looking for. We moved into a small flat[6] together in 2010. I thought of the nights I spent there on the laptop as being a pastime, like playing computer games. But Lisa says that even then, with our relationship in full swing, I was **obsessive**. Looking back, I can see that this was true.

24   After all the years of my story being in my thoughts and dreams, I felt I was closing in on the reality. I decided this time I wasn't going to listen to anybody who said, "It might be time to move on," or "It's just not possible to find your hometown in

---

6. **flat** *n.* apartment.

obsessive (uhb SEHS ihv) *adj.* tending to think or worry so much about something that you cannot think about anything else

all of India like this." Lisa never said those things, and with her support, I became even more determined to succeed.

25   I didn't tell many people what I was doing anyway. And I decided not to tell my parents. I was worried they might misunderstand my intentions. I didn't want them to think that the **intensity** of my search revealed an unhappiness with the life they'd given me or the way they'd raised me. I also didn't want them to think that I was wasting time. So even as it took up more and more of my life, I kept it mostly to myself. I finished work with Dad at five p.m., and by five-thirty I would be back at the laptop, slowly advancing along train tracks and studying the towns they led to. This went on for months—it had been over a year since I started. But I reasoned that even if it took years . . . or decades . . . it was possible to eventually sift completely through a haystack. The needle would have to show up if I persisted.

26   Slowly, over several more months, I eliminated whole areas of India. I traced all the connections within the northeastern states without finding anything familiar, and I was confident that I could rule out Orissa, too. Determined to be thorough, no matter how long it took, I started following lines farther out than my original thousand-kilometer zone. South beyond Orissa, I eliminated Andhra Pradesh, five hundred kilometers farther down the east coast. Jharkhand and Bihar didn't offer up anything promising, either, and as I wound up in Uttar Pradesh, I thought I'd keep going to cover most of the state. In fact, the states eventually replaced my zone boundary as a way of marking my progress. Ruling out areas state by state provided a series of goals that spurred me on.

27   Unless I had something pressing to do for work, or some other unbreakable commitment, I was on the laptop seven nights a week. I went out with Lisa sometimes, of course, but the moment we got home I was back on the computer. Sometimes I caught her looking at me strangely, as though she thought I might have gone a bit crazy. She'd say, "You're at it again!" but I would reply, "I have to . . . I'm really sorry!" I think Lisa knew she simply had to let me exhaust myself of the interest. I became distant during that time, and although Lisa would have been within her rights to feel alone in this still-new relationship, we worked through it. Perhaps to some extent sharing something so fundamental to me strengthened our connection—and that came through when we sometimes talked about what it all meant. It wasn't always easy for me to articulate,[7] especially as I was trying to keep a lid on my expectations, trying to convince myself it was a fascinating exercise, not a deeply meaningful personal quest. Talking to Lisa

---
7. **articulate** (ahr TIHK yuh layt) *v.* express clearly using words.

intensity (ihn TEHN suh tee) *n.* great focus or concentration; strong commitment

CLOSE READ

ANNOTATE: In paragraph 27, mark details that show how often Brierley is searching for his hometown at this point.

QUESTION: What do these details reveal about how his search is progressing?

CONCLUDE: How do these details help the reader to better understand Brierley's state of mind?

sometimes revealed the underlying importance of the search to me: that I was looking for my home to provide closure and to understand my past and perhaps myself better as a result, in the hope that I might somehow reconnect with my Indian family so they would know what had happened to me. Lisa understood all this and didn't resent it, even if there were times when she wanted to ban me from staring at the screen for my own sake. Once in a while she would simply come over and shut my laptop and place it on the floor because I was becoming so obsessive about my search.

28   At times Lisa admitted her own greatest fear: that I would find what I thought I was looking for, go back to India, and somehow be wrong or fail to find my family there. Would I return to Hobart[8] and simply start again, obsessively searching online? I couldn't answer her questions any more than I could allay her fears. I couldn't allow myself to think about failure.

29   If anything, I became more intense about my search as 2010 drew to a close, and the speed of our newly acquired broadband connection made it quicker to refresh the images and zoom in and out. But I still had to take it slowly—if I rushed, I'd leave myself open to wondering later if I'd missed anything and then going back in an endless cycle. And I had to try not to bend my memories to fit what I was looking at.

30   By early 2011, I was concentrating more on areas within India's center, in Chhattisgarh and Madhya Pradesh. I spent months poring over them, relentlessly, methodically.

31   Of course, there were times when I doubted the wisdom, and even the sanity, of what I was doing. Night after night, with the day's last reserves of energy and willpower, I sat staring at railway lines, searching for places my five-year-old mind might recognize. It was a repetitive, forensic[9] exercise, and sometimes it started to feel claustrophobic, as if I were trapped and looking out at the world through a small window, unable to break free of my course in a mind-twisting echo of my childhood ordeal.

32   And then one night in March around one in the morning, in just such a mood, spent with frustration, I took a wild dive into the haystack, and it changed everything.

33   As always, on March 31, 2011, I had come home from work, grabbed my laptop, opened Google Earth, and settled in for a session on the sofa, stopping only briefly for dinner when Lisa got home. I was examining the central west at this time, so I picked up there, "traveling" a train line near my former search zone

relentlessly (rih LEHNT lihs lee) *adv.* without stopping; with determination

---

8. **Hobart** capital of Tasmania, an island state of Australia, where Brierley lives.
9. **forensic** (fuh REHN sihk) *adj.* careful and detailed, similar to the scientific methods used to solve a crime.

boundary. Even with quicker broadband, it was still slow going. I continued for what seemed like ages, looking at a few stations, but as usual, when I zoomed out, I found I'd only covered a tiny area. I thought that the countryside looked a bit green for my dusty old town, but I knew by now that India's landscape changed appearance regularly as you moved across it.

34   After a few hours, I had followed a line to a junction. I took a break, checking Facebook for a while before rubbing my eyes, stretching my back, and returning to my task.

35   Before zooming in, I idly flicked the map along to get a quick picture of where the westerly line out of the junction headed, and watched hills, forests, and river sweep by, a seemingly endless terrain of reasonably similar features. I was distracted by a large river that fed into what looked like a massive, deep blue lake called Nal Damayanti Sagar, which was surrounded by some lush country and had mountains to its north. For a while, I enjoyed this little exploration, indulgently unrelated to my search, like a recreational hike of grand proportions. It was getting late, after all, and I'd turn in soon.

36   There didn't seem to be any train lines in this part of the country, which might have been why it was relaxing to look at. But once I'd noticed that, I found myself almost subconsciously looking for one. There were villages and towns dotted around here and there, and I wondered how the people traveled without rail—perhaps they didn't move around much? And farther west, still no tracks! Then as the countryside flattened out into farmland, I finally came across a little blue symbol denoting a train station. I was so attuned to looking for them, I was somehow relieved to find this one, and I checked out the tiny wayside station, just a few buildings to the side of a reasonably major train line with several tracks. Out of habit, I started tracing the route as it wound southwest. I quickly came across another station, a bit bigger, again with a platform on only one side of the tracks, but some areas of the township on either side. That explained the overpass, and was that . . . was that a water tower just nearby?

37   Holding my breath, I zoomed in for a closer look. Sure enough, it was a municipal water tank just across from the platform, and not far from a large pedestrian overpass spanning the railway line. I scrolled over to the town side and saw something incredible—a horseshoe-shaped road around a square immediately outside the station. Could it be—perhaps it was the ring road I used to be able to see from the platform! Was it possible? I closed my

> Could it be—perhaps it was the ring road I used to be able to see from the platform! Was it possible?

ANNOTATE: In paragraph 37, mark the words the author emphasizes with italics.

QUESTION: Why does the author choose to emphasize these words?

CONCLUDE: How does this emphasis help the reader understand Brierley's thoughts and emotions?

eyes and went back twenty four years in time to when I would walk to the station's exit and see the ring road with an island in the middle. I thought to myself, *This is unique; I haven't seen this before.* I zoomed out, discovering that the train line skimmed the northwestern edge of a really large town. I clicked on the blue train station symbol to reveal its name . . . Burhanpur. My heart nearly stopped. *Burhanpur!*

38   I didn't recognize the town itself, but then I'd never been in it—I'd never left the platform. I zoomed back in and re-examined the ring road, the water tower, the overpass, and they were all positioned where I remembered them. That meant that not far away, just up the line, I should find my hometown, "Ginestlay."

39   Almost afraid to do so, I dragged the cursor to pull the image north along the train line. When I saw that the track crossed a gorge just on the edge of the built-up area, I was flooded with adrenaline—I remembered in a flash that the train I took with my brothers traveled on a small bridge over a gorge like that before pulling into the station. I pushed on more urgently, east then northeast, in just moments zooming over seventy kilometers

of green farms, forested hills, and small rivers. Then I passed across some dry, flat land, broken up by a patchwork of irrigated farmland and the occasional small village, before I hit a bridge over a substantial river. Ahead I was able to see the town's outskirts. The river's flow was significantly reduced below the bridge by dam walls on either side. If this was the right place, this was the river I used to play in, and there should be a bigger concrete dam wall to my right a little farther from the bridge . . .

40   There it was!

41   I sat staring at the screen for what seemed like an eternity. What I was looking at matched the picture in my head exactly. I couldn't think straight; I was frozen with excitement, terrified to go on.

42   Finally, after a couple of minutes, I forced myself to take the next step, slowly, nervously. I tried to calm myself so I didn't jump to any rash conclusions. If I really was looking at "Ginestlay" for the first time in twenty-four years, then I should be able to follow the path I remembered from the river back to the train station, only a short way up ahead. I began to drag the cursor again, slowly rolling the map to trace the course of the path, which wound gently alongside a tributary stream, left and right, around a field, under a street overpass and then . . . the station. I clicked on the blue symbol and the name came up on the screen: Khandwa Railway Station.

43   The name meant nothing to me.

44   My stomach knotted. How could this be?

45   Things had looked so right all the way from Burhanpur, which had to be the "B" town I had tried to remember. But if the bridge and the river were correct, where was "Ginestlay"? I tried not to despair. I had spent a lot of time in and around our local train station as a boy, so I checked off what I remembered—the three platforms, the covered pedestrian overpass that connected them, an underpass road beneath the tracks at the northern end. But it wasn't so much the existence of these reasonably common features but their position in relation to each other that would identify the specific place that I was looking for. It all checked out. I also remembered a huge fountain in a park near the underpass, and I went looking. Sure enough, it was a little indistinct, but I thought I detected its familiar circular shape in a central clearing, surrounded by trees.

46   From here, I knew the route to where my home should be. This was why I'd gone over and over it in my head since I was a little boy: so that I would never forget it.

47   Now, as a man, I followed the road up from the fountain and along the route of the underpass, and then the streets and alleys I had walked as a child—the way I used to imagine myself walking

CLOSE READ

ANNOTATE: In paragraph 41, mark the words that show Brierley's reaction to the image on his screen.

QUESTION: Why might Brierley react with these feelings?

CONCLUDE: How does the description of his reaction add suspense to Brierley's narrative?

when I lay in bed at night, in the safe comfort of my house in Hobart, trying to project myself back to my village home to let my mother know I was okay. Before I realized I'd gone far enough, I was looking down at the neighborhood I knew as a boy.

48   Still, nothing like "Ginestlay" came up on the map. It was the strangest feeling, and one that I became familiar with over the next year or so—part of me was certain, but still another part of me doubted. I was sure this was the right place, but for all this time I'd also been sure of the name "Ginestlay." Khandwa rang no bells whatsoever. Maybe "Ginestlay" was a part of Khandwa? A suburb? That seemed possible. I looked through the maze of alleys where my family lived, and although the image wasn't as clear as what I would get when I looked at where I lived in Hobart, I was sure I could see the little rectangular roof of my childhood home. Of course, I'd never seen the place from above, but the building was the right shape and in precisely the correct location. I hovered over the streets for a while, astonished, trying to take it all in. Finally I couldn't contain my excitement any longer.

49   I called out to Lisa, "I've found my hometown! You've gotta come and see this!" It was only then that I realized the time. I'd been at the computer for over seven hours nonstop, except for dinner.

50   Lisa poked her head around the corner, yawning, in her nightie. It took her a moment to wake up properly, but even half-asleep she could see my excitement. "Are you sure?" she asked.

51   "This is it, this is it!" I replied.

52   In that moment, I was convinced. "This is my hometown!"

53   It had taken eight months of intense searching, and it was nearly five years since I'd first downloaded Google Earth.

54   Lisa grinned and hugged me tightly. "That's so great! You did it, Saroo!" ❧

Response

1. Personal Connections If you didn't know your address or even the state or town you came from, what landmarks might you use to find your home on Google Earth? Explain.

> Answer the questions in your notebook. Use text evidence to support your responses.

Comprehension

2. Reading Check (a) What is the goal of Saroo Brierley's search? **(b)** What is the main resource Brierley uses to conduct his search? **(c)** What is "Ginestlay"?

3. Strategy: Make Predictions (a) How did you use text features of the memoir to make predictions about the content? **(b)** Were you able to confirm your predictions, or did you have to correct them? Explain.

Analysis

4. (a) Connect How does Brierley emphasize the importance of his search method and process throughout the excerpt? **(b) Make Inferences** What does that evidence tell you about Brierley's personality? **(c) Analyze** Why do you think Brierley didn't give up on his search? Support your answer with text evidence.

5. (a) Analyze In paragraph 10, what insight does Brierley have? **(b) Analyze Cause and Effect** Explain how this insight affects Brierley's character and ultimately changes his life.

6. (a) Interpret In paragraph 29, what does Brierley mean when he writes, "And I had to try not to bend my memories to fit what I was looking at"? **(b) Speculate** What do you think Brierley would have done if he hadn't found his childhood village? Explain.

EQ Notes ▶ What drives people to explore?

What have you learned about exploration from reading this memoir? Go to your Essential Question Notes and record your observations and thoughts about *A Long Way Home*.

⚙ TEKS

6.A. Describe personal connections to a variety of sources including self-selected texts.

6.C. Use text evidence to support an appropriate response.

Close Read

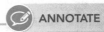 ANNOTATE

1. The model passage and annotation show how one reader analyzed part of paragraph 13 of the memoir. Find another detail in the passage to annotate. Then, write your own question and conclusion. If you need support, ask your peers or teachers for help.

CLOSE-READ MODEL

> It was a staggering amount of territory, covering some 962,300 square kilometers…. Within its bounds lived 345 million people. I tried to keep my emotions out of the exercise, but I couldn't help but wonder: Is it possible to find four family members among these 345 million?

ANNOTATE: The author has included numerical data in this passage.

QUESTION: Why does the author use specific numbers rather than general terms?

CONCLUDE: The numbers emphasize the magnitude of Brierley's project and show how difficult it will be.

MY QUESTION:

MY CONCLUSION:

2. For more practice, answer the Close-Read notes in the selection.

3. Choose a section of the memoir you found especially important. Mark important details. Then, jot down questions and write your conclusions in the open space next to the text.

Inquiry and Research

 RESEARCH

 NOTEBOOK

Research and Extend Often, you have to generate your own research questions. Sometimes, however, your teacher will give you research questions to explore. Practice responding to teacher-guided questions by conducting a brief, informal inquiry to find facts about the author of this memoir:

What did Saroo Brierley do after he found his childhood village online?

Write a summary of the information you find.

 TEKS

8.D.i. Analyze characteristics and structural elements of informational text, including the controlling idea or thesis with supporting evidence.

12.A. Generate student-selected and teacher-guided questions for formal and informal inquiry.

Genre / Text Elements

Controlling Idea and Evidence The **controlling idea** is the author's message or main point. In narrative nonfiction, such as this memoir, the controlling idea is an insight the author shares about his or her own life:

- how the author changes and what he or she learns

- what the author finds important in life

- how the author relates to his or her environment and the world

- how the author faces dramatic conflicts, or personal struggles

In narrative nonfiction, the author may not simply state the controlling idea or provide obvious evidence. Instead, he or she uses details that lead readers to an understanding of the message.

📓 NOTEBOOK

✋ INTERACTIVITY

PRACTICE Complete the activity and answer the questions.

1. **(a) Analyze** Complete the chart by identifying details that reveal what the author thinks and feels and determining the main point of each passage indicated. **(b) Interpret** What larger, controlling idea do these passages combine to express? Explain.

PARAGRAPH(S)	DETAILS THAT REVEAL AUTHOR'S THOUGHTS AND FEELINGS	MAIN POINT OF PASSAGE
10		
17–18		
31		

2. **Compare and Contrast** What comparisons does Brierley make between his childhood journey and his quest to find his hometown as an adult?

3. **(a) Analyze** What role do Brierley's childhood memories play in his search? **(b) Synthesize** What do they reveal about Brierley's goals?

from A LONG WAY HOME

Concept Vocabulary

 NOTEBOOK

Why These Words? The vocabulary words relate to the idea of searching or exploring. Saroo Brierley uses these words as he describes his search for his childhood home. For example, Brierley discusses how his search must be *deliberate*, or carefully planned, if he has any chance of succeeding.

deliberate	thorough	intensity
quest	obsessive	relentlessly

PRACTICE **Answer the question and complete the activity.**

1. How do the vocabulary words sharpen your understanding of the nature of Brierley's search?

2. Demonstrate your understanding of the vocabulary words by writing a paragraph in which you describe an imaginary quest. For example, you may write about a quest to find a mythical creature or a hidden treasure. Include all of the vocabulary words in your paragraph.

Word Study

 NOTEBOOK

Latin Suffix: *-ive* The Latin suffix *-ive* means "pertaining to," "tending to," or "serving to do." Words that contain this suffix are usually adjectives. In *A Long Way Home*, Brierley describes his behavior and attitude as *obsessive* because he tended to think about his search so much that he neglected his personal relationships.

1. Find another word in paragraph 23 that contains the Latin suffix *-ive*, and write a brief definition of it.

2. Use your prior knowledge as well as your understanding of the suffix *-ive* to write definitions for the following words: *active, creative, secretive.*

WORD NETWORK

Add words that are related to the idea of exploration from the text to your Word Network.

 TEKS

6.F. Respond using newly acquired vocabulary as appropriate.

10.D.ii. Edit drafts using standard English conventions, including consistent, appropriate use of verb tenses.

Conventions

Verb Tenses A **verb** expresses an action or a state of being. A verb's **tense** indicates when an action happens or a state exists.

VERB TENSE	EXAMPLE
Present tense indicates an action that is happening now or happens regularly.	I <u>use</u> software to explore.
Past tense indicates an action that has already happened.	I <u>used</u> software to explore.
Future tense indicates an action that will happen.	I <u>will use</u> software to explore.
Present perfect tense indicates an action that happened in the past and may still be happening now.	I <u>have used</u> software to explore.
Past perfect tense indicates an action that ended before another action in the past.	I <u>had used</u> software to explore before I traveled.
Future perfect tense indicates an action that will have ended before a specific time.	I <u>will have used</u> software to explore by the time I leave.

TIP: In English, there are six common verb tenses: present, past, future, present perfect, past perfect, and future perfect.

 INTERACTIVITY  NOTEBOOK

READ IT Work with a partner to identify sentences in the excerpt that include past and past perfect tense verbs. Write your examples in the chart. Then, choose one example for each verb tense, and rewrite the sentence using a different tense.

Past	
Past Perfect	

WRITE IT With your partner, choose a verb from the memoir, such as *travel, find,* or *remember*. Write two sentences using the verb in the present and past tenses. Then, edit your sentences, changing the tenses of all the verbs. Share your work with a partner, and challenge him or her to identify the verb tenses you used in your second set of sentences.

from A LONG WAY HOME

Composition

An **argumentative essay** is a brief nonfiction work in which you state a claim, or position, and use logical reasons and evidence to support it.

ASSIGNMENT

Write an **argumentative essay** in response to this question:

Is Saroo Brierley an explorer? Why, or why not?

- First, explain what you think it means to explore or to be an explorer. For example, must an explorer go somewhere no one else has ever been, or can exploration happen in familiar places?

- State your opinion about whether or not Brierley is an explorer. This is your claim.

- Support your claim with reasons and evidence from the text.

- Use transitional words and phrases to connect your ideas in logical ways. Be sure to use a comma after transitions used in introductory phrases.

- Include a strong conclusion that restates your claim in a new way and provides an additional insight.

Use New Words

Try to use one or more of the vocabulary words in your writing.
deliberate, thorough, intensity, quest, obsessive, relentlessly

EDITING TIP

Review your draft and make sure the transitional words and phrases you use show logical connections among your ideas. For example, if you want to indicate an effect, use specific transitions such as *consequently, as a result,* or *therefore.*

 NOTEBOOK

Reflect on Your Writing

PRACTICE After you have written your essay, answer the following questions.

1. What was the most challenging part of the assignment?

2. How would you revise your argument to improve it?

3. WHY THESE WORDS? The words you choose make a difference in your writing. Which words did you choose to help you convey precise ideas?

TEKS

6.C. Use text evidence to support an appropriate response.

6.E. Interact with sources in meaningful ways such as notetaking, annotating, freewriting, or illustrating.

10.D.viii. Edit drafts using standard English conventions, including punctuation marks, including commas in complex sentences, transitions, and introductory elements.

11.C. Compose multi-paragraph argumentative texts using genre characteristics and craft.

Speaking and Listening

When you **annotate,** you add notes to a text to provide additional information. An **annotated map** is a type of map that includes brief descriptions and explanations of locations.

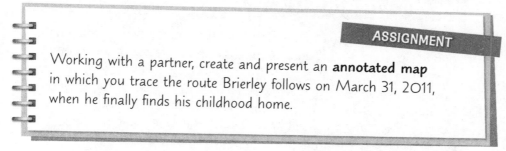

ASSIGNMENT

Working with a partner, create and present an **annotated map** in which you trace the route Brierley follows on March 31, 2011, when he finally finds his childhood home.

INTERACTIVITY

List and Paraphrase Reread paragraphs 33–54 and list the locations Brierley finds during his March 31st search. Paraphrase, or restate in your own words, Brierley's descriptions of the area. Include details he remembers as well as what he sees as he zooms in on his hometown. Make sure your paraphrases maintain the meaning and logical order of Brierley's descriptions.

PLACE	PARAPHRASE

EQ Notes Before moving on to a new selection, go to your Essential Question Notes and record any additional thoughts or observations you may have about the excerpt from *A Long Way Home.*

Annotate Locate a map of India and mark the places from your list. Annotate the map with your paraphrased descriptions. If you work on paper, use sticky notes or notecards and tape. If you work digitally, create text boxes and type in your paraphrases.

Create Illustrations Make illustrations or find images of some of the places and objects Brierley describes. Add them in the appropriate spots on your map.

Present and Discuss Take turns sharing your annotated maps with the class. Use these questions to guide your discussions:

- How does the map help you visualize Brierley's search?
- How does creating a map of India enable you to grasp the enormous scope of his search?
- How did the process of annotating your map deepen your understanding of the text?

About the Narrator

The Irish comedian **Dara Ó Briain** (b. 1972) is a self-described "geek." He attended University College, Dublin, and studied math and theoretical physics. Ó Briain is best known, however, for his comedy and for his hosting of many popular television shows, including the British version of *The Apprentice: You're Fired* and *Mock the Week.*

BBC Science Club: All About Exploration

Media Vocabulary

These words describe characteristics of animation, a type of multimodal genre. Use them as you analyze, discuss, and write about the video.

cut-out animation: technique that uses flat characters, backgrounds, and props cut from materials such as paper, cardboard, and fabric	Cut-out animation involves moving cut-out objects in small steps and taking a picture of each step to create an illusion of natural movement.
object animation: form that involves the movement of actual objects, such as a book or a pen	• The objects are generally not designed to look like a human or animal character. • Animated objects are not made of flexible materials, such as clay or wax.
real-time animation: style in which animated events seem to move at the same speed they would in real life	• Interactive video games commonly use real-time animation. • Animated movies also use real-time animation to create an impression of real life.

Comprehension Strategy

 NOTEBOOK

Monitor Comprehension

As you watch a video, monitor your comprehension, making sure you understand the ideas, and make adjustments if you don't. For example, use your **background knowledge,** or information you already know, to better understand new ideas expressed in this video.

- Read the Background section and consider what you already know about the subject.
- Discuss the topic with your peers or teacher and gain more background information from them.
- As you play the video, listen for new ideas and decide if they add to, change, or contradict your background knowledge.

PRACTICE As you watch the video, monitor your comprehension and make sure you fully understand all the ideas and details. If your understanding breaks down, make adjustments, such as using your background knowledge. Use the Take Notes sections to capture your thoughts.

 TEKS

5.I. Monitor comprehension and make adjustments such as re-reading, using background knowledge, asking questions, and annotating when understanding breaks down.

8.F. Analyze characteristics of multimodal and digital texts.

BBC Science Club:
All About Exploration

BACKGROUND

In the video, the narrator mentions the pioneering scientist Dr. Robert Goddard, who invented liquid-fueled rockets in the early 20th century. Goddard devoted his life to researching and developing rockets, laying the groundwork for space exploration. An insightful physicist and inventor, Goddard envisioned the possibility of space flight, and his contributions were essential to making space travel a reality. The Goddard Space Flight Center in Maryland, a major NASA research laboratory, was established in his memory.

 AUDIO

NOTEBOOK

TAKE NOTES As you watch the video, look for images that reinforce word meanings. Write down your observations and questions, making sure to note time codes so you can easily revisit sections later.

NOTEBOOK

Answer the questions in your notebook. Use text evidence to support your responses.

Response

1. **Personal Connections** **(a)** What personal qualities do you think it takes to be an explorer? **(b)** Do you think most people have those qualities? Explain.

Comprehension

2. **Strategy: Monitor Comprehension** How did you monitor your comprehension as you watched the video? Did you need to make any adjustments? If so, what actions did you take and how did they help?

Analysis

3. **(a) Generalize** In general, how has our ability to explore been affected by advancements in navigation? **(b) Make a Judgment** Which type of advancements—technological or navigational—do you think were most important? Explain.

4. **Interpret** At the beginning of the video, the narrator says that people need "effective means and methods" to explore. What does he mean by this statement?

5. **Evaluate** How effective do you find the use of animation in conveying information? Explain.

6. **Essential Question** *What drives people to explore?* What have you learned about exploration from watching the video? Go to your Essential Question Notes and record your observations and thoughts.

Close Review

 ANNOTATE

Watch the video again. As you watch, take notes about important details and jot down your observations. Note time codes so you can find information later. Then, write a question and your conclusion.

MY QUESTION:

MY CONCLUSION:

MEDIA VOCABULARY

Use these terms as you discuss and write about the video.

cut-out animation
object animation
real-time animation

 TEKS

5.I. Monitor comprehension and make adjustments such as re-reading, using background knowledge, asking questions, and annotating when understanding breaks down.

Research

A **storyboard** is a sequence of drawings that shows the camera shots planned for a film.

ASSIGNMENT

Research an explorer whose accomplishments could be added to the BBC Science Club video. Then, create a **storyboard** to show how you would present the information in a video.

BBC SCIENCE CLUB: ALL ABOUT EXPLORATION

 INTERACTIVITY

Research and Plan Generate two questions about explorers who aren't featured in this video. Briefly research each explorer. Then, choose one and research that person in depth. Consult a variety of sources and gather relevant information, including dates, explorers' goals, explanations, and other details.

Focus the Information Decide which aspects of the explorer's life and achievements will be the focus of your storyboard. List three main points.

Draft a Storyboard Use the storyboard form given here, or one like it, to organize your ideas. Add illustrations of the scenes you will show in your video to the boxes. Write captions or narration beneath each box.

EQ Notes Before moving on to a new selection, go to your Essential Question Notes and record what you learned from the video.

STORYBOARD

Present If possible, use digital tools to make a video of your storyboard and record the narration. Play the video for the class. Otherwise, simply present your storyboard and read the captions aloud.

 TEKS

6.E. Interact with sources in meaningful ways such as notetaking, annotating, freewriting, or illustrating.

12.A. Generate student-selected and teacher-guided questions for formal and informal inquiry.

12.D. Identify and gather relevant information from a variety of sources.

Write a Formal Research Paper

A **research paper** is a report in which a writer combines research from outside sources with his or her own ideas to answer a research question.

Write a **research paper** in which you answer a focused research question about one of the following broad topics:

an explorer from history

someone who is exploring new frontiers today

Combine, or synthesize, information to create an engaging and informative text. Include elements of research writing in your paper.

ELEMENTS OF RESEARCH WRITING

Purpose: to answer a focused research question

Characteristics
- a controlling idea, or thesis
- varied types of evidence gathered from a variety of reliable sources
- citations that follow an accepted format, including a Works Cited page or bibliography
- elements of craft, including word choices that are precise and appropriate for the intended audience, or reader
- correct spelling, capitalization, and punctuation

Structure
- logical organization that includes an introduction and a conclusion
- well-chosen transitions, and coherence within and across paragraphs

TEKS
11.B. Compose informational texts, including multi-paragraph essays that convey information about a topic, using a clear controlling idea or thesis statement and genre characteristics and craft.

Take a Closer Look at the Assignment

1. Do I understand the basic vocabulary of the assignment? What is it asking me to do (in my own words)?

 NOTEBOOK

2. Is a specific **audience** mentioned in the assignment?

◯ Yes   If "yes," who is my main audience?

◯ No   If "no," who do I think my audience is or should be?

AUDIENCE

Always keep your **audience,** or readers, in mind.

- Choose words your audience will understand.
- Explain any information that may be unfamiliar to your audience.

3. Is my **purpose** for writing specified in the assignment?

◯ Yes   If "yes," what is the purpose?

◯ No   If "no," why am I writing this research paper (not just because it's an assignment)?

PURPOSE

A specific **purpose,** or reason for writing, will lead to a stronger paper.

- **General Purpose:** *In this paper, I'll write about an explorer.*
- **Specific Purpose:** *In this paper, I'll write about Jane Goodall's first trip to Africa to live among chimpanzees.*

4. (a) Does the assignment require that I use specific **types of sources**?

◯ Yes   If "yes," what are they?

◯ No   If "no," what types of sources might I use?

(b) Where will I find these sources?

SOURCES

Varied **types of sources** will make your research paper more accurate and interesting.

- **Primary Sources:** firsthand accounts of events, such as diaries, letters, and original maps
- **Secondary Sources:** sources that discuss information originally presented in primary sources; includes articles and reference works

5. Does the assignment ask me to organize my ideas a certain way?

◯ Yes   If "yes," what structure does it require?

◯ No   If "no," how can I best order my ideas?

Planning and Prewriting

In order to choose your topic and generate a meaningful research question, you need to do some preliminary work.

Generate Questions to Develop a Plan

- Do a quick online search to gather background information about the broad topic. You may discuss specific topics that interest you with a partner.
- List aspects of the topic that spark your curiosity. Write them as questions. Try to use "how" and "why" questions. Write quickly and freely.
- Go back through your list of questions and mark the ones you find most exciting. Cross out the ones that don't interest you.

SAMPLE RESEARCH QUESTIONS

- How did ancient seafaring cultures, such as the Polynesians or Vikings, explore?
- How did new technology, such as the quadrant, change exploration?
- How are people still exploring the unknown today?

NOTEBOOK

WRITE IT Generate questions about your topic.

 TEKS

12.A. Generate student-selected and teacher-guided questions for formal and informal inquiry; **12.C.** Refine the major research question, if necessary, guided by answers to a secondary set of questions.

Refine the Major Research Question

 NOTEBOOK

A. Write Your Question Pick the question you generated that you like the most. Write it here. Also, jot down any secondary questions you might want to use.

_____

_____

_____

> **TIP:** Your major research question will focus your work. You may also use secondary questions that are more detailed or involve a related topic. Answers you find to these secondary questions may lead you to modify your original question and alter the focus of your research.

B. Evaluate Your Question A good question will provide a clear path for your research. A weak question will result in either too much or too little information. Use the checklist to make sure your question is narrow enough to be interesting and answerable.

Research Question Checklist

Complexity

◯ I can't answer the question with a simple "yes" or "no."

Clarity and Focus

◯ The question is precise.

◯ Information related to the question is plentiful but not overwhelming.

◯ The question will point me in a clear direction for finding information.

Significance

◯ The question matters to me.

◯ The question will matter to my readers.

STRONG RESEARCH QUESTIONS

A strong research question has certain qualities.

- **Level of Complexity:** The question is complex enough to warrant research, but not so complex that it becomes impossible to answer.

- **Clarity and Focus:** The question is focused enough that you're able to identify sources that will help you answer it.

- **Significance:** The question is important enough to warrant researching in the first place and is something that readers will find interesting.

C. Refine Your Question If your question doesn't meet all the checklist items, revise it so that it does. Write your revised question here.

_____

_____

_____

_____

Planning and Prewriting

Gather your research sources from the school or local library, reputable online sites, and local experts, such as history teachers.

A. Identify and Gather a Variety of Sources

List sources you might use to gather information that is relevant to your research question. Plan to use at least one source from each category.

Type of Source	Title of Source
Primary Sources: texts created at the time of the events • Diaries or journals • Research studies • Original newspaper articles • Eyewitness accounts • Public records • Ads or cartoons from the time period	
Secondary Sources: accounts or interpretations of events by later writers • Newspaper or magazine articles • Encyclopedia entries • Historical writing • Media (documentaries, TV programs, etc.)	
Your Own Research: organized information-gathering you do yourself • Online surveys • In-person surveys • Interviews	

 TEKS

6.E. Interact with sources in meaningful ways such as notetaking, annotating, freewriting, or illustrating; **9.G.** Explain the differences between rhetorical devices and logical fallacies; **12.D.** Identify and gather relevant information from a variety of sources; **12.E.** Differentiate between primary and secondary sources; **12.H.i.** Examine sources for reliability, credibility, and bias; **12.H.ii.** Examine sources for faulty reasoning such as hyperbole, emotional appeals, and stereotype.

B. Evaluate Sources

Plan to use only those sources that are credible, reliable, unbiased, and show clear reasoning. Use these guidelines to evaluate each source on your list. After your evaluation, add or delete sources, as necessary.

Guidelines for Evaluating Sources

○ **Credibility: Is the information believable?**

Does the author have deep knowledge of the topic?

Source Title: _____   Yes ○ No ○

Source Title: _____   Yes ○ No ○

Source Title: _____   Yes ○ No ○

○ **Reliability: Is the information accurate?**

Can you confirm the author's findings with at least one other source?

Source Title: _____   Yes ○ No ○

Source Title: _____   Yes ○ No ○

Source Title: _____   Yes ○ No ○

○ **Bias: Are the author's views fair?**

Does the author have unjustified negative or positive feelings about something?

Source Title: _____   Yes ○ No ○

Source Title: _____   Yes ○ No ○

Source Title: _____   Yes ○ No ○

○ **Reasoning: Is the author's logic sound?**

Writers may use rhetorical devices, such as parallelism, to clarify ideas and add emotional power to a text. Some writers, however, use logical fallacies, or faulty reasoning. The deliberate use of fallacies serves one purpose: to mislead readers. Evaluate potential sources for their uses of such devices, including the ones shown here. If you find fallacies, avoid the source.

- *hyperbole*: exaggeration that distorts the facts (*They were always wrong in every way.*)

- *stereotype*: unfair generalization of someone's qualities based on his or her membership in a specific group

Source Title/Explanation: _____   ○ Yes ○ No

Source Title/Explanation: _____   ○ Yes ○ No

Source Title/Explanation: _____   ○ Yes ○ No

CHECK ONLINE SOURCES

Some websites are reliable, but some are not.

- Consult sites from established institutions and those with expertise (.edu, .gov).

- Avoid commercial sites (.com).

- Question personal blogs and avoid anonymous sites or pages.

TAKE NOTES

Try different ways to take notes and capture information.

- Use notecards.
- Use software.
- Use digital tools, such as screenshots or bookmarks.

Choose a logical way to organize your notes.

- by source
- by topic

Be sure to record citation information for every source you consult.

REVISE YOUR PLAN

Allow enough time for your initial research. Then, review your findings and decide if you need more information. Identify your resources and leave time to gather them.

- Visit the library.
- Research online.
- Interview experts.

Drafting

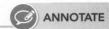 ANNOTATE

Now that you've gathered the information you need, organize it and write a first draft.

Write Your Thesis

Turn your research question into an answer. This is your thesis, or controlling idea.

Sample Thesis: New technology adds to our ability to explore and advance our knowledge.

My Thesis: _____

_____

Make an Outline

List the points you want to make and the evidence that will support each one. Use the Outline Model as a guide.

> **OUTLINE MODEL**
> Title of Your Report
> I. Introduction
>   Thesis Statement
> II. First main point
>   A. Supporting detail #1
>   1. Example
>   2. Example
>   3. Example
>   B. Supporting detail #2
>   C. Supporting detail #3
> III. Second main point

📓 NOTEBOOK

WRITE IT ▶ Make an outline for your paper.

DEPTH OF THOUGHT / SYNTHESIZE INFORMATION

As you draft, show that you have synthesized research to express your own insights.

- **Audience** Explain any specialized words or concepts that may be unfamiliar to your readers.
- **Development** Integrate facts, details, and examples from sources and use them to support your own point of view.
- **Citations** Mark ideas and phrases that come directly from sources so you can easily add citations when you have finished drafting.

 TEKS

10.B.i. Develop drafts into a focused, structured, and coherent piece of writing by organizing with purposeful structure, including an introduction, transitions, coherence within and across paragraphs, and a conclusion; **12.F.** Synthesize information from a variety of sources; **12.G.** Differentiate between paraphrasing and plagiarism when using source materials; **12.I.** Display academic citations and use source materials ethically.

Create Coherence

There are different ethical ways to include information from sources. Decide how you will use specific pieces of evidence. Then, add **transitions** (words that connect ideas) to create coherence both within and across paragraphs.

USE SOURCE MATERIALS ETHICALLY

Use of Source	Definition	Examples
Direct Quotation	source's exact words, set off in quotation marks	Professor Marcus explains: "We can use Mars...as a laboratory for studying other rocky planets" (40).
Paraphrase NOTE: Even when you reword ideas, they are still not yours. Cite paraphrases accurately to avoid plagiarism.	restatement of another's ideas in your own words	Scientists think that we can learn about other rocky planets by studying Mars ("Mars Mission" 40).
Summary	brief statement of the main ideas and key details of a text	Many processes depleted the atmosphere on Mars. By exploring Mars, we learn about these effects on other planets (Alton 34).

TIP: Place in-text citations in parentheses.
- Author Indicated: cite the page number
- Author Not Indicated: cite the author's last name and page number
- No Author: cite short version of the title and the page number
- No Page Number: cite short title or author only

When to Cite information

As you use information from sources, err on the side of caution and create a citation. Otherwise, you risk **plagiarizing**, or using someone else's words and ideas as your own.

- **Citation Not Needed:** your own ideas; common knowledge
- **Citation Needed:** direct quote, paraphrase, or summary of someone else's idea; specialized information

Provide full information about your sources in a Works Cited list at the end of your paper. Follow the format your teacher prefers.

 NOTEBOOK

WRITE IT ▸ Write a paragraph of your paper here. Use one direct quotation and one paraphrase of information. Cite both correctly.

USE TRANSITIONS

Once you have included evidence, add transitions, such as *for example* or *as a result* that clarify connections to your ideas. To create coherence across paragraphs, use transitions that suggest bigger ideas, such as *In a different way.*

Revising

 ANNOTATE

Now that you have a first draft, revise it to be sure it is as clear and informative as possible. When you revise, you "re-see" your writing, checking for the following elements:

Clarity: sharpness of your ideas; clear controlling idea or thesis statement

Development: full explanations and strong evidence; ethical use of researched information, including paraphrases that are accurately cited to avoid plagiarism

Organization: logical flow of ideas

Style and Tone: a variety of well-written sentence types, lengths, and patterns; precise, well-chosen words; a level of formality that suits your audience and purpose

Read Like a Writer

Review the revisions made to the Model Text. Then, answer the question in the white box.

MODEL TEXT

from On Top of the World

At its summit, Mount Everest measures almost 30,000 feet. To put that in perspective, the highest mountain in Texas, Mt. Guadalupe, is not even a third of Everest's height. *As many climbers have noted, from Everest's summit, one can actually see the curve of the planet (McRae 122).*

> Why did the author add this detail?

The view is breathtaking, but the dangers of climbing Everest are very serious. In fact, 1977 was the last year without a recorded death on the mountain (*WorldBook* 42). What draws people to risk death for a chance at a view? Malavath Poorna, the thirteen-year-old who became the youngest girl ever to scale Mount Everest, ~~was overwhelmed by emotion after her climb.~~ *said, "When I reached the top, I felt too much emotion, too much joy"* (Chen 2).

> The author replaces paraphrased information with a direct quotation because it is more powerful.

⭐ TEKS
10.C. Revise drafts for clarity, development, organization, style, word choice, and sentence variety.

Take a Closer Look at Your Draft

Now, revise your draft. Use the Revision Guide for Research Writing to evaluate and strengthen your paper.

REVISION GUIDE FOR RESEARCH WRITING

EVALUATE	TAKE ACTION
Clarity	
Is my thesis, or controlling idea, concise and clear?	If your thesis isn't clear, **summarize** the main point you want to make. Use that statement to sharpen your thesis.
Have I cited ideas that are not my own, including any paraphrases?	Review your paper, and **mark** any ideas you paraphrased. **Add** any missing citations to those passages to make sure you avoid plagiarism.
Development	
Have I used researched information to support my own ideas?	Mark sourced information in your paper in one way and your own ideas in another. If you see too few of your own ideas, consider the reasons you are using each piece of sourced evidence. Then, **add** explanations of those reasons.
Do I rely too much on one source?	If most of the evidence you use is from the same source, **add** variety. • Review your source list and **integrate** relevant evidence from a different text. • Do more research, using sources you may have overlooked. Then, **replace** existing details with new evidence.
Organization	
Does every paragraph add meaningfully to my thesis?	In the margins of your paper, jot down a few words that state how each paragraph relates to the next and supports your thesis. For example, "gives example" or "shows similarity." **Add** explanations to reinforce any missing connections.
Do the sentences within each paragraph all relate to the topic sentence?	Mark the topic sentence in each paragraph, Then, analyze each supporting sentence to ensure it relates to the topic sentence. **Delete** any sentences that are off topic.
Style and Tone	
Does my introduction engage readers?	**Add** a question, anecdote, quotation, or strong detail to interest your audience.
Is my conclusion strong and memorable?	**Add** a quotation, a call to action, an insight, or a strong statement to conclude.
Are my word choices precise?	Review your draft and mark any vague words, such as *nice, good, bad,* or *important*. **Replace** these words with precise words that will convey your ideas more exactly.

Editing

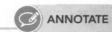 ANNOTATE

Don't let errors distract readers from your ideas and information. Reread your draft and fix mistakes to create a finished informative work.

Read Like a Writer

Look at how the writer of the model text edited the draft. Then, follow the directions in the white box.

MODEL TEXT

from On Top of the World

Located in the Asian countries of Tibet and Nepal, temperatures at its top can plummet to -40°F year-round, while snowy clouds blast by at hurricane speeds *(Christopher 187).* Snowstorms can blind hikers, causing them to lose their way or seek shelter for hours in the deathly cold; avalanches occur without warning. Both new climers and ~~expertly~~ *expert guides* can suffer fatal falls. In fact, the month before Malavath's climb, 16 hikers were killed in a sudden avalanche (*Climber News*).

> The writer added a citation to identify the source of a specific specialized detail.

> Find and fix a spelling error.

Focus on Sentences

Correlative Conjunctions **Correlative conjunctions** are pairs of conjunctions, or joining words, that link words, phrases, or clauses. They include *both/and, either/or, neither/nor,* and *not only/but also.* They always connect two elements that are parallel, or grammatically the same. For example, if a noun follows *either*, a noun must also follow *or*.

Correct: The climbers were *either* <u>fearless</u> *or* <u>foolish</u>. (parallel adjectives)
Incorrect: The climbers were *either* <u>fearless</u> *or* <u>fools</u>. (incorrectly connects the adjective *fearless* and the noun *fools*)

Correct: *Neither* <u>experience</u> *nor* <u>luck</u> can guarantee safety. (parallel nouns)
Incorrect: *Neither* <u>experience</u> *nor* <u>being lucky</u> can guarantee safety. (incorrectly connects the noun *experience* and the gerund phrase *being lucky*)

PRACTICE Edit each item to ensure that the correlative conjunctions link parallel elements in a correct sentence pattern.

1. An explorer should be *both* skilled *and* organize well.

2. *Neither* the mountain's size *nor* how cold it is kept her from wanting to climb.

> **EDITING TIPS**
> 1. Mark the correlative conjunctions in a sentence.
> 2. Make sure the terms following each conjunction are the same grammatical form.
> 3. If the terms are not parallel, replace one or both with items that are grammatically the same.

🔅 TEKS

10.D.vi. Edit drafts using standard English conventions, including subordinating conjunctions to form complex sentences and correlative conjunctions such as *either/or* and *neither/nor*. **12.I.** Display academic citations and use source materials ethically; **12.J.** Use an appropriate mode of delivery, whether written, oral, or multimodal, to present results.

Rules for Proper Citation

Works Cited List A Works Cited list is just what the name suggests—a list of all the sources you cite in your paper. There are different styles for the formatting of these lists. The rules shown here represent MLA style.

- **Capitalization of Titles:** Don't capitalize articles (*a, an, the*), prepositions, or conjunctions unless they are the first words in a title.
  Book Title: *The Mountainous West: Historical Explorations*
  Magazine Article Title: "To the Heights of the World"

- **Punctuation of Author Names:** Follow these models to punctuate author names correctly.
  Single Author: Antigua, Maia. *Everest Bound.* Random House, 2012.
  Multiple Authors: Kay, Jayne, and Samuel Asher. *Beyond the Sky.* Random House, 2017.

- **Formatting Titles:** Place the titles of shorter texts—for example, short stories, articles, poems, songs, or episodes of a show—in quotation marks. Set the titles of full-length works in italics.
  Shorter Work: Campion, Mary. "Exploring Mars." *Spaceflight Magazine,* May 2017, pp. 24–27.
  Full-Length Work: Argenti, Nicole. *Journeys That Changed the World.* 3rd ed., Longman, 2011.

> **EDITING TIPS**
> **Spelling** The *us* sound at the end of a word is spelled *ous* when it represents the suffix *-ous*, meaning "full of." For example, *joyous* means "full of joy." Make sure you have spelled words that contain this suffix correctly. Use a dictionary to confirm your spelling.

> For complete information about Works Cited lists, see the **Research** section of the **Tool Kit** in this program.

> **PRACTICE** Correct the citations.
>
> **1.** Peter Compound. The wonders Of Wandering. Bent Hill Press. 2017.
>
> **2.** St. Pierre, Barbara, St. Pierre, Stowe. *"Musical movements From sea to land."* Wanderlust Wonderings Magazine (pp. 52–56) May 2017.

Publishing and Presenting

Share With a Broader Audience

Share your paper with your class or school community. Choose one of these options:

OPTION 1 Post your paper to a class or school website. If you choose this option, include images and captions.

OPTION 2 Create a book of the class's research papers. Write an introduction and give the book a title. Then, print multiple copies to share with other classes or to place in the school library.

Essential Question

What drives people to explore?

Human beings investigate the world in many different ways and for many different reasons, including curiosity, survival, and adventure. You will read selections that examine how and why we explore. Work in a small group to continue your explorations about the idea of exploration itself.

▶ VIDEO

👆 INTERACTIVITY

Peer-Group Learning Strategies

Throughout your life, in school, in your community, and in your career, you will continue to learn and work with others. Review these strategies and the actions you can take to practice them as you work in small groups. Add ideas of your own for each category. Use these strategies during Peer-Group Learning.

STRATEGY	MY PEER-GROUP ACTION PLAN
Prepare • Complete your assignments so that you are prepared for group work. • Take notes on your reading to share with your group.	
Participate fully • Volunteer information and use verbal and nonverbal forms of communication to get your points across. • Use text evidence when making a point.	
Support others • Build off ideas from others in your group. • Ask others who have not yet spoken to do so.	
Clarify • Paraphrase the ideas of others to check your own understanding. • Ask follow-up questions.	

CONTENTS

PERFORMANCE TASK: SPEAKING AND LISTENING

Deliver a Research Presentation

The Peer-Group readings feature people, both real and imaginary, who explore the world in different ways. After reading, your group will research, write, and present an infomercial in which you try to persuade an audience to join one of these explorers in their adventures.

Working as a Group

 NOTEBOOK

1. Take a Position
In your group, discuss the following question:

> Would you rather explore an ancient civilization in the middle of a desert or an island in the middle of the ocean?

As you take turns sharing your positions, provide reasons for your choices. After all group members have shared, come to a consensus, or agreement, as to the pros and cons of each option.

2. Use Text Evidence
In this section, make sure that everyone in the group uses text evidence to support responses in both speaking and writing activities. Work to identify textual evidence in ways that reflect the demands of a question or activity:

- **Comprehension:** Identify specific, explicitly stated details.
- **Analysis:** Choose text evidence that fits the criteria for analysis.
- **Inference:** Identify clues that hint at meaning but do not directly state it.
- **Interpretation:** Draw connections among multiple details and show how they lead to deeper meanings.
- **Evaluation:** Identify textual evidence and consider it in relationship to other texts, your own values, or another measure.

3. Name Your Group
Choose a name that reflects the unit topic.

Our group's name: _____

4. Create a Communication Plan
Decide how you want to communicate with one another. For example, you might use online collaboration tools, email, or instant messaging.

Our group's plan:

_____

_____

_____

_____

 TEKS

1.D. Participate in student-led discussions by eliciting and considering suggestions from other group members, taking notes, and identifying points of agreement and disagreement; **6.C.** Use text evidence to support an appropriate response.

Making a Schedule

First, find out the due dates for the Peer-Group activities. Then, preview the texts and activities with your group and make a schedule for completing the tasks.

SELECTION	ACTIVITIES	DUE DATE
Ada and the Thinking Machine		
The King of Mazy May		
from Sacajawea		
from Lewis & Clark		

NOTEBOOK

Working on Group Projects

As your group works together, you'll find it more effective if each person has a specific role. Different projects require different roles. Before beginning a project, discuss the necessary roles and choose one for each group member. Some possible roles are listed here. Add your own ideas to the list.

Project Manager: monitors the schedule and keeps everyone on task
Researcher: organizes research activities
Recorder: takes notes during group meetings

_____

_____

_____

_____

ADA AND THE THINKING MACHINES

The selection you are about to read is a biography.

Reading Biographies

A **biography** is a type of narrative nonfiction. It tells the story of a real person's life.

BIOGRAPHY

Author's Purpose
- to tell the story of a person's life

Characteristics
- often, the subject is a famous figure, but may also be an unknown person
- written in the third person point of view, by an author who is not the subject
- presents the author's view of the subject's life
- may appear in different formats, from a magazine article to a full-length book
- may include print and graphic text features that add interest and structure

Structure
- usually written in narrative form, so it reads like a story; usually uses time order
- may have chapters or sections

Take a Minute!

 NOTEBOOK

LIST IT With a partner, choose two people whose biographies you would like to read. Discuss the qualities—such as their personality traits, achievements, and life experiences—that would make each person an interesting subject.

© Pearson Education, Inc., or its affiliates. All rights reserved.

 TEKS
9.C. Analyze the author's use of print and graphic features to achieve specific purposes.

Genre / Text Elements

Print and Graphic Features Nonfiction texts often include print and graphic features that add information, create visual interest, and clarify the organization of ideas. **Print features** are mainly verbal (words). **Graphic features** are mainly visual, and include photographs, illustrations, charts, tables, graphs, and maps.

PRINT AND GRAPHIC FEATURES	
Subheads	groups of words that are set off visually from the main text to identify specific sections
Captions	text that appears with photos or illustrations to explain the content of a picture
Sidebars	mini-articles that are set off from the main text and provide information on a related topic; may include pictures
Timelines	dates and basic information about key events set in a line to show the passage of time; may also include pictures

INTERACTIVITY

PRACTICE Suppose an author is writing a biography of a famous musician. Work with your group to choose the feature that would best accomplish each objective.

OBJECTIVE

_____ **1.** identify when the musician was born, got her first guitar, and released her first recording

_____ **2.** provide information about another band that influenced the musician

_____ **3.** organize the main text into sections focused on each part of the musician's life

_____ **4.** show how the musician looked before she was famous

_____ **5.** explain pictures included with the main text

FEATURE

A. Photograph

B. Timeline

C. Subheads

D. Caption

E. Sidebar

About the Author

Kathleen Krull (b. 1952) worked briefly as a part-time librarian in Wilmette, Illinois. However, she read books while she was supposed to be working and was fired. She now writes books for children. Her book, *Harvesting Hope: The Story of Cesar Chavez,* was selected as a Pura Belpré Honor Book and an ALA Notable Book. Her series *Giants of Science* explores the lives of famous scientists, including Sir Isaac Newton and Leonardo da Vinci.

Ada and the Thinking Machines

Concept Vocabulary

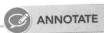 ANNOTATE

As you read the biography, you will encounter these words.

rebelliousness	exception	visionary

Context Clues The context of a word is the other words and phrases that appear close to it in the text. Clues in the context can help you figure out a word's meaning. There are different types of context clues.

An **analogy** is a comparison between two seemingly different things. Authors make analogies to clarify or explain an idea. These analogies can also be context clues.

EXAMPLE Her **disproportionate** reaction was like that of a child screaming over a lost toy.

ANALYSIS: If a child loses a toy, he or she may get more upset than seems reasonable. *Disproportionate* must mean "too extreme for the circumstances."

PRACTICE As you read "Ada and the Thinking Machines," study the context to determine the meanings of unknown words. Mark your observations in the open space next to the text.

Comprehension Strategy

 ANNOTATE

Make Predictions

Predictions are guesses you make about the types of ideas and information a writer will share in a text. The structures and features of a text offer meaningful clues. Consider these elements of biographies:

- **Time Order:** Most biographies have a chronological, or time-order, structure. You can predict that the beginning will focus on childhood and later sections will focus on adulthood.
- **Connections:** A biography explores themes in the subject's life. You can predict that related ideas will be repeated.
- **Sections:** Biographies often have sections that focus on specific parts of the subject's life. Subheads and other text features may indicate these sections. You can scan a text and predict the focus of each section.

PRACTICE As you read, use the text's structures and features to make specific predictions about the content. Confirm or correct your predictions as you read on.

 TEKS

2.B. Use context such as definition, analogy, and examples to clarify the meaning of words.

5.C. Make, correct, or confirm predictions using text features, characteristics of genre, and structures.

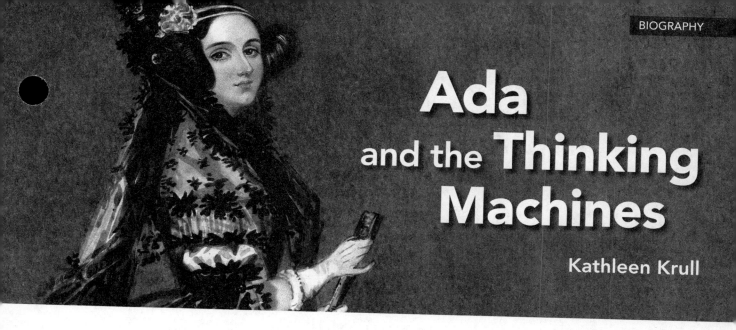

Ada
and the Thinking Machines

Kathleen Krull

BACKGROUND

Ada Lovelace (1815–1852), the subject of this biography, grew up during a historical period known as the Industrial Revolution, when people began developing advanced machinery to do work. Goods that had been made at home by hand were now manufactured on a large scale in factories. Many of the tools and technology we use today originated in this innovative time period. In this article, the author describes the life and achievements of Lovelace, one of the period's most creative thinkers.

 AUDIO

 ANNOTATE

Preface

Computers are an important part of many people's lives, and I was curious to learn more about them and how they originated. During my research on the creation and evolution of computing, I learned of Ada Lovelace, a brilliant woman who played a significant role in the development of what is widely considered to be the world's first computer. I wrote this biographical profile because I felt it was important for more people to know about this remarkable and unique person.

—Kathleen Krull

1   Ada Lovelace (1815–1852) grew up in a seriously unusual way. It was more like a science experiment than a childhood: how could her mother, Lady Annabella Byron, raise Ada to be as unlike her father as possible?

2   Ada never knew her dad, who left England when she was still a baby. Annabella refused to tell her daughter anything about him until after he died in Greece, when Ada was eight. Lord Byron was

BUILD YOUR VOCABULARY

Concept and other higher-level words aren't the only ones that matter. As you read, actively build your understanding of sight and basic words. Listen to the audio and note words you've mastered and those you are still acquiring.

^ Ada's parents, Annabella and the poet Lord Byron, had a short and unhappy marriage. Byron's temper and need for excitement dismayed Annabella, and her prim ways drove him crazy.

Use context clues or indicate another strategy you used that helped you determine meaning.

rebelliousness (rih BEHL yuhs nehss) *n.*

MEANING:

one of England's most famous poets. But he was also, in the words of a former girlfriend, "mad,[1] bad, and dangerous to know"—the very opposite of Ada's very proper mother.

3   Annabella's friends were horrified when she married the wild Byron, and soon, so was she. During their brief marriage, Byron dubbed his wife the Princess of Parallelograms for her love of geometrical shapes. Annabella was a well-educated woman for her day, especially in math and science, and logical to a fault. She thought she could rescue Byron from his wild life—but shortly after Ada was born Byron fled, never to return.

No Poetry!

4   Annabella was determined to save her daughter from the dangerous imagination she thought had driven Byron mad. She kept an iron grip on Ada's days from the moment Ada awoke at 6:00 a.m. until bedtime. She hired scholars to educate Ada at home on every subject—except poetry. They taught Ada only facts, logic, math, languages, and other useful subjects.

5   Poor Ada had no siblings or playmates. Instead, a group of her mother's unmarried friends watched over her. If she showed any **rebelliousness** or bad behavior, like talking too much or riding her horse too often, they reported back to her mother. Ada called them "the Furies"[2] and hated them.

6   If Ada had a moment to herself, she could be found on the lawn, her cat Puff on her lap, reading a big book like *Bingley's Useful Knowledge.* Even her meals were strictly controlled.

7   Ada decided early on that she was a genius. By the age of eight, she was in love with numbers. Equations and calculations became her delight, and she read all the latest news in science.

8   One day Puff the cat dragged in a bird he had killed. The 12-year-old Ada carefully studied its wing. For the next year, she did experiments and research on bird anatomy. She became obsessed with finding a way for humans to fly, even designing wings for herself of paper and wire. She dreamed of a new branch of science, which she called Flyology.

---

1. **mad** (mad) *adj.* British slang for *crazy.*
2. **the Furies** In Greek myths, the Furies were three goddesses of vengeance, or revenge, who hunted down and punished wrong-doers. They were feared for their cruelty.

9   At 13 she drew a complete map of the stars. At 17 one of her tutors gushed that Ada could become "an original mathematical investigator." Ada felt she was destined for a brilliant future in science—it was just a matter of focusing. Despite her mother's efforts, she was quite a passionate and imaginative person—just the thing for a scientist.

Marvelous Thinking Machines

10   When she was 18, Ada met Charles Babbage, mathematician, inventor, and social butterfly. Every Saturday he invited a crowd of fashionable people to his home to marvel at his collection of amazing machines. Soon Ada was a regular guest.

11   One of his marvels was the "Silver Dancer," a beautiful metal automaton (a doll moved by clockwork) that danced on a table holding a flapping metal bird. Visitors loved to watch it twirl, but Ada was more interested in the machinery inside.

12   Babbage was thrilled by new inventions like steam engines and gas lamps.[3] He was also fascinated by a new French invention, the Jacquard loom. Controlled by a series of cards with holes punched in them, these looms could automatically weave complicated patterns in fabrics. This gave Babbage an idea for a similar machine that could be used to solve math problems.

13   People called his ideas "thinking machines," but few really understood how they would work. Ada was an **exception**. She asked for copies of the plans so she could study them. Babbage, in turn, was impressed by Ada. He called her "The Enchantress of Numbers." They took long walks together, discussing science and math.

14   When she was 20, Ada married the Earl of Lovelace, a gentleman approved by her mom. He was a bit of an inventor

BABBAGE'S THINKING MACHINES

Charles Babbage was not the first to make a machine to add up numbers—this idea had been around since the ancient Greeks. But Babbage took it to a whole new level.

His first machine, called the Difference Engine, could add, subtract, multiply, and divide. Ada was fascinated by the way it looked—like the inside of a clock, but bigger, with hundreds of gears and levers.

Babbage's second machine, the Analytical Engine, was something entirely new. It had many different parts to do different kinds of math.

It could store numbers and transfer them between different parts of the machine. It could be programmed to do any kind of math problem, even algebra. A series of punched cards would control what the machine did and in what order by blocking different gears and levers. Changing the cards changed what the machine did. In fact, it was like a modern computer in many ways.

Unfortunately, Babbage never managed to completely build either of his machines. But in 1991 the Science Museum of London used his plans to build a Difference Engine—and it worked!

Babbage kept this small part of the Difference Engine on a table in his home to show people how it worked. The whole machine would have been the size of a car, with 25,000 parts.

Use context clues or indicate another strategy you used that helped you determine meaning.

exception (ehk SEHP shuhn) *n*.

MEANING:

---

3. **steam engines and gas lamps** During the Industrial Revolution, engines that were powered by steam and lamps that used gas to stay lit were new inventions.

himself. Having three children didn't slow Ada down. She kept up her math studies and visited Babbage whenever she could.

15   Meanwhile, Babbage was having a lot of trouble raising money to build his complicated machines. "A very costly toy ... worthless," sniffed the prime minster. Without funds, Babbage's work stalled.

Ada Sees the Future

16   In 1842 Babbage went to Italy to give a talk about his machines. An Italian engineer wrote an article about it in French—a language that Ada knew. Babbage asked her to translate the article into English and invited her to add her own notes.

17   Ada's notes ended up being much longer than the original article! She explained exactly how the new Analytical Engine worked and what made it different—a challenge that had defeated other scientists.

18   Ada did get frustrated—"I am in much dismay at having got into so amazing a quagmire[4] & botheration with these Numbers," she wrote in one letter to Babbage. But she stuck to it until she understood. She even wrote out a set of rules for it to use to solve an algebra problem—an early version of a computer program. It would weave "algebraical patterns just as the Jacquard loom weaves flowers and leaves," she wrote.

19   Then she leaped ahead of Babbage. She saw that the machine might be able to do a lot more than crunch numbers. "It can do whatever we *know how to order it* to perform," she declared. She envisioned all kinds of uses, from writing new music to figuring out how much fabric to buy for a gown. She was talking about the modern computer in a way no one else was at the time. It was all about information, not just numbers. It was an imaginative leap worthy of her poet father.

20   When the notes were published, she felt satisfied that at 28 she had at last become "a completely *professional* person."

21   Unfortunately, Ada's later life was mostly unhappy. She tried to use math to bet on horse races and lost a lot of money. Often ill, she finally died of cancer at the young age of 36. At her own request, Ada was buried in the Byron family vault, beside the father she had never known.

22   It took almost 100 years for Ada's and Babbage's ideas to catch on. In the 1940s, the first modern computers were built using much quicker electric signals instead of gears—but as Ada had envisioned, they could do much more than just math. And when the United States Department of Defense created a new computer language in 1980, they called it Ada, in honor of the **visionary** Countess Ada Lovelace.

Use context clues or indicate another strategy you used that helped you determine meaning.

visionary (VIHZH uh nehr ee) *adj.*

MEANING:

---

4. **quagmire** (KWAG myr) *n.* confusing situation with no clear answer.

 **NOTEBOOK**

Response

1. **Personal Connections** Early in her life, Ada Lovelace decided she was a "genius." Do you think we can decide things about ourselves and make them true? Explain.

> Work on your own to answer the questions in your notebook. Use text evidence to support your responses.

Comprehension

2. **Reading Check** **(a)** Why does Ada's mother discourage her daughter's interest in poetry? **(b)** What sparks Ada's interest in human flight? **(c)** What new way of thinking about mathematical machines does Ada imagine?

3. **Strategy: Make Predictions** Cite at least one prediction you made about this selection based on its structure and text features. Were you able to confirm your prediction or did you have to correct it?

Analysis and Discussion

4. **Analyze** Cite two aspects of Ada's childhood that lead to her interests in science and technology. Explain your answer.

5. **(a) Make Inferences** Reread paragraphs 7–9. How would you describe Ada's personality? Which text evidence supports your inference? **(b) Analyze** How did Ada's personality reflect the influences of both her parents?

6. **Interpret** Explain what Ada means in paragraph 18 when she describes Babbage's machine weaving "algebraic patterns just as the Jacquard loom weaves flowers and leaves."

7. **Get Ready for Close Reading** Choose a passage from the text that you find especially interesting or important. You'll discuss the passage with your group during Close-Read activities.

> **WORKING AS A GROUP**
> Discuss your responses to the Analysis and Discussion questions with your group.
> - Note agreements and disagreements.
> - Summarize insights.
> - Consider changes of opinion.
>
> If necessary, revise your original answers to reflect what you learn from your discussion.

EQ Notes **What drives people to explore?**

What have you learned about exploration from reading this biography? Go to your Essential Question Notes and record your observations and thoughts about "Ada and the Thinking Machines".

 TEKS

5.C. Make, correct, or confirm predictions using text features, characteristics of genre, and structures.

6.A. Describe personal connections to a variety of sources including self-selected texts.

6.C. Use text evidence to support an appropriate response.

ADA AND THE THINKING
MACHINES

Close Read

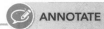

PRACTICE Complete the following activities.
Use text evidence to support your responses.

1. **Present and Discuss** With your group, share the passages from the biography that you found especially interesting. Discuss what you notice, the questions you have, and the conclusions you reach. For example, you might focus on the following:

   • **Paragraphs 13–16:** Discuss Ada and Babbage's professional relationship and what each gained from it.

   • **Paragraph 19:** Discuss how Ada "leaped ahead" of Babbage.

2. **Reflect on Your Learning** What new ideas or insights did you uncover during your second reading of the text?

WORD NETWORK

Add words that are related to the idea of exploration from the text to your Word Network.

NOTEBOOK

LANGUAGE STUDY

Concept Vocabulary

Why These Words? The vocabulary words are related.

| rebelliousness | exception | visionary |

1. With your group, determine what the words have in common. Write your ideas.

2. Add another word that fits the category. _____

3. Use the vocabulary words to complete the paragraph. Use each word only once.

   A _____ person, such as a great artist or scientist, may be misunderstood. Often, such people have a _____ that makes others uneasy. Where everyone else follows the rules, they see the _____.

Word Study

Latin Root: -vis- The Latin root -vis-/-vid- means "see, look at." It forms the basis of the vocabulary word *visionary*.

PRACTICE Complete each item.

1. Explain how the meaning of *visionary* involves the idea of sight.

2. Explain how the root contributes to the meanings of the following words: *visit, video, revise.*

TEKS
2.C. Determine the meaning and usage of grade-level academic English words derived from Greek and Latin roots such as *mis/mit, bene, man, vac, scrib/script,* and *jur/jus.*

9.C. Analyze the author's use of print and graphic features to achieve specific purposes.

Genre / Text Elements

Print and Graphic Features In this biography, the author uses a variety of **print and graphic features** that serve specific purposes.

Subheads: text that is visually set apart and identifies the focus of specific sections

Images: paintings or photographs that depict people, places, or things

Captions: explanatory text that goes with a photograph or other image

Sidebar: mini-article or feature about a related topic that is visually set off from the main article

NOTEBOOK

INTERACTIVITY

PRACTICE Work on your own to answer the questions. Then, share your responses with your group.

1. **Connect** In the chart, list the three subheads used in the article. Explain how each subhead connects to the information that appears after it.

SUBHEAD	CONNECTION TO CONTENT

2. **Analyze** If you wanted to find information related to Ada Lovelace's influence on later generations, which subhead would guide you to the right details? Explain.

3. **(a)** What is the topic of the sidebar that accompanies the main article? **(b) Connect** How does this topic relate to the main article? **(c) Evaluate** What purpose does the sidebar serve? Explain.

4. **(a)** List the subjects of the three images that appear in the article, including the sidebar. **(b) Analyze** What purpose is served by the inclusion of these particular images? Explain.

ADA AND THE THINKING MACHINES

Conventions

Conjunctive Adverbs **Conjunctive adverbs** are words that join independent clauses. They are used as transitions, connecting complete ideas by indicating comparisons, contrasts, results, and other relationships.

TYPE OF CONNECTION	EXAMPLE CONJUNCTIVE ADVERBS
add information	additionally furthermore
show comparison	likewise comparatively
show contrast	however otherwise
indicate time	meanwhile subsequently
show cause or effect	consequently therefore
add emphasis	certainly indeed

Conjunctive adverbs can be used at the beginning, middle, or end of an independent clause, but the beginning or middle is preferable. Punctuation is required both before and after conjunctive adverbs. Notice the correct punctuation in these examples:

Beginning: _Indeed_, Ada Lovelace should be more famous.

Middle: Babbage's machines were never used; _however_, they are still important inventions.

> **TIP:** When two independent clauses are connected, a semicolon comes before the conjunctive adverb and a comma comes after it. Otherwise, only a comma follows the conjunctive adverb.

 ANNOTATE — NOTEBOOK

READ IT

1. Reread paragraph 5 of the biography. Mark the conjunctive adverb. Explain the type of connection between ideas it indicates.

2. Reread paragraph 15. Mark the conjunctive adverb. Explain the type of connection between ideas it indicates.

WRITE IT Work on your own to write a paragraph in which you describe a sequence of events. Do not use conjunctive adverbs. When you finish, switch papers with a partner. Edit each other's paragraphs to include appropriate conjunctive adverbs. Make sure to use proper punctuation before and after each conjunctive adverb you add.

TEKS

1.B. Follow and give oral instructions that include multiple action steps.

10.D.iii. Edit drafts using standard English conventions, including conjunctive adverbs.

10.D.viii. Edit drafts using standard English conventions, including punctuation marks, including commas in complex sentences, transitions, and introductory elements.

Speaking and Listening

Oral instructions are an organized set of steps that a speaker explains to one or more listeners to help them accomplish a specific task.

ASSIGNMENT

When Ada Lovelace was twelve years old, she designed a set of wings using paper and wire. With your group, deliver **oral instructions** about how to make your own set of wings. Then, follow the oral instructions other groups deliver. Choose one of these options:

○ build wings using materials on-hand

○ use software to design and print wings

○ design a set of wings directly on poster board or paper

Identify the Steps First, work together to find wing designs you like and to choose one. Then, using the design you chose, write instructions that clearly spell out how to make a set of wings:

- Provide a list of materials.
- List each step on its own line.
- Start each step with an action word, such as "twist" or "trace."
- Write in a positive way. For example, instead of saying "don't curve the wire," say "keep the wire straight."

Test Your Instructions Before your give the instructions, make sure they are accurate by following them yourselves. Adjust any details that need to be clarified.

Give Your Instructions Consider having one or two members of your group model the process as other members give the instructions. Then, switch places so that everyone has a chance to both speak and model. Even if you are speaking rather than modeling, use gestures as needed to clarify your meaning.

Follow the Instructions When it is your turn to follow instructions, listen for key words. Notice non-verbal cues, such as gestures, that clarify how to do something. Ask for help if you don't understand.

Make a Display Make a class display of the wings all the groups made and discuss the experience.

EQ Notes Before moving on to a new selection, go to your Essential Question Notes and record any additional thoughts or observations you may have about "Ada and the Thinking Machines."

THE KING OF MAZY MAY

The selection you are about to read is an adventure story.

Reading Adventure Stories

An **adventure story** is a type of fiction in which action is one of the most important elements. Many adventure stories feature heroes on journeys and the conflicts they face along the way.

ADVENTURE STORIES

Author's Purpose
- to thrill or excite readers

Characteristics
- setting that presents physical danger and fuels conflict
- a main character who must face and overcome dangers
- one or more characters that threaten or attempt to thwart the hero
- an action-filled plot that moves at a fast pace
- dialogue that reveals characters' personalities and propels the action

Structure
- plot is centered around a conflict that involves danger or violence
- plot involves a journey or quest to accomplish a goal

TEKS

7.C. Analyze plot elements, including rising action, climax, falling action, resolution, and non-linear elements such as flashback.

8.A. Demonstrate knowledge of literary genres such as realistic fiction, adventure stories, historical fiction, mysteries, humor, and myths.

Take a Minute!

 NOTEBOOK

LIST IT Many action films may be considered adventure stories. Name three movies you have seen that might be categorized as adventure stories and explain why.

Genre / Text Elements

Elements of Plot To *plot* something is to plan it: Who will be there, what do we expect to happen, when will it happen, where will it happen, and why is it important? A story's **plot** is a series of related events that unfolds around a conflict.

Here are the basic elements of plot and how they engage readers:

> **TIP** There is no set length for any plot element: A story's exposition, for example, could be very short or even skipped, plunging readers directly into the action.

PLOT ELEMENTS	READER ENGAGEMENT
Exposition: Like the opening shots of a movie, the exposition orients readers to the setting and characters.	*"Where are we? Who lives here?"*
Rising Action: Things start to happen as the story's main conflict becomes evident. Events escalate the conflict.	*"Which characters are friends? Which are enemies?"*
Climax: This is the part of the story when suspense is at its highest. The climax ends when readers learn the outcome of the conflict.	*"Who will win? Will good triumph over evil?"*
Falling Action: These are the events that take place after the climax, when the immediate threat is over.	*"Is everyone safe? Will life return to normal?"*
Resolution: Final part of the story; we learn how any lingering minor issues have been resolved.	*"Is there a happy ending for all? Has justice been served?"*

 INTERACTIVITY

PRACTICE The plot events shown here are out of order. Read each passage and identify its correct order. Then, write the plot element each passage represents. The first item has been done for you.

SUMMARIZED PASSAGE	ORDER OF EVENTS	PLOT ELEMENT
The lead bandit, Marcus, crept into the mine and grabbed sacks of gold. Manny fell and was unable to stop him.	1 ②3 4 5	*rising action*
The valley was at peace. Never again would they be troubled by gold bandits.	1 2 3 4 5	
The sun rose on the sleepy mountain village. Manny waited impatiently for the day to begin so he could start his mission.	1 2 3 4 5	
Exhausted, Manny used his last ounce of strength and captured Marcus for good.	1 2 3 4 5	
Triumphant, Manny left the scene of the fight to find his family and tell them the happy news.	1 2 3 4 5	

About the Author

Jack London (1876–1916) was born in San Francisco and led an adventurous life, pirating oysters, riding freight trains around the U.S., and traveling to Japan as a sailor. At 17, he won a writing contest and decided to make writing his career. His adventure novels *White Fang* and *The Call of the Wild* are among the most popular adventure stories of all time.

The King of Mazy May

Concept Vocabulary

 ANNOTATE

As you read "The King of Mazy May," you will encounter these words.

endured	perilously	suspense

Print Resources You can use a dictionary to look up the meaning, syllabication, pronunciation, part of speech, and word origin of an unfamiliar word. Here's an example entry for *hybrid:*

> **SAMPLE DICTIONARY ENTRY**
>
> entry   pronunciation/   part of
> word   syllabication   speech   definition   context sentence
>
> **hybrid** (HY brid) *noun* **1.** a thing made by combining two different elements; a mixture. *"Did you know that a pluot is a hybrid created from a mixture of plum and apricot?"*
> ***Word Origin:*** early 17th c. (as a noun): from Latin *hybrida*

PRACTICE As you read, use a dictionary to determine the meanings of unfamiliar words. Mark your findings in the open space next to the text.

Comprehension Strategy

 NOTEBOOK

Make Predictions

Predictions are a type of guess you make about events that will happen later in a story. You can use the characteristics of the genre you are reading to make predictions. For example, adventure stories like this one feature certain kinds of conflicts.

 TEKS

2.A. Use print or digital resources to determine the meaning, syllabication, pronunciation, word origin, and part of speech.

5.I. Monitor comprehension and make adjustments such as re-reading, using background knowledge, asking questions, and annotating when understanding breaks down.

PASSAGE	GENRE CHARACTERISTIC	SAMPLE PREDICTION
Alida shot out of the water as if propelled by a rocket. She gasped for air, and then dived under again. She *had* to get the locked chest up from the lake bottom before it was too late.	Conflicts in adventure stories involve both physical threats and characters' emotions.	Alida will find a way to retrieve the locked chest.

PRACTICE As you read, write predictions in the open space next to the text. Read on and decide whether the story fulfills the predictions you made based on genre characteristics. If it does, confirm your predictions. If it doesn't, correct your predictions.

The King of Mazy May

Jack London

BACKGROUND

In 1896, a group of men discovered gold near the Klondike River, located in the Yukon region of Canada. By 1897, huge swarms of adventurers seeking their fortune set out for the Klondike. However, much of the area had already been staked, or claimed by those who had arrived before them. The result? The area was stampeded, or overrun with people. Stores were left with no supplies, and those who had staked claims had to be careful that gold was not mined from right under their noses.

 AUDIO

 ANNOTATE

1   **W**alt Masters is not a very large boy, but there is manliness in his make-up, and he himself, although he does not know a great deal that most boys know, knows much that other boys do not know. He has never seen a train of cars or an elevator in his life, and for that matter, he has never once looked upon a corn-field, a plow, a cow, or even a chicken. He has never had a pair of shoes on his feet, nor gone to a picnic or a party, nor talked to a girl. But he has seen the sun at midnight, watched the ice jams on one of the mightiest of rivers, and played beneath the northern lights,[1] the one white child in thousands of square miles of frozen wilderness.

---

1. **northern lights** glowing bands or streamers of light, sometimes appearing in the night sky of the Northern Hemisphere.

Use a print dictionary or indicate another strategy that helped you determine meaning.

endured (ehn DOORD) *v.*

MEANING:

2   Walt has walked all the fourteen years of his life in sun tanned, moose-hide moccasins, and he can go to the Indian camps and "talk big" with the men, and trade calico and beads with them for their precious furs. He can make bread without baking powder, yeast, or hops, shoot a moose at three hundred yards, and drive the wild wolf dogs fifty miles a day on the packed trail.

3   Last of all, he has a good heart, and is not afraid of the darkness and loneliness, of man or beast or thing. His father is a good man, strong and brave, and Walt is growing up like him.

4   Walt was born a thousand miles or so down the Yukon,[2] in a trading post below the Ramparts. After his mother died, his father and he came on up the river, step by step, from camp to camp, till now they are settled down on the Mazy May Creek in the Klondike country. Last year they and several others had spent much toil and time on the Mazy May, and **endured** great hardships; the creek, in turn, was just beginning to show up its richness and to reward them for their heavy labor. But with the news of their discoveries, strange men began to come and go through the short days and long nights, and many unjust things they did to the men who had worked so long upon the creek.

5   Si Hartman had gone away on a moose hunt, to return and find new stakes driven and his claim jumped.[3] George Lukens and his brother had lost their claims in a like manner, having delayed too long on the way to Dawson to record them. In short, it was the old story, and quite a number of the earnest, industrious prospectors had suffered similar losses.

6   But Walt Masters's father had recorded his claim at the start, so Walt had nothing to fear now that his father had gone on a short trip up the White River prospecting for quartz. Walt was well able to stay by himself in the cabin, cook his three meals a day, and look after things. Not only did he look after his father's claim, but he had agreed to keep an eye on the adjoining one of Loren Hall, who had started for Dawson to record it.

7   Loren Hall was an old man, and he had no dogs, so he had to travel very slowly. After he had been gone some time, word came up the river that he had broken through the ice at Rosebud Creek and frozen his feet so badly that he would not be able to travel for a couple of weeks. Then Walt Masters received the news that old Loren was nearly all right again, and about to move on afoot for Dawson as fast as a weakened man could.

---

2. **Yukon** (YOO kahn) river flowing through the Yukon Territory of northwest Canada.
3. **claim jumped** A claim is a piece of land marked with stakes by a miner to show where the borders are. A jumped claim is one that has been stolen by someone else.

8   Walt was worried, however; the claim was liable to be jumped at any moment because of this delay, and a fresh stampede had started in on the Mazy May. He did not like the looks of the newcomers, and one day, when five of them came by with crack dog teams and the lightest of camping outfits, he could see that they were prepared to make speed, and resolved to keep an eye on them. So he locked up the cabin and followed them, being at the same time careful to remain hidden.

9   He had not watched them long before he was sure that they were professional stampeders, bent on jumping all the claims in sight. Walt crept along the snow at the rim of the creek and saw them change many stakes, destroy old ones, and set up new ones.

10   In the afternoon, with Walt always trailing on their heels, they came back down the creek, unharnessed their dogs, and went into camp within two claims of his cabin. When he saw them make preparations to cook, he hurried home to get something to eat himself, and then hurried back. He crept so close that he could hear them talking quite plainly, and by pushing the underbrush aside he could catch occasional glimpses of them. They had finished eating and were smoking around the fire.

11   "The creek is all right, boys," a large, black-bearded man, evidently the leader, said, "and I think the best thing we can do is to pull out to-night. The dogs can follow the trail; besides, it's going to be moonlight. What say you?"

12   "But it's going to be beastly cold," objected one of the party. "It's forty below zero now."

13   "An' sure, can't ye keep warm by jumpin' off the sleds an' runnin' after the dogs?" cried an Irishman. "An' who wouldn't? The creek's as rich as a United States mint! Faith, it's an ilegant chanst to be gettin' a run fer yer money! An' if ye don't run, it's mebbe you'll not get the money at all, at all."

14   "That's it," said the leader. "If we can get to Dawson and record, we're rich men; and there's no telling who's been sneaking along in our tracks, watching us, and perhaps now off to give the alarm. The thing for us to do is to rest the dogs a bit, and then hit the trail as hard as we can. What do you say?"

15   Evidently the men had agreed with their leader, for Walt Masters could hear nothing but the rattle of the tin dishes which were being washed. Peering out cautiously, he could see the leader studying a piece of paper. Walt knew what it was at a glance—a list of all the unrecorded claims on Mazy May. Any man could get these lists by applying to the gold commissioner at Dawson.

16   "Thirty-two," the leader said, lifting his face to the men. "Thirty-two isn't recorded, and this is thirty-three. Come on; let's take a look at it. I saw somebody had been working on it when we came up this morning."

17   Three of the men went with him, leaving one to remain in camp. Walt crept carefully after them till they came to Loren Hall's shaft. One of the men went down and built a fire on the bottom to thaw out the frozen gravel, while the others built another fire on the dump and melted water in a couple of gold pans. This they poured into a piece of canvas stretched between two logs, used by Loren Hall in which to wash his gold.

18   In a short time, a couple of buckets of dirt were sent up by the man in the shaft, and Walt could see the others grouped anxiously about their leader as he proceeded to wash it. When this was finished, they stared at the broad streak of black sand and yellow gold grains on the bottom of the pan, and one of them called excitedly for the man who had remained in camp to come. Loren Hall had struck it rich and his claim was not yet recorded. It was plain that they were going to jump it.

19   Walt lay in the snow, thinking rapidly. He was only a boy, but in the face of the threatened injustice to old lame Loren Hall he felt that he must do something. He waited and watched, with his mind made up, till he saw the men begin to square up new stakes. Then he crawled away till out of hearing, and broke into a run for

the camp of the stampeders. Walt's father had taken their own dogs with him prospecting, and the boy knew how impossible it was for him to undertake the seventy miles to Dawson without the aid of dogs.

20   Gaining the camp, he picked out, with an experienced eye, the easiest running sled and started to harness up the stampeders' dogs. There were three teams of six each, and from these he chose ten of the best. Realizing how necessary it was to have a good head dog, he strove to discover a leader amongst them; but he had little time in which to do it, for he could hear the voices of the returning men. By the time the team was in shape and everything ready, the claim-jumpers came into sight in an open place not more than a hundred yards from the trail, which ran down the bed of the creek. They cried out to Walt, but instead of giving heed to them he grabbed up one of their fur sleeping robes, which lay loosely in the snow, and leaped upon the sled.

21   "Mush! Hi! Mush on!" he cried to the animals, snapping the keen-lashed whip among them.

22   The dogs sprang against the yoke straps, and the sled jerked under way so suddenly as to almost throw him off. Then it curved into the creek, poising **perilously** on the runner. He was almost breathless with **suspense**, when it finally righted with a bound and sprang ahead again. The creek bank was high and he could not see the men, although he could hear their cries and knew they were running to cut him off. He did not dare to think what would happen if they caught him; he just clung to the sled, his heart beating wildly, and watched the snow rim of the bank above him.

23   Suddenly, over this snow rim came the flying body of the Irishman, who had leaped straight for the sled in a desperate attempt to capture it; but he was an instant too late. Striking on the very rear of it, he was thrown from his feet, backward, into the snow. Yet, with the quickness of a cat, he had clutched the end of the sled with one hand, turned over, and was dragging behind on his breast, swearing at the boy and threatening all kinds of terrible things if he did not stop the dogs; but Walt cracked him sharply across the knuckles with the butt of the dog whip till he let go.

24   It was eight miles from Walt's claim to the Yukon—eight very crooked miles, for the creek wound back and forth like a snake, "tying knots in itself," as George Lukens said. And because it was so crooked, the dogs could not get up their best speed, while the sled ground heavily on its side against the curves, now to the right, now to the left.

25   Travelers who had come up and down the Mazy May on foot, with packs on their backs, had declined to go round all the bends,

Use a print dictionary or indicate another strategy that helped you determine meaning.

perilously (PEHR uh luhs lee) *adv.*

MEANING:

suspense (suh SPEHNS) *n.*

MEANING:

and instead had made shortcuts across the narrow necks of creek bottom. Two of his pursuers had gone back to harness the remaining dogs, but the others took advantage of these shortcuts, running on foot, and before he knew it they had almost overtaken him.

26 "Halt!" they cried after him. "Stop, or we'll shoot!"

27 But Walt only yelled the harder at the dogs, and dashed around the bend with a couple of revolver bullets singing after him. At the next bend they had drawn up closer still, and the bullets struck uncomfortably near him but at this point the Mazy May straightened out and ran for half a mile as the crow flies. Here the dogs stretched out in their long wolf swing, and the stampeders, quickly winded, slowed down and waited for their own sled to come up.

28 Looking over his shoulder, Walt reasoned that they had not given up the chase for good, and that they would soon be after him again. So he wrapped the fur robe about him to shut out the stinging air, and lay flat on the empty sled, encouraging the dogs, as he well knew how.

29 At last, twisting abruptly between two river islands, he came upon the mighty Yukon sweeping grandly to the north. He could not see from bank to bank, and in the quick-falling twilight it loomed a great white sea of frozen stillness. There was not a sound, save the breathing of the dogs, and the churn of the steel-shod sled.

30 No snow had fallen for several weeks, and the traffic had packed the main river trail till it was hard and glassy as glare ice. Over this the sled flew along, and the dogs kept the trail fairly well, although Walt quickly discovered that he had made a mistake in choosing the leader. As they were driven in single file, without reins, he had to guide them by his voice, and it was evident the head dog had never learned the meaning of "gee" and "haw." He hugged the inside of the curves too closely, often forcing his comrades behind him into the soft snow, while several times he thus capsized the sled.

31 There was no wind, but the speed at which he traveled created a bitter blast, and with the thermometer down to forty below, this bit through fur and flesh to the very bones. Aware that if he remained constantly upon the sled he would freeze to death, and knowing the practice of Arctic travelers, Walt shortened up one of the lashing thongs, and whenever he felt chilled, seized hold of it, jumped off, and ran behind till warmth was restored. Then he would climb on and rest till the process had to be repeated.

32 Looking back he could see the sled of his pursuers, drawn by eight dogs, rising and falling over the ice hummocks like a boat in a seaway. The Irishman and the black-bearded leader were with it, taking turns in running and riding.

33   Night fell, and in the blackness of the first hour or so Walt toiled desperately with his dogs. On account of the poor lead dog, they were continually floundering off the beaten track into the soft snow, and the sled was as often riding on its side or top as it was in the proper way. This work and strain tried his strength sorely. Had he not been in such haste he could have avoided much of it, but he feared the stampeders would creep up in the darkness and overtake him. However, he could hear them yelling to their dogs, and knew from the sounds that they were coming up very slowly.

34   When the moon rose he was off Sixty Mile, and Dawson was only fifty miles away. He was almost exhausted, and breathed a sigh of relief as he climbed on the sled again. Looking back, he saw his enemies had crawled up within four hundred yards. At this space they remained, a black speck of motion on the white river breast. Strive as they would, they could not shorten this distance, and strive as he would, he could not increase it.

35   Walt had now discovered the proper lead dog, and he knew he could easily run away from them if he could only change the bad leader for the good one. But this was impossible, for a moment's delay, at the speed they were running, would bring the men behind upon him.

36   When he was off the mouth of Rosebud Creek, just as he was topping a rise, the report of a gun and ping of a bullet on the ice beside him told him that they were this time shooting at him with a rifle. And from then on, as he cleared the summit of each ice jam, he stretched flat on the leaping sled till the rifle shot from the rear warned him that he was safe till the next ice jam was reached.

37   Now it is very hard to lie on a moving sled, jumping and plunging and yawing[4] like a boat before the wind, and to shoot through the deceiving moonlight at an object four hundred yards away on another moving sled performing equally wild antics. So it is not to be wondered at that the black-bearded leader did not hit him.

38   After several hours of this, during which, perhaps, a score of bullets had struck about him, their ammunition began to give out and their fire slackened. They took greater care, and only whipped a shot at him at the most favorable opportunities. He was also leaving them behind, the distance slowly increasing to six hundred yards.

39   Lifting clear on the crest of a great jam off Indian River, Walt Masters met with his first accident. A bullet sang past his ears, and struck the bad lead dog.

40   The poor brute plunged in a heap, with the rest of the team on top of him.

---

4. **yawing** (YAW ihng) *v.* moving from side to side.

The King of Mazy May **561**

41   Like a flash Walt was by the leader. Cutting the traces[5] with his hunting knife, he dragged the dying animal to one side and straightened out the team.

42   He glanced back. The other sled was coming up like an express train. With half the dogs still over their traces, he cried, "Mush on!" and leaped upon the sled just as the pursuers dashed abreast of him.

43   The Irishman was just preparing to spring for him—they were so sure they had him that they did not shoot—when Walt turned fiercely upon them with his whip.

44   He struck at their faces, and men must save their faces with their hands. So there was no shooting just then. Before they could recover from the hot rain of blows, Walt reached out from his sled, catching their wheel dog by the forelegs in midspring, and throwing him heavily. This brought snarled the team, capsizing the sled and tangling his enemies up beautifully.

45   Away Walt flew, the runners of his sled fairly screaming as they bounded over the frozen surface. And what had seemed an accident proved to be a blessing in disguise. The proper lead dog was now to the fore, and he stretched low and whined with joy as he jerked his comrades along.

46   By the time he reached Ainslie's Creek, seventeen miles from Dawson, Walt had left his pursuers, a tiny speck, far behind. At Monte Cristo Island, he could no longer see them. And at Swede Creek, just as daylight was silvering the pines, he ran plump into the camp of old Loren Hall.

47   Almost as quick as it takes to tell it, Loren had his sleeping furs rolled up, and had joined Walt on the sled. They permitted the dogs to travel more slowly, as there was no sign of the chase in the rear, and just as they pulled up at the gold commissioner's office in Dawson, Walt, who had kept his eyes open to the last, fell asleep.

48   And because of what Walt Masters did on this night, the men of the Yukon have become very proud of him, and speak of him now as the King of Mazy May.

---

5. **traces** (TRAY sihz) *n.* leather straps that connect sled dogs together, and to the sled.

Response

NOTEBOOK

1. Personal Connections Would you enjoy Walt's way of life? Why or why not?

> Work on your own to answer the questions in your notebook. Use text evidence to support your responses.

Comprehension

2. Reading Check (a) What special skills does Walt possess? **(b)** What made the stampeders excited about Loren's claim? **(c)** Why does Walt steal the stampeders' dogs and sled?

3. Strategy: Make Predictions (a) What adventure story characteristics did you apply to make predictions? Give two examples. **(b)** Were you able to confirm your predictions, or did you have to correct them?

Analysis and Discussion

4. Analyze Name three adjectives that describe Walt. Use text evidence to support your response.

5. (a) Make Inferences What can you infer about Walt's father? Support your inferences with evidence. **(b) Speculate** Based on your inferences about Walt and his father, how do you think his father would react to hearing the story about Walt's adventure?

6. (a) Connect Why do the men of the Yukon start referring to Walt as "The King of Mazy May"? **(b) Make a Judgment** Is that title well earned? Why or why not?

7. Get Ready for Close Reading Choose a passage from the text that you find especially interesting or important. You'll discuss the passage with your group during Close-Read activities.

> ## WORKING AS A GROUP
> Discuss your responses to the Analysis and Discussion questions with your group. Work together to make sure everyone comes to a deeper understanding of the text. Ask your teacher for guidance if you need it.

EQ Notes **What drives people to explore?**

What have you learned about exploration from reading this story? Go to your Essential Question Notes and record your observations and thoughts about "The King of Mazy May."

 TEKS

5.C. Make, correct, or confirm predictions using text features, characteristics of genre, and structures.

6.A. Describe personal connections to a variety of sources including self-selected texts.

6.C. Use text evidence to support an appropriate response.

6.G. Discuss and write about the explicit or implicit meanings of text.

THE KING OF MAZY MAY

Close Read

PRACTICE Complete the following activities.
Use text evidence to support your responses.

1. **Present and Discuss** With your group, share the passages from the story that you found especially interesting. Discuss what you notice, the questions you have, and the conclusions you reach. For example, you might focus on the following passages:

   • Paragraph 1: Discuss the effectiveness of the author's decision to introduce Walt by comparing his knowledge to that of other boys his age.

   • Paragraph 22: Discuss London's choice of verbs in this paragraph and their effect.

   • Paragraphs 29–30: Discuss London's description of the trail and the effect it has on readers' abilities to form mental pictures.

2. **Reflect on Your Learning** What new ideas or insights did you uncover during your second reading of the text?

WORD NETWORK

Add words that are related to the idea of exploration from the text to your Word Network.

LANGUAGE STUDY

NOTEBOOK

Concept Vocabulary

Why These Words? The vocabulary words are related.

| endured | perilously | suspense |

1. With your group, discuss what the words have in common. Write your ideas.

2. Add another word that fits the category. _____

3. Write a sentence for each concept vocabulary word in which the meaning of the word is evident. Exchange sentences with your group.

Word Study

Latin Root: -pend- Develop your vocabulary by learning word roots. For example, the word *suspense* is built on the Latin root *-pend-*, which means "to hang." A person in suspense is "left hanging" until a problem is resolved. Work with your group to find the meanings of these words containing the root *-pend-*: *pendant; appendage; depend.* Figure out what resources might give you the right information, and consult your teacher if you need help.

 TEKS

2.C. Determine the meaning and usage of grade-level academic English words derived from Greek and Latin roots such as *mis/mit, bene, man, vac, scrib/script,* and *jur/jus.*

6.F. Respond using newly acquired vocabulary as appropriate.

7.C. Analyze plot elements, including rising action, climax, falling action, resolution, and non-linear elements such as flashback.

Genre / Text Elements

Plot and Conflict Reading an adventure story, like "The King of Mazy May," is like going on an adventure along with the story's main character. The plot moves quickly, and most of the story centers around actions that fuel or escalate the conflict. Adventure stories often feature these two types of conflict: person versus person, and person versus nature.

Once you finish reading a story, analyze it to understand what the writer did to generate excitement and suspense.

> **TIP:** The **protagonist** of a story is the hero, the character you root for. The **antagonist** is the character or force of nature that conflicts with the protagonist.

 NOTEBOOK

INTERACTIVITY

PRACTICE Work alone to complete the chart. Then, work with a partner to answer the questions.

1. Note which paragraphs from the story correspond to each plot segment, and briefly summarize each section.

PLOT SEGMENT	MY NOTES
Exposition	
Rising Action	
Climax	
Falling Action	
Resolution	

2. (a) Analyze What is the main conflict in "The King of Mazy May"?
(b) Analyze Cause and Effect How does the story's conflict begin and then drive the events of the plot? Use text evidence in your answer.

3. Analyze (a) When does the climax of the story occur? Explain.
(b) What events happen during the story's falling action?

4. Evaluate Does the story's resolution provide a satisfying end to Walt's adventure? Why or why not?

THE KING OF MAZY MAY

Research

An **informational report** provides facts and details that increase readers' knowledge and offer insight into a topic.

With your group, prepare a coherent **informational report** about the Klondike Gold Rush that Jack London personally experienced and in which he set his stories. Choose one of the following options:

○ **physical challenges:** difficulties prospectors faced from the Klondike environment

○ **social dimensions:** impact the Klondike Gold Rush had on people in the area's small towns

You may choose to deliver your findings as a written report, an oral talk, or a multimodal presentation that includes audio or video.

TIP: A specific example of a primary source related to the gold rush would be a newspaper article about a prospector's death from the cold. An example of a secondary source would be a biography of a Klondike prospector.

Find Primary and Secondary Sources Locate a variety of sources to make your report balanced, accurate, and interesting. Differentiate between these two types of sources in your search:

• **Primary sources** are documents, letters, diaries, recordings, and other items from a historical moment. They provide a firsthand look at the period.

• **Secondary sources** are articles and books written by later historians.

Use the chart to record your sources.

PRIMARY SOURCES	SECONDARY SOURCES

Synthesize Research Synthesize the information you gather by using evidence to support your own insights. For example, think about what the sources tell you about the lives of prospectors: what would the process of panning for gold have felt like?

Draft and Deliver a Coherent Report Regardless of your choice of delivery, make sure your report is coherent, which means that it holds together and conveys a unified message. Make sure every paragraph builds toward a main idea, and that every sentence belongs in the paragraph. Use transitions to clarify connections within and across paragraphs.

⊕ TEKS

11.D. Compose correspondence that reflects an opinion, registers a complaint, or requests information in a business or friendly structure.

12.D. Identify and gather relevant information from a variety of sources.

12.E. Differentiate between primary and secondary sources.

12.F. Synthesize information from a variety of sources.

12.J. Use an appropriate mode of delivery, whether written, oral, or multimodal, to present results.

Composition

A **business letter** is a letter between two companies or between an organization and a customer or client.

ASSIGNMENT

The Department of Resources, Government of Yukon is the office that regulates gold-mining claims. Work with a partner to write a **business letter** to this office in which you do one of the following:

- Request information about how to register a claim. Include details about the location of your claim and the reason you need to register it.

- Register a complaint about the claim jumpers who have come to Mazy May. Include a suggestion to resolve the problem.

You may write in either your own voice, or from Walt's point of view. Include details from the story to add to its authenticity.

Plan With your partner, decide which letter you'd like to write. Then, look up story details you'd like to include.

Draft Model your letter after the sample template shown here. Remember to use more formal language than you would in a letter to a friend. Address the recipient as *Mr., Mrs., Miss,* or *Sir* or *Madam,* and close with a polite word or phrase such as *Sincerely.*

Capitalize Correctly Even when proper nouns appear in shortened forms—such as **abbreviations** or **initials**—they are capitalized. An **acronym** is a special type of abbreviation that uses the first letters of a long term to form a pronounceable word. Even if the long form is not a proper noun, the acronym is capitalized. Follow these examples as you draft your letter.

[Your Street]
[Your City, Town, Zip]
[Date]

Department of Resources
1234 Main Street,
Mazy May, AK 54321

Dear Sir or Madam:

- Introduction: why you are writing
- Body Paragraphs: Explain important information. Give at least one paragraph to each idea.
- Conclusion: Restate your main point and thank your reader.

Sincerely yours,
[your signature]

PUBLISHING TIP: Fold your letter and put it in an envelope. Write the recipient's address in the center and your address in the upper left corner. Place your letters in a bag. Then, take turns choosing letters and reading them aloud.

TYPE OF TERM	FULL FORM	SHORTENED FORM
Proper Name	Leigh Ann Garcia	Initials: L. A. Garcia
Company Name	Yukon Gold Mining, Inc.	Abbreviation: YGM
Organization	Miners Against Stake Stealers	Acronym: MASS

from SACAJAWEA

Fiction and Nonfiction

Historical fiction is an imagined story about real historical events, settings, or people. A **graphic "novel" history** is a true account of historical events told in comic book form.

from LEWIS & CLARK

HISTORICAL FICTION

Author's Purpose
- → to tell a story that combines true historical events or settings with imagined elements

Characteristics
- → actual, historical settings, or places that could have existed in real life
- → characters who are actual historical people or modeled on them
- → conflicts based on true historical situations
- → dialogue that reflects how people spoke in the time and place of the story's action
- → theme, or deeper message

Structure
- → plot that features actual historical events or events that could have happened
- → may include imaginary events that fit in with the historical ones

GRAPHIC "NOVEL" HISTORY

Author's Purpose
- → to use comic-book format to tell a true, historically important story

Characteristics
- → real-life, historical places, people, and events
- → may include dialogue that was actually spoken
- → factual information synthesized from multiple sources
- → author's interpretation of events

Structure
- → illustrations set in panels that appear in time order
- → comic book conventions, including speech bubbles, splash screens, special effects lettering, etc.

Genre / Text Elements

Historical and Cultural Setting The **setting** of a story is the time and place in which it occurs. It includes all the details of the physical location, such as the type of place (wilderness? city?) and weather. Some stories, such as works of historical fiction, are set in specific historical and cultural places and times. These types of settings include elements that are less obvious than the physical location but just as important:

- a people's beliefs, values, traditions, and customs
- how the society is organized; what types of people have status or power and what types of people don't
- problems, such as war or poverty

These aspects of history and culture may influence the development of the characters and plot even more than the physical setting does.

EXAMPLE SETTING: ANCIENT GREECE

Value	Hospitality is the highest value.
Situation	A criminal arrives in a town. People are suspicious, but welcome him because of their value of hospitality.
Character and Plot	A child overhears the man plotting a crime, and figures out a way to trick him and get him to leave. The child becomes a leader, famous for his cleverness.

 INTERACTIVITY NOTEBOOK

PRACTICE Work on your own to read the passage and answer the questions. Share your responses with your group.

Ethan ran through the snow. The fire had gone out and he had to fetch embers from the nearest neighbor, three miles off. Still, he paused at the edge of the field. Once an apple orchard, Washington's soldiers had cut down the trees for fuel and left behind a blackened mess. Ethan remembered the tired soldiers. The cause is glorious—freedom, colonial self-rule! But the soldiers' faces were awful. The memories scared him, but he had to keep going. Ethan kept running.

1. **(a)** Mark details that show the physical setting. **(b)** Mark other details that show aspects of the historical and cultural setting.

2. **(a)** How does the historical and cultural setting influence the character? **(b)** Given this influence, what kinds of plot events might happen after this scene? Explain.

⊙ **TEKS**
7.D. Analyze how the setting, including historical and cultural settings, influences character and plot development.

Compare Fiction and Nonfiction

In this lesson, you will read a work of historical fiction that imagines real-life events from a different point of view. You will then compare the work of fiction to a work of nonfiction told in graphic-novel format.

from SACAJAWEA

from LEWIS & CLARK

About the Author

A professional storyteller and writer from New York State, **Joseph Bruchac** (b. 1942) often draws on the traditions of his Native American ancestry, the Abenaki people. He has written more than 120 books for children and adults and has performed worldwide as a teller of Native American folk tales.

from Sacajawea

Concept Vocabulary

ANNOTATE

As you read the excerpt from *Sacajawea*, you will encounter these words.

journey	seeking	scouting

Multiple-Meaning Words and Context Clues Many words have more than one meaning. To determine which meaning of a word is being used in a text, look for context clues in the surrounding words and phrases.

EXAMPLE: *Her **initial** fear of the dangerous river went away when she saw the calm, peaceful water.*

Analysis: The word *initial* can be a noun, a verb, or an adjective. Here, context clues show that it is an adjective that means "first." The person's *initial* fear goes away when she sees there is no danger.

PRACTICE As you read, use context clues to determine the meanings of any multiple-meaning words as they are used in the excerpt.

Comprehension Strategy

ANNOTATE

Monitor Comprehension

As you read a text, monitor your comprehension and make adjustments if you feel that you are missing important connections. For example, use your **background knowledge** and prior experiences to fill in details in a story that the author may not explain. Ask yourself:

- What do I know about this type of event or time in history?
- How does that knowledge help explain the situation?
- What do my own experiences tell me about the types of problems the characters face?

PRACTICE As you read, monitor your comprehension and make adjustments to better understand the characters and events. Jot down your ideas and observations in the open space next to the text.

 TEKS

2.B. Use context such as definition, analogy, and examples to clarify the meaning of words.

5.I. Monitor comprehension and make adjustments such as re-reading, using background knowledge, asking questions, and annotating when understanding breaks down.

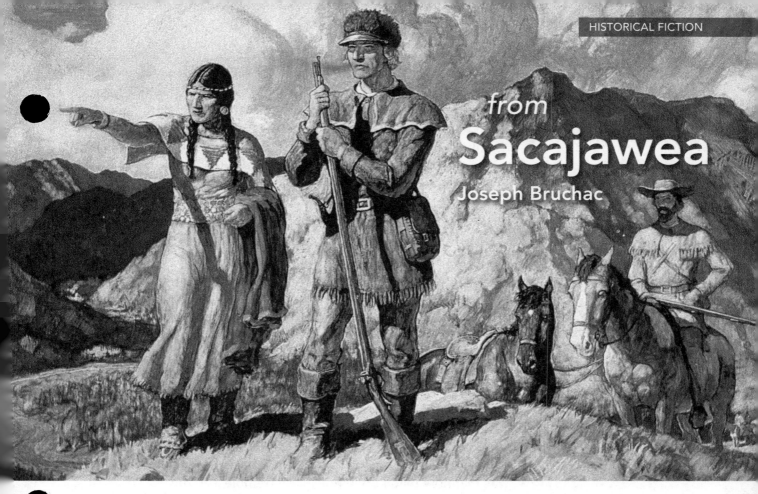

from
Sacajawea

Joseph Bruchac

BACKGROUND

The narrator of this excerpt of Bruchac's novel is Sacajawea, relating the story to her son Pomp. Sacajawea was a Shoshone interpreter on the Lewis and Clark Corps of Discovery expedition in the early 1800s, and was the only woman among the explorers. She proved invaluable in the expedition's dealings with the Shoshone, and her presence—and that of her infant son—convinced many of the other tribes they met that the explorers were not a war party.

AUDIO

ANNOTATE

Long ago, many of our people were sick. So our chiefs called on a medicine man to help them. His name was Man from the Sky. He went into his lodge, opened his medicine bundle, and prayed. When he was done, he told the people to bring all those who were sick to him. He would take them on a **journey**. *He led the people up the Snake River to a place in the hills. Then he went up the hill and tapped a rock with his stick. Healing water flowed from that rock. The people bathed in that water and grew well again.*

1   Your good uncle[1] had made himself ill. With all of his walking through the prickly pear cactus, his feet were covered with open wounds and blisters. He was so tired that it was an effort for him to stand again after he sat upon the ground. Yet he did not wish to stop. His heart told him to keep **seeking** my people, even after Captain Lewis begged him to rest.

1. **good uncle** Captain William Clark.

Use context clues or indicate another strategy you used that helped you determine meaning.

journey (JUR nee) *n.*

MEANING:

seeking (SEE kihng) *v.*

MEANING:

2   Although we had not yet found my relatives, we had come to the lands that I remembered. They were as clear in the eye of my heart as if I had slept but a single night without seeing them, even though it had been five winters. My heart pounded and it seemed as if it would burst from my chest when I first recognized a place where the river bent around a little island filled with wild onions.

3   But I could not tell if I was filled with happiness at returning home or if my heart was beating so fast because I was afraid of what I might find. What had happened to those close to my heart when the Minnetarees raided on that harsh day?[2] Were any of them still alive? Was my mother among the living? My brother, Stays Here? What of my friends? Would I ever again see the face of anyone from my childhood other than Otter Woman?

4   It had been many moons since I had seen Otter Woman. It was so long now since those nights in the Minnetaree village where we had sat with our heads close together, speaking to each other in our own language. Our language is one that your father[3] has never wished to learn.

5   There were so many questions in my mind, so many voices speaking to me from within, I could not answer them all.

6   So I showed no emotion, for I did not know what emotion it was that now made my whole body tremble as it did.

7   "This is the river on which my relations live," I told them. My voice stayed calm. "The Three Forks are no great distance from here."

8   All of them were made happy by my words. Though he was ill, your good uncle hugged me, and Captain Lewis looked at me with a brief smile and nodded his head.

9   Such a serious man, Captain Lewis was. It always seemed as if there was something that made him doubt himself, even though he was good and strong. It is not that way with your good uncle. He always knows who he is. The red of his hair is a sign of the sunshine that lives in his heart. The spirit power in his heart is his friend. It never confuses him.

10   Now I could tell them where we were going and help show them the way. The captains were so pleased that they gave me a beautiful string of the blue beads that everyone loves. I used them as a belt. I did not own that belt long, but I still remember how good it felt to my touch, how proud I was to be useful. Now I was not just the one who set up the tent, who found the good roots to eat. I was also the one who could show them the way to my people, the one who could help them get horses.

2. **that harsh day** When she was about twelve years old, Sacajawea and her friend Otter Woman were kidnapped by an enemy tribe.
3. **father** Sacajawea's husband, Toussaint Charbonneau, a French-Canadian fur trader.

11   Yes, Firstborn Son, your good uncle told you they expected this of me all along. But perhaps their hopes would not have come true. I might have been like that iron boat, unable to carry the load. Now it seemed all they hoped of me would come true. My heart was singing.

12   But we still had not met with my people.

❋ ❋ ❋

13   As we went along I showed them things. There was the creek where we got the earth from which we made our white paint. I taught them how a friend would paint the cheeks of someone he or she met. I told them that they should carry paint with them. If they ever met any of my people, they should use the vermilion paint to honor them in this way. I explained how we would greet friends. You know how it is done, Firstborn Son. We put the arms closest to our hearts around each other's shoulders, we press our cheeks together like this. And what do we say? Uh-huh. We say *"Ah-hi-e, ah-hi-e." I am so pleased, I am so pleased*.

14   They listened closely to me and nodded. But Captain Lewis needed to know something else. Captain Lewis was trying to find words to speak in other languages. Though he sometimes got them wrong, as soon as he was able to turn them into his marks on white leaves he was sure he understood perfectly.

15   "What do you call us?" Captain Lewis asked.

16   "You are the Red-Haired Captains," I answered.

17   "No," he said, looking unhappy. "That is not what I mean," he said, speaking very slowly, as if it were his words, not his question, that confused me. "All of us." He gestured with his hands. Then he looked at our little party. He motioned for York[4] to take Seaman[5] and lead him off to the side. He had your father join them. Then he made a circling motion, including him, your good uncle, and the other men who came from far away. "All of *us*," he said.

18   He wanted our word for white men. But I still could not understand. Your father looked worried. Captain Clark caught my eye. He held out one of his hands and raised an eyebrow.

19   "Janey?"[6] he said.

20   I had to say something or Captain Lewis would have been unhappy all that day. I remained silent, though, until Captain

---

4. **York** William Clark's slave who was an important member of the expedition.
5. **Seaman** Newfoundland dog that Meriwether Lews purchased in Pittsburgh to take on the expedition.
6. **Janey** nickname that William Clark gave Sacajawea.

Lewis asked one more question. He made the motion in sign language that stands for our people.

21   "What would your people, the Snakes, call us?"

22   At last I thought I understood. *"Ta-ba-bone,"* I said. *"Ta-ba-bone."* It is a word for those who are strangers, who might be enemies.

23   *"Ta-ba-bone,"* Captain Lewis said. He was very pleased. He smiled as he turned *it* into black lines on a white leaf. *"Ta-ba-bone."*

24   Despite his sickness, your good uncle kept **scouting** ahead, walking far along the shore and farther inland as we came down the river in the cottonwood canoes. Your father had sprained his ankle some days before, but he assured Captain Clark he was better now. He begged to go with him. You know how your father always wants to see something new. So your good uncle agreed. And I remained behind.

Use context clues or indicate another strategy you used that helped you determine meaning.

scouting (SKOW tihng) *v.*

MEANING:

25   The mountains were so close to the river now that we could no longer see the ranges of peaks beyond them. Captain Lewis was greatly worried that we would come to waterfalls or dangerous rapids.

26   "No," I told him, "our river has no such places. It flows all the way just as it does now."

27   He did not believe me, or at least he was not ready to let go of his worries. He was troubled so much by the insects that bit him. His eyes and face were always swollen, even though he covered his head each night within the thin cloth you can see through. He also kept urging your good uncle to cease his walking and allow him to take a turn looking for our people. But everyone in our party, including Captain Lewis, knew that your good uncle was the better of the two men at speaking with Indians. You could see in his face how he enjoyed meeting our people, sharing their food, and hearing their stories. Captain Lewis only showed such excitement when he looked at some small plant he had never seen before or when an animal or bird new to him was brought in. Then he would spend much time making his marks on white leaves, sometimes even drawing the exact shape of that fish or animal or bird.

* * *

28   It was a fine day when we came to the place where I had been taken captive. There were the Three Forks of the river, that same river I had spoken to on that day long ago when I made my foolish wish to travel. The river had certainly heard me then. I whispered to it again.

29   "Help my friends," I said in a very soft voice. Then I stood quietly on the banks and looked.

30   Now your good uncle was so sick that he had no wish to eat. Yet he wanted to walk. He walked along the north branch of the three rivers with only your father and one other man by his side.

31   The river almost took your father that day, Firstborn Son. They were wading together out to a large island when your father lost his footing. He was pulled into the deep water by the fast current. Weak though he was, your good uncle came into the river after him and pulled him to safety. Then they continued on to the island, where Captain Clark decided to camp for the night. His scout for my people had not succeeded. ❧

NOTEBOOK

Work on your own to answer the questions in your notebook. Use text evidence to support your responses.

Response

1. Personal Connections Have you ever felt like Sacajawea, torn between different feelings or responsibilities? Explain.

Comprehension

2. Reading Check (a) How has the "good uncle," Captain William Clark, made himself ill? **(b)** Why do the captains give Sacajawea blue beads? **(c)** Who saves Firstborn Son's father from the fast current of the river?

3. Strategy: Monitor Comprehension At what point in the narrative did you pause to monitor your comprehension? Why? In what ways did applying background knowledge improve your understanding? Explain.

WORKING AS A GROUP

Discuss your responses to the Analysis and Discussion questions with your group.

- Note agreements and disagreements.
- Summarize insights.
- Consider changes of opinion.

If necessary, revise your original answers to reflect what you learn from your discussion.

Analysis and Discussion

4. Analyze Does Sacajawea seem to have a close relationship with Lewis and Clark or a distant one? Explain using evidence from the text.

5. Contrast In what ways are Captains Clark and Lewis different in their interests and in their abilities to communicate with Sacajawea's people? Explain.

6. Make Inferences Do you think Captain Lewis understands the meaning of *Ta-ba-bone,* the word Sacajawea says her people would use to identify white people? Cite text evidence to support your response.

7. Get Ready for Close Reading Choose a passage from the text that you find especially interesting or important. You'll discuss the passage with your group during Close-Read activities.

⊙ TEKS

5.I. Monitor comprehension and make adjustments such as re-reading, using background knowledge, asking questions, and annotating when understanding breaks down.

6.A. Describe personal connections to a variety of sources including self-selected texts.

6.C. Use text evidence to support an appropriate response.

6.F. Respond using newly acquired vocabulary as appropriate.

6.G. Discuss and write about the explicit or implicit meanings of text.

EQ Notes **What drives people to explore?**

What have you learned about exploration from reading this novel excerpt? Go to your Essential Question Notes and record your observations and thoughts about the excerpt from *Sacajawea.*

Close Read

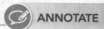 ANNOTATE

from SACAJAWEA

PRACTICE Complete the following activities.
Use text evidence to support your responses.

1. **Present and Discuss** With your group, share the passages from the text that you found especially interesting. Discuss what you notice, the questions you have, and the conclusions you reach. For example, you might focus on the following passages:

   • Paragraph 13: Discuss what the reader learns about Sacajawea's people.

   • Paragraph 27: Discuss Sacajawea's comparison of Lewis and Clark.

2. **Reflect on Your Learning** What new ideas or insights did you uncover during your second reading of the text?

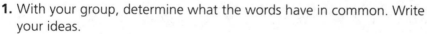

📝 NOTEBOOK

LANGUAGE STUDY

Concept Vocabulary

Why These Words? The vocabulary words are related.

journey	seeking	scouting

1. With your group, determine what the words have in common. Write your ideas.

2. Add another word that fits the category. _____

3. Think of a place you would like to explore. Use the vocabulary words in a paragraph that describes the trip you would take.

- -

Word Study

Synonyms The vocabulary word *scouting* is a precise word choice that has specific nuances, or shades of meaning. Synonyms for *scouting* have similar basic meanings, but may have very different nuances.

1. Use a thesaurus to find two synonyms for *scouting* (use the base word *scout*). Then, use a dictionary to learn the nuances of the synonyms. Explain your findings.

2. Replace *scouting* in the sentence from the text with each synonym you chose. Explain how each word affects the meaning of the sentence.

> **WORD NETWORK**
>
> Add words that are related to the idea of exploration from the text to your Word Network.

from SACAJAWEA

Genre/Text Elements

Historical and Cultural Setting In historical fiction, the historical and cultural elements of the **setting** may influence the characters and plot even more than the physical environment. Historical and cultural elements include people's values, beliefs, and customs, as well as the conflicts or problems they face as a society.

 NOTEBOOK

INTERACTIVITY

PRACTICE Work with your group to answer the questions. As you discuss your responses, use vocabulary you have learned, such as *cultural* and *customs*.

1. **(a)** What is the historical and cultural setting for this excerpt? **(b) Analyze** In this specific section of the novel, where is the expedition trying to go?

2. **(a) Distinguish** Reread paragraphs 1, 9, 27, and 31. Use the chart to list details that Sacajawea notices about Captain Clark. **(b) Generalize** What admirable qualities do these details suggest he has? **(c) Connect** Why would someone with these qualities be especially valuable in the story's setting? Explain.

DETAILS	ADMIRABLE QUALITIES

3. **(a) Make Inferences** What does Sacajawea's experience with the Minnetarees tell you about cultural problems her people face? **(b) Analyze Cause and Effect** How does Sacajawea's experience with the Minnetarees affect her feelings toward her journey with Lewis and Clark? Explain.

4. **(a)** Who is York? (see footnote 4) **(b) Make Inferences** In paragraph 17, what does Lewis ask York to do and for what reason? **(c) Connect** What tensions in the cultural setting does this detail reveal? Explain.

5. **(a) Make Inferences** In paragraph 14, how does Sacajawea seem to feel about Lewis's certainty that he understood other languages "perfectly"? **(b) Connect** How does this connect to the detail in paragraph 23 about the word *Ta-ba-bone*? **(c) Predict** What conflicts between the native people and the expedition do these historical and cultural details suggest might happen later in the plot? Explain.

⊙ TEKS

6.F. Respond using newly acquired vocabulary as appropriate.

7.D. Analyze how the setting, including historical and cultural settings, influences character and plot development.

9.D. Describe how the author's use of figurative language such as metaphor and personification achieves specific purposes.

Author's Craft

Figurative Language to Develop Character **Figurative language** is language that is used imaginatively rather than literally. It includes specific kinds of figures of speech, such as personification, simile, and metaphor.

- **Personification** presents nonhuman things as though they have human qualities: *The sky misses the birds*.

- **Metaphors** imply a similarity between two unlike things: *In the morning, the river is a ribbon of sunlight*.

- **Similes** use the words "like" or "as" to state a similarity between two unlike things: *In the morning, the river looks like a ribbon of light*.

In this selection, the author's use of figurative language helps to develop Sacajawea's character.

NOTEBOOK

PRACTICE Work with your group to complete the activity and answer the questions. As you write and discuss your responses, use new vocabulary, such as *metaphor*.

 INTERACTIVITY

1. **Analyze** Explain why each passage listed in the chart is an example of the figure of speech indicated.

PASSAGE	EXPLANATION
Personification: *the eye of my heart* (paragraph 2)	
Metaphor: *the sunshine that lives in his heart* (paragraph 9)	
Simile: *I might have been like that iron boat, unable to carry the load.* (paragraph 11)	

2. **Analyze** What type of figure of speech is each of these examples?
   (a) My heart was singing
   (b) The river almost took your father that day

3. In paragraph 28, Sacajawea says: "The river had certainly heard me then." **(a) Analyze** Explain how this is an example of personification. **(b) Interpret** Explain why this passage is also literal and shows the nature of Sacajawea's religion.

4. **Interpret** How does figurative language in this selection help to develop Sacajawea's character, showing how she sees connections between people, emotions, and nature.

from SACAJAWEA

Fiction and Nonfiction

The work of historical fiction and this history told in graphic-novel format focus on the same exploration and feature some of the same real historical figures.

from LEWIS & CLARK

About the Author

Nick Bertozzi's (b.1970) father introduced him to comics before he could read. As an adult, he developed his own mini-comic while working in the marketing department at DC Comics. Besides being an illustrator and an author of graphic novels, Bertozzi is also a computer programmer and an educator who has taught his craft at several prestigious art schools.

from Lewis & Clark

Media Vocabulary

These words will be useful to you as you analyze, discuss, and write about graphic novels, a type of multimodal text.

penciler: artist who sketches the basic layout for each panel	• A penciler shows the figures, expressions, objects, and backgrounds in each panel. • The amount of detail in the drawings varies from penciler to penciler.
inker: artist who goes over the penciled art in ink	• An inker uses pen and brush with ink to create an image that will print well. • The amount of detail left for the inker to fill in depends on how much detail was done by the penciler.
letterer: artist who letters the dialogue and captions	• A letterer fills in the speech balloons and may also place them in the panel. • Different weights, shapes, and sizes of letters can convey different emotions and meanings.

Comprehension Strategy

 NOTEBOOK

Make Connections

Deepen your appreciation of a text by **making connections** to the ideas in other texts you have read. Ask yourself questions, such as *What does this remind me of?* and *How is this different from other works on the subject?* Doing so will add to your understanding of the text you are reading and the topic as a whole. Consider various elements of other texts as you make connections:

- ideas, themes, or messages in other works
- people or characters in other works
- events in other works
- structural elements or styles in other works

PRACTICE As you read this graphic "novel" history, jot down connections you make to the ideas in other texts you have read.

 TEKS

5.E. Make connections to personal experiences, ideas in other texts, and society.

8.F. Analyze characteristics of multimodal and digital texts.

Lewis & Clark

Nick Bertozzi

BACKGROUND

The Lewis and Clark expedition (1804–1806) was a major exploration of the northwestern United States that allowed the government to later claim the area. The band of explorers and their co-leaders, Captain Meriwether Lewis and Lieutenant William Clark, were known as the Corps of Discovery.

 AUDIO

 NOTEBOOK

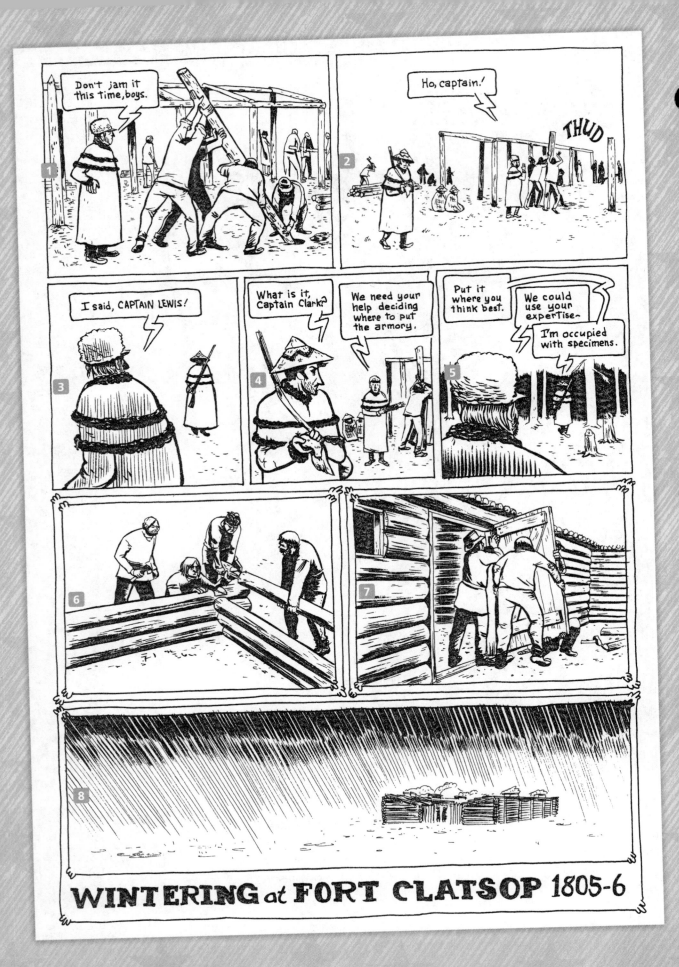

WINTERING at FORT CLATSOP 1805-6

NOTEBOOK

> Work on your own to answer the questions in your notebook. Use text evidence to support your responses.

Response

1. **Personal Connections** Does this graphic "novel" history help you better understand some of the hardships the men of the Corps of Discovery endured? Explain.

Comprehension

2. **Reading Check** **(a)** In panels 1–7, what are the men building? **(b)** What is the weather like during the winter of 1805–6? **(c)** What do the men of the Corps of Discovery do to thank the Native Americans for their help?

3. **Strategy: Make Connections (a)** What connections did you make between this graphic "novel" history and other texts about the Lewis and Clark expedition that you have read? **(b)** Did making these connections help you better understand the graphic "novel" excerpt? Explain.

Analysis and Discussion

4. **(a) Analyze** Explain what happens in panels 1–8. **(b) Interpret** How do details in panel 8 help establish the historical setting?

5. **Interpret** What do panels 21–32 show about the relations between people who belong to different cultural groups? Explain, citing details from both the dialogue and illustrations.

6. **Modify** How would you retell this graphic "novel" as a narrative? Choose one panel and retell it in story form, using dialogue and description.

7. **Get Ready for Close Reading** Choose one or more panels from the graphic "novel" history that you find especially interesting or important. You'll discuss the panel or panels with your group during Close-Read activities.

> **WORKING AS A GROUP**
>
> With your group, respond to items 4–6 orally.
> - Note agreements and disagreements.
> - Summarize insights.
> - Consider changes of opinion.
>
> If necessary, revise your original answers to reflect what you learn from your discussion.

TEKS

5.E. Make connections to personal experiences, ideas in other texts, and society.

6.C. Use text evidence to support an appropriate response.

6.F. Respond using newly acquired vocabulary as appropriate.

8.F. Analyze characteristics of multimodal and digital texts.

> **EQ Notes** **What drives people to explore?**
>
> What have you learned about exploration from reading this graphic "novel" history? Go to your Essential Question Notes and record your observations and thoughts about the excerpt from *Lewis & Clark*.

Close Read

 ANNOTATE

from LEWIS & CLARK

PRACTICE Complete the following activities. Use text evidence to support your responses.

1. **Present and Discuss** With your group, share the panels from the text that you find especially interesting. Discuss what you notice, the questions you have, and the conclusions you reach. For example, you might focus on the following sections:

   • Whole Excerpt: Discuss the use of wordless panels. What do they show that words do not?

   • Panels 13–30: Discuss what the Native Americans may have felt about the party of explorers.

2. **Reflect on Your Learning** What new ideas or insights did you uncover during your second reading of the text?

Inquiry and Research

 RESEARCH

 NOTEBOOK

Research and Extend Practice responding to teacher-guided questions by conducting a formal inquiry about this topic: What happened to York during and after the expedition? Write a brief, well-organized report on your findings. Challenge yourself to identify and gather information from both primary and secondary sources.

 WORD NETWORK

Add words that are related to the idea of exploration from the text to your Word Network.

Media Vocabulary

NOTEBOOK

These words describe characteristics of multimodal texts. Practice using them in your responses.

| penciler | inker | letterer |

1. In panels 10–13, why do you think the artist chose to draw the men without adding words?

2. What contrast do you see between the cover of the graphic "novel" history and the interior?

3. Choose several panels and explain the contributions each type of artist made to their creation.

EQ Notes Before moving on to a new selection, go to your Essential Question Notes and record what you learned from the excerpt from *Lewis & Clark*.

from SACAJAWEA

from LEWIS & CLARK

Compare Fiction and Nonfiction

Multiple Choice

📄 NOTEBOOK

These questions are based on the excerpts from
Sacajawea and *Lewis & Clark*. Choose the best answer to each question.

1. What do the two selections have in common?

    A Episodes or events

    B General topic

    C Text type

    D Narrator

2. Which text more clearly shows York's experiences with both the Corps of Discovery and the Native peoples?

    F the excerpt from *Sacajawea*

    G the graphic "novel" history

    H Both texts equally highlight York's experiences.

    J Neither text highlights York's experiences.

3. Which answer choice best describes the perspective from which events in each text are shown?

    A Both texts show events from many different characters' perspectives.

    B The excerpt from *Sacajawea* shows events through Sacajawea's eyes, and the excerpt from *Lewis & Clark* shows events entirely through York's eyes.

    C The excerpt from *Sacajawea* shows events through Clark's eyes, and the excerpt from *Lewis & Clark* shows events through Lewis's eyes.

    D The excerpt from *Sacajawea* shows events through Sacajawea's eyes, but the excerpt from *Lewis & Clark* does not show one person's perspective.

 TEKS

6.B. Write responses that demonstrate understanding of texts, including comparing sources within and across genres.

Short Response

Answer the questions in your notebook. Use text evidence to support your responses.

1. **Generalize** Which aspects of the Lewis and Clark expedition do you think might have been fun and exciting, and which were probably very difficult? Explain, citing or describing details from both texts.

2. **Interpret** How would you describe the relationship between the Corps of Discovery and the native people they encounter? Explain, citing or describing details from both texts.

3. **Evaluate** Which text do you think more accurately conveys historical information? Explain, citing or describing details from both works.

Timed Writing

A **response to literature** is a type of essay in which you explain your understanding of one or more works of literature and use details from the text to support your ideas.

ASSIGNMENT

Write a **response to literature** in which you compare what these two texts of different genres can teach readers about the Lewis and Clark expedition. Include your opinion, supported with reasons and details, about which text conveys deeper insights.

5-MINUTE PLANNER

1. Read the assignment carefully and completely.
2. Decide what you want to say—your controlling idea.
3. Decide which examples you'll use from the two works.
4. Organize your ideas, making sure to address these points:
   - Explain specific information and insights a reader can gain from each text.
   - Consider the genres of the two texts, and explain differences in the types of information and insights each one provides.
   - Take a position about which text you think teaches readers more about this event in history.

- Ada and the Thinking Machines
- The King of Mazy May
- *from* Sacajawea
- *from* Lewis & Clark

Deliver a Research Presentation

ASSIGNMENT

With your group, conduct research to learn more about the people, places, and objects discussed in these selections. Then, write and present an **infomercial.** An infomercial is a long TV commercial that provides information and tries to convince audiences to buy a product or invest their time and money in a particular activity.

Plan With Your Group

INTERACTIVITY

Choose a Focus With your group, discuss and choose one of these options:

○ "Ada and the Thinking Machines": Research Charles Babbage's Difference Engine. Try to convince viewers to buy it.

○ "The King of Mazy May": Research the Yukon Gold Rush and try to convince viewers to join up.

○ from *Sacajawea*/from *Lewis & Clark*: Research the Corps of Discovery. Try to convince viewers to sign up.

Conduct Research Use at least three sources to research your topic. Take careful notes, identifying details that make your product or experience sound like a great investment of listeners' time and money. Collect interesting images that you can include in your presentation.

Organize and Assign Roles

Establish an Effective Sequence Gather the information, pictures, and music you want to use and plan a logical sequence. Brainstorm for interesting ways to introduce your topic to viewers and engage their interest. Decide how you will develop ideas, and choose an ending that will leave viewers with a strong impression.

Assign Roles Many infomercials are set up like TV talk shows with a host, guest speakers, and interviews. Assign roles to group members and decide which information each person will present.

Draft and Revise

 INTERACTIVITY

Choose Language Devices Advertisers often use specific language techniques to move viewers' emotions and make them want a product or service.

- **Rhetorical devices** are patterns of words and ideas that create emphasis and stir emotion. In general, rhetorical devices engage viewers' emotions but don't present falsehoods.

- **Logical fallacies** are errors in reasoning that lead to faulty conclusions. They may sound convincing but don't make sense when closely examined.

Study the examples and think about which techniques you will use in your infomercial. Then, write your script.

DEVICE/FALLACY	EXAMPLE
(device) **Repetition:** re-use of the same words or phrases	Call *now* before it's too late. Time is running out, so call *now*!
(device) **Rhetorical Questions:** questions asked for effect, not to be answered	Do you *like* paying more? Do you *want* to be left out?
(fallacy) **Bandwagon Appeal:** false idea that if everyone likes something, you should, too	Everyone loves this product. It has a 125% approval rating from everyone!
(fallacy) **Slippery Slope:** false idea that a terrible result is inevitable	If you don't call now, this offer is over! You'll never have a chance like this again, and you'll be disappointed forever.

Rehearse and Present

After you write your script, rehearse your infomercial with your group members. Offer each other constructive feedback on speaking clearly and correctly at an appropriate volume and rate, making eye contact, and using gestures to enhance your delivery. Once you are happy with both your content and presentation skills, deliver your infomercial to your class.

Listen and Evaluate

Discuss Presentations Hold a question-and-answer session after each presentation.

1. For Presenters: Describe the techniques you chose and the effects you wanted to achieve. Listen closely to questions and take requests from your audience. Respond with clear explanations.

2. For Listeners: Provide feedback and explain the different effects created by the rhetorical devices and the logical fallacies presenters used.

 TEKS

1.C. Give an organized presentation with a specific stance and position, employing eye contact, speaking rate, volume, enunciation, natural gestures, and conventions of language to communicate ideas effectively.

9.G. Explain the differences between rhetorical devices and logical fallacies.

Essential Question

What drives people to explore?

What challenges do explorers face in unfamiliar environments? In this section, you will choose a selection about exploration to read independently. Get the most from this section by establishing a purpose for reading. Ask yourself, "What do I hope to gain from my independent reading?" Here are just a few purposes you might consider:

Read to Learn Think about the selections you have already read. What questions do you still have about the unit topic?

Read to Enjoy Read the descriptions of the texts. Which one seems most interesting and appealing to you?

Read to Form a Position Consider your thoughts and feelings about the Essential Question. Are you still undecided about some aspect of the topic?

Reading Digital Texts

Digital texts, like the ones you will read in this section, are electronic versions of print texts. They have a variety of characteristics:

- can be read on various devices
- text can be resized
- may include highlighting or other annotation tools
- may have bookmarks, audio links, and other helpful features

 VIDEO

 INTERACTIVITY

Independent Learning Strategies

Throughout your life, in school, in your community, and in your career, you will need to rely on yourself to learn and work on your own. Use these strategies to keep your focus as you read independently for sustained periods of time. Add ideas of your own for each category.

STRATEGY	MY ACTION PLAN
Create a schedule • Be aware of your deadlines. • Make a plan for each day's activities.	
Read with purpose • Use a variety of comprehension strategies to deepen your understanding. • Think about the text and how it adds to your knowledge.	
Take notes • Record key ideas and information. • Review your notes before sharing what you've learned.	

TEKS
4. Self-select text and read independently for a sustained period of time; **5.A.** Establish purpose for reading assigned and self-selected text; **8.F.** Analyze characteristics of multimodal and digital texts.

CONTENTS

 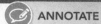

Choose one selection. Selections are available online only.

SHARE YOUR INDEPENDENT LEARNING

Reflect on and evaluate the information you gained from your Independent Reading selection. Then, share what you learned with others.

Close-Read Guide

Tool Kit
Close-Read Guide and
Model Annotation

Establish your purpose for reading. Then, read the selection through at least once. Use this page to record your Close-Read ideas.

Selection Title: _____   Purpose for Reading: _____

Minutes Read: _____

INTERACTIVITY

Close Read the Text

Zoom in on sections you found interesting. **Annotate** what you notice. Ask yourself **questions** about the text. What can you **conclude?**

_____

_____

_____

_____

_____

_____

Analyze the Text

1. Think about the author's choices of literary elements, techniques, and structures. Select one and record your thoughts.

_____

_____

_____

2. What characteristics of digital texts did you use as you read this selection, and in what ways? How do the characteristics of a digital text affect your reading experience? Explain.

_____

_____

QuickWrite

Choose a paragraph from the text that grabbed your interest. Explain the power of this passage.

_____

_____

_____

_____

_____

_____

_____

Share Your Independent Learning

What drives people to explore?

When you read something independently, your understanding continues to grow as you share what you have learned with others.

 NOTEBOOK

Prepare to Share

CONNECT IT One of the most important ways to respond to a text is to notice and describe your personal reactions. Think about the text you explored independently and the ways in which it connects to your own experiences.

- What similarities and differences do you see between the text and your own life? Describe your observations.

- How do you think this text connects to the Essential Question? Describe your ideas.

Learn From Your Classmates

DISCUSS IT Share your ideas about the text you explored on your own. As you talk with others in your class, take notes about new ideas that seem important.

Reflect

EXPLAIN IT Review your notes, and mark the most important insight you gained from these writing and discussion activities. Explain how this idea adds to your understanding of why some people are driven to explore.

 TEKS

6.A. Describe personal connections to a variety of sources, including self-selected texts.
6.E. Interact with sources in meaningful ways such as notetaking, annotating, freewriting, or illustrating.

Research-Based Essay

ASSIGNMENT

In this unit, you read about many different explorers and types of exploration. You also practiced writing research-based texts. Now, apply what you have learned.

Write a **research-based essay** in which you synthesize information and your own ideas to answer the Essential Question:

Essential Question
What drives people to explore?

Review and Evaluate Evidence

INTERACTIVITY

Review your Essential Question Notes and your QuickWrite from the beginning of the unit. Have your ideas changed?

⬤ YES	⬤ NO
Identify at least three pieces of evidence that changed your thinking.	Identify at least three pieces of evidence that reinforced your initial thinking.
1.	1.
2.	2.
3.	3.

State your ideas now:

What other evidence might you need to develop your ideas?

Share Your Perspective

The **Research-Based Essay Checklist** will help you stay on track.

PLAN Before you write, read the Checklist and make sure you understand all the items.

DRAFT As you write, pause occasionally to make sure you're meeting the Checklist requirements.

Use New Words Refer to your Word Network to vary your word choice. Also, consider using one or more of the Academic Vocabulary terms you learned at the beginning of the unit: *critical, manual, omit, valid, coherent.*

REVIEW AND EDIT After you have written a first draft, evaluate it against the Checklist. Make any changes needed to strengthen your controlling idea, structure, transitions, and language. Then, reread your essay and fix any errors you find.

EQ Notes Make sure you have synthesized information from your Essential Question Notes to support your controlling idea.

INTERACTIVITY

RESEARCH-BASED ESSAY CHECKLIST

My essay clearly contains . . .

○ a controlling idea that is supported by evidence.

○ supporting evidence from a variety of reliable sources.

○ clearly credited sources after quotes or paraphrases.

○ a purposeful structure that includes an introduction, logical connections among body paragraphs, and a strong conclusion.

○ use of transitional words and phrases that accurately show how ideas are related.

○ precise word choices.

○ correct use of standard English conventions, including consistent verb tenses.

○ no punctuation or spelling errors.

TEKS
11.B. Compose informational texts, including multi-paragraph essays that convey information about a topic, using a clear controlling idea or thesis statement and genre characteristics and craft.

Revising and Editing

Read this draft and think about corrections the writer might make. Then, answer the questions that follow.

[1] Just east of the small desert town of marfa, texas, strange lights sometimes appears in the sky. [2] Observers have reported these "Marfa Lights" for nearly a century. [3] They have said the lights, which are often red or blue, dance around the sky or zoom by. [4] Surprisingly, both scientists or citizens really know what causes them. [5] Some Native Americans thought the lights were fallen stars likewise some people believe the lights are UFOs. [6] Physics students from the University of Texas found that the lights correspond with car headlights passing on the highway. [7] They will have said that water droplets in the atmosphere reflect the beams from passing cars, creating the effect (Linnet 7). [8] One problem with that theory? [9] The first sighting was reported in 1883—long before cars roamed the highways (Linnet 8).

1. What correction, if any, should be made to correct capitalization in sentence 1?

   A Change *east* to *East*.

   B Change *desert town* to *Desert Town*.

   C Change *marfa, texas* to *Marfa, Texas*.

   D Make no change.

2. In sentence 4, what correction, if any, should be made to correct the use of correlative conjunctions?

   F Change *both* to *not only*.

   G Change *or* to *and*.

   H Change *or* to *nor*.

   J Make no change.

3. What punctuation should be added to correct sentence 5?

   A Add a comma after *likewise*.

   B Add a comma after *Native Americans*.

   C Add a semicolon after *stars* and a comma after *likewise*.

   D Add a comma after *stars* and a semicolon after *likewise*.

4. How should sentence 7 be corrected?

   F Add a comma after *atmosphere*.

   G Change *droplets* to *droplet*.

   H Delete the comma after *cars*.

   J Change *will have said* to *say*.

Reflect on the Unit

 NOTEBOOK

 INTERACTIVITY

Reflect on the Unit Goals

Review your Unit Goals chart from the beginning of the unit. Then, complete the activity and answer the question.

1. In the Unit Goals chart, rate how well you meet each goal now.

2. In which goals were you most and least successful?

Reflect on the Texts

VOTE! Which exploration portrayed in this unit would you most like to have joined in real life, and which one would you have wanted to avoid? Mark your choices, and then discuss your reasons.

SELECTION TITLE	JOIN OR NOT JOIN
A Long Way Home	
BBC Science Club: All About Exploration	
Ada and the Thinking Machines	
The King of Mazy May	
from Sacajawea and *from* Louis & Clark	
Your Independent Reading Selection:	

Reflect On the | Essential Question

Journal Entry Explorers often keep journals of their experiences. As you read the selections and completed the activities in this unit, you, too, were an explorer. Write a journal entry that captures your experiences as you worked through the unit and shows your understanding of the Essential Question: **What drives people to explore?**

✦ TEKS

10.D.vi. Edit drafts using standard English conventions, including subordinating conjunctions to form complex sentences and correlative conjunctions such as *either/or* and *neither/nor*; **10.D.vii.** Edit drafts using standard English conventions, including capitalization of proper nouns, including abbreviations, initials, acronyms, and organizations; **10.D.viii.** Edit drafts using standard English conventions, including punctuation marks, including commas in complex sentences, transitions, and introductory elements.

RESOURCES

Marking the Text: Strategies and Tips for Annotation

When you close read a text, you read for comprehension and then reread to unlock layers of meaning and to analyze a writer's style and techniques. Marking a text as you read it enables you to participate more fully in the close-reading process.

Following are some strategies for text mark-ups, along with samples of how the strategies can be applied. These mark-ups are suggestions; you and your teacher may want to use other mark-up strategies.

✱	Key Idea
!	I love it!
?	I have questions
◯	Unfamiliar or important word
—	Context Clues
▨	Highlight

SUGGESTED MARK-UP NOTES

WHAT I NOTICE	HOW TO MARK UP	QUESTIONS TO ASK
Key Ideas and Details	• Highlight key ideas or claims. • Underline supporting details or evidence.	• What does the text say? What does it leave unsaid? • What inferences do you need to make? • What details lead you to make your inferences?
Word Choice	• Circle unfamiliar words. • Put a dotted line under context clues, if any exist. • Put an exclamation point beside especially rich or poetic passages.	• What inferences about word meaning can you make? • What tone and mood are created by word choice? • What alternate word choices might the author have made?
Text Structure	• Highlight passages that show key details supporting the main idea. • Use arrows to indicate how sentences and paragraphs work together to build ideas. • Use a right-facing arrow to indicate foreshadowing. • Use a left-facing arrow to indicate flashback.	• Is the text logically structured? • What emotional impact do the structural choices create?
Author's Craft	• Circle or highlight instances of repetition, either of words, phrases, consonants, or vowel sounds. • Mark rhythmic beats in poetry using checkmarks and slashes. • Underline instances of symbolism or figurative language.	• Does the author's style enrich or detract from the reading experience? • What levels of meaning are created by the author's techniques?

TOOL KIT: CLOSE READING

Close-Reading Model

When close reading, take the time to analyze not only the author's ideas but the way that those ideas are conveyed. Consider the genre of the text, the author's word choice, the writer's unique style, and the message of the text.

Here is how one reader close read this text. You will use different mark-up tools when working digitally.

Key

* *   Key Idea
* !   I love it!
* ?   I have questions
* ◯   Unfamiliar or important word
* —   Context Clues
* ▬   Highlight

MODEL

INFORMATIONAL TEXT

NOTES

explanation of sunlight and starlight

What is light and where do the colors come from?

This paragraph is about Newton and the prism.

What discoveries helped us understand light?

Fraunhofer and gaps in spectrum

from Classifying the Stars

Cecilia H. Payne

1   Sunlight and starlight are composed of waves of various lengths, which the eye, even aided by a telescope, is unable to separate. We must use more than a telescope. In order to sort out the component colors, the light must be dispersed by a prism, or split up by some other means. For instance, sunbeams passing through rain drops are transformed into the myriad-tinted rainbow. The familiar rainbow spanning the sky is Nature's most glorious demonstration that light is composed of many colors.

2   The very beginning of our knowledge of the nature of a star dates back to 1672, when Isaac Newton gave to the world the results of his experiments on passing sunlight through a prism. To describe the beautiful band of rainbow tints, produced when sunlight was dispersed by his three-cornered piece of glass, he took from the Latin the word *spectrum*, meaning an appearance. The rainbow is the spectrum of the Sun. . . .

3   In 1814, more than a century after Newton, the spectrum of the Sun was obtained in such purity that an amazing detail was seen and studied by the German optician, Fraunhofer. He saw that the multiple spectral tints, ranging from delicate violet to deep red, were crossed by hundreds of fine dark lines. In other words, there were narrow gaps in the spectrum where certain shades were wholly blotted out. We must remember that the word spectrum is applied not only to sunlight, but also to the light of any glowing substance when its rays are sorted out by a prism or a grating.

MODEL

Close-Read Guide

Use this page to record your close-read ideas.

Selection Title: _Classifying the Stars_

Close Read the Text

Revisit sections of the text you marked during your first read. Read these sections closely and **annotate** what you notice. Ask yourself **questions** about the text. What can you **conclude?** Write down your ideas.

Paragraph 3: Light is composed of waves of various lengths. Prisms let us see different colors in light. This is called the spectrum. Fraunhofer proved that there are gaps in the spectrum, where certain shades are blotted out.

More than one researcher studied this and each built off the ideas that were already discovered.

Analyze the Text

Think about the author's choices of patterns, structure, techniques, and ideas included in the text. Select one, and record your thoughts about what this choice conveys.

The author showed the development of human knowledge of the spectrum chronologically. Helped me see how ideas were built upon earlier understandings.
Used dates and "more than a century after Newton" to show time.

QuickWrite

Pick a paragraph from the text that grabbed your interest. Explain the power of this passage.

The first paragraph grabbed my attention, specifically the sentence "The familiar rainbow spanning the sky is Nature's most glorious demonstration that light is composed of many colors." The paragraph began as a straightforward scientific explanation. When I read the word "glorious," I had to stop and deeply consider what was being said. It is a word loaded with personal feelings. With that one word, the author let the reader know what was important to her.

TOOL KIT: CLOSE READING

Close-Reading Model **R3**

Argument

When you think of the word *argument,* you might think of a disagreement between two people, but the word has another meaning, too. An argument is a logical way of presenting a belief, conclusion, or stance. A good argument is supported with reasoning and evidence.

Argument writing can be used for many purposes, such as changing a reader's opinion or bringing about an action or a response from a reader.

ARGUMENT

Your Purpose: to explain and defend your position

Characteristics

- a clear claim that relates to an engaging idea and shows depth of thought
- a consideration of other opinions or positions
- varied types of evidence, including specific facts, details, and examples
- language that makes a connection to your reader
- well-chosen transitions
- standard English conventions

Structure

- a well-organized structure that includes:
  - an interesting introduction
  - a logical flow of ideas from paragraph to paragraph
  - a strong conclusion

Celebrities Should Try to Be Better Role Models

A lot of Celebrities are singers or actors or actresses or athletes. Kids spend tons of time watching Celebrities on TV. They listen to their songs. They read about them. They watch them play and perform. No matter weather the Celebrities are good people or bad people. Kids still spend time watching them. The kids will try to imitate what they do. Some of them have parents or brothers and sisters who are famous also.

Celebrities don't seem to watch out what they do and how they live. Some say, "Why do I care? It's none of you're business"! Well, that's true. But it's bad on them if they do all kinds of stupid things. Because this is bad for the kids who look up to them.

Sometimes celebrity's say they wish they are not role models. *"I'm just an actor!"* *"I'm just a singer"*! they say. But the choice is not really up to them. If their on TV all the time, then kids' will look up to them, no matter what. It's stupid when Celebrities mess up and then nothing bad happens to them. That gives kids a bad lesson. Kids will think that you can do stupid things and be fine. That is not being a good role model.

Some Celebrities give money to charity. That's a good way to be a good role model. But sometimes it seems like Celebrities are just totally messed up. It's hard always being in the spotlight. That can drive Celebrities kind of crazy. Then they act out.

It is a good idea to support charities when you are rich and famous. You can do a lot of good. For a lot of people. Some Celebrities give out cars or houses or free scholarships. You can even give away your dresses and people can have an auction to see who will pay the most money for them. This can help for example the Humane Society. Or whatever charity or cause the celebrity wants to support.

Celebrities are fun to watch and follow, even when they mess up. I think they don't realize that when they do bad things, they give teens wrong ideas about how to live. They should try to keep that under control. So many teens look up to them and copy them, no matter what.

The claim is not clearly stated in the introduction or elsewhere.

Some of the ideas in the essay do not relate to the claim or focus on the issue.

The writer ineffectively addresses other positions.

The word choice in the essay is not effective and lends it an informal tone.

The progression of ideas is not logical or purposeful.

Errors in spelling, capitalization, punctuation, grammar, usage, and sentence boundaries are frequent. The effectiveness of the essay is affected by these errors.

The conclusion does not clearly restate the claim.

TOOL KIT: WRITING MODELS AND RUBRICS

MODEL

ARGUMENT: SCORE 2

Celebrities Should Try to Be Better Role Models

Most kids spend tons of time watching celebrities on TV, listening to their songs, and reading about them. No matter how celebrities behave—whether they do good things or bad—they are role models for kids. They often do really dumb things, and that is not good considering they are role models.

Sometimes celebrity's say they wish they were not role models. "I'm just an actor!" or, "I'm just a singer!" they say. But the choice is not really up to them. If they are on TV all the time, then kids' will look up to them. No matter what. It's really bad when celebrities mess up and then nothing bad happens to them. That gives kids a false lesson because in reality there are bad things when you mess up. That's why celebrities should think more about what they are doing and what lessons they are giving to kids.

Some celebrities might say, *"Why do I care? Why should I be bothered?"* Well, they don't have to. But it's bad on them if they do all kinds of stupid things and don't think about how this affects the kids who look up to them. Plus, they get tons of money, much more even than inventors or scientists or other important people. Being a good role model should be part of what they have to do to get so much money.

When you are famous it is a good idea to support charities. Some celebrities give out cars, or houses, or free scholarships. They even sometimes give away their dresses and people have an auction to see who will pay the most money for them. This can help for example the Humane Society, or whatever charity or cause the celebrity wants to support.

Sometimes it seems like celebrities are more messed up than anyone else. That's in their personal lives. Imagine if people wanted to take pictures of you wherever you went, and you could never get away. That can drive celebrities kind of crazy, and then they act out.

Celebrities can do good things and they can do bad things. They don't realize that when they do bad things, they give teens wrong ideas about how to live. So many teens look up to them and copy them, no matter what. They should make an effort to be better role models.

The introduction does not state the claim clearly enough.

The writer ineffectively addresses other positions.

Errors in spelling, grammar, and sentence boundaries decrease the effectiveness of the essay.

The word choice in the essay contributes to an informal tone.

The writer does not make use of transitions and sentence connections.

Some of the ideas in the essay do not relate to the claim or focus on the issue.

The essay has a clear conclusion.

Celebrities Should Try to Be Better Role Models

Kids look up to the celebrities they see on TV and want to be like them. Parents may not *want* celebrities to be role models for their children, but they are anyway. Therefore, celebrities should think about what they say and do and live lives that are worth copying. Celebrities should think about how they act because they are role models.

"I'm just an actor!" or, "I'm just a singer!" celebrities sometimes say. "Their parents and teachers are the ones who should be the role models!" But it would be foolish to misjudge the impact that celebrities have on youth. Kids spend hours every day digitally hanging with their favorite stars. Children learn by imitation, so, for better or worse, celebrities are role models. That's why celebrities should start modeling good decision-making and good citizenship.

With all that they are given by society, celebrities owe a lot back to their communities and the world. Celebrities get a lot of attention, time, and money. Often they get all that for doing not very much: acting, singing, or playing a sport. It's true; some of them work very hard. But even if they work very hard, do they deserve to be in the news all the time and earn 100 or even 1000 times more than equally hard-working teachers, scientists, or nurses? I don't think so. After receiving all that, it seems only fair that celebrities take on the important job of being good role models for the young people who look up to them.

Celebrities can serve as good role models is by giving back. Quite a few use their fame and fortune to do just that. They give scholarships, or even build and run schools; they help veterans; they visit hospitals; they support important causes such as conservation, and women's rights. They donate not just money but their time and talents too. This is a great way to be a role model.

Celebrities should recognize that as role models, they have a responsibility to try to make good decisions and be honest. Celebrities should step up so they can be a force for good in people's lives and in the world.

The writer's word choice is good but could be better.

The introduction mostly states the claim.

The writer addresses other positions.

The ideas relate to the stated claim and focus on the issue.

The sentences are varied and coherent and enhance the effectiveness of the essay.

The progression of ideas is logical, but there could be better transitions and sentence connections to show how ideas are related.

The conclusion mostly follows from the claim.

TOOL KIT: WRITING MODELS AND RUBRICS

Writing Models and Rubrics

ARGUMENT: SCORE 4

Celebrities Should Try to Be Better Role Models

Like it or not, kids look up to the celebrities they see on TV and want to be like them. Parents may not *want* celebrities to be role models for their children, but the fact is that they are. With such an oversized influence on young people, celebrities have a responsibility to think about what they say and do and to live lives that are worth emulating. In short, they should make an effort to be better role models.

Sometimes celebrities say they don't want to be role models. "I'm just an actor!" or "I'm just a singer!" they protest. "Their parents and teachers are the ones who should be guiding them and showing them the right way to live!" That is all very well, but it would be foolish to underestimate the impact that celebrities have on children. Kids spend hours every day digitally hanging out with their favorite stars. Children learn by imitation, so for better or worse, celebrities act as role models.

Celebrities are given a lot of attention, time, and money. They get all that for doing very little: acting, singing, or playing a sport very well. It's true some of them work very hard. But even if they work hard, do they deserve to be in the news all the time and earn 100 or even 1,000 times more than equally hardworking teachers, scientists, or nurses? I don't think so.

With all that they are given, celebrities owe a lot to their communities and the world. One way they can serve as good role models is by giving back, and quite a few celebrities use their fame and fortune to do just that. They give scholarships or even build and run schools; they help veterans; they entertain kids who are sick; they support important causes such as conservation and women's rights. They donate not just money but their time and talents too.

Celebrities don't have to be perfect. They are people too and make mistakes. But they should recognize that as role models for youth, they have a responsibility to try to make good decisions and be honest about their struggles. Celebrities should step up so they can be a force for good in people's lives.

The writer has chosen words that contribute to the clarity of the essay.

The writer clearly states the claim in the introduction.

The writer addresses other positions.

There are no errors to distract the reader from the effectiveness of the essay.

The writer uses transitions and sentence connections to show how ideas are related.

The writer clearly restates the claim and the most powerful idea presented in the essay.

Argument Rubric

	1 (POOR)	**2** (WEAK)	**3** (GOOD)	**4** (EXCELLENT)
Clarity and Purpose	The claim is unstated or unclear. Evidence is absent or irrelevant to the purpose. The argument is unfocused and the intended audience is not addressed.	The claim is unclear or lacks power. Evidence is weak and does not build the argument. The argument is often unfocused and not suited to its audience.	The claim is stated, but could be more powerful. The argument is mostly focused and supported by evidence. It is somewhat suited to its audience.	The claim is clear and powerful. The argument is focused and supported by ample and varied evidence. It is totally suited to the audience.
Organization	The argument has no purposeful structure. The ideas presented do not relate to one another.	The argument has a weak structure. The organization is unclear and does not help build the argument.	The structure of the argument is evident. Ideas are clearly linked with transitions.	A purposeful structure clearly builds the argument. The ideas presented are coherent and powerful.
Development of Ideas	The argument lacks specific facts, details, and examples to support the claim. Sources are not cited. Transitions are not used to link ideas. Other positions are not addressed.	The argument has few facts, details, and examples to support the claim. Sources are often unidentified. Transitions are usually absent. Other positions are ineffectively addressed.	The claim is mostly supported by facts, details, and examples. Most sources are identified. Most ideas are linked using transitions. Other positions are addressed.	Varied facts, details, and examples fully support the claim. Sources are always identified. Transitions link ideas within and among paragraphs. Other positions are addressed.
Language and Style	Word choice is vague, repetitive, or misleading. Sentences lack variety and impact.	Word choice is often vague, repetitive, or misleading. There is little sentence variety.	Word choice is often precise and to the point. Most passages contain a variety of sentence types.	Word choices are precise and purposeful. A variety of sentence types help focus and maintain the audience's attention.
Conventions	Misspellings and errors in grammar detract from the argument. Punctuation is lacking or incorrect.	The argument is weakened by occasional errors in spelling, punctuation, and grammar.	The argument contains few errors in spelling, punctuation, and grammar.	The argument is free from errors in spelling, punctuation, and grammar.

TOOL KIT: WRITING MODELS AND RUBRICS

Informational Text

Informational writing should present facts, details, data, and other kinds of evidence to communicate information about a topic. Informative writing serves several purposes: to increase readers' knowledge of a subject, to help readers better understand a procedure or process, or to provide readers with enhanced comprehension of a concept. It should also feature a clear introduction, body, and conclusion.

INFORMATIONAL TEXT

Your Purpose: to communicate information about a topic

Characteristics

- a clear thesis statement or controlling idea
- varied types of evidence
- precise language and well-chosen transitions
- definitions of unfamiliar or technical terms
- an objective tone
- standard English grammar and conventions

Structure

- an engaging introduction with a clear thesis statement
- a logical flow of ideas from paragraph to paragraph
- a strong conclusion

Kids, School, and Exercise: Problems and Solutions

In the past, children ran around and even did hard physical labor. Today most kid's just sit most of the time. They don't know the old Outdoor Games. Like tether ball. and th ve hard chores to do. Like milking the cows. But children should be Physically Active quite a bit every day. That doesn't happen very much any more. Not as much as it should anyway.

Even at home when kid's have a chance to run around, they choose to sit and play video games, for example. Some schools understand that it's a problem when students don't get enough exercise. Even though they have had to cut Physical Education classes. Some also had to make recess shorter.

But lots of schools are working hard to find ways to get kid's moving around again. Like they used to long ago.

Schools use volunteers to teach kid's old-fashioned games. Old-fashioned games are an awesome way to get kid's moving around like crazy people.

Some schools have before school activities. Such as games in the gym. Other schools have after school activities. Such as bike riding or outdoor games. They can't count on kid's to be active. Not even on their own or at home. So they do the activities all together. Kids enjoy doing stuff with their friends. So that works out really well.

If you don't exercise you get overweight. You can end up with high blood pressure and too much colesterol. Of course its also a problem if you eat too much junk food all the time. But not getting enough exercise is part of the problem too. That's why schools need to try to be part of the solution.

A break during class to move around helps. Good teachers know how to use exercise during classes. There are all kinds of ways to move in the classroom that don't mean you have to change your clothes. Classes don't have to be just about math and science.

Schools are doing what they can to get kids moving, doing exercise, being active. Getting enough exercise also helps kid's do better in school. Being active also helps kids get strong.

There are extensive errors in spelling, capitalization, punctuation, grammar, usage, and sentence boundaries.

Many of the ideas in the essay do not focus on the topic and are not supported by evidence. The thesis is unclear.

The word choice shows the writer's lack of awareness of the essay's purpose and tone.

The essay's sentences are not purposeful, varied, or well-controlled. The writer's sentences decrease the effectiveness of the essay.

The essay is not well organized. Its structure does not support its purpose, and ideas do not flow logically from one paragraph to the next.

The conclusion is not insightful or engaging.

TOOL KIT: WRITING MODELS AND RUBRICS

Writing Models and Rubrics

MODEL

INFORMATIONAL: SCORE 2

Kids, School, and Exercise: Problems and Solutions

In the past, children ran around a lot and did chores and other physical work. Today most kid's sit by a TV or computer screen or play with their phones. But children should be active for at least 60 minutes a day. Sadly, most don't get nearly that much exercise. And that's a big problem.

Some schools understand that it's a problem when students don't get enough exercise. Even though they have had to cut Physical Education classes due to budget cuts. Some also had to make recess shorter because there isn't enough time in the schedule. But they are working hard to find creative ways that don't cost too much or take up too much time to get kid's moving. Because there's only so much money in the budget, and only so much time in the day, and preparing to take tests takes lots of time.

Schools can use parent volunteers to teach kid's old-fashioned games such as kick-the-can, hopscotch, foursquare, tetherball, or jump rope. Kid's nowadays often don't know these games! Old-fashioned games are a great way to get kid's moving. Some schools have before school activities, such as games in the gym. Other schools have after school activities, such as bike riding or outdoor games. They can't count on kid's to be active on their own or at home.

A break during class can help students concentrate when they go back to work. There are all kinds of ways to move in the classroom. And you don't have to change your clothes or anything. Wiggling, stretching, and playing a short active game are all good ideas. Good teachers know how to squeeze in time during academic classes like math and language arts.

Not getting enough exercise is linked to many problems. For example, unhealthy wait, and high blood pressure and colesterol. When students don't' get enough exercise, they end up overweight.

Physical activity also helps kid's do better in school. Kids who exercise have better attendance rates. They have increased attention span. They act out less. They have less stress and learn more. Being active also helps muscles and bones. It increases strength and stamina.

Schools today are doing what they can to find a solution by being creative and making time for physical activity before, during, and after school. They understand that it is a problem when kid's don't get enough exercise.

Not all the ideas in the essay focus on the topic or are supported by evidence. The thesis is not completely clear.

The writer uses some transitions and sentence connections.

Some ideas are well developed. Some examples and details are well chosen and specific and add substance to the essay.

Ideas do not always flow logically from one paragraph to the next.

There are errors in spelling, punctuation, grammar, usage, and sentence boundaries that decrease the effectiveness of the essay.

The essay's organizing structure does not effectively support its purpose.

The conclusion lacks focus and insight.

Kids, School, and Exercise: Problems and Solutions

A 2008 report said school-age children should be physically active for at least 60 minutes a day. Sadly, most children don't get nearly that much exercise. Lots of schools have cut Physical Education classes because of money and time pressures. And there's less recess than there used to be. Even at home when kids have a chance to run around, many choose screen time instead. No wonder so many of us are turning into chubby couch potatoes!

Not getting exercise is linked to many problems, for example unhealthy weight, and high blood pressure and cholesterol. Studies show physical activity also helps students do better in school: it means better attendance rates, increased attention span, fewer behavioral problems, less stress, and more learning. Being active helps develop strong muscles and bones. It increases strength and stamina.

Many schools around the country get that there are problems when students are inactive. They are working hard to find creative solutions that don't cost too much or take up precious time in the school schedule.

Some schools are using parent volunteers to teach kids active games such as kick-the-can, hopscotch, foursquare, tetherball, or jump rope. These games are more likely to get kids moving than just sitting gossiping with your friends or staring at your phone. Some schools have before school activities such as run-around games in the gym. Other schools have after school activities such as bike riding or outdoor games. They can't count on kids to be active on their own.

There are all kinds of fun and healthy ways to move in the classroom, without changing clothes. An active break during class can help students concentrate when they go back to work. Creative teachers know how to squeeze in active time even during academic classes. Wiggling, stretching, and playing a short active game are all good ideas.

Schools today understand that it is a problem when kids don't get enough exercise. They are doing what they can to find a solution by being creative and making time for physical activity before, during, and after school.

The essay is fairly thoughtful and engaging.

Almost all the ideas focus on the topic, and the thesis is clear.

The ideas in the essay are well developed, with well-chosen evidence.

The writer uses transitions and connections between sentences and paragraphs, such as "Not getting exercise is linked…" "Many schools …" "Some schools…" "Other schools…"

Ideas in the essay are mostly well developed and flow logically.

Words are chosen carefully and contribute to the clarity of the essay.

TOOL KIT: WRITING MODELS AND RUBRICS

MODEL

INFORMATIONAL: SCORE 4

Kids, School, and Exercise: Problems and Solutions

In 2008, the U.S. Department of Health and Human Services published a report stating that all school-age children need to be physically active for at least 60 minutes a day. Sadly, most children don't get nearly the recommended amount of exercise. Due to budget cuts and time pressure, many schools have cut Physical Education classes. Even recess is being squeezed to make room for more tests and test preparation.

> The writer explains the problem and its causes in the thesis and provides evidence.

Lack of exercise can lead to many problems, such as unhealthy weight, high blood pressure, and high cholesterol. Physical activity helps develop strong muscles and bones, and it increases strength and stamina. Studies show physical activity leads to better attendance rates, increased attention span, fewer behavioral problems, less stress, and more learning. When kids don't get enough physical activity, a lot is at stake!

> The writer clearly lays out the effects of the problem.

Many schools around the country are stepping up to find innovative solutions—even when they don't have time or money to spare. Some have started before-school activities such as active games in the gym. Others have after-school activities such as bike riding or outdoor games. Just a few extra minutes a day can make a big difference!

> The writer turns to the solution. The essay's organizing structure supports its purpose.

Some schools try to make the most of recess by using parent volunteers to teach kids active games such as kick-the-can, hopscotch, foursquare, tetherball, or jump rope. Volunteers can also organize races or tournaments—anything to get the kids going! At the end of recess, everyone should be a little bit out of breath.

> The writer includes specific examples and well-chosen details.

> The progression of ideas is logical.

Creative educators squeeze in active time even during academic classes. It could be a quick "brain break" to stretch in the middle of class, imaginary jump rope, or a game of rock-paper-scissors with legs instead of fingers. There are all kinds of imaginative ways to move in the classroom, without moving furniture or changing clothes. And research shows that an active break during class can help students focus when they go back to work.

> Details and examples add substance to the essay.

Schools today understand the problems that can arise when kids don't have enough physical activity in their lives. They are meeting the challenge by finding opportunities for exercise before, during, and after school. After all, if students do well on tests but end up unhealthy and unhappy, what is the point?

> The conclusion is insightful and engaging.

Informational Text Rubric

	1 (POOR)	2 (WEAK)	3 (GOOD)	4 (EXCELLENT)
Clarity and Purpose	The thesis is unstated or unclear. Evidence is absent or irrelevant to the purpose. Ideas are unfocused.	The thesis is unclear. Ideas are often unfocused and not supported by evidence.	The thesis is clear. Most of the ideas are focused and supported by evidence.	The thesis is completely clear. The ideas are focused and are supported by ample and varied evidence.
Organization	The topic is not clearly stated, and ideas do not follow a logical progression. The conclusion does not follow from the rest of the essay.	The introduction sets forth the topic. Ideas often do not progress logically, and the conclusion does not completely follow from the rest of the essay.	The introduction is somewhat engaging and compelling. Ideas progress somewhat logically. The conclusion does not completely follow from the rest of the essay.	The introduction is engaging and sets forth the topic in a compelling way. Ideas progress logically. The conclusion is insightful and follows from the rest of the essay.
Development of Ideas	The topic is not developed with reliable or relevant evidence. Sources are not cited. Transitions are not used to link ideas.	The topic is supported with few facts, details, and examples. Sources are often unidentified. Transitions are usually absent.	The topic is supported by facts, details, and examples. Most sources are identified. Transitions are often used to link ideas.	Varied facts, details, and examples fully support the topic. Sources are always identified. Transitions consistently link ideas.
Language and Style	Word choice is vague or repetitive. Sentences lack variety and impact. Technical words are not defined. The tone is not objective.	Word choice is often vague or repetitive. There is little sentence variety. Most technical words are not defined. The tone is often not objective.	Word choice is often precise and varied. Most passages contain a variety of sentence types. Most technical words are defined. The tone is usually objective.	Word choice is precise and varied. Sentences types are varied throughout. Technical words are defined. The tone is consistently objective.
Conventions	The essay contains numerous misspellings and errors in standard English conventions. Punctuation is lacking or incorrect.	The essay contains some misspellings and errors in standard English conventions. Punctuation is sometimes lacking or incorrect.	The essay contains few misspellings and errors in standard English conventions. Punctuation is usually correct.	The essay is free from errors in spelling, punctuation, and standard English conventions.

TOOL KIT: WRITING MODELS AND RUBRICS

Narrative Text

Narrative writing conveys an experience, either real or imaginary, and uses time order to provide structure. Usually its purpose is to entertain, but it can also instruct, persuade, or inform. Whenever writers tell a story, they are using narrative writing. Most types of narrative writing share certain elements, such as characters, setting, a sequence of events, and, often, a theme.

NARRATIVE TEXT

Your Purpose: To tell a fiction or nonfiction story that expresses an insight

Characteristics

→ a clear sequence of events

→ details that show time and place

→ well-developed, interesting characters (fiction) or real people (nonfiction)

→ a conflict, or problem, and a resolution (fiction) or clear main idea (nonfiction)

→ description and dialogue

→ a clear narrative point of view
  - first-person (fiction or nonfiction)
  - third-person (fiction or nonfiction)
  - third-person omniscient (usually fiction)

→ word choices and sensory details that paint a picture for readers

→ standard English conventions

Structure

→ a well-organized structure that includes
  - an engaging beginning
  - a chronological organization of events
  - a strong ending that expresses an insight

Mind Scissors

There's a bike race. Right away people start losing. But me and Thad were winning. Thad is the kid who always wins is who is also popular. I don't like Thad. I pumped pumping hard at my pedals, I knew the end was coming. I looked ahead and all I could see was Thad, and the woods.

I pedaled harder and then I was up to Thad. That was swinging at me, I swerved, I kept looking at him, I was worried!

That's stick had untied my shoelace and it was wrapped around my pedal! But I didn't know it yet.

We were out of the woods. I still wanted to win, I pedaled even faster. than my pedals stopped!

I saw with my mind the shoelace was caught in my pedal. No worries, I have the superpower of mind scissors. That's when my mind looked down and I used my mind scissors. I used the mind scissors to cut the shoelace my right foot was free.

That's how I became a superhero. I save people with my mind scissors now.

The story's beginning is not clear or engaging. The conflict is not well established.

The narrative does not include sensory language or precise words to convey experiences and develop characters.

Events do not progress logically. The ideas seem disconnected, and the sentences do not include transitions.

The narrative contains mistakes in standard English conventions of usage and mechanics.

The resolution does not connect to the narrative.

TOOL KIT: WRITING MODELS AND RUBRICS

Writing Models and Rubrics

MODEL

NARRATIVE: SCORE 2

Mind-Scissors

When I was a baby I wound up with a tiny pair of scissors in my head. What the doctors couldn't have predicted is the uncanny ability they would give me. This past summer that was when I discovered what I could do with my mind-scissors.

Every summer there's a bike race. The kid who always wins is Thad who is popular.

The race starts. Right away racers start losing. After a long time pumping hard at my pedals, I knew the end was coming. I looked ahead and all I could see was Thad, and the woods.

I pedaled harder than ever. I was up to Thad. I turned my head to look at him. He was swinging a stick at me, I swerved, I kept looking at him, boy was I worried.

We were now out of the woods. Still hopeful I could win, I pedaled even faster. Suddenly, my pedals stopped!

Oh no! Thad's stick had untied my shoelace and it was wrapped around my pedal!

I was going to crash my bike. That's when my mind looked down. That's when I knew I could use my mind-scissors. I used the mind scissors to cut the shoelace my right foot was free.

That's how I won the race.

The story's beginning introduces the main character.

Events in the narrative progress somewhat logically, but the conflict is not completely clear. The writer uses some transition words.

The writer uses some description in the narrative.

The narrative demonstrates some accuracy in standard English conventions of usage and mechanics.

The words vary between vague and precise. The writer uses some sensory language.

The resolution is weak and adds very little to the narrative.

Mind-Scissors

When I was a baby I wound up with a tiny pair of scissors in my head. Lots of people live with pieces of metal in their heads. We just have to be careful. What the doctors couldn't have predicted is the uncanny ability they would give me.

Every summer there's a bike race that ends at the lake. The kid who always wins is Thad Thomas the Third, who is popular. This past summer that was about to change. It's also when I discovered what I could do with my mind-scissors.

The race starts. Right away racers start falling behind. After what seemed an eternity pumping hard at my pedals, I knew the end had to be in sight. I looked ahead and all I could see was Thad, and the opening to the woods—the last leg of the race.

I felt like steam was coming off my legs. I could see Thad's helmet. I turned my head to flash him a look. Only, Thad was the one who was gloating! And then I saw it—he was holding a stick he had pulled off a low-hanging branch.

He jabbed it toward me. I swerved out of the way. I kept pedaling, shifting my eyes to the right, to see what he was going to do.

But I waited too long. Then Thad made a slashing motion. Then he tossed the stick aside, yelled, "Yes!" and zoomed forward.

What happened? I felt nothing. We were now out of the woods and into the clearing before the finish line. Still hopeful I could win, I pedaled even faster. Suddenly, there was a jerk. My pedals had stopped!

I looked down. Oh no! My shoelace was wrapped around my pedal! Thad's stick had untied it!

I looked for a place to crash. That's when my head started tingling. I looked down at the shoelace. I concentrated really hard. I could see the scissors in my mind, floating just beside the pedal. Snip! The shoelace broke and my foot was free.

Thad was too busy listening to his fans cheer him on as I rode past him. Thanks to the mind-scissors, I won.

The story's beginning is engaging and clearly introduces the main character and situation.

Events in the narrative progress logically, and the conflict is clear. The writer uses transition words frequently.

The writer uses precise words and some sensory language to convey the experiences in the narrative and to describe the characters and scenes.

The writer uses some description and dialogue to add interest to the narrative and develop experiences and events.

The narrative demonstrates accuracy in standard English conventions of usage and mechanics.

The resolution follows from the rest of the narrative.

TOOL KIT: WRITING MODELS AND RUBRICS

Writing Models and Rubrics

MODEL

NARRATIVE: SCORE 4

Mind-Scissors

As long as I wear my bike helmet, they say I'll be okay. Lots of people live with pieces of metal in their heads. We just have to be careful. When I was a baby I wound up with a tiny pair of scissors in mine. What the doctors couldn't have predicted is the uncanny ability they would give me.

Every summer there's a bike race that ends at the lake. The kid who always wins is Thad Thomas the Third, who is popular, but if you ask me, it's because he knows how to sweet-talk everyone. This past summer that was about to change. It's also when I discovered what I could do with my mind-scissors.

The race starts. Right away, racers start falling behind. After what seemed an eternity pumping hard at my pedals, I knew the end had to be in sight. I looked ahead and all I could see was Thad and the opening to the woods—the last leg of the race.

I put my stamina to the test—pedaling harder than ever, I felt like steam was coming off my legs. Thad's red helmet came into view. As I could sense I was going to overtake him any second, I turned my head to flash him a look. Only, to my befuddlement, Thad was the one who was gloating! And then I saw it—he was holding a stick he had pulled off a low-hanging branch.

He jabbed it toward me. I swerved out of the way. Was he trying to poke me with it? I kept pedaling, shifting my eyes to the right, to see what he was going to do.

But I waited too long. Thad made a slashing motion. Then he tossed the stick aside, yelled, "Yes!" and zoomed forward.

What happened? I felt nothing. We were now out of the woods and into the clearing before the finish line. Still hopeful I could win, I pedaled even faster. Suddenly, there was a jerk. My pedals had stopped!

I looked down. Oh no! My shoelace was wrapped around my pedal! Thad's stick had untied the shoelace!

I coasted as I looked for a place to crash. That's when my head started tingling. I got this funny notion to try something. I looked down. I had the tangled shoelace in my sights. I concentrated really hard. I could see the scissors in my mind, floating just beside the pedal. Snip! The shoelace broke and my right foot was free.

Thad was busy motioning his fans to cheer him on as I made my greatest effort to pedal back up to speed. Guess who made it to the finish line first?

The story's beginning is engaging and introduces the main character and situation in a way that appeals to a reader.

The writer uses techniques such as dialogue and description to add interest to the narrative and to develop the characters and events.

Events in the narrative progress in logical order and are linked by clear transitions. The conflict is well established.

The writer uses vivid description and sensory language to convey the experiences in the narrative and to help the reader imagine the characters and scenes.

The writer uses standard English conventions of usage and mechanics.

The resolution follows from the events in the narrative.

Narrative Rubric

	1 (POOR)	**2** (WEAK)	**3** (GOOD)	**4** (EXCELLENT)
Clarity and Purpose	The beginning does not introduce characters or a situation. The conflict is unclear.	The beginning does not clearly introduce the situation or characters. The conflict is not well established.	The beginning introduces the characters and the situation. The conflict is established, but is not entirely developed.	An engaging beginning introduces the characters and situation in an appealing way. The conflict is well established and developed.
Organization	Events are jumbled and hard to follow and do not progress in chronological order.	Events are sometimes difficult to follow. They often do not progress in chronological order.	Most events are easy to follow and appear to progress in chronological order.	Events are easy to follow and clearly progress in chronological order.
Development of Ideas	Events do not progress logically and ideas seem disconnected. Sentences are not linked using transitions. The ending does not connect to the narrative or present an insight.	Events progress somewhat logically. Ideas are sometimes connected using transitions. The ending adds little to the narrative and provides a weak insight.	Most events progress logically. Ideas are often linked using transitions. The ending mostly follows from the narrative and provides an insight.	Events progress logically and are linked using clear transitions. The ending effectively follows from the narrative and provides and interesting insight.
Language and Style	Dialogue and description are absent. The narrative does not include sensory language or precise words to convey experiences and develop characters. The point of view is inconsistent.	The narrative includes some dialogue and description. Some precise words and sensory language are included. The point of view is not always consistent.	Dialogue and description are use to develop the story. Most words are precise and sensory language is included. The point of view is consistent.	Dialogue and description are used to add interest and develop the story. Word choice and sensory language are effectively used. The point of view is consistent.
Conventions	The narrative contains numerous misspellings and errors in standard English conventions. Punctuation is lacking or incorrect.	The narrative contains some misspellings and errors in standard English conventions. Punctuation is sometimes lacking or incorrect.	The narrative contains few misspellings and errors in standard English conventions. Punctuation is usually correct.	The narrative is free of errors in spelling, punctuation, and standard English conventions.

TOOL KIT: WRITING MODELS AND RUBRICS

Conducting Research

You can conduct research to gain more knowledge about a topic. Sources such as articles, books, interviews, or the Internet have the facts and explanations that you need. Not all of the information that you find, however, will be useful—or reliable. Strong research skills will help you find accurate information about your topic.

Narrowing or Broadening a Topic

The first step in any research is finding your topic. Choose a topic that is narrow enough to cover completely. If you can name your topic in just one or two words, it is probably too broad. Topics such as mythology, hip hop music, or Italy are too broad to cover in a single report. Narrow a broad topic into smaller subcategories.

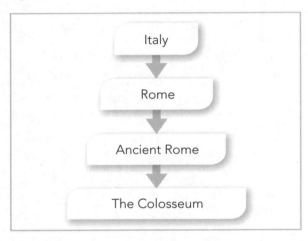

When you begin to research, pay attention to the amount of information available. If there is way too much information on your topic, you may need to narrow your topic further.

You might also need to broaden a topic if there is not enough information for your purpose. A topic is too narrow when it can be thoroughly presented in less space than the required size of your assignment. It might also be too narrow if you can find little or no information in library and media sources. Broaden your topic by including other related ideas.

Generating Research Questions

Use research questions to focus your research. Specific questions can help you avoid wasting time. For example, instead of simply hunting for information about Peter Pan, you might ask, "What inspired J. M. Barrie to write the story of Peter Pan?" or "How have different artists depicted Peter Pan?"

A research question may lead you to find your topic sentence. The question can also help you focus your research plan. Write your question down and keep it in mind while you hunt for facts. Your question can prevent you from gathering unnecessary information. As you learn more about your topic, you may need to refine your original question.

© Pearson Education, Inc., or its affiliates. All rights reserved.

Consulting Print and Digital Sources

An effective research project combines information from multiple sources. It is important not to rely too heavily on a single source. The creativity and originality of your research depends on how you synthesize, or combine, ideas from many places. Plan to include a variety of these resources:

- **Primary and Secondary Sources:** Use both primary sources (firsthand or original accounts, such as interview transcripts and newspaper articles) and secondary sources (accounts that are not created at the time of an event, such as encyclopedia entries).
- **Print and Digital Resources:** The Internet allows fast access to data, but print resources are often edited more carefully. Plan to include both print and digital resources in order to guarantee that your work is accurate.
- **Media Resources:** You can find valuable information in media resources such as documentaries, television programs, podcasts, and museum exhibitions.
- **Original Research:** Depending on your topic, you may wish to conduct original research to include among your sources. For example, you might interview experts or eyewitnesses or conduct a survey of people in your community.

Using Online Encyclopedias

Online encyclopedias are often written by anonymous contributors who are not required to fact-check information. These sites can be very useful as a launching point for research, but should not be considered accurate. Look for footnotes, endnotes, or hyperlinks that support facts with reliable sources that have been carefully checked by editors.

Evaluating Sources It is important to evaluate the credibility and accuracy of any information you find. Ask yourself questions such as these to evaluate sources:

- **Reliability and Credibility:** Is the author well known? What are the author's credentials? Does the source include references to other reliable sources? Does the author's tone win your confidence? Why or why not?
- **Bias:** Does the author have any obvious biases? What is the author's purpose for writing? Who is the target audience?
- **Currency:** When was the work created? Has it been revised? Is there more current information available?

Using Search Terms

Finding information on the Internet is easy, but it can be a challenge to find facts that are useful and trustworthy. If you type a word or phrase into a search engine, you will probably get hundreds—or thousands—of results. However, those results are not guaranteed to be relevant or accurate.

These strategies can help you find information from the Internet:

- Create a list of topic keywords before you begin using a search engine. Use a thesaurus to expand your list.
- Enter six to eight keywords.
- Choose unique nouns. Most search engines ignore articles and prepositions. Verbs may lead to sources that are not useful. Use modifiers, such as adjectives, when necessary to specify a category. For example, you might enter "ancient Rome" instead of "Rome."
- Use quotation marks to focus a search. Place a phrase in quotation marks to find pages that include exactly that phrase. Add several phrases in quotation marks to narrow your results.
- Spell carefully. Many search engines correct spelling automatically, but they cannot catch every spelling error.
- Scan search results before you click them. The first result isn't always the most useful. Read the text and notice the domain before you make a choice.
- Consult more than one search engine.

Evaluating Internet Domains

Not everything you read on the Internet is true, so you have to evaluate sources carefully. The last three letters of an Internet URL identify the site's domain, which can help you evaluate the information on the site.

- **.gov**—Government sites are sponsored by a branch of the United States federal government and are considered reliable.
- **.edu**—Information from an educational research center or department is likely to be carefully checked, but may include student pages that are not edited or monitored.
- **.org**—Organizations are often nonprofit groups and usually maintain a high level of credibility but may still reflect strong biases.
- **.com and .net**—Commercial sites exist to make a profit. Information might be biased to show a product or service in a good light.

Taking Notes

Use different strategies to take notes:

- Use index cards to create notecards and source cards. On each source card, record information about each source you use—author, title, publisher, date of publication, and relevant page numbers. On each notecard, record information to use in your writing. Use quotation marks when you copy exact words, and indicate the page number(s) on which the information appears.

- Photocopy articles and copyright pages. Then, highlight relevant information. Remember to include the Web addresses of printouts from online sources.

- Print articles from the Internet or copy them directly into a "notes" folder.

You will use these notes to help you write original text.

Source Card

> Papp, Joseph
> and Kirkland, Elizabeth
>
> **Shakespeare Alive!**
>
> New York: Bantam Books, 1988

Notecard

> Education
> Papp, p.5
>
> Only the upper classes could read.
>
> Most of the common people in Shakespeare's time could not read.

Quote Accurately Responsible research begins with the first note you take. Be sure to quote and paraphrase your sources accurately so you can identify these sources later. In your notes, circle all quotations and paraphrases to distinguish them from your own comments. When photocopying from a source, include the copyright information. Include the Web addresses of printouts from online sources.

Reviewing Research Findings

You will need to review your findings to be sure that you have collected enough accurate and appropriate information.

Considering Audience and Purpose

Always keep your audience in mind as you gather information. Different audiences may have very different needs. For example, if you are writing a report for your class about a topic you have studied together, you will not need to provide background information in your writing. However, if you are writing about the topic for a national student magazine, you cannot assume that all of your readers have the same information. You will need to provide background facts from reliable sources to help inform those readers about your subject. When thinking about your research and your audience, ask yourself:

- Who am I writing for?
- Have I collected enough information to explain my topic to this audience?
- Do I need to conduct more research to explain my topic clearly?
- Are there details in my research that I can leave out because they are already familiar to my audience?

Your purpose for writing will also affect your research review. If you are researching to satisfy your own curiosity, you can stop researching when you feel you understand the answer completely. If you are writing a research report that will be graded, you need to think about your assignment. When thinking about whether or not you have enough information, ask yourself:

- What is my purpose for writing?
- Will the information I've gathered be enough to achieve my purpose?
- If I need more information, where might I find it?

Synthesizing Sources

Effective research writing is more than just a list of facts and details. Good research synthesizes—gathers, orders, and interprets—those elements. These strategies will help you synthesize effectively:

- Review your notes. Look for connections and patterns among the details you have collected.
- Organize notes or notecards to help you plan how you will combine details.
- Pay close attention to details that emphasize the same main idea.
- Also look for details that challenge one another. For many topics, there is no single correct opinion. You might decide to conduct additional research to help you decide which side of the issue has more support.

Types of Evidence

When reviewing your research, also think about the kinds of evidence you have collected. The strongest writing combines a variety of evidence. This chart describes three of the most common types of evidence.

TYPE OF EVIDENCE	DESCRIPTION	EXAMPLE
Statistical evidence includes facts and other numerical data used to support a claim or explain a topic.	Statistical evidence are facts about a topic, such as historical dates, descriptions about size and number, and poll results.	Jane Goodall began to study chimpanzees when she was 26 years old.
Testimonial evidence includes any ideas or opinions presented by others. Testimonies might come from experts or people with special knowledge about a topic.	Firsthand testimonies present ideas from eyewitnesses to events or subjects being discussed.	Goodall's view of chimps has changed: "When I first started at Gombe, I thought the chimps were nicer than we are. But time has revealed that they are not. They can be just as awful."
	Secondary testimonies include commentaries on events by people who were not directly involved.	Science writer David Quammen points out that Goodall "set a new standard, a very high standard, for behavioral study of apes in the wild."
Anecdotal evidence presents one person's view of the world, often by describing specific events or incidents.	An anecdote is a story about something that happened. Personal stories can be part of effective research, but they should not be the only kind of evidence presented. Anecdotes are particularly useful for proving that broad generalizations are not accurate.	It is not fair to say that it is impossible for dogs to use tools. One researcher reports the story of a dog that learned to use a large bone as a back scratcher.

Incorporating Research Into Writing

Avoiding Plagiarism

Whether you are presenting a formal research paper or an opinion paper on a current event, you must be careful to give credit for any ideas or opinions that are not your own. Presenting someone else's ideas, research, or opinion as your own—even if you have phrased it in different words—is plagiarism, the equivalent of academic stealing, or fraud.

Do not use the ideas or research of others in place of your own. Read from several sources to draw your own conclusions and form your own opinions. Incorporate the ideas and research of others to support your points. Credit the source of the following types of support:

- Statistics
- Direct quotations
- Indirectly quoted statements of opinions
- Conclusions presented by an expert
- Facts available in only one or two sources

When you are drafting and revising, circle any words or ideas that are not your own. Follow the instructions on pages R30 and R31 to correctly cite those passages.

Reviewing for Plagiarism Take time to review your writing for accidental plagiarism. Read what you have written and take note of any ideas that do not have your personal writing voice. Compare those passages with your resource materials. You might have copied them without remembering the exact source. Add a correct citation to give credit to the original author. If you cannot find the questionable phrase in your notes, think about revising your word choices. You want to be sure that your final writing reflects your own thinking and not someone else's work.

Quoting and Paraphrasing

When including ideas from research in your writing, you will decide to quote directly or paraphrase.

Direct Quotation Use the author's exact words when they are interesting or persuasive. You might decide to include direct quotations in these situations:

- to share a strong statement
- to reference a historically significant passage
- to show that an expert agrees with your position
- to present an argument to which you will respond

Include complete quotations, without deleting or changing words. If you need to leave out words for space or clarity, use ellipsis points to show where you removed words. Enclose direct quotations in quotation marks.

Paraphrase A paraphrase restates an author's ideas in your own words. Be careful to paraphrase accurately. Beware of making sweeping generalizations in a paraphrase that were not made by the original author. You may use some words from the original source, but a good paraphrase does more than simply rearrange an author's phrases, or replace a few words with synonyms.

Original Text	"Some teens doing homework while listening to music and juggling tweets and texts may actually work better that way, according to an intriguing new study performed by two high-school seniors." *Sumathi Reddy, "Teen Researchers Defend Media Multitasking"*
Patchwork Plagiarism phrases from the original are rearranged, but they too closely follow the original text.	An intriguing new study conducted by two high-school seniors suggests that teens work better when they are listening to music and juggling texts and tweets.
Good Paraphrase	Two high-school students studied homework habits. They concluded that some people do better work while multitasking, such as studying and listening to music or checking text messages at the same time.

Maintaining the Flow of Ideas

Effective research writing is much more than just a list of facts. Maintain the flow of ideas by connecting research information to your own ideas. Instead of simply stating a piece of evidence, use transitions to connect information you found from outside resources with your own thinking. The transitions shown here can be used to introduce, compare, contrast, and clarify.

Choosing an effective organizational strategy for your writing will help you create a logical flow of ideas. Once you have chosen a clear organization, add research in appropriate places to provide evidence and support.

Useful Transitions

When providing examples:

for example   for instance   to illustrate   in [name of resource], [author]

When comparing and contrasting ideas or information:

in the same way   similarly   however   on the other hand

When clarifying ideas or opinions:

in other words   that is   to explain   to put it another way

ORGANIZATIONAL STRUCTURE	USES
Chronological order presents information in the sequence in which it happens.	historical topics; science experiments; analysis of narratives
Part-to-whole order examines how several categories affect a larger subject.	analysis of social issues; historical topics
Order of importance presents information in order of increasing or decreasing importance.	persuasive arguments; supporting a bold or challenging thesis
Comparison-and-contrast organization presents similarities and differences.	addressing two or more subjects

Formats for Citing Sources

When you cite a source, you acknowledge where you found your information and you give your readers the details necessary for locating the source themselves. Within the body of a paper, you provide a short citation, a footnote number linked to a footnote, or an endnote number linked to an endnote reference. These brief references show the page numbers on which you found the information. Prepare a reference list at the end of a research report to provide full bibliographic information on your sources. These are two common types of reference lists:

- A bibliography provides a listing of all the resources you consulted during your research.
- A works-cited list indicates the works you have referenced in your writing.

The chart on the next page shows the Modern Language Association format for crediting sources. This is the most common format for papers written in the content areas in middle school and high school. Unless instructed otherwise by your teacher, use this format for crediting sources.

Focus on Citations When you revise your writing, check that you cite the sources for quotations, factual information, and ideas that are not your own. Most word-processing programs have features that allow you to create footnotes and endnotes.

Identifying Missing Citations These strategies can help you find facts and details that should be cited in your writing:

- Look for facts that are not general knowledge. If a fact was unique to one source, it needs a citation.
- Read your report aloud. Listen for words and phrases that do not sound like your writing style. You might have picked them up from a source. If so, use your notes to find the source, place the words in quotation marks, and give credit.
- Review your notes. Look for ideas that you used in your writing but did not cite.

MLA (8th Edition) Style for Listing Sources

Book with one author	Pyles, Thomas. *The Origins and Development of the English Language.* 2nd ed., Harcourt Brace Jovanovich, 1971. [Indicate the edition or version number when relevant.]
Book with two authors	Pyles, Thomas, and John Algeo. *The Origins and Development of the English Language.* 5th ed., Cengage Learning, 2004.
Book with three or more authors	Donald, Robert B., et al. *Writing Clear Essays.* Prentice Hall, 1983.
Book with an editor	Truth, Sojourner. *Narrative of Sojourner Truth.* Edited by Margaret Washington, Vintage Books, 1993.
Introduction to a work in a published edition	Washington, Margaret. Introduction. *Narrative of Sojourner Truth,* by Sojourner Truth, edited by Washington, Vintage Books, 1993, pp. v–xi.
Single work in an anthology	Hawthorne, Nathaniel. "Young Goodman Brown." *Literature: An Introduction to Reading and Writing,* edited by Edgar V. Roberts and Henry E. Jacobs, 5th ed., Prentice Hall, 1998, pp. 376–385. [Indicate pages for the entire selection.]
Signed article from an encyclopedia	Askeland, Donald R. "Welding." *World Book Encyclopedia,* vol. 21, World Book, 1991, p. 58.
Signed article in a weekly magazine	Wallace, Charles. "A Vodacious Deal." *Time,* 14 Feb. 2000, p. 63.
Signed article in a monthly magazine	Gustaitis, Joseph. "The Sticky History of Chewing Gum." *American History,* Oct. 1998, pp. 30–38.
Newspaper article	Thurow, Roger. "South Africans Who Fought for Sanctions Now Scrap for Investors." *Wall Street Journal,* 11 Feb. 2000, pp. A1+. [For a multipage article that does not appear on consecutive pages, write only the first page number on which it appears, followed by the plus sign.]
Unsigned editorial or story	"Selective Silence." Editorial. *Wall Street Journal,* 11 Feb. 2000, p. A14. [If the editorial or story is signed, begin with the author's name.]
Signed pamphlet or brochure	[Treat the pamphlet as though it were a book.]
Work from a library subscription service	Ertman, Earl L. "Nefertiti's Eyes." *Archaeology,* Mar.–Apr. 2008, pp. 28–32. *Kids Search,* EBSCO, New York Public Library. Accessed 7 Jan. 2017. [Indicating the date you accessed the information is optional but recommended.]
Filmstrips, slide programs, videocassettes, DVDs, and other audiovisual media	*The Diary of Anne Frank.* 1959. Directed by George Stevens, performances by Millie Perkins, Shelley Winters, Joseph Schildkraut, Lou Jacobi, and Richard Beymer, Twentieth Century Fox, 2004. [Indicating the original release date after the title is optional but recommended.]
CD-ROM (with multiple publishers)	Simms, James, editor. *Romeo and Juliet.* By William Shakespeare, Attica Cybernetics / BBC Education / Harper, 1995.
Radio or television program transcript	"Washington's Crossing of the Delaware." *Weekend Edition Sunday,* National Public Radio, 23 Dec. 2013. Transcript.
Web page	"Fun Facts About Gum." ICGA, 2005–2017, www.gumassociation.org/index.cfm/facts-figures/fun-facts-about-gum. Accessed 19 Feb. 2017. [Indicating the date you accessed the information is optional but recommended.]
Personal interview	Smith, Jane. Personal interview, 10 Feb. 2017.

All examples follow the style given in the MLA Handbook, 8th edition, published in 2016.

EQ Notes / Word Network Model

MODEL

EQ Notes

Unit Title: _Discovery_

Perfomance-Based Assessment Prompt:
Do all discoveries benefit humanity?

My initial thoughts:
Yes - all knowledge moves us forward.

As you read multiple texts about a topic, your thinking may change. Create EQ Notes like these to record your thoughts, to track details you might use in later writing or discussion, and to make further connections.

Here is a sample to show how one reader's ideas deepened as she read two texts.

TITLE	MY IDEAS/OBSERVATIONS	TEXT EVIDENCE/INFORMATION
Classifying the Stars	Newton shared his discoveries and then other scientists built on his discoveries.	Paragraph 2: "Isaac Newton gave to the world the results of his experiments on passing sunlight through a prism." Paragraph 3: "In 1814 . . . the German optician, Fraunhofer . . . saw that the multiple spectral tints . . . were crossed by hundreds of fine dark lines."

How does this text change or add to my thinking? This confirms what I think.　　Date: _Sept. 20_

TITLE	MY IDEAS/OBSERVATIONS	TEXT EVIDENCE/INFORMATION
Cell Phone Mania	Cell phones have made some forms of communication easier, but people don't talk to each other as much as they did in the past.	Paragraph 7: "Over 80% of young adults state that texting is their primary method of communicating with friends. This contrasts with older adults who state that they prefer a phone call."

How does this text change or add to my thinking?　　Date: _Sept. 25_

Maybe there are some downsides to discoveries. I still think that knowledge moves us forward, but sometimes there are negative effects.

Word Network

A word network is a collection of words related to a topic. As you read the selections in a unit, identify interesting theme-related words and build your vocabulary by adding them to your Word Network.

Use your Word Network as a resource for your discussions and writings. Here is an example:

challenge

uncovered

perseverance

achieve/achievement

novel

research/search

explore/exploration

reveal/revelation

results

DISCOVERY

experiment

observe/observation

scientific

scrutinize/scrutiny

innovate

ground-breaking

investigation

expeditions

inquiry

Academic vocabulary appears in **blue type**.

Pronunciation Key

Symbol	Sample Words	Symbol	Sample Words
a	at, catapult, Alabama	oo	boot, soup, crucial
ah	heart, charms, argue	ow	now, stout, flounder
ai	care, various, hair	oy	boy, toil, oyster
aw	law, maraud, caution	s	say, nice, press
awr	pour, organism, forewarn	sh	she, abolition, motion
ay	ape, sails, implication	u	full, put, book
ee	even, teeth, really	uh	ago, focus, contemplation
eh	ten, repel, elephant	ur	bird, urgent, perforation
ehr	merry, verify, terribly	y	by, delight, identify
ih	it, pin, hymn	yoo	music, confuse, few
o	shot, hopscotch, condo	zh	pleasure, treasure, vision
oh	own, parole, rowboat		

A

abandoned (uh BAN duhnd) *adj.* left behind; tossed aside

admired (uhd MYRD) *v.* respected or approved of

agile (AJ uhl) *adj.* able to move quickly and easily

animation (an uh MAY shuhn) *n.* process of making films or cartoons from drawings, computer graphics, or photos

apologetically (uh pol uh JEHT ihk lee) *adv.* in a way that shows someone is sorry for having done or said something; regretfully

askance (uh SKANS) *adv.* with an attitude of suspicion or disapproval

audio (AW dee oh) *n.* recorded sound

B

background (BAK grownd) *n.* the part of an image farthest from the observer

benefit (BEHN uh fiht) *n.* positive result; fundraising event

beware (bee WAIR) *v.* act carefully in case there is danger

breaches (BREE chuhz) *n.* gaps in a line of defense

bypassed (BY past) *v.* gotten around or avoided

C

camera angle (KAM ruh) (AN guhl) *n.* position from which a photograph is taken

certain (SUR tuhn) *adj.* without a doubt; reliable; particular

coherent (koh HIHR uhnt) *adj.* logical; clearly communicated

composition (kom puh ZIH shuhn) *n.* arrangement of different elements in a work of art

compromise (KOM pruh myz) *n.* settlement of a disagreement in which each side gives up part of what it wanted

consequently (kon suh KWEHNT lee) *adv.* as a result; therefore

consumed (kuhn SOOMD) *adj.* absorbed; occupied

consideration (kuhn sihd uh RAY shuhn) *n.* careful thought

continuation (kuhn tihn yoo AY shuhn) *n.* state of going on without interruption; unbroken action

contribute (kuhn TRIHB yoot) *v.* give or provide along with others

convince (kuhn VIHNS) *v.* persuade

criminals (KRIHM uh nuhlz) *n.* people who break the law

critical (KRIHT uh kuhl) *adj.* disapproving or having a negative opinion about; very important

cumbersome (KUHM buhr suhm) *adj.* difficult to carry or wear because of heaviness and bulk

cut-out animation (KUHT owt) (an uh MAY shuhn) *n.* technique that uses flat characters, backgrounds, and props cut from materials such as paper, cardboard, and fabric

D

darting (DAHRT ihng) *v.* moving suddenly or rapidly

declare (dih KLAIR) *v.* make a statement; announce

deliberate (dih LIHB uhr iht) *adj.* carefully thought over in advance; planned

description (dih SKRIHP shuhn) *n.* words meant to evoke a detailed image in the listener's or reader's mind

desperate (DEHS puhr iht) *adj.* suffering extreme need or frustration; with little hope

detached (dih TACHT) *adj.* separated, not attached

devouring (dih VOW rihng) *v.* taking in greedily

dialogue (DY uh log) *n.* conversation

dignified (DIHG nuh fyd) *adj.* in a manner worthy of respect

disguise (dihs GYZ) *v.* change or hide appearance

disgusted (dihs GUHS tihd) *adj.* feeling a strong dislike; annoyed

distressed (dih STREHST) *adj.* troubled; upset

domesticated (duh MEHS tuh kay tuhd) *adj.* changed from a wild state to a tame state

dominate (DOM uh nayt) *v.* rule or control

drained (draynd) *v.* used up; emptied of energy

E

elaborate (ih LAB uh rayt) *v.* explain by adding more details

encapsulation (ehn kap suh LAY shuhn) *n.* choice of important scenes to display in each panel

endured (ehn DOORD) *v.* underwent without giving in; suffered

envied (EHN veed) *v.* badly wanted something someone else had

evaluate (ee VAL yoo ayt) *v.* determine the value or condition of someone or something in a careful and thoughtful way

exception (ehk SEHP shuhn) *n.* case to which a rule does not apply

exclude (ehk SKLOOD) *v.* shut out; keep from entering, happening, or being

exploiting (ehk SPLOYT ihng) *v.* taking unfair advantage of

F

fearlessly (FEER lihs lee) *adv.* without fear

feathery (FEHTH uhr ee) *adj.* light and airy, like the touch of a feather

foreground (FAWR grownd) *n.* the part of an image closest to the observer

forged (fawrjd) *v.* made falsely with intent to trick

forlorn (fawr LAWRN) *adj.* sad, hopeless, abandoned, and lonely

fraud (frawd) *n.* a crime that involves deception and fakery

G

gradually (GRAJ oo uhl ee) *adv.* in a way that is little by little

H

hacked (hakt) *v.* gained illegal access to private information

host (hohst) *n.* someone who introduces and talks to the guests on a television or radio program

hostile (HOS tuhl) *adj.* dangerous or hazardous

hover (HUH vuhr) *v.* remain in one place in the air

humming (HUHM ihng) *v.* singing with closed lips and without words

I

ignorance (IHG nuhr uhns) *n.* state of lacking knowledge, learning, or information

illustrate (IHL uh strayt) *v.* provide pictures, diagrams or maps that explain or decorate; provide an example that demonstrates an idea

images or graphics (IHM uh jihz) (GRAF ihks) *n.* representations of a person or thing

impetuous (ihm PEHCH yoo uhs) *adj.* acting suddenly with little thought

impostor (ihm POS tuhr) *n.* a person who pretends to be someone else in order to deceive people

inker (IHNGK uhr) *n.* artist who goes over the penciled art in ink

insincerity (ihn sihn SEHR uh tee) *n.* lack of honesty; untruthfulness

intelligent (ihn TEH luh juhnt) *adj.* able to learn and understand things

intensity (ihn TEHN suh tee) *n.* great focus or concentration; strong commitment

interpret (ihn TUR pruht) *v.* explain the meaning of something

interview (IHN tuhr vyoo) *n.* recorded conversation in which someone is asked questions about his or her life, experiences, or opinions

investigation (ihn vehs tuh GAY shuhn) *n.* careful examination of something, especially to discover the truth about it

irritable (IHR uh tuh buhl) *adj.* easily annoyed or angered

J

journey (JUR nee) *n.* trip from one place to another

justify (JUHS tuh fy) *v.* show or prove to be right or reasonable

K

keen (keen) *adj.* extremely clear or sharp in perception

L

lamented (luh MEHN tihd) *v.* said in a way that showed sadness or sorrow

letterer (LEHT uhr uhr) *n.* artist who letters the dialogue and captions

loftily (LAWF tih lee) *adv.* in a superior manner

M

malice (MAL ihs) *n.* meanness; ill will

malicious (muh LIHSH uhs) *adj.* having or showing bad intentions

manual (MAN yoo uhl) *adj.* of, relating to, or involving the hands; *n.* instructional text

masquerade (mas kuh RAYD) *v.* pretend to be someone or something else

measurable (MEH zhuhr uh buhl) *adj.* having a size or quantity that can be dtermined

memorize (MEHM uh ryz) *v.* learn well enough to later recall; learn by heart

milled (mihld) *v.* moved about in a confused way

misapprehension (mihs ap ree HEHN shuhn) *n.* incorrect understanding; wrong idea

miserable (MIHZ uhr uh buhl) *adj.* extremely unhappy or uncomfortable

mission (MIH shuhn) *n.* ambition or goal

model (MOD uhl) *n.* set of ideas to be followed as a plan or an example

mournfully (MAWRN fuh lee) *adv.* in a way that expresses grief or sadness

N

narrator (NA ray tuhr) *n.* person who tells a story

nonchalantly (non shuh LONT lee) *adv.* in an unconcerned way

nostalgic (nuhs TAL jihk) *adj.* longing for the past

novelty (NOV uhl tee) *n.* something new, fresh, or unusual; *adj.* unusual and mainly for fun

O

object animation (OB jehkt) (an uh MAY shuhn) *n.* form that involves the movement of non-drawn objects, such as a book or a pen

objective (uhb JEHK tihv) *n.* aim or goal

observing (uhb ZUR vihng) *v.* watching carefully

obsessive (uhb SEHS ihv) *adj.* tending to think or worry so much about something that you cannot think about anything else

obstacle (OB stuh kuhl) *n.* something that stands in the way or stops progress

omit (oh MIHT) *v.* leave out

opposable (uh POH zuh buhl) *adj.* able to be placed against one or more of the other fingers on the same hand or foot

P

pacing (PAYS ihng) *n.* rate at which one speaks

panel (PAN uhl) *n.* individual frame of a comic, depicting a single moment

parameters (puh RAM uh tuhrz) *n.* boundaries; characteristics

pathetically (puh THEHT ihk lee) *adv.* in a way that causes someone to feel pity

penciler (PEHN suhl uhr) *n.* artist who sketches the basic layout for each panel

performance (puhr FAWR muhns) *n.* entertainment presented before an audience

perilously (PAIR uh luhs lee) *adv.* involving peril or danger

personal account (PUR suh nuhl) (uh KOWNT) *n.* account of a personal experience told from the first-person point of view

pessimistic (pehs uh MIHS tihk) *adj.* expecting the worst; focusing on the bad aspects of a situation

phenomenon (fuh NOM uh NON) *n.* rare or important fact or event

podcast (POD kast) *n.* digital audio or video file or recording, usually part of a series, that can be downloaded from the Internet

prehensile (pree HEHN suhl) *adj.* able to grab or hold something by wrapping around it

presume (prih ZOOM) *v.* take for granted; assume something to be the case

primary source (PRY mair ee) (SAWRS) *n.* source that provides firsthand evidence about an event, object, person, or work of art

process (PROS ehs) *v.* gain an understanding

Q

quest (kwehst) *n.* long search undertaken in order to find or realize something

quivering (KWIHV uhr ihng) *n.* trembling; shivering

R

real-time animation (REEL tym) (an uh MAY shuhn) *n.* style in which animated events or objects are reproduced so that they appear to be occurring or moving at the same speed they would in real life

rebelliousness (rih BEHL yuhs nihs) *n.* refusal to obey

recognize (REHK uhg nyz) *v.* identify something from memory or description; acknowledge as worthy of appreciation; honor

reflect (rih FLEHKT) *v.* think carefully; show or give back an image

relentlessly (rih LEHNT lihs lee) *adv.* without stopping; with determination

respected (rih SPEHK tihd) *adj.* honored; treated with esteem

righteous (RY chuhs) *adj.* morally right or justifiable; virtuous

S

scorched (skawrcht) *v.* burned with extreme heat

scouting (SKOWT ihng) *v.* exploring to obtain information

security (suh KYOOR uh tee) *n.* protection, safety measure

seeking (SEE kihng) *v.* searching for

sensible (SEHN suh buhl) *adj.* reasonable, practical

sensitive (SEHN suh tihv) *adj.* able to easily detect stimulation

shun (shuhn) *v.* persistently avoid, ignore, or reject

shushes (SHUHSH ihz) *v.* tells or signals someone to be quiet

skittered (SKIHT uhrd) *v.* moved lightly or quickly

sorrowfully (SAWR oh fuhl ee) *adv.* done with sadness

speculate (SPEHK yuh layt) *v.* guess, using information that is uncertain or incomplete

speech balloon (speech) (buh LOON) *n.* display of what a character is speaking or thinking

squish (skwihsh) *n.* spongy, cushioned feeling when walking on a flexible surface

sufficient (suh FIHSH uhnt) *adj.* as much as needed

surmise (suhr MYZ) *v.* guess, using only intuition or imagination

suspended (suh SPEHND ihd) *v.* hung

suspense (suh SPEHNS) *n.* uncertainty and excitement about an outcome

suspiciously (suh SPIHSH uhs lee) *adv.* based on a lack of trust or belief; disbelievingly; cautiously

swiftly (SWIHFT lee) *adv.* without delay or quickly

T

template (TEHM pliht) *n.* pattern or shape to be used as an example

thorough (THUR oh) *adj.* including everything possible; careful and complete

threateningly (THREHT uhn ihng lee) *adv.* in a frightening or alarming way

transform (trans FAWRM) *v.* convert or change

twirl (twurl) *v.* turn around and around quickly

twist (twihst) *v.* wind or spin around one another

U

unprotected (uhn pruh TEHKT ihd) *adj.* not kept safe from harm; not protected

V

valiant (VAL yuhnt) *adj.* possessing or showing courage or determination

valid (VAL ihd) *adj.* acceptable; based on and supported by facts

vanished (VAN ihsht) *v.* disappeared

visionary (VIH zhuh nair ee) *adj.* marked by foresight and imagination

voiceover (VOYS oh vuhr) *n.* voice commenting on the action or narrating a film off-camera

volume (VOL yoom) *n.* softness or loudness of voice

vulnerabilities (vuhl nuhr uh BIHL uh teez) *n.* areas of weakness

El vocabulario académico está en **letra azul**.

A

abandoned / abandonado *adj.* dejado atrás; descartado

admired / admiró *v.* respetó o aprobó

agile / ágil *adj.* capaz de moverse con rapidez y facilidad

animation / animación *s.* proceso de crear películas o caricaturas a partir de dibujos, gráficas de computadora o fotos

apologetically / arrepentido *adv.* de una manera que muestra sentimiento de pesar por haber hecho o dicho algo

askance / con recelo *adv.* con actitud de sospecha o desconfianza

audio / audio *s.* sonido grabado

B

background / fondo *s.* la parte de una imagen que está más lejos del observador

benefit / beneficio; acto benéfico *s.* resultado positivo; evento realizado para recaudar fondos

beware / cuidarse de *v.* actuar con cuidado por si hay peligro

breaches / rupturas *s.* aperturas en una línea de defensa

bypassed / rodeó *v.* evitó al ir por otro camino

C

camera angle / ángulo de la cámara *s.* posición desde la que se toma una fotografía

certain / incuestionable *adj.* que no presenta dudas; fiable

coherent / coherente *adj.* comunica con claridad y lógica

composition / composición *s.* disposición de distintos elementos en una obra de arte

compromise / mutuo acuerdo *s.* acuerdo alcanzado por partes distintas o enfrentadas en el que cada parte cede en algo

consequently / por consiguiente *adv.* en consecuencia; por lo tanto

consumed / abstraído *adj.* absorto en, ocupado con

consideration / consideración *s.* pensar sobre algo y analizarlo con atención

continuation / continuación *s.* acción de seguir sin interrupción; acción que no se detiene

contribute / contribuir *v.* dar o aportar junto con otras personas

convince / convencer *v.* persuadir

criminals / delincuentes *s.* personas que violan la ley

critical / crítico crucial *adj.* que suele estar en contra de hechos e ideas / muy importante

cumbersome / engorroso *adj.* difícil de llevar o de usar por pesado y abultado

cut-out animation / animación con recortes *s.* técnica que utiliza figuras planas, fondos y objetos recortados de materiales tales como papel, cartón y tela

D

darting / disparando *v.* moviéndose con rapidez o repentinamente

declare / declarar *v.* decir algo públicamente; anunciar

deliberate / meditado *adj.* pensado de antemano; que se ha reflexionado qué hacer atenta y detenidamente

description / descripción *s.* palabras con las que se procura evocar una imagen detallada en la mente del oyente o lector

desperate / desesperado *adj.* que sufre necesidad o frustración extrema y con poca esperanza

detached / desconectado *adj.* separado, no conectado

devouring / devorando *v.* consumiendo de manera voraz

dialogue / diálogo *s.* conversación

dignified / digno *adj.* que merece respeto

disguise / disfrazar *v.* cambiar u ocultar la apariencia

disgusted / indignado *adj.* con un fuerte sentimiento de desaprobación; molesto

distressed / consternado *adj.* apenado; molesto

domesticated / domesticado *adj.* que cambió de un estado salvaje a uno manso

dominate / dominar *v.* dirigir o controlar

drained / agotó *v.* consumió; usó toda la energía

E

elaborate / profundizar *v.* explicar incluyendo muchos detalles

encapsulation / encapsulación *s.* selección de las escenas importantes que van a aparecer en cada viñeta

endured / toleró *v.* padeció sin rendirse; soportó

envied / envidió *v.* deseó mucho algo que tenía otro

evaluate / evaluar *v.* determinar el valor o la condición de alguien o algo de manera atenta y concienzuda

exception / excepción *s.* caso al que no se aplica una regla

exclude / excluir *v.* dejar fuera; impedir que entre, que ocurra o que esté

exploiting / explotando *v.* sacando ventaja de algo injustamente

F

fearlessly / intrépidamente *adv.* sin miedo

feathery / ligero *adj.* que no pesa mucho y es vaporoso, como una pluma de ave

foreground / frente *s.* la parte de una imagen que está más cerca del observador

forged / falsificó *v.* fabricó con intención de engañar

forlorn / desolado *adj.* triste, sin esperanzas, abandonado y solo

fraud / fraude *s.* delito que involucra engaño y falsificación

G

gradually / gradualmente *adv.* que ocurre poco a poco

H

hacked / hackeó *v.* obtuvo acceso ilegal a información privada

host / presentador *s.* persona que presenta y habla con los invitados en un programa de televisión o de radio

hostile / hostil *adj.* peligroso o adverso

hover / cernerse *v.* permanecer en un mismo lugar en el aire

humming / tarareo *s.* acción de cantar con los labios cerrados y sin palabras

I

ignorance / ignorancia *s.* falta de conocimiento, educación o información

illustrate / ilustrar *v.* hacer dibujos, diagramas o mapas para explicar o decorar una historia; proveer un ejemplo que demuestre una idea

images or graphics / imágenes o gráficas *s.* representaciones de una persona o cosa

impetuous / impulsivo *adj.* que actúa repentinamente y con poca reflexión

impostor / impostor *s.* persona que simula ser otra para engañar

inker / entintador *s.* artista que repasa con tinta un dibujo hecho a lápiz

insincerity / insinceridad *s.* falta de honestidad; falsedad

intelligent / inteligente *adj.* capaz de aprender y entender

intensity / intensidad *s.* cualidad de concentrarse o comprometerse del todo

interpret / interpretar *v.* explicar el significado o sentido de algo

interview / entrevista *s.* conversación grabada en la cual se hacen preguntas a una persona sobre su vida, sus experiencias o sus opiniones

investigation / investigación *s.* examen minucioso de un asunto, especialmente para descubrir la verdad acerca de él

irritable / irritable *adj.* que se enoja o indigna fácilmente

J

journey / travesía *s.* viaje de un lugar a otro

justify / justificar *v.* demostrar que es correcto o razonable

K

keen / sagaz *adj.* de percepción sumamente clara o aguda

L

lamented / lamentó *v.* expresó pena o tristeza

letterer / rotulista *s.* artista que escribe los textos de los diálogos y las leyendas

loftily / altivamente *adv.* con aire de superioridad

M

malice / malicia *s.* maldad; mala voluntad

malicious / malicioso *adj.* que tiene o demuestra malas intenciones

manual / manual *adj.* relativo a las manos o que se hace con ellas; *n.* texto de enseñanza

masquerade / aparentar *v.* simular ser alguien o algo distinto de lo que se es

measurable / mensurable *adj.* de tamaño o cantidad determinable

memorize / memorizar *v.* aprender algo de manera que pueda recordarse perfectamente luego

milled / vagó *v.* se movió desplazándose sin orden ni dirección

misapprehension / malentendido *s.* confusión

miserable / miserable *adj.* profundamente infeliz e incómodo

mission / misión *s.* ambición o meta

model / modelo *s.* conjunto de ideas que se deben seguir como plan de acción o ejemplo

mournfully / tristemente *adv.* de una manera que manifiesta pena y desconsuelo

N

narrator / narrador *s.* persona que cuenta una historia

nonchalantly / con aire despreocupado *adv.* hecho de manera indiferente

nostalgic / nostálgico *adj.* que extraña el pasado

novelty / novedad *s.* algo nuevo, fresco o infrecuente; *adj.* inusual y principalmente para diversión

O

object animation / animación de objetos *s.* técnica que utiliza los movimientos de objetos que no han sido dibujados, como un libro o una pluma

objective / objetivo *s.* finalidad o meta

observing / observando *v.* mirando con detenimiento

obsessive / obsesivo *adj.* que se preocupa tanto por algo que no puede pensar en otra cosa

obstacle / obstáculo *s.* algo que se cruza en nuestro camino o nos impide progresar

omit / omitir *v.* pasar por alto

opposable / oponible *adj.* que puede colocarse frente a uno o más de los demás dedos de la misma mano o pie

P

pacing / ritmo *s.* velocidad a la que se habla

panel / viñeta *s.* cada uno de los recuadros de un cómic, mostrando un momento individual

parameters / parámetros *s.* límites; características

pathetically / patéticamente *adv.* de manera que provoca pena a una persona

penciler / dibujante *s.* artista que bosqueja las viñetas en una página

performance / actuación *s.* entretenimiento que se presenta frente a un público

perilously / peligrosamente *adv.* con peligro o riesgo

personal account / relato personal *s.* relato de una experiencia personal contado en primera persona

pessimistic / pesimista *adj.* que espera lo peor; que se concentra en los aspectos negativos de una situación

phenomenon / fenómeno *s.* hecho o suceso poco común o importante

podcast / podcast *s.* archivo digital o de audio o de video, que forma normalmente parte de una serie y se puede descargar de Internet

prehensile / prensil *adj.* que puede enroscarse sobre algo para asirlo o tomarlo

presume / presumir *v.* suponer que algo es cierto; asumir

primary source / fuente primaria *s.* fuente que proporciona evidencia de primera mano acerca de un suceso, objeto, persona u obra de arte

process / procesar *v.* lograr el entendimiento de información

Q

quest / búsqueda *s.* acción de ir en busca de algo, expedición larga

quivering / temblor *s.* estremecimiento

R

real-time animation / animación en tiempo real *s.* técnica que consiste en simular que eventos u objetos animados ocurran o se muevan a la misma velocidad que en la vida real

rebelliousness / rebeldía *s.* negativa a obedecer

recognize / reconocer *v.* identificar algo a través de la memoria o mediante una descripción

reflect / reflejar; reflexionar *v.* mostrar o devolver una imagen; pensar detenidamente

relentlessly / implacablemente *adv.* sin detenerse; con determinación

respected / respetado *adj.* venerado; tratado con aprecio

righteous / recto *adj.* moralmente correcto o justificable; virtuoso

S

scorched / chamuscó *v.* quemó con calor extremo

scouting / explorando *v.* recorriendo para obtener información

security / seguridad *s.* protección, medida preventiva

seeking / buscando *v.* procurando encontrar

sensible / sensato *adj.* razonable, práctico

sensitive / sensible *adj.* que detecta el estímulo con facilidad

shun / evitar *v.* ignorar o rechazar persistentemente

shushes / hace callar *v.* manda o señala a alguien que guarde silencio

skittered / se escabulló *v.* se movió sutil y rápidamente

sorrowfully / tristemente *adv.* hecho con pena

speculate / especular *v.* pensar sobre algo y formar una idea sin tener información definitiva

speech balloon / globo de diálogo *s.* espacio donde se escribe lo que el personaje dice o piensa

squish / blandura *s.* sensación suave y esponjosa que se tiene al caminar en una superficie flexible y mullida

sufficient / suficiente *adj.* bastante para cubrir lo necesario

surmise / conjeturar *v.* adivinar; pensar algo sin tener datos definitivos en que basarse

suspended / suspendió *v.* colgó

suspense / suspenso *s.* emoción acerca de un resultado desconocido

suspiciously / sospechosamente *adv.* con recelo, que causa desconfianza

swiftly / raudamente *adv.* enseguida, sin demoras

template / patrón *s.* plantilla o forma fija que se usa como ejemplo

thorough / riguroso *adj.* meticuloso; completo; incluyendo cada detalle posible

threateningly / amenazadoramente *adv.* de manera que da miedo o alarmante

transform / transformar *v.* convertir o cambiar

twirl / dar vueltas *v.* girar sobre sí mismo rápidamente

twist / girar *v.* enrollarse o dar vueltas alrededor de sí mismo

U

unprotected / desprotegido *adj.* sin resguardo contra el daño; sin protección

V

valiant / valeroso *adj.* que tiene o demuestra valentía o determinación

valid / válido *adj.* aceptable; que se basa o respalda con hechos

vanished / desapareció *v.* se esfumó, dejó de estar a la vista

visionary / visionario *adj.* que se caracteriza por su visión de futuro y su imaginación

voiceover / voz en off *s.* voz que comenta sobre la acción o narra una película detrás de la cámara

volume / volumen *s.* intensidad del sonido

vulnerabilities / vulnerabilidades *s.* aspectos que muestran debilidad

GLOSARIO: VOCABULARIO ACADÉMICO / VOCABULARIO DE CONCEPTOS

ANALOGY An *analogy* makes a comparison between two or more things that are similar in some ways but otherwise unalike.

ANECDOTE An *anecdote* is a brief nonfiction story about an interesting, amusing, or strange event. Writers tell anecdotes to entertain or to make a point.

ARGUMENT In an *argument*, the writer states and supports a claim, or opinion, based on factual evidence and logical reasoning. Most arguments are composed of an *introduction*, in which a claim is stated; the *body*, in which the claim is supported by evidence; and the *conclusion*, in which the claim is summarized or restated.

AUDIENCE The *audience* of a literary work is the person or people that a writer or speaker is addressing. The writer or speaker must consider the interests, knowledge, and education of his or her intended audience, which will help shape the work.

AUTHOR'S POINT OF VIEW The attitude toward a topic an author reveals in a piece of nonfiction writing shows the *author's point of view*.

AUTHOR'S PURPOSE An *author's purpose* is his or her main reason for writing. For example, an author may want to entertain, inform, or persuade the reader. Sometimes an author is trying to teach a moral lesson or reflect on an experience. An author may have more than one purpose for writing.

AUTOBIOGRAPHY An *autobiography* is the story of the writer's own life, told by the writer. Autobiographical writing may tell about the person's whole life or only a part of it.

Because autobiographies are about real people and events, they are a form of nonfiction. Most autobiographies are written in the *first-person point of view*.

BIOGRAPHY A *biography* is a form of nonfiction in which a writer tells the life story of another person. Most biographies are written about famous or admirable people. Although biographies are nonfiction, the most effective ones share the qualities of good narrative writing.

BLOG A *blog post* is a piece of online writing added to an online journal, called a *blog*. Writers of blogs provide information or express thoughts on various subjects.

BOOK FEATURES *Book features* can include acknowledgements, a foreword, a preface, an introduction, and references to help the audience gain background information. In an *acknowledgements* section, the author of a book expresses gratitude to all those who have helped him or her in researching, writing, and editing the book. A *foreword* is an introductory note that is written by a person other than the author. A *preface* is the author's own statement about the book. It usually includes reasons

why he or she wrote the book, the type of research used, and any other background information that may help readers understand the book. An *introduction* appears either in the front of the book or at the beginning of the text. It focuses on the content of the book, rather than its origins and background. *References* for a book usually appear in the back of the book before the index, if there is one. They provide all the necessary documentation for the work.

CHARACTER A *character* is a person or an animal that takes part in the action of a literary work. The main, or *major,* character is the most important character in a story, poem, or play. A *minor* character is one who takes part in the action but is not the focus of attention. Character qualities include the characteristics, attitudes and values that a character possesses—such as dependability, intelligence, selfishness, or stubbornness. These qualities influence the resolution of the conflict in the story.

Characters are sometimes classified as flat or round. A *flat character* is one-sided and often stereotypical. A *round character,* on the other hand, is fully developed and exhibits many traits—often both faults and virtues. Characters can also be classified as dynamic or static. A *dynamic character* is one who changes or grows during the course of the work. A *static character* is one who does not change.

CHARACTER TRAITS *Character traits* are the individual qualities that make each character unique.

CHARACTERIZATION *Characterization* is the act of creating and developing a character. Authors use two major methods of characterization—*direct* and *indirect.* When using direct characterization, a writer states the *characters' traits,* or characteristics.

When describing a character indirectly, a writer depends on the reader to draw conclusions about the character's traits. Sometimes the writer tells what other participants in the story say and think about the character.

CITATION A *citation* gives credit in the body of a research paper to an author whose ideas are either quoted directly or paraphrased. It usually gives the author's last name, the year of publication, and a page number or range in parentheses after the words or ideas that are borrowed. To complete the citation, the entire bibliographic entry is included in the References at the end of the research paper. *Footnotes* are numbered notes that are placed at the foot or bottom of a page. They cite sources and references or comment on a particular part of the text on the page. *Endnotes* are numbered notes that are placed at the end of the article or book and provide the source of the information quoted within it.

CLAIM A *claim* is a statement of the author's position on an issue. In an argument, an author supports his or her claim with data, examples, or other types of evidence.

CLIMAX The *climax,* also called the turning point, is the high point in the action of the plot. It is the moment of greatest tension, when the outcome of the plot hangs in the balance. See *Plot.*

COLLABORATIVE DISCUSSION The exploration of a topic in a group setting in which all individuals participate is called a *collaborative discussion.*

COMEDY A *comedy* is a literary work, especially a play, which is light, often humorous or satirical, and ends happily. Comedies frequently depict ordinary characters faced with temporary difficulties and conflicts. Types of comedy include *romantic comedy,* which involves problems between lovers, and the *comedy of manners,* which satirically challenges social customs of a society.

CONFLICT A *conflict* is a struggle between opposing forces. Conflict is one of the most important elements of stories, novels, and plays because it causes the action. There are two kinds of conflict: external and internal. An *external conflict* is one in which a character struggles against some outside force, such as another person. Another kind of external conflict may occur between a character and some force in nature.

An *internal conflict* takes place within the mind of a character. The character struggles to make a decision, take an action, or overcome a feeling.

CONNOTATIONS The *connotation* of a word is the set of ideas associated with it in addition to its explicit meaning. The connotation of a word can be personal, based on individual experiences. More often, cultural connotations—those recognizable by most people in a group—determine a writer's word choices.

CONTROLLING IDEA The *controlling idea* is a statement of the main idea or purpose of an informational text or research paper. See *Thesis*.

COUNTERCLAIM An opposing view to the main claim of an argument is called a *counterclaim*. Another name for counterclaim is *counterargument.*

CONSTRUCTIVE CRITCISM Respectful disagreements and critiques, meant to improve an outcome, are referred to as *constructive criticism*.

CULTURAL CONTEXT The *cultural context* of a literary work is the economic, social, and historical environment of the characters. This includes the attitudes and customs of that culture and historical period.

DENOTATION The *denotation* of a word is its dictionary meaning, independent of other associations, that the word may have. The denotation of the word *lake,* for example, is "an inland body of water." "Vacation spot" and "place where the fishing is good" are connotations of the word *lake.*

DESCRIPTION A *description* is a portrait, in words, of a person, place, or object. Descriptive writing uses images that appeal to the five senses—sight, hearing, touch, taste, and smell.

DIALECT *Dialect* is the form of a language spoken by people in a particular region or group. Dialects differ in pronunciation, grammar, and word choice. The English language is divided into many dialects. British English differs from American English.

DIALOGUE A *dialogue* is a conversation between characters. In poems, novels, and short stories, dialogue is usually set off by quotation marks to indicate a speaker's exact words.

In a play, dialogue follows the names of the characters, and no quotation marks are used.

DICTION *Diction* is a writer's word choice and the way the writer puts those words together. Diction is part of a writer's style and may be described as formal or informal, plain or fancy, ordinary or technical, sophisticated or down-to-earth, old-fashioned or modern.

DIGITAL TEXT *Digital text* is the electronic version of a written text. Digital text is accessed on the Internet or on a computer or other electronic device.

DIRECT QUOTATIONS Quotations that show a person's exact words in quotation marks are *direct quotations. Personal interviews* are a research method often used by authors as a source of direct quotations.

DRAMA A *drama* is a story written to be performed by actors. Although a drama is meant to be performed, one can also read the script, or written version, and imagine the action. The *script* of a drama is made up of dialogue and stage directions. The *dialogue* is the words spoken by the actors. The *stage directions,* usually printed in italics, tell how the actors should look, move, and speak. They also describe the setting, sound effects, and lighting.

Dramas are often divided into parts called *acts.* The acts are often divided into smaller parts called *scenes.*

EDITORIAL An *editorial* is a type of argument that typically appears in a newspaper and takes a position on a specific topic.

ESSAY An *essay* is a short nonfiction work about a particular subject. Most essays have a single major focus and a clear introduction, body, and conclusion.

There are many types of essays. An *informal essay* uses casual, conversational language. A *historical essay* gives facts, explanations, and insights about historical events. An *expository essay* explains an idea by breaking it down. A *narrative essay* tells a story about a real-life experience. An *informational essay* explains a process. A *persuasive essay* offers an opinion and supports it. A *humorous essay* uses humor to achieve the author's purpose. A *descriptive essay* creates an engaging picture of a subject, by using vivid, sensory details. A *how-to essay* is a step-by-step explanation of how to make or do something. An *explanatory essay* is a short piece of nonfiction in which the author explains, defines, or interprets ideas, events, or processes. A *reflective essay* is a brief prose work in which an author presents his or her thoughts or feelings—or reflections—about an experience or an idea.

An *objective point of view* is based on fact. It does not relate opinions, feelings, or emotions. A *subjective point of view,* on the other hand, may include personal opinions, emotions, and feelings. A persuasive essay is an example of subjective point of view, or *bias.* The persuasive essay writer attempts to get the reader to agree with his or her opinion.

EVIDENCE *Evidence* is all the information that is used to support an argument. Various types of evidence include facts, examples, statistics, quotations, expert testimony, observations, or personal experiences.

EXAMPLE An *example* is a fact, idea or event that supports an idea or insight.

EXPOSITION In the plot of a story or a drama, the *exposition,* or introduction, is the part of the work that introduces the characters, setting, and basic situation.

EXPOSITORY WRITING *Expository writing* is writing that explains or informs.

FANTASY A *fantasy* is highly imaginative writing that contains elements not found in real life. Examples of fantasy include stories that involve supernatural elements, stories that resemble fairy tales, stories that deal with imaginary places and creatures, and science-fiction stories.

FICTION *Fiction* is prose writing that tells about imaginary characters and events. Short stories and novels are works of fiction. Some writers base their fiction on actual events and people, adding invented characters, dialogue, settings, and plots. Other writers rely on imagination alone.

There are many types of fiction. An *adventure story* describes an event that happens outside a character's ordinary life. It is often characterized by danger and much action, with a plot that moves quickly. A *fantasy* is highly imaginative writing that contains elements not found in real life. Examples of fantasy include stories that involve supernatural elements, stories that resemble fairy tales,

stories that deal with imaginary places and creatures, and science-fiction stories. A *mystery* usually involves a mysterious death or other crime that must be solved. Each suspect must have a reasonable motive and opportunity to commit the crime. The main character must work as a detective who solves the mystery from the facts that are presented in the story. A *myth* is an tale meant to explain the actions of gods (and the human heroes who interact with them) or the causes of natural phenomena. *Science fiction* combines elements of fiction and fantasy with scientific fact. Many science-fiction stories are set in the future. *Historical fiction* is set in the past during a particular historical time period, but with fictional characters or a combination of historical and fictional characters.

FIGURATIVE LANGUAGE *Figurative language* is writing or speech that is not meant to be taken literally. The many types of figurative language are known as *figures of speech.* Common figures of speech include metaphor, personification, and simile. Writers use figurative language to state ideas in vivid and imaginative ways.

FLASHBACK A *flashback* is a scene within a narrative that interrupts the sequence of events to relate events that happened in the past. Writers use flashbacks to show what motivates a character or to reveal something about a character's past. A flashback is part of a *nonlinear plot* since it interrupts the normal chronological order of events to go back into the past. In a *linear plot*, all the events are told in chronological order.

FORESHADOWING *Foreshadowing* is the use of clues hinting at events that are going to happen later in the plot of a narrative. This technique helps create suspense, which keeps the reader wondering what will happen next.

FRAME STORY A *frame story* is a story that brackets— or frames—another story or group of stories. This framing device creates a story-within-a-story narrative structure.

FREE VERSE *Free verse* is poetry not written with a *formal structure*, or in a regular, rhythmical pattern, or meter. The poet is free to write lines of any length or with any number of stresses, or beats. Free verse is therefore less constraining than *metrical verse,* in which every line must have a certain length and a certain number of stresses.

GENRE A *genre* is a division or type of literature. Literature is commonly divided into three major genres: poetry, prose, and drama. Each major genre is, in turn, divided into lesser genres, as follows:

1. *Poetry:* lyric poetry, concrete poetry, dramatic poetry, narrative poetry, epic poetry
2. *Prose:* fiction (novels and short stories) and nonfiction (biography, autobiography, letters, essays, and reports)

3. *Drama:* serious drama and tragedy, comic drama, melodrama, and farce

GRAPHIC FEATURE A *graphic feature* is a visual aid that helps the reader better understand information in a text. Graphic features can include images, graphs, charts, type treatments, icons, and other visual elements that organize, emphasize, or augment certain aspects of a text. Authors use these features to achieve a certain purpose.

HISTORICAL CONTEXT The *historical context* of a literary work includes the actual political and social events and trends of the time. When a work takes place in the past, knowledge about that historical time period can help the reader understand its setting, background, culture, and message, as well as the attitudes and actions of its characters. A reader must also take into account the historical context in which the writer was creating the work, which may be different from the time period of the work's setting.

HUMOR *Humor* is writing intended to evoke laughter. While most humorists try to entertain, humor can also be used to convey a serious theme.

HYPERBOLE *Hyperbole* is a form of figurative language that uses exaggeration for effect.

IDIOM An *idiom* is an expression that has a meaning particular to a language or region.

IMAGERY *Imagery* is a technique of writing with images.

IMAGES *Images* are words or phrases that appeal to one or more of the five senses. Writers use images to describe how their subjects look, sound, feel, taste, and smell. Poets often paint images, or word pictures, that appeal to the senses. These pictures help you to experience the poem fully.

INFERENCES An *inference* is a guess based on clues. Very often in literature, authors leave some details unstated; it is up to readers to "fill in the blanks" and infer details about characters, events, and setting.

IRONY *Irony* is a contradiction between what happens and what is expected. There are three main types of irony. *Situational irony* occurs when something happens that directly contradicts the expectations of the characters or the audience. *Verbal irony* is created when words are used to suggest the opposite of their meaning. In *dramatic irony,* the audience is aware of something that the character or speaker is not aware of. The result is suspense or humor.

JOURNAL A *journal* is a daily or periodic account of events and the writer's thoughts and feelings about those events. Personal journals are not normally written for publication, but sometimes they do get published later with permission from the author or the author's family.

LETTERS A *letter* is a written communication from one person to another. In personal letters, the writer shares information and his or her thoughts and feelings with one other person or group. Although letters are not normally written for publication, they sometimes do get published later with the permission of the author or the author's family.

LOGICAL FALLACY A *logical fallacy* is an argument that may appear to be logical but is actually based on a faulty assumption. There are many types of logical fallacies. *Loaded language* is a specific choice of words designed to persuade an audience by appealing to emotions or stereotypes. A *sweeping generalization* applies a general rule to a specific instance without sufficient evidence. A *bandwagon appeal* argues that if something is popular and everybody else is doing it, so should you. *Circular reasoning* asserts its conclusion as one of the premises of the argument, thus expecting the listener to accept the conclusion when it has not been proven.

MAIN IDEA The *main idea* is the *central idea* or most important point in a text.

MEDIA Stories and information are shared using different forms of *media*. Books and magazines are a type of media. Film, video, and digital are other forms of media. A *multimedia presentation* is created from a combination of words, images, sounds, and video.

MEDIA ACCOUNTS *Media accounts* are reports, explanations, opinions, or descriptions written for television, radio, newspapers, and magazines. While some media accounts report only facts, others include the writer's thoughts and reflections.

METAPHOR A *metaphor* is a figure of speech in which something is described as though it were something else. A metaphor, like a simile, works by pointing out a similarity between two unlike things. An *extended metaphor* is a metaphor that is sustained and developed over several lines or an entire poem.

METER The *meter* of a poem is its rhythmical pattern. In poetry with a regular meter, this pattern is based on the number and arrangement of strong and weak beats, or stresses, in each line.

MONOLOGUE A *monologue* is a dramatic speech presented by a single character in a play. The character speaks from the first-person point of view and relates his or her thoughts and feelings.

GLOSSARY: LITERARY TERMS HANDBOOK

MOOD The *mood* is the feeling created in a reader by a piece of writing. Writers create mood by using imagery, word choice and descriptive details.

MOTIVE A *motive* is a reason that explains or partially explains a character's thoughts, feelings, actions, or speech. Writers try to make their characters' motives, or motivations, as clear as possible. If the motives of a main character are not clear, then the character will not be believable.

Characters are often motivated by needs, such as food and shelter. They are also motivated by feelings, such as fear, love, and pride. Motives may be obvious or hidden.

MULTIMODAL TEXT A *multimodal text* uses two or more modes of communication to convey meaning—for example, images, spoken language, sound effects, and music in addition to written language. Examples of multimodal texts include picture books that have both images and text and web pages with oral language, sound effects, images, animations, and written language.

NARRATION *Narration* is writing that tells a story. The act of telling a story is also called narration. Any story told in fiction, nonfiction, poetry, or even drama is called a narrative.

Writers of narratives employ many techniques to bring their stories to life. For example, most narratives contain a plot, setting, characters, and theme. The readers' experience can be enhanced by varied **narrative pacing**, in which the writer speeds up or slows down the plot events to create effects such as suspense.

NARRATIVE A *narrative* is a story. Novels and short stories are types of fictional narratives. Biographies and autobiographies are nonfiction narratives.

NARRATOR A *narrator* is a speaker or a character who tells a story. The narrator's perspective is the way he or she sees things. A *third-person narrator* is one who stands outside the action and speaks about it. A *first-person narrator* is one who tells a story and participates in its action.

NONFICTION *Nonfiction* is prose writing that presents and explains ideas or that tells about real people, places, objects, or events. Autobiographies, biographies, essays, reports, letters, memos, and newspaper articles are all types of nonfiction.

NOVEL A *novel* is a long work of fiction. Novels contain such elements as characters, plot, conflict, and setting. The writer of novels, or novelist, develops these elements. In addition to its main plot, a novel may contain one or more subplots, or independent, related stories. A novel may also have several themes. See *Fiction* and *Short Story.*

ONOMATOPOEIA *Onomatopoeia* is the use of words that imitate sounds. *Crash, buzz, screech, hiss, neigh, jingle,* and *cluck* are examples of onomatopoeia. *Chickadee, towhee,* and *whippoorwill* are onomatopoeic names of birds.

ORGANIZATION The structure of a text or media presentation is referred to as its **organization**. Common organizational structures are cause-and-effect, comparison-and-contrast, order of importance, and chronological order. Writers choose organizational structures that best suit their topic and purpose.

OXYMORON An *oxymoron* (pl. *oxymora*) is a figure of speech that links two opposite or contradictory words in order to point out an idea or situation that seems contradictory or inconsistent but on closer inspection turns out to be somehow true.

PARAPHRASE When you *paraphrase*, you restate a text using your own words.

PERSONIFICATION *Personification* is a type of figurative language in which a nonhuman subject is given human characteristics.

PERSUASION *Persuasion* is used in writing or speech that attempts to convince the reader or listener to adopt a particular opinion or course of action. Newspaper editorials and letters to the editor use persuasion. So do advertisements and campaign speeches given by political candidates.

Writers use a combination of persuasive techniques to argue their point of view. *Appeals to authority* use the statements of experts. *Appeals to emotion* use words that convey strong feelings. *Appeals to reason* use logical arguments backed by facts.

PLAYWRIGHT A *playwright* is a person who writes plays. William Shakespeare is regarded as the greatest playwright in English literature.

PLOT *Plot* is the sequence of events in which each event results from a previous one and causes the next. In most novels, dramas, short stories, and narrative poems, the plot involves both characters and a central conflict. The plot usually begins with an *exposition* that introduces the setting, the characters, and the basic situation. This is followed by the *inciting incident,* which introduces the central conflict. The conflict then increases during the *development* until it reaches a high point of interest or suspense, the *climax.* The climax is followed by the *falling action,* or end, of the central conflict. Any events that occur during the *falling action* make up the *resolution* or *denouement.* A *subplot* is a secondary story line that complicates or adds depth to the main plot in a narrative. For example, a novel or play may have one or more subplots, or minor stories, in addition to the central conflict.

Some plots do not have all of these parts. Some stories begin with the inciting incident and end with the resolution. See *Conflict.*

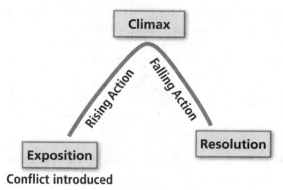

POETRY *Poetry* is one of the three classic types of literature, the others being prose and drama. Most poems make use of highly concise, musical, and emotionally charged language. Many also make use of imagery, figurative language, and special devices of sound such as rhyme. Poems often make use of graphical elements in language such as punctuation and capitalization. Some poems may have no punctuation at all. Types of poetry include *lyric poetry, narrative poetry, epic poetry,* and *humorous poetry.*

A *lyric poem* is a highly musical verse that expresses the observations and feelings of a single speaker. It creates a single, unified impression. A *narrative poem* is a story told in verse. Narrative poems often have all the elements of short stories, including characters, conflict, and plot. An *epic poem* is a long narrative poem about a larger-than-life hero engaged in a dangerous journey, or quest, that is important to the history of a nation or culture. *Humorous poems* are written to make the reader laugh. They are usually brief and often contain word play, puns, interesting rhyme, and alliteration.

POINT OF VIEW *Point of view* is the perspective, or vantage point, from which a story is told. It is either a narrator outside the story or a character in the story. *First-person point of view* is told by a character who uses the first-person pronoun "I."

The two kinds of *third-person point of view,* limited and omniscient, are called "third person" because the narrator uses third-person pronouns such as *he* and *she* to refer to the characters. There is no "I" telling the story.

In stories told from the *omniscient third-person point of view,* the narrator knows and tells about what each character feels and thinks.

In stories told from the *limited third-person point of view,* the narrator relates the inner thoughts and feelings of only one character, and everything is viewed from this character's perspective.

PRESENTATION A presentation is the act of showing or demonstrating something to an audience. *Oral presentations,* spoken aloud to a live audience, may include other *visual presentation* forms, such as charts, diagrams, illustrations, and photos. Video clips and slide shows often are key parts of *digital presentations,* which are created partly or entirely on a computer.

PROSE *Prose* is the ordinary form of written language. Most writing that is not poetry, drama, or song is considered prose. Prose is one of the major genres of literature and occurs in fiction and nonfiction.

QUOTATION *Quotations* are groups of words that are taken from a text, a speech, or an interview and are used or repeated by someone other than the original author or speaker. Quotations must be attributed to the original writer or speaker.

READ CLOSELY To *read closely* involves careful analysis of a text, its ideas, and the ways in which the author chooses to express those ideas.

REPETITION *Repetition* is the use, more than once, of any element of language—a sound, word, phrase, clause, or sentence. Repetition is used in both prose and poetry.

RESEARCH PAPER A *research paper* provides detailed information on a topic or thesis. Effective research papers are built on information from a variety of credible sources, which are credited.

RESOLUTION The *resolution* is the outcome of the conflict in a plot.

RETELLING A *retelling* of a story can be either written or oral and should include a clear sequence of events and narrative techniques such as dialogue and description.

RHETORICAL DEVICES *Rhetorical devices* are special patterns of words and ideas that create emphasis and stir emotion, especially in speeches or other oral presentations. Some of the most common rhetorical devices include *rhetorical questions,* or questions asked in order to make a point or create a dramatic affect rather than to get an answer. *Direct address* is a rhetorical device wherein a speaker or writer directs a message directly to an individual or a group of people. An *analogy* is a comparison that points out the similarities between two things, often explaining something unfamiliar by likening it to something familiar. Analogies are usually extended comparisons. *Juxtaposition* as a rhetorical device places two or more ideas or characters side by side for the purpose of comparing and contrasting them.

RHYME *Rhyme* is the repetition of sounds at the ends of words. Poets use rhyme to lend a songlike quality to their verses and to emphasize certain words and ideas. Many traditional poems contain *end rhymes,* or rhyming words at the ends of lines.

Another common device is the use of *internal rhymes,* or rhyming words within lines. Internal rhyme also emphasizes the flowing nature of a poem.

RHYTHM *Rhythm* is the pattern of stressed and unstressed syllables in spoken or written language.

SCAN To *scan* is to run your eyes over the text to find answers to questions, to clarify, or to find supporting details.

SCENE A *scene* is a section of uninterrupted action in the act of a drama.

SCRIPT A *script* is the written version of a play or film. It includes *dialogue* and *stage directions*.

SENSORY LANGUAGE *Sensory language* is writing or speech that appeals to one or more of the five senses.

SETTING The *setting* of a literary work is the time and place of the action. The setting includes all the details of a place and time—the year, the time of day, even the weather. The place may be a specific country, state, region, community, neighborhood, building, institution, or home. Details such as dialects, clothing, customs, and modes of transportation are often used to establish setting. In most stories, the setting serves as a backdrop—a context in which the characters interact. Setting can also help to create a feeling, or atmosphere.

SHORT STORY A *short story* is a brief work of fiction. Like a novel, a short story presents a sequence of events, or plot. The plot usually deals with a central conflict faced by a main character, or protagonist. The events in a short story usually communicate a message about life or human nature. This message, or central idea, is the story's theme.

SIMILE A *simile* is a figure of speech that uses *like* or *as* to make a direct comparison between two unlike ideas. Everyday speech often contains similes, such as "pale as a ghost," "good as gold," "spread like wildfire," and "clever as a fox."

SKIM To *skim* is to look over the text quickly, to get a sense of important ideas before reading.

SOUND DEVICES *Sound devices* are techniques used by writers to give musical effects to their writing. Some of these include *onomatopoeia, alliteration, rhyme, meter,* and *repetition.*

SPEAKER The *speaker* is the imaginary voice a poet uses when writing a poem. The speaker is the character who tells the poem. This character, or voice, often is not identified by name. There can be important differences between the poet and the poem's speaker.

SPEECH A *speech* is a work that is delivered orally to an audience. There are many kinds of speeches suiting almost every kind of public gathering. Types of speeches include *dramatic, persuasive,* and *informative.*

STAGE DIRECTIONS *Stage directions* are notes included in a drama to describe how the work is to be performed or staged. Stage directions are usually printed in italics and enclosed within parentheses or brackets. Some stage directions describe the movements, costumes, emotional states, and ways of speaking of the characters.

STAGING *Staging* includes the setting, lighting, costumes, special effects, and music that go into a stage performance of a drama.

SUMMARY A *summary* is a short, clear description of the main ideas of something, such as a text, a film, or a presentation. Effective summaries are objective—free from bias or evaluation.

SUSPENSE *Suspense* is the growing curiosity, tension, or anxiety the reader feels about the outcome of events in a literary work. Suspense builds until the *climax,* the high point of tension in the plot, when the conflict reaches a peak. The tension of suspense is part of what keeps the reader engaged in a story and anxious to find out what will happen next.

SYMBOL A *symbol* is anything that stands for or represents something else. Symbols are common in everyday life. A dove with an olive branch in its beak is a symbol of peace. A blindfolded woman holding a balanced scale is a symbol of justice. A crown is a symbol of a king's status and authority.

SYMBOLISM *Symbolism* is the use of symbols. Symbolism plays an important role in many different types of literature. It can highlight certain elements the author wishes to emphasize and also add levels of meaning.

TEXT FEATURE A *text feature*, which can also be called a *print feature*, is a design element that helps to show or augment the organization of a text. Text features can include headings, subheadings, captions, and sidebars.

TEXT STRUCTURE *Text structure* is the way in which information in a text is organized or put together. An author chooses a particular text structure according to his or her purpose. An *advantage and disadvantage* structure addresses the positive and negative aspects of a topic and then gives an opinion. *Cause-and-effect* text structure examines the relationship between events. It provides reasons or an explanation for why something has happened. *Chronological order* text relates events in the order in which they happened. *Classification* text structure creates categories and then provides examples of things that fit into each category. In *comparison and contrast* text structure, an author presents the similarities and differences between two subjects. A comparison and contrast text can be organized using **point-by-point organization** in which one aspect of both subjects is discussed, then another aspect, and so on. **Block method organization** presents all the details of one subject, and then all the details about the next subject.

THEME A *theme* is a central message in a literary work that can usually be expressed in a general statement about human beings or about life. The theme of a work is not a summary of its plot.

Although a theme may be stated directly in the text, it is more often presented indirectly. When the theme is stated indirectly, or implied, the reader must figure out what the theme is by looking at what the work reveals about people or life. A single text may have multiple themes. The various sub-themes are usually closely related to the central theme.

THESIS The *thesis* of a text is the main idea or purpose of an essay or research paper. See *Controlling Idea.*

TONE The *tone* of a literary work is the writer's attitude toward his or her audience and subject. The tone can often be described by a single adjective, such as *formal* or *informal, serious* or *playful, bitter* or *ironic.* Factors that contribute to the tone are word choice, sentence structure, line length, rhyme, rhythm, and repetition.

UNIVERSAL THEME A *universal theme* is a message about life that is expressed regularly in many different cultures and time periods. Folk tales, epics, and romances often address universal themes like the importance of courage, the power of love, or the danger of greed.

VOICE *Voice* is the author's individual writing style or manner of expression that make his or her writing distinctive or unique. *Voice* can also refer to the speech and thought patterns of the narrator of a work of fiction.

WEIGHTED WORDS Words that have strong emotional associations beyond their basic meanings are *weighted words.*

WORD CHOICE A writer's *word choice* is the way the writer puts those words together. Diction is part of a writer's style and may be described as formal or informal, plain or fancy, ordinary or technical, sophisticated or down-to-earth, old-fashioned or modern.

ANALOGY / ANALOGÍA Una *analogía* establece una comparación entre dos o varias cosas que comparten similitudes, pero son distintas en todo lo demás.

ANECDOTE / ANÉCDOTA Una *anécdota* es un relato corto de no ficción sobre un acontecimiento extraño, interesante o divertido. Los escritores cuentan anécdotas para entretener o explicar algo importante.

ARGUMENT / ARGUMENTO En un *argumento* los escritores exponen y defienden una afirmación o una opinión, para lo cual se basan en hechos probados o razonamientos lógicos. Casi todos los argumentos tienen una *introducción*, en la que se expone una afirmación; un *desarrollo*, en el que se respalda la afirmación con evidencia; y una *conclusión*, en la que se resume o replantea la afirmación.

AUDIENCE / PÚBLICO El *público* de una obra literaria es la persona o el conjunto de personas a quienes se dirige un escritor u orador. Tomar en cuenta los intereses, los conocimientos y la educación del público destinatario ayuda al escritor u orador a dar forma a la obra.

AUTHOR'S POINT OF VIEW / PUNTO DE VISTA DEL AUTOR La postura hacia el tema que revela el autor de un texto de no ficción muestra el *punto de vista del autor*.

AUTHOR'S PURPOSE / PROPÓSITO DEL AUTOR El *propósito del autor* es la razón principal por la que este autor o autora escribe. Por ejemplo, un autor puede buscar entretener, informar o persuadir al lector. En ocasiones un autor intenta enseñarnos una lección moral o reflexionar sobre una experiencia. Un autor puede tener más de un propósito por los que escribir.

AUTOBIOGRAPHY / AUTOBIOGRAFÍA Una *autobiografía* es la historia de la vida del propio autor. Los textos autobiográficos pueden hablar de la vida completa del autor o solo de una parte.

Como las autobiografías tratan sobre gente y acontecimientos reales, son consideradas como no ficción. La mayoría de las autobiografías están escritas en narrador en primera persona.

BIOGRAPHY / BIOGRAFÍA Una *biografía* es un tipo de texto de no ficción donde el escritor explica la historia de la vida de otra persona. La mayoría de las biografías son sobre gente famosa y admirable. Aunque las biografías están consideradas libros de no ficción, las de mayor calidad suelen compartir cualidades con los buenos textos narrativos.

BLOG / BLOG Una *entrada de blog* es un texto en línea que se aporta a un diario en línea llamado *blog*. Los autores de blogs ofrecen información o expresan su opinión sobre distintos temas.

BOOK FEATURES / SECCIONES ESPECIALES Las *secciones especiales* de los libros son partes tales como los agradecimientos, el prólogo, el prefacio, la introducción y las referencias, que ayudan al público a obtener información general. En la sección de *agradecimientos*, el autor expresa su gratitud a todos aquellos que lo ayudaron a investigar, escribir y editar el libro. El *prólogo* es una nota preliminar que escribe alguien que no es el autor. El *prefacio* es lo que dice el autor acerca de su propio libro. Allí suele mencionar los motivos por los que lo escribió, el tipo de investigación que usó y demás información general que pueda ayudar a los lectores a entender la obra. La *introducción* aparece en las primeras páginas del libro o al comienzo del texto principal. Trata del contenido del libro, en lugar de sus orígenes o su contexto. Las *referencias* suelen estar al final del libro, antes del índice, cuando lo hay. Proporcionan toda la documentación necesaria para la obra.

CHARACTER / PERSONAJE Un *personaje* es una persona o un animal que participa en la acción de una obra literaria. El personaje *principal* o protagonista es el más importante de una historia, poema u obra teatral. El personaje *secundario* participa también en la acción pero no es el centro de atención. Las cualidades de un personaje son sus características, actitudes y valores; por ejemplo, confiabilidad, inteligencia, egoísmo o terquedad. Estas cualidades influyen en la resolución del conflicto de la historia.

A menudo se clasifican los personajes como planos o redondos.

Un *personaje plano* es unilateral y a menudo estereotipado.

Un *personaje redondo*, por el contrario, está desarrollado completamente y presenta muchos rasgos (a menudo tanto defectos como virtudes). También se pueden clasificar a los personajes como dinámicos o estáticos. Un *personaje dinámico* es aquel que cambia o evoluciona a lo largo de la obra. Un *personaje estático* es aquel que no cambia.

CHARACTER TRAITS / RASGOS DEL PERSONAJE Los *rasgos del personaje* son las características particulares que hacen que cada personaje sea único.

CHARACTERIZATION / CARACTERIZACIÓN La *caracterización* es la acción de crear y desarrollar un personaje. Los autores utilizan dos métodos principales de caracterización: *directa* e *indirecta*. Cuando se utiliza la caracterización directa, el escritor describe los *rasgos del personaje* o sus características.

En cambio, cuando se describe a un personaje indirectamente, el escritor depende del lector para que pueda extraer conclusiones sobre los rasgos del personaje. A veces el escritor cuenta lo que otros personajes que participan en la historia dicen o piensan sobre el personaje en cuestión.

CITATION / CITA Las *citas* reconocen, en el cuerpo de un trabajo de investigación, a un autor cuyas ideas se tomaron textualmente o se parafrasearon. Por lo general, la cita incluye el nombre del autor, el año de publicación de su obra, y un número o un rango de páginas entre paréntesis, después de las palabras o ideas que se tomaron de allí. Para completar la cita, la nota bibliográfica íntegra se incorpora en las Referencias, al final del trabajo de investigación. Las *notas al pie* son notas numeradas que se ubican en el pie de página, es decir, abajo de todo el texto. En ellas se mencionan fuentes y referencias, o se comenta una parte determinada del texto de la página. Las *notas al final* son notas numeradas que se ubican al final del artículo o libro, y que proporcionan la fuente de la información mencionada en él.

CLAIM / AFIRMACIÓN Una *afirmación* es donde el autor expone su posición sobre una cuestión determinada. Se usa como punto principal para demostrar un argumento. En su argumento, el autor defiende su afirmación con datos, ejemplos u otros tipos de evidencia.

CLIMAX / CLÍMAX El *clímax,* también llamado momento culminante, es el punto más elevado de la acción de una trama. Es el momento de mayor tensión, es decir, cuando el desenlace de la trama pende de un hilo.
Ver *Trama.*

COLLABORATIVE DISCUSSION / DISCUSIÓN COLABORATIVA Se conoce como *discusión colaborativa* a la exploración de un tema en grupo, con la participación de todos los miembros del grupo.

COMEDY / COMEDIA Una *comedia* es una obra literaria, especialmente una obra de teatro, que es ligera, a menudo cómica o satírica y tiene un final feliz. Las comedias describen a personajes normales que se enfrentan a dificultades y conflictos temporales. Algunos tipos de comedia incluyen la *comedia romántica*, que contiene problemas entre amantes, y la *comedia de costumbres,* que cuestiona satíricamente las costumbres sociales de un sector de la sociedad.

CONFLICT / CONFLICTO Un *conflicto* es una lucha entre fuerzas opuestas. El conflicto es uno de los elementos más importantes de los cuentos, novelas y obras de teatro porque provoca la acción. Hay dos tipos de conflictos: externos e internos.

Un *conflicto externo* se da cuando un personaje lucha contra una fuerza ajena a él, como por ejemplo otra persona. Otro tipo de conflicto externo puedo ocurrir entre un personaje y una fuerza de la naturaleza.

Un *conflicto interno* tiene lugar en la mente de un personaje. El personaje lucha por tomar una decisión, llevar a cabo una acción o frenar un sentimiento.

CONNOTATIONS / CONNOTACIONES La *connotación* de una palabra es el conjunto de ideas que se asocian con esta, más allá de su significado explícito. La connotación de una palabra puede ser personal, basada en una experiencia individual. Con frecuencia son las connotaciones culturales, aquellas que son reconocibles por la mayoría de las personas de un grupo, las que determinan la elección de palabras de un autor.

CONTROLLING IDEA / IDEA CONTROL La *idea control* es la exposición de la idea principal o el propósito de un texto informativo o un trabajo de investigación.
Ver *Tesis*.

COUNTERCLAIM / CONTRAARGUMENTO Se llama *contraargumento* a una opinión contraria a la afirmación principal de un argumento.

CONSTRUCTIVE CRITICISM / CRÍTICA CONSTRUCTIVA Se conoce como *crítica constructiva* a las diferencias de opinión que se exponen de manera respetuosa y que tienen como fin mejorar un resultado.

CULTURAL CONTEXT / CONTEXTO CULTURAL El *contexto cultural* de una obra literaria es el entorno económico, social e histórico de los personajes. Este incluye los comportamientos y costumbres de dicho período cultural e histórico.

DENOTATION / DENOTACIÓN La *denotación* de una palabra es su significado del diccionario, independientemente de otras asociaciones que se le puedan otorgar. La denotación de la palabra *lago* sería "una masa de agua que se acumula en un terreno". "Un lugar de vacaciones" o "un lugar adonde se puede ir de pesca" son connotaciones de la palabra *lago.*

DESCRIPTION / DESCRIPCIÓN Una *descripción* es un retrato en palabras de una persona, lugar u objeto. Los textos descriptivos utilizan imágenes que se relacionan con los cinco sentidos: vista, oído, tacto, gusto y olfato.

DIALECT / DIALECTO Un *dialecto* es la variedad de una lengua que habla un grupo o las personas de una región particular. Los dialectos se diferencian en la pronunciación, gramática y elección de las palabras utilizadas. La lengua inglesa está dividida en muchos dialectos. Por ejemplo, el inglés británico es distinto del inglés estadounidense.

DIALOGUE / DIÁLOGO Un *diálogo* es una conversación entre personajes. En los poemas, novelas y cuentos en inglés, los diálogos se indican normalmente entre comillas para señalar que estas son las palabras exactas que dice un personaje.

En una obra de teatro, los diálogos se colocan después de los nombres de los personajes y no se utilizan comillas.

DICTION / DICCIÓN La *dicción* es tanto la elección de las palabras que hace un escritor como la manera de combinarlas. La dicción forma parte del estilo de un escritor y puede ser descrita como formal o informal, sencilla o elegante, corriente o técnica, sofisticada o popular, anticuada o moderna.

DIGITAL TEXT / TEXTO DIGITAL Un *texto digital* es la versión electrónica de un texto escrito. Se accede a los textos digitales por Internet, con una computadora o con otro aparato electrónico.

DIRECT QUOTATIONS / CITAS DIRECTAS Las *citas directas* presentan las palabras exactas que dijo alguien y se ponen entre comillas. Las *entrevistas personales* son uno de los métodos de investigación que utilizan los autores como fuente de citas directas.

DRAMA / DRAMA Un *drama* es una historia escrita para ser representada por actores. Aunque está destinada a ser representada, también se puede, únicamente, leer su texto e imaginar la acción. El *texto dramático*, o guión, está compuesto de diálogos y acotaciones. Los *diálogos* son palabras que dicen los personajes. Las *acotaciones* aparecen normalmente en cursiva e indican cómo deben verse, moverse o hablar los personajes. También describen el decorado, los efectos de sonido y la iluminación.

Los dramas suelen estar divididos en distintas partes denominadas *actos.* Los actos aparecen a menudo divididos en partes más pequeñas denominadas *escenas.*

EDITORIAL / EDITORIAL Un *editorial* es un tipo de argumento que suele aparecer en los periódicos y que adopta una postura en un asunto determinado.

ESSAY / ENSAYO Un *ensayo* es un texto de no ficción corto sobre un tema particular. La mayoría de los ensayos se concentran en un único aspecto fundamental y tienen una introducción clara, un desarrollo y una conclusión.

Hay muchos tipos de ensayos. Un *ensayo informal* emplea lenguaje coloquial y conversacional. Un *ensayo histórico* nos presenta hechos, explicaciones y conocimientos sobre acontecimientos históricos. Un *ensayo expositivo* expone una idea desglosándola. Un *ensayo narrativo* cuenta una historia sobre una experiencia real. Un *ensayo informativo* explica un proceso. Un *ensayo argumentativo* ofrece una opinión y la argumenta. Un *ensayo humorístico* utiliza el humor para lograr el propósito del autor. Un *ensayo descriptivo* crea un retrato cautivador del sujeto, usando detalles vívidos y sensoriales. Un *ensayo instructivo* explica paso por paso cómo crear o hacer algo. Un *ensayo explicativo* es una obra de no-ficción corta en la que el autor aclara, define e interpreta ideas, acontecimientos o procesos. Un *ensayo reflexivo* es una obra de prosa corta en la que el autor presenta sus pensamientos y sentimientos, es decir, sus reflexiones, sobre una experiencia o idea.

Punto de vista objetivo es aquel que se apoya en los hechos. No hace mención de opiniones, sentimientos ni emociones. El *punto de vista subjetivo,* en cambio, puede incorporar opiniones personales, emociones y sentimientos. El ensayo persuasivo es un ejemplo de punto de vista subjetivo, también llamado *sesgo.* El autor de un ensayo persuasivo procura conseguir que el lector concuerde con su opinión.

EVIDENCE / EVIDENCIA La *evidencia* es toda la información que se usa para defender un argumento. Hay diversos tipos de evidencia, como los datos, los ejemplos, las estadísticas, las citas, los testimonios de especialistas, las observaciones y las experiencias personales.

EXAMPLE / EJEMPLO Un *ejemplo* es un dato, idea o suceso que respalda un concepto o una visión de las cosas.

EXPOSITION / PLANTEAMIENTO En el argumento de una historia o drama, el *planteamiento* o introducción es la parte de la obra que presenta a los personajes, escenarios y situación básica.

EXPOSITORY WRITING / TEXTO EXPOSITIVO Un *texto expositivo* es un texto que explica e informa.

FANTASY / LITERATURA FANTÁSTICA La *literatura fantástica* son textos con elementos muy imaginativos que no pueden encontrarse en la vida real. Algunos ejemplos de literatura fantástica incluyen historias que contienen elementos supernaturales, historias que recuerdan a los cuentos de hadas, historias que tratan de lugares y criaturas imaginarias e historias de ciencia ficción.

FICTION / FICCIÓN La *ficción* son obras en prosa que hablan de sucesos y personajes imaginarios. Los cuentos y las novelas son obras de ficción. Algunos escritores se inspiran para sus obras de ficción en sucesos y personas reales, a los que añaden también personajes, diálogos, escenarios y tramas inventados. Otros escritores se sirven únicamente de la imaginación.

Existen muchos tipos de ficción. Las *historias de aventuras* describen sucesos fuera de lo común que ocurren en la vida de un personaje. Suelen caracterizarse por situaciones de peligro y mucha acción, y por una trama que avanza con rapidez. La *literatura fantástica* incluye textos muy imaginativos que contienen elementos que no pueden hallarse en la vida real. Las historias con elementos sobrenaturales, las que recuerdan a los cuentos de hadas, las que tratan de lugares y criaturas imaginarios, y las de ciencia ficción son ejemplos de literatura fantástica.

Las **historias de misterio** generalmente tratan de una muerte misteriosa u otro crimen que hay que resolver. Cada sospechoso tiene que tener un móvil y una oportunidad razonable para haber cometido el crimen. El personaje principal debe trabajar como detective que resuelve el misterio a partir de los hechos que se le presentan en la historia. Los **mitos** son relatos que intentan explicar los actos de los dioses (y de los héroes humanos que interactúan con ellos) o las causas de fenómenos naturales. La **ciencia ficción** combina elementos de la ficción y la literatura fantástica con datos científicos. Muchas historias de ciencia ficción están situadas en el futuro. La **ficción histórica** se sitúa en el pasado, durante un período histórico particular, pero se desarrolla con personajes ficticios o con una combinación de personajes históricos y ficticios.

FIGURATIVE LANGUAGE / LENGUAJE FIGURADO El **lenguaje figurado** es un texto o diálogo que no se debe interpretar literalmente. A los numerosos tipos de lenguaje figurado se los llama **figuras retóricas.** Algunas de las más comunes son las metáforas, las personificaciones y los símiles. Los escritores utilizan el lenguaje figurado para expresar ideas de una manera imaginativa y vívida.

FLASHBACK / FLASHBACK Un **flashback** es una escena de un relato que interrumpe la secuencia de acontecimientos para narrar sucesos ocurridos en el pasado. Los escritores usan los *flashbacks* para mostrar lo que motiva a un personaje o para revelar algo de su historia personal. Los *flashbacks* son parte de una **trama no lineal**, puesto que interrumpen el orden cronológico normal de los acontecimientos para volver al pasado. En una **trama lineal,** todos los acontecimientos se cuentan en orden cronológico.

FORESHADOWING / PRESAGIO El **presagio** es el uso de indicios de sucesos que van a ocurrir más adelante en la trama de un relato. Esta técnica ayuda a crear suspenso, que hace que el lector no deje de preguntarse cómo seguirá la historia.

FRAME STORY / NARRACIÓN ENMARCADA Una **narración enmarcada** es una historia que pone entre paréntesis o enmarca otra historia o grupo de historias. Este recurso literario crea la estructura narrativa de una historia dentro de otra historia.

FREE VERSE / VERSO LIBRE El **verso libre** es poesía que no tiene una **estructura formal**; es decir, que no sigue un patrón rítmico ni métrico normal. El poeta es libre de escribir versos de la extensión que prefiera y con un número libre de acentos. Por consiguiente, el verso libre es menos restrictivo que el **verso métrico**, en el que cada verso debe ser de determinada extensión y contener un número concreto de acentos.

GENRE / GÉNERO Un **género** es una clase o tipo de literatura. La literatura se divide normalmente en tres géneros principales: poesía, prosa y drama. Cada uno de estos géneros está, a su vez, dividido en otros géneros menores:

1. **Poesía:** poesía lírica, poesía concreta, poesía dramática, poesía narrativa, poesía épica

2. **Prosa:** ficción (novelas y cuentos cortos) y no ficción (biografías, autobiografías, cartas, ensayos y reportajes)

3. **Drama:** drama serio y tragedia, comedia, melodrama y farsa

GRAPHIC FEATURE / ELEMENTO GRÁFICO Un **elemento gráfico** es un recurso visual que ayuda al lector a entender mejor la información contenida en un texto. Los elementos gráficos pueden ser imágenes, diagramas, gráficos, tratamientos tipográficos, íconos y otros recursos visuales que organizan, enfatizan o hacen foco en ciertos aspectos de un texto. El autor usa esos elementos para lograr un objetivo determinado.

HISTORICAL CONTEXT / CONTEXTO HISTÓRICO El **contexto histórico** de una obra literaria lo constituyen los verdaderos acontecimientos y tendencias político-sociales de la época. Cuando una obra tiene lugar en el pasado, el conocimiento previo sobre ese período histórico puede ayudar al lector a comprender la ambientación, trasfondo, cultura y mensaje, así como las actitudes y acciones de sus personajes. Un lector también debe tener en cuenta el contexto histórico en el que el escritor creó su obra, ya que puede ser distinto del contexto real en el que se desarrolla la obra.

HUMOR / HUMOR El **humor** es una forma de escribir que incita a la risa. Si bien es cierto que la mayoría de los humoristas tratan de entretener, también se puede utilizar el humor para transmitir un tema serio.

HYPERBOLE / HIPÉRBOLE La **hipérbole** es un tipo de figura retórica que utiliza la exageración para provocar un efecto en el lector.

IDIOM / MODISMOS Los **modismos** son expresiones idiomáticas que tienen un significado particular en una lengua o región.

IMAGERY / IMAGINERÍA La **imaginería** es la técnica de escribir con imágenes.

IMAGES / IMÁGENES La **imágenes** son palabras o frases que se relacionan con uno o varios de los cinco sentidos. Los escritores utilizan imágenes para describir qué apariencia tienen, cómo suenan, sienten, saben y huelen las personas u objetos descritos. Los poetas suelen dibujar imágenes o hacer una descripción visual que se vincula con los sentidos. Estas descripciones visuales nos ayudan a experimentar el poema en su totalidad.

INFERENCES / INFERENCIAS Una *inferencia* es una suposición que se basa en pistas. Es frecuente en la literatura que los autores no lo expliquen todo; les corresponde a los lectores "llenar los espacios en blanco" e inferir detalles sobre los personajes, sucesos y ambiente.

IRONY / IRONÍA Una *ironía* es una contradicción entre lo que ocurre realmente y lo que se espera que pase. Hay tres tipos principales de ironía. La *ironía situacional* se da cuando ocurre algo que se contradice directamente con aquello que los personajes o el público espera. La *ironía verbal* se crea cuando se usan las palabras para insinuar algo opuesto a su significado literal. En la *ironía dramática,* el público conoce algo que el personaje o la persona que habla no sabe. El resultado es el suspenso o el humor.

JOURNAL / DIARIO Un *diario* es un relato periódico o diario de acontecimientos y reflexiones u opiniones que el escritor tiene sobre esos acontecimientos. Los diarios personales no se escriben normalmente para ser publicados, pero en ocasiones se publican más tarde con el permiso del autor o de la familia del autor.

LETTERS / CARTAS Una *carta* es una comunicación escrita de una persona a otra. En las cartas personales, los escritores comparten información, así como sus opiniones y sentimientos, con otra persona o grupo. Aunque las cartas no se escriben normalmente para ser publicadas, a veces se publican más tarde con el permiso del autor o de la familia del autor.

LOGICAL FALLACY / FALACIA LÓGICA Una *falacia lógica* es un argumento que puede parecer lógico pero que, en realidad, se apoya en un supuesto incorrecto. Hay muchos tipos de falacias lógicas. El *vocabulario emotivo* es una elección de palabras diseñada para persuadir al público apelando a emociones y a estereotipos. La *generalización indiscriminada* consiste en aplicar una regla general a una instancia específica sin suficiente evidencia. La *apelación a la tendencia* sostiene que, si algo es popular y todos lo hacen, uno también debería. El *razonamiento circular* afirma su conclusión entre las premisas del argumento, y así pretende que el interlocutor acepte una conclusión sin que se la haya demostrado.

MAIN IDEA / IDEA PRINCIPAL La *idea principal* es la *idea central* o lo más importante de un texto.

MEDIA / MEDIOS Los relatos y la información se transmiten usando distintos *medios*. Los libros y las revistas son un tipo de medios. El cine, el video y el formato digital son otras formas de medios. Las *presentaciones multimedios* son las que combinan palabras, imágenes, sonidos y video.

MEDIA ACCOUNTS / REPORTAJES PERIODÍSTICOS Los *reportajes periodísticos* son relatos, explicaciones, opiniones o descripciones escritas para televisión, radio, periódicos o revistas. Si bien algunos reportajes periodísticos solo relatan hechos, otros incluyen también las opiniones y reflexiones del autor.

METAPHOR / METÁFORA Una *metáfora* es una figura retórica que se utiliza para identificar una cosa con algo distinto. Una metáfora, al igual que un símil, se obtiene analizando las similitudes que comparten dos cosas distintas. Una *metáfora ampliada* es una metáfora que se sostiene y desarrolla a lo largo de varios versos o de un poema entero.

METER / MÉTRICA La *métrica* de un poema es su estructura rítmica. En la poesía con métrica regular, esa estructura consiste en la cantidad y disposición de pulsos fuertes y débiles, o acentos, en cada verso.

MONOLOGUE / MONÓLOGO Un *monólogo* en una obra de teatro es un discurso dramático por parte de un personaje. El personaje habla desde el punto de vista de primera persona y comparte sus pensamientos y sentimientos.

MOOD / ATMÓSFERA La *atmósfera* es la sensación que un texto produce en el lector. Los escritores crean la atmósfera mediante el uso de imaginería, su elección de palabras y los detalles descriptivos.

MOTIVE / MOTIVACIÓN Una *motivación* es una razón que explica total o parcialmente las opiniones, sentimientos, acciones o diálogos de los personajes. El escritor intenta exponer las motivaciones o motivos de sus personajes de la manera más clara posible. Si las motivaciones de un personaje principal no están claras, el personaje no será creíble.

Las motivaciones que mueven con frecuencia a los personajes son necesidades tales como encontrar comida o un refugio. Además les pueden motivar también sentimientos como el miedo, el amor y el orgullo. Las motivaciones pueden ser claras u ocultas.

MULTIMODAL TEXT / TEXTO MULTIMODAL *Texto multimodal* es el que utiliza dos o más modos de comunicación para transmitir sentido: por ejemplo, imágenes, lenguaje oral, efectos sonoros y música, además de lenguaje escrito. Los libros ilustrados, que tienen tanto imágenes como texto, y las páginas web que contienen lenguaje oral, efectos sonoros, imágenes, animaciones y lenguaje escrito son ejemplos de texto multimodal.

NARRATION / NARRACIÓN Una *narración* es un texto que cuenta una historia. También se denomina narración a la acción de contar una historia. Una historia contada en ficción, no ficción, poesía o incluso en drama es conocida como narración.

Los escritores emplean distintas técnicas para darles vida a sus historias. Por ejemplo, las narraciones suelen tener una trama, un escenario, varios personajes y un tema. La experiencia de los lectores se enriquece con el uso de distintos *ritmos narrativos*, mediante los que el escritor acelera o desacelera los sucesos de la narración para crear una variedad de efectos como el suspenso.

NARRATIVE / TEXTO NARRATIVO Un *texto narrativo* es una historia. Las novelas y los cuentos son tipos de textos narrativos de ficción. Las biografías y las autobiografías son textos narrativos de no ficción.

NARRATOR / NARRADOR Un *narrador* es la persona o personaje que cuenta una historia. El punto de vista del narrador es la manera en la que él o ella ve las cosas. Un *narrador en tercera persona* es aquel que solo habla de la acción sin implicarse en ella. Un *narrador en primera persona* es aquel que cuenta una historia y además participa en su acción.

NONFICTION / NO FICCIÓN Un texto de *no ficción* es un texto en prosa que presenta y explica ideas, o que trata de personas, lugares, objetos o acontecimientos de la vida real. Las autobiografías, biografías, ensayos, reportajes, cartas, memorandos y artículos periodísticos son todos diferentes tipos de no ficción.

NOVEL / NOVELA Una *novela* es una obra larga de ficción. Las novelas contienen elementos tales como los personajes, la trama, el conflicto y los escenarios. Los escritores de novelas, o novelistas, desarrollan estos elementos. Aparte de su trama principal, una novela puede contener una o varias subtramas, o narraciones independientes o relacionadas con la trama principal. Una novela puede contener también diversos temas.

Ver *Ficción* y *Cuento*.

ONOMATOPOEIA / ONOMATOPEYA Una *onomatopeya* es el uso de las palabras que imitan sonidos. *Cataplam, zzzzzz, zas, din don, glu glu glu, achís* y *crag* son ejemplos de onomatopeyas. El *cuco,* la *urraca* y el *pitirre* son nombres onomatopéyicos de aves.

ORGANIZATION / ORGANIZACIÓN La estructura de un texto o de una presentación audiovisual es lo que se conoce como su *organización*. Algunas estructuras organizativas comunes son: causa y efecto, comparación y contraste, orden de importancia y orden cronológico. Los escritores eligen la organización que mejor se adapte al tema y propósito de su texto.

OXYMORON / OXÍMORON Un *oxímoron* es una figura retórica que vincula dos palabras contrarias u opuestas con el fin de indicar que una idea o situación, que parece contradictoria o incoherente a simple vista, encierra algo de verdad cuando la analizamos detenidamente.

PARAPHRASE / PARÁFRASIS Una *paráfrasis* ocurre cuando explicamos un texto con nuestras propias palabras.

PERSONIFICATION / PERSONIFICACIÓN La *personificación* es una figura retórica con la que se atribuyen características humanas a un animal o una cosa.

PERSUASION / PERSUASIÓN La *persuasión* se utiliza cuando escribimos o hablamos para convencer a nuestro lector o interlocutor de que debe adoptar una opinión concreta o tomar un rumbo determinado en sus decisiones. Los editoriales periodísticos y las cartas al editor emplean la persuasión. Asimismo, la publicidad y los discursos electorales que los políticos pronuncian en campaña también la utilizan.

Los escritores emplean distintas técnicas persuasivas para defender sus opiniones. Las *apelaciones a la autoridad* usan lo que han dicho diversos expertos. Las *apelaciones a las emociones* usan palabras que transmiten sentimientos profundos. Las *apelaciones a la razón* utilizan argumentos lógicos fundamentados con datos.

PLAYWRIGHT / DRAMATURGO Un *dramaturgo* es una persona que escribe obras de teatro. Muchos consideran a William Shakespeare el mejor dramaturgo de la literatura inglesa.

PLOT / TRAMA Una *trama* es la secuencia de acontecimientos en la cual cada acontecimiento es el resultado de otro acontecimiento anterior y la causa de uno nuevo que lo sigue. En la mayoría de novelas, dramas, cuentos y poemas narrativos, la trama contiene personajes y un conflicto central. La trama suele comenzar con un *planteamiento* o introducción que presenta el escenario, los personajes y la situación básica. A esto le sigue el *suceso desencadenante*, que presenta el conflicto central. El conflico va aumentando durante el *desarrollo* hasta que alcanza el punto más elevado de interés o suspenso, el *clímax.* El clímax va seguido de una *acción descendente* del conflicto central. Todos los acontecimientos que ocurren durante la acción descendente forman el *desenlace.* La *subtrama* es una línea narrativa secundaria que complica o profundiza la trama principal de un relato. Por ejemplo, una novela u obra de teatro puede tener una o más subtramas, o historias secundarias, además del conflicto central.

Algunas tramas no tienen todas estas partes. Algunas historias comienzan con el suceso desencadenante y acaban con un desenlace.

Ver **Conflicto.**

Presentación del conflicto

POETRY / POESÍA La *poesía* es uno de los tres géneros clásicos de la literatura junto con la prosa y el drama. La mayoría de los poemas utilizan lenguaje muy conciso, musical y cargado de emoción. Muchos también emplean imágenes, lenguaje figurado y recursos sonoros especiales como la rima. En la poesía también suele hacerse uso de elementos gráficos del lenguaje, como la puntuación y las mayúsculas. Algunos poemas pueden omitir toda puntuación. Algunos tipos de poesía son: la *poesía lírica,* la *poesía narrativa,* la *poesía épica* y la *poesía humorística.*

Un *poema lírico* es una obra en verso muy musical que expresa las observaciones y los sentimientos de un solo yo poético, lo que da como resultado una impresión unificada. Un *poema narrativo* es una historia contada en verso. Los poemas narrativos suelen tener todos los elementos de los cuentos, como personajes, conflicto y trama. Un *poema épico* es un poema narrativo extenso sobre un héroe extraordinario que se embarca en una peligrosa travesía o misión importante para la historia de una nación o una cultura. Los *poemas humorísticos* se escriben para hacer reír al lector. Suelen ser cortos y a menudo contienen juegos de palabras, rimas interesantes y aliteración.

POINT OF VIEW / PUNTO DE VISTA El *punto de vista* es la perspectiva, o el punto de observación, desde la que se cuenta una historia. Puede tratarse de un narrador situado fuera de la historia o un personaje dentro de ella. El *punto de vista en primera persona* corresponde a un personaje que utiliza el pronombre "yo" o la conjugación de los verbos en primera persona de singular. Los dos tipos de *punto de vista en tercera persona*, limitado y omnisciente, son conocidos como "tercera persona" porque el narrador utiliza los pronombres de tercera persona como "él" y "ella" y la conjugación de los verbos en tercera

persona para referirse a los personajes. Por el contrario, no se utiliza el pronombre "yo".

En las historias contadas desde el *punto de vista en tercera persona omnisciente*, el narrador sabe y cuenta todo lo que sienten y piensan los personajes.

En las historia contadas desde el *punto de vista en tercera persona limitado*, el narrador relata los pensamientos y sentimientos de solo un personaje, y se cuenta todo desde la perspectiva de ese personaje.

PRESENTATION / PRESENTACIÓN Una *presentación* es el acto de mostrar o enseñar algo a un público. Las *presentaciones orales*, que se comunican a un público en vivo, pueden incluir *presentaciones visuales* como tablas, diagramas, ilustraciones y fotografías. Los videoclips y las diapositivas suelen ser parte de las *presentaciones digitales*, que se crean parcial o totalmente en computadora.

PROSE / PROSA La *prosa* es la forma más corriente del lenguaje escrito. La mayoría de los textos escritos que no se consideran poesía, drama o canción son textos en prosa. La prosa es uno de los géneros más importantes de la literatura y puede ser de ficción o de no ficción.

QUOTATION / CITA Las *citas* son grupos de palabras que se toman de un texto, de un discurso o de una entrevista y que son usadas o repetidas por alguien distinto al autor original. Siempre se debe atribuir una cita al autor original.

READ CLOSELY / LEER CON ATENCIÓN *Leer con atención* conlleva un análisis cuidadoso del texto, sus ideas y la manera en la que el autor expresa esas ideas.

REPETITION / REPETICIÓN La *repetición* se da cuando se utiliza más de una vez cualquier elemento del lenguaje (un sonido, una palabra, una expresión, un sintagma o una oración). La repetición se emplea tanto en prosa como en poesía.

RESEARCH PAPER / DOCUMENTO DE INVESTIGACIÓN Un *documento de investigación* brinda información detallada acerca de un tema o una tesis. Los documentos de investigación eficaces se elaboran a partir de información tomada de diversas fuentes creíbles, que se citan en el documento.

RESOLUTION / DESENLACE El *desenlace* es la resolución del conflicto en una trama.

RETELLING / VOLVER A CONTAR Las historias se pueden *volver a contar* de manera escrita u oral. Al volverse a contar una historia, se debe seguir una secuencia clara de los sucesos y utilizar técnicas narrativas como el diálogo y la descripción.

RHETORICAL DEVICES / FIGURAS RETÓRICAS Las *figuras retóricas* son formas especiales de organizar palabras e ideas para producir énfasis y provocar emoción, especialmente en discursos y otras presentaciones orales. Algunas de las figuras retóricas más frecuentes son las *preguntas retóricas,* que se formulan para insistir en una idea o para producir un efecto dramático más que para obtener una respuesta. La *apelación directa* es una figura retórica en la que el orador o escritor apunta un mensaje directamente a una persona o a un grupo de personas. La *analogía* es una comparación que destaca las semejanzas entre dos cosas, a menudo para explicar algo con lo que el público está poco familiarizado equiparándolo a algo más conocido. Muchas veces, las analogías son comparaciones ampliadas. La *yuxtaposición* es una figura retórica que coloca dos o más ideas o personajes uno al lado del otro para compararlos y contrastarlos.

RHYME / RIMA La *rima* es la repetición de los sonidos finales de las palabras. Los poetas emplean la rima para revestir de musicalidad sus versos y resaltar ciertas palabras e ideas. Muchos poemas tradicionales contienen *rimas finales* o palabras rimadas al final de los versos.

Otro recurso muy común es el uso de *rimas internas* o palabras que riman entre ellas en un mismo verso. La rima interna también resalta la fluidez propia de un poema.

RHYTHM / RITMO El *ritmo* es el patrón de sílabas acentuadas y no acentuadas en el lenguaje hablado o escrito.

SCAN / OJEAR *Ojear* es mirar por encima un texto para buscar la respuesta a una pregunta, clarificar algo o buscar detalles de apoyo.

SCENE / ESCENA Una *escena* es una sección de acción ininterrumpida dentro de uno de los actos de un drama.

SCRIPT / GUIÓN Un *guión* es la versión escrita de una obra de teatro o de una película. Los guiones se componen de *diálogos* y *acotaciones*.

SENSORY LANGUAGE / LENGUAJE SENSORIAL El *lenguaje sensorial* es texto o diálogo que tiene relación con uno o varios de los cinco sentidos.

SETTING / ESCENARIO El *escenario* de una obra literaria es el tiempo y lugar en los que ocurre la acción. El escenario incluye todos los detalles sobre el tiempo y el lugar: el año, el momento del día o incluso el tiempo atmosférico. El lugar puede ser un país concreto, un estado, una región, una comunidad, un barrio, un edificio, una institución o el propio hogar. Los detalles como los dialectos, ropa, costumbres y medios de trasporte se emplean con frecuencia para componer el escenario. En la mayoría de historias, los escenarios sirven de telón de fondo, es decir, de contexto en el que los personajes interactúan. El escenario también puede contribuir a crear una determinada sensación o un ambiente.

SHORT STORY / CUENTO Un *cuento* es una obra corta de ficción. Al igual que una novela, los cuentos presentan una secuencia de acontecimientos o trama. La trama suele contener un conflico central al que se enfrenta un personaje principal o protagonista. Los acontecimientos en un cuento normalmente comunican un mensaje sobre la vida o la naturaleza humana. Este mensaje o idea central es el tema del cuento.

SIMILE / SÍMIL Un *símil* es una figura retórica que utiliza *como* o *igual que* para establecer una comparación entre dos ideas distintas. Las conversaciones que mantenemos a diario también contienen símiles como, por ejemplo, "pálido como un muerto", "se propaga igual que un incendio" y "listo como un zorro".

SKIM / ECHAR UN VISTAZO *Echar un vistazo* a un texto es mirarlo rápidamente para tener una idea de lo más importante antes de comenzar a leerlo.

SOUND DEVICES / RECURSOS SONOROS Los *recursos sonoros* o fónicos son técnicas utilizadas por los escritores para dotar de musicalidad a sus textos. Entre ellos se incluyen la *onomatopeya,* la *aliteración,* la *rima,* la *métrica* y la *repetición.*

SPEAKER / YO POÉTICO El *yo poético* es la voz imaginaria que emplea un poeta cuando escribe un poema. El yo poético es el personaje que cuenta el poema. Este personaje o voz no suele identificarse con un nombre. Pueden existir notables diferencias entre el poeta y el yo poético.

SPEECH / DISCURSO Un *discurso* es una creación que se pronuncia de manera oral ante un público. Hay muchas clases de discursos que se ajustan a diversos tipos de reuniones y actos públicos. Algunos tipos de discursos son el *dramático,* el *persuasivo* y el *informativo.*

STAGE DIRECTIONS / ACOTACIONES Las *acotaciones* son las notas de un texto dramático en las que se describe como se debe interpretar o escenificar la obra. Las acotaciones suelen aparecer en cursiva y encerradas entre paréntesis o corchetes. Algunas acotaciones describen los movimientos, el vestuario, los estados de ánimo y el modo en el que deben hablar los personajes.

STAGING / ESCENOGRAFÍA La *escenografía* incluye la ambientación, iluminación, vestuario, efectos especiales y música que debe aparecer en el escenario donde se representa un drama.

SUMMARY / RESUMEN Un *resumen* es una descripción corta y clara de las ideas principales de algo como un texto, una película o una presentación. Los resúmenes eficaces son objetivos; es decir, son imparciales y no ofrecen valoraciones.

SUSPENSE / SUSPENSO El *suspenso* es la curiosidad, tensión o ansiedad en aumento que siente el lector por el devenir de la trama en una obra literaria. El suspenso se acrecienta hasta llegar al *clímax*, el punto máximo de tensión en la trama, cuando el conflicto alcanza su pico. La tensión del suspenso es parte de lo que mantiene al lector interesado en una historia y deseoso de descubrir cómo seguirá.

SYMBOL / SÍMBOLO Un *símbolo* es algo que representa una cosa diferente. Los símbolos son muy comunes en nuestra vida diaria. Una paloma con una rama de olivo en el pico es un símbolo de la paz. Una mujer con los ojos vendados sujetando una balanza es un símbolo de la justicia. Una corona es un símbolo del poder y la autoridad de un rey.

SYMBOLISM / SIMBOLISMO El *simbolismo* es el uso de los símbolos. El simbolismo juega un papel importante en muchos tipos de literatura. Puede ayudar a destacar algunos elementos que el autor quiere subrayar y añadir otros niveles de significado.

TEXT FEATURE / ELEMENTO TEXTUAL Un *elemento textual* es un elemento de diseño que ayuda a mostrar o incrementar la organización de un texto. Los títulos, subtítulos, pies de ilustración y apartados son ejemplos de elementos textuales.

TEXT STRUCTURE / ESTRUCTURA TEXTUAL La *estructura textual* es el modo en que está organizada la información en un texto. El autor elige una estructura textual determinada en función de su propósito. La estructura de *ventajas y desventajas* aborda los aspectos positivos y negativos de un tema, y luego da una opinión. La estructura de *causa y efecto* examina la relación entre distintos sucesos. Proporciona razones o una explicación de algo que ocurrió. El texto estructurado en *orden cronológico* narra una serie de sucesos en el orden en que ocurrieron. La estructura de *clasificación* crea categorías y luego da ejemplos de cosas que corresponden a cada una de ellas. En un texto estructurado como *comparación y contraste,* el autor presenta las semejanzas y diferencias entre dos asuntos. Los textos de comparación y contraste pueden adoptar una *organización punto por punto,* en la que se analiza un aspecto de ambos asuntos, luego otro, y así sucesivamente. En la *organización en bloque,* en cambio, se presentan todos los detalles sobre uno de los asuntos, seguidos de todos los detalles sobre el otro.

THEME / TEMA El *tema* es el mensaje central de una obra literaria. Se puede entender como una generalización sobre los seres humanos o la vida. El tema de una obra no es el resumen de su trama.

Aunque el tema puede exponerse directamente en el texto, se suele presentar indirectamente. Cuando se expone el tema indirecta o implícitamente, el lector lo podrá deducir al observar lo que se muestra en la obra sobre la vida y las personas. Un texto puede tener muchos temas. Los diversos subtemas suelen estar estrechamente relacionados con el tema central.

THESIS / TESIS La *tesis* de un texto es la idea principal o el propósito de un ensayo o trabajo de investigación.

Ver *Idea control.*

TONE / TONO El *tono* de una obra literaria es la actitud del escritor hacia sus lectores o hacia aquello sobre lo que escribe. El tono se puede describir con un único adjetivo como, por ejemplo, *formal* o *informal, serio* o *jocoso, amargo* o *irónico.* Los factores que contribuyen a crear el tono son la elección de las palabras, la estructura de la oración, la longitud de un verso, la rima, el ritmo y la repetición.

UNIVERSAL THEME / TEMA UNIVERSAL Un *tema universal* es un mensaje sobre la vida que se expresa habitualmente en muchas culturas y períodos históricos diferentes. Los cuentos populares, las epopeyas y los romances suelen abordar temas universales como la importancia de la valentía, el poder del amor o el peligro de la avaricia.

VOICE / VOZ La *voz* es el estilo personal del autor, la forma de expresarse que distingue su escritura de la de los demás. *Voz* puede referirse también a la organización del habla y el pensamiento del narrador de una obra de ficción.

WEIGHTED WORDS / PALABRAS EMOCIONALMENTE CARGADAS Las palabras que producen fuertes asociaciones emocionales que van más allá de sus significados básicos son *palabras emocionalmente cargadas.*

WORD CHOICE / ELECCIÓN DE PALABRAS La *elección de palabras* es la forma que tiene un escritor de escoger su lenguaje. La dicción es parte del estilo de un escritor y se describe como formal o informal, llana o elaborada, común o técnica, sofisticada o popular, anticuada o moderna.

PARTS OF SPEECH

Every English word, depending on its meaning and its use in a sentence, can be identified as one of the eight parts of speech. These are nouns, pronouns, verbs, adjectives, adverbs, prepositions, conjunctions, and interjections. Understanding the parts of speech will help you learn the rules of English grammar and usage.

Nouns A **noun** names a person, place, or thing. A **common noun** names any one of a class of persons, places, or things. A **proper noun** names a specific person, place, or thing.

Common Noun	Proper Noun
writer, country, novel	Charles Dickens, Great Britain, *Hard Times*

Pronouns A **pronoun** is a word that stands for one or more nouns. The word to which a pronoun refers (whose place it takes) is the **antecedent** of the pronoun.

A **personal pronoun** refers to the person speaking (first person); the person spoken to (second person); or the person, place, or thing spoken about (third person).

	Singular	Plural
First Person	I, me, my, mine	we, us, our, ours
Second Person	you, your, yours	you, your, yours
Third Person	he, him, his, she, her, hers, it, its	they, them, their, theirs

A **reflexive pronoun** reflects the action of a verb back on its subject. It indicates that the person or thing performing the action also is receiving the action.

I keep *myself* fit by taking a walk every day.

An **intensive pronoun** adds emphasis to a noun or pronoun.

It took the work of the president *himself* to pass the law.

A **demonstrative** pronoun points out a specific person(s), place(s), or thing(s).

this, that, these, those

A **relative pronoun** begins a subordinate clause and connects it to another idea in the sentence.

that, which, who, whom, whose

An **interrogative pronoun** begins a question.

what, which, who, whom, whose

An **indefinite pronoun** refers to a person, place, or thing that may or may not be specifically named.

all, another, any, anybody, both, each, everyone, few, most, much, none, no one, several, somebody

Verbs A **verb** expresses action or the existence of a state or condition.

An **action verb** tells what action someone or something is performing.

gather, read, work, jump, imagine, analyze, conclude

A **linking verb** connects the subject with another word that identifies or describes the subject. The most common linking verb is *be*.

appear, be, become, feel, look, remain, seem, smell, sound, stay, taste

A **helping verb**, or **auxiliary verb,** is added to a main verb to make a verb phrase.

be, can, could, do, have, may, might, must, shall, should, will, would

Adjectives An **adjective** modifies a noun or pronoun by describing it or giving it a more specific meaning. An adjective answers the questions:

What kind?	*purple* hat, *happy* face, *loud* sound
Which one?	*this* bowl
How many?	*three* cars
How much?	*enough* food

The articles *the, a,* and *an* are adjectives.

A **proper adjective** is an adjective derived from a proper noun.

French, Shakespearean

Adverbs An **adverb** modifies a verb, an adjective, or another adverb by telling *where, when, how,* or *to what extent*.

will answer *soon, extremely* sad, calls *more* often

Prepositions A **preposition** relates a noun or pronoun that appears with it to another word in the sentence.

Dad made a meal *for* us. We talked *till* dusk. Bo missed school *because of* his illness.

Conjunctions A **conjunction** connects words or groups of words.

A **coordinating conjunction** joins words or groups of words of equal rank.

bread *and* cheese, brief *but* powerful, milk *or* water

Correlative conjunctions are used in pairs to connect words or groups of words of equal importance.

both Luis *and* Rosa, *neither* you *nor* I, *either* Jon *or* his sister

Subordinating conjunctions indicate the connection between two ideas by placing one below the other in rank or importance. A subordinating conjunction introduces a subordinate, or dependent, clause (in a complex or compound-complex sentence).

   We will miss her *if* she leaves. Hank shrieked *when* he slipped on the ice.

Conjunctive adverbs do not subordinate a clause. Rather, they connect independent clauses of equal importance. They show the relationship between the two clauses and provide a smooth transition between the two ideas.

I love skiing; *however*, my sister hates the snow and cold weather. [*However* shows a contrast relationship between the two clauses.]
Skiing can be dangerous; *therefore*, I always wear a helmet. [*Therefore* shows a cause-and-effect relationship between the two clauses.]

Interjections An **interjection** expresses feeling or emotion. It is not related to other words in the sentence.
   ah, hey, oh, ouch, well, wow, ugh, yippee

PHRASES AND CLAUSES

Phrases A **phrase** is a group of words that does not have both a subject and a verb and that functions as one part of speech. A phrase expresses an idea but cannot stand alone.

Prepositional Phrases A **prepositional phrase** is a group of words that begins with a preposition and ends with a noun or pronoun that is the **object of the preposition.**
   before dawn   as a result of the rain

An **adjective phrase** is a prepositional phrase that modifies a noun or pronoun.
   Eliza appreciates the beauty **of a well-crafted poem.**

An **adverb phrase** is a prepositional phrase that modifies a verb, an adjective, or an adverb.
   She reads Spenser's sonnets **with great pleasure.**

Appositive Phrases An **appositive** is a noun or pronoun placed next to another noun or pronoun to add information about it. An **appositive phrase** consists of an appositive and its modifiers.
   Mr. Roth, **my music teacher,** is sick.

Verbal Phrases A **verbal** is a verb form that functions as a different part of speech (not as a verb) in a sentence. **Participles, gerunds,** and **infinitives** are verbals.

A **verbal phrase** includes a verbal and any modifiers or complements it may have. Verbal phrases may function as nouns, as adjectives, or as adverbs.

A **participle** is a verb form that can act as an adjective. Present participles end in *-ing;* past participles of regular verbs end in *-ed*.

A **participial phrase** consists of a participle and its

modifiers or complements. The entire phrase acts as an adjective.
   Jenna's backpack, **loaded with equipment,** was heavy.
   Barking incessantly, the dogs chased the squirrels out of sight.

A **gerund** is a verb form that ends in *-ing* and is used as a noun.

A **gerund phrase** consists of a gerund with any modifiers or complements, all acting together as a noun.
   Taking photographs of wildlife is her main hobby. [acts as subject]
   We always enjoy **listening to live music.** [acts as object]

An **infinitive** is a verb form, usually preceded by *to,* that can act as a noun, an adjective, or an adverb.

An **infinitive phrase** consists of an infinitive and its modifiers or complements, and sometimes its subject, all acting together as a single part of speech.
   She tries **to get out into the wilderness often.** [acts as a noun; direct object of *tries*]
   The Tigers are the team **to beat.** [acts as an adjective; describes *team*]
   I drove twenty miles **to witness the event.** [acts as an adverb; tells why I drove]

Clauses A **clause** is a group of words with its own subject and verb.

Independent Clauses An **independent clause** can stand by itself as a complete sentence.
   George Orwell wrote with extraordinary insight.

Subordinate Clauses

Subordinate Clauses A **subordinate clause** cannot stand by itself as a complete sentence. Subordinate clauses always appear connected in some way with one or more independent clauses.

> George Orwell, **who wrote with extraordinary insight,** produced many politically relevant works.

An **adjective clause** is a subordinate clause that acts as an adjective. It modifies a noun or a pronoun by telling *what kind* or *which one*. Also called relative clauses, adjective clauses usually begin with a **relative pronoun:** *who, which, that, whom,* or *whose*.

> "The Lamb" is the poem **that I memorized for class.**

An **adverb clause** is a subordinate clause that, like an adverb, modifies a verb, an adjective, or an adverb. An adverb clause tells *where, when, in what way, to what extent, under what condition,* or *why*.

> The students will read another poetry collection **if their schedule allows.**
> **When I recited the poem,** Mr. Lopez was impressed.

A **noun clause** is a subordinate clause that acts as a noun.

> William Blake survived on **whatever he made as an engraver.**

SENTENCE STRUCTURE

Subject and Predicate A **sentence** is a group of words that expresses a complete thought. A sentence has two main parts: a *subject* and a *predicate*.

The **subject** tells *whom* or *what* the sentence is about. The **predicate** tells what the subject of the sentence does or is.

A subject or a predicate can consist of a single word or of many words. All the words in the subject make up the **complete subject.** All the words in the predicate make up the **complete predicate.**

> **Complete Subject**   **Complete Predicate**
> Both of those girls | have already read *Macbeth*.

The **simple subject** is the essential noun, pronoun, or group of words acting as a noun that cannot be left out of the complete subject. The **simple predicate** is the essential verb or verb phrase that cannot be left out of the complete predicate.

> **Both** of those girls | **have** already **read** *Macbeth*.
> [Simple subject: *Both;* simple predicate: *have read*]

A **compound subject** is two or more subjects that have the same verb and are joined by a conjunction.

> **Neither the horse nor the driver** looked tired.

A **compound predicate** is two or more verbs that have the same subject and are joined by a conjunction.

> She **sneezed and coughed** throughout the trip.

Complements A **complement** is a word or word group that completes the meaning of the subject or verb in a sentence. There are four kinds: *direct objects, indirect objects, object complements,* and *subject complements*.

A **direct object** is a noun, a pronoun, or a group of words acting as a noun that receives the action of a transitive verb.

> She drove **Zach** to the launch site.
> We watched **how the rocket lifted off.**

An **indirect object** is a noun or pronoun that appears with a direct object and names the person or thing to which or for which something is done.

> He sold the **family** a mirror. [The direct object is *mirror.*]

An **object complement** is an adjective or noun that appears with a direct object and describes or renames it.

> The decision made her **unhappy**.
> [The direct object is *her*.]
> Many consider Shakespeare the greatest **playwright**. [The direct object is *Shakespeare*.]

A **subject complement** follows a linking verb and tells something about the subject. There are two kinds: *predicate nominatives* and *predicate adjectives*.

A **predicate nominative** is a noun or pronoun that follows a linking verb and identifies or renames the subject.

> "A Modest Proposal" is a **pamphlet.**

A **predicate adjective** is an adjective that follows a linking verb and describes the subject of the sentence.

> "A Modest Proposal" is **satirical.**

Classifying Sentences by Structure

Sentences can be classified according to the kind and number of clauses they contain. The four basic sentence structures are *simple, compound, complex,* and *compound-complex*.

A **simple sentence** consists of one independent clause.

> Terrence enjoys modern British literature.

A **compound sentence** consists of two or more independent clauses. The clauses are joined by a conjunction or by a semicolon.

> Terrence enjoys modern British literature, but his brother prefers the classics.

A **complex sentence** consists of one independent clause and one or more subordinate clauses.

Terrence, who reads voraciously, enjoys modern British literature.

A **compound-complex sentence** consists of two or more independent clauses and one or more subordinate clauses.

Terrence, who reads voraciously, enjoys modern British literature, but his brother prefers the classics.

Classifying Sentences by Function

Sentences can be classified according to their function or purpose. The four types are *declarative, interrogative, imperative,* and *exclamatory.*

A **declarative sentence** states an idea and ends with a period.

An **interrogative sentence** asks a question and ends with a question mark.

An **imperative sentence** gives an order or a direction and ends with either a period or an exclamation mark.

An **exclamatory sentence** conveys a strong emotion and ends with an exclamation mark.

Errors in Sentence Structure

A **fragment** is a group of words that does not express a complete thought. It lacks a subject, a predicate, or both.

A **run-on** sentence is made of two or more independent clauses run together as a single sentence.

A **comma splice** is a type of run-on sentence. It contains two independent clauses joined only by a comma. Independent clauses should be joined either by a semicolon or by a comma plus a coordinating conjunction. Independent clauses may also stand alone as sentences.

AGREEMENT

Subject and Verb Agreement

A singular subject must have a singular verb. A plural subject must have a plural verb.

Dr. Boone uses a telescope to view the night sky.
The **students use** a telescope to view the night sky.

A verb always agrees with its subject, not its object.
Incorrect: The best part of the show were the jugglers.
Correct: The best part of the show was the jugglers.

A phrase or clause that comes between a subject and verb does not affect subject-verb agreement.

His **theory** about black holes **lacks** support. [prepositional phrase in simple sentence]
The library **books,** which are on the table, **are** due tomorrow. [subordinate clause in complex sentence]

Two subjects joined by *and* usually take a plural verb.
The **dog** and the **cat are** healthy.

Two singular subjects joined by *or* or *nor* take a singular verb.
The **dog** or the **cat is** hiding.

Two plural subjects joined by *or* or *nor* take a plural verb.
The **dogs** or the **cats are** coming home with us.

When a singular and a plural subject are joined by *or* or *nor,* the verb agrees with the closer subject.
Either the **dogs** or the **cat is** behind the door.
Either the **cat** or the **dogs are** behind the door.

Pronoun and Antecedent Agreement

Pronouns must agree with their antecedents in number and gender. Use singular pronouns with singular antecedents and plural pronouns with plural antecedents.

Doris Lessing uses **her** writing to challenge ideas about women's roles.
Writers often use **their** skills to promote social change.

Use a singular pronoun when the antecedent is a singular indefinite pronoun such as *anybody, each, either, everybody, neither, no one, one,* or *someone.*
Judge **each** of the articles on **its** merits.

Use a plural pronoun when the antecedent is a plural indefinite pronoun such as *both, few, many,* or *several.*
Both of the articles have **their** flaws.

The indefinite pronouns *all, any, more, most, none,* and *some* can be singular or plural depending on the number of the word to which they refer.
Most of the *books* are in **their** proper places.
Most of the *book* has been torn from **its** binding.

Principal Parts of Regular and Irregular Verbs

A verb has four principal parts:

Present	Present Participle	Past	Past Participle
learn	learning	learned	learned
discuss	discussing	discussed	discussed
stand	standing	stood	stood
begin	beginning	began	begun

Regular verbs such as *learn* and *discuss* form the past and past participle by adding *-ed* to the present form. **Irregular verbs** such as *stand* and *begin* form the past and past participle in other ways. If you are in doubt about the principal parts of an irregular verb, check a dictionary.

Verb Tense

The different tenses of verbs indicate the time in which an action or condition occurs.

The **present tense** expresses an action that happens regularly or states a current condition or general truth.

> Tourists **flock** to the site yearly.
> Daily exercise **is** good for your heallth.

The **past tense** expresses a completed action or a condition that is no longer true.

> The squirrel **dropped** the nut and **ran** up the tree.
> I **was** very tired last night by 9:00.

The **future tense** indicates an action that will happen in the future or a condition that will be true.

> The Glazers **will visit** us tomorrow.
> They **will be** glad to arrive from their long journey.

The **present perfect tense** expresses an action that happened at an indefinite time in the past or an action that began in the past and continues into the present.

> Someone **has cleaned** the trash from the park.
> The puppy **has been** under the bed all day.

The **past perfect tense** shows an action that was completed before another action in the past.

> Gerard **had revised** his essay before he turned it in.

The **future perfect tense** indicates an action that will have been completed before another action takes place.

> Mimi **will have painted** the kitchen by the time we finish the shutters.

Unnecessary Shift in Verb Tense

A shift in verb tense is a change in verb tense—for example, from past tense to present tense, or from present to past. Shifting from one tense to another unnecessarily can cause confusion. Use a single verb tense unless there is a good reason to shift.

> The cat **is** hungry, so Margot **fed** her. [confusing shift from present tense to past tense]
> The cat **was** hungry, so Margot **fed** her. [consistent use of past tense]

Verb Voice

The **voice** of a verb shows whether the subject of a sentence is performing the action or receiving the action.

Active voice shows that the subject of the verb is performing the action.

> Josephine Baker **bought** her chateau in southern France in 1947.

Passive voice shows that the subject of the verb is receiving the action. It is often used when the person or thing doing the action is unknown or unimportant.

> The chateau **was built** in the fifteenth century.

Unnecessary Shift in Verb Voice

Do not shift needlessly from active voice to passive voice in your use of verbs.

> Elena and I **searched** the trail for evidence, but no clues **were found**. [shift from active voice to passive voice]
> Elena and I **searched** the trail for evidence, but we **found** no clues. [consistent use of active voice]

Degrees of Comparison

Adjectives and adverbs take different forms to show the three degrees of comparison: the *positive*, the *comparative*, and the *superlative*.

Positive	Comparative	Superlative
fast	faster	fastest
crafty	craftier	craftiest
abruptly	more abruptly	most abruptly
badly	worse	worst

Using Comparative and Superlative Adjectives and Adverbs

Use comparative adjectives and adverbs to compare two things. Use superlative adjectives and adverbs to compare three or more things.

> This season's weather was **drier** than last year's.
> This season has been one of the **driest** on record.
> Jake practices **more often** than Jamal.
> Of everyone in the band, Jake practices **most often.**

USING PRONOUNS

Pronoun Case

The **case** of a pronoun is the form it takes to show its function in a sentence. There are three pronoun cases: *nominative*, *objective*, and *possessive*.

Nominative	Objective	Possessive
I, you, he, she, it, we, you, they	me, you, him, her, it, us, you, them	my, mine, your, yours, his, her, hers, its, our, ours, their, theirs

Use the **nominative case** when a pronoun functions as a *subject* or as a *predicate nominative*.

They are going to the movies. [subject]
The biggest movie fan is **she**. [predicate nominative]

Use the **objective case** for a pronoun acting as a *direct object*, an *indirect object,* or the *object of a preposition.*

The ending of the play surprised **me**. [direct object]
Mary gave **us** two tickets to the play. [indirect object]
The audience cheered for **him**. [object of preposition]

Use the **possessive case** to show ownership.

The red suitcase is **hers.**

COMMONLY CONFUSED WORDS

Diction The words you choose contribute to the overall effectiveness of your writing. **Diction** refers to word choice and to the clearness and correctness of those words. You can improve one aspect of your diction by choosing carefully between commonly confused words, such as the sets of words listed below.

accept, except

Accept is a verb that means "to receive" or "to agree to." *Except* is a preposition that means "other than" or "leaving out."

Please **accept** my offer to buy you lunch this weekend.
He is busy every day **except** the weekends.

affect, effect

Affect is usually a verb meaning "to influence" or "to bring about a change in." *Effect* is usually a noun meaning "result."

The distractions outside **affect** Steven's ability to concentrate.
The teacher's remedies had a positive **effect** on Steven's ability to concentrate.

among, between

Among is usually used with three or more items, and it emphasizes collective relationships or indicates distribution. *Between* is generally used with only two items, but it can be used with more than two if the emphasis is on individual (one-to-one) relationships within the group.

I had to choose a snack **among** the various vegetables.
He handed out the booklets **among** the conference participants.
Our school is **between** a park and an old barn.
The tournament included matches **between** France, Spain, Mexico, and the United States.

amount, number

Amount refers to overall quantity and is mainly used with mass nouns (those that can't be counted). *Number* refers to individual items that can be counted.

The **amount** of attention that great writers have paid to Shakespeare is remarkable.
A **number** of important English writers have been fascinated by the legend of King Arthur.

assure, ensure, insure

Assure means "to convince [someone of something]; to guarantee." *Ensure* means "to make certain [that something happens]." *Insure* means "to arrange for payment in case of loss."

The attorney **assured** us we'd win the case.
The rules **ensure** that no one gets treated unfairly.
Many professional musicians **insure** their valuable instruments.

bad, badly

Use the adjective *bad* before a noun or after linking verbs such as *feel, look,* and *seem*. Use *badly* whenever an adverb is required.

The situation may seem **bad**, but it will improve over time.
Though our team played **badly** today, we will focus on practicing for the next match.

beside, besides

Beside means "at the side of" or "close to." *Besides* means "in addition to."

The stapler sits **beside** the pencil sharpener in our classroom.
Besides being very clean, the classroom is very organized.

can, may

The helping verb *can* generally refers to the ability to do something. The helping verb *may* generally refers to permission to do something.

I **can** run one mile in six minutes.
May we have a race during recess?

complement, compliment

The verb *complement* means "to enhance"; the verb *compliment* means "to praise."

    Online exercises **complement** the textbook lessons.

    Ms. Lewis **complimented** our team on our excellent debate.

compose, comprise

Compose means "to make up; constitute." *Comprise* means "to include or contain." The whole comprises its parts or is composed of its parts, and the parts compose the whole.

    The assignment **comprises** three different tasks.

    The assignment is **composed** of three different tasks.

    Three different tasks **compose** the assignment.

different from, different than

Different from is generally preferred over *different than*, but *different than* can be used before a clause. Use *different from* before a noun or pronoun.

    Your point of view is so **different from** mine.

    His idea was so **different from** [or **different than**] what we had expected.

farther, further

Use *farther* to refer to distance. Use *further* to mean "to a greater degree or extent" or "additional."

    Chiang has traveled **farther** than anybody else in the class.

    If I want **further** details about his travels, I can read his blog.

fewer, less

Use *fewer* for things that can be counted. Use *less* for amounts or quantities that cannot be counted. *Fewer* must be followed by a plural noun.

    Fewer students drive to school since the weather improved.

    There is **less** noise outside in the mornings.

good, well

Use the adjective *good* before a noun or after a linking verb. Use *well* whenever an adverb is required, such as when modifying a verb.

    I feel **good** after sleeping for eight hours.

    I did **well** on my test, and my soccer team played **well** in that afternoon's game. It was a **good** day!

its, it's

The word *its* with no apostrophe is a possessive pronoun. The word *it's* is a contraction of "it is."

    Angelica will try to fix the computer and **its** keyboard.

    It's a difficult job, but she can do it.

lay, lie

Lay is a transitive verb meaning "to set or put something down." Its principal parts are *lay, laying, laid, laid. Lie* is an intransitive verb meaning "to recline" or "to exist in a certain place." Its principal parts are *lie, lying, lay, lain.*

    Please **lay** that box down and help me with the sofa.

    When we are done moving, I am going to **lie** down.

    My hometown **lies** sixty miles north of here.

like, as

Like is a preposition that usually means "similar to" and precedes a noun or pronoun. The conjunction *as* means "in the way that" and usually precedes a clause.

    Like the other students, I was prepared for a quiz.

    As I said yesterday, we expect to finish before noon.

Use **such as,** not **like,** before a series of examples.

    Foods **such as** apples, nuts, and pretzels make good snacks.

of, have

Do not use *of* in place of *have* after auxiliary verbs such as *would, could, should, might,* or *must.* The contraction of *have* is formed by adding *-ve* after these verbs.

    I **would have** stayed after school today, but I had to help cook at home.

    Mom **must've** called while I was still in the gym.

principal, principle

Principal can be an adjective meaning "main; most important." It can also be a noun meaning "chief officer of a school." *Principle* is a noun meaning "moral rule" or "fundamental truth."

    His strange behavior was the **principal** reason for our concern.

    Democratic **principles** form the basis of our country's laws.

raise, rise

Raise is a transitive verb that usually takes a direct object. *Rise* is intransitive and never takes a direct object.

    Iliana and Josef **raise** the flag every morning.

    They **rise** from their seats and volunteer immediately whenever help is needed.

than, then

The conjunction *than* is used to connect the two parts of a comparison. The adverb *then* usually refers to time.

    My backpack is heavier **than** hers.

    I will finish my homework and **then** meet my friends at the park.

GLOSSARY: GRAMMAR HANDBOOK

that, which, who

Use the relative pronoun *that* to refer to things or people. Use *which* only for things and *who* only for people.

That introduces a restrictive phrase or clause, that is, one that is essential to the meaning of the sentence. *Which* introduces a nonrestrictive phrase or clause—one that adds information but could be deleted from the sentence—and is preceded by a comma.

> Ben ran to the park **that** just reopened.
> The park, **which** just reopened, has many attractions.
> The man **who** built the park loves to see people smiling.

their, there, they're *Their* is a possessive pronoun. *There* is an adverb that shows location. *They're* is the contraction of "they are."

> **They're** meeting **their** friends over **there.**

to, too, two *To* is a preposition that can mean "in the direction toward." *To* is also the first part of an infinitive. *Too* means "also" or "excessively." *Two* is the number after one.

> The **two** friends were careful not **to** wave **to** each other **too** quickly.

who, whom

In formal writing, use *who* only as a subject in clauses and sentences. Use *whom* only as the object of a verb or of a preposition.

> **Who** paid for the tickets?
> I wonder **who** was able to get them.
> **Whom** should I pay for the tickets?
> I can't recall to **whom** I gave the money for the tickets.

your, you're

Your is a possessive pronoun expressing ownership. *You're* is the contraction of "you are."

> Have you finished writing **your** informative essay?
> **You're** supposed to turn it in tomorrow. If **you're** late, **your** grade will be affected.

EDITING FOR ENGLISH LANGUAGE CONVENTIONS

Capitalization

First Words

Capitalize the first word of a sentence.

> **S**tories about knights and their deeds interest me.

Capitalize the first word of direct speech.

> **S**haron asked, "**D**o you like stories about knights?"

Capitalize the first word of a quotation that is a complete sentence.

> **E**instein said, "**A**nyone who has never made a mistake has never tried anything new."

Proper Nouns and Proper Adjectives

Capitalize all proper nouns, including geographical names, historical events and periods, and names of organizations.

> **T**hames **R**iver   **J**ohn **K**eats   the **R**enaissance
> **U**nited **N**ations   **W**orld **W**ar II   **S**ierra **N**evada

Capitalize all proper adjectives.

> **S**hakespearean play   **B**ritish invasion
> **A**merican citizen   **L**atin **A**merican literature

Abbreviations

An **abbreviation** is the shortened form of a word or a phrase.

Capitalize the first letter of many common abbreviations.

> **D**r.   **M**r.   **M**s.   **D**ept.
> **I**nc.   **A**ve.   **B**lvd.   **S**t.

Capitalize the first letter of the traditional abbreviations for states and both letters of the postal abbreviation.

> **C**alif.   **CA** (California)   **F**la.   **FL** (Florida)

An **acronym** is a type of abbreviation that is created from the first letters or from parts of a compound term. An acronym is read or spoken as a single word.

Capitalize all the letters in most acronyms.

> **NASA** (National Aeronautics and Space Administration)
> **NATO** (North Atlantic Treaty Organization)
> **SAT** (Scholastic Aptitude Test)
> **UNESCO** (United Nations Educational, Scientific, and Cultural Organization)

Some acronyms have become words and are not capitalized, such as *radar* (radio detection and ranging), and *scuba* (self-contained underwater breathing apparatus).

Initialisms are another type of abbreviation made from the first letters of a compound term. However, they are spoken letter by letter, not as one word.

Capitalize all the letters in most initialisms.

> **DVD** (Digital Video Disk)
> **FBI** (Federal Bureau of Investigation)
> **FDA** (Food and Drug Administration)
> **UN** (United Nations)
> **URL** (Uniform Resource Locator)

Academic Course Names

Capitalize course names only if they are language courses, are followed by a number, or are preceded by a proper noun or adjective.

Spanish   **H**onors **C**hemistry   **H**istory 101
geology   **a**lgebra   **s**ocial **s**tudies

Titles

Capitalize personal titles when followed by the person's name.

Senator Pérez   **K**ing George
At the time, George was **k**ing.

Capitalize titles showing family relationships when they are followed by a specific person's name, unless they are preceded by a possessive noun or pronoun.

Uncle Oscar   Mangan's **s**ister   his **a**unt Tessa

Capitalize the first word and all other key words in the titles of books, stories, songs, and other works of art.

Frankenstein   "**S**hooting an **E**lephant"

Punctuation

End Marks

Use a **period** to end a declarative sentence or an imperative sentence.

We are studying the structure of sonnets.
Read the biography of Mary Shelley.

Use periods with initials and abbreviations.

D. H. Lawrence   Mrs. Browning
Mt. Everest   Maple St.

Use a **question mark** to end an interrogative sentence.

What is Macbeth's fatal flaw?

Use an **exclamation mark** after an exclamatory sentence or a forceful imperative sentence.

That's a beautiful painting!   Let me go now!

Commas

Use a **comma** before a coordinating conjunction to separate two independent clauses in a compound sentence.

The game was very close, but we were victorious.

Use a comma in a complex sentence if the subordinate clause precedes the independent clause.

If it rains, we will cancel the game.

Do not use a comma if the subordinate clause follows the independent clause.

We will cancel the game if it rains.

Use commas to separate three or more words, phrases, or clauses in a series.

William Blake was a writer, artist, and printer.

Use commas to separate coordinate adjectives.

It was a witty, amusing novel.

Use a comma after an introductory word, phrase, or interjection. Use a comma in direct address, after the noun that names the person(s) being addressed.

Well, I haven't decided yet.
Carmen, have you made up your mind?

Use a comma after a transition word or phrase at the beginning of a sentence.

Last week, I studied for my math exam. This week, I will study for my science exam and finish my research project.

Use commas to set off nonrestrictive phrases and clauses in the middle of a sentence.

Old English, of course, requires translation.
Middle English, which was spoken from about 1100 to 1500, eventually became Modern English.

Use commas with places and dates.

Coventry, England   September 1, 1939

Semicolons

Use a **semicolon** to join closely related independent clauses that are not already joined by a conjunction.

Tanya likes to write poetry; Heather prefers prose.

Use semicolons to avoid confusion when items in a series contain commas.

They traveled to London, England; Madrid, Spain; and Rome, Italy.

Colons

Use a **colon** before a list of items following an independent clause.

Notable Victorian poets include the following: Tennyson, Arnold, Housman, and Hopkins.

Use a colon to introduce information that summarizes or explains the independent clause before it.

She just wanted to do one thing: rest.
Malcolm loves volunteering: He reads to sick children every Saturday afternoon.

Quotation Marks

Use **quotation marks** to enclose a direct quotation.

"Short stories," Ms. Hildebrand said, "should have rich, well-developed characters."

An **indirect quotation** does not require quotation marks.

Ms. Hildebrand said that short stories should have well-developed characters.

Use quotation marks around the titles of short written works, episodes in a series, songs, and works mentioned as parts of collections.

"The Lagoon"   "Boswell Meets Johnson"

GLOSSARY: GRAMMAR HANDBOOK

Italics

Italicize the titles of long written works, movies, television and radio shows, lengthy works of music, paintings, and sculptures.

Howards End   *60 Minutes*   *Guernica*

For handwritten material, you can use underlining instead of italics.

The Princess Bride   Mona Lisa

Dashes

Use **dashes** to indicate an abrupt change of thought, an interrupting idea, or a summary statement.

I read the entire first act of *Macbeth*—you won't believe what happens next.

The director—what's her name again?—attended the movie premiere.

Hyphens

Use a **hyphen** with certain numbers, after certain prefixes, with two or more words used as one word, and with a compound modifier that comes before a noun.

seventy-two
pre-Columbian
president-elect
five-year contract

Parentheses

Use **parentheses** to set off asides and explanations when the material is not essential or when it consists of one or more sentences. When the sentence in parentheses interrupts the larger sentence, it does not have a capital letter or a period.

He listened intently (it was too dark to see who was speaking) to try to identify the voices.

When a sentence in parentheses falls between two other complete sentences, it should start with a capital letter and end with a period.

The quarterback threw three touchdown passes. (We knew he could do it.) Our team won the game by two points.

Apostrophes

Add an **apostrophe** and an *s* to show the possessive case of most singular nouns and of plural nouns that do not end in *-s* or *-es*.

Blake's poems   the mice's whiskers

Names ending in *s* form their possessives in the same way, except for classical and biblical names, which add only an apostrophe to form the possessive.

Dickens's   Hercules'

Add an apostrophe to show the possessive case of plural nouns ending in *-s* and *-es*.

the girls' songs   the Ortizes' car

Use an apostrophe in a contraction to indicate the position of the missing letter or letters.

She's never read a Coleridge poem she didn't like.

Brackets

Use **brackets** to enclose clarifying information inserted within a quotation.

Columbus's journal entry from October 21, 1492, begins as follows: "At 10 o'clock, we arrived at a cape of the island [San Salvador], and anchored, the other vessels in company."

Ellipses

Use three ellipsis points, also known as an **ellipsis,** to indicate where you have omitted words from quoted material.

Wollestonecraft wrote, "The education of women has of late been more attended to than formerly; yet they are still . . . ridiculed or pitied. . . ."

In the example above, the four dots at the end of the sentence are the three ellipsis points plus the period from the original sentence.

Use an ellipsis to indicate a pause or interruption in speech.

"When he told me the news," said the coach, "I was . . . I was shocked . . . completely shocked."

Spelling

Spelling Rules

Learning the rules of English spelling will help you make **generalizations** about how to spell words.

Word Parts

The three word parts that can combine to form a word are roots, prefixes, and suffixes. Many of these word parts come from the Greek, Latin, and Anglo-Saxon languages.

The **root** carries a word's basic meaning.

Root and Origin	Meaning	Examples
-log- [Gr.]	word, discourse	*logic, monologue*
-pel- [L.]	force, drive	*expel, compel*

A **prefix** is one or more syllables added to the beginning of a word that alter the meaning of the root.

Prefix and Origin	Meaning	Example
anti- [Gr.]	against	*antipathy*
inter- [L.]	between	*international*
mis- [A.S.]	wrong	*misplace*

A **suffix** is a letter or group of letters added to the end of a word that changes the word's meaning or part of speech.

Suffix and Origin	Meaning and Example	Part of Speech
-ful [A.S.]	full of: *scornful*	adjective
-ity [L.]	state of being: *adversity*	noun
-ize (-ise) [Gr.]	to make: *idolize*	verb
-ly [A.S.]	in a manner: *calmly*	adverb

Rules for Adding Suffixes to Words

When adding a suffix to a word ending in *y* preceded by a consonant, change *y* to *i* unless the suffix begins with *i*.

ply + -able = pliable   happy + -ness = happiness
defy + -ing = defying   cry + -ing = crying

For a word ending in *e*, drop the *e* when adding a suffix beginning with a vowel.

drive + -ing = driving   move + -able = movable
SOME EXCEPTIONS: traceable, seeing, dyeing

For words ending with a consonant + vowel + consonant in a stressed syllable, double the final consonant when adding a suffix that begins with a vowel.

mud + -y = muddy   submit + -ed = submitted
SOME EXCEPTIONS: mixing, fixed

Rules for Adding Prefixes to Words

When a prefix is added to a word, the spelling of the word remains the same.

un- + certain = uncertain   mis- + spell = misspell

When a prefix is added to a proper noun, add a hyphen before the noun.

pro- + Europe = pro-Europe
post- + Victorian = post-Victorian

Orthographic Patterns

Certain letter combinations in English make certain sounds. For instance, *ph* sounds like *f*, *eigh* usually makes a long *a* sound, and the *k* before an *n* is often silent.

pharmacy   n**eigh**bor   **k**nowledge

Understanding **orthographic patterns** such as these can help you improve your spelling.

Forming Plurals

The plural form of most nouns is formed by adding *-s* to the singular.

computer**s**   gadget**s**   Washington**s**

For words ending in *s, ss, x, z, sh,* or *ch,* add *-es*.

circus**es**   tax**es**   wish**es**   bench**es**

For words ending in *y* or *o* preceded by a vowel, add *-s*.

key**s**   patio**s**

For words ending in *y* preceded by a consonant, change the *y* to an *i* and add *-es*.

cit**ies**   enem**ies**   troph**ies**

For most words ending in *o* preceded by a consonant, add *-es*.

echo**es**   tomato**es**

Some words form the plural in irregular ways.

women   oxen   children   teeth   deer

Foreign Words Used in English

Some words used in English are actually foreign words that have been adopted. Learning to spell these words requires memorization. When in doubt, check a dictionary.

sushi   enchilada   au pair   fiancé
laissez faire   croissant   al fresco   piñata

characteristics
  adventure stories, 552
  argumentative essay, 258
  autobiography, 128
  biography, 212, 540
  drama, 360
  graphic "novel" history, 568
  historical fiction, 568
  informational article, 258
  lyric poetry, 190
  memoir, 12, 64, 498
  myths, 202
  narrative poem, 454
  persuasive essays, 308
  realistic short story, 78
  reflective essay, 298, 468
  retellings, 442
  science article, 148
  science fiction, 34, 244, 318
  song, 454
claim, 259, 275, 309, 315
comic strip, 28
conflict, 565
controlling idea, 65, 71, 259, 267, 469, 475, 499, 515
cultural setting, 569, 578
dialogue, 361, 389
diction, 299, 305
drama, 360
essay
  argumentative, 258, 271
  personal, Unit 1:IL18
  persuasive, 311
  reflective, 298, 301, Unit 2:IL4
evidence, 65, 309
  anecdotes, 65
  descriptions, 65
  details, 65
  dialogue, 65
  reflections, 65
  supporting evidence, 71, 315, 475
expository nonfiction, Unit 5:IL18
fantasy, Unit 1:IL1, Unit 4:IL1, Unit 4:IL16
fiction
  adventure stories, 552, 555
  historical fiction, 568, 571
  realistic fiction, 78, 80, Unit 1:IL21, Unit 1:IL24
  science fiction, 244, 246, 247, 318, 321
  short story, Unit 4:IL7
    realistic, 78, 80
first-person point of view, 13, 23, 79
flashback, 35, 45
graphic features, 541

captions, 549
photographs, 549
sidebar, 549
subheads, 541, 549
graphic novel, Unit 5:IL25
graphic "novel" history, 581
historical fiction, 571
historical setting, 569, 578
informational article, 258, 261
informational text, Unit 2:IL8, Unit 2:IL11
lyric poetry, 190, 194, 195, 196
magazine article, Unit 5:IL14
memoir, 12, 64, 498, 501
message, 129, 143, 299, 305
  explicit, 213, 221
  implicit, 213, 221
myths, 202, 204, 205
narrative point of view, 79, 92, 104
  first-person, 13, 23, 79
  purpose achieved by, 79
  third-person limited, 79, 92
  third-person omniscient, 79, 104
narrator, 92, 104
nonfiction
  argumentative essay, 258, 260
  graphic "novel" history, 568
  informational article, 258, 260
  narrative, Unit 5:IL8
  science article, 148, 150, 151, 164, 165, 174
organizational patterns, 149, 259, 275
  advantage/disadvantage, 267
  classification, 149, 171
  definition, 149, 161
personal essay, Unit 1:IL18
persuasive essays, 308, 311
plot, 35, 45, 443, 451, 553, 565
  climax, 553
  exposition, 553
  falling action, 553
  resolution, 553
  rising action, 553
plot development, 319, 327
poetry, 456, 466, Unit 1:IL13, Unit 1:IL15, Unit 2:IL1, Unit 4:IL4, Unit 4:IL6
  lyric, 190, 194, 195, 196
  meter, 455, 464
    anapestic, 455, 464
    iambic, 455, 464
    trochaic, 455, 464
  structural elements, 191, 455, 464
    line breaks, 199
    lines, 199
    rhyme scheme, 191

stanzas, 191
print features
  captions, 541, 549
  photographs, 549
  sidebars, 541, 549
  subheads, 541, 549
  timelines, 541
realistic fiction, Unit 1:IL21, Unit 1:IL24
realistic short story, 78, 80
reflective essay, 298, 301, 468, Unit 2:IL4, IL4
retellings, 442, 445
rhetorical questions, 305
science fiction, 34, 36, 37, 246, 247, 318, 321
setting, 319, 327
  cultural, 569, 578
  historical, 569, 578
short story, Unit 4:IL7
  realistic, 78, 80
song, 456
stage directions, 361, 423
structure
  adventure stories, 552
  argumentative essay, 258
  autobiography, 128
  biography, 212, 540
  drama, 360
  graphic "novel" history, 568
  historical fiction, 568
  informational article, 258
  lyric poetry, 190
  memoir, 12, 64, 498
  myths, 202
  narrative poem, 454
  persuasive essays, 308
  realistic short story, 78
  reflective essay, 298, 468
  retellings, 442
  science article, 148
  science fiction, 34, 244, 318
  song, 454
subheads, 161
supporting details, 515
  descriptions, 499
  emotional response, 499
  events, 499
  lessons learned, 499
  title, 499
supporting evidence, 71, 259, 315, 475
themes, 253
  characters, 245, 253
  conflicts, 245, 253
  multiple, 203, 209, 245

complete, 184
correlative conjunctions, 534
run-on, 184
sentence fragments, 184
sentence variety, 436
subject-verb agreement, 58
spelling, 185
plurals of words ending in *-f* or *-fe*, 437
EQ Notes, 357
review and evaluate, 114, 230, 346, 484
Essay
argumentative, 256, 284, 346, 518
cause-and-effect, 477
comparison-and-contrast, 175, 477
explanatory, 477
how-to, 146
informational, 176, 230
research-based, 596
Evidence, 177, 285
anecdotes, 285
examples, 285
expert opinion, 285
facts, 285
transitions, 181
Examples, 180, 285
Expert opinion, 285
Explanatory essay, 477
Facts, 285
specific, 180
First-person point of view, 429
Freewrite, 52, 178, 286, 430
Friendly letter, 201
drafting, 201
planning, 201
Genre, 429
Homophones, 185
How-to essay, 146
Independent clause, 433
Informational essay, 176, 230
drafting, 180
editing, 184, 232
elements of, 176
Informational Essay Checklist, 231
planning and prewriting, 178
publishing and presenting, 185
review and evaluate EQ Notes, 230
revising, 182, 232
Letter
business letter, 567
friendly letter, 201
Mood, 429

Narration, 55
Narrative
characteristics, 51
personal, 50, 114
retelling, 426
Objective summary, 283
Organization, 56, 57, 182, 183, 290, 291, 532, 533
Outline, 530
Personal narrative, 50, 114
drafting, 54
editing, 58, 116
elements of, 50
Personal Narrative Checklist, 115
planning and prewriting, 52
publishing and presenting, 59
review and evaluate EQ Notes, 114
revising, 56, 116
Planning and prewriting, 52, 178, 286, 430, 528
clarity, 527
complexity, 527
controlling idea, 179
evaluate sources, 529
focus, 527
freewrite, 52, 178, 286, 430
generate questions, 526
identify sources, 528
refine research question, 527
significance, 527
structure, 53, 179
claim, 287
counterclaim, 287
rebuttal, 287
support, 287
Plot, 48, 431
Poetry, 26
sensory language, 26
Point of view,
first-person, 429
third-person, 429
Portrayals, 55
Prepositional phrases, 277, 289
Publishing and presenting, multimodal, 59, 185, 293, 437, 535
Punctuation, 55
comma, 293, 433, 437
comma splice, 184
dialogue, 59
transitions, 185
varying, 55
Purpose, 51, 177, 285, 429
general, 285, 525
specific, 285, 525

QuickWrite, 9, 112, 125, 228, 241, 357, 482, 495, 594
Rebuttal, 287, 340
Reflect on writing, 26, 48, 146, 201, 256, 392, 426, 518
Research-based essay, 596
Research-Based Essay Checklist, 597
review and evaluate evidence, 596
revising and editing, 598
Research paper, 524
drafting, 530
editing, 534
elements, 524
planning and prewriting, 526
publishing and presenting, 535
revising, 532
Research report, 335
Response to literature, 107, 467, 589
Revising
clarity, 56, 57, 182, 183, 290, 291, 434, 435, 532, 533
development, 56, 57, 182, 183, 290, 291, 434, 435, 532, 533
organization, 56, 57, 182, 183, 290, 291, 532, 533
structure, 434, 435
style and tone, 56, 57, 182, 183, 290, 291, 434, 435, 532, 533
Run-on sentences, 184
Sensory details, 432
Sensory language, 26
Sentence fragments, 184
Sentences
comma splice, 184
complete, 184
complex, 433
compound, 210
correlative conjunctions, 391, 433, 534
run-on, 184
sentence fragments, 184, 436
sentence variety, 56, 57
simple, 210
subject-verb agreement, 58, 306, 452
topic sentence, 181
Sentence variety, 436
Sequence of events, 53
climax, 53
falling action, 53
inciting incident, 53
resolution, 53
rising action, 53
Setting, 54, 431
Short story, 48, 428, 478, 484
character, 48

Speaking and Listening

Annotate, 519

Annotated map, 519

Bandwagon appeal, 591

Class discussion, 147

Debate, 340
- discuss and evaluate, 341
- four-corner, 494
- prepare, 340
- rehearse and debate, 341
- walk-around debate, 240

Discussion, 124
- class discussion, 147
- group discussion, 8, 77, 307, 356
- partner discussion, 27

Dramatic reading, 393

Evaluate presentations, 257

Four-corner debate, 494

Group discussion, 8, 77, 307, 356

Infomercial, 590
- draft and revise, 591
- evaluate, 591
- plan, 590
- rehearse and present, 591

Language devices
- logical fallacies, 591
- rhetorical devices, 591

Logical fallacies, 591
- bandwagon appeal, 591
- slippery slope, 591

Media presentation, 257

Narrative presentation, retelling, 108

Oral instructions, 224, 551
- listen actively, 225
- plan, 224
- rehearse, 225

Oral reading, 49

Oral report, 283

Partner discussion, 27

Peer-group learning
- analyzing meanings
  - explicit meanings, 189
  - implicit meanings, 189
  - paraphrase, 189
- making a schedule, 63, 189, 297, 441, 539
- roles on group projects, 539
- strategies
  - clarify, 60, 186, 294, 438, 536
  - participate fully, 60, 186, 294, 438, 536
  - prepare, 60, 186, 294, 438, 536
  - support others, 60, 186, 294, 438, 536

using text evidence
- evaluate your choices, 63
- notice key details, 63
- understand the question, 63

working as a group
- apply the rules, 62, 296, 440, 538
- create a communication plan, 62, 188, 296, 440, 538
- list your rules, 62, 188, 296, 440, 538
- name your group, 62, 188, 296, 440, 538
- take a position, 62, 188, 296, 440, 538

Presentations
- infomercial, 590
- retelling, 108
- short story, 478

Repetition, 591

Research presentation, infomercial, 590

Retelling, 108
- listen and evaluate, 109
- plan, 108
- rehearse and present, 109

Rhetorical devices, 591
- repetition, 591
- rhetorical questions, 591

Rhetorical questions, 591

Short story, 478
- listen and evaluate, 479
- plan and write, 478
- prepare to share, 479
- rehearse and present, 479

Slippery slope, 591

Speech, 427

Walk-around debate, 240

Whole-class learning strategies
- demonstrate respect, 10, 126, 242, 358, 496
- interact and share ideas, 10, 126, 242, 358, 496
- listen actively, 10, 126, 242, 358, 496
- show interest, 10, 126, 242, 358, 496

Vocabulary

Academic vocabulary
- benefit, 121
- certain, 237
- coherent, 491
- consequently, 353
- contribute, 5
- convince, 237
- critical, 491
- declare, 237
- description, 353

dialogue, 353

elaborate, 121

exclude, 121

illustrate, 121

justify, 237

manual, 491

memorize, 5

mission, 5

novelty, 353

objective, 121

omit, 491

recognize, 5

reflect, 5

sufficient, 237

transform, 353

valid, 491

Concept vocabulary
- abandoned, 94, 101, 103
- admired, 80, 84, 91
- agile, 164, 166, 172
- apologetically, 246, 249, 254
- askance, 456, 461, 463
- beware, 456, 458, 463
- breaches, 270, 272, 276
- bypassed, 270, 272, 276
- compromise, 394, 415, 424
- consideration, 362, 373, 390
- consumed, 310, 311, 314
- continuation, 300, 303, 304
- criminals, 260, 263, 268
- cumbersome, 36, 39, 46
- darting, 204, 206, 208
- deliberate, 500, 503, 516
- desperate, 66, 68, 70
- detached, 94, 99, 103
- devouring, 310, 311, 314
- dignified, 192, 195, 198
- disguise, 260, 263, 268
- disgusted, 66, 69, 70
- distressed, 246, 249, 254
- domesticated, 192, 194, 198
- dominate, 130, 139, 144
- drained, 36, 40, 46
- endured, 554, 556, 564
- envied, 80, 81, 91
- evaluate, 150, 152, 162
- exception, 542, 545, 548
- exploiting, 270, 271, 276
- fearlessly, 444, 445, 450
- feathery, 14, 20, 24
- forged, 260, 263, 268
- forlorn, 36, 40, 46
- fraud, 260, 261, 268
- gradually, 300, 302, 304
- hacked, 270, 272, 276

Assessment

INDEX OF AUTHORS AND TITLES

The following authors and titles appear in the print and online versions of myPerspectives.

The following Independent Learning titles appear only in the online version of myPerspectives.

The following selections appear in Grade 6 of *myPerspectives*. Some selections appear online only.

Asimov Holdings LLC "The Fun They Had" from *Isaac Asimov: The Complete Stories, Vol. I* by Isaac Asimov. Copyright ©1954 by Isaac Asimov. Reprinted with permission of Asimov Holdings LLC.

Associated Press ©The Associated Press, Reprinted with permission of the YGS Group; "High-tech backpacks open world of whales to deaf students" by AP staff on 3/17/2017. Used with permission from Wright's Media.

BBC News Online "The girl who gets gifts from birds" from BBC, February 25, 2015. Used with permission.

BBC Worldwide Americas, Inc. "The Secret Life of the Dog," ©Two BBC Worldwide Learning; Animation of the history of exploration ©BBC Worldwide Learning.

Bilingual Review Press, Hispanic Research Center "The Sand Castle" by Alma Luz Villanueva from *Weeping Woman: La Llorona and Other Stories* by Alma Luz Villanueva, Bilingual Review Press, 1994

Byron Preiss Visual Publications, Inc. Reprinted with the permission of Byrn Preiss Visual Publications, Inc., from *My Life With the Chimpanzees* by Jane Goodall. Copyright 1988, 1996 Byron Preiss Visual Publications, Inc. Text copyright ©1988, 1996 Jane Goodall.

Candlewick Press Copyright ©2009 by Amnesty International UK. "Prince Francis," copyright ©2009 by Roddy Doyle. Reproduced by permission of the publisher, Candlewick Press, on behalf of Walker Books, London.

Chhabra, Esha "The Importance of Imagination" by Esha Chhabra. Used with permission.

Chronicle Books "Oranges" from *New and Selected Poems* by Gary Soto. Copyright ©1995 by Gary Soto. Visit www.chroniclebooks.com. Used with permission of Chronicle Books LLC, San Francisco.

Creative Book Services From *Lewis & Clark* by Nick Bertozzi. Copyright ©2011 by Nick Bertozzi. Used with permission of Macmillan Publishing Group.

Cricket Media "So What Is A Primate?" by Faith Hickman Brynie/Cricket Media; "The Biometric Body" by Kathiann M. Kowalski/Cricket Media; "Ada and the Thinking Machines" by Kathleen Krull/Cricket Media.

Don Congdon Associates, Inc. "The Sound of Summer Running" by Ray Bradbury. Reprinted by permission of Don Congdon Associates, Inc. Copyright ©1956 by the Curtis Publishing Co., renewed 1984 by Ray Bradbury.

Faber & Faber, Ltd. (UK) "The Naming of Cats" from *Old Possum's Book of Practical Cats* by T.S. Eliot. ©1939 by T.S. Eliot and renewed 1967 by Esme Valerie Eliot. Reprinted by permission of Faber and Faber Ltd.

Hanging Loose Press "Sonnet, Without Salmon" reprinted from *What I've Stolen, What I've Earned* ©2014 by Sherman Alexie, by permission of Hanging Loose Press.

HarperCollins Publishers From *Bad Boy* by Walter Dean Myers. Copyright ©1998 by Walter Dean Myers. Used with permission of HarperCollins Publishers.

Hogan, Linda E "Predators" by Linda E. Hogan, from *9 Poems*. Used with permission of the author.

Houghton Mifflin Harcourt Publishing Co. "All Watched Over by Machines of Loving Grace" from *The Pill Versus the Springhill Mine Disaster* by Richard Brautigan. Copyright ©1968 by Richard Brautigan. Reproduced by permission for Houghton Mifflin Harcourt Publishing Company. All rights reserved; Excerpt from *Sacajawea: The Story of Bird Woman and the Lewis and Clark Expedition* by Joseph Bruchac. Copyright ©2000 by Joseph Bruchac. Reprinted by permission of Houghton Mifflin Harcourt Publishing Company. All rights reserved; Excerpt from *How Smart Are Animals?* by Dorothy Hinshaw Patent. Text copyright ©1990 by Dorothy Hinshaw Patent. Reprint by permission of Houghton Mifflin Harcourt; "The Naming of Cats" from *Old Possum's Book of Practical Cats* by T.S. Eliot. Copyright 1939 by T.S. Eliot and renewed 1967 by Esme Valerie Eliot. Reprint by permission of Houghton Mifflin Harcourt Publishing Company. All rights reserved.

Khan, Leena "The Black Hole of Technology" by Leena Khan, from Huffington Post, January 20, 2015. Used with permission of the author.

Lerner Publishing Group, Inc. *The Hero Twins: Against the Lords of Death, a Mayan Myth* by Dan Jolley, illustrated by David Witt. Copyright ©2008 by Lerner Publishing Group, Inc. Reprinted with the permission of Graphic Universe™, a division of Lerner Publishing Group, Inc. All rights reserved. No part of this excerpt may be used or reproduced in any manner whatsoever without the prior written permission of Lerner Publishing Group, Inc.

LinguaText, Ltd. From *The Misadventures of Don Quixote* Printed with permission from LinguaText, LLC.

Loesch, Cailin "Is Our Gain Also Our Loss?" by Cailin Loesch, originally appeared in Huffington Post, November 14, 2014.

Macmillan Children's Publishing Group From *Lewis & Clark* by Nick Bertozzi. Copyright ©2011 by Nick Bertozzi. Used with permission of Macmillan Publishing Group.

The Moth The Moth Presents: Aleeza Kazmi © The Moth.

Mountaineers Books "The Legacy of Arctic Explorer Matthew Henson" ©2014. Reprinted with permission of the publisher from *The Adventure Gap: Changing the Face of the Outdoors* by James Edward Mills, Mountaineers Books, Seattle.

National Geographic Magazine "Barrington Irving, Pilot and Educator" from *National Geographic: Explorers;* NG Staff/ National Geographic Creative.

New York Public Radio NPR Bored and Brilliant: A Production of WNYC Studios.

NPR (National Public Radio) ©2012 National Public Radio, Inc. News report titled "Pet Therapy: How Animals And Humans Heal Each Other" by Julie Rovner was originally published on NPR.org on March 5, 2012, and is used with the permission of NPR. Any unauthorized duplication is strictly prohibited.

Penguin Books For Young Readers From *Black Cowboy, Wild Horses* by Julius Lester. Copyright ©1998. Used with permission of Penguin Random House.

Penguin Books Ltd. (Canada) From *A Long Way Home* by Saroo Brierley, copyright ©2013 by Saroo Brierley. Used by permission of Penguin Random House Canada.

Penguin Books, Ltd. (UK) "The Shah of Blah," from *Haroun and the Sea of Stories* by Salman Rushdie, copyright ©1990 by Salman Rushdie. Used by permission of Penguin Books, Ltd.; From *A Long Way Home* by Saroo Brierley, copyright ©2013 by Saroo Brierley. Used by permission of Penguin Books, Ltd.

Penguin Group (Australia) From *A Long Way Home* by Saroo Brierley, copyright ©2013 by Saroo Brierley. Used by permission of Penguin Australia.

Penguin Publishing Group "Brooklyn Rain," "Another Way," "Gifted," "Sometimes," "Uncle Robert," and "Believing" from *Brown Girl Dreaming* by Jacqueline Woodson. Copyright ©2014 by Jacqueline Woodson. Used with permission of Penguin Random House.

Penguin Publishing Group "The Shah of Blah," from *Haroun and the Sea of Stories* by Salman Rushdie, copyright ©1990 by Salman Rushdie. Used by permission of Viking Books, an imprint of Penguin Publishing Group, a division of Penguin Random House LLC.; From *A Long Way Home* by Saroo Brierley, copyright ©2013 by Saroo Brierley. Used by permission of G. P. Putnam's Sons, an imprint of Penguin Publishing Group, a division of Penguin Random House LLC; "The Legend of the Hummingbird" from *Once in Puerto Rico* by Pura Belpré, copyright ©1973 by Pura Belpré. Used by permission of Frederick Warne, an imprint of Penguin Young Readers Group, a division of Penguin Random House LLC. All rights reserved.

Public Domain *Peter Pan* by J. M. Barrie (1911); *Alice's Adventures in Wonderland* (1865) by Lewis Carroll; "Jabberwocky" by Lewis Carroll, from *Through the Looking-Glass, and What Alice Found There* (1871); *The Wonderful Wizard of Oz* (1900) by L. Frank Baum; "Fantasy" by Gwendolyn Bennett, originally appeared in *Caroling Dusk: An Anthology of Verse by Negro Poets* (1927), "The King of Mazy May" by Jack London, 1899; "The Mock Turtle's Song" from *Alice's Adventures in Wonderland* by Lewis Carroll, 1865.

Random House, Inc. "Raymond's Run," copyright ©1971 by Toni Cade Bambara; "The Fun They Had" from *Isaac Asimov: The Complete Stories, Vol. I* by Isaac Asimov. Copyright ©1954 by Isaac Asimov. Reprinted with permission of Random House; "Into the Boats" from *Shipwreck at the Bottom of the World: The Extraordinary True Story of Shackleton and the Endurance* by Jennifer Armstrong, copyright ©1998 by Jennifer M. Armstrong. Used by permission of Crown Publishers, an imprint of Random House Children's Books, a division of Penguin Random House LLC. All rights reserved. Any third party use of this material, outside of this publication, is prohibited. Interested parties must apply directly to Penguin Random House LLC for permission.

Ringgold, Faith "The Boy Nobody Knew" Faith Ringgold ©2003.

Samantha Larson "To the Top of Everest" by Samantha Larson, from http://www.samanthalarson.blogspot.com/. Used with permission of the author.

Samuel French, Inc. *The Phantom Tollbooth: A Children's Play in Two Acts* by Susan Nanus and Norton Juster. Copyright ©1977 by Susan Nanus and Norton Juster. Used by permission of Samuel French, Inc. All rights reserved. CAUTION NOTICE: Professionals and amateurs are hereby warned that *The Phantom Tollbooth*, being fully protected under the copyright laws of the United States of America, the British Commonwealth countries, including Canada, and the other countries of the Copyright Union, is subject to royalty. All rights, including professional, amateur, motion picture, recitation, lecturing, public reading, radio, television and cable broadcasting, and the rights of translation into foreign languages, are strictly reserved. Any inquiry regarding the availability of performance rights, or the purchase of individual copies of the authorized acting edition, must be directed to Samuel French, Inc., 45 West 25th Street, NY, NY 10010 with other locations in Hollywood and Toronto, Canada.

Scovil Galen Ghosh Literary Agency, Inc. "Feathered Friend" reprinted by permission of the author's estate and the author's agents, Scovil Galen Ghosh Literary Agency, Inc.

Shotorov, Vacille "YoHoHo and a Rubber Ducky" © Vasil Shotorov.

Sheep Meadow Press "Nikita" by Alberto Ríos, published with permission of the Sheep Meadow Press.

Simon & Schuster, Inc. Reprinted with the permission of Simon & Schuster Books for Young Readers, an imprint of Simon & Schuster Children's Publishing Division. From *My Life With the Chimpanzees* by Jane Goodall. Copyright 1988, 1996 Byron Preiss Visual Publications, Inc. Text copyright 1988, 1996 Jane Goodall.

Society for Science & the Public "Screen Time Can Mess With the Body's Clock" from *Student Science, Science News for Students*, February 9, 2015 by Andrew Bridges. Used with permission.

Susan Bergholz Literary Services "Eleven," from *Woman Hollering Creek.* Copyright ©1991 by Sandra Cisneros. Published by Vintage Books, a division of Penguin Random House, and originally in hardcover by Random House. By permission of Susan Bergholz Literary Services, New York, NY and Lamy, NM. All rights reserved.

Texas Monthly "All the Pretty Ponies" Reprinted with permission from the March 2014 issue of *Texas Monthly*.

University of Pennsylvania Press "Our Wreath of Rosebuds," from *Changing is Not Vanishing: A Collection of American Indian Poetry to 1930* by Corrinne, edited by Robert Dale Parker. Copyright ©2011. Reprinted with permission of the University of Pennsylvania Press.

Villanueva, Alma Luz "I Was a Skinny Tomboy Kid" by Alma Luz Villanueva. Used with permission of the author.

Wall Street Journal "Teen Researchers Defend Media Multitasking," republished with permission of Dow Jones, Inc, from Wall Street Journal, October 13, 2014; permission conveyed through Copyright Clearance Center, Inc.

Wesleyan University Press Wright, James. "A Blessing" from *Above the River* ©1990 by James Wright. Reprinted with permission of Wesleyan University Press, www.wesleyan.edu/wespress.

White Mountain Films "The Endurance" ©White Mountain Films.

WNET "Jabberwocky" from *Through the Looking Glass* by Lewis Carroll ©WNET.

Wylie Agency "The Shah of Blah," from *Haroun and the Sea of Stories* by Salman Rushdie, copyright ©1990 by Salman Rushdie. Used by permission of Wylie Agency, LLC.

ACKNOWLEDGEMENTS AND CREDITS

Photo locators denoted as follows: Top (T), Center (C), Bottom (B), Left (L), Right (R), Background (Bkgd)

Amarillo/Shutterstock; 270 TR: enotpoloskun/Getty Images; 271: enotpoloskun/Getty Images; 274: enotpoloskun/Getty Images; 276: enotpoloskun/Getty Images; 278 TCL: enotpoloskun/Getty Images; 278 TL: Carlos Amarillo/Shutterstock; 281: IBM External Submissions; 283: IBM External Submissions; 288: Van1981Roo/Shutterstock; 290: Van1981Roo/Shutterstock; 292: Van1981Roo/Shutterstock; 295 BCR: SEFT-1 project. Andrés Padilla Domene and Ivan Puig.; 295 BR: Bikeriderlondon/Shutterstock; 295 CR: Kirill_Makarov/Shutterstock; 295 TCR: Karinkamon/Shutterstock; 295 TR: H. Armstrong Roberts/ClassicStock/Getty Images; 295 TR: R. Gino Santa Maria/Shutterstock; 298 TCL: R. Gino Santa Maria/Shutterstock; 298 TL: H. Armstrong Roberts/ClassicStock/Getty Images; 300: Robin Platzer/Twin Images/LFI/Photoshot/Newscom; 301 TCR: R. Gino Santa Maria/Shutterstock; 301 TR: H. Armstrong Roberts/ClassicStock/Getty Images; 304 TCL: R. Gino Santa Maria/Shutterstock; 304 TL: H. Armstrong Roberts/ClassicStock/Getty Images; 306 TCL: R. Gino Santa Maria/Shutterstock; 306 TL: H. Armstrong Roberts/ClassicStock/Getty Images; 308: Karinkamon/Shutterstock; 310: © Leena A. Khan; 311: Karinkamon/Shutterstock; 314: Karinkamon/Shutterstock; 316: Karinkamon/Shutterstock; 318: Kirill_Makarov/Shutterstock; 320: Marty Lederhandler/AP Images; 321: Kirill_Makarov/Shutterstock; 326: Kirill_Makarov/Shutterstock; 328: Kirill_Makarov/Shutterstock; 331: SEFT-1 project. Andrés Padilla Domene and Ivan Puig.; 332 B: SEFT-1 project. Andrés Padilla Domene and Ivan Puig.; 332 T: SEFT-1 project. Andrés Padilla Domene and Ivan Puig.; 333 B: SEFT-1 project. Andrés Padilla Domene and Ivan Puig.; 333 T: SEFT-1 project. Andrés Padilla Domene and Ivan Puig.; 337: Bikeriderlondon/Shutterstock; 339: Bikeriderlondon/Shutterstock; 341 BCR: David Crockett/Shutterstock; 341 BR: Dgmata/Shutterstock; 341 TCR: M Swiet Productions/Getty Images; 341 TR: Damian Dovarganes/AP Images; IL1: Damian Dovarganes/AP Images; IL11: Dgmata/Shutterstock; IL4: M Swiet Productions/Getty Images; IL7 C: Michael Ochs Archives/Moviepix/Getty Images; IL7 T: David Crockett/Shutterstock; IL9 C: Chris Felver/Archive Photos/Getty Images; IL9 T: LeshaBu/Shutterstock; NPR Bored and Brilliant: A Production of WNYC Studios; 350 Bkgrd: Jamesteohart/Shutterstock; 350 BL: © Vasil Shotarov; 351 BL: Melis/Shutterstock; 351 BR: Duncan Walker/iStock/Getty Images; 351 C: AF Fotografie/Alamy Stock Photo; 351 CR: Kristin Smith/Shutterstock; 351 T: Dotshock/Shutterstock; 351 TCL: Duncan1890/iStock/Getty Images; 351 TCR: Painting/Alamy Stock Photo; 351 TR: Ryan Etter/Ikon Images/Superstock; 354: Dotshock/Shutterstock; 434: Dotshock/Shutterstock; 436: Dotshock/Shutterstock; 439 BR: Melis/Shutterstock; 439 CR: AF Fotografie/Alamy Stock Photo; 439 TCR: Duncan1890/iStock/Getty Images; 444: FALKENSTEINFOTO/Alamy Stock Photo; 445: *The Misadventures of Don Quxiote,* illustrations by Jack Davis. Copyright Gerald & Cullen Rapp.; 446: *The Misadventures of Don Quxiote,* illustrations by Jack Davis. Copyright Gerald & Cullen Rapp.; 448: *The Misadventures of Don Quxiote,* illustrations by Jack Davis. Copyright Gerald & Cullen Rapp.; 454 TL: Duncan1890/iStock/Getty Images; 454 TR: AF Fotografie/Alamy Stock Photo; 456 TL: Duncan1890/iStock/Getty Images; 456 TR: AF Fotografie/Alamy Stock Photo; 457: New York Public Library/Science Source/Getty Images; 458: Duncan1890/iStock/Getty Images; 459: WNET; 460: AF Fotografie/Alamy Stock Photo; 463 TCR: AF Fotografie/Alamy Stock Photo; 463 TR: Duncan1890/iStock/Getty Images; 464 TCL: AF Fotografie/Alamy Stock Photo; 464 TL: Duncan1890/iStock/Getty Images; 466 TCL: AF Fotografie/Alamy Stock Photo; 466 TL: Duncan1890/iStock/Getty Images; 468: Melis/Shutterstock; 471: Melis/Shutterstock; 474: Melis/Shutterstock; 476: Melis/Shutterstock; 481 BR: Duncan Walker/iStock/Getty Images; 481 CR: Kristin Smith/Shutterstock; 481 TCR: Painting/Alamy Stock Photo; 481 TR:

Ryan Etter/Ikon Images/Superstock; IL1 C: Interim Archives/Archive Photos/Getty Images; IL1 T: Ryan Etter/Ikon Images/Superstock; IL14: Taiga; IL16 C: New York Public Library/Science Source/Getty Images; IL16 T: Duncan Walker/iStock/Getty Images; IL4: Painting/Alamy Stock Photo; IL6: Fotomaster03/Shutterstock; IL7 C: David Levenson/Getty Images; IL7 T: Kristin Smith/Shutterstock; 488 Bkgrd: Paul Nicklen/National Geographic/Getty Images; 488 BL: Ryan Deboodt; 489 BC: Newell Convers Wyeth (18821945)/Private Collection/Peter Newark American Pictures/Bridgeman Images; 489 BCR: PhotoQuest/Archive Photos/Getty Images; 489 CL: BBC Worldwide Learning; 489 CR: MA1/MA1 Wenn Photos/Newscom; 489 T: Universal Images Group/DeAgostini/Alamy Stock Photo; 489 TC: GL Archive/Alamy Stock Photo; 489 TCR: Royal Geographical Society/Alamy Stock Photo; 489 TL: Pjhpix/Fotolia; 489 TR: "To the Top of Everest" by Samantha Larson, from http://www.samanthalarson.blogspot.com/. Used with permission of the author.; 492: Universal Images Group/DeAgostini/Alamy Stock Photo; 497 C: BBC Worldwide Learning; 497 T: Pjhpix/fotolia; 498: Pjhpix/fotolia; 500: Saroo Brierly; 501: Pjhpix/fotolia; 504: Universal Images Group Limited/Alamy Stock Photo; 510: Pep Roig/Alamy Stock Photo; 514: Pjhpix/fotolia; 516: Pjhpix/fotolia; 518: Pjhpix/fotolia; 520: WENN Ltd/Alamy Stock Photo; 521: BBC Worldwide Learning; 523: BBC Worldwide Learning; 532: Universal Images Group/DeAgostini/Alamy; 534: Universal Images Group/DeAgostini/Alamy; 537 BCR: Newell Convers Wyeth (18821945)/Private Collection/Peter Newark American Pictures/Bridgeman Images; 537 TR: GL Archive/Alamy Stock Photo; 540: GL Archive/Alamy Stock Photo; 543: GL Archive/Alamy Stock Photo; 544 TC: World History Archive/Alamy Stock Photo; 544 TL: Paul Fearn/Alamy Stock Photo; 545: Clive Streeter/Dorling Kindersley/Science Museum, London/Science Source; 548: GL Archive/Alamy Stock Photo; 550: GL Archive/Alamy Stock Photo; 554: Bettmann Archive/Getty Images; 568: Newell Convers Wyeth (18821945)/Private Collection/Peter Newark American Pictures/Bridgeman Images; 570 C: © Eric Jenks, Awasos Entertainment; 570 T: Newell Convers Wyeth (18821945)/Private Collection/Peter Newark American Pictures/Bridgeman Images; 571: Newell Convers Wyeth (18821945)/Private Collection/Peter Newark American Pictures/Bridgeman Images; 574: Danita Delimont/Alamy Stock Photo; 577: Newell Convers Wyeth (18821945)/Private Collection/Peter Newark American Pictures/Bridgeman Images; 578: Newell Convers Wyeth (18821945)/Private Collection/Peter Newark American Pictures/Bridgeman Images; 580 C: © Creative Book Services; 580 T: Newell Convers Wyeth (18821945)/Private Collection/Peter Newark American Pictures/Bridgeman Images; 588: Newell Convers Wyeth (18821945)/Private Collection/Peter Newark American Pictures/Bridgeman Images; 593 BCR: PhotoQuest/Archive Photos/Getty Images; 593 CR: MA1/MA1 Wenn Photos/Newscom; 593 TCR: Royal Geographical Society/Alamy Stock Photo; 593 TR: "To the Top of Everest" by Samantha Larson, from http://www.samanthalarson.blogspot.com/. Used with permission of the author.; IL1 C: Scott Smeltzer/The PressTelegram/AP Images; IL1 T: "To the Top of Everest" by Samantha Larson, from http://www.samanthalarson.blogspot.com/. Used with permission of the author.; IL14: MA1/MA1 Wenn Photos/Newscom; IL18 C: Nick Berard; IL18 T: PhotoQuest/Archive Photos/Getty Images; IL4: "To the Top of Everest" by Samantha Larson, from http://www.samanthalarson.blogspot.com/. Used with permission of the author.; IL7: "To the Top of Everest" by Samantha Larson, from http://www.samanthalarson.blogspot.com/. Used with permission of the author.; IL8: Royal Geographical Society/Alamy Stock Photo